T0254164

Real World Windows 10 Development

Second Edition

Edward Moemeka
Elizabeth Moemeka

Apress®

Real World Windows 10 Development

ISBN-13 (pbk): 978-1-4842-1450-3

ISBN-13 (electronic): 978-1-4842-1449-7

Managing Director: Welmoed Spahr
Lead Editor: James DeWolf
Technical Reviewer: Fabio Cladio Ferracchiati
Editorial Board: Steve Anglin, Pramila Balen, Louise Corrigan, Jim DeWolf, Jonathan Gennick, Robert Hutchinson, Celestin Suresh John, Michelle Lowman, James Markham, Susan McDermott, Matthew Moodie, Jeffrey Pepper, Douglas Pundick, Ben Renow-Clarke, Gwenan Spearing
Coordinating Editor: Melissa Maldonado
Copy Editor: Mary Behr
Compositor: SPi Global
Indexer: SPi Global
Artist: SPi Global

Distributed to the book trade worldwide by Springer Science+Business Media New York, 233 Spring Street, 6th Floor, New York, NY 10013. Phone 1-800-SPRINGER, fax (201) 348-4505, e-mail orders-ny@springer-sbm.com, or visit www.springer.com. Apress Media, LLC is a California LLC and the sole member (owner) is Springer Science + Business Media Finance Inc (SSBM Finance Inc). SSBM Finance Inc is a Delaware corporation.

For information on translations, please e-mail rights@apress.com, or visit www.apress.com.

Apress and friends of ED books may be purchased in bulk for academic, corporate, or promotional use. eBook versions and licenses are also available for most titles. For more information, reference our Special Bulk Sales–eBook Licensing web page at www.apress.com/bulk-sales.

Any source code or other supplementary material referenced by the author in this text is available to readers at www.apress.com. For detailed information about how to locate your book's source code, go to www.apress.com/source-code/.

This book is dedicated to my father, Professor Andrew Azukaego Moemeka, who has been my greatest inspiration.

—Edward Moemeka

We also both dedicate this book, in loving memory, to William "Bill" Brown.

Contents at a Glance

Contents

About the Authors

Edward Moemeka is an enterprise architect with a career spanning two decades. His experience in building, integrating, and delivering high-profile, large-scale applications for clients has made him a known commodity in the technology field. He is the Principal Architect at e-builder, a class leader in project management software for large-scale capital projects. Follow Edward at Twitter handle @moemeka, on YouTube at www.youtube.com/user/sineofreason, and on Facebook at www.facebook.com/edwardmoemeka.

Elizabeth Moemeka is a communications specialist whose experience spans writing, marketing, and project support. She has used her creative expertise towards designing Windows apps. She blogs on technology and other subjects of personal interest. She has spent time in many parts of the United States and currently lives with her husband, two sons, and cat in Connecticut.

About the Technical Reviewers

Fabio Claudio Ferracchiati is a senior consultant and a senior analyst/developer using Microsoft technologies. He works for Blu Arancio (`www.bluarancio.com`). He is a Microsoft Certified Solution Developer for .NET, a Microsoft Certified Application Developer for .NET, a Microsoft Certified Professional, and a prolific author and technical reviewer. Over the past ten years, he's written articles for Italian and international magazines and co-authored more than ten books on a variety of computer topics.

Damien Foggon is a developer, writer, and technical reviewer of cutting-edge technologies and has contributed to more than 50 books on .NET, C#, Visual Basic, and ASP.NET. He is the co-founder of the Newcastle-based user group NEBytes (online at `www.nebytes.net`), is a multiple MCPD in .NET 2.0 onwards, and can be found online at `http://blog.fasm.co.uk`.

Acknowledgments

We would like to thank Nick Spano, Mike Soranno, John Leum, and Jonner Londono for their help and support. We would also like to thank the staff at Apress for this opportunity and for putting their faith in us, with special thanks to Melissa Maldonado, Damien Foggon, and Fabio Claudio Ferracchiati for their involvement in this process.

Introduction

Welcome to *Real World App Development for Windows 10*, your step-by-step, one-stop guide to going from a great idea to a published app in the Windows desktop and mobile platforms. Windows 10, already a hugely successful implementation of the venerable Microsoft operating system, offers great potential for effective and innovative apps.

Who This Book Is For

Maybe you've been a lifelong fan and follower of Microsoft. Maybe you're taking a look at the Windows OS for the first time. Either way, Windows 10 and, specifically, its dynamic environment for app inclusion in the overlapping spheres of desktop and mobile, lends itself to an expansive environment, replete with creative potential for developers and practical potential for users.

If you have a passion for cutting-edge technology, a working knowledge of HTML, and creative ideas about how we can better interface with technological tools daily in our lives, this book is for you. The following chapters hold a rich store of knowledge to get you on your way creating, developing, and publishing apps in the Windows 10 platform. The approach of this book is to lay out the steps towards app publication clearly, concisely, and systematically to make the process as simple as possible.

What This Book Covers

While this book covers an end-to-end explanation of app development in the Windows 10 environment, its reach is more comprehensive than this. First, we begin with a thorough introduction to the Windows 10 environment. Following the app development process, we expand into the ins and outs of the submission process, even touching on monetizing your app and making you app successful in other respects as well. As the book takes you through app development, instruction is given for every step of the process. In addition, the instruction relies heavily upon samples in which you are also given the code to build, thus making the text an interactive, hands-on process. While you can utilize this book as a desktop reference text, referring to chapters, sections, and topics as needed, we believe it is worthwhile to read front-to-back; by building the examples in order you'll build a thorough knowledge of exactly how to create a fully realized app in the Windows 10 platform in the process.

The pages ahead contain a comprehensive curriculum that, with a solid foundation in technology and a working knowledge of Windows 10, will answer all the questions you will come across as your build you own Windows app. So sit back, crack open the book, and get on your way to creating your very own Windows platform application!

All content for this book can be downloaded from `www.apress.com/9781484214503?gtmf=s`.

CHAPTER 1

The Windows 10 Ethos and Environment

RIP Windows 8

In July, 2013, Windows 8, an operating system as innovative as it is disjointed, turned the computing world upside down with a boldly reimagined user experience that focused on touch as a first-class citizen. Windows 8 introduced us to the start screen, the charms bar, tiles, and dedicated full screen applications. For many, this was a dream come true, a fast and fluid version of Windows with far fewer hardware requirements, a beautiful touch-first user interface complete with fluid, intuitive edge-driven interaction patterns, and access to the legacy desktop when needed for running old-school Win32 applications. Despite the forward progress Microsoft made with Windows 8, however, it was widely panned as an operating system fit only for the schizophrenic; see Figure 1-1.

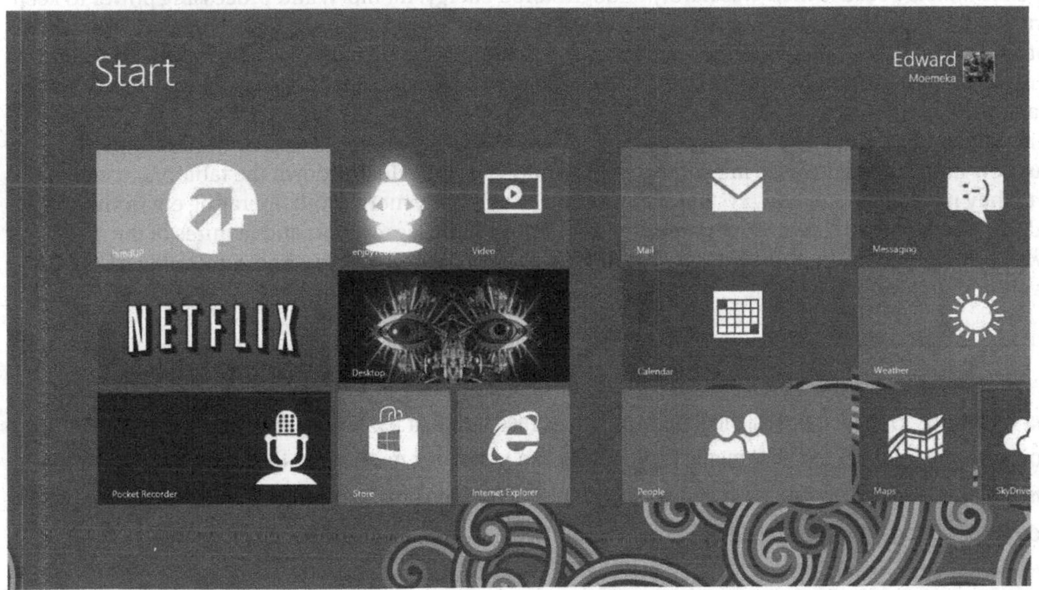

Figure 1-1. Windows 8 Start screen

Many found that although it offered great innovations, the lack of consistency between the two operating environments running within the overarching OS made using it quite confusing at times. Users would open files that would launch them into a full screen experience in one situation, while other file types would jarringly bring them out of the full screen immersive experience into the desktop! The touch-first nature of Windows 8 was another common complaint, as it appeared that Microsoft had foregone any consideration for users working with a mouse and keyboard. Indeed, what seemed easy to do with the finger proved laborious when working with a Windows 8 device that had no touch interface included. Finally, and probably most importantly, the choice to do away from the Start menu proved to be too much of a deviation from what users were comfortable with.

■ **Note** There are some third-party applications that can be purchased to enhance the Windows 8 experience with a Start menu, such as Start8 from Stardock.

The arguments from all sides were the same. Customers wanted input into the decision-making process for features of the Microsoft operating system; they had largely been shunned by Microsoft all through the Windows 8 development cycle despite months of clamoring for the inclusion of a Start menu feature and windowed Modern apps running on the desktop (after all, the OS *was* called "Windows"). Despite all the metrics Microsoft consistently threw at Windows 7 users who wanted to see a Start menu, customers still felt quite strongly that a Start menu was needed–or they at least wanted the freedom to pick one option (having a Start menu) versus the other (using the Start screen).

Windowed applications were also a critical ask from customers and a reason behind Windows 8 not being fully embraced. The shift to full screen applications that Windows 8 introduced seemed to most like a gigantic step backwards from all the innovations of the Windows-of-old genre. Microsoft, it seemed, had ventured too far towards the tablet world for really no reason at all. Tablet operating systems had that limitation because the hardware they ran on (screen, chip, memory) had that limitation, not because it was an innovation on user experience. It worked for phones because the screens were too small for multitasking. It worked for tablets because there was hardly enough stored energy, memory, and processing power to keep things running the way windowed applications required them to be kept running. Full-fledged workstations and laptops had no such constraints: they had large enough screens to do multiple things at one time, they had plenty of processing power, and they were not intended to be used in full fidelity mobility scenarios like tablets and phones are.

What Microsoft needed with its next operating system endeavor was an OS that continued with the powerful new innovations they had introduced with Windows 8 while dialing down the tablet-focused mindset. They needed an operating system that was able to smoothly merge both operating environments: the modern, touch-friendly, secure operating environment with the legacy tools and features of the Windows 7 paradigm. Windows 10 unites these two worlds seamlessly into one while continuing on the path of innovation that Windows 8 began.

■ **Note** Microsoft published a comprehensive blog outlining the details or the rationale behind many of the Windows 8 features. One blog post highlights the complex research that led Microsoft to using the Start screen in Windows 8 in favor of the old Start menu. If you would like to find out more about this, head to the Building Windows 8 blog at `http://blogs.msdn.com/b/b8/`. The specific blog post that walks through the evolution of the Windows Start screen can be found at `http://blogs.msdn.com/b/b8/archive/2011/10/03/evolving-the-start-menu.aspx`.

Hello, Windows 10

Welcome to the brave new world of Windows 10! In this introductory chapter, you will take a walk through yet another "new user interface" for Windows that might appear familiar to some and drastically, even jarringly, different to others. If you are coming from Windows 7 or anything previous, Windows 10 will seem like a major upgrade to you, but one that you will quite possibly cognitively recognize from the standpoint of usability and user experience. Unfortunately for Windows 8/8.1 users, Windows has once again been reimagined, but this time for the better.

An interesting thing happened between the end of development of Windows 8/8.1 and the beginning of Windows 10 development. For whatever reason, Microsoft finally decided that perhaps their customers knew a thing or two about how they would like to use the operating system, so Microsoft began listening! As a result, Windows 10 reintroduces the Start menu as a combination of both the original Windows 7 Start menu and the Windows 8 Start screen, adds support for windowed applications, merges the operating environments, standardizing on the continued use of the desktop, and even adds back transparency, Aero blurs, and depth to the operating system! And it doesn't stop there. Windows 10 continues with the legacy of innovation initiated with Windows 8/8.1 by building out a one-OS architecture which not only allows Windows 10 to be installed on a wide variety of devices, but also allows Modern apps built to target Windows 10 to run on any of the many devices that Windows 10 can run on. Figure 1-2 shows the reincarnated Start menu in Windows 10.

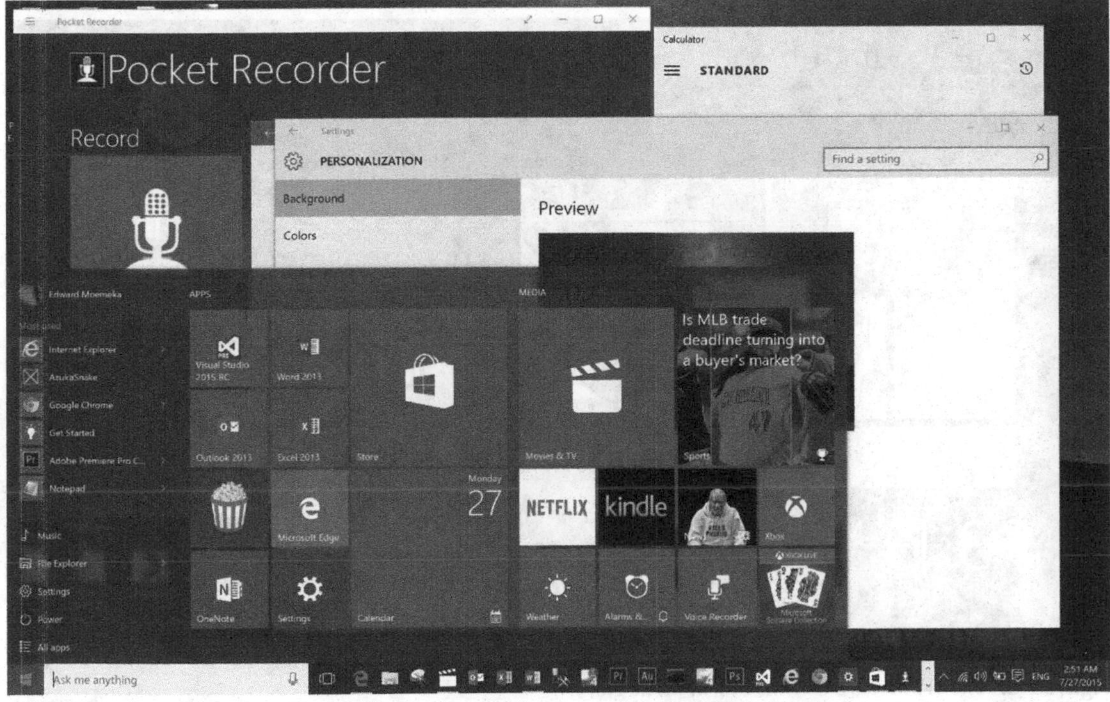

Figure 1-2. Windows 10 Start menu

■ **Note** Presently, Windows 10 is the only operating system that can run on an IOT device, phone, tablet, workstation, Surface Hub, HoloLense, and even Xbox.

The new Windows 10 Start menu functions basically the same as the Start screen from Windows 8/8.1 but does not automatically take up the full screen. Note that the Start menu is transparent with a blur applied to it, similar to the aero look from Windows Vista/7. Figure 1-2 also shows a number of Modern apps running on the desktop. As can be seen from the image, these apps run within a Windows 10 window, meaning they can be treated like any other system window. One of the shortcomings of Windows 8/8.1 was in the forcing of drastic paradigm shifts onto the masses without providing many ways to fall back to previous approaches. Indeed, this author recalls using the "Windows 2000 theme" on Windows XP for a good three years following its release before finally making a switch to the standard XP theme. In fact, I don't believe I would have ever purchased a Windows XP license had the option to continue to use an old approach not been available to me.

The evidence of an awareness of this resistance to change is clear in Windows 10 in a number of ways, but two major inclusions in the operating system drive this mindset home. Firstly, although the legacy charms bar is not present in this release, Modern apps that were written using the Windows 8 SDK can still access the bar through the app's hamburger menu (located on the top left corner of the app title bar). This allows apps that were built in the previous application development model to be available for use within Windows 10 without the need for recompilation. Figure 1-3 shows the Windows 8 charms bar as displayed when a user activates it by swiping in from the right edge of their tablet. From the top, the icons will invoke the search experience, sharing, launch the Start screen, launch interactions with devices, or open the Settings pane. Apps that were developed with Windows 8 in mind would undoubtedly be dependent on any one of these features to function as intended. It is safe to say that making sure that all of the popular Modern apps worked with the new OS was a good idea.

***Figure 1-3.** The Windows 8 charms bar in all its glory*

■ **Note** Mouse and keyboard gestures were also available for accessing the Windows 8 charms bar. Discussion on these is beyond the scope of this book but can be found in Chapter 1 of ***Real World Windows 8 App Development with JavaScript*** (Apress).

Not only would users be frustrated by the presumed failure of the operating system to run their apps, but the developers of the given apps would be frustrated by having to, at the very least, recompile and republish their perfectly fine Windows 8 Modern apps to the Windows 10 platform. Having the charms bar accessible when running these apps alleviates this. It provides a stop-gap solution to the software upgrade problem so developers can take their time and republish to the Windows 10 platform when they have the bandwidth to so. Figure 1-4 shows a Windows 8 Modern app running on Windows 10. Note that the charms bar now appears within the app instead of as a fly-out overlay to the right of the screen. Also note that only three of the original five charms are available.

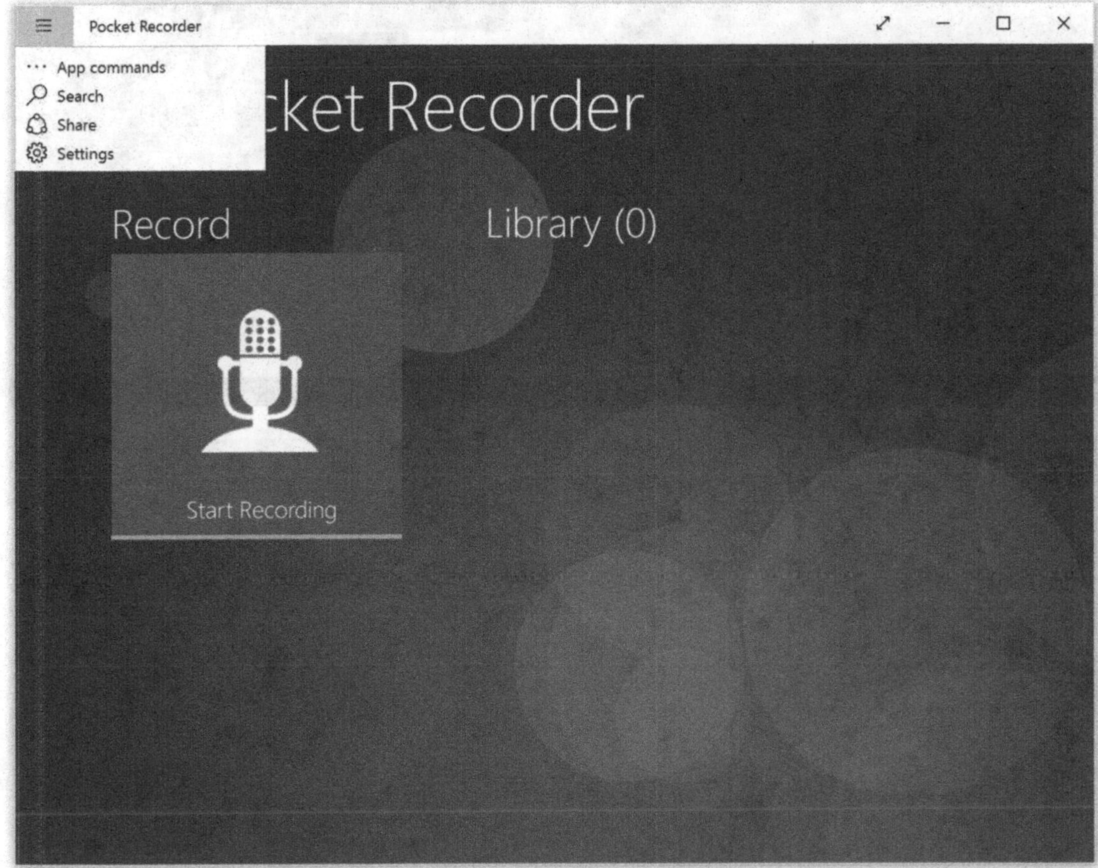

***Figure 1-4.** The Windows 8 charms bar now shows within the Windows 8 Modern app hamburger menu when running on Windows 10*

The second major evidence of an awareness of backwards compatibility is the inclusion of a "Tablet Mode" in Windows 10 across all workstation form factors. Tablet Mode brings your Windows 10 device back in line with the Windows 8 user experience by locking the user into the same single-full-screen-app-at-a-time model that Windows 8/8.1 utilized. Figure 1-5 shows a desktop in Tablet Mode. Note that the taskbar has been cleared of any running items and that no taskbar shortcuts are present. In Tablet Mode, they are removed to streamline the user experience, but many of these behaviors can be modified through various settings in the operating system.

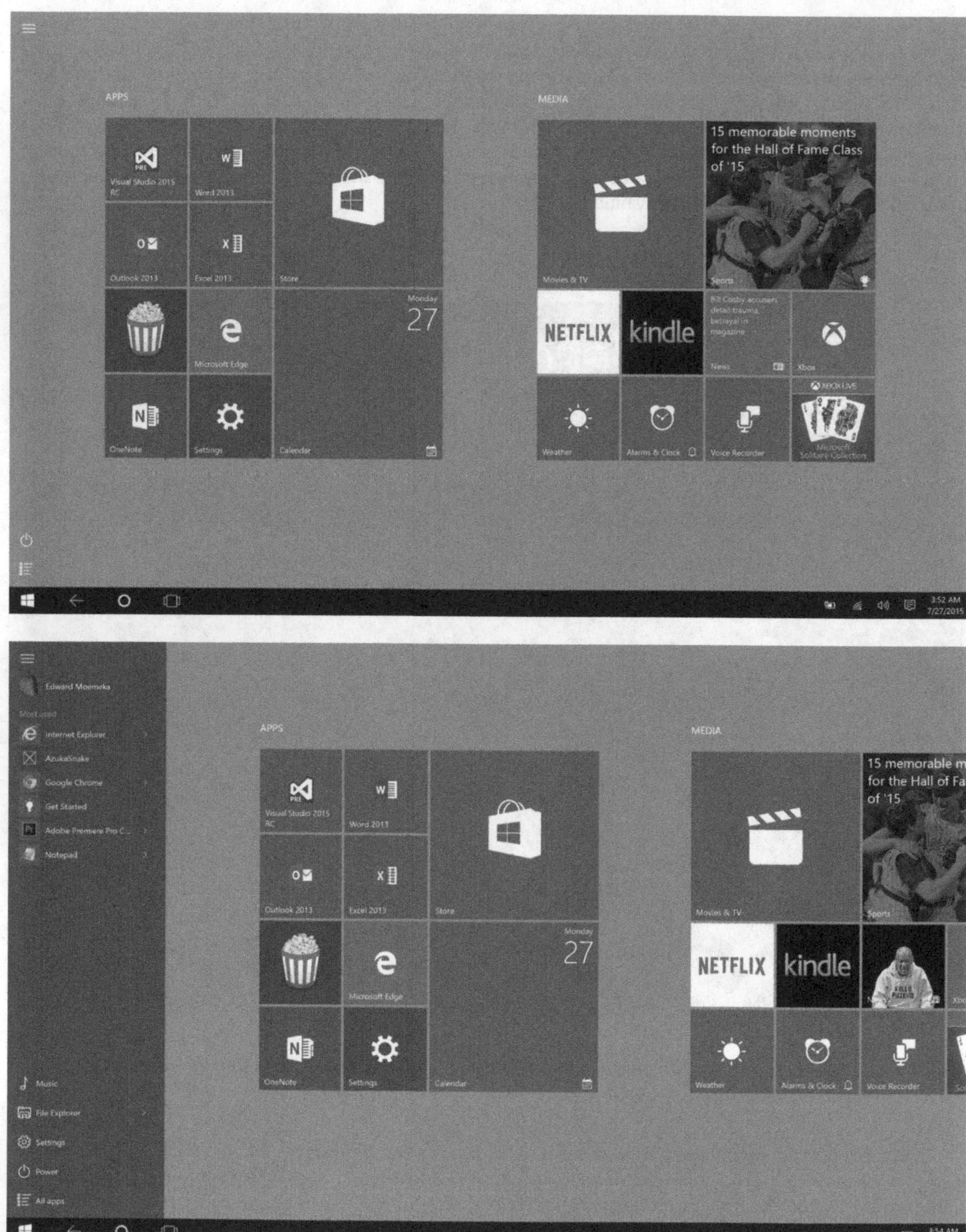

Figure 1-5. Windows 10 Start screen (Tablet Mode)

In our last book, *Real World Windows 8 App Development with JavaScript,* we claimed that Windows 8 was a hugely significant opportunity for developers. Windows 10 is a continuation, an expansion, on this vast realm of possibilities. Not only does Windows 10 allow you to capitalize on the billion plus devices that will be running the operating system within the next three years, it also allows those who have built Windows 8 Modern apps to benefit from Windows 10 with literally no additional work. Windows 10 allows you to develop for it not only using a diverse set of languages like C#, JavaScript, and C++, but also allows iOS and Android applications to be cross-compiled to it so that they run natively in the Windows 10 environment, no emulation needed. This book explores the languages and technologies that can be used to build modern Windows 10 apps, and how you as a Windows 10 developer can use them to build powerful and immersive Windows 10 applications and experiences.

A Not-So-Brief Introduction

Now that we have given a brief, high-level overview of Windows 10, its driving principles (as we understand them to be), and how it matches up to and exceeds on the promise of Windows 8, it is important to provide an introduction to Windows 10 from a developer's perspective, specifically focusing on how Modern apps work and are managed by the system. The discussion isn't exhaustive, because the subject could probably span multiple books, but it should provide you with a baseline of information in order to understand the basics of Windows 10 and Windows 10 app development using the Windows SDK and Runtime.

For the purpose of explanation, let's walk through the Windows 10 UI artifacts, not because you don't already understand how Windows works, but for those of you who may not yet have access to the operating system. The Windows 10 shell has taken the Windows 8 "digital reverse mullet" theme (party time in the front, and good old-fashioned business behind that) and converged it into a single user experience across all application types. Whether they be legacy Win32 applications, Windows 8 Modern apps, or Windows 10 Universal Windows Platform apps, the user experience is the same, save a few nuances.

■ **Note** As you've already seen, Windows 8 Modern apps running on Windows 10 have an additional title bar Item, a hamburger menu at the top left of the window can be used to access the Search, Share, and Settings charms, and the Modern app's command bars.

At first glimpse, in Windows 10 you should see the good old Windows desktop with what will appear to you as a well-overdue user interface touch up. Unless you are on a device that has been specifically earmarked by the manufacturer as a tablet, the default experience for a laptop is to take you to the desktop once signed in. Figure 1-6 shows the default Windows 10 desktop with the Start menu activated.

Figure 1-6. *Windows 10 Desktop with Start menu showing*

The new Windows 10 Start menu, which for the most part is the Windows 8 start screen with a few additional capabilities (first and foremost being that it no longer needs to run exclusively in full screen mode), continues to serve as a powerful launch pad for applications. In Figure 1-6, the colored rectangles with images in them are a combo launch-point for applications. These magical rectangular surfaces are commonly referred to as *live tiles* and combine the application shortcut, particularly the version of the shortcut you might find on your Windows desktop, with the representation of the notification mechanism of your applications, found in the system tray area. Figure 1-7 shows two states of the Calendar application live tile. The image to the left is the default state; when a meeting is approaching, the tile takes on a different appearance (right).

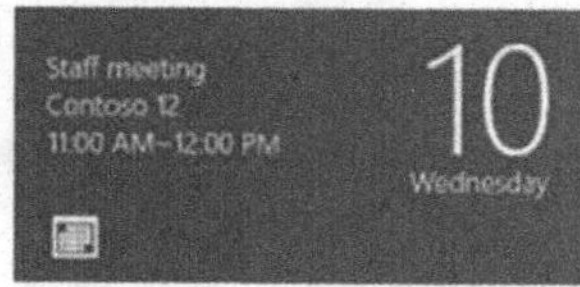

Figure 1-7. *Two states of a Windows 10 Modern app tile*

Let's take a real world case where live tiles can consolidate these kinds of functions. Skype, for instance, may have a system tray icon that changes appearance when it switches from online to offline, a beautiful shortcut on the Windows desktop. The Windows 10 live tile encapsulates those two functions in one. Through the live tile, you can of course launch the application, but as shown in Figure 1-7 tiles can also display notifications based on things happening in the application or even things happening while the application is not running.

Not all tiles on the Start screen are live tiles. Legacy applications such as Visual Studio, Microsoft Word, and Adobe Photoshop can also appear on the Start screen as tiles, but these tiles aren't "live;" they don't possess the ability to present dynamic content on their surface. Legacy Windows application tiles function more or less like the application icons of old (we say "more or less" because Windows 10 exposes some shortcut features to these sorts of tiles that follow patterns similar to their live alternatives, such as being able to launch in administrator mode). Applications built using the new paradigm, which can express themselves through live tiles, are referred to by Microsoft as *Universal Windows Platform (UWP) apps*. For the remainder of this book, we use this terminology to refer to them. Figure 1-8 shows the look of a launched Windows 10 UWP application.

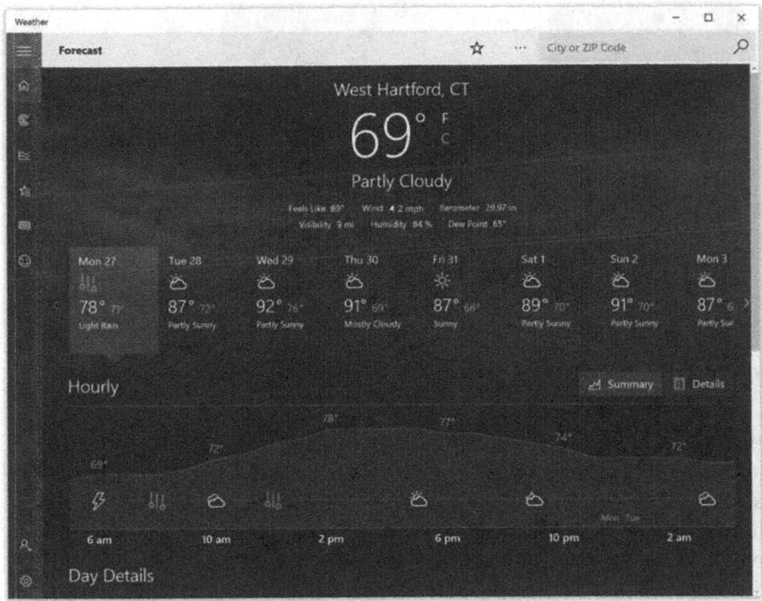

Figure 1-8. *A Windows 10 app*

Notice something? The ubiquitous *close, minimize, and maximize/restore* buttons are back! Unlike in Windows 8/8.1 where apps take up the entire screen at all times, Windows 10 apps (with the exception of when windows is in Tablet Mode) present themselves like standard windowed applications. Developers coming from the Windows 8 paradigm will likely have questions on how to handle the various layout sizes that windowed apps introduce. Because of the non-deterministic nature of a given app's Window mode and hence its size, it is important to build apps with an agnostic viewpoint on both size and layout. Even if the plan is to build a simple utility window, you as the developer must consider how you intend to lay things out in a manner that reduces negative space and flows in accordance with the present size (as determined by the end user) of the app window. It's a tough problem, compounded by the variety of screen resolutions your application must support even when in Tablet Mode. Later chapters delve more into this as we talk about style guidelines and how to pass certification.

Another question that might arise while looking at a launched application in Windows 10 is, how do you close it? On the face of it, providing a close button for UWP apps gives the impression they follow the same life cycle management strategy as legacy applications. Traditional Windows development typically delegated application lifecycle management to the user, meaning the user had to explicitly click the close button at the upper right to end the application process and remove it from memory. If they didn't, the application continued running. Applications such as Skype rely on this. Because the system provides no mechanism for automatically closing an application that is no longer in use (or has not been in use for some time), applications like Skype can treat a user's *close* request as a *hide* request and continue to run with an invisible window in the background. This wouldn't be a problem if everyone acted with honor and compassion, but it does create security concerns. It also consumes system resources, if not unnecessarily, then at least without the user's consent.

Windows 10 strives to *reimagine* this situation by introducing an application lifecycle management model that takes both the user and system resources into account (see Figure 1-9).

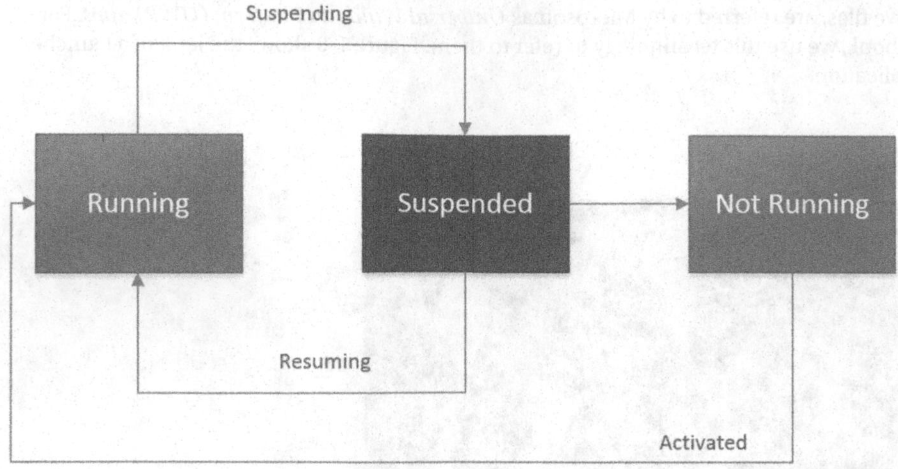

***Figure 1-9.** A Windows 10 app's lifecycle*

In Windows 10, only the presently running and un-minimized UWP apps and, potentially, UWP apps that have been chosen by the user to run in the background are guaranteed to be active at any given time. All other UWP apps may be in the *suspended* state, meaning their memory is intact and in the specified order, but no active threads are running that are owned by the UWP app. As with a saved file, a suspended application is intact just as it was left. And also like a saved file, which can be opened at any time and continues right where it left off, switching back to a UWP app (or launching it again from the Start menu) takes you right back into it. Future chapters talk more about the Windows 10 app lifecycle.

■ **Note** A UWP application can be forcibly closed by dragging from the top of the application screen to the bottom of the screen ("throwing it away"), by clicking the close button, using the task manager, or by using Alt+F4. Mobile family apps are suspended when the user switched to another application, and desktop family apps (apps that target a full fidelity desktop experience) are suspended when the user minimizes them (they can also be suspended when they are no longer the active windows).

The final question one might have concerns something else missing from the app, something that is perhaps not as ubiquitous as the close and minimize/maximize buttons, but certainly is a well-known Windows application feature. This missing component is the *main menu bar*. Regardless of whether the app takes up the full screen or not, there will continue to be a need to represent important application commands somewhere. The obvious choice is to put it onscreen, and to be sure, many applications do just that. But this pattern can create confusion with the user since content and control mechanisms are presented in the same area. (The practice was, in fact, against style guidelines prescribed by Microsoft for Windows 8/8.1 apps).

The Windows 8/8.1 system provided two areas, the *bottom app bar* and the *top app bar*, from which application commands could be launched. Figure 1-10 shows how Windows 8/8/1 Modern apps use the app bar concept to segregate command functionality into a central location within the app. From here, an end user can launch searches, group recordings by category, clear their entire library, or pin the activity of starting a recording directly to the Windows Start screen. (Pinning and the concept of secondary tiles are discussed in more detail in Chapter 6.

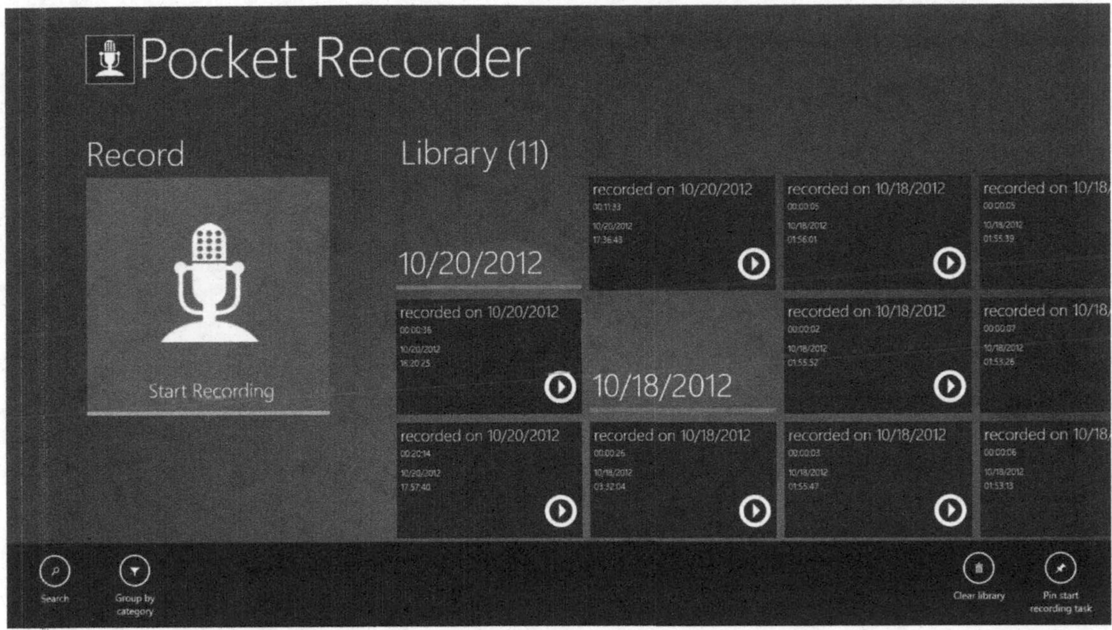

Figure 1-10. *Windows 8 app with the bottom app bar enabled*

In any Windows 8 app, the bottom/top app bar could be activated (made visible) by swiping from either the bottom or the top of the device screen upward or downward, respectively, if touch was enabled. Since those edge gestures have been removed in Windows 10, the only access to them is by a mouse right-click or by using the keyboard combination of the Windows logo key + Z.

■ **Note** Not all Windows 8 devices come touch enabled–or have a mouse, for that matter–so it was important that legacy devices continue to be usable when they upgrade to Windows 8. For this reason, Windows 8 provides mouse and keyboard support for all touch-related functions. To activate the app bar of any application using the mouse, right-click in the application. Using the keyboard, press Windows logo key + Z.

Windows 10 refines the idea of the app bar introduced in Windows 8/8.1 Modern apps, adding two new constructs to their presentation. Firstly, the app bar is now at least partially visible at all times. Unlike in Windows 8/8.1 where the only way to know if an app had app bars was to attempt to invoke it with any one of the invocation methods highlighted above, Windows 10 UWP apps let you know immediately if an app has any app bars by showing a portion of it with an ellipses that can be used to expand the app bar to its full height. Figures 1-11 and 1-12 show a simple UWP app with the app bars in their collapsed and expanded states. As you can see in Figure 1-11, in the collapsed state, the app bar show a portion of its user interface along with an ellipsis that can be used to expand it to its full height. The app bars can be expanded independently using their individual ellipses or expanded together with the mouse right-click. Windows 10 does not respond the swipe up gestures of Windows 8/8.1, so don't expect to use those gestures when in Tablet Mode.

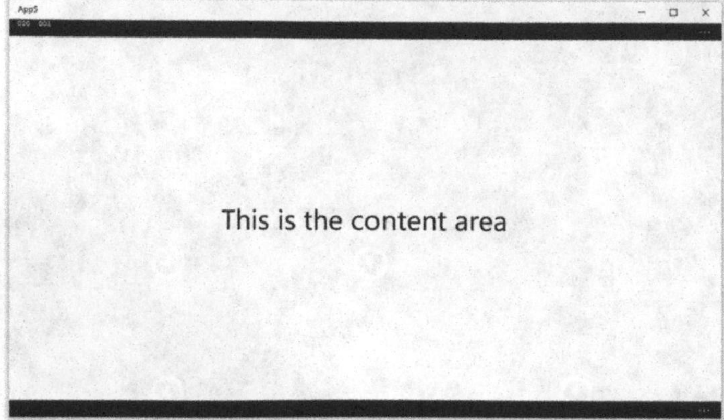

Figure 1-11. *Windows 10 UWP app with new app bar UI*

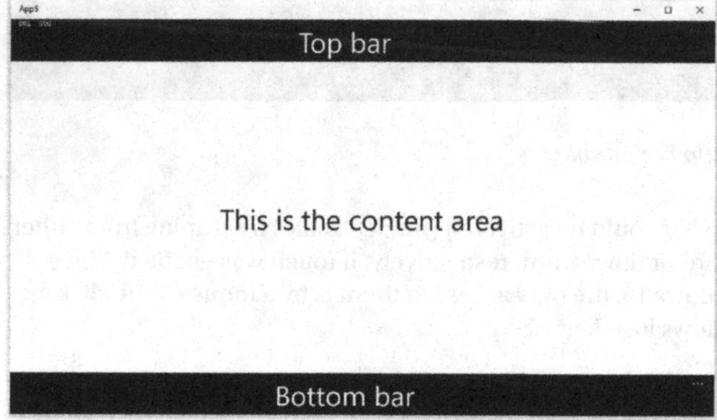

Figure 1-12. *Windows 10 UWP app with app bars enabled*

The New All-New Taskbar

Windows 10 introduces two new components to its taskbar area. Using the task switching button (or Windows logo key + Tab) gives the user access to all applications, suspended or running, across all virtual desktops presently available. From this view the user can also add new desktops as needed (see Figure 1-13).

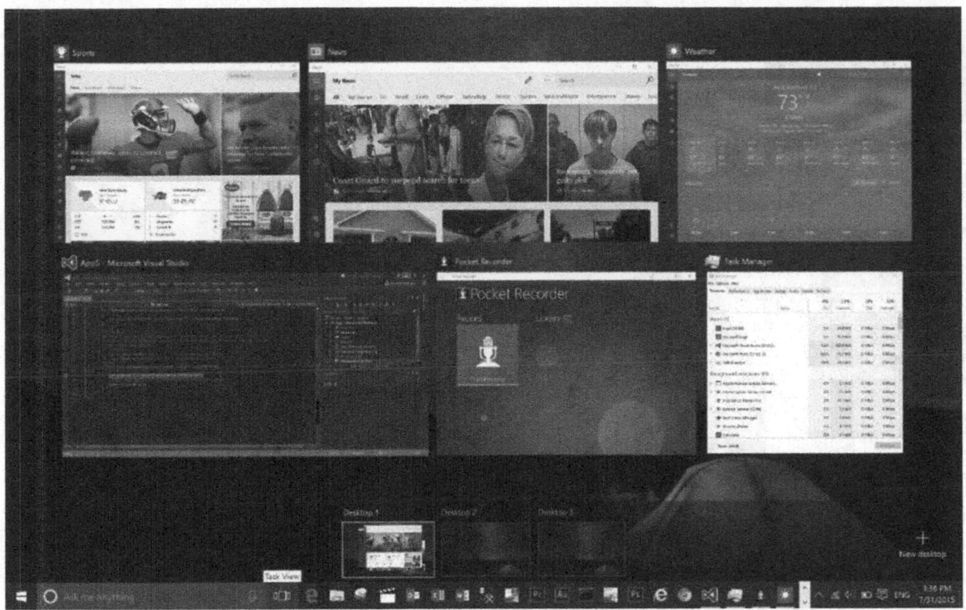

Figure 1-13. *Windows 10 task switcher*

■ **Note** Yes, you guessed it: Windows 10 introduces the concept of virtual desktops to the platform! Virtual desktops allow you to segregate application windows into their own private desktops. Put Facebook and the Xbox app on one desktop and your work Excel spreadsheet and Visual Studio on the other. You can then easily toggle between the two whenever your boss comes around!

The other big addition to the taskbar is the all new, Halo-like, voice assistant aptly named Cortana (Figures 1-14 and 1-15). If you have used a Windows 8.1 phone, you will already be familiar with this utility. Cortana functions like similar voice assistant technologies such as Siri and Google Now. It can help with appointments, reminders, changing settings on your computer, searches, and many more things beyond the scope of this book. Depending on how the user's taskbar is configured, Cortana may show up as a full textbox (like Figure 1-13), just an icon, or not at all. Regardless of how Cortana is presented it can be accessed with the keyboard combination of the Windows logo key + C.

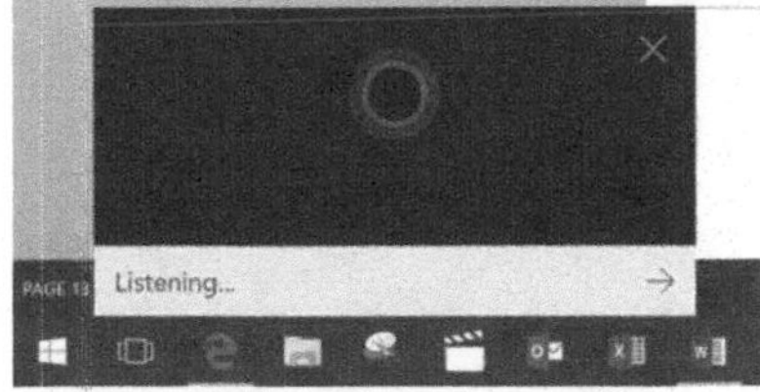

Figure 1-14. *Cortana "compact UI" on Windows 10 listening for instructions*

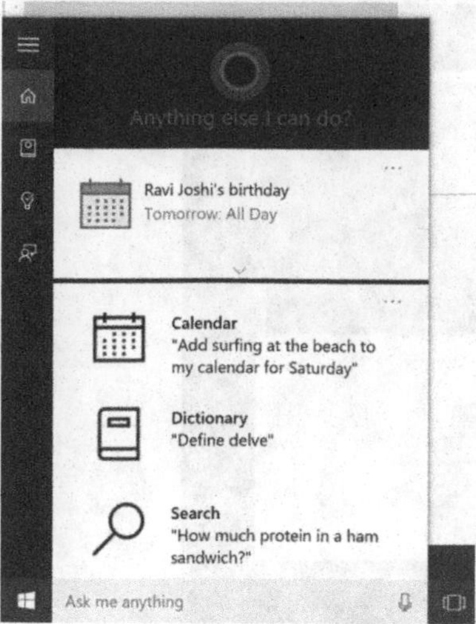

Figure 1-15. *Cortana "full UI" on Windows 10*

The Windows 10 Cortana feature is an extremely important innovation. It provides users with the ability to search across all applications on the system and the Web on top of all the personal assistant functionality inherited from its mobile version.

A developer building UWP apps must contend with various system environment changes that applications developed using older frameworks simply don't have to worry about. This is because applications built using the Universal Windows Platform have a level of connectivity to the native OS that hasn't previously existed by default. One instance of this is with the application *view state*. On devices that support rotation, UWP apps can query the current layout of the system and adjust their UI accordingly. This way, an application can use vertical space that might not be available in landscape mode and horizontal space that might not be available in portrait mode. This is a carry-over from the manner in which Windows 8 functions but it has been vastly enhanced in Windows 10 to support any size. Since UWP apps can be windowed, sizing is now no longer locked to the system but can be controlled directly by the end user; because of this, UWP apps must be able to support multiple layouts. To help facilitate this layout transitioning that must occur as either the user changes window sizes or a UWP app shifts from form factor to form factor, the platform includes adaptive layout tools. The following figures show the Sports UWP app of Windows 10 in two user-controlled sizes; Figure 1-16 is a larger width and Figure 1-17 is a smaller width.

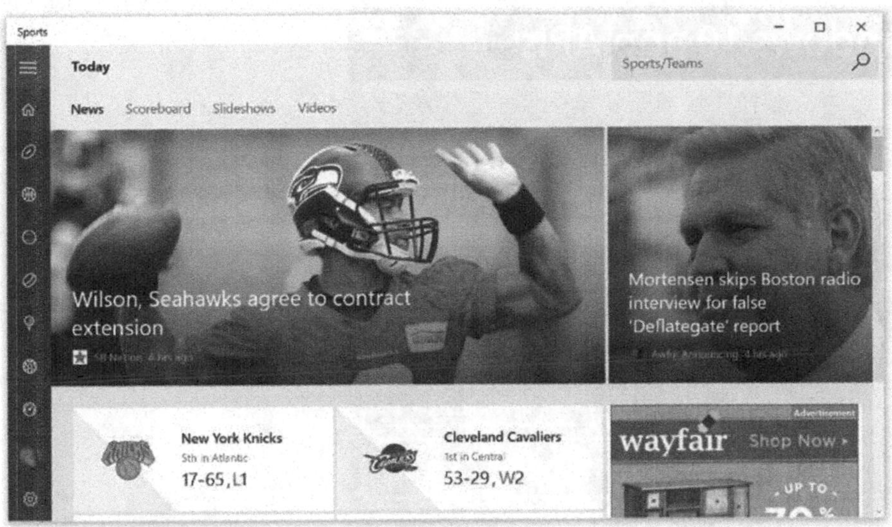

Figure 1-16. *Sports app in a larger width*

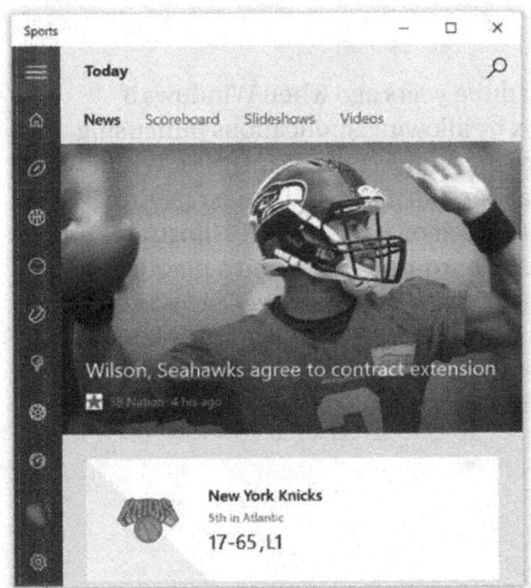

Figure 1-17. *Sports app in a smaller width*

Building Windows 10 UWP Apps

Windows 10 apps can be built using HTML/JavaScript, .NET languages (C# and VB), or native C/C++ through an extension of C++ called C++/Cx. Regardless of the technology used to develop the application, the Windows team has done a good job of providing a core set of APIs that are projected into each of the target languages. Figure 1-18 provides a layered view of the Windows 10 UWP (Universal Windows Platform) interface.

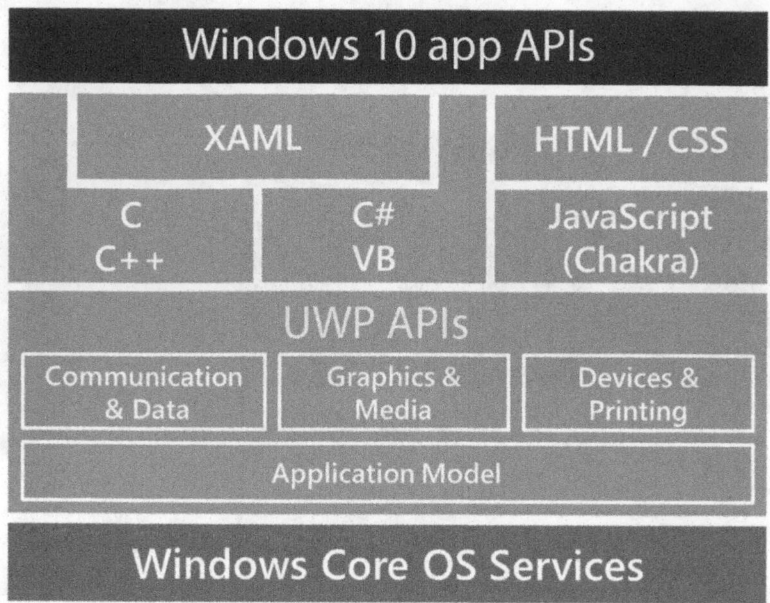

Figure 1-18. *Window 10 app API landscape*

Conceptually, this is really no different than what was offered three years ago when Windows 8 launched with the Windows Runtime. Windows 10 adds to this mix by allowing applications built using this platform to run on all windows devices moving forward, hence the "universal" in Universal Windows Platform. The "windows" part of the name comes from the fact that once an app is built to target this platform, it will work on all Windows devices with that platform deployed on it. Figure 1-19 illustrates the device families and services that are exposed by the UWP. You will be hard-pressed to find a platform that can deliver this kind of end-to-end solution to developers targeting it. If you take the other two competing platforms (iOS and Android), you will find that neither provides the broad reach a UWP app does. Sure, you can build an iOS app for the iPhone and iPad but such an app does not target the broader OSX workstation. The Android world is less consistent even within the mobility device family and offers no true workstation experience.

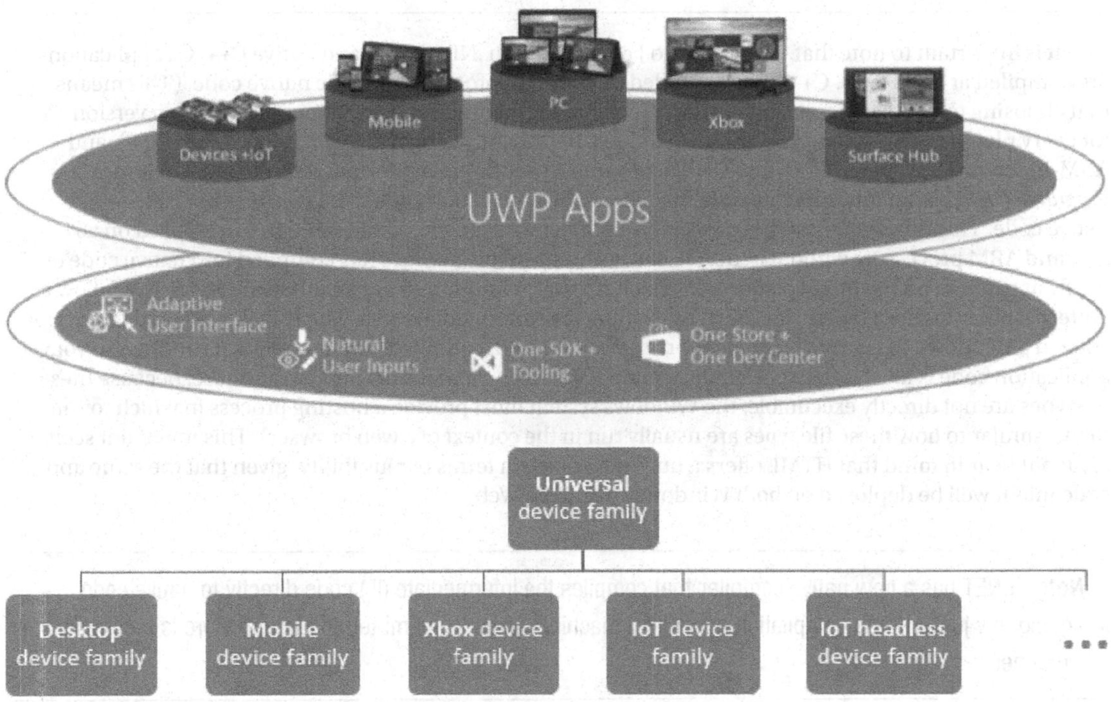

Figure 1-19. *Window 10 unified distribution channel and device families*

For all UWP developers, regardless of technology or language used, applications built using these projected APIs end up in a package containing an application's code (in binary or text format); resources; libraries; and a *manifest* that describes the app (names, logos, and so on), its *capabilities* (such as areas of the file system or specific devices like cameras), and everything else that's needed to make the app work (such as *file associations*, declaration of *background tasks*, and so forth). The manifest describes the application to the Windows Store and also to potential Windows clients that download it from the store. The manifest is a critical component of the development story for Windows 10. The exact workings of the app manifest (as it relates to publishing your application and setting up its permissions) are discussed in the section entitled "Developing for Windows 10 UWP Apps."

Supported Languages

Regardless of language choice, UWP development offers a great full fidelity experience that allows developers who target a specific technology set to work in a way that is both natural to them and consistent with the common approaches to development that those technologies provide. Native C++ development and .NET are great platforms for building UWP apps and do offer some distinct advantages for building Windows 10 apps; the most notable is access to a subset of legacy Win32 APIs.

■ **Note** Win32 is the previous programming platform for building Windows applications. Programs like Adobe Photoshop, Microsoft Word, and Internet Explorer are at least partially built using this technology, and it is still available for building Windows 10 applications that target the desktop experience alone.

It is important to note that, in contrast to JavaScript, both .NET-based and native C++/Cx applications are compiled at build time. C++/Cx is compiled directly into processor-specific native code. (This means that choosing to build an application using this technology requires the developer to compile a version for every platform they intend to support. Windows 10 presently supports 64-bit (x64), 32-bit (x86), and ARM-based processors.) .NET compiles the code into a pseudo-binary format referred to as *intermediate language (IL)*. IL is an intermediate state that allows the application code to be far more portable than native code. This is because the IL is processor-architecture agnostic, so the same IL can be used on x64, x86, and ARM processors without issue. (IL can accomplish this because it is compiled into native code on the fly at runtime on the target platform in which it's run.) Windows 10 apps built using JavaScript follow a pattern similar to those built using .NET, but without the intermediate step. The HTML, CSS, and JavaScript code in a Windows 10 JavaScript application is always parsed, compiled, and rendered at runtime, so your application code is always transported in its entirety to every client it runs on. Furthermore, because these file types are not directly executable, the Windows system must provide a hosting process in which to run them (similar to how these file types are usually run in the context of a web browser). This might not seem ideal but bear in mind that HTML offers a huge advantage in terms of reusability, given that the same app code might well be deployed on both Windows 10 and the Web.

■ **Note** .NET has a new native compiler that compiles the intermediate (IL) code directly to native code, foregoing any just-in-time compilation on a client machine. All code submitted to the app store is recompiled in this manner.

Whereas JavaScript developers use HTML and CSS to lay out the user interface for their apps, UWP apps built using native or .NET-based technologies lay out their user interfaces and build/access system controls using a technology called Extensible Application Markup Language (XAML for short). Listing 1-1 shows some XAML markup.

Listing 1-1. XAML Markup

```
<Page x:Class="AllLearnings.Samples.ApplicationBars.AppBarSamples"
    xmlns="http://schemas.microsoft.com/winfx/2006/xaml/presentation"
    xmlns:x="http://schemas.microsoft.com/winfx/2006/xaml"
    xmlns:d="http://schemas.microsoft.com/expression/blend/2008"
    xmlns:mc="http://schemas.openxmlformats.org/markup-compatibility/2006"
    mc:Ignorable="d"
    >
    <Page.BottomAppBar>
        <AppBar x:Name="appbar_bottom" VerticalAlignment="Bottom" Height="100" >
```

```
            <Grid>
                <Button x:Name="btn_bottomone" Visibility="Visible" Content="&#x002b;" ➥
                          AutomationProperties.Name="Add"  HorizontalAlignment="Right" ➥
                     VerticalAlignment="Top" Style="{StaticResource AppBarButtonStyle}"
                          />
            </Grid>
        </AppBar>
    </Page.BottomAppBar>
    <Grid x:Name="LayoutRoot" >
        <TextBlock>This sample tests the app bar functionality, right click or swipe from ➥
             the bottom to open the bottom app bar.</TextBlock>
    </Grid>
</Page>
```

Listing 1-2 contains the same user interface designed with HTML/CSS as the layout engine!

Listing 1-2. HTML Markup

```
<!DOCTYPE html>
<html>
<head>
        <meta charset="utf-8" />
        <title>TestAppBars</title>

        <!-- WinJS references -->
        <link href="WinJS/css/ui-dark.css" rel="stylesheet" />
    <script src="WinJS/js/base.js"></script>
    <script src="WinJS/js/ui.js"></script></head>
<body>

  <section aria-label="Main content" role="main" style="margin-left: 100px;">
    <p>This sample tests the app bar functionality, right click or ➥
       swipe from the bottom to open the bottom app bar.</p>
  </section>
      <div data-win-control="WinJS.UI.AppBar" >
       <button id="btn_bottomone" data-win-control="WinJS.UI.AppBarCommand" ➥
               data-win-options="{id:'cmdAdd',label:'Add',icon:'add', ➥
                   section:'global',tooltip:'Add item'}">
                 </button>
        </div>
</body>
</html>
```

Additionally, the developer is free to use whatever third-party modules desired (again, in the same manner as is customary to an HTML/CSS/JavaScript developer). For a detailed discussion on the use of HTML/CSS/JavaScript to build modern Windows apps, please see our previous book, *Real World Windows 8 Development with JavaScript*.

Developing for Windows 10 UWP Apps

Now that you have a basic introduction to Windows 10, what Windows 10 UWP apps look like, and what technologies are out there for building Windows 10 apps, you're ready to start building samples and getting on your way to being the next Instagram.

Setting Up Your Environment

Before you begin, you'll need a couple of things. First, to build Windows UWP apps and work through the samples in this book, you will need a copy of Windows 10. You will also need the Windows 10 SDK and, at the very least, a copy of Visual Studio Community Edition 2015. The download links for the required tools are listed in Table 1-1. Please note that installing the Visual Studio Community Edition installs everything you need. The other items are included in the table in case you ever need a specific component. If you have access to an MSDN license, you can download any one of the full featured versions of Visual Studio 2015 directly from the MSDN site

Table 1-1. *Baseline Windows 10 Development Environment Setup*

Tool	Location
Windows 10	`https://www.microsoft.com/en-us/software-download/windows10`
Visual Studio Community Edition	`https://go.microsoft.com/fwlink/?LinkId=532606&clcid=0x409`
Windows 10 SDK (Standalone)	`https://go.microsoft.com/fwlink/p/?LinkId=619296`

Of course, if you plan on using HTML/JavaScript for development, much of the layout and functionality can potentially be achieved without any of this. If you have a simple text editor and web browser, you can follow along to a certain extent; however, you will still need Visual Studio to package your code into a UWP app so we recommend just downloading it; the Community Edition is free.

The Visual Studio IDE

Figure 1-20 shows the Visual Studio 2015 Enterprise Edition IDE with a C#-based UWP project loaded. There are six primary areas that will concern you as a UWP developer, regardless of language choice: the toolbox area, the document outline, the Solution Explorer, the design surface XAML and Design tabs, and the Properties window.

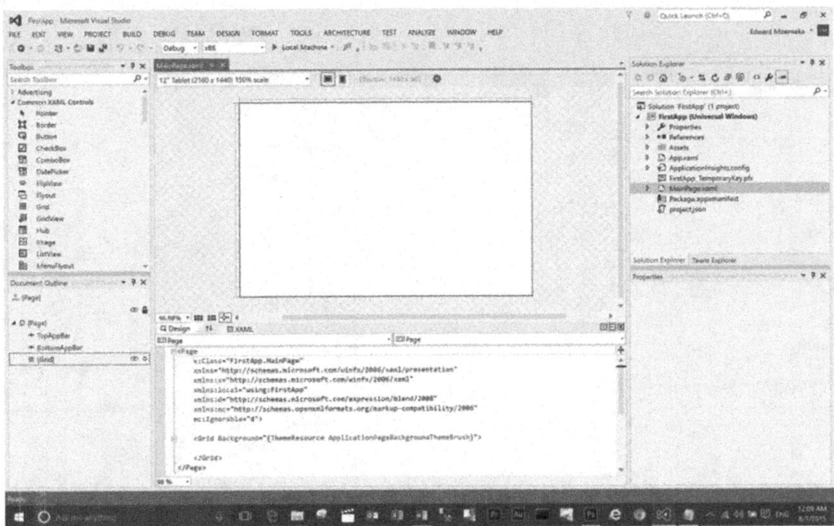

Figure 1-20. *Visual Studio 2015 Enterprise Edition with C# Universal project loaded*

The design surface is the stage where your user interface is composed. It is broken into two parts: the XAML tab contains the markup used to constitute the design surface while the Design tab shows a real-time view of what the user interface will look like. The Design tab allows you to do drag-and-drop designing, meaning you can drag items directly onto its surface and even move things around within it. Figure 1-21 shows the design surface. Note the highlighted drop-down used to simulate various resolutions and form factors.

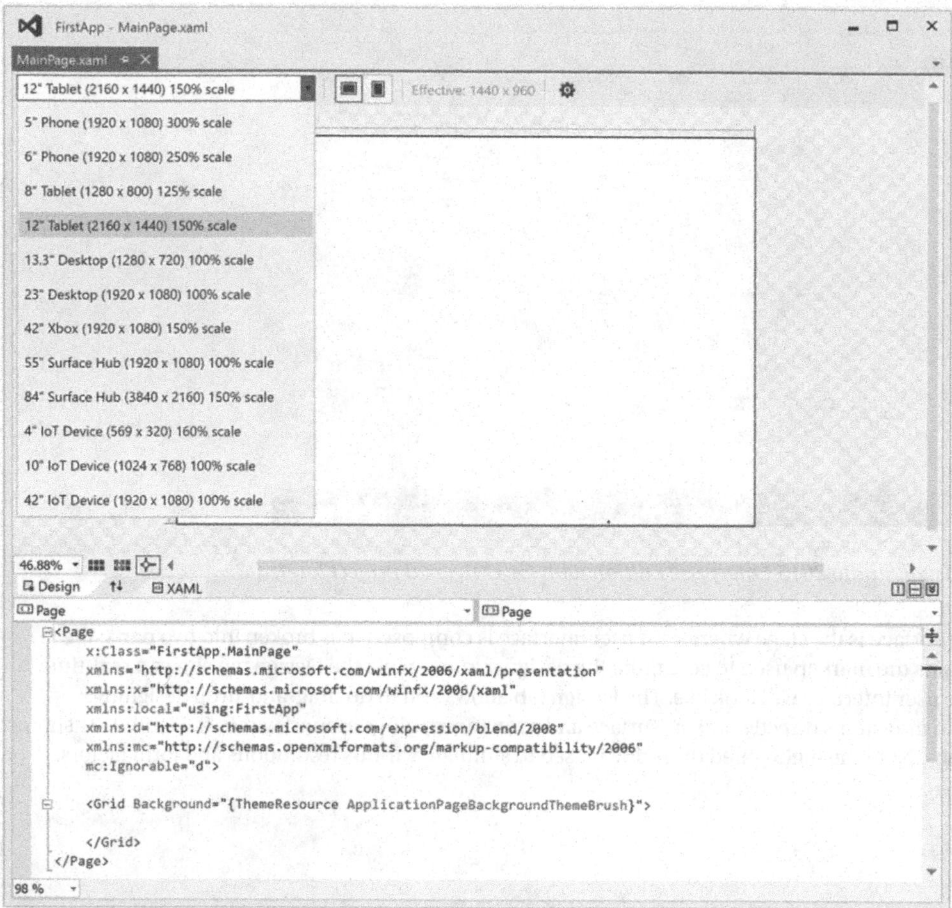

Figure 1-21. *XAML-based Universal project design surface*

To speed up this design process, the Toolbox can be used. If you have previous familiarity with Visual Studio, especially if you have built WinForms, WPF, or Silverlight applications, the Toolbox should be familiar to you. It principally provides an area from which controls can be dragged onto the design surface. It doesn't get much credit for this, but the Toolbox is also a subliminal teacher as it contains a list of all controls that can be dropped onto a given design target. You can quickly use it to seek out controls that you might want to use, similar to how IntelliSense is used, eventually teaching you all the controls available to you. The document outline area presents a hierarchical outline of the controls on the given screen. Content presented inside other content is said to be a child of that content. This relationship is represented in graphical form on the document outline pane. Figure 1-22 shows the Toolbox and the document outline area.

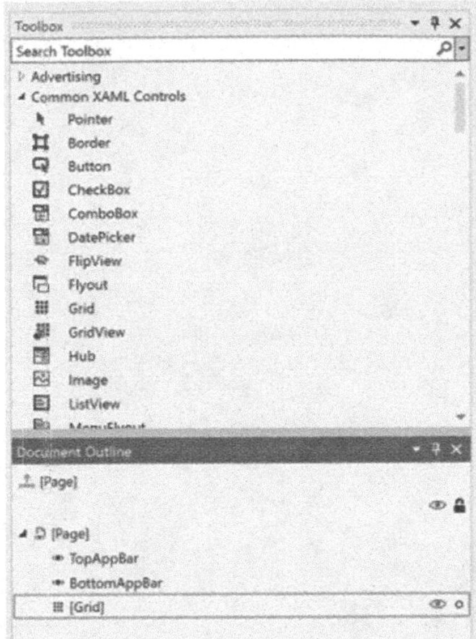

Figure 1-22. *Toolbox and Document Outline panes*

■ **Note** If you examine the images in Figure 1-21 and Figure 1-22 you should be able to see just how the Document Outline pane works. The XAML pane of Figure 1-21 contains a document with a Grid element inside a Page element. This relationship is represented in a tree format within the Document Outline pane in Figure 1-22.

Finally, on the right side of the design surface you can find the Solution Explorer and Properties window. The Solution Explorer maintains a tree-like representation of all the files and folders that are a part of a Universal project. In Visual Studio 2015 (as with all previous versions of Visual Studio since Visual Studio .NET), a solution is a collection of projects. Visual Studio treats solutions as the highest organizational unit within a given instance of the application. Projects are always represented as part of a solution and can only be opened in the context of an overarching solution. Solutions may have virtual folders, loosely coupled files, and projects of varying types within them. Ideally, a solution would contain the various project types: database projects, web application projects, installation projects, Azure projects, and universal projects, along with any build instructions and source control bindings needed to deliver a given solution to a customer, hence the name Solution.

The Properties window works with the document outline and design surface to tweak items that have been placed onto the design surface. Any item selected either through the document outline or directly on the design surface will have its relevant properties displayed in the Properties window. Figure 1-23 shows the Solution Explorer and Properties windows. You can see how the background color of an item on the design surface might be modified using this pane.

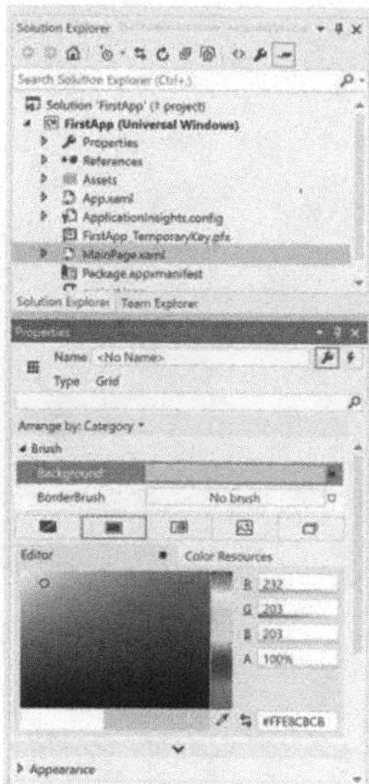

Figure 1-23. *Toolbox and Document Outline panes, again*

Creating Your First Project

Now that you have some acclamation to the Visual Studio 2015 environment, it's time to create your very first project. You will be building a very simple attendance counter UWP app that can be used to keep track of how many people have entered a space. It should have three buttons: one for incrementing the count, one for decrementing the count, and one for resetting the count to zero. It should also have a content area where the current count of people in attendance is presented.

(Don't worry; the samples get more elaborate and complicated as you go along. In the beginning, it is important to minimize complexity so we can focus on getting the primary points you need to understand through quickly.)

Start by firing up Visual Studio 2015. This sample (along with all other samples in this book) was developed using Visual Studio 2015 Enterprise Edition, but the Community Edition will work just as well for any of them.

Select File ➤ New ➤ Project **from the main menu to open up the Visual Studio project selection dialog**. You should now be seeing the Visual Studio project selection dialog in some form. Figure 1-24 shows how the dialog appears on my computer. You will be using Visual C# as the language of choice for this exercise but any one of the supported languages may be used to develop UWP apps.

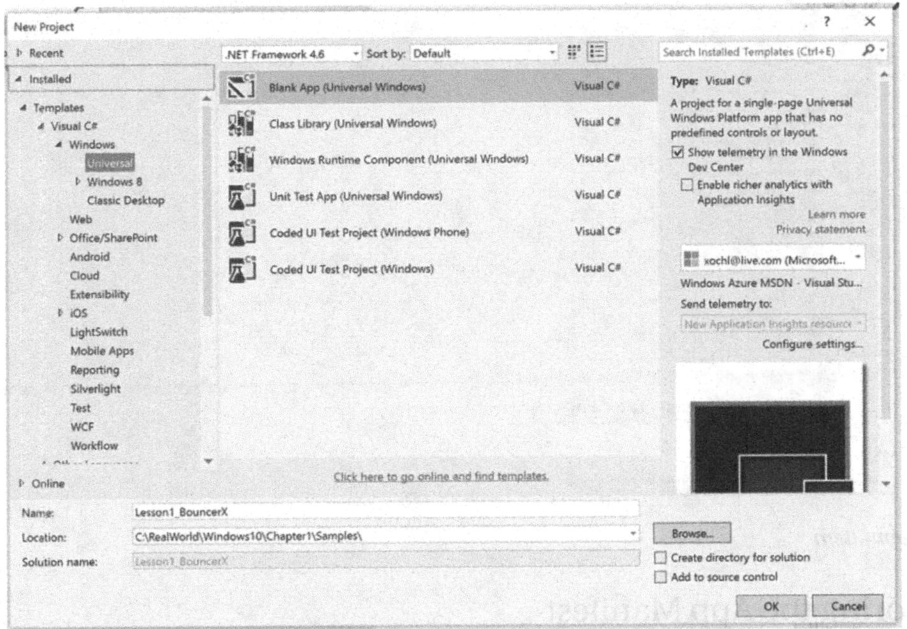

***Figure 1-24.** Project selection dialog*

■ **Note** Presently UWP development can be divided into two layout categories, XAML and HTML. C#, Visual Basic, and C++/Cx all use the same XAML layout engine for rendering their user interfaces. JavaScript uses HTML. Visual Basic and C# have near feature parity in terms of the UWP, meaning both access the same APIs and controls. C++/Cx functions differently but again accesses the same APIs and controls. Because of the difference in technology between XAML and HTML/CSS there are marked differences in the approach to development between these two technologies.

Select Blank App (Universal Windows) and give the project the name *Lesson1_BouncerX* and a suitable location on your workstation. Select OK to generate the project. Once the solution and project are loaded, use the *View* menu item (from the main menu) to ensure that the Toolbox, Document Outline, Solution Explorer, and Properties window are all visible. Figure 1-25 shows the various panes that can be enabled via the View menu item. The document outline option can be found in a sub-menu of view called Other Windows.

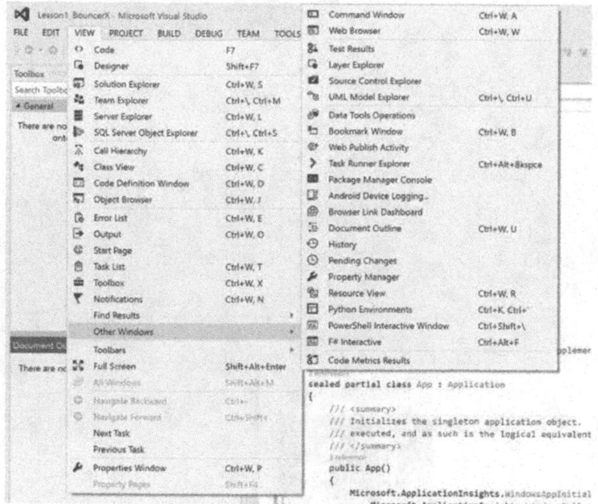

Figure 1-25. *View menu item*

Sidebar: Exploring the App Manifest

At this point, you should have a loaded project with the `App.xaml.cs` file open in the code window. Before you get into the layout or coding of the app, however, you need explore some housekeeping options regarding the type of app this will be, what it will do when installed, how it will look, and the many more things that the manifest allows you to declare.

Look in the Solution Explorer for a file called `Package.appxmanifest`. This is the manifest for the app you are presently working on, so double-click it to open it up. Hopefully the UI representation of this file appears (in my version of Visual Studio 2015 Enterprise Edition I found that the Apache Cordova tools interfered with the product's ability to open this file. Once I uninstalled those specific tools I was once again able to use the designer for manifest files.) Figure 1-26 shows the app manifest user interface that appears when you open `package.appxmanifest`. The app manifest consists of six tabs grouped by the function they serve in helping define your app to the Windows Store and end user machines that install it.

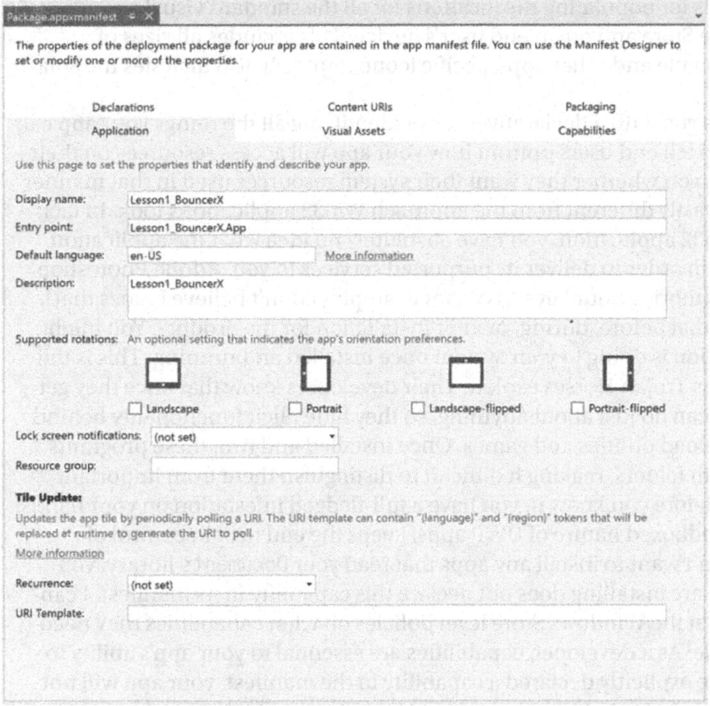

Figure 1-26. App Manifest user interface

The **Application tab** allows you to enter general information about your app. Table 1-2 provides a brief description of some notable items in this tab.

Table 1-2. Application Tab Fields

Name	Description
`Display Name`	The full name of the app. This is the name that will be displayed on the application title bar and will serve as the "name" of the app.
`Entry Point`	According to the documentation, this field is meant to identify the class that runs when the application is started. In practice, we have found that regardless of the value entered here, marking `app.xaml` (or the application startup XAML of your choice) as the application definition for the app will invoke it and ignore this value.
`Description`	Description for the app. The text here is used in the "Set Default Programs" Windows 10 UI.
`Supported Rotations`	Identifies the orientations supported by an app.

The last two fields, Recurrence and URI template, are used as part of the tile update functionality (Live tiles will be covered in greater detail in Chapter 10.) These fields allow you to specify a URI where a template used to render a given app's tile should be pulled from. These templates are XML snippets that the Windows 10 system uses to determine what to display on a given tile with what layout and animation. The Recurrence field tells the system how often the URI specified in the URI Template field should be polled. It has a minimum of every half hour and a maximum poll time of daily.

The **Visual Assets** tab contains fields for populating the locations for all the standard visual assets needed to display your application in the Store and on an end user's device. This includes all sizes of application logos used for the application tile and other app-specific iconography. It also includes the splash screen image.

The next tab, **Capabilities**, provides you with a declarative way of identifying all the things your app can do. Capabilities are a great way for you to tell end users upfront how your app will access resources on their system; it allows them to make a decision on whether they want their system resources used in that manner before installing your UWP app. This is vastly different from the approach Win32 applications took. In fact, for the most part, when you install a Win32 application, you have absolutely no idea what the application might possibly be doing on your system in order to deliver its purported services to you. Adobe Photoshop could be running in the background monitoring your keystrokes, for example (I don't believe it does that), and you would have no way of knowing that before, during, or after installation for the product. You might never know what a given Win32 application is doing to your system once installed and running. This is the area of vulnerability that malware such as Trojan Horses exploit. Their developers know that once they get on your machine as an executable, they can do just about anything, so they hide illicit functionality behind seemingly harmless programs like download utilities and games. Once installed and run, these programs copy malicious software onto your system folders, making it difficult to distinguish them from important components of your operating system. Before you know it, you have a full-fledged infestation on your hands!

Capabilities, combined with the sandboxed nature of UWP apps, keeps the end user in control of the resources apps can access. If you don't want to install any apps that read your `Documents` library, you simply check to ensure that any app you are installing does not declare this capability in its manifest. I can even foresee a day when one can define at the Windows Store level policies on what capabilities they need declared before an install is even possible! As a developer, capabilities are essential to your app's ability to access resources as well. Unless you have explicitly declared a capability in the manifest, your app will not be able to access any APIs associated with that capability at runtime. Hence you can only use what you have specified to your potential end users that you intend on using. At the store level, this security constraint is also enforced. Apps deployed to the store that use undeclared APIs will fail certification and will not make it to the Windows Store. Figure 1-27 shows the Capabilities tab.

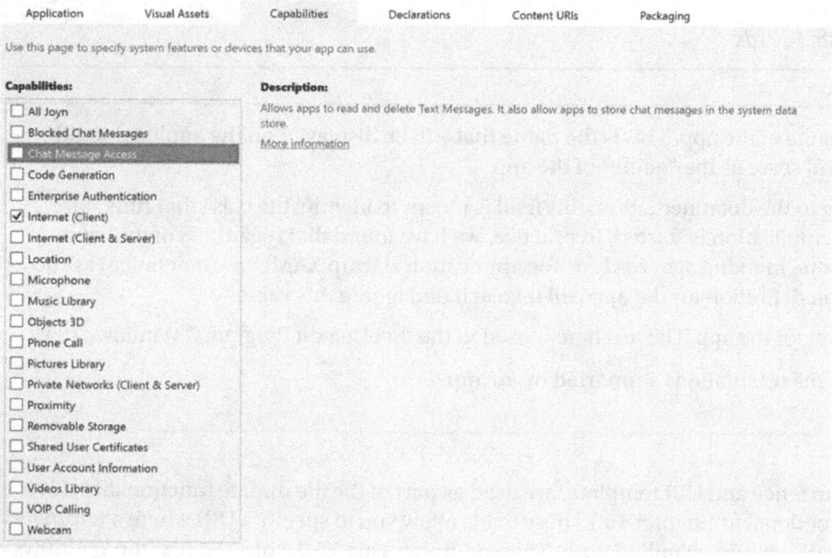

***Figure 1-27.** Capabilities tab of the app manifest*

Table 1-3 itemizes some of the capabilities that can be declared in a UWP app. Please go to `https://msdn.microsoft.com/en-us/library/windows/apps/Hh464936.aspx` for more detailed information on the various capabilities.

Table 1-3. *Capabilities That Can Be Declared in a UWP App*

Name	Description
All Joyn	Allows AllJoyn-enabled apps and devices on a network to discover and interact with each other. AllJoyn is a system that allows devices to advertise and share their abilities with other devices around them. A simple example would be a motion sensor letting a light bulb know no one is in the room it is lighting.
Blocked Chat Messages	Allows apps to read SMS and MMS messages that have been blocked by the Spam Filter app.
Chat Message Access	Allows apps to read and delete text messages. This capability will also allow apps to store text messages in the system data store.
Code Generation	Apps that declare this capability can dynamically generate code.
Internet (Client)	Allows apps to have outbound access the Internet (selected by default). If your app uses the Internet, ensure that this capability is declared.
Internet (Client and Server)	Provides both inbound and outbound access to the Internet. If you are building a server (for instance, for peer-to-peer purposes), this capability is a must. Note that critical ports are always blocked.
Location	Provides the app with access to the GPS location information.
Microphone	Provides the app with access to the microphone's audio feed.
Music Library	Provides management access to files in the Music library.
Phone Call	Allows apps to access all of the phone lines on the device and perform the following functions: Place a call on the phone line and show the system dialer without prompting the user. Access line-related metadata. Access line-related triggers. Allows the user-selected spam filter app to set and check block list and call origin information.
Pictures Library	Provides management access to files in the Pictures library.
Proximity	Allows apps to use NFC or Wi-Fi directly to APIs for connecting to other devices.
Removable Storage	Provides management access to files in removable storage media that is connected to the device.
User Account Information	Gives the app access to the current user's name and picture.
Videos Library	Provides management access to files in the Videos library.
VOIP Calling	Allows the app to access the VOIP calling APIs.
Webcam	Provides the app with access to the webcam's video feed. This capability is necessary for capturing images as well as video.

Capabilities are great in some respects but limiting in others. They provide access to resources but fall short in scenarios where further configuration is needed. This can be good in certain scenarios but lacking in others. Take the case of access to the file system, the Music Library for example. The capability to access this folder is only the beginning of the story; there is also the question of what file types can be accessed, perhaps even what file sizes or file names. **Declarations** round out the capability story given that they are capabilities that require further configuration for them to work. Starting in Chapter 6, you will be using declarations extensively to enable many of the features we will be discussing.

The next tab, **Content URIs**, allows you to specify URIs that can use the `window.external.notify` JavaScript function to send a `ScriptNotify` event to the app. When an app has a certain control called a WebView (essentially a web browser hosted within the app) as part of its user interface, messages may be passed from the web page being viewed by the WebView to the app. WebView has an event, `ScriptNotify`, that is fired when `window.external.notify` is invoked on the web page. This can allow for instances where part (if not all) of your app's user interface is rendered from a web site and, when native UWP functionality is required, your app serves as a broker to the device running it by invoking the appropriate APIs and passing the results back to the web page being hosted. This type of application is sometimes referred to as a hybrid app. To enable this type of interaction in UWP apps, you must declare the URIs that will be using this functionality explicitly.

The final tab, **Packaging**, can be used to specify the properties that identify and describe your app package when it is deployed. Figure 1-28 shows this page.

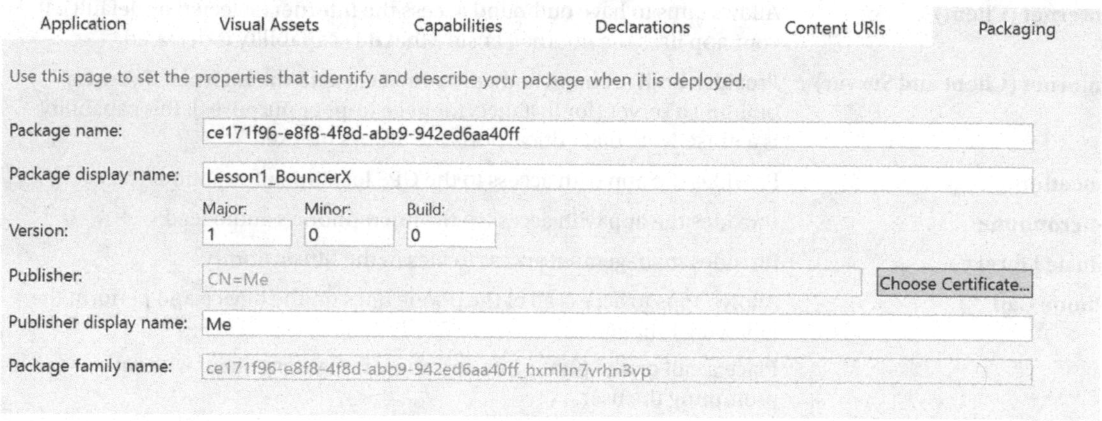

Figure 1-28. *Packaging tab of the app manifest*

Table 1-4 itemizes some relevant fields on the Packaging tab of the `package.appxmanifest` file.

Table 1-4. *Fields in The Packaging Tab*

Name	Description
Package Name	Unique name that identifies the package on the development/test system. This name is replaced when deployed to the Windows Store.
Package Display Name	App name that appears in the Windows Store, also replaced when deployed.
Version	Version string following the format <major>.<minor>.<build>.<revision>
Publisher	Temporarily represents the subject field of the certificate used to sign the app package. Replaced once the app is deployed to the Windows Store.
Publisher Display Name	Name from the Publisher name of the developer web portal.
Package Family	Unique name that identifies the package on the system.

Back to Your First Project

Now that you have a decent understanding of the settings defined in the app manifest, let's get back to building your awesome bouncer UWP app. Close the package.appxmanifest file and open the file called MainPage.xaml.

In the XAML tab, add the bolded sections from Listing 1-3 to the markup.

Listing 1-3. User Interface for BouncerX Attendant Counter

```
<Page x:Class="Lesson1_BouncerX.MainPage"
      xmlns="http://schemas.microsoft.com/winfx/2006/xaml/presentation"
      xmlns:x="http://schemas.microsoft.com/winfx/2006/xaml"
      xmlns:local="using:Lesson1_BouncerX"
      xmlns:d="http://schemas.microsoft.com/expression/blend/2008"
      xmlns:mc="http://schemas.openxmlformats.org/markup-compatibility/2006"
      mc:Ignorable="d">

    <Grid Background="{ThemeResource ApplicationPageBackgroundThemeBrush}">
        <StackPanel Orientation="Vertical"
                    HorizontalAlignment="Center"
                    VerticalAlignment="Center">
            <TextBlock x:Name="txt_attendants"
                       HorizontalAlignment="Center"
                       Text="0 Attendants"
                       FontSize="42"
                       FontFamily="Segoe UI"
                       FontWeight="ExtraLight" />
            <StackPanel Orientation="Horizontal"
                        Margin="0,20,0,0"
                        HorizontalAlignment="Center">
                <Button x:Name="btn_reset"
                        Content="Reset Attendants"
                        Width="200"
                        Height="100"
                        Margin="5" />
                <Button x:Name="btn_remove"
                        Content="Remove Attendant"
                        Width="200"
                        Height="100"
                        Margin="5" />
            </StackPanel>
            <Button x:Name="btn_add"
                    Content="Add Attendant"
                    Width="410"
                    Height="100"
                    Margin="5,50,5,5" />
        </StackPanel>
    </Grid>
</Page>
```

If you are familiar with Silverlight, Windows Phone development, WPF, or you've built some Windows 8 Modern apps, you will probably have a good understanding of what Listing 1-3 is all about. If you have not, don't fret; we will be getting into the controls available to UWP apps and all their uses in the next three chapters. Don't worry so much about what this all means right now. The important thing to note here is that you have added the appropriate controls to the surface and identified all the controls you plan to use in an interactive manner. At this point, the Design tab of your design surface should look something like Figure 1-29. As mentioned, the great thing about the Visual Studio 2015 design surface is that it allows you to see (within limits) how your app will look at runtime. I say "within limits" because this is not a true runtime view of your application, meaning if part of your app user interface relies on data that comes from a web service, it will not be rendered in the design surface at all. For such scenarios, you will have to run the application. Your application stores all information in memory and really does not have much in terms of a user interface so the design surface works fine. We have found that very elaborate user interfaces can give the design surface some trouble, so be warned.

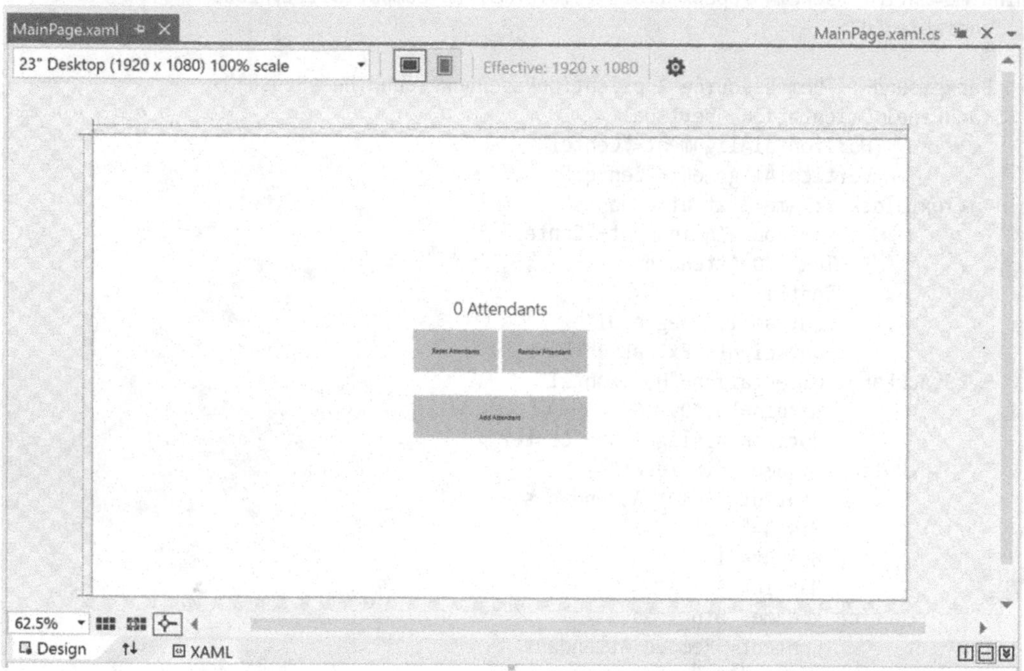

Figure 1-29. *BouncerX design surface*

Visual Studio 2015 comes with a separate tool called Microsoft Blend that can be used for designer-specific workflows that the main IDE cannot handle. These workflows include animations, visual state management, vector graphics drawing, and deep integration into UI styling. Blend provides a far richer designer experience that Visual Studio; it started its life as a competitor to Adobe Flash toolset, so for advanced layout and styling we recommend using Blend. You can use Blend to design your XAML file or open your Visual Studio 2015 project in Blend 2015 at any time by right-clicking the specified project item (click any XAML file in your project or the project itself) and select "Design with Blend."

Right-click anywhere in the main content area of the design surface and select View Code to open the code behind for this page. You should now have the file `MainPage.xaml.cs` open. You need to do a couple of things in this file to enable the functionality you require. First, let's create a centralized method that you can use to display the number of attendants. Listing 1-4 provides the code for a `DisplayAttendants` method that does just this. Add it as a method to the `MainPage` class.

Listing 1-4. Centralized Method for Displaying the Current Number of Attendants

```
private void DisplayAttendants()
        {
            txt_attendants.Text = $"{_attendant_count} attendants";
        }
```

The code in Listing 1-4 is quite straightforward. Given that a class level field `_attendant_count` is defined, this method will display a string in the Text property of the Textbox you previously added to MainPage using a concatenation of the value of `_attendant_count` and the literal string " attendants" (note the space).

Now define the `_attendant_count` variable as an integer field with a default value of zero and then add the following lines in Listing 1-5 to the constructor of MainPage (from Listing 1-4):

Listing 1-5. Event Handler Code for MainPage.xaml.cs Constructor

```
this.Loaded += MainPage_Loaded;
btn_add.Click += Btn_add_Click;
```

Finally add the code from Listing 1-6 to `MainPage.xaml.cs`.

Listing 1-6. Event Handlers for the Page Load and Add Button's Button Clicked Events

```
private void MainPage_Loaded(object sender, RoutedEventArgs e)
{
     DisplayAttendants();
}

private void Btn_add_Click(object sender, RoutedEventArgs e)
{
     _attendant_count++;
     DisplayAttendants();
}
```

The code in Listing 1-6 is also quite self-explanatory. Loaded events are fired when a page first loads; `MianPage_Loaded` simply presents the current number of attendants by invoking `DisplayAttendants` every time a MainPage loads. The other even handler, `btn_add_Click`, is called whenever the Add button is clicked. Whenever this happens, the attendant count is incremented by one and `DisplayAttendants` is once again called. Compiling and running the app at this time should yield an image similar to Figure 1-30. At the time this screenshot was taken, the Add Attendant button had been clicked 13 times.

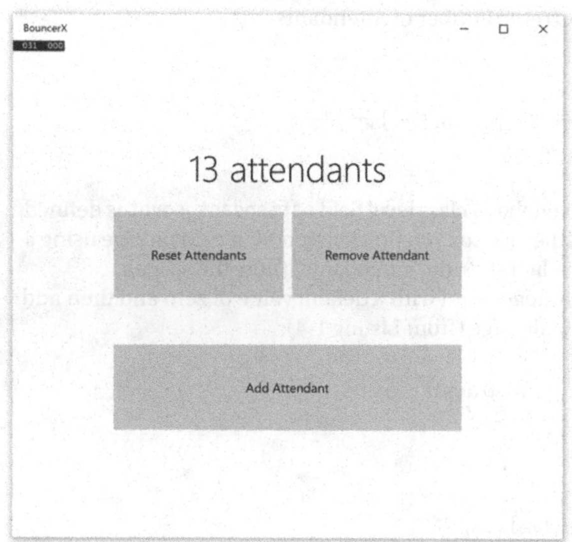

Figure 1-30. *BouncerX running after 13 clicks of the Add Attendant button*

Let's tackle the Remove Attendant button next. When enabling the Add Attendant functionality from the earlier sample, you exclusively used the code behind file to programmatically attach an event handler to the Add Attendant button. For Remove Attendants, we will show how you can accomplish connecting event handlers to the buttons directly from the XAML. This is one of the many triumphs of flexibility that XAML provides to developers. Close `MainPage.xaml.cs` and reopen `MainPage.xaml`. Now alter the definition for `btn_remove` to match the code in Listing 1-7.

Listing 1-7. Adding Event Handling into XAML Markup

```
<Button x:Name="btn_remove"
        Content="Remove Attendant"
        Width="200"
        Height="100"
        Margin="5" Click="RemoveAttendant" />
```

Not much has changed here except for the addition of a new attribute to `btn_remove`. Adding this attribute generates the same functionality as programmatically hooking into the Click event, as you did with `btn_add`. You are not done, though. As it stands, the XAML is aware of the fact that `btn_remove` handles the click event using the method `RemoveAttendant`; however, there is presently no method such as this in the code behind file. You can, of course, open `MainPage.xaml.cs` and add a definition for this event but there is an easier way to do this from here: simply right-click the text `RemoveAttendant` and select **Go to Definition**. Doing so automatically opens `MainPage.xaml.cs` and adds a new method with the same name as the one specified within the XAML Click event. Listing 1-8 provides the full implementation of the `RemoveAttendant` method. Replace the generated stub with it.

Listing 1-8. Event Handler for Remove Button's Clicked Events

```
private void RemoveAttendant(object sender, RoutedEventArgs e)
        {
        if(_attendant_count > 0)
                _attendant_count--;
            DisplayAttendants();
        }
```

Listing 1-8 functions similarly to the event handler for adding attendants with one minor change. Since you are dealing with actual individuals, the attendant count can never be less than zero. Because of this, a Boolean guard condition is used to prevent the value of `_attendant_count` from dropping below zero. At this point, if you run the app, you should be able to both add and remove attendants. The basic function of the app is complete. The final stage is providing the ability to quickly reset the counter so one does not have to restart the app or tediously click the remove attendant button repeatedly until zero is hit. For this last bit of functionality, you will use the design surface provided by Blend, the companion tool for Visual Studio.

Right-click `MainPage.xaml` and select Design in Blend to launch Blend for Visual Studio 2015. Figure 1-31 shows the Blend for Visual Studio 2015 IDE.

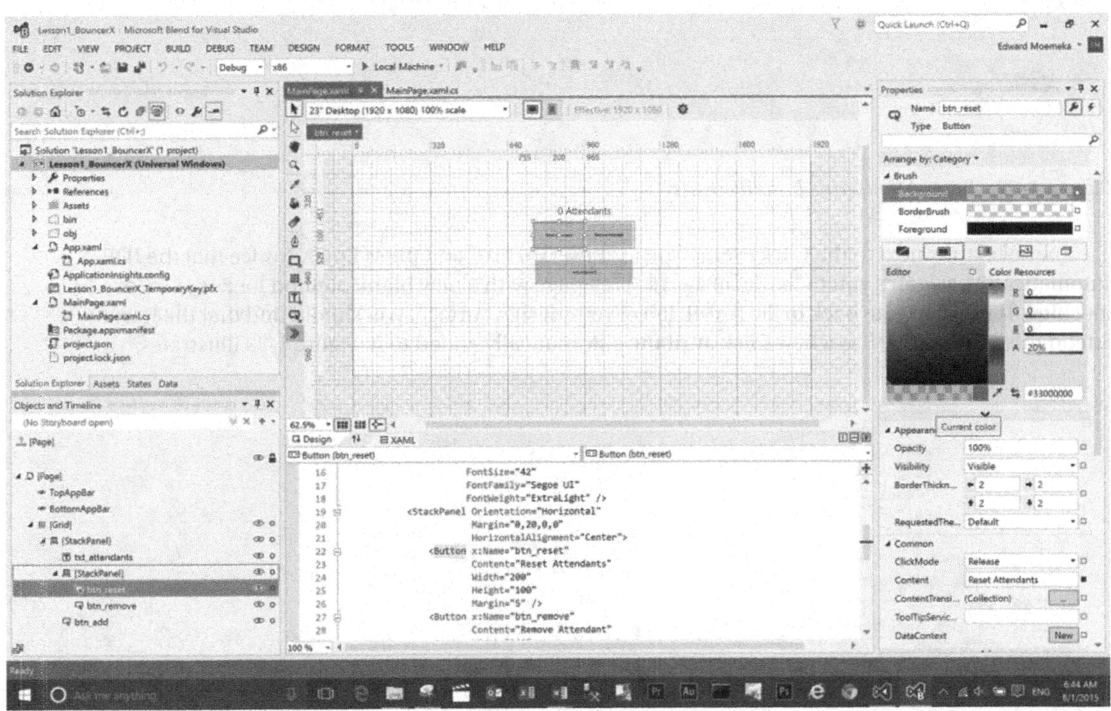

Figure 1-31. *BouncerX project opened in Blend for Visual Studio 2015*

You won't find much difference style-wise between Blend and Visual Studio; this is because the Blend interface has been rebuilt from the ground up on top of the Visual Studio IDE platform. This approach is so integrated that you can accomplish many of the same developer workflows directly in Blend! Be sure to once again use the *View* main menu item to ensure the Solution Explorer, Document Outline, and Properties pane are enabled. You will need them for this exercise.

Let's use Blend now to attach interactivity to the last button in your user interface. Start by selecting the button, Reset Attendants, from the Blend design surface. The Properties window should now show all the properties associated with this control. At the top of the Properties window, to the right of the Name text box, are two buttons, one with a wrench and the other with a lightning bolt. The wrench represents properties of the currently selected design surface item while the lightning bolt represents events of the same item. Click the event button to reveal a Properties pane view similar to the one in Figure 1-32. (The green arrow points to the button to click.)

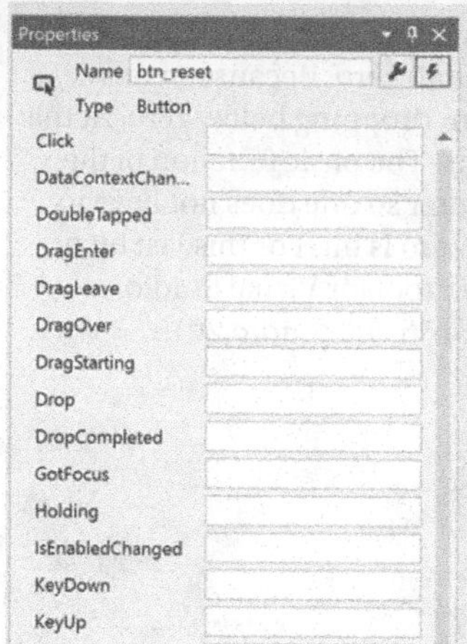

***Figure 1-32.** Reset Attendants button events*

In the textbox next to the Click event, type in "ResetToZero" and press Enter. Notice that the IDE automatically navigates you to the `MainPage.xal.cs` page with a new blank method for `ResetToZero` specified. If you navigate back to the XAML tab of your design surface, you should find that the Reset Attendants button now has a new Click attribute automatically added to it. Figure 1-33 illustrates.

```
<StackPanel Orientation="Horizontal"
            Margin="0,20,0,0"
            HorizontalAlignment="Center">
    <Button x:Name="btn_reset"
            Content="Reset Attendants"
            Width="200"
            Height="100"
            Margin="5"
            Click="ResetToZero" />
    <Button x:Name="btn_remove"
            Content="Remove Attendant"
            Width="200"
            Height="100"
            Margin="5" Click="RemoveAttendant" />
</StackPanel>
```

***Figure 1-33.** Reset Attendants markup with new event handler added automatically by the IDE*

■ **Note** Both Blend and Visual Studio 2015 possess the ability to use the Properties window Events section to attach events to items selected in the design surface. Using this feature is a shortcut to directly adding the events in XAML and then writing the handler in the code behind for the XAML.

Replace ResetToZero with the code in Listing 1-9 to complete the app functionality. If you build and run this app now, you should be able to add attendants, remove them, and also reset the attendant count to zero.

Listing 1-9. Resetting Attendants to Zero

```
private void ResetToZero(object sender, RoutedEventArgs e)
        {
            _attendant_count = 0;
            DisplayAttendants();
        }
```

Listing 1-10 provides the full code for the application.

Listing 1-10. BouncerX App Code Behind

```
using System;
using System.Collections.Generic;
using System.IO;
using System.Linq;
using System.Runtime.InteropServices.WindowsRuntime;
using Windows.Foundation;
using Windows.Foundation.Collections;
using Windows.UI.Xaml;
using Windows.UI.Xaml.Controls;
using Windows.UI.Xaml.Controls.Primitives;
using Windows.UI.Xaml.Data;
using Windows.UI.Xaml.Input;
using Windows.UI.Xaml.Media;
using Windows.UI.Xaml.Navigation;

namespace Lesson1_BouncerX
{
    public sealed partial class MainPage : Page
    {
        int _attendant_count = 0;
        public MainPage()
        {
            this.InitializeComponent();
            this.Loaded += MainPage_Loaded;
            btn_add.Click += Btn_add_Click;
        }

        private void MainPage_Loaded(object sender, RoutedEventArgs e)
        {
            DisplayAttendants();
        }
        private void Btn_add_Click(object sender, RoutedEventArgs e)
        {
            _attendant_count++;
            DisplayAttendants();
        }
```

```
        private void DisplayAttendants()
        {
            txt_attendants.Text = $"{_attendant_count} attendants";
        }

        private void RemoveAttendant(object sender, RoutedEventArgs e)
        {
            if (_attendant_count > 0)
                _attendant_count--;
            DisplayAttendants();
        }

        private void ResetToZero(object sender, RoutedEventArgs e)
        {
            _attendant_count = 0;
            DisplayAttendants();
        }
    }
}
```

Notes on XAML

In the previous section, we pointed out that there are two distinct layout description languages for building UWP app user interfaces. HTML/CSS is one and XAML the other. They both serve the same purpose: giving developers a markup-based declarative technology for representing a user interface. While HTML gives you the best of breed in terms of interoperability and not much more beyond that, XAML offers a rational expression of the layout innovations promised but ultimately never delivered by HTML. You can't have your cake and eat it too, though. While XAML is as powerful and expressive as HTML with complete predictability as far as layout results, an app built using this technology will likely never run anywhere else unless a rewrite occurs.

■ **Note** Don't be too hard on HTML. Building technologies to a specification is quite difficult. Check out the various implementations of XAML within Microsoft if you doubt this point. You will find the same kind of nuanced deviation between WPF, Silverlight, and UWP apps.

Namespaces

One distinction between HTML and XAML is with the explicit reliance on XML namespaces. To see this in action, let's take a look at the top level page element from Listing 1-1. In Listing 1-11, we have highlighted the relevant attributes, those specific to namespace definition.

Listing 1-11. Top-Level XAML Element with Default Namespaces Defined

```
<Page x:Class="Lesson1_BouncerX.MainPage"
      xmlns="http://schemas.microsoft.com/winfx/2006/xaml/presentation"
      xmlns:x="http://schemas.microsoft.com/winfx/2006/xaml"
      xmlns:local="using:Lesson1_BouncerX"
      xmlns:d="http://schemas.microsoft.com/expression/blend/2008"
      xmlns:mc="http://schemas.openxmlformats.org/markup-compatibility/2006"
      mc:Ignorable="d">
```

Two of the namespaces defined in Listing 1-11 are necessary for all XAML UI documents: `xmlns=http://schemas.microsoft.com/winfx/2006/xaml/presentation` and `xmlns:x="http://schemas.microsoft.com/winfx/2006/xaml"`. The first of the two namespaces is the standard user interface namespace; it contains the elements used to represent all the user interface controls that are packaged as part of the Universal Windows Platform. XAML follows standard XML syntax, so although these are represented here without a prefix, it is only by convention. You *could* apply a prefix to the `xmlns=http://schemas.microsoft.com/winfx/2006/xaml/presentation` namespace but that would mean every UI element you specify would need to use that prefix. So if `xmlns=http://schemas.microsoft.com/winfx/2006/xaml/presentation` was defined as `xmlns:ui=http://schemas.microsoft.com/winfx/2006/xaml/presentation`, you would have to define `<Page />` as `<ui:Page />`.

The second default required namespace is often referred to as the XAML language namespace. It contains keywords such as `Name`, `Key`, and `Class` and is used to bind a XAML document to the underlying technology that a specific implementation represents. Unlike HTML, which is primarily used to define user interfaces in a very specific way, XAML has been developed so that it can be used to declaratively represent just about anything. You need look no further that the `App.xaml` file to see this flexibility in action. Whereas `MainPage.xaml` is used to define the layout and user interface for that specific page, `App.xaml` is used to define the application as a whole and is not concerned with any specific user interface at all. XAML can do this because it has been designed such that almost anything expressed in the XAML language can also be represented in a standard procedural language. In many cases, the XAML document is in fact first converted to its procedural counterpart and then executed. In UWPs, XAML follows this code generation pattern such that elements within a XAML document are instantiated into objects at runtime, with the attributes of those elements used to set the corresponding properties of the underlying objects.

Using this approach, in most cases the `Name` attribute will be translated into the name of a variable containing the instantiated object that a XAML element represents while the `Class` attribute maps to a class broken into two parts. One part is system generated and contains the procedural expression of the XAML document while the other is a user-controlled counterpart used for adding user-controlled behavior. Listing 1-12 shows the XAML definition for `MainPage.xaml` once again.

■ **Note** The process of converting XAML documents to an object structure is far more involved than this and well beyond the scope of this text. More importantly, because this is an abstraction technology, understanding the inner workings of how it provides its services is far less important that understanding the services it actually provides.

Listing 1-12. User Interface for BouncerX Attendant Counter

```
<Page x:Class="Lesson1_BouncerX.MainPage"
      xmlns="http://schemas.microsoft.com/winfx/2006/xaml/presentation"
      xmlns:x="http://schemas.microsoft.com/winfx/2006/xaml"
      xmlns:local="using:Lesson1_BouncerX"
      xmlns:d="http://schemas.microsoft.com/expression/blend/2008"
      xmlns:mc="http://schemas.openxmlformats.org/markup-compatibility/2006"
      mc:Ignorable="d">

    <Grid Background="{ThemeResource ApplicationPageBackgroundThemeBrush}">
        <StackPanel Orientation="Vertical"
                    HorizontalAlignment="Center"
                    VerticalAlignment="Center">
```

```
            <TextBlock x:Name="txt_attendants"
                       HorizontalAlignment="Center"
                       Text="0 Attendants"
                       FontSize="42"
                       FontFamily="Segoe UI"
                       FontWeight="ExtraLight" />
            <StackPanel Orientation="Horizontal"
                        Margin="0,20,0,0"
                        HorizontalAlignment="Center">
                <Button x:Name="btn_reset"
                        Content="Reset Attendants"
                        Width="200"
                        Height="100"
                        Margin="5" />
                <Button x:Name="btn_remove"
                        Content="Remove Attendant"
                        Width="200"
                        Height="100"
                        Margin="5" />
            </StackPanel>
            <Button x:Name="btn_add"
                    Content="Add Attendant"
                    Width="410"
                    Height="100"
                    Margin="5,50,5,5" />
        </StackPanel>
    </Grid>
</Page>
```

Listing 1-12 shows the procedural expression of this XAML document in C# code. Note that each element with an x:Name attribute defined in Listing 1-12 has a corresponding field in Listing 1-13.

Listing 1-13. Procedural Expression of MainPage.xaml in C#

```
namespace Lesson1_BouncerX
{
    partial class MainPage : Page
    {

        [GeneratedCodeAttribute("Microsoft.Windows.UI.Xaml.Build.Tasks"," 14.0.0.0")]
        private TextBlock txt_attendants;
        [GeneratedCodeAttribute("Microsoft.Windows.UI.Xaml.Build.Tasks"," 14.0.0.0")]
        private Button btn_add;
        [GeneratedCodeAttribute("Microsoft.Windows.UI.Xaml.Build.Tasks"," 14.0.0.0")]
        private Button btn_reset;
        [GeneratedCodeAttribute("Microsoft.Windows.UI.Xaml.Build.Tasks"," 14.0.0.0")]
        private Button btn_remove;
        [GeneratedCodeAttribute("Microsoft.Windows.UI.Xaml.Build.Tasks"," 14.0.0.0")]
        private bool _contentLoaded;

        /// <summary>
        /// InitializeComponent()
        /// </summary>
```

```
        [GeneratedCodeAttribute("Microsoft.Windows.UI.Xaml.Build.Tasks"," 14.0.0.0")]
        [DebuggerNonUserCodeAttribute()]
        public void InitializeComponent()
        {
            if (_contentLoaded)
                return;

            _contentLoaded = true;

            Uri resourceLocator = new global::System.Uri("ms-appx:///MainPage.xaml");
            Application.LoadComponent(this, resourceLocator, ComponentResourceLocation.
            Application);
        }

    }
}
```

The other two namespaces are far less important. `xmlns:mc="http://schemas.openxmlformats.org/markup-compatibility/2006"` is primarily used for compatibility. In the case of the document in Listing 1-12, the `mc:Ignorable="d"` attribute is used to ignore any items from the `xmlns:d=http://schemas.microsoft.com/expression/blend/2008` namespace, which is a namespace for design time tools to use for storing information in the XAML document to help with the design process.

Microsoft has done a great job of including many of the user interface elements a developer will need to build their UWP apps but there are always instances where you want to utilize a custom component, whether created by yourself or a third party. Since XAML elements are representations of object instances, it calls to question how a developer might include new objects not already defined in the UWP control set or any of the other default namespaces XAML automatically provides. As you have seen thus far, XAML rightfully uses namespaces to achieve this for the built in controls, thus making it 100% XML compliant in this regard. In the case of custom components, namespace takes on an additional meaning, referring here to the actual procedural language namespace that the object is a part of. In the old days of Silverlight and WPF, namespaces were declared into scope using the notation `clr-namespace:<namespace name>` so it was clear to developers that in this case the namespace being imported was an actual CLR namespace. This changed in Windows 8/8.1 to the more consistent `using:<namespace name>`, the pattern used to import namespaces in C# and C++. This later notation is what Windows 10 UWP apps use as well. In Listing 1-12, all classes associated with the current project's default namespace Lesson1_BouncerX are imported into the XAML document using the notation `xmlns:local="using:Lesson1_BouncerX"`. If you defined a class, Bounce, as a user interface component, you could then use it in the document as follows: `<local:Bounce />`.

Elements

We briefly explored the relationship between elements and the objects they represent in the last section. In general, two key features separate element definition in XAML from the same in HTML. Firstly, an element specified in a XAML document is functionally the same as instantiating its corresponding class by calling that class' default constructor. Secondly, an attribute defined on a XAML element with a value specified is functionally the same as setting the value of the property on the corresponding object that shares its name. The implications of this general rule are quite clear. Every element in a XAML document must have a corresponding object that it represents. This object must have its class definition in scope in the document through the use of the namespace import feature discussed in the previous section. Similarly, every attribute defined in a XAML document must have a corresponding public property defined in the class its element represents. Listing 1-14 shows the TextBlock element in Listing 1-12 and how it could be defined programmatically.

Listing 1-14. Programmatic Definition of a TextBlock

```
<TextBlock x:Name="txt_attendants"
                    HorizontalAlignment="Center"
                    Text="0 Attendants"
                    FontSize="42"
                    FontFamily="Segoe UI"
                    FontWeight="ExtraLight" />

TextBlock txt_attendants_prog = new TextBlock();
txt_attendants_prog.HorizontalAlignment = HorizontalAlignment.Center;
txt_attendants_prog.Text = "0 attendants";
txt_attendants_prog.FontFamily = new FontFamily("Segoe UI");
txt_attendants_prog.FontSize = 42;
txt_attendants_prog.FontWeight = Windows.UI.Text.FontWeights.ExtraLight;
```

Attributes are a fast and easy way of associating properties to object elements but they can be impossible to use in scenarios where rich composition in required. Another highlight of XAML in comparison to a technology such as WinForms is its ability to facilitate rich composition. In Listing 1-12, you saw the use of several buttons to enable incrementing, decrementing, and resetting of the attendance counter. These buttons express their purpose with the text content they contain. If you examine the `Content` property of the `Button` class, however, you will note that it is of type `Object`, meaning any type may be set to the `Content` property of a `Button`. Exposing the content of a `Button` in this manner allows the presentation of a `Button` to be composed in any number of ways. You could, for instance, use an Image as the content for the button. The problem is that Image is an element while the `Content` property is exposed as an attribute on the TextBlock element.

To help alleviate this, a new class of element, called a Property Element, can be used. Property Elements have two defining characteristics. As with attributes, they represent the assignment of a value to a property on an overarching element in a XAML document. As such, Property Elements must be contained within the element they are representing an assignment to.

Let's explore a scenario where this would come in handy. One major problem with the previous implementation of BouncerX is that all the buttons look the same. This could potentially lead to any number of hitting-the-wrong-button-at-the-wrong-instance class problems, most notably the catastrophic instance where the Reset Attendants button is mistakenly hit. Let's present the various buttons of the app with a subtle distinguishing characteristic so an end user can easily tell the difference between each button. Setting the entire background color for each button to a different value would work but would deviate too far from the overall. An ideal compromise would be to include a color coded underline for the text in each button. This type of addition would be impossible in WinForms without rolling you own custom button. In XAML, with Property elements you can simply compose the content of each button such that it contains an underlined TextBlock. Listing 1-15 shows the BouncerX user interface from Listing 1-12 expanded to use a property element and to utilize rich composition.

Listing 1-15. Rich Composition with Property Elements

```
<Page x:Class="Lesson1_BouncerX.MainPage"
    xmlns="http://schemas.microsoft.com/winfx/2006/xaml/presentation"
    xmlns:x="http://schemas.microsoft.com/winfx/2006/xaml"
    xmlns:local="using:Lesson1_BouncerX"
    xmlns:d="http://schemas.microsoft.com/expression/blend/2008"
    xmlns:mc="http://schemas.openxmlformats.org/markup-compatibility/2006"
    mc:Ignorable="d">
```

```
<Grid Background="{ThemeResource ApplicationPageBackgroundThemeBrush}">
    <StackPanel Orientation="Vertical"
                HorizontalAlignment="Center"
                VerticalAlignment="Center">
        <TextBlock x:Name="txt_attendants"
                   HorizontalAlignment="Center"
                   Text="0 Attendants"
                   FontSize="42"
                   FontFamily="Segoe UI"
                   FontWeight="ExtraLight" />
        <StackPanel Orientation="Horizontal"
                    Margin="0,20,0,0"
                    HorizontalAlignment="Center">
            <Button x:Name="btn_reset"
                    Width="200"
                    Height="100"
                    Margin="5"
                    Click="ResetToZero">
                <Button.Content>
                    <Border Padding="20"
                            BorderThickness="0,0,0,5"
                            BorderBrush="Red">
                        <TextBlock Text="Reset Attendants" />
                    </Border>
                </Button.Content>
            </Button>
            <Button x:Name="btn_remove"
                    Width="200"
                    Height="100"
                    Margin="5"
                    Click="RemoveAttendant">
                <Button.Content>
                    <Border Padding="20"
                            BorderThickness="0,0,0,5"
                            BorderBrush="Yellow">
                        <TextBlock Text="Remove Attendant" />
                    </Border>
                </Button.Content>
            </Button>
        </StackPanel>
        <Button x:Name="btn_add"
                Width="410"
                Height="100"
                Margin="5,50,5,5">
            <Button.Content>
                <Border Padding="100,20,100,20"
                        BorderThickness="0,0,0,5"
                        BorderBrush="Green">
                    <TextBlock Text="Add Attendant" />
                </Border>
            </Button.Content>
```

```
            </Button>
        </StackPanel>
    </Grid>
</Page>
```

You haven't done anything too fancy in Listing 1-15. First, instead of setting the Content attribute on the Button elements themselves, you use a Button.Content property element within the element's tags. Inside this element you then layout the new user interface for the button's content (again, we will be going over the various controls and how they work in Chapters 2, 3, and 4, so don't worry if you don't understand what these controls do right now.) If you run the BouncerX project, you should now see a view similar to Figure 1-34.

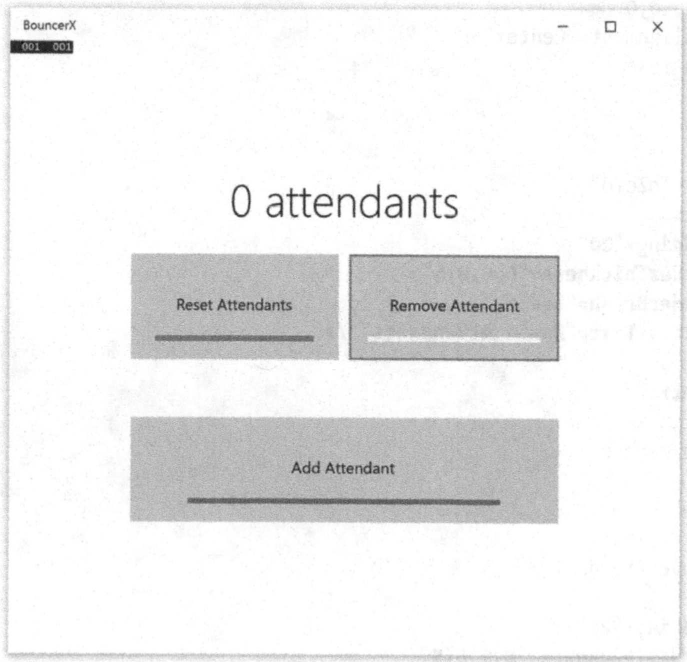

Figure 1-34. *BouncerX UWP app with rich composition applied to buttons*

Binding and Value Converters

So far your BouncerX UWP is looking great, but it falls short of the mark in terms of using standard object-oriented patterns and practices. The very critical attendance count has been left "open" within the MainPage.xaml.cs class. MainPage should provide the functionality to increment, decrement, and reset the attendance count but should it "know" how to do those things. If the programming logic needed to accomplish these functions is directly embedded into your UI controller class, MainPage.xaml.cs, there is no telling how complicated and convoluted the code base within this file might become once you begin to enhance BouncerX. You might want to move the storage of the attendance count to a database or web service in the future. Conventional thinking is that this kind of information, while important, is irrelevant to MainPage.xaml.cs. Its job is to connect the user's interactions with the components that perform the actual actions. Let's create a new class, Occasion, which will represent a given occasion that our end user might be monitoring. To get started, right-click your project in Visual Studio and select Add ➤ New Item. From the Add New Item dialog, select Class. Name the file Occasion.cs and click Add to add it to your project. Figure 1-35 illustrates.

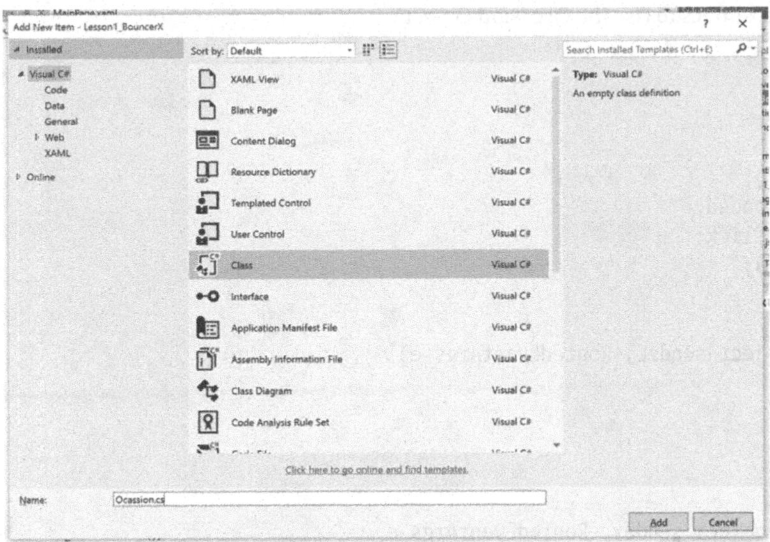

Figure 1-35. Adding a new item to a project

Place the code from Listing 1-16 into the occasion file.

Listing 1-16. The Occasion Class Definition

```
public class Occasion
{
    public int AttendanceCount { get; private set; }

    public void Enter()
    {
        AttendanceCount++;
    }

    public void Leave()
    {
        if (AttendanceCount > 0)
            AttendanceCount--;
    }
}
```

The `Occasion` class simply encapsulates the function of entering or leaving an event so that a consumer of this object does not have to know anything about how attendance is internally kept. You might in the future choose to persist the value to the file system so catastrophic failures do not wipe out your counts. This is the business of the `Occasion` class, not `MainPage`. To fully remove all knowledge of the counts, you must also modify `MainPage.xaml.cs` so that it uses the `Occasion` class rather than using the class level field `_attendance_count`. Listing 1-17 shows the changes that need to be made.

Listing 1-17. Changing MainPage.xaml.cs to Use the Occasion Object

```
Occasion _occasion;

public MainPage()
{
    this.InitializeComponent();
    this.Loaded += MainPage_Loaded;
    btn_add.Click += Btn_add_Click;
    _occasion = new Occasion();
}

private void Btn_add_Click(object sender, RoutedEventArgs e)
{
    _occasion.Enter();
    DisplayAttendants();
}

private void RemoveAttendant(object sender, RoutedEventArgs e)
{
    _occasion.Leave();
    DisplayAttendants();
}

private void ResetToZero(object sender, RoutedEventArgs e)
{
    _occasion = new Occasion();
    DisplayAttendants();
}
```

In Listing 1-17, you replace the int variable `_attendance_count` with an `Occasion` variable. You initialize `_occasion` in the constructor and recreate it each time `ResetToZero` is called. You then map `Btn_add_Click` and `RemoveAttendant` to `_occasion.Enter()` and `_occasion.Leave()`, respectively. Looking at this code, it is easy to see what occasion does without exposing how it does it, but you still have work to do. `DisplayAttendants` needs to be modified to support this new approach. One simple change assignment operation within this method satisfies this: `txt_attendants.Text = $"{_occasion.AttendanceCount} attendants"`.

It might not seem so to the "untrained eye," but this type of explicit assignment is less than ideal. In many cases, multiple attributes of a XAML element will need to be set to present a meaningful user interface to the user. Exposing the values to be assigned to the code behind class file `MainPage.xaml.cs` would once again break encapsulation. Even if these values are bundled into related objects (as you did with the `Occasion` class), forcing MainPage to "know" what values within that object correspond to the designated attributes in the XAML can be confusing, difficult to maintain, and prohibitive towards enhancement. Finally, using this technique diminishes the declarative nature of XAML. A more ideal approach would be to connect the elements themselves with an object that represents all the data the element needs to present itself. The developer can then declaratively decide, in XAML, which attributes it wants populated with which data values. Databinding does just that.

Data binding is a technology in XAML/UWP that allows you to connect the underlying object of a XAML element to a generic data source, called a DataContext, such that attributes of that element can use data from that data source to populate the underlying object's properties. Using this technique, rather than directly setting the value of `Text` on `txt_attendance`, you can just bind the occasion instance `_occasion` to `txt_attendance`. Listing 1-18 shows how `DisplayAttendants` now looks.

Listing 1-18. DisplayAttendants Method Definition

```
private void DisplayAttendants()
{
    txt_attendants.DataContext = null;
    txt_attendants.DataContext = _occasion;
}
```

In Listing 1-14, you set the DataContext for `txt_attendants` to the class level instance of `_occasion` immediately after setting it to null. This pattern essentially refreshes the DataContext values. The final step to enable this change is to modify the TextBlock definition such that it enables data binding. Listing 1-19 shows the changes you make to `MainPage.xaml` to facilitate data binding for `txt_attendants`.

Listing 1-19. Enabling Data Binding on the Attendance Count Text Block

```
<TextBlock x:Name="txt_attendants"
                        HorizontalAlignment="Center"
                        Text="{Binding AttendanceCount}"
                        FontSize="42"
                        FontFamily="Segoe UI"
                        FontWeight="ExtraLight" />
```

You can see from Listing 1-8 and 1-18 the power in approaching attribute assignment with a declarative mindset. Once again, `MainPage.xaml.cs` has been left to simply connect things. All assignment is now happening where it should, in the XAML file itself. There is still one more problem you have to face, though. Figure 1-36 shows the app when it is run.

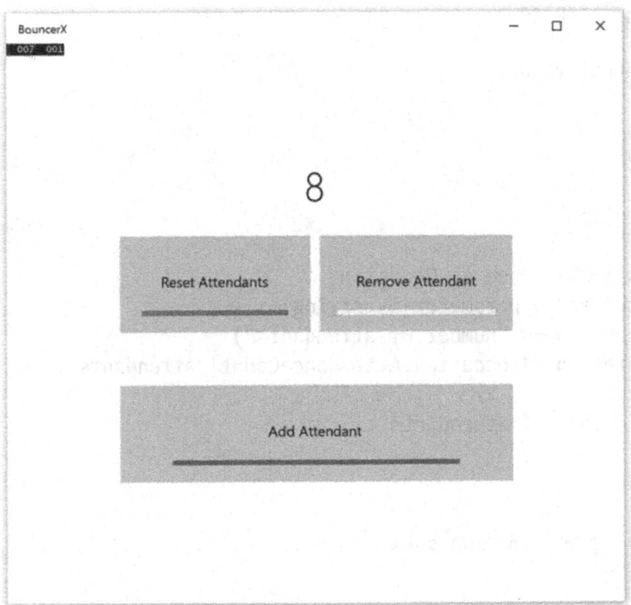

Figure 1-36. *BouncerX after binding is enabled*

The "attendants" part of your attendants display string is now gone. This makes sense since you were concatenating it to the attendance count previously and that bit of functionality has changed. The encapsulation story is also yet to be fully realized. Yes, you have moved the assignment of attributes from a procedural approach to a declarative one but the problem of having to "know" is still not solved. Looking at Listing 1-19, you should see the problem. The property `AttendantsCount` is now being directly referenced in the XAML, meaning you have now propagated the procedural-ness of the procedural part of your UWP app onto your user interface! **Value converters** provide an elegant mechanism for solving both of these problems.

XAML/UWP value converters are objects that can be called upon to perform custom conversions from type to another. They are used in binding scenarios where the value being set does not match the type expected by the attribute/property being bound to. Because they are applied in a declarative manner and because they provide a mechanism to pass parameters into the converter (you can use the parameter to conditionally perform multiple kinds of conversions within the same converter), they are an ideal final step to create a truly code-agnostic XAML user interface. Listing 1-20 shows the code for an `OccasionConverter` class. Add a new class to your project and populate it with this code.

Listing 1-20. A Simple Value Converter

```
public class OccasionConverter : IValueConverter
    {
        /// <summary>
        /// For when converting the databound object into a
        /// value that can be displayed
        /// </summary>
        /// <param name="value"></param>
        /// <param name="targetType"></param>
        /// <param name="parameter"></param>
        /// <param name="language"></param>
        /// <returns></returns>
        public object Convert(object value,
            Type targetType,
            object parameter,
            string language)
        {
            if (value is Occasion)
            {
                var occasion = value as Occasion;
                var ui_command = parameter as string;
                if (ui_command == "number of attendants")
                    return $"{occasion.AttendanceCount} attendants";
            }
            return "Unknown number of attendants";
        }

        /// <summary>
        /// For when saving binding information back to
        /// the databound object
        /// </summary>
        /// <param name="value"></param>
        /// <param name="targetType"></param>
        /// <param name="parameter"></param>
        /// <param name="language"></param>
```

```
        /// <returns></returns>
        public object ConvertBack(object value,
                Type targetType,
                object parameter,
                string language)
        {
                throw new NotImplementedException();
        }
    }
```

Listing 1-20 illustrates a sample implementation of a value converter. Value converters must implement the interface IValueConverter. This interface expects instantiable classes that support it to have two concretely functions defined: Convert and ConvertBack. Convert converts the value bound to a format that the attribute doing the binding can support. ConvertBack does the reverse: it applies to controls that allow user input. Convert does a number of important things: first, it checks to ensure that the value being passed into it, the value you set DataContext to, is an instance of Occassion. If so, it casts the instance to Occassion and also casts the parameter argument to a local string object ui_command. You do this in order to abstract the XAML declaration away from any aspects of the data providing the object model. You now test to see the value of ui_command and, based on that value, do a conversion based on the appropriate property of Occassion. If it isn't obvious yet, what you are doing here is abstracting away the need for anyone defining this user interface to explicitly know structural details of the objects that provide it data. The other thing happening here is the ability to format what is presented as data to the attribute doing the binding. When you bound directly to AttendantsCount property in Occassion, you lost the ability to control how that value was presented. Because value converters sit between the data being bound and the attribute doing the binding, you are free to format that data as needed (or even throw it away entirely).

As you can see from Listing 1-21, by using this pattern your XAML now has no knowledge of Occassion or any of its properties. Run this app now and it should look like Figure 1-25.

Listing 1-21. Modified MainPage.xaml. Changes Are in Bold

```
<Page x:Class="Lesson1_BouncerX.MainPage"
    xmlns="http://schemas.microsoft.com/winfx/2006/xaml/presentation"
    xmlns:x="http://schemas.microsoft.com/winfx/2006/xaml"
    xmlns:local="using:Lesson1_BouncerX"
    xmlns:d="http://schemas.microsoft.com/expression/blend/2008"
    xmlns:mc="http://schemas.openxmlformats.org/markup-compatibility/2006"
    mc:Ignorable="d">
  <Page.Resources>
    <local:OccassionConverter x:Key="attendant_ext" />
  </Page.Resources>
  <Grid Background="{ThemeResource ApplicationPageBackgroundThemeBrush}">
    <StackPanel Orientation="Vertical"
                HorizontalAlignment="Center"
                VerticalAlignment="Center">
      <TextBlock x:Name="txt_attendants"
                 HorizontalAlignment="Center"
                 Text="{Binding Converter={StaticResource attendant_ext},
                        ConverterParameter='number of attendants'}"
                 FontSize="42"
                 FontFamily="Segoe UI"
                 FontWeight="ExtraLight" />
      <StackPanel Orientation="Horizontal"
```

```
                    Margin="0,20,0,0"
                    HorizontalAlignment="Center">
                <Button x:Name="btn_reset"
                    Width="200"
                    Height="100"
                    Margin="5"
                    Click="ResetToZero">
                    <Button.Content>
                        <Border Padding="20"
                                BorderThickness="0,0,0,5"
                                BorderBrush="Red">
                            <TextBlock Text="Reset Attendants"
                                       HorizontalAlignment="Left"
                                       VerticalAlignment="Center" />
                        </Border>
                    </Button.Content>
                </Button>
                <Button x:Name="btn_remove"
                    Width="200"
                    Height="100"
                    Margin="5"
                    Click="RemoveAttendant">
                    <Button.Content>
                        <Border Padding="20"
                                BorderThickness="0,0,0,5"
                                BorderBrush="Yellow">
                            <TextBlock Text="Remove Attendant"
                                       HorizontalAlignment="Left"
                                       VerticalAlignment="Center" />

                        </Border>
                    </Button.Content>
                </Button>
            </StackPanel>
            <Button x:Name="btn_add"
                    Width="410"
                    Height="100"
                    Margin="5,50,5,5">
                <Button.Content>
                    <Border Padding="100,20,100,20"
                            BorderThickness="0,0,0,5"
                            BorderBrush="Green">
                        <TextBlock Text="Add Attendant" />
                    </Border>
                </Button.Content>
            </Button>
        </StackPanel>
    </Grid>
</Page>
```

Summary

Although what you see what on the surface looks like a sensible incremental upgrade (read boring), Windows 10 is undoubtedly a powerful, innovative platform that brings enterprises, device users, gamers, developers, and general purpose computing lovers together in one service-centric community. Developing for it is also somewhat so. The broad review of Windows 10 in this chapter should prepare you for the basics covered in the next chapter and give you the foundational knowledge you need for Windows 10 app development. You learned the following:

- The traits, features, and properties of interacting with the Windows 10 UI
- The various technologies that can be used in Windows 10 development
- Where to access the tools you need to develop for Windows 10
- How to build a Windows 10 UWP app
- What XAML is and how it is used in Windows 10 development

CHAPTER 2

Basic Controls

Modern Windows user interface programming has always involved some form of control use. Controls can be described as reusable user interface elements that encapsulate predictable behavior in the form of user experience. This tenet of Windows development hasn't changed with Windows 10. In this chapter, you will learn about the basic controls that are exposed to you as a Windows 10 UWP developer. In the next chapter, you will focus on data controls, which are controls that represent data in a structured, meaningful way.

As stated in Chapter 1, Windows 10 UWP development can be approached using one of two user interface rendering engines available to Windows 10 developers, HTML5 and XAML. The samples in this chapter build on concepts introduced in Chapter 1 and will utilize XAML and C# as the main languages. Many of them can be easily ported to any other UWP-supported language.

Setting Up a Project

Let's start this chapter with a quick walkthrough of creating a Universal Windows Platform (UWP) project. You will create the proverbial "Hello World" application, in this case, "Hello Windows 10!"

Although you can do most of your development and user interface layout with any XML-compatible application (or Notepad, if you desire), you need Visual Studio 2015 to compile your app into the app package discussed in Chapter 1. Visual Studio also provides some deployment workflow automation tools that can be invaluable to a Windows 10 developer building apps for the Windows Store.

To start, launch Visual Studio 2015. Figure 2-1 shows how the Visual Studio 2015 IDE looks on my machine. If you've changed the color scheme for Visual Studio 2015, modified your preferences, or installed add-ins for various other technologies, you might get a different view.

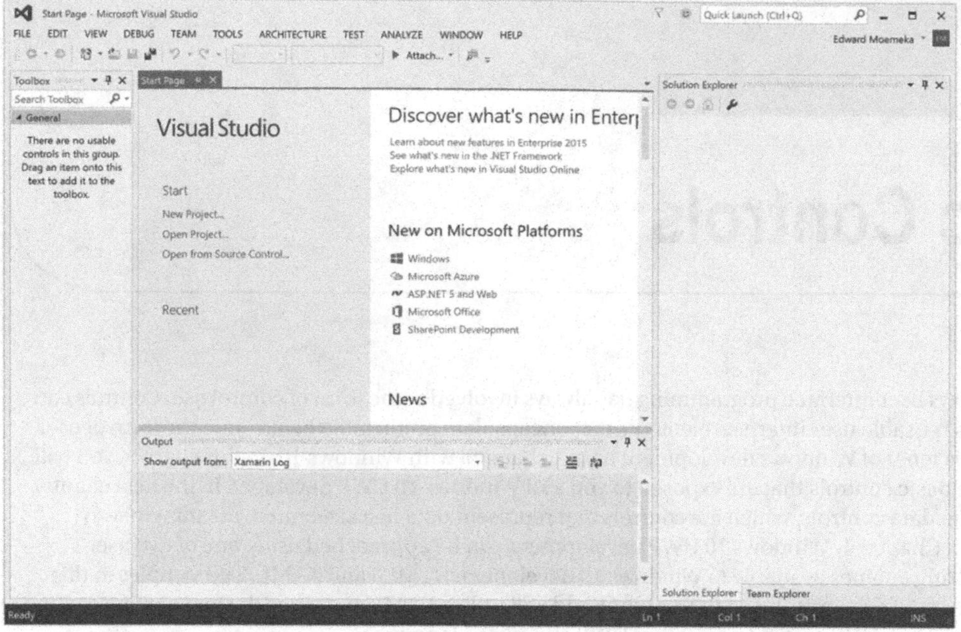

Figure 2-1. Visual Studio 2015 Enterprise edition

This chapter doesn't spend time walking through the various pieces of the IDE; for that, please consult *Pro Visual Studio 2012* by Adam Freeman (Apress 2012). For the purpose of this exercise, the important sections to note are the central content area, the Toolbox to the left of that, and the Solution Explorer to the right of it. In a moment, you'll create a new project and see how these areas on the screen "light up" when a project is in scope. This is because they are, like many of the other views in Visual Studio 2015, context aware. Before you move on to the next steps, take a moment to play around with the IDE layout. You can shift, resize, detach, attach, pin, and unpin most panes in Visual Studio 2015. You can even drag the entire content area to another screen and maximize it, effectively dedicating an entire screen to content with no menus, toolbars, or distractions.

You can create a new project by selecting File ➤ New ➤ Project. The resulting dialog looks like Figure 2-2 on my machine.

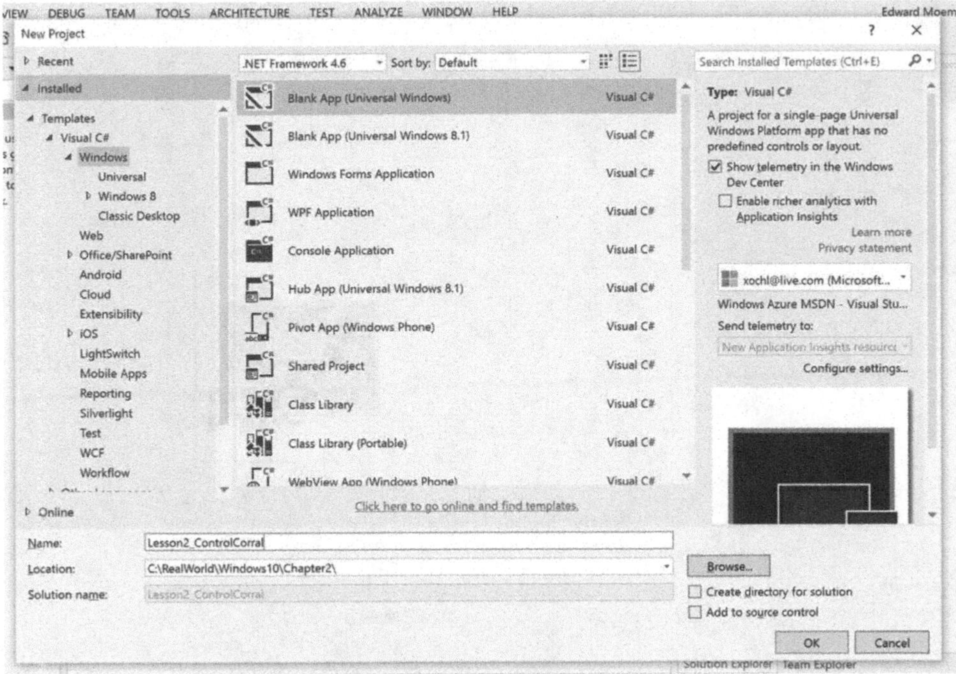

Figure 2-2. *New Project dialog in Visual Studio 2015*

■ **Note** The C# profile in Visual Studio 2015 contains far more project types than are relevant to this text. With C#, you can create just about anything, from a Windows device driver to Windows Phone applications. These days, companies like Xamarin have taken the C#/Visual Studio 2015 platform even further with plug-ins that allow C# developers to develop iOS and Android apps.

Visual Studio 2015 employs a usage profile mechanism to feature activities you are most interested in. Depending on the initial setup of your environment, you may be locked in as a C# developer, a Web developer, a database developer, or any number of other profile types. On my machine, C# is the default profile I use; as a result, Visual C# projects are front and center for me to pick from when I launch the New Project activity. If I wanted to build Visual Basic, Visual C++, or JavaScript UWP apps, I'd have to look in the Other Languages section of the New Project dialog box. In case you were wondering, Figure 2-3 shows the same dialog, this time with the Other Languages section expanded to reveal the project types available for building UWP apps with JavaScript.

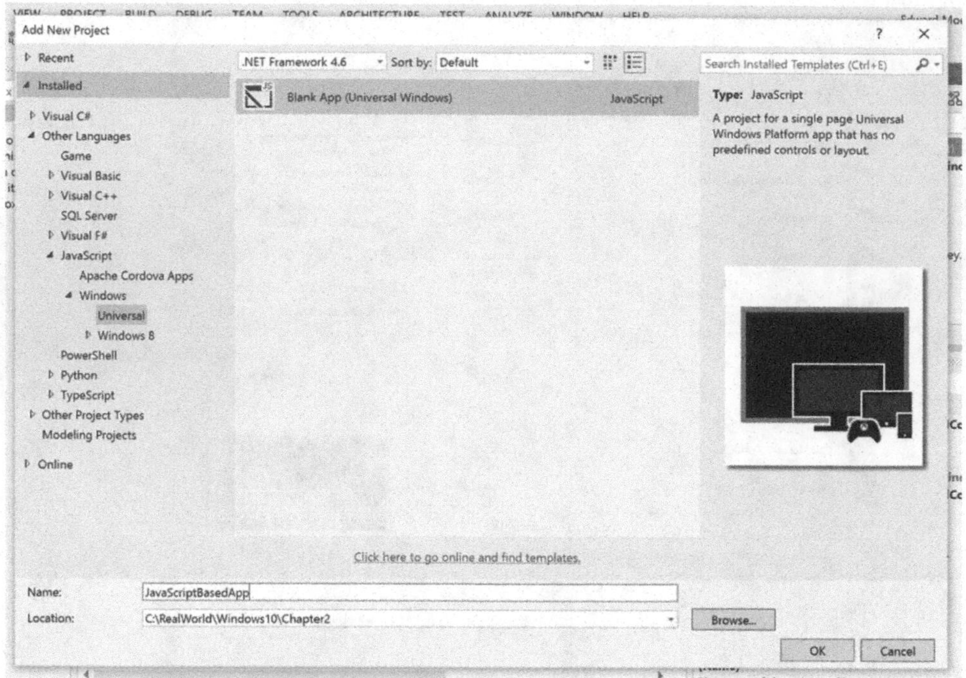

Figure 2-3. *New project template for JavaScript-based Windows 10 UWP app*

■ **Note** The samples in this book are not designed for deployment to the Windows Store. Be sure to uncheck the checkbox labelled "Show Telemetry in the Windows Dev Center" to disable the app insights functionality. You won't need it for what you are doing.

Enter the name *Lesson2_ControlCorral* in the Name text field along with a location where the project files will be stored, and then click the OK button to generate the project. Figure 2-4 shows the Solution Explorer window after the project has been created.

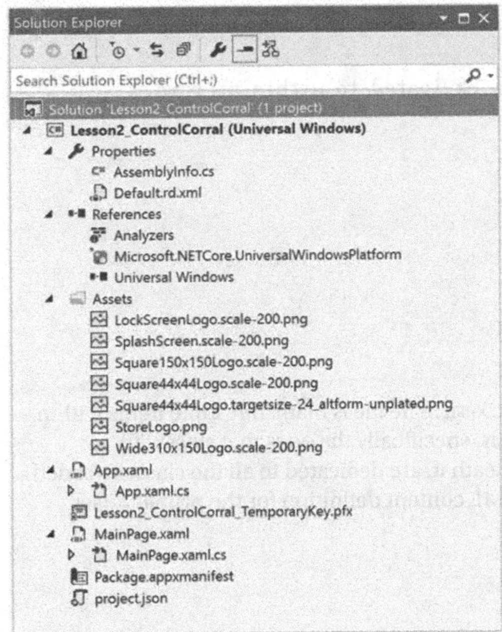

Figure 2-4. *Project items of a newly created WinJS project*

As is to be expected, the project contains C# and XAML files, with image assets included to help with default app branding. Listing 2-1 shows the contents of the default C# file, `MainPage.xaml.cs`.

Listing 2-1. Default C# File of the New Project

```
using System;
using System.Collections.Generic;
using System.IO;
using System.Linq;
using System.Runtime.InteropServices.WindowsRuntime;
using Windows.Foundation;
using Windows.Foundation.Collections;
using Windows.UI.Xaml;
using Windows.UI.Xaml.Controls;
using Windows.UI.Xaml.Controls.Primitives;
using Windows.UI.Xaml.Data;
using Windows.UI.Xaml.Input;
using Windows.UI.Xaml.Media;
using Windows.UI.Xaml.Navigation;

// The Blank Page item template is documented at http://go.microsoft.com/fwlink/?
LinkId=402352&clcid=0x409
```

```
namespace Lesson2_ControlCorral
{
    /// <summary>
    /// An empty page that can be used on its own or navigated to within a Frame.
    /// </summary>
    public sealed partial class MainPage : Page
    {
        public MainPage()
        {
            this.InitializeComponent();
        }
    }
}
```

Listing 2-1 shows the code file associated with MainPage.xaml. The file is blank but some items within it are still of interest to us. Take a look at the using declarations, specifically the ones that start with Windows.UI.Xaml. This namespace, and the namespaces beneath it, are dedicated to all the classes needed to use XAML for defining a user interface. The associated XAML content definition for the primary user interface of the app is shown in Listing 2-2.

Listing 2-2. Default HTML File of the New Project

```
<Page
    x:Class="Lesson2_ControlCorral.MainPage"
    xmlns="http://schemas.microsoft.com/winfx/2006/xaml/presentation"
    xmlns:x="http://schemas.microsoft.com/winfx/2006/xaml"
    xmlns:local="using:Lesson2_ControlCorral"
    xmlns:d="http://schemas.microsoft.com/expression/blend/2008"
    xmlns:mc="http://schemas.openxmlformats.org/markup-compatibility/2006"
    mc:Ignorable="d">

    <Grid Background="{ThemeResource ApplicationPageBackgroundThemeBrush}">

    </Grid>
</Page>
```

In Listing 2-2, the Background property of the main grid is not set to a color string; rather it is set to a special kind of string value used in XAML called a markup extension. A markup extension evaluates the value contained in an attribute and returns an appropriate object instance representation of it. It functions very similarly to the value converters discussed in Chapter 1, the difference being that markup extensions always go from a string value to an object instance while value converters do a more general conversion from one object instance to another. XAML already has something similar to this, something that is integral to the ability of XAML to represent strings as object or enum values. It is what allows us to set the Background attribute of the above grid to "Green", for instance, and have XAML set the underlying property to new SolidColorBrush(Windows.UI.Color.Green). To achieve this level of flexibility, XAML uses type converters.

Type converters are the functional equivalent to markup extensions. Unlike markup extensions, however, type converters function implicitly (there is no need to explicitly tell XAML that the string "Green" should be converted, it just does it). In contrast, markup extensions utilize specific notation to activate their conversion feature. There are only a handful of possible extensions presently available. In Chapter 1, you got a taste of the Binding markup extension; there is also RelativeSource, CustomResource, StaticResource, and ThemeResource.

The extension used in this case, ThemeResource, is a good launch point into another new feature exposed in Listing 2-2: resources. In XAML, resources are a collection of declaratively defined elements that can be referenced via a key. (Remember the x:Key attribute from Chapter 1? Here is where it is used.) Not surprisingly, the collection that contains resources is called a resource dictionary.

■ **Note** When you think of a resource dictionary, think of it as a Dictionary object defined as follows: *Dictionary<string, object>*. A resource in a resource dictionary can be the declarative representation of any XAML-instantiable object (for objects not in the default namespaces provided to work, they must be imported into the resource dictionary via the using keyword).

ThemeResource, CustomResource, and StaticResource can all be used to access resources in the resource dictionary that is currently in scope by specifying the key of the resource they are targeting. In Listing 2-2, the value of the background color of the main grid is being read from a resource with the key name ApplicationPageBackgroundThemeBrush. Listing 2-3 provides the definition of the resource in question.

Listing 2-3. A SolidColorBrush Resource

```
<SolidColorBrush
        x:Key="ApplicationPageBackgroundThemeBrush"
        Color="#FFFFFFFF" />
```

Press F5 to run this app. The project should build successfully and, if you haven't deviated from the steps provided above, launch the app with a blank white screen.

Now that you've prepared a basic project for use in exploring what UWP has to offer in terms of controls, let's proceed with a brief discussion on how they work in Windows 10.

So Just What Are Controls?

If you have ever worked with HTML, WPF, WinForms, Visual Basic 6, ATL, MFC, Power Builder, or any other user interface-driven WISYWG designer and technology, you will probably be quite familiar with the concept of controls. Put simply, a control is an encapsulated piece of user interface that combines layout, content, and behavior to create a distinct experience within the construct of the surface that contains it. All controls strictly adhere to the three tenets identified in the previous statement. Regardless of their function, they must all present a user interface that is isolated from their parent. They must all include behavior that is again isolated from behavioral traits of their parent. And finally, they must all utilize a layout system that is sequestered from the overarching layout system of the parent surface they reside in.

Incorporating Controls

Controls in XAML can be generally broken up into four main categories: basic controls, layout controls, data controls, and custom controls. Basic controls can broadly be classified as controls that contribute to the viewable content of a given screen. Buttons, checkboxes, sliders, and pickers are examples of this. Data controls, like basic controls, are primarily meant to be part of a screen's viewable content. However, data controls vary from their basic counterparts in that they are specifically designed with the problem of generically representing collections of objects in mind. Layout controls are not ideally intended to be a part of the viewable surface. Rather, they share the primary purpose of managing the location, position, and dimensions of all controls. One unique feature of layout controls is that they support adding multiple children as their content. (Some data controls theoretically can support multiple children; this is not their intended use, however.) Almost all of the popular layout controls are completely invisible in their default implementation. Finally, custom controls can be a combination of any of the aforementioned control classifications. They are controls created by you.

The BouncerX sample in Chapter 1 was your first foray into the realm of controls. The app used a TextBlock and three Button controls to compose a dashboard for maintaining a count of the number of attendees for a given occasion. This section builds on the knowledge you acquired through that exercise, going into more detail on the controls themselves. Over the next three chapters (this one and the next two), you will be building out a reservation system for an imaginary massage parlor. You will use this to frame discussions around the purpose and usage instructions of a number of important controls. The process starts with continuing the foundational work you started earlier in this chapter. Before you begin designing your user interface, let's take some time to think through the requirements of such a reservation system.

In order to satisfy the base functionality of being a reservation system, your sample app must, at a minimum, provide the ability to take and store reservations. Assuming you treat reservations like appointments, this app will need to gather information about the date and time when a massage takes place; expect information about the customer; and perhaps also take information about special requests a given customer might have. Listing 2-4 contains the primary class you will use for storing this information. Create a new C# file class named `ReservationInfo` and add the code here into it.

Listing 2-4. ReservationInfo Class Definition

```
using System;
using System.Collections.Generic;
using System.Linq;
using System.Text;
using System.Threading.Tasks;

namespace Lesson2_ControlCorral
{
        public class ReservationInfo
        {
                public DateTime AppointmentDay { get; set; }

                public DateTime DOB { get; set; }

                public bool HasPaid { get; set; } = true;

                public string Passphrase { get; set; }

                public string Procedure { get; set; }

                public TimeSpan AppointmentTime { get; set; }

                public string CustomerName { get; set; }

                public byte[] CustomerImage { get; set; }

                public double MassageIntensity { get; set; }

        }
}
```

In Listing 2-4, you design a simple data class that can be used to store all the captured information from your user interface. In Listing 2-5, you modify MainPage.xaml.cs to include this class. Because a user of this system will undoubtedly be creating multiple reservations over the course of its use, you store the reservations made in a List object. The relevant changes are in bold.

Listing 2-5. Modified MainPage.xaml.cs to Include ReservationInfo

```
...
    public sealed partial class MainPage : Page
    {
        List<ReservationInfo> _reservations;

        public MainPage()
        {

            this.InitializeComponent();
            _reservations = new List<ReservationInfo>();
        }
    }

...
```

As each reservation is made, you create a new instance of the ReservationInfo object, populate it with values from the user interface, and then add it to the list _reservations. You now have everything you need to get started.

Window

The Window object is not a control but it will be difficult to describe some controls-or fully understanding UWP programming-without having some sort of conversation about it. In the UWP, this class is used to represent the primary window of the current application. You can retrieve an instance to your UWP app's Window object through the static Current property it defines. This object instance must be used to do two things in order for your user interface to be presented. First, you must assign a user interface object to its Content property; any object that derives from UIElement will suffice. Second, you must call its Activate method.

In your project, open up the file App.xaml.cs and navigate to the method OnLaunched. Delete everything in that method and run the application. You should see something close to Figure 2-5.

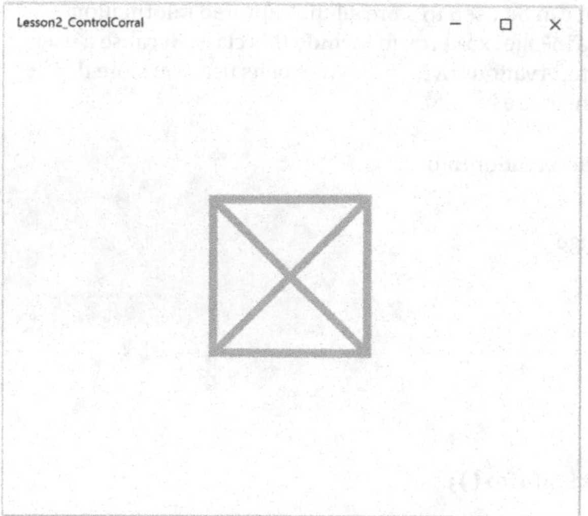

Figure 2-5. *A window that has not been activated*

The grey square with the X in the middle is actually the default splash screen image for the app. If either of the conditions specified above are not met, the system will show this image. (Try it out; add `Window.Current.Activate();` to the method and run the project again. You will still get the splash screen). Now set the `Content` property as specified in Listing 2-6 and run the project.

Listing 2-6. Specifying the Content of an App's Window

```
protected override void OnLaunched(LaunchActivatedEventArgs e)
{
        Window.Current.Content = new Button() {
                Content = "This button is the root content for this application's window",
                HorizontalAlignment = HorizontalAlignment.Center };
        Window.Current.Activate();
}
```

In the previous listing, you set the content of the app's window to a `Button` object. Because `UIElement` is the base class for all user interface elements, any of the controls you will talk about, and just about any XAML element with a user interface, can be assigned to this property. Figure 2-6 shows how the app now looks when it is run.

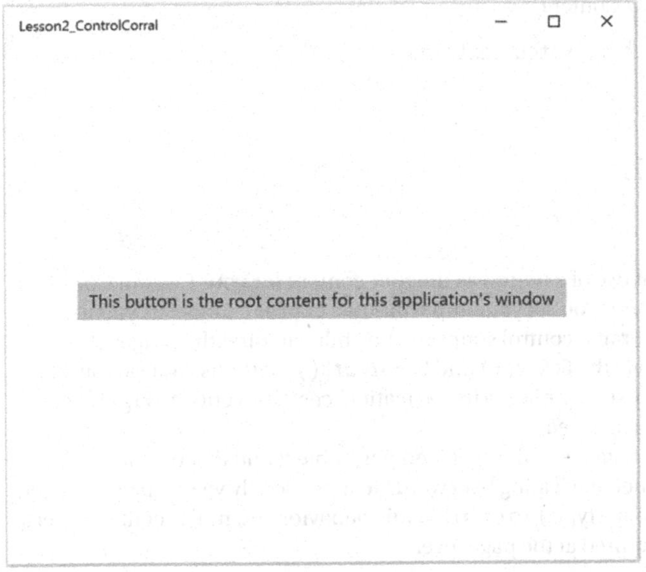

***Figure 2-6.** A UWP app window with a Button control assigned as the root content*

Frame

Because the content of an app's window can be changed through the lifetime of the application, you might be tempted to use it as a mechanism for implementing screen segregation patterns like those involved in navigation. This type of thing has been used in past frameworks to break up functionality into separate screens that the user gains access to based on their interactions with the app. This is the very pattern that HTML browsers use, but such an approach does not natively translate well to the use of a window's content as the primary navigation mechanism. History and scope come to mind as reasons to avoid this practice. All the mechanisms used to track the history of screens navigated to and the simplicity of just "going back" is lost when you choose to constantly set `Window.Current.Content`. The scope of the navigation is also always locked to that of the entire application (meaning "navigating" will always affect the entire app and not just portions of it).

Unlike other legacy UI technologies like WinForms and Win32 programming, XAML, like HTML, is built with the notion of navigation in mind. The Frame control helps facilitate this by providing a way to present the content and behavior of an otherwise external page within itself. So far, you have only had to create one page in the apps you have been developing, but in a typical UWP application you will probably want to have numerous pages, with each page designed to service a specific function. Frames free you to organize your UWP apps in this manner. Using them, you can create as many different page types as needed by your app, and then navigate to those pages by calling the `Navigate` method, passing in the type of the page to navigate to. (You can optionally pass in a parameter object to initialize the page to a particular state.)

Let's change Listing 2-6 so that it uses a Frame as the root content of the app window. Listing 2-7 shows the code for the revamped `OnLoaded` method.

Listing 2-7. Using a Frame as an App's Window Content

```
protected override void OnLaunched(LaunchActivatedEventArgs e)
{
        var frame = new Frame();
        Window.Current.Content = frame;
        frame.Navigate(typeof(MainPage));
        Window.Current.Activate();
}
```

In Listing 2-7, you remove the nonsensical use of a button as the root content for your Control Corral app, replacing it instead with a Frame object. After you set your app window's `Content` property, you use navigate to transfer the user to MainPage. The Frame control supports the ability to directly navigate to pages as well as use a linear navigation model via the `GoBack()` and `GoForward()` methods. You can observe the navigation activities any Frame performs by subscribing to its navigation-centric events: `Navigating`, `Navigated`, `NavigationStopped`, and `NavigationFailed`.

By default, each navigation creates a new instance of the specified page object and disposes the previous page instance. (This happens even when navigating backwards to a previously visited page or when the new page type is the same as the previous page type.) To override this behavior you must set the property `NavigationCacheMode` to either Enabled or Required at the page level.

Page

Although Page is a control, it is used in a special kind of way in the world of the UWP. Frames can only navigate to Page objects, but because Page is meant to encapsulate content that the Frame control can navigate to, and because that content will invariable be different from Page to Page, you will almost always work with pages that are subclasses of the base Page control. It is this subclass that renders inside the Frame's display area.

You can override the Page's `OnNavigatedTo`, `OnNavigatedFrom`, and `OnNavigationFrom` methods to perform tasks such as initializing and saving the Page state. `OnNavigatingFrom` can be used to cancel a navigation by setting a `Cancel` property in the event data from your handler. Pages that are navigated to as part of an activation are generally passed data from the activation. Other navigation scenarios such as search result pages also have expectations of what info will be contained in the parameter.

Like most basic controls, the Page control is an example of what are called content controls. Content controls have one property within them that represents the content area they are providing. Within this property, only one element, the content of the control, can be added. Normally this would translate to element declarations like what is shown in Listing 2-8, where a layout control (we will discuss layout controls in Chapter 4) is placed inside the Page control's `Content` property using property element syntax.

Listing 2-8. Setting the Content Property of Page Using Property Element Syntax

```
<Page x:Class="Lesson2_ControlCorral.MainPage"
     xmlns="http://schemas.microsoft.com/winfx/2006/xaml/presentation"
     xmlns:x="http://schemas.microsoft.com/winfx/2006/xaml"
     xmlns:local="using:Lesson2_ControlCorral"
     xmlns:d="http://schemas.microsoft.com/expression/blend/2008"
     xmlns:mc="http://schemas.openxmlformats.org/markup-compatibility/2006"
     mc:Ignorable="d">
   <Page.Content>
       <Grid Background="{ThemeResource ApplicationPageBackgroundThemeBrush}">

       </Grid>
   </Page.Content>
</Page>
```

XAML, however, allows for certain properties of the underlying control to be earmarked as the default content property of the element. This allows you to use the more conventional approach to declaring an element, the one seen in Listing 2-2 earlier.

■ **Note** You might have guessed this already, but you have been using Page all along. It is the surface on which the user interface of your BouncerX UWP app from Chapter 1 was built. What might come as a surprise to you is that you have also been using Frame from the beginning. If you open the `App.xaml.cs` file of a new, blank, XAML-based UWP project and examine the `OnLaunched` method, you will see that a Frame is used as the root content for the application window.

Button

The `Button` class is one of the most basic types of controls. In its simplest form, it represents an area that when tapped with a finger or stylus, or when a mouse button is pressed while the mouse pointer is over this area, raises a click event. (If a button has keyboard focus, pressing the Enter key or the Spacebar key also fires the click event). Let's modify Listing 2-2 to include a new button for making the actual reservation. When this button is hit, a new `ReservationInfo` object should be created and added to the list of reservations being tracked on the page. Listing 2-9 shows the new markup followed by the method that needs to be added to the code-behind file.

Listing 2-9. Button Added to Page

```
<Page x:Class="Lesson2_ControlCorral.MainPage"
      xmlns="http://schemas.microsoft.com/winfx/2006/xaml/presentation"
      xmlns:x="http://schemas.microsoft.com/winfx/2006/xaml"
      xmlns:local="using:Lesson2_ControlCorral"
      xmlns:d="http://schemas.microsoft.com/expression/blend/2008"
      xmlns:mc="http://schemas.openxmlformats.org/markup-compatibility/2006"
      mc:Ignorable="d">

    <Grid Background="{ThemeResource ApplicationPageBackgroundThemeBrush}">
        <Button
                Content="Reserve Room"
                HorizontalAlignment="Center"
                VerticalAlignment="Center"
                Click="ReserveMassage" />
    </Grid>
</Page>

//code
private void ReserveMassage(object sender, RoutedEventArgs e)
{
        var new_reservation = new ReservationInfo();
        _reservations.Add(new_reservation);
}
```

In Chapter 1, we talked about disconnecting the user interface from the programming logic used to build its interactivity wherever possible. You went from a sample where procedural code was being used to set the value of a text field to one that was almost completely disconnected from the code driving its values to change. The sample in Listing 2-9 continues this approach by using a click event defined in the markup instead of programmatically defining it in the code-behind file. This is a great way to shift the behavior specification of the button to as declarative an approach as possible. Let's take it a step further.

Command Binding

UWP command binding is a technique that allows you to essentially divorce the user interface from the code-behind. Setting up command binding is a three-step process: first, you define the command object; second, you set it to the `DataContext` of the `Button` being bound to (or any parent of that `Button`); and finally you declaratively bind to it in your XAML. Add a new class file to your project called `GenericCommand` and place the code from Listing 2-10 into it.

Listing 2-10. A Simple Command

```
public class GenericCommand : System.Windows.Input.ICommand
{
        public event EventHandler CanExecuteChanged;
        public event Action<string> DoSomething;

        public bool CanExecute(object parameter)
        {
                return true;
        }

        public void Execute(object parameter)
        {
                var command = parameter as string;
                DoSomething?.Invoke(command);
        }
}
```

The code here does nothing but delegate the results of a command execution to anyone listening for the `DoSomething` event. The next step is to modify the code-behind file to utilize this command class. Listing 2-11 illustrates. Items marked in bold are the changes.

Listing 2-11. Applying Command to code behind

```
...
public sealed partial class MainPage : Page
    {
        List<ReservationInfo> _reservations;
        GenericCommand _command;

                public MainPage()
                {
                        this.InitializeComponent();
```

```
            _reservations = new List<ReservationInfo>();
                        this.Loaded += MainPage_Loaded;
            _command = new GenericCommand();
            _command.DoSomething += _command_DoSomething;
            }

        private void MainPage_Loaded(object sender, RoutedEventArgs e)
        {
                this.DataContext = _command;
        }

        async private void _command_DoSomething(string command)
        {
                if (command.ToLower() == "make a reservation")
                {
                        var new_reservation = new ReservationInfo();
                        _reservations.Add(new_reservation);
                        MessageDialog md =
                        new MessageDialog($"{_reservations.Count} massages reserved");
                        await md.ShowAsync();
                }
        }
}
...
```

In Listing 2-11, you instantiate and apply the GenericCommand object to MainPage. To get commanding to work in this example, you are data binding the command directly to the page. In real-life scenarios, the command object would be a part of a much larger data object that the page binds to. That way, specific controls on the page could declaratively decide which properties of the full data object to bind to. The new method, _command_DoSomething serves as a general purpose handler for any command parameters passed into it. Be sure to include the namespace Windows.UI.Popups.

The commands being processed in _command_DoSomething come directly from the user interface. They are parameters declared in XAML now being passed into the binding subsystem so as to differentiate one class of command execution from another. This is necessary since you are using a generic command object to handle all your commands. Let's modify MainPage.xaml so it matches Listing 2-12. Changes are in bold.

Listing 2-12. Utilizing Command Bindings in XAML

```
<Button Content="Reserve Room"
                HorizontalAlignment="Center"
                VerticalAlignment="Center"
                Command="{Binding}"
        CommandParameter="make a reservation"/>
```

Notice that the click event handler has been removed. On the face of it, this element declaration has no idea what code is occurring in the code-behind to facilitate its functionality. All it knows is that it represents the "make a reservation" command. This could not be said for the previous implementation, though. Assigning to the click event means the UI has knowledge of at least one method of its corresponding code-behind class. Figure 2-7 shows how the app looks when it is run and the Reserve Room button is clicked (in this case, clicked a second time).

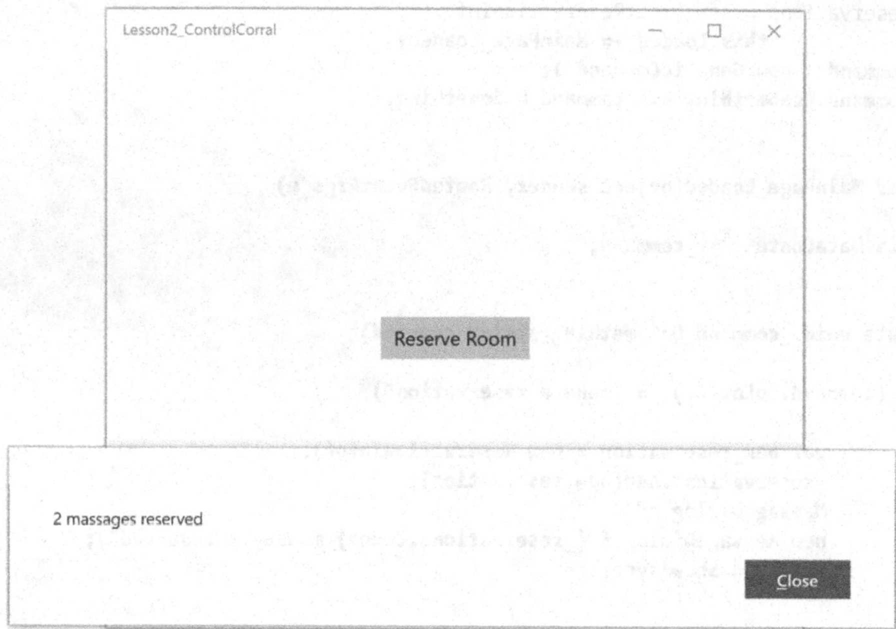

Figure 2-7. *Control Corral with control binding in action*

Templates

Buttons, like other UWP XAML controls, rely on templates to describe their user interface. Templates are XAML snippets that describe how a control should be rendered. This not only includes the view of the control, but also any animations or state change effects that the control should implement. The great thing about XAML, something that makes it even better than HTML, is that any one of these templates can be overridden. This means that you can create your own user interface from the ground up, even for controls that were packaged with the UWP!

Listing 2-13 shows how the button you have been working with can be re-templated to create a rounded rectangle button. If you run this sample, you will notice that all the mouse interaction effects have been lost. This is because those effects are defined on the default template for Button. Play around with the template for some time and see what kinds of buttons you can make. Once you are done, return the button code to Listing 2-13.

Listing 2-13. Re-Templated Button Sample

```
<Button Content="Reserve Room"
        HorizontalAlignment="Center"
        VerticalAlignment="Center"
        Command="{Binding}"
        CommandParameter="make a reservation" >
            <Button.Template>
            <ControlTemplate TargetType="Button">
                    <Border Width="200"
                            Height="100"
                            CornerRadius="20"
                            Background="{TemplateBinding Background}">
```

```
                        <ContentControl Content="{TemplateBinding Content}"
                                        HorizontalAlignment="Center"
                                        VerticalAlignment="Center" />
                </Border>
            </ControlTemplate>
        </Button.Template>
</Button>
```

CalendarDatePicker

There are two date selection scenarios in general use in the computing world today. One is when you know the exact date you are selecting, for instance if you need to select your birthdate. The other is if you don't and are looking for a date to select, for instance when a person is looking to select a date in an appointment book to do something. In such a scenario, contextual information like the day of the week or fullness of the calendar becomes very important. The CalendarDatePicker is optimized to support the latter case.

The Date property is used for retrieving or setting the selected date. End users can clear the value of this property by clicking the selected date in the calendar view to deselect it.

Listing 2-14 shows the updated MainPage.xaml for Control Corral along with the changes that need to be made to its code-behind in order to incorporate this control. There are changes to the layout style for the controls, so pay close attention.

Listing 2-14. CalendarDatePicker Control in Action

```
        <Button Content="Reserve Room"
                HorizontalAlignment="Left"
                VerticalAlignment="Top"
                Command="{Binding}"
                CommandParameter="make a reservation"
                Margin="223,164,0,0">
        </Button>
        <CalendarDatePicker x:Name="control_calendar"
                            HorizontalAlignment="Left"
                            Margin="91,165,0,0"
                            VerticalAlignment="Top"
               PlaceholderText="What day works for you?" />

//code
if (command.ToLower() == "make a reservation")
{
        if (control_calendar.Date != null)
        {
                var new_reservation = new ReservationInfo()
                {
                        AppointmentDay = control_calendar.Date.Value.Date,
                };
                _reservations.Add(new_reservation);
                MessageDialog md =
                        new MessageDialog($"{_reservations.Count} massages reserved");
                await md.ShowAsync();
                control_calendar.Date = null;
        }
```

```
        else
        {
                MessageDialog md =
                        new MessageDialog("Select a day first");
                await md.ShowAsync();
        }
}
```

There are a few things worth mentioning in Listing 2-14. The alignment for the Reserve Room button is switched to Top/Left so laying it out in the root grid would be more predictable. Since there is more than one control, now you want to make sure that things align properly with each other. As part of this process, you've also added a `Margin` attribute to the button. `Margin` can be used to set the margins on a given control. You will find out more about margins and laying out a grid in Chapter 4.

In the code-behind, you first check to see if a date has been selected, prompting the user if this is not the case. If a date has been selected, you set it to the `AppointmentDay` property of your newly created `ReservationInfo` object. Figure 2-8 shows the updated app when it is run.

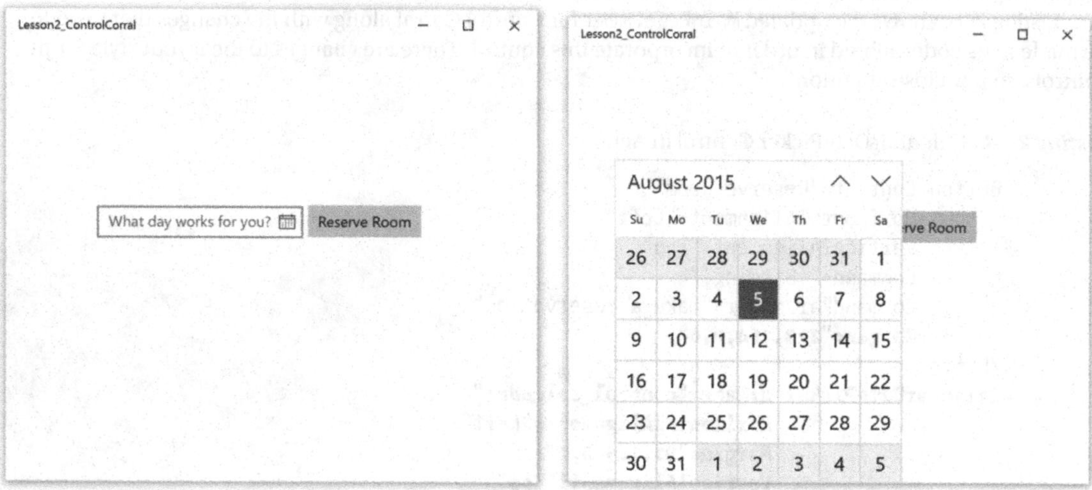

Figure 2-8. *CalendarDatePicker in action*

TimePicker

Your requirement must also specify that you need to capture the time of day the user would like to reserve. The TimePicker is the UWP XAML control designed to allow a user to pick a time value. Listing 2-15 shows the changes that need to be made to `MainPage.xaml` and its code-behind to enable the TimePicker functionality.

Listing 2-15. Enabling the TimePicker Control

```
<Grid Background="{ThemeResource ApplicationPageBackgroundThemeBrush}">
    <Button Content="Reserve Room"
            HorizontalAlignment="Right"
            VerticalAlignment="Bottom"
            Command="{Binding}"
            CommandParameter="make a reservation"
            Margin="0,0,10,10"
            Width="114"
            Height="32">
    </Button>
    <CalendarDatePicker x:Name="control_calendar"
                        HorizontalAlignment="Left"
                        Margin="91,165,0,0"
                        VerticalAlignment="Top"
                        PlaceholderText="What day works for you?"
                        Width="242" />
    <TimePicker x:Name="control_time" Header="What time works for you?"
                Margin="91,202,0,0"
                VerticalAlignment="Top" />

</Grid>
//code
if (command.ToLower() == "make a reservation")
{
        if (control_calendar.Date != null)
        {
                var new_reservation = new ReservationInfo()
                {
                        AppointmentDay = control_calendar.Date.Value.Date,
                        AppointmentTime = control_time.Time,
                };
                _reservations.Add(new_reservation);
                MessageDialog md =
                        new MessageDialog
                        ($"{_reservations.Count} massages reserved\n" +
                                $"Newest is on {new_reservation.AppointmentDay.Month}/" +
                                $"{new_reservation.AppointmentDay.Day}/" +
                                $"{new_reservation.AppointmentDay.Year}" +
                                $" at {new_reservation.AppointmentTime}");
                await md.ShowAsync();
                control_calendar.Date = null;
        }
```

```
        else
        {
                MessageDialog md =
                        new MessageDialog("Select a day first");
                await md.ShowAsync();
        }
}
```

You are making some more changes to the layout to support new controls being added in Listing 2-15. In the code-behind, you've expanded the content that the MessageDialog shows when a reservation completes. It now not only displays how many reservations have been made, it also tells you the date and time of the most recent reservation.

AutoSuggestBox

AutoSuggestBox gives the user a list of suggestions to select from as they type. To use it, your code needs to handle three of its events: `TextChanged`, `SuggestionChosen`, and `QuerySubmitted`. The idea is to use the `TextChanged` event to limit the scope of the search being performed to the items that match the current text in the control. When a selection is made from one of the suggestions presented, `SuggestionChosen` can be used to update the text box associated with this control. Finally, when the user invokes a search by either clicking the search button associated with the control or pressing the Enter key, `QuerySubmitted` can be used to run a search to determine if the search term exists. Listing 2-16 shows the updated layout for the page. Update your page and code-behind to match.

Listing 2-16. AutoSuggestBox in Action

```
<Grid Background="{ThemeResource ApplicationPageBackgroundThemeBrush}">
    <Button Content="Reserve Room"
            HorizontalAlignment="Right"
            VerticalAlignment="Bottom"
            Command="{Binding}"
            CommandParameter="make a reservation"
            Margin="0,0,10,10"
            Width="114"
            Height="32">
    </Button>
    <CalendarDatePicker x:Name="control_calendar"
                        HorizontalAlignment="Left"
                        Margin="10,10,0,0"
                        VerticalAlignment="Top"
                        PlaceholderText="What day works for you?"
                        Width="242" />
    <TimePicker x:Name="control_time" Header="What time works for you?"
                Margin="10,47,0,0"
                VerticalAlignment="Top" />
    <AutoSuggestBox x:Name="control_name"
                    HorizontalAlignment="Left" Header="What's your name?"
                    Margin="10,112,0,0"
                    VerticalAlignment="Top"
                    Width="242" QueryIcon="Find" />
</Grid>
```

```
//code

public sealed partial class MainPage : Page
{
        List<ReservationInfo> _reservations;
        GenericCommand _command;
        List<string> _usuals = new List<string>();
        public MainPage()
        {
                this.InitializeComponent();
                this.Loaded += MainPage_Loaded;
                _reservations = new List<ReservationInfo>();
                _command = new GenericCommand();
                _command.DoSomething += _command_DoSomething;
                control_name.QuerySubmitted += Control_name_QuerySubmitted;
                control_name.TextChanged += Control_name_TextChanged;
                control_name.SuggestionChosen += Control_name_SuggestionChosen;
        }

        private void Control_name_SuggestionChosen(AutoSuggestBox sender,
                AutoSuggestBoxSuggestionChosenEventArgs args)
        {
                control_name.Text = args.SelectedItem as string;
        }

        private void Control_name_TextChanged(AutoSuggestBox sender,
                AutoSuggestBoxTextChangedEventArgs args)
        {
                if (args.CheckCurrent())
                {
                        var search_term = control_name.Text.ToLower();
                        var results = _usuals.
                                Where(i => i.Contains(search_term.ToLower())).ToList();
                        control_name.ItemsSource = results;

                }
        }

        private void Control_name_QuerySubmitted(AutoSuggestBox sender,
                AutoSuggestBoxQuerySubmittedEventArgs args)
        {
                var search_term = args.QueryText.ToLower();
                var results = _usuals.
                        Where(i => i.Contains(search_term.ToLower())).ToList();
                control_name.ItemsSource = results;
                control_name.IsSuggestionListOpen = true;
        }
```

```
        private void MainPage_Loaded(object sender, RoutedEventArgs e)
        {
            this.DataContext = _command;
            _usuals = new List<string> {"alex",
                "azuka",
                "elizabeth",
                "ahmed","josh","allan", "john","david","chris","jack",
                "bobby","ike","emeka","tobe","chidi","mason","andrew" };
            control_name.ItemsSource = _usuals;
        }

        async private void _command_DoSomething(string command)
        {

            if (command.ToLower() == "make a reservation")
            {
                if (control_calendar.Date != null)
                {
                    var new_reservation = new ReservationInfo()
                    {
                        AppointmentDay = control_calendar.Date.Value.Date,
                        AppointmentTime = control_time.Time,
                        CustomerName = control_name.Text,
                    };
                    _reservations.Add(new_reservation);
                    MessageDialog md =
                    new MessageDialog
                    ($"{_reservations.Count} massages reserved\n" +
                    $"Newest is on {new_reservation.AppointmentDay.Month}/" +
                        $"{new_reservation.AppointmentDay.Day}/" +
                        $"{new_reservation.AppointmentDay.Year}" +
                        $" at {new_reservation.AppointmentTime}\n" +
                        $"for {new_reservation.CustomerName}");
                    await md.ShowAsync();
                    control_calendar.Date = null;
                }
                else
                {
                    MessageDialog md =
                        new MessageDialog("Select a day first");
                    await md.ShowAsync();
                }
            }
        }
}
```

Although there is a lot of added code, you haven't done much in Listing 2-16. Let's start with the code-behind. You add a new list of strings to represent the list of usual customers, and in the loaded event, you populate it with a generic sample list. You then databind this list to the AutoSuggestBox. This is the manner with which suggestions are added to the drop-down list of this control. In the `TextChanged` and `QuerySubmitted` event handlers, you query the `_usuals` list and retrieve the results that match to the text presently in the suggestion box. You then simply databind the filtered results back into the AutoSuggestBox, thus creating the filtered list effect.

CommandBar

The CommandBar is used to give end users quick access to an app's most common tasks. It is a general purpose, flexible, lightweight control that can display complex content (such as images, progress bars, or text blocks) and simple commands. It replaces the AppBar control from Windows 8/8.1 lore. (Even though AppBar is still present in the UWP, it is recommended that you use CommandBar instead.)

The CommandBar is divided into four main areas. The content area is shown on the left; the More button is shown on the right; the primary commands are shown to the left of the More button; and an overflow menu is shown only when the CommandBar is open and contains secondary commands.

When elements are added directly to the CommandBar's content, it essentially behaves like an additional user interface surface that you must lay out as you see fit. In Listing 2-17, you move the Reserve Room button out of the main page user interface and place it into a CommandBar's content area. This sample also shows how CommandBars are added to a page.

Listing 2-17. CommandBar in Action

```
<Page x:Class="Lesson2_ControlCorral.MainPage"
    xmlns="http://schemas.microsoft.com/winfx/2006/xaml/presentation"
    xmlns:x="http://schemas.microsoft.com/winfx/2006/xaml"
    xmlns:local="using:Lesson2_ControlCorral"
    xmlns:d="http://schemas.microsoft.com/expression/blend/2008"
    xmlns:mc="http://schemas.openxmlformats.org/markup-compatibility/2006"
    mc:Ignorable="d">
  <Page.BottomAppBar>
    <CommandBar>
      <CommandBar.Content>
        <StackPanel Orientation="Horizontal">
          <Button Content="Reserve Room"
                  Command="{Binding}"
                  CommandParameter="make a reservation"
                  Width="114"
                  Height="32">
          </Button>
        </StackPanel>
    </CommandBar.Content>
    </CommandBar>
   </Page.BottomAppBar>
...
</Page>
```

In Listing 2-17, a CommandBar is added to your MainPage using the `BottomAppBar` property via the property element `Page.BottomAppBar`. Page has two areas where CommandBars can be added, the top of the page and the bottom of the page. Can you guess what the property for adding a CommandBar to the top of the page is? For those of you who might not be paying attention, it is `TopAppBar`. Figure 2-9 shows how the app looks with the CommandBar in place.

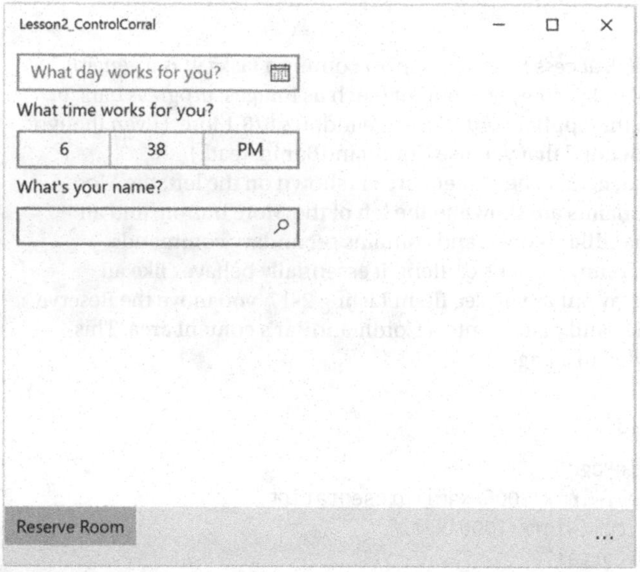

Figure 2-9. *CommandBar user interface*

You can add elements as direct children of the CommandBar, but only the `AppBarButton`, `AppBarToggleButton`, and `AppBarSeparator` elements are supported. This is because the default content added to a CommandBar maps to its `PrimaryCommands` property, and this property as well as its counterpart, `SecondaryCommands`, only support the aforementioned controls. If you need to know when your page's CommandBar has been opened or closed, you can handle the `Opening`, `Opened`, `Closing`, and `Closed` events. You can programmatically set the CommandBar to either state with the `IsOpen` property. When open, the primary command buttons are shown with text labels; the overflow menu is open only if secondary commands are present.

One of the key benefits of using a CommandBar is reducing the amount of space taken up by controls on the screen. However, at present, the Reserve Room button is still showing when the application launches. By default, CommandBar shows in what is referred to as its Compact mode, with content, icons without labels, and the More button. Using the property `ClosedDisplayMode`, you can change this behavior. You can set the mode to Minimal to show only a thin bar that acts as the More button. (This is the behavior an AppBar utilizes when in a closed state.) The other choice is Hidden, in which case the CommandBar is not displayed. Modify the code in Listing 2-17 by adding the following attribute, `ClosedDisplayMode = "Minimal"`, to the CommandBar element and then run the same. The app should now look like Figure 2-10.

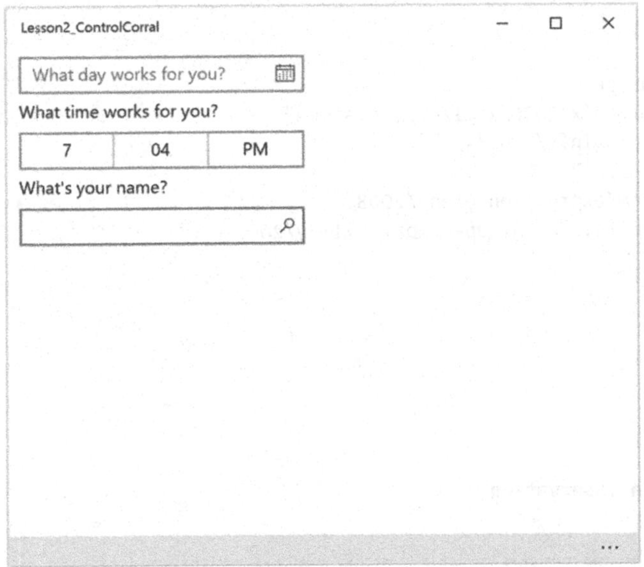

***Figure 2-10.** CommandBar in "Minimal" user interface*

You might have noticed that the CommandBar is automatically returned to closed state after you interact with anything in your app (including the buttons inside it). For some apps, this might not be ideal behavior. To prevent this from happening, set the value of the `IsSticky` property to true.

AppBarButton

The AppBarButton is a specialized kind of button designed to be primarily used in concert with a UWP CommandBar (it does not need to be placed in a CommandBar, it is just designed to be used with one). Two distinguishing characteristics of the AppBarButton are that it has a full fidelity and compact view, and that its content is set through two properties: `Label` and `Icon`. You can set the `Label` property to a string to specify the text label; however, be mindful of the fact that it will be hidden when the button is in its compact state (accomplished by setting the `IsCompact` property appropriately). To ensure that a user can still derive meaning from the button when in compact mode, be sure to define a meaningful icon. You can define the AppBarButton icon by setting the `Icon` property to any element derived from the `IconElement` class. The UWP provides four kinds of icon elements at the present time:

- FontIcon: The icon is based on a glyph from the specified font family.
- BitmapIcon: The icon is based on a bitmap image file with the specified URI.
- PathIcon: The icon is based on Path data.
- SymbolIcon: The icon is based on a glyph from the Segoe MDL2 Assets font as listed in the Symbol enumeration.

You previously had the Reserve Room button designed as a standard UWP button sitting in the CommandBar for the page. Let's change it to an AppBarButton. Listing 2-18 shows the changes that need to be made to the XAML to do this. No code-behind changes are necessary.

Listing 2-18. AppBarButton in Action

```
<Page
    x:Class="Lesson2_ControlCorral.MainPage"
    xmlns="http://schemas.microsoft.com/winfx/2006/xaml/presentation"
    xmlns:x="http://schemas.microsoft.com/winfx/2006/xaml"
    xmlns:local="using:Lesson2_ControlCorral"
    xmlns:d="http://schemas.microsoft.com/expression/blend/2008"
    xmlns:mc="http://schemas.openxmlformats.org/markup-compatibility/2006"
    mc:Ignorable="d">
    <Page.BottomAppBar>
        <CommandBar
            ClosedDisplayMode="Compact"
            IsSticky="True">

            <AppBarButton
                Command="{Binding}"
                CommandParameter="make a reservation"
                Label="Reserve"
                Icon="Calendar">
            </AppBarButton>
        </CommandBar>
    </Page.BottomAppBar>
...
</Page>
```

In Listing 2-18, you convert the Button control you have been using for making reservations to an AppBarButton control. You also move it out of the Content section of the CommandBar and into the PrimaryCommands section. Since the Reserve Room button is now following the layout rules of the CommandBar, you no longer need size or layout information on the button. You also no longer need to place it inside of a layout control. If you run the app, it should now look like Figure 2-11 when the CommandBar is expanded.

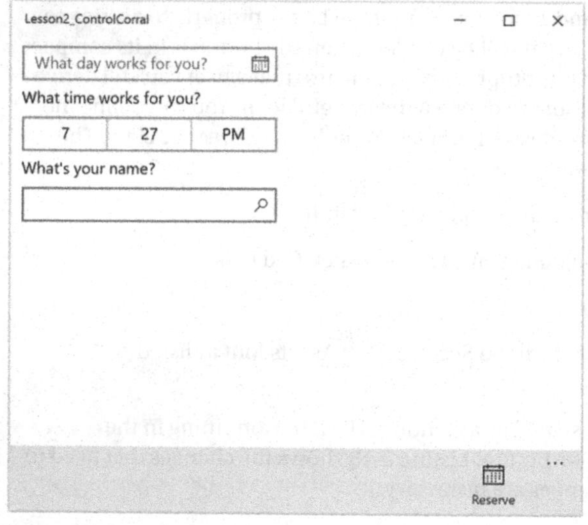

Figure 2-11. *CommandBar with AppBarButton primary command*

■ **Note** Even though CommandBar contains a `Content` property, child elements of CommandBar are placed into the PrimaryCommands collection by default. This is because the PrimaryCommands, and not Content, is the default content property defined for CommandBar.

DatePicker

A DatePicker control is used in scenarios where your app needs to allow a user to easily enter a known date value. The user picks the date using ComboBox selection for month, day, and year values. You can then programmatically access the date value selected by the user through the `Date` property. You will use the DatePicker to capture the date of birth of potential massage clients. Add the DatePicker control to the Control Corral user interface and code-behind as shown in Listing 2-19.

Listing 2-19. DatePicker in Action

```
<Grid>
...
<DatePicker
            x:Name="control_dob"
            Header="When were you born?"
            HorizontalAlignment="Left"
            Margin="10,177,0,0"
            VerticalAlignment="Top" />
...
</Grid>

//code
var new_reservation = new ReservationInfo()
{
        AppointmentDay = control_calendar.Date.Value.Date,
        AppointmentTime = control_time.Time,
        CustomerName = control_name.Text,
        DOB = control_dob.Date.Date,
};
```

Figure 2-12 shows how Control Corral looks on my machine when I try to enter a date of birth.

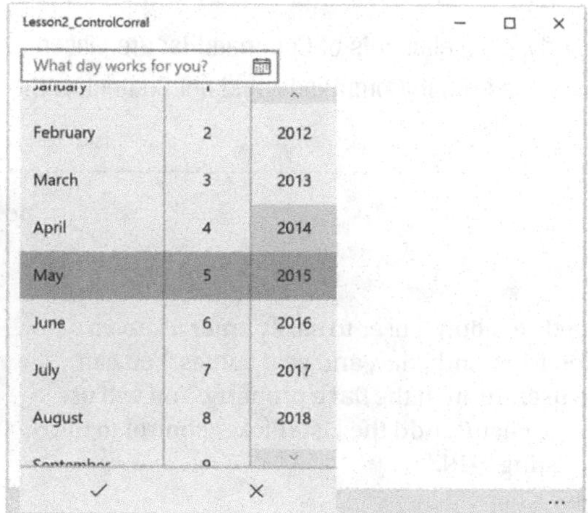

Figure 2-12. *DatePicker user interface*

MenuFlyout

MenuFlyout functions somewhat similar to context menus. It temporarily displays a list of commands related to what the user is currently doing. MenuFlyouts are usually set in XAML as the value of the property `Button.Flyout` for all button types and `FlyoutBase.AttachedFlyout` for all other controls. When specified on a button type, the MenuFlyout displays when the button is invoked. When assigned to any other UI elements, you must call either the `ShowAt` method or the static `ShowAttachedFlyout` method to display the flyout. Let's do some refactoring of your app user interface to enable the flyout functionality. Listing 2-20 shows how the command bar should now be specified; the areas in bold are the changes.

Listing 2-20. MenuFlyout in Action

```
<Page.BottomAppBar>
    <CommandBar
        ClosedDisplayMode="Minimal"
        IsSticky="True">

        <AppBarButton
            Label="Reserve"
            Icon="Calendar">
            <AppBarButton.Flyout>
                <MenuFlyout>
                    <MenuFlyoutItem
                        Command="{Binding}"
                        CommandParameter="make a reservation"
                        Text="Pay Now" />
                    <MenuFlyoutItem
                        Text="Pay Later"
                        Command="{Binding}"
                        CommandParameter="hold my spot" />
                </MenuFlyout>
```

```
            </AppBarButton.Flyout>
        </AppBarButton>
    </CommandBar>
</Page.BottomAppBar>
```

Notice from this sample that you have shifted the point at which a reservation happens from the AppBarButton itself and placed it on the menu items of its MenuFlyout. The command and command parameter property have also been shifted down to the menu items of the flyout. Now when a user clicks the reserve button, they get two choices: they can decide to pay upfront or pay when they show up for a massage. To support the Pay Later scenario, a new command parameter and declaration have been added to the Pay Later menu item. The exercise of moving these properties between the three control types you have now used, from Button to AppBarButton and now to MenuFlyoutItem, without the need to modify event handlers in the code-behind, should highlight the benefits of using commands versus programmatically wiring interactivity.

In the code-behind, some changes must also be made. First, let's add a new centralized location for displaying reservation summary information. Presumably any activity that generates a reservation would need to have a summary displayed; having one method service all these potential scenarios is far more ideal than having multiple copies of the same basic code spread around the app. Listing 2-21 shows the code for a `ShowSummary` method; add it to the `MainPage` class.

Listing 2-21. Centralizing the Display of Summary Information

```
async void ShowSummary(ReservationInfo new_reservation,
                                string reservation_tag = "")
{
    MessageDialog md =
        new MessageDialog
          ($"{_reservations.Count} massages reserved\n" +
              $"Newest is {reservation_tag} on {new_reservation.AppointmentDay.Month}/" +
         $"{new_reservation.AppointmentDay.Day}/" +
         $"{new_reservation.AppointmentDay.Year}" +
         $" at {new_reservation.AppointmentTime}\n" +
         $"for {new_reservation.CustomerName}\n" +
         $"born {new_reservation.DOB}");
    await md.ShowAsync();
    control_calendar.Date = null;
}
```

The only change to the code from its previous version is the addition of a `reservation_tag` value to the summary display string. For the purposes of this sample, that value will be used to indicate what kind of reservation has been made during summary presentation. Listing 2-22 shows the updated code for the `_command_DoSomething` event handler. Modify your code base to match it.

Listing 2-22. Connecting Your New MenuFlyout

```
async private void _command_DoSomething(string command)
{
        if (control_calendar.Date == null)
        {
                MessageDialog md =
                        new MessageDialog("Select a day first");
                await md.ShowAsync();
                return;
        }
```

```
        if (command.ToLower() == "make a reservation")
        {
                var new_reservation = new ReservationInfo()
                {
                        AppointmentDay = control_calendar.Date.Value.Date,
                        AppointmentTime = control_time.Time,
                        CustomerName = control_name.Text,
                        DOB = control_dob.Date.Date,
                };
                _reservations.Add(new_reservation);
                ShowSummary(new_reservation, "confirmed");
        }
        else if (command.ToLower() == "hold my spot")
        {
                var new_reservation = new ReservationInfo()
                {
                        AppointmentDay = control_calendar.Date.Value.Date,
                        AppointmentTime = control_time.Time,
                        CustomerName = control_name.Text,
                        DOB = control_dob.Date.Date,
                        HasPaid = false,
                };
                _reservations.Add(new_reservation);
                ShowSummary(new_reservation, "**tentatively**");
        }
        control_calendar.Date = null;
}
```

Now that you have more than one command to work with, it makes sense to start refactoring the code base for readability and efficiency. You've moved the null checking for the CalendarDatePicker outside of the logic for any one specific command as it will apply regardless of command. You are now also using ShowSummary to present a summary of the reservation rather than have a slightly different copy of the contents of ShowSummary present for each command implement.

Finally, you are passing a contextual string into ShowSummary so the user can tell whether it is a confirmed reservation or a tentative one. For a confirmed reservation, you pass "confirmed" and for a tentative one you pass "**tentative**". This string will be combined with the summary string in ShowSummary to present a message to the user that gives an indication of what kind of reservation has been made. An example of a tentative summary is below.

```
"100 massages reserved
Newest is **tentative** on 10/15/2015 at 05:00:00
for Azuka M.
Born 7/7/1997"
```

Figure 2-13 shows the various states of the app now.

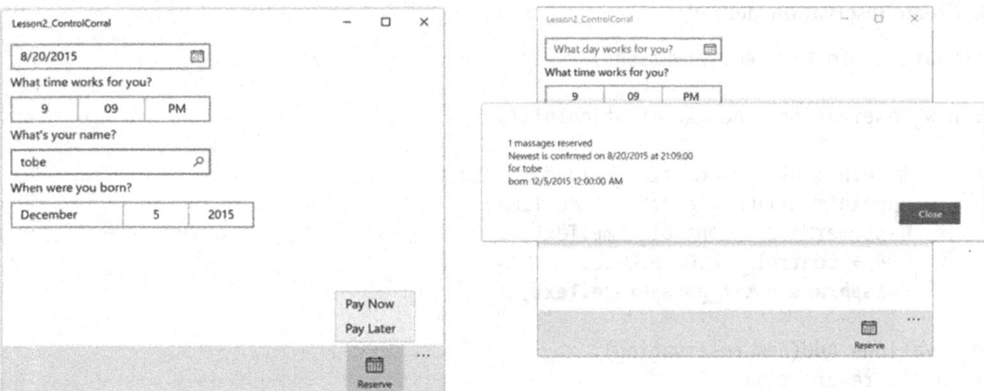

Figure 2-13. *MenuFlyout in action*

TextBox

The TextBox control, commonly used to accept data input, provides the ability to display and edit plain text in single or multi-line form. You previously used a kind of TextBox called an AutoSuggestBox.

To access the contents of a textbox, use the `Text` property. If your code needs to be notified as text in the textbox changes, you can handle the TextChanged event. You can restrict the number of characters the user can type by setting the `MaxLength` property. However, `MaxLength` does not restrict the length of pasted text. You can customize how the text is displayed in the TextBox through the standard Control properties like `FontFamily`, `FontSize`, `FontStyle`, `Background`, `Foreground`, and `CharacterSpacing`.

To enable multi-line input, set the `AcceptsReturn` property to true. If multiline input is enabled, you can enable text wrapping by setting the `TextWrap` property to Wrap. A multi-line TextBox will continue to grow vertically unless it is constrained by its `Height` or `MaxHeight` property, or by a parent container. When in multi-line mode, vertical scrollbars are not shown by default. You can show the vertical scrollbars by setting the attached property `ScrollViewer.VerticalScrollBarVisibility` to Auto. You can make a TextBox read-only by setting the `IsReadOnly` property to true.

Let's use a TextBox control to capture a passphrase that can be used to identify a user when they come for their appointment. Listing 2-23 shows the changes that need to be made to the XAML.

Listing 2-23. TextBox in Action

```
<TextBox
            x:Name="txt_passphrase"
            Header="Enter a passphrase"
            HorizontalAlignment="Left"
            Margin="10,242,0,0"
            TextWrapping="Wrap"
            PlaceholderText="keep it a secret"
            VerticalAlignment="Top"
            Width="296" />
```

In Listing 2-24, you continue your refactoring efforts by moving the reservation creation process into its own method, `MakeReservation`. Add the code to the `MainPage` class.

Listing 2-24. CreateReservation Method

```
private ReservationInfo CreateReservation()
{
        var new_reservation = new ReservationInfo()
        {
                AppointmentDay = control_calendar.Date.Value.Date,
                AppointmentTime = control_time.Time,
                CustomerName = control_name.Text,
                DOB = control_dob.Date.Date,
                Passphrase = txt_passphrase.Text,
        };
        _reservations.Add(new_reservation);
        return new_reservation;
}
```

Note that you have added the setting of Passphrase to the method. Now modify `_command_DoSomething` so that it now looks like Listing 2-25.

Listing 2-25. Refactored _command_DoSomething Event Handler

```
async private void _command_DoSomething(string command)
{
        if (control_calendar.Date == null)
        {
                MessageDialog md =
                        new MessageDialog("Select a day first");
                await md.ShowAsync();
                return;
        }
        if (command.ToLower() == "make a reservation")
        {
                var new_reservation = CreateReservation();
                ShowSummary(new_reservation, "confirmed");
        }
        else if (command.ToLower() == "hold my spot")
        {
                var new_reservation = CreateReservation();
                ShowSummary(new_reservation, "**tentatively**");
        }
        control_calendar.Date = null;
}
```

PasswordBox

PasswordBox is basically a TextBox that lets a user enter a single line of masked, non-wrapping text into it. It offers a more secure approach to entering content since the text entered cannot be read. Password uses a masking character to obfuscate the text entered into it. If you don't like the default masking character, you can modify it by setting the `PasswordChar` property. To access the contents of the PasswordBox, use the `Password` property.

In the previous section, you added a passphrase TextBox into your Control Corral screen. This item was meant to capture and store a secret passphrase that will be used as an additional identification factor when the user goes to get their massage. As you might imagine, using a TextBox to store this kind of information is less than ideal. In Listing 2-26, you convert your user interface and code-behind to support PasswordBox.

Listing 2-26. PasswordBox in Action

```
<PasswordBox
            x:Name="txt_passphrase"
            Header="Enter a passphrase"
            HorizontalAlignment="Left"
            Margin="10,242,0,0"
            PlaceholderText="keep it a secret"
            VerticalAlignment="Top"
            Width="296" />

//code
private ReservationInfo CreateReservation()
{
        var new_reservation = new ReservationInfo()
        {
                AppointmentDay = control_calendar.Date.Value.Date,
                AppointmentTime = control_time.Time,
                CustomerName = control_name.Text,
                DOB = control_dob.Date.Date,
                Passphrase = txt_passphrase.Password,
        };
        _reservations.Add(new_reservation);
        return new_reservation;
}
```

Figure 2-14 shows what it looks like when this app is run and some text is entered into the PasswordBox field.

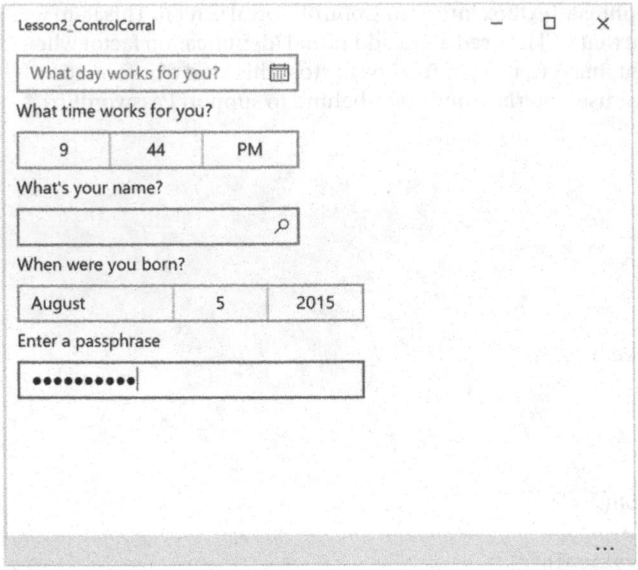

Figure 2-14. *PasswordBox in action*

ComboBox

The ComboBox control is unique in that it can be thought of as a basic control but also as a data control. This is because it is used to present a list of items that a user can select from, more specifically because this list can be populated in one of two ways. You can manually add objects directly to the ComboBox's Items collection or you can use databinding. It is that latter approach that shifts the categorization of a ComboBox away from just a simple control.

Two properties are critical to working with the ComboBox control: `SelectedItem` and `SelectedIndex`. Using either you can get or set its currently selected item. Modify `MainPage.xaml` and its code-behind incorporate ComboBox, as shown in Listing 2-27.

Listing 2-27. ComboBox in Action

```
<ComboBox
            x:Name="control_procedure"
            Header="Select a procedure"
            HorizontalAlignment="Left"
            Margin="10,307,0,0"
            VerticalAlignment="Top"
            Width="296" SelectedIndex="0">
            <ComboBoxItem
                Content="Swedish" />
            <ComboBoxItem
                Content="Hot Stone" />
            <ComboBoxItem
                Content="Shiatsu" />
            <ComboBoxItem
                Content="Deep Tissue" />
```

```
        <ComboBoxItem
            Content="Trigger Point" />
        <ComboBoxItem
            Content="Thai" />
    </ComboBox>

//code
async void ShowSummary(ReservationInfo new_reservation,
                                string reservation_tag = "")
{
        MessageDialog md =
                new MessageDialog
                ($"{_reservations.Count} massages reserved\n" +
                        $"Newest is {reservation_tag} on" +
                        "{new_reservation.AppointmentDay.Month}/" +
                        $"{new_reservation.AppointmentDay.Day}/" +
                        $"{new_reservation.AppointmentDay.Year}" +
                        $" at {new_reservation.AppointmentTime}\n" +
                        $"for {new_reservation.CustomerName}\n" +
                        $"born {new_reservation.DOB}\n" +
                        $"Massage Type: {new_reservation.Procedure}"
                        );
        await md.ShowAsync();
        control_calendar.Date = null;
}

private ReservationInfo CreateReservation()
{
        var new_reservation = new ReservationInfo()
        {
                AppointmentDay = control_calendar.Date.Value.Date,
                AppointmentTime = control_time.Time,
                CustomerName = control_name.Text,
                DOB = control_dob.Date.Date,
                Passphrase = txt_passphrase.Password,
                Procedure = (control_procedure.SelectedItem
                                as ComboBoxItem).Content as string,
        };
        _reservations.Add(new_reservation);
        return new_reservation;
}
```

Slider

The Slider lets the user select from a range of values by moving a Thumb control along a track. It is a great choice in scenarios where exact values are less useful than their visual representation. Sliders expose the `Minimum` and `Maximum` properties to help set the range of values a user is picking from. You can use the `Value` property to retrieve the currently selected value of the slider. Let's use a slider to capture the intensity of massage pressure a potential customer thinks they are comfortable with. Listing 2-28 shows how you can add a slider to your app. Modify MainPage and its code-behind to match it.

Listing 2-28. Slider in Action

```
<Slider
    x:Name="control_intensity"
    Header="Massage Intensity"
    HorizontalAlignment="Left"
    Margin="10,375,0,0"
    VerticalAlignment="Top"
    Width="296" />

//code
private ReservationInfo CreateReservation()
{
        var new_reservation = new ReservationInfo()
        {
                AppointmentDay = control_calendar.Date.Value.Date,
                AppointmentTime = control_time.Time,
                CustomerName = control_name.Text,
                DOB = control_dob.Date.Date,
                Passphrase = txt_passphrase.Password,
                Procedure = (control_procedure.SelectedItem
                                as ComboBoxItem).Content as string,
                MassageIntensity = control_intensity.Value,
        };
        _reservations.Add(new_reservation);
        return new_reservation;
}
```

Image

The Image control can be used to display images of the following image file formats:

- Joint Photographic Experts Group (JPEG)
- Portable Network Graphics (PNG)
- Bitmap (BMP)
- Graphics Interchange Format (GIF)
- Tagged Image File Format (TIFF)
- JPEG XR
- Icons (ICO)

You can specify the source URI that an Image control displays via the Source attribute. In XAML, this field expects an HTTP or ms-appx-based URI to the specified image resource. Typically, the images you load are from image files included as part of your app package, but in situations where you need to get files from an external server, the Image control has built in support for it. Listing 2-29 shows the basic use of an Image control.

Listing 2-29. Image in Action

```
<Image
                x:Name="control_image"
                Source="/assets/storelogo.png" />
```

This code snippet displays an image directly from your app's app package. When an image is referenced in XAML, the shorthand notation used here can be utilized. The source attribute could have also been specified as `ms-appx:/assets/storelogo.png` and it would be the same result.

Displaying an image file programmatically is a bit more involved. Listing 2-30 illustrates how it can be done. It requires the using statement `using Windows.UI.Xaml.Media.Imaging;` for it to work.

Listing 2-30. Setting the Source to an Image Programmatically

```
BitmapImage image = new BitmapImage();
image.UriSource = new Uri("ms-appx:///assets/storelogo.png");
control_image.Source = image;
```

Your image source might also be a stream, in which case you can call the `SetSourceAsync` method of `BitmapImage`. Using a stream for an image source is fairly common. For example, if your app enables a user to choose an image file using a FileOpenPicker control, the object you get that represents the file the user chose can only be opened as a stream. Let's add a control to capture and store the user's picture. Listing 2-31 shows the changes that need to be made to `MainPage.xaml` to enable displaying an image.

Listing 2-31. Image in Action

```
<Button
           Click="ReplaceImage"
            HorizontalAlignment="Left"
            Height="227"
            Margin="353,10,0,0"
            VerticalAlignment="Top"
            Width="225"
            BorderThickness="1"
            BorderBrush="Gray"
            Background="Gainsboro">
            <Image
                x:Name="control_image"
Source="/alex.jpg"
                />
        </Button>
```

As you can see, rather than simply placing an image on the screen, you are using content composition to place the image directly inside a Button control.

This sample will utilize features you won't be exploring until Chapter 7, but it should be straightforward enough for you to understand. Again, if you don't quite get anything, don't worry; you will get into it later in this book.

You will be using a class called the `CameraCaptureUI` to invoke the camera app as a dialog. You will then be able to take a picture and have that picture sent back to your app for rendering and storing. This will all be kicked off when the user clicks the Replace Image button.

Open the code-behind for MainPage and define ReplaceImage as follows, making sure to add all appropriate namespace declarations, class level fields, and modifications to CreateReservation. Listing 2-32 illustrates.

Listing 2-32. Wiring Up the Image Control

```
...
CameraCaptureUI ccui = new CameraCaptureUI();
byte[] _user_image;
...
async private void ReplaceImage(object sender, RoutedEventArgs e)
{
        BitmapImage image = new BitmapImage();
        control_image.Source = image;

        ccui.PhotoSettings.AllowCropping = true;
        ccui.PhotoSettings.MaxResolution =
                CameraCaptureUIMaxPhotoResolution.HighestAvailable;
        var result = await ccui.CaptureFileAsync(CameraCaptureUIMode.Photo);
        if (result != null)
        {
                var stream = await result.OpenReadAsync();
                await image.SetSourceAsync(stream);

                //get the image data and store it
                stream.Seek(0);
                BinaryReader reader = new BinaryReader(stream.AsStreamForRead());
                _user_image = new byte[stream.Size];
                reader.Read(_user_image, 0, _user_image.Length);
        }
}

...

private ReservationInfo CreateReservation()
{
        var new_reservation = new ReservationInfo()
        {
                AppointmentDay = control_calendar.Date.Value.Date,
                AppointmentTime = control_time.Time,
                CustomerName = control_name.Text,
                DOB = control_dob.Date.Date,
                Passphrase = txt_passphrase.Password,
                Procedure = (control_procedure.SelectedItem
                                as ComboBoxItem).Content as string,
                MassageIntensity = control_intensity.Value,
                CustomerImage = _user_image,
        };
        _reservations.Add(new_reservation);
        return new_reservation;
}
```

After a user takes a picture using the `CameraCaptureUI` class, `ReplaceImage` reads the image as a stream and passes it into `SetSourceAsync`. This takes care of showing the image that the user has picked but does nothing to store the information for future use. To do this, you read the stream into a buffer that you maintain at the class level. When `CreateReservation` is called, this buffer is used to set the reservation's `CustomerImage` property. Figure 2-15 shows what the app looks like during the image selection process.

Figure 2-15. *CamerCaptureUI in action*

Figure 2-16 shows how the user interface looks after an image has been selected.

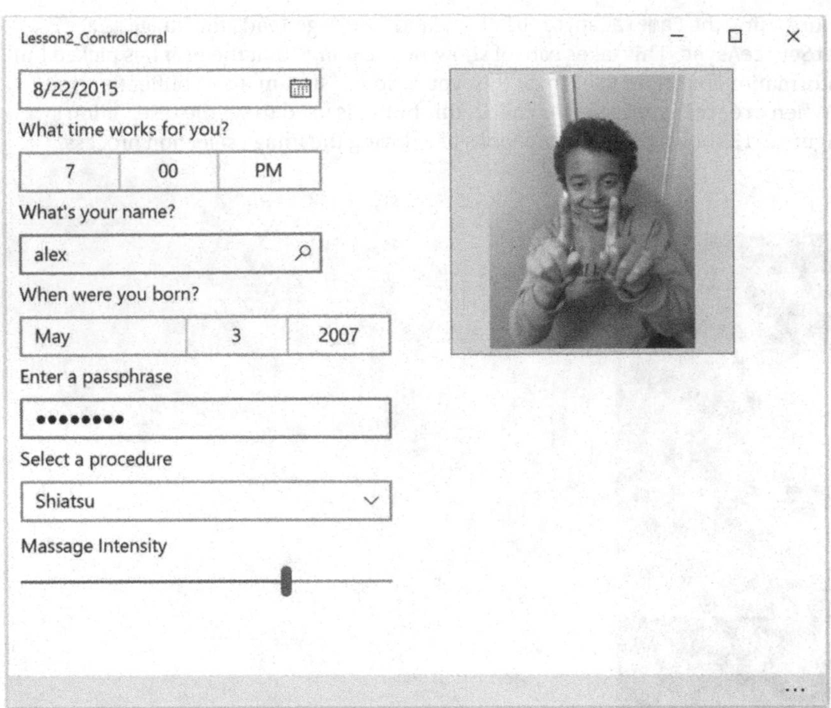

Figure 2-16. *Image control in action*

Even if you were not storing the binary data of the image in a class level field, it's a safe bet to say that large image files can impact performance. Images load into memory, so if you are referencing an image file where you know that the source file is a large, high-resolution image, but your app is displaying it in a UI region that's smaller than the image's natural size, you should set the `DecodePixelWidth` property, or `DecodePixelHeight`. The `DecodePixel*` properties enable you to pass information directly to the format-specific codec, and the codec can use this information to decode more efficiently and to a smaller memory footprint. Set `DecodePixelWidth` to the same pixel width of the area that you want your app to actually display. In other words, `DecodePixelWidth` for the BitmapImage source should be the same value as the `Width` or `ActualWidth` of the Image control that displays that source.

WebView

The WebView control can be used to host HTML content on your screen. This content can come from the Web, your local app package, or even a programmatically-specified string in your code-behind. There are a number of things to keep in mind when working with the WebView. The list below highlights some notable differences from a standard browser:

- WebView is not a control; rather, it is a UIElement.
- WebView doesn't support most of the user input events inherited from UIElement.
- WebView always uses Internet Explorer 11 in document mode.

- WebView does not support any ActiveX controls or plug-ins, nor does it support some HTML5 features including AppCache, IndexedDB, programmatic access to the Clipboard, and geolocation.
- WebView only supports navigation with the HTTP, HTTPS, ms-appx-web, and ms-appdata schemes.

Like the Frame control, WebView provides several APIs for basic navigation that can be used to add typical web browsing capabilities to your app. These include: `GoBack`, `GoForward`, `Stop`, `Refresh`, `CanGoBack`, and `CanGoForward`. To set the content of the WebView, set the `Source` property in XAML or use any one of the `Navigate` methods in code. For more advanced navigation scenarios, like using specific VERBS as part of a navigation request or setting headers, use the `NavigateWithHttpRequestMessage` method.

Loading Content

WebView supports the loading of uncompressed and unencrypted content from your app's LocalFolder or TemporaryFolder data stores using the ms-appdata scheme (you will discuss these folder locations in detail in Chapter 6). To load compressed or encrypted files, use the `NavigateToLocalStreamUri` method with a custom resolver. The WebView support for this scheme requires you to place your content in a subfolder under the local or temporary folder. These subfolders are completely isolated from each other so that hyperlinks from a page in one folder cannot take a user to a page in another folder. The following are examples of URIs that map to these locations:

```
ms-appdata:///local/folder/file.html
ms-appdata:///temp/folder/file.html.
```

WebView also supports loading content directly from your app package. To do this, use the `Navigate` method with a URI that uses the ms-appx-web scheme. This scheme follows the same format as ms-appdata.

```
ms-appx-web:///folder/file.html
```

And of course, WebView supports accessing HTML content from a remote web location using HTTP/HTTPS.

Handling Events

WebView provides several events that you can use to respond to navigation and content loading states. These events occur in the following order for the root WebView content:

- `NavigationStarting`: Occurs before the WebView navigates to new content. You can cancel navigation in the event handler by setting the `WebViewNavigationStartingEventArg` parameter's `Cancel` property to true.
- `ContentLoading`: Occurs when the WebView has started loading new content.
- `DOMContentLoaded`: Occurs when the WebView has finished parsing the current HTML content.
- `NavigationCompleted`: Occurs when the WebView has finished loading the current content or if navigation has failed. To determine whether navigation has failed, check the `IsSuccess` property on the `WebViewNavigationCompletedEventArgs` parameter.

Similar events occur in the same order for each iframe loaded within the WebView content. These events names are prefixed by the word Frame so the `ContentLoading` event for an iframe inside a WebView would be `FrameContentLoading`.

Interoperability with WebView Content

WebView supports the ability to programmatically interact with the content of the WebView by using the `InvokeScriptAsync` method to either invoke or inject script into the WebView content. If a JavaScript function is called, it cannot return anything but a string value. Additionally, functions that require a secondary window to operate (for instance `prompt()` or `alert()`) cannot be successfully called.

To get information back from the HTML document in a WebView, your page code must handle the `ScriptNotify` event. On the HTML side, the executing script must make a call to `window.external.notify` with a string parameter to send information back to your app. This functionality must be enabled in the app manifest for it to function. Specifically, the URI where the call to `window.external.notify` is coming from must be included in the ApplicationContentUriRules section of the app manifest. This manifest requirement does not apply to content that originates from the app package, uses an ms-local-stream schemed URI, or is loaded using NavigateToString.

Figure 2-17 shows the app manifest configuration window for setting this value.

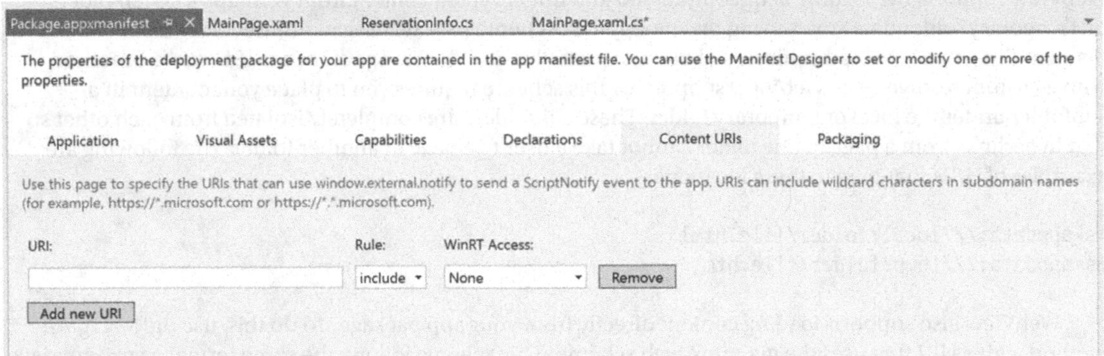

Figure 2-17. *The Content URIs section of App manifest*

The URIs in this list must use HTTPS, and may contain subdomain wildcards (for example, `https://*.microsoft.com`), but they cannot contain domain wildcards.

One cool feature the WebView control supports is the ability to take a snapshot of the content it is currently presenting using the `CapturePreviewToStreamAsync` method. You can also enable the sharing of WebView content using `CaptureSelectedContentToDataPackageAsync` method.

Noteworthy Mentions

The following controls are not very popular for every day use but do satisfy specific scenarios where their unique features are required.

ProgressBar

The ProgressBar control visually indicates progress of an operation with one of two styles: a bar that displays a repeating pattern (when the `IsIndeterminate` property is set to true), or a bar that fills based on a value. When `IsIndeterminate` is false, you specify the range with the `Minimum` and `Maximum` properties. By default `Minimum` is 0 and `Maximum` is 1. To specify the progress value, you set the `Value` property. You can alternatively use a ProgressRing control to indicate indeterminate progress. A progress ring does the same thing as an indeterminate progress bar but uses an animated ring instead of a line. See Listing 2-33 and Figure 2-18.

Listing 2-33. Defining a ProgressBar Control in XAML

```
<ProgressBar
            HorizontalAlignment="Left"
            Height="10"
            Margin="754,215,0,0"
            VerticalAlignment="Top"
            Width="100"
            Minimum="0"
            Maximum="100"
            Value="45" />
<ProgressRing IsActive="True" />
```

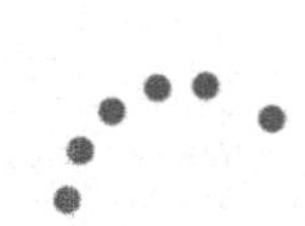

Figure 2-18. *The ProgressBar and ProgressRing user interfaces*

■ **Note** When the ProgressBar is indeterminate, the progress animation continues even if it's not visible on the screen, such as when the ProgressBar `Visibility` is `Collapsed`. This can keep the UI thread awake, use resources, and impair app performance. When the ProgressBar is not visible, you should disable the animation by setting `IsIndeterminate` to `False`.

HyperlinkButton

One handy kind of button you will probably use as some point in your UWP app is the HyperlinkButton. These controls are designed to open the URI specified in their `NavigateUri` property when a user clicks them (the defaults defined on the machine will determine what program/app is used to handle the URI launch request). If a `NavigateUri` is not specified and the Click event is, HyperlinkButton will function like a normal button. See Listing 2-34 and Figure 2-19.

Listing 2-34. Defining a HyperlinkButton Control in XAML

```
<HyperlinkButton
            Content="Publishers Website"
            NavigateUri="http://www.thethinkmine.com"
            HorizontalAlignment="Left"
            Margin="353,242,0,0"
            VerticalAlignment="Top" />
```

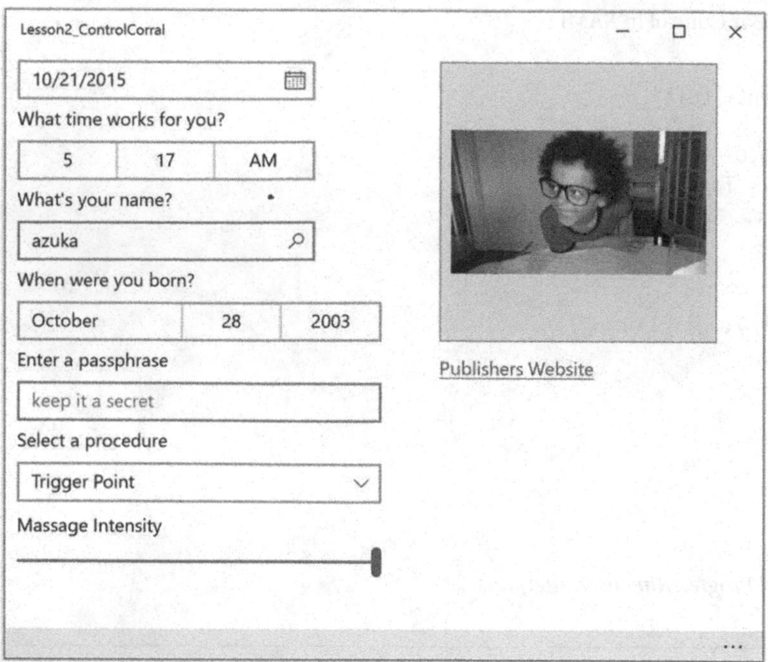

Figure 2-19. *HyperlinkButton in action*

CheckBox

Both CheckBox and RadioButton controls allow the user to select from a list of options. CheckBox controls allow the user to select a combination of options. In contrast, RadioButton controls allow the user to select from mutually exclusive options. UWP checkboxes can report an intermediate state when the property `IsThreeState` is set to true. You can use the `IsChecked` property to determine if a given checkbox is in the checked state. See Listing 2-35 and Figure 2-20.

Listing 2-35. Defining a Checkbox Control in XAML

```
<CheckBox
            x:Name="checkBox"
            IsChecked="True"
            Content="Send me useless information"
            HorizontalAlignment="Left"
            Margin="10,439,0,0"
            VerticalAlignment="Top" />
```

Send me useless information

Figure 2-20. *The Checkbox control*

RadioButton

The RadioButton can be used to limit a user's selection to a single choice within a set of related, but mutually exclusive, choices. You group RadioButton controls by putting them inside the same parent container or by setting the GroupName property on each RadioButton to the same value. Like a CheckBox, you can use the IsChecked property of a RadioButton to determine if it has been selected.

A RadioButton can be cleared by clicking another RadioButton in the same group, but it cannot be cleared by clicking it again like a checkbox can. See Listing 2-36 and Figure 2-21.

Listing 2-36. RadioButton Control in Action

```
<Grid
    Margin="10,483,0,0"
    Height="130" VerticalAlignment="Top"
    HorizontalAlignment="Left" Width="296">
    <Border
        BorderThickness="1" BorderBrush="Black" Padding="10">
        <Grid>
            <RadioButton
                Content="Female" HorizontalAlignment="Left"
                Margin="0,31,0,0" GroupName="Gender"
                VerticalAlignment="Top" Width="219" />
            <RadioButton
                Content="Male" HorizontalAlignment="Left"
                GroupName="Gender" VerticalAlignment="Top"
                Width="219" />
            <RadioButton
                Content="Unspecified" HorizontalAlignment="Left"
                Margin="0,62,0,0" GroupName="Gender"
                IsChecked="True" VerticalAlignment="Top"
                Width="219" />
        </Grid>
    </Border>
    <Border
        HorizontalAlignment="Right" Margin="0,-10,14,0"
        VerticalAlignment="Top" Background="White"
        Width="63">
        <TextBlock
            HorizontalAlignment="Center" TextAlignment="Center"
            TextWrapping="Wrap"  Text="Gender"
            Height="20" Width="62" />
    </Border>
</Grid>
```

Figure 2-21. *The RadioButton controls in action*

ToggleSwitch

The ToggleSwitch lets the user switch between on and off states. To determine the current state of the switch, use the `IsOn` property. To know immediately when the toggle state has been modified, use the `Toggled` event. See Listing 2-37 and Figure 2-22.

Listing 2-37. Defining a ToggleSwitch Control in XAML

```
<ToggleSwitch

            Header="Make recurring appointment"
            HorizontalAlignment="Left"
            Margin="10,630,0,0"
            VerticalAlignment="Top" />
```

Make recurring appointment

 On

Figure 2-22. *The ToggleSwitch control*

Border

Border draws a border and or background around a single child object. You can specify basic properties of a Border by setting its `Width`, `Height`, `BorderBrush`, `BorderThickness`, and `Background` color. Additionally, you can round the border corners by setting the `CornerRadius` property, and you can position the object inside the Border by setting the `Padding` property. You used a border object earlier in this chapter when you re-templated a button; you also used one in Chapter 1 when you used content composition to style the content inside your attendee counting buttons. Although this control does not technically stand alone as screen content, it can be an invaluable asset when building UWP user interfaces.

Summary

You just completed a meaty chapter with a comprehensive and in-depth investigation into incorporating basic controls into your UWP apps. Here's a review of some key points:

- Controls are encapsulated pieces of user interface that combine layout, content, and behavior to create distinct experiences within the construct of the surface that contains them.
- The four main classes of controls are basic controls, layout controls, data controls, and custom controls that the UWP provides.
- Controls are made up of their user interface (in the form of templates or composed content) and the behaviors that bind their user interface in meaningful ways.
- The UWP app window has a `Content` property that is the primary surface upon which XAML-based user interfaces are presented. Additionally, Frame and Page controls facilitate navigation within a XAML-based UWP app.

- Command binding is a technique that allows us to bind behavior to abstract commands such that the user interface declaration of a command-generating control is not rigidly connected to the code-behind that implements that behavior.
- Controls can be re-templated to enable a more tailored user experiences.
- You learned how to use many of the major controls exposed by the UWP platform.
- Custom controls give you the ability to create reusable user interfaces. This allows you to use controls that have the same layout and behavior in repeated instances.

CHAPTER 3

Data Controls

In the previous chapter, you learned about the basic controls available to a developer. This chapter continues the control discussion with data controls. Data controls, like basic controls, are designed with presentation and interaction with the end user in mind. They are meant to be seen by the end user. What separates data controls from basic controls is that data controls are tailored to present sets of data to the user in an optimized manner, while most basic controls are meant to either take input from the user or present scalar information to the user.

As you did in the previous chapter, you will be using the UWP app you are building for the Control Corral imaginary business to frame the conversation. Chapter 2's implementation of the Control Corral app was a great start on a useful massage reservation system, but it lacked a number of key features. To get it to the next level, reservations and their associated information need to be properly persisted so that all the data captured isn't lost once the app is closed. The app also needs more screens. Most applications that work with data expose SCRUD interfaces to the end user (SCRUD stands for Search, Create, Read, Update, and Delete.) Right now the app only has the ability to capture and store reservations, satisfying the "Create" part of SCRUD. You must add new pages to the app to support the various other activities that must be performed on the captured data. Let's get started with changing the persistence model

Modifying the Project

You'll need to do some initial project setup that has little to do with data controls to get your environment in place to properly add functionality. One of the first activities is to change the persistence model that Control Corral uses.

Creating a Control Corral Model

You are going to be navigating between multiple pages in this example, using the same data to present different views to the user based on the page. This means that a primitive approach of storing the reservations in a class level field will no longer suffice. Instead, you will need a global location where the data can be accessed. You also need to expand the definition of the data and make it more normalized. Normalizing the data minimizes the amount of data that must be stored. If you consider that ReservationInfo stores the Name and Image of a customer and that a customer might make multiple appointments, you begin to see the problem. As it stands, the same customer would be represented for each appointment, with an image buffer for each one. Yikes! Let's create a `CustomerInfo` class with `CustomerName`, `DOB`, `CustomerImage`, and `MassageIntensity` preference properties. Listing 3-1 does this.

Listing 3-1. CustomerInfo Class Definition

```
namespace Lesson2_ControlCorral
{
        public class CustomerInfo
        {
                public string CustomerName { get; set; }
                public byte[] CustomerImage { get; set; }
                public double MassageIntensity { get; set; }
                public DateTime DOB { get; set; }
        }
}
```

Because you are now using `CustomerInfo` to store the customer-related data, `ReservationInfo` must be changed to reference this class rather than directly storing the customer field within it. Keep the massage intensity value here as well so that the user has the choice to override the value they might have specified as a preference. See Listing 3-2.

Listing 3-2. ReservationInfo Class Definition

```
public class ReservationInfo
{
        public DateTime AppointmentDay { get; set; }
        public TimeSpan AppointmentTime { get; set; }
        public bool HasPaid { get; set; } = true;
        public string Passphrase { get; set; }
        public string Procedure { get; set; }
        public double MassageIntensity { get; set; }
        public CustomerInfo Customer { get; set; }
}
```

Next, you define a class `MassageType` that can be used to store a list of the types of massages offered. Presently the list of massage types is hard-coded into the UI, a bad practice. Using this type allows a user to add or remove massage types as needed. See Listing 3-3.

Listing 3-3. MassageType Class Definition

```
namespace Lesson2_ControlCorral
{
        public class MassageType
        {
                public string Name { get; set; }
                public string Description { get; set; }
        }
}
```

The system now has three data lists that it needs to track: the list of reservations, the list of known customers, and the list of massage types that the business supports. One good practice in developing with data is to encapsulate the various data sets your application uses into a single model or data context object so that that there is a single point of access to all data being used by the system. To do so, create a new class `ControlCorralModel` as shown in Listing 3-4.

Listing 3-4. ControlCorralModel Class Definition

```
namespace Lesson2_ControlCorral
{
        public class ControlCorralModel
        {
                public List<CustomerInfo> Customers { get; set; } = new
                List<CustomerInfo>();
                public List<ReservationInfo> Reservations { get; set; } = new
                List<ReservationInfo>();
                public List<MassageType> MassageTypes { get; set; } = new
                List<MassageType>();
        }
}
```

In Listing 3-4, you add the various data lists being tracked by the app as properties in the ControlCorralModel class. You now have a central place where application data is defined, so let's connect that class with the app. Because you know that this app will have multiple pages which will need access to the model, you will use the Application object as the location for this instance (the application object is available to all pages in a UWP app). Add the code in Listing 3-5 to the app object's OnLaunched event handler in App.xaml.cs. The new code is highlighted in bold.

Listing 3-5. Implementing the Model

```
public static ControlCorralModel Model { get; set; }

protected override void OnLaunched(LaunchActivatedEventArgs e)
{
        //instantiate model
        Model = new ControlCorralModel();

        //add default massage types
        Model.MassageTypes.AddRange(
                new List<string>
                {
                        "Swedish","Hot Stone",
                        "Shiatsu","Deep Tissue",
                        "Trigger Point","Thai",
                }.Select(i => new MassageType
                {
                        Name = i,
                }).ToList());

        //add sample customers
        Model.Customers.AddRange(
                new List<string> {"alex",
                        "azuka",
                        "elizabeth",
                        "ahmed","josh","allan", "john","david",
                        "chris","jack","bobby","ike","emeka",
```

```
                        "tobe","chidi","mason","andrew" }.
                                Select(i => new CustomerInfo
                                {
                                        CustomerName = i,
                                }).ToList());

        var frame = new Frame();
        Window.Current.Content = frame;
        frame.Navigate(typeof(MainPage));
        Window.Current.Activate();
}
```

In Listing 3-5, you instantiate the app's model and populate it with the same default values you used in the previous chapter. Rather than add these values one item at a time, you use LINQ to query into a string list you create and project out the collection of objects you are interested in using. This is a great technique to quickly create a collection of objects from a list of strings (it saves you the trouble of manually creating each object in code).

Now that you have this configured, you can go back to MainPage and modify it to use the new storage paradigm. First, you modify the `OnLoad` event for the MainPage so that it uses the data from your model and not data created here. See Listing 3-6.

Listing 3-6. DataBinding to Model

```
//MainPage Load event
private void MainPage_Loaded(object sender, RoutedEventArgs e)
{
        this.DataContext = _command;
        control_name.ItemsSource = App.Model.Customers;
}
```

Using the data from the model means you no longer need the `_usuals` field, so let's remove it from the class by modifying the `AutoSuggestBox` event handlers used to filter the user list. They should now also point to the model. See Listing 3-7.

Listing 3-7. Changing AutoSuggestBox to Use Model

```
private void Control_name_TextChanged(AutoSuggestBox sender,
        AutoSuggestBoxTextChangedEventArgs args)
{
        if (args.CheckCurrent())
        {
                var search_term = control_name.Text.ToLower();
                var results = App.Model.Customers
                        .Where(i => i.CustomerName.ToLower()
                        .Contains(search_term.ToLower())).ToList();
                control_name.ItemsSource = results;

        }
}
```

```
private void Control_name_QuerySubmitted(AutoSuggestBox sender,
        AutoSuggestBoxQuerySubmittedEventArgs args)
{
        var search_term = args.QueryText.ToLower();
        var results = App.Model.Customers
                .Where(i => i.CustomerName
                .Contains(search_term.ToLower())).ToList();
        control_name.ItemsSource = results;
        control_name.IsSuggestionListOpen = true;
}

private void Control_name_SuggestionChosen(AutoSuggestBox sender,
        AutoSuggestBoxSuggestionChosenEventArgs args)
{
        control_name.Text = (args.SelectedItem as CustomerInfo).CustomerName;
}
```

In Listing 3-7, the AutoSuggestBox event handlers are modified to use your app's model rather than a local one. Because the type of your app model is CustomerInfo and not just a generic string, you also make some changes to the where clause used.

You next modify CreateReservation so that it is using the new paradigm. The older ReservationInfo object had customer-related properties that were used elsewhere (in display, for instance). In an effort to encapsulate this data in its relevant containing types, the properties were moved to CustomerInfo. All previous references to these fields through the ReservationInfo class will now have to change. You start with the reservation creation process.

Because you are now tracking customers in their own list (and because you want to reuse the same customer instance for multiple reservations if needed) this method will now create new customers if and only if they do not already exist in the model. Listing 3-8 illustrates.

Listing 3-8. Updating Reservation Creation to Use Model

```
private ReservationInfo CreateReservation()
{
        var customer = App.Model.Customers
                .Where(i =>
                i.CustomerName.ToLower() == control_name.Text.ToLower())
                .FirstOrDefault();
        if (customer == null)
        {
                //create and add a new customer if
                //none exist with that name
                customer = new CustomerInfo
                {
                        CustomerName = control_name.Text,
                        DOB = control_dob.Date.Date,
                        MassageIntensity = control_intensity.Value,
                        CustomerImage = _user_image,
                };
                App.Model.Customers.Add(customer);
        }
```

```
        var new_reservation = new ReservationInfo()
        {
                AppointmentDay = control_calendar.Date.Value.Date,
                AppointmentTime = control_time.Time,
                Passphrase = txt_passphrase.Password,
                Procedure = (control_procedure.SelectedItem
                                as ComboBoxItem).Content as string,
                MassageIntensity = control_intensity.Value,
                Customer = customer,  //connect the customer
        };
        _reservations.Add(new_reservation);
        return new_reservation;
}
```

The next step is to change ShowSummary to support using the Customer property on ReservationInfo to access the customer's name and date of birth. See Listing 3-9.

Listing 3-9. Updating Summary Dialog to Use Model

```
async void ShowSummary(ReservationInfo new_reservation,
                                string reservation_tag = "")
{
        MessageDialog md =
                new MessageDialog
                ($"{_reservations.Count} massages reserved\n" +
                        $"Newest is {reservation_tag} on" +
                        $"{new_reservation.AppointmentDay.Month}/" +
                        $"{new_reservation.AppointmentDay.Day}/" +
                        $"{new_reservation.AppointmentDay.Year}" +
                        $" at {new_reservation.AppointmentTime}\n" +
                        $"for {new_reservation.Customer.CustomerName}\n" +
                        $"born {new_reservation.Customer.DOB}\n" +
                        $"Massage Type: {new_reservation.Procedure}"
                        );
        await md.ShowAsync();
        control_calendar.Date = null;
        Frame.GoBack();
}
```

You then modify _command_DoSomething to store the created reservations to your model. Later, you will create the implementations for the SaveModelAsync method. For now, just add it (you know it won't compile). Listing 3-10 illustrates.

Listing 3-10. Updating Command Handler to Use Model

```
async private void _command_DoSomething(string command)
{
        if (control_calendar.Date == null)
        {
                MessageDialog md =
                        new MessageDialog("Select a day first");
                await md.ShowAsync();
                return;
        }
```

```
        if (command.ToLower() == "make a reservation")
        {
                var new_reservation = CreateReservation();
                App.Model.Reservations.Add(new_reservation);
                await App.SaveModelAsync();
                ShowSummary(new_reservation, "confirmed");
        }
        else if (command.ToLower() == "hold my spot")
        {
                var new_reservation = CreateReservation();
                App.Model.Reservations.Add(new_reservation);
                await App.SaveModelAsync();
                ShowSummary(new_reservation, "**tentatively**");
        }
        control_calendar.Date = null;
}
```

Finally, you must modify the user interface for MainPage.xaml so that the AutoSuggestBox is properly connected to the back-end data that it displays. Previously this control directly bound to a list of users (as a string). With this new change, customers are no longer stored as a string, rather as a rich set of properties represent the massage parlor's data. Listing 3-11 shows the changes that must be made to the AutoSuggestBox to complete reservations.

Listing 3-11. AutoSuggestBox Modifications (in Bold)

```
<AutoSuggestBox
        x:Name="control_name"
        HorizontalAlignment="Left"
        Header="What's your name?"
        DisplayMemberPath="CustomerName"
        Margin="10,112,0,0"
        VerticalAlignment="Top"
        Width="242"
        QueryIcon="Find" />
```

DisplayMemberPath is used to identify to the data binding runtime what property of the underlying bound object instance to display. The line in Listing 3-9 highlighted in bold means that the CustomerName property of your CustomerInfo object it is bound to is displayed.

Persisting to the File System

You haven't yet solved the persistence problem introduced in the version of Control Corral from Chapter 2; you've merely propagated it to the next level. Shifting the storage of the control corral data model items from MainPage to the application object allows you to access the model from any page in the application. But what happens if the app crashes?

Because the model is presently stored in memory, any changes to it will be lost once the memory is reclaimed by the system (when the application is closed). This means that every time you close and reopen the app, you are starting from scratch. This is not ideal. One solution is to maintain the model information outside of the app itself. When the app starts, you read the data from the external store and populate your in-memory model with that information. While the app is running you maintain a copy of the model data in memory but also push changes down to the external store as they happen. This way the external store is always up to date, thus preventing data loss as a result of catastrophic failure.

This process can be accomplished in two steps. You start by writing the contents of the app's model to an external store, specifically the file system. You use the app's local storage area, accessed via the `Windows.ApplicationData.LocalFolder` property, and two classes, `StorageFolder` and `StorageFile`, to accomplish the persistence model. You saw `StorageFile` in action in the previous chapter. When you read the contents of an image taken by the user, it was a `StorageFile` you were working with. In general, these classes can be thought of as representations of a File and Folder. (These topics will be covered in greater detail in Chapter 5; for now, just go with it.)

The sample relies on serialization as a means to convert an instance of the model into text that can be stored in the file system. This approach is a shortcut that prevents you from having to manually copy the data over and back. Add the static function `SaveModelAsync` to the `App` class. For the code destined for `App.xaml.cs` to work, a few namespace declarations must be added to the file. Listing 3-12 illustrates.

Listing 3-12. Implementing Persistent Save Method

```
async public static Task SaveModelAsync()
{
        //serialize the model object to a memory stream
        DataContractSerializer dcs = new DataContractSerializer(Model.GetType());

        //write model string to file
        var file = await ApplicationData.Current
                                    .LocalFolder
                                    .CreateFileAsync("corralmodel.xml",
                                    CreationCollisionOption.OpenIfExists);
        var transaction = await file.OpenTransactedWriteAsync();
        var opn = transaction.Stream;
        var ostream = opn.GetOutputStreamAt(0);
        var stream = ostream.AsStreamForWrite();
        dcs.WriteObject(stream, Model);
        stream.Flush();
        stream.Dispose();
        await transaction.CommitAsync();
        transaction.Dispose();
}
```

Basically, Listing 3-12 uses the built-in `DataContractSerializer` class to write the state of your model to a stream.

Now modify the Create reservation part so that it calls `SaveModelAsync` after adding a new reservation. Open and run the app, create a new reservation, and then close the app. You should now have one reservation stored in your model. Let's see if you can load it back into the app. Add a new static method called `LoadModelAsync` to the `App` class that follows Listing 3-13.

Listing 3-13. Implementing Load Model That Loads from Persistent Store

```
async public static Task<ControlCorralModel> LoadModelAsync()
{
        //read the target file's text
        try
        {
                var file = await ApplicationData
                        .Current
                        .LocalFolder.GetFileAsync("corralmodel.xml");
```

```
            var opn = await file
                    .OpenAsync(Windows.Storage.FileAccessMode.Read);
            var stream = opn.GetInputStreamAt(0);
            var reader = new DataReader(stream);
            var size = (await file
                    .GetBasicPropertiesAsync()).Size;
            await reader.LoadAsync((uint)size);
            var model_text = reader.ReadString((uint)size);

            //before attempting deserialize, ensure the string is valid
            if (string.IsNullOrWhiteSpace(model_text))
                    return null;

            //deserialize the text
            var ms = new MemoryStream(Encoding
                    .UTF8.GetBytes(model_text));
            var dsc =
                    new DataContractSerializer(typeof(ControlCorralModel));
            var ret_val = dsc.ReadObject(ms) as ControlCorralModel;
            return ret_val;
        }
        catch (Exception ex)
        {
            return null;
        }
}
```

In Listing 3-13, you are doing the reverse of Listing 3-12. You read the contents of `corralmodel.xml` into a string and use that string to construct a stream, which you can then use to deserialize your model back into its object form. You must now modify the instantiation of your model object so that it tries to load from the file system each time the application starts. Let's modify `OnLaunched` so it is like Listing 3-14. The relevant change is highlighted in bold.

Listing 3-14. Updating App Launch to Use Persistence

```
async protected override void OnLaunched(LaunchActivatedEventArgs e)
{
        //instantiate model
        Model = await LoadModelAsync();
        if (Model == null)
        {
                Model = new ControlCorralModel();

                //add default massage types
                Model.MassageTypes.AddRange(
                        new List<string>
                        {
                        "Swedish","Hot Stone",
                        "Shiatsu","Deep Tissue",
                        "Trigger Point","Thai",
                        }.Select(i => new MassageType
```

```
                        {
                                Name = i,
                        }).ToList());
        }

        var frame = new Frame();
        Window.Current.Content = frame;
        frame.Navigate(typeof(MainPage));
        Window.Current.Activate();
}
```

Place a breakpoint on the line right after your model object is created and run the app. You should see that the Model property has been correctly populated with the one reservation. Figure 3-1 shows this.

```
0 references
async protected override void OnLaunched(LaunchActivatedEventArgs e)
{
    //instantiate model
    Model = await LoadModelAsync();
    if ( ◢ Model {Lesson2_ControlCorral.ControlCorralModel}
    {     ▷ Customers      Count = 2
        Mo▷ MassageTypes Count = 6  l();
          ▷ Reservations   Count = 1
        //add default massage types
        Model.MassageTypes.AddRange(
            new List<string>
            {
    "Swedish","Hot Stone",
    "Shiatsu","Deep Tissue",
    "Trigger Point","Thai",
```

***Figure 3-1.** Persistent storage in action*

Setting Up the Pages

As it stands, the Control Corral app is made up of just one page, `MainPage.xaml`. Although it is technically feasible to do in one page, the various actions that need to be performed in order to satisfy the SCRUD requirements make splitting the app up into multiple pages more sensible. The list below outlines the new pages you will be adding to the app, mapping them to the SCRUD-based requirement they satisfy. Add each item as a page to your project.

- `Dashboard.xaml`
- `ListReservations.xaml`
- `ManageReservation.xaml`
- `ManageCustomer.xaml`
- `RootHost.xaml`

Once added, your project files should look like Figure 3-2.

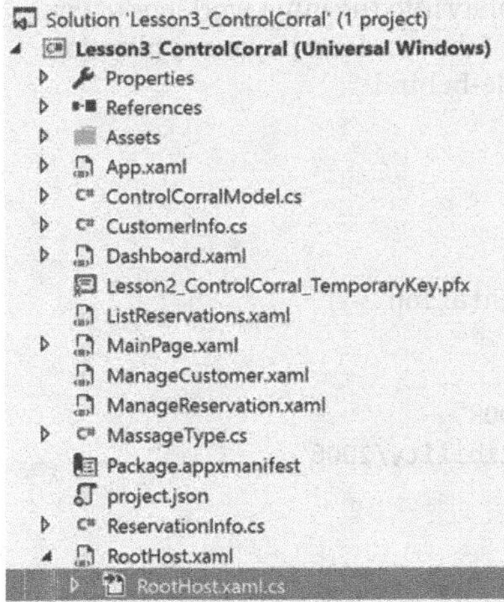

Figure 3-2. *Project files*

You now need to go back into the app's App object and modify the first page launched by the app. Presently the root frame for the app initially navigates to MainPage, which-despite its name-is used solely for creating new ReservationInfo objects. First, to help with encapsulating navigation functionality, replace the use of a Frame as the main content with a RootHost instance. Listing 3-15 shows how OnLaunched should now look.

Listing 3-15. Changing Root Host for App

```
async protected override void OnLaunched(LaunchActivatedEventArgs e)
{
        //instantiate model
        Model = await LoadModelAsync();
        if (Model == null)
        {
                Model = new ControlCorralModel();

                //add default massage types
                Model.MassageTypes.AddRange(
                        new List<string>
                        {
        "Swedish","Hot Stone",
        "Shiatsu","Deep Tissue",
        "Trigger Point","Thai",
                        }.Select(i => new MassageType
                        {
                                Name = i,
                        }).ToList());
        }

        var root_host = new RootHost();
        Window.Current.Content = root_host;
        Window.Current.Activate();
}
```

RootHost serves as a proxy to a frame object so you have some visibility into the inner workings of your Frame host. It also gives you the ability to overlay content on top of any of the windows in your application. Listing 3-16 shows the contents of `RootHost.xaml` and its associated code-behind.

Listing 3-16. RootHost XAML Definition and Code-Behind

```
<Page
    x:Class="Lesson2_ControlCorral.RootHost"
    xmlns="http://schemas.microsoft.com/winfx/2006/xaml/presentation"
    xmlns:x="http://schemas.microsoft.com/winfx/2006/xaml"
    xmlns:local="using:Lesson2_ControlCorral"
    xmlns:d="http://schemas.microsoft.com/expression/blend/2008"
    xmlns:mc="http://schemas.openxmlformats.org/markup-compatibility/2006"
    mc:Ignorable="d">

    <Frame x:Name="rootframe" />
</Page>

namespace Lesson2_ControlCorral
{
        /// <summary>
        /// An empty page that can be used on its own or navigated to within a Frame.
        /// </summary>
        public sealed partial class RootHost : Page
        {
                public RootHost()
                {
                        this.InitializeComponent();
                        SystemNavigationManager
                                .GetForCurrentView()
                                .AppViewBackButtonVisibility
                                = AppViewBackButtonVisibility.Visible;
                        SystemNavigationManager
                                .GetForCurrentView()
                                .BackRequested += RootHost_BackRequested;
                        this.Loaded += RootHost_Loaded;
                }

                private void RootHost_Loaded(object sender, RoutedEventArgs e)
                {
                        rootframe.Navigate(typeof(Dashboard));
                }

                private void RootHost_BackRequested(object sender,
                        BackRequestedEventArgs e)
                {
                        if (rootframe.CanGoBack)
                        {
                                e.Handled = true;
                                rootframe.GoBack();
                        }
```

```
                else
                        e.Handled = false;
            }
        }
}
```

Note the use of the SystemNavigationManager in the constructor of this class. SystemNavigationManager will present a global back button on Windows 10 UWP app's title bar when AppViewBackButtonVisibility is set to Visible. The code-behind also navigates the user directly to Dashboard. This way the dashboard is the first thing a user sees when they start the application.

Now open Dashboard.xaml and add a new button to it. Then set its content to "New Reservation". This button will be used to navigate from the Dashboard to the MainPage. Listing 3-17 shows the layout for the new button and the code-behind for it.

Listing 3-17. New Reservation Button Implementation

```
<Button
        Content="New Reservation"
        HorizontalAlignment="Left"
        Height="55"
        Margin="10,10,0,0"
        VerticalAlignment="Top"
        Click="OnReservation" />

namespace Lesson2_ControlCorral
{

        public sealed partial class Dashboard : Page
        {
                public Dashboard()
                {
                        this.InitializeComponent();
                        this.Loaded += Dashboard_Loaded;
                }

                private void Dashboard_Loaded
                        (object sender, RoutedEventArgs e)
                {

                }

                private void OnReservation(object sender, RoutedEventArgs e)
                {
                        this.Frame.Navigate(typeof(MainPage));
                }
        }
}
```

Use F5 to fire up the application, and you should now see the dashboard. Clicking the New Reservation button should now take you to the same screen you used in Chapter 2: the MainPage screen. You should also now be able to use the global back button on the title bar for the UWP to navigate backwards (if the navigation stack has items to navigate backwards to).

At this point, you have all you need to begin learning about data controls. The remainder of this chapter will focus on introducing the various data controls available to the UWP with a focus on using each control to satisfy the SCRUD requirements outlined earlier.

Listing Reservations with ListBox

Like a ComboBox, a ListBox is used to present a list of items that a user can select from. Unlike a ComboBox, a ListBox can display, and allow the selection of, more than one item at a time. To populate a ListBox, you can either manually add items its Items collection or use data binding to bind to its `ItemSource` property. Selections made by a user can be retrieved via the `SelectedIndex`, `SelectedItem`, or `SelectedValue` properties. When multiple selection is enabled, `SelectedItems` must be used to iterate through the user's selections. (Multiple selection is not enabled by default; to enable it, use the `SelectionMode` property.)

The ListBox control has quite a few similarities with two other controls you will be exploring in this chapter, ListView and GridView. They share some functionality but ultimately the ListBox, like ComboBox, is best for general UI composition, while those other controls are best for data binding.

You will be using a ListBox to populate the ListReservations page. Open ListReservations and rewrite the main grid as follows in Listing 3-18.

Listing 3-18. ListReservations XAML Layout

```
<Grid
        Background="{ThemeResource ApplicationPageBackgroundThemeBrush}">
        <TextBlock
            Text="List Reservations"
            HorizontalAlignment="Left"
            FontSize="40"
            FontWeight="ExtraLight"
            VerticalAlignment="Top"
            Margin="20,0,0,0" />
        <ListBox
            x:Name="list_reservations"
            Margin="20,58,20,20"
            ItemsSource="{Binding}">
            <ListBox.ItemTemplate>
                <DataTemplate>
                    <StackPanel
                        Orientation="Horizontal">
                        <TextBlock
                            Text="{Binding Procedure}"
                            Margin="0,0,10,0" />
                        <TextBlock
                            Text="{Binding AppointmentDay.Month}" />
                        <TextBlock
                            Text="/" />
                        <TextBlock
                            Text="{Binding AppointmentDay.Day}"
                            Margin="0,0,10,0" />
                        <TextBlock
                            Text="{Binding AppointmentTime}"
                            Margin="0,0,10,0" />
```

```
                    <TextBlock
                        Text="{Binding Customer.CustomerName}"
                        Margin="0,0,10,0" />
                </StackPanel>
            </DataTemplate>
        </ListBox.ItemTemplate>
    </ListBox>
</Grid>
```

The ListBox is using a special kind of template called a DataTemplate to define its contents. We identified templates in the previous chapter as user interfaces that can be applied to controls. When dealing with plain old objects bound to data controls, templates can be used to define the user interface of each item. In the case of Listing 3-18, you have defined an item template for the ListBox that will be used to render each `ReservationInfo` object in the collection it represents. When a given item in the list comes into view, the template is used to render the user interface for the item, with each {Binding} defined serving as a placeholder for the content that should be there at runtime. Add the code-behind that populates the ListBox as follows in Listing 3-19.

Listing 3-19. ListReservations Code-Behind

```
namespace Lesson2_ControlCorral
{

        public sealed partial class ListReservations : Page
        {
                List<ReservationInfo> _current_list;
                public ListReservations()
                {
                        this.InitializeComponent();
                        this.Loaded += ListReservations_Loaded;
                }

                private void ListReservations_Loaded(object sender,
                        RoutedEventArgs e)
                {
                        list_reservations.DataContext = _current_list;
                }

                protected override void OnNavigatedTo(NavigationEventArgs e)
                {
                        var list = e.Parameter as List<ReservationInfo>;
                        if (list != null)
                                _current_list = list;
                }
        }
}
```

The important thing to note in this code-behind sample is that you are not directly pulling the list of reservations from your model; rather you are expecting it to be passed in through the `Parameter` property of `OnNavigatedTo`. The value proposition here is flexibility. Using this pattern makes this page a general purpose view for `ReservationInfo` lists rather than just a view of one specific class of `ReservationInfo` lists, the “all” class. You will see this at work later in the chapter when you explore displaying specific views on the ReservationInfo list (like just seeing the reservations slated for the current day). For now, let’s open up the Dashboard.xaml file and add an All Reservations button to it. The layout and code-behind are shown in Listing 3-20.

Listing 3-20. Incorporating ListReservations

```
<Button
            Content="List Reservations"
            HorizontalAlignment="Left"
            Height="55"
            Margin="10,70,0,0"
            VerticalAlignment="Top"
            Click="ListReservations" />

private void ListReservations(object sender,
        RoutedEventArgs e)
{
        this.Frame.Navigate(typeof(ListReservations),
                App.Model.Reservations);
}
```

Running the app and clicking the All Reservations button should product a screen like Figure 3-3.

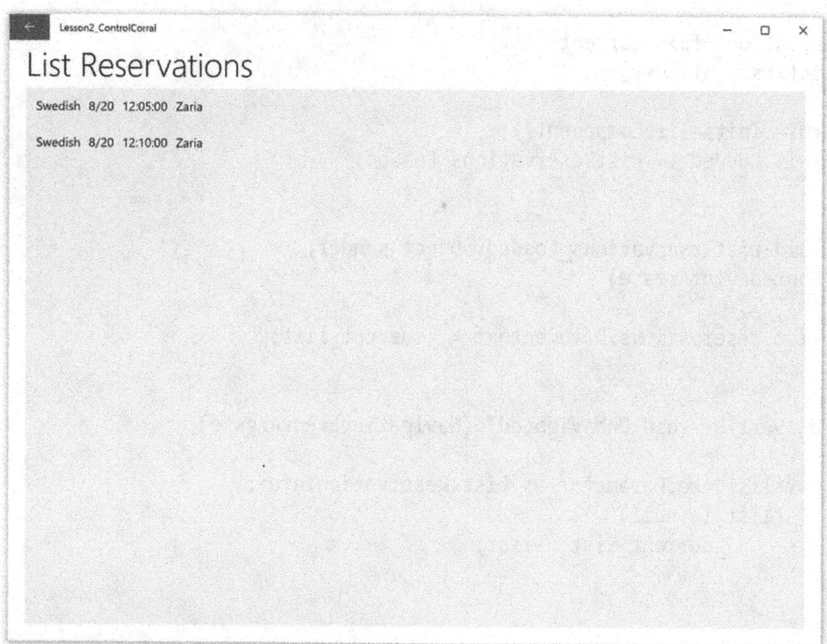

Figure 3-3. *Reservation list page in action*

Viewing Individual Reservations with FlipView

A FlipView presents a collection of items that the user views sequentially, one at a time. It's useful for displaying a gallery of images or the pages of a magazine. In your app, you will use it to display the detail information for the reservation list, allowing users to quickly go from one reservation to the next. You will be adding a view button to the template you created in the previous section and wiring it up. Listing 3-21 shows how the DataTemplate for your `list_reservations` ListBox should now look. The new parts are highlighted in bold.

Listing 3-21. DataTemplate for the list_reservations ListBox

```
<DataTemplate>
    <StackPanel
        Orientation="Horizontal">
        <TextBlock
            Text="{Binding Procedure}"
            Margin="0,0,10,0" />
        <TextBlock
            Text="{Binding AppointmentDay.Month}" />
        <TextBlock
            Text="/" />
        <TextBlock
            Text="{Binding AppointmentDay.Day}"
            Margin="0,0,10,0" />
        <TextBlock
            Text="{Binding AppointmentTime}"
            Margin="0,0,10,0" />
        <TextBlock
            Text="{Binding Customer.CustomerName}"
            Margin="0,0,10,0" />
        <Button
            Content="View Reservation"
            Margin="0,0,10,0"
            Click="ViewReservation" />
    </StackPanel>
</DataTemplate>
```

You now update the click event for that button so that it points you to the ManageReservation page you previously created. Listing 3-22 shows the code for this.

Listing 3-22. Updating the Click Event

```
private void ViewReservation(object sender, RoutedEventArgs e)
{
        var control = sender as FrameworkElement;
        var reservation_info = control.DataContext as ReservationInfo;

        Frame.Navigate(typeof(ManageReservation), new
        {
                Selection = reservation_info,
                List = _current_list,
        });
}
```

In Listing 3-22 you once again see the pattern of passing parameters into the Navigate method. Again, this is so the page being navigated to has some context on what to present. In this case, you pass in an anonymous object with two properties, one for storing the selection the user made and the other for storing the list that was selected from (as discussed in the previous section, this list can change depending on the situation). Because FlipView shows items one at a time, you will use the selection value to indicate which item in the list should be displayed first; however, you will still allow users to navigate to the other items in the list on an item-by-item basis. Listing 3-23 shows the ManageReservation layout.

Listing 3-23. ManageReservation XAML Layout

```
<Grid
        Background="{ThemeResource ApplicationPageBackgroundThemeBrush}">
        <FlipView
            x:Name="flipview_reservations"
            ItemsSource="{Binding}">
            <FlipView.ItemTemplate>
                <DataTemplate>
                    <Grid>
                        <TextBlock
                            Loaded="MassageDateLoaded"
                            HorizontalAlignment="Left"
                            Margin="10,10,0,0"
                            FontSize="30"
                            VerticalAlignment="Top" />
                        <TextBlock
                            HorizontalAlignment="Left"
                            Text="{Binding Customer.CustomerName}"
                            Margin="10,55,0,0"
                            FontWeight="Bold"
                            VerticalAlignment="Top"
                            Width="242" />
                        <DatePicker
                            Header="DOB:"
                            HorizontalAlignment="Left"
                            Margin="10,80,0,0"
                            Date="{Binding Customer.DOB}"
                            VerticalAlignment="Top"
                            IsEnabled="False" />
                        <TextBlock
                            HorizontalAlignment="Left"
                            Margin="10,145,0,0"
                            Text="{Binding Passphrase}"
                            VerticalAlignment="Top"
                            Width="296"
                            Foreground="Red" />
                        <TextBlock
                            HorizontalAlignment="Left"
                            Margin="10,237,0,0"
                            VerticalAlignment="Top"
                            Width="296"
                            Text="{Binding Procedure}" />
```

```
                    <Slider
                        Header="Massage Intensity"
                        HorizontalAlignment="Left"
                        Loaded="MassageIntensityLoaded"
                        Minimum="20"
                        Maximum="100"
                        Margin="10,173,0,0"
                        VerticalAlignment="Top"
                        IsEnabled="True"
                        Width="296" />
                    <Border
                        HorizontalAlignment="Left"
                        Height="227"
                        Margin="353,10,0,0"
                        VerticalAlignment="Top"
                        Width="225"
                        BorderThickness="1"
                        BorderBrush="Gray"
                        Background="Gainsboro">
                        <Image
                            Loaded="CustomerImageLoaded" />
                    </Border>
                    <Button
                        Content="Cancel Reservation"
                        HorizontalAlignment="Left"
                        Margin="353,242,0,0"
                        VerticalAlignment="Top" />
                </Grid>
            </DataTemplate>
        </FlipView.ItemTemplate>
    </FlipView>
</Grid>
```

There is nothing too unique here. You implement a DataTemplate for the FlipView that you use to lay out each individual presentation of a reservation using binding in some cases and code-behind in others. For controls like an image, there is no direct binding to a byte array or memory buffer, so you need to handle the specific control's Loaded event, and in that event perform whatever gymnastics are necessary to present to the user. When laid out, the user interface should look something like Figure 3-4. To get to the template designer in Visual Studio 2015, right-click the control of interest from the document outline pane and select Edit Addition Templates ➤ Edit Generated Items (Item Template) ➤ Edit Current. This option is only visible to you if a template has already been defined. Otherwise, you can use this context menu to create an empty template or edit a copy of a template.

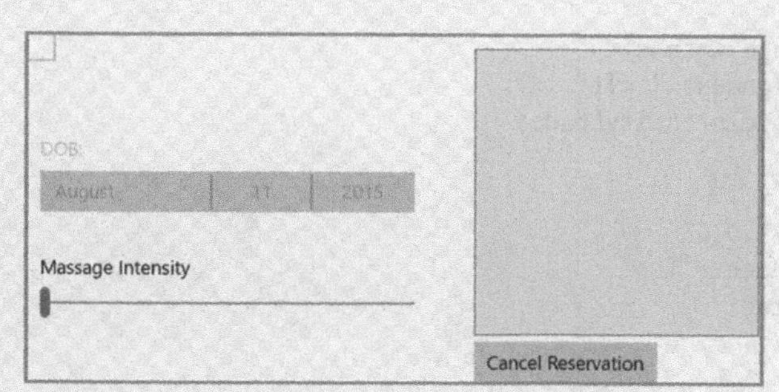

Figure 3-4. *Template designer in Visual Studio 2015*

The code-behind for ManageReservation starts with adding class level fields for maintaining the values passed in from the previous page:

```
List<ReservationInfo> _current_list;
ReservationInfo _selected_reservation;
```

Listing 3-24 shows the implementation of the `OnNavigated` method.

Listing 3-24. ManageReservation OnNavigated Method

```
protected override void OnNavigatedTo(NavigationEventArgs e)
{
        dynamic param = e.Parameter;
        if (param != null)
        {
                _current_list = param.List;
                _selected_reservation = param.Selection;
        }
}
```

Listing 3-24 uses a dynamic object to capture the value of the parameter passed into the page and then assigns the individual values from that parameter to the field level values `_current_list` and `_selected_reservation`.

The next step is to add the event handlers for the various controls defined in your DataTemplate. Listing 3-25 shows the implementation of these methods.

Listing 3-25. Implementing ManageReservation Event Handlers

```
private void MassageDateLoaded(object sender, RoutedEventArgs e)
{
        var txt_date = sender as TextBlock;
        var reservation_info = txt_date.DataContext as ReservationInfo;

        txt_date.Text = $"{reservation_info.AppointmentDay.Month}/" +
                        $"{reservation_info.AppointmentDay.Day}/" +
                        $"{reservation_info.AppointmentDay.Year}" +
                        $" at {reservation_info.AppointmentTime}";
}
```

```
async private void CustomerImageLoaded(object sender,
        RoutedEventArgs e)
{
        var control_image = sender as Image;
        var reservation_info = control_image.DataContext as ReservationInfo;

        if (reservation_info.Customer.CustomerImage != null)
        {
                BitmapImage image = new BitmapImage();
                control_image.Source = image;
                MemoryStream stream =
                        new MemoryStream(reservation_info.Customer.CustomerImage);
                await image.SetSourceAsync(stream.AsRandomAccessStream());
        }
}

private void MassageIntensityLoaded(object sender,
        RoutedEventArgs e)
{
        var control_slider = sender as Slider;
        var reservation_info = control_slider.DataContext as ReservationInfo;
        control_slider.Value = reservation_info.MassageIntensity;
}
```

The event handler methods in Listing 3-25 follow the same basic pattern. The sender is cast back to the control that fired it, the DataContext for that control is read and casts the ReservationInfo object, and finally some specific behavior is implemented. The conclusion to be drawn from this pattern (particularly the retrieval of the given control's DataContext) is that whereas the list as a whole was applied to the data control, each element in the list has as its DataContext the object it represents. The remainder of ManageReservation code-behind is implemented in Listing 3-26.

Listing 3-26. Implementing Constructor and Loaded Event Handler

```
public ManageReservation()
{
        this.InitializeComponent();
        this.Loaded += ManageReservation_Loaded;
}

private void ManageReservation_Loaded(object sender, RoutedEventArgs e)
{
        flipview_reservations.DataContext = _current_list;
        flipview_reservations.SelectedItem = _selected_reservation;
}
```

Your ManageReservation screen should look something like Figure 3-5 when you run the app.

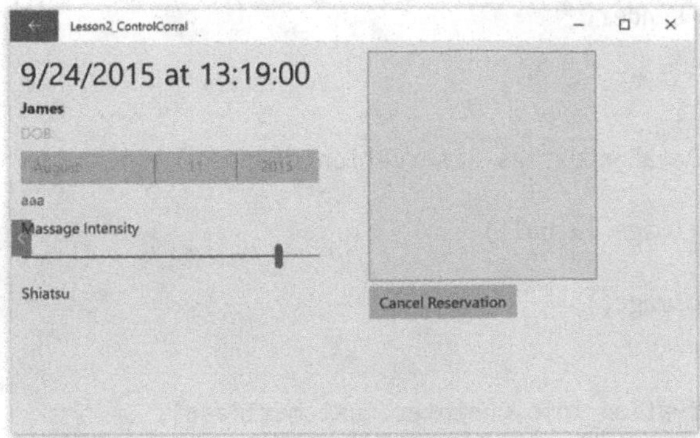

Figure 3-5. FlipView control in action

The final step is to implement the Cancel Reservation button. Clicking this button should delete the reservation but keep the associated customer information. Listing 3-27 shows the layout and code-behind for this.

Listing 3-27. Cancel Reservation Button Definition and Implementation

```
                <Button
                    Content="Cancel Reservation"
        Click="CancelReservation"
                    HorizontalAlignment="Left"
                    Margin="353,242,0,0"
                    VerticalAlignment="Top" />

async private void CancelReservation(object sender, RoutedEventArgs e)
{
        App.Model.Reservations.Remove(_selected_reservation);
        await App.SaveModelAsync();
        Frame.GoBack();
}
```

Revisiting AutoSuggestBox

When you first looked at the AutoSuggestBox, you used a statically created a list to populate it. Now that you are storing actual users, let's go back and update it to use values from the Users collection. You previously used databinding with the `DisplayMemberPath` property of this control to display just the customer's name on the control's search result list. But you can do better. The ListBox section introduced you to databinding and DataTemplates. Using this feature set, you can now make the reservation screen a tad more user friendly and slick by adding the user's picture to the drop-down that appears when AutoSuggestBox utilized. Open MainPage and apply the following changes highlighted in Listing 3-28. Note that since you are using a data template, you no longer need to have `DisplayMemberPath` set (both cannot be set at the same time).

Listing 3-28. Modernizing AutoSuggestBox

```
<AutoSuggestBox
        x:Name="control_name"
        HorizontalAlignment="Left"
        Header="What's your name?"
        Margin="10,112,0,0"
```

```
        VerticalAlignment="Top"
        Width="242"
        QueryIcon="Find">
        <AutoSuggestBox.ItemTemplate>
            <DataTemplate>
                <StackPanel
                    Orientation="Horizontal">
                    <Border
                        HorizontalAlignment="Left"
                        Height="100"
                        Margin="5"
                        Width="100"
                        BorderThickness="1"
                        BorderBrush="Gray"
                        Background="Gainsboro">
                        <Image
                            Loaded="CustomerImageLoaded" />
                    </Border>
                    <TextBlock
                        Text="{Binding CustomerName}"
                        VerticalAlignment="Center" />
                </StackPanel>
            </DataTemplate>
        </AutoSuggestBox.ItemTemplate>
    </AutoSuggestBox>
```

DisplayMemberPath has been removed and a full scale item template has been added instead. Now the user interface for the drop-down can be completely customized. In this case, you use a simple panel to arrange an image and a textbox horizontally from left to right. You will learn more about the StackPanel and all the other powerful layout controls in the next chapter.

To enable the image load functionality, you must now implement the code-behind. The code here follows the identical pattern to what you did for your ManageReservation sample with one exception. ManageReservation binds to a list of `ReservationInfo` objects, meaning that within the loaded even a `ReservationInfo` object is the DataContext. This control binds to a list of `CustomerInfo` objects, meaning that a `CustomerInfo` is the result of `control_image.DataContext`. Listing 3-29 illustrates.

Listing 3-29. CustomerImageLoaded Event Handler

```
async private void CustomerImageLoaded(object sender,
            RoutedEventArgs e)
{
        var control_image = sender as Image;
        var customer_info = control_image.DataContext as CustomerInfo;

        if (customer_info.CustomerImage != null)
        {
                BitmapImage image = new BitmapImage();
                control_image.Source = image;
                MemoryStream stream =
                        new MemoryStream(customer_info.CustomerImage);
                await image.SetSourceAsync(stream.AsRandomAccessStream());
        }
}
```

Figure 3-6 shows how the AutoSuggestBox looks based on the information I entered in my instance of the Control Corral app.

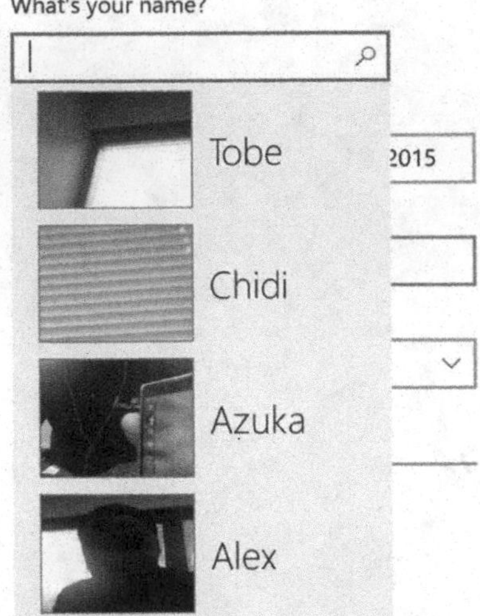

Figure 3-6. *The re-templated AutoSuggestBox in action*

Revisiting ComboBox

While you are revisiting previous controls that can be classified as both data and basic, let's take a second look at the ComboBox. In the previous approach to designing MainPage, the contents of the MassageType ComboBox were not only hard-coded, but specified in the XAML! Since the object defines text primarily, let's change this to use the `DisplayMemberPath` property of the ComboBox to show this information.

When you first looked at the AutoSuggestBox, you used a statically created list to populate it. Now that you are storing actual users, let's go back and update it to use values from the Users collection. You will add the user's picture to the drop-down that appears when AutoSuggestBox is hit. Open MainPage and apply the following changes. Listing 3-30 shows the changes that must be made to the layout and code-behind methods `MainPage_Loaded` and `CreateReservation` to do this.

Listing 3-30. Updating ComboBox

```
<ComboBox
            x:Name="control_procedure"
            Header="Select a procedure"
            HorizontalAlignment="Left"
            Margin="10,307,0,0"
            VerticalAlignment="Top"
            Width="296"
            ItemsSource="{Binding}"
            DisplayMemberPath="Name"
            />
```

```
private void MainPage_Loaded(object sender, RoutedEventArgs e)
{
        this.DataContext = _command;
        control_name.ItemsSource = App.Model.Customers;
        control_procedure.DataContext = App.Model.MassageTypes;
}

private ReservationInfo CreateReservation()
{

        var customer = App.Model.Customers
                .Where(i =>
                i.CustomerName.ToLower() == control_name.Text.ToLower())
                .FirstOrDefault();
        if (customer == null)
        {
                //create and add a new customer if
                //none exist with that name
                customer = new CustomerInfo
                {
                        CustomerName = control_name.Text,
                        DOB = control_dob.Date.Date,
                        MassageIntensity = control_intensity.Value,
                        CustomerImage = _user_image,
                };
                App.Model.Customers.Add(customer);
        }

        var new_reservation = new ReservationInfo()
        {
                AppointmentDay = control_calendar.Date.Value.Date,
                AppointmentTime = control_time.Time,
                Passphrase = txt_passphrase.Password,
                Procedure = (control_procedure.SelectedItem
                                as MassageType).Name as string,
                MassageIntensity = control_intensity.Value,
                Customer = customer,  //connect the customer
        };
        _reservations.Add(new_reservation);
        return new_reservation;
}
```

In Listing 3-30, you remove all of the ComboBoxItems from the ComboBox. Since you will now be using databinding to populate it, you set the ItemSource to binding and also set what property you want the framework to use for displaying content for each line item in the underlying list.

In the Loaded code-behind method, you now simply set the DataContext for the ComboBox. Finally, because you are no longer using ComboBoxItems explicitly, the SelectedItem property will map to the instance of the object being presented at a given time in the ComboBox. Because you have bound to a list of MassageType objects, this will always be a MassageType object. You cast SelectedItem to this and set the value of procedure using the Name property of this object.

Showing Customers with GridView

The GridView control is used to display a collection of data in rows and columns that can scroll vertically. Like the ListBox and every other ItemsControl, it represents a collection of items of any type and is most often used to display multiple items at a time.

By default, a user can select a single item in a GridView. You can set the `SelectionMode` property to a ListViewSelectionMode enumeration value to allow multi-selection or to disable selection. You can also change the GridView interaction mode to make items respond to a user clicks—like a button. This requires setting the `IsItemClickable` property to true.

You will be using this control to display a list of customers with some summary info. You will be using the same template you used in the previous sample, just to illustrate the reusability of templates. As long as the type being bound to is the same and the control displaying the template has the available space, a template can be used anywhere binding occurs. Listing 3-31 shows the user list implementation on the Dashboard page.

Listing 3-31. GridView XAML Layout

```
<Border
    Margin="156,54,10,0"
    Height="184" BorderThickness="0,2,0,1"
                BorderBrush="Gray"
    VerticalAlignment="Top">
    <GridView
        x:Name="gridview_customers"
        SelectionMode="Single"
        ItemsSource="{Binding}"
        ItemClick="CustomerSelected"
        IsItemClickEnabled="True">
        <GridView.ItemTemplate>
            <DataTemplate>
                <StackPanel
                    Orientation="Horizontal">
                    <Border
                        HorizontalAlignment="Left"
                        Height="75"
                        Margin="5,5,10,5"
                        Width="100"
                        BorderThickness="1"
                        BorderBrush="Gray"
                        Background="Gainsboro">
                        <Image
                            Stretch="Fill"
                            Loaded="CustomerImageLoaded" />
                    </Border>
                    <TextBlock
                        Text="{Binding CustomerName}"
                        FontSize="24"
                        FontWeight="ExtraLight"
                        VerticalAlignment="Center" />
                </StackPanel>
            </DataTemplate>
```

```
        </GridView.ItemTemplate>
    </GridView>
</Border>
<TextBlock Text="Customers"
    HorizontalAlignment="Right"
    FontSize="40"
    FontWeight="ExtraLight"
    VerticalAlignment="Top" />
...
```

Now open Dashboard.xaml.cs and add Listing 3-32 to the Dashboard class.

Listing 3-32. GridView Code-Behind Event Handlers

```
async private void CustomerImageLoaded(object sender, RoutedEventArgs e)
{
        var control_image = sender as Image;
        var customer_info = control_image.DataContext as CustomerInfo;

        if (customer_info.CustomerImage != null)
        {
                BitmapImage image = new BitmapImage();
                control_image.Source = image;
                MemoryStream stream =
                        new MemoryStream(customer_info.CustomerImage);
                await image.SetSourceAsync(stream.AsRandomAccessStream());
        }
}

private void CustomerSelected(object sender, ItemClickEventArgs e)
{
        var selected_customer = e.ClickedItem as CustomerInfo;
        Frame.Navigate(typeof(ManageCustomer), selected_customer);
}
```

Implementing ManageCustomer should be a piece of cake at this point, given that the same patterns you have been utilizing will be once again used. Listing 3-33 shows the layout page.

Listing 3-33. ManageCustomer Layout

```
<Page
    x:Class="Lesson2_ControlCorral.ManageCustomer"
    xmlns="http://schemas.microsoft.com/winfx/2006/xaml/presentation"
    xmlns:x="http://schemas.microsoft.com/winfx/2006/xaml"
    xmlns:local="using:Lesson2_ControlCorral"
    xmlns:d="http://schemas.microsoft.com/expression/blend/2008"
    xmlns:mc="http://schemas.openxmlformats.org/markup-compatibility/2006"
    mc:Ignorable="d">
```

```
    <ScrollViewer>
        <StackPanel Margin="20"
            Orientation="Vertical"
            Background="{ThemeResource ApplicationPageBackgroundThemeBrush}">
            <TextBlock
                HorizontalAlignment="Left"
                Text="{Binding CustomerName}"
                Margin="10,10,0,10"
                FontWeight="Bold"
                VerticalAlignment="Top"
                Width="225"
                Height="22" />
            <Button
                Click="ReplaceImage"
                HorizontalAlignment="Left"
                Height="227"
                Margin="10"
                VerticalAlignment="Top"
                Width="225"
                BorderThickness="1"
                BorderBrush="Gray"
                Background="Gainsboro">
                <Image
                    x:Name="control_image"
                    Source="/alex.jpg" />
            </Button>
            <Slider
                x:Name="control_intensity"
                Header="Massage Intensity"
                HorizontalAlignment="Left"
                Minimum="20"
                Maximum="100"
                Margin="10,10,0,10"
                VerticalAlignment="Top"
                Width="225" />
            <DatePicker
                x:Name="control_dob"
                Header="When were you born?"
                HorizontalAlignment="Left"
                VerticalAlignment="Top" />
            <Button
                Margin="0,05,0,0"
                Content="Save"
                Click="SaveCustomer" />
        </StackPanel>
    </ScrollViewer>

</Page>
```

The two points of difference, highlighted in bold, are the use of a StackPanel rather than a grid and the introduction of a new control type, the ScrollViewer. ScrollViewer is another example of the power and flexibility of layout controls (see Chapter 4). The code-behind for this file is in Listing 3-34.

Listing 3-34. ManageCustomer Code-Behind

```
public sealed partial class ManageCustomer : Page
{
        CameraCaptureUI ccui = new CameraCaptureUI();
        CustomerInfo _customer;
        public ManageCustomer()
        {
                this.InitializeComponent();
                this.Loaded += ManageCustomer_Loaded;
        }

        async private void ManageCustomer_Loaded(object sender, RoutedEventArgs e)
        {
                if (_customer.CustomerImage != null)
                {
                        BitmapImage image = new BitmapImage();
                        control_image.Source = image;
                        MemoryStream stream =
                                new MemoryStream(_customer.CustomerImage);
                        await image.SetSourceAsync(stream.AsRandomAccessStream());
                }
                this.DataContext = _customer;
                control_intensity.Value = _customer.MassageIntensity;
                control_dob.Date = _customer.DOB;
        }

        async private void SaveCustomer(object sender, RoutedEventArgs e)
        {
                _customer.MassageIntensity = control_intensity.Value;
                _customer.DOB = control_dob.Date.Date;
                await App.SaveModelAsync();
                Frame.GoBack();
        }

        protected override void OnNavigatedTo(NavigationEventArgs e)
        {
                _customer = e.Parameter as CustomerInfo;
        }

        async private void ReplaceImage(object sender, RoutedEventArgs e)
        {
                BitmapImage image = new BitmapImage();
                control_image.Source = image;

                ccui.PhotoSettings.AllowCropping = true;
                ccui.PhotoSettings.MaxResolution =
                        CameraCaptureUIMaxPhotoResolution.HighestAvailable;
```

```
            var result =
                    await ccui.CaptureFileAsync(CameraCaptureUIMode.Photo);
            if (result != null)
            {
                    var stream = await result.OpenReadAsync();
                    await image.SetSourceAsync(stream);

                    //get the image data and store it
                    stream.Seek(0);
                    BinaryReader reader =
                            new BinaryReader(stream.AsStreamForRead());
                    _customer.CustomerImage = new byte[stream.Size];
                    reader.Read(_customer.CustomerImage,
                            0,
                            _customer.CustomerImage.Length);
            }
    }
}
```

Displaying Today's Reservations with ListView

Like a GridView, ListView is used to display a collection of items, in this case stacked vertically. Beyond this difference, the two controls are virtually identical.

The final sample you will create will use the ListView to list out the reservations for the day. You'll place it in the dashboard so users can see what reservations still need to be completed for a given day. As with the previous reservations, you will link this back to the reservation view. In this case, however, the reservation view will be limited to the items from this list, not the entire list of reservations. This illustrates how passing the list to be presented in a list presentation page like ListReservations is superior to locking a page to a single list. Let's examine the layout changes in Listing 3-35. Add the code to the main grid view.

Listing 3-35. ListView XAML Definition

```
<Border
            Margin="156,296,10,-120"
            Height="184"
            BorderThickness="0,2,0,1"
            BorderBrush="Gray"
            VerticalAlignment="Top">
            <ListView
                x:Name="listview_reservations"
                SelectionMode="Single"
                ItemsSource="{Binding}"
                IsItemClickEnabled="True"
                ItemClick="ReservationSelected">
                <ListView.ItemTemplate>
                    <DataTemplate>
                        <StackPanel
                            Orientation="Horizontal">
                            <TextBlock
                                Text="{Binding Procedure}"
                                Margin="0,0,10,0" />
```

```
                    <TextBlock
                        Text="{Binding AppointmentDay.Month}" />
                    <TextBlock
                        Text="/" />
                    <TextBlock
                        Text="{Binding AppointmentDay.Day}"
                        Margin="0,0,10,0" />
                    <TextBlock
                        Text="{Binding AppointmentTime}"
                        Margin="0,0,10,0" />
                    <TextBlock
                        Text="{Binding Customer.CustomerName}"
                        Margin="0,0,10,0" />

                </StackPanel>
            </DataTemplate>
        </ListView.ItemTemplate>
    </ListView>
</Border>
<TextBlock
    Text="Today's Appointments"
    HorizontalAlignment="Left"
    FontSize="40"
    FontWeight="ExtraLight"
    VerticalAlignment="Top"
    Margin="156,243,0,0" />
```

The code-behind for this is in Listing 3-36 with additions highlighted in bold.

Listing 3-36. Updated Dashboard Code-Behind

```
public sealed partial class Dashboard : Page
{
        public Dashboard()
        {
                this.InitializeComponent();
                this.Loaded += Dashboard_Loaded;
        }

        private void Dashboard_Loaded
                (object sender, RoutedEventArgs e)
        {
                gridview_customers.DataContext = App.Model.Customers;
                listview_reservations.DataContext =
                        App.Model.Reservations
                        .Where(i => i.AppointmentDay.Date == DateTime.Now.Date)
                        .ToList();
        }
```

```
        private void OnReservation(object sender, RoutedEventArgs e)
        {
                this.Frame.Navigate(typeof(MainPage));
        }

        private void ListReservations(object sender,
                RoutedEventArgs e)
        {
                this.Frame.Navigate(typeof(ListReservations),
                        App.Model.Reservations);
        }

        async private void CustomerImageLoaded
                (object sender, RoutedEventArgs e)
        {
                var control_image = sender as Image;
                var customer_info = control_image
                        .DataContext as CustomerInfo;

                if (customer_info.CustomerImage != null)
                {
                        BitmapImage image = new BitmapImage();
                        control_image.Source = image;
                        MemoryStream stream =
                                new MemoryStream(customer_info.CustomerImage);
                        await image.SetSourceAsync(stream.AsRandomAccessStream());
                }
        }

        private void CustomerSelected(object sender, ItemClickEventArgs e)
        {
                var selected_customer = e.ClickedItem as CustomerInfo;
                Frame.Navigate(typeof(ManageCustomer), selected_customer);
        }

        private void ReservationSelected(object sender, ItemClickEventArgs e)
        {
                var selected_reservation = e.ClickedItem as ReservationInfo;
                this.Frame.Navigate(typeof(ManageReservation),
                        new
                        {
                                List = listview_reservations.DataContext,
                                Selection = selected_reservation,
                        });
        }
}
```

Listing 3-36 finishes off this discussion on data controls with the final feature set Control Corral requires: a list of today's reservations so the user can quickly see how busy a given day might be. The loaded method is updated to include a databinding the ListView to a filtered list of reservations. `ReservationSelected` is called when the user clicks any of the reservations on in this list. Using the same pattern established previously, you make a call directly to `ManageReservation`, this time passing in just the filtered list of today's reservations along with the reservation presently selected. A user clicking any reservation item from the "Today" list will not only see the detail of that specific reservation but can also go through each of the reservations for that day. On my machine, after spending some time populating my instance of Control Corral with all the names of my wonderful niece and nephews, the dashboard page looks like Figure 3-7.

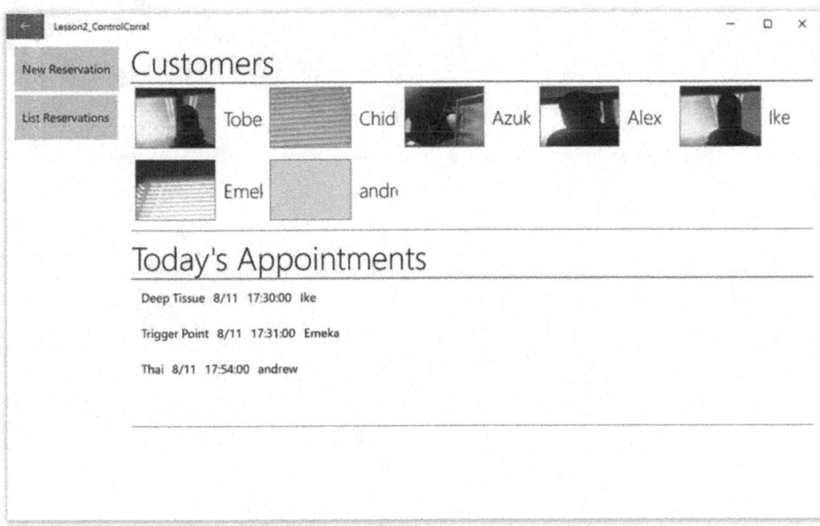

Figure 3-7. *Control Corral user interface*

Summary

Controls are encapsulated pieces of user interface that combine layout, content, and behavior to create distinct experiences within the construct of the surface that contains them, creating a tailored user experience. In this chapter, you covered data controls. These controls, tailored to show sets of data to the user in an optimized manner, were presented in this chapter. With this information on data controls, you increase your ability to present data collections to the user in various modes. Here are some important points to remember:

- SCRUD (Search, Create, Read, Update, Delete) operations are exposed by most applications that work with data that interfaces to the end user. The UWP app window has a `Content` property that is the primary surface upon which XAML-based user interfaces are presented. Additionally, Frame and Page controls facilitate navigation within a XAML based UWP app.
- A ListBox is used to present a list of items that a user can select from. A ListBox can display and allow a selection of multiple items at a time.
- Several data controls are available to the UWP to satisfy the SCRUD requirements. ListView, FlipView, and GridView are controls used to display a collection of data. ListView displays data in rows and columns that can scroll horizontally. GridView is used to display a collection of items vertically. FlipView presents a collection of items sequentially, one at a time, as would be used for an image gallery.

Summary

CHAPTER 4

Layout and Custom Controls

So far you have looked at controls that serve as content for entering data and controls that are primarily designed for viewing data (either in individual form or as a list). In this chapter, you will learn about the last two classes of controls: layout controls and custom controls.

You've been using layout controls all along. In fact, there is very little that can be done in terms of working with multiple controls without the use of layout controls. In the past few chapters, you utilized both the Grid and the StackPanel to lay out some of the samples we discussed. In this chapter, we will go into greater detail on many of the layout controls you can use for building your UWP apps.

Layout Controls

The first thing you should be asking yourself before getting into a discussion about layout controls is, what do we mean when we say layout? By layout, we mean basically mean the location and display characteristics of a control. Layout is used to structure a user interface such that it has some intended meaning. Layout controls affect the location on the screen where the controls they directly contain appear.

So why encapsulate the layout of controls into a set of controls themselves? Previous technologies have traditionally locked the developer into one primary layout engine. WinForms used a Cartesian style coordinate system that required developers to position controls based on X and Y coordinates, with the point of origin at the top left corner. This worked well in certain respects but lacked flexibility in scenarios where controls needed to be laid out in a non-traditional manner (for instance, if a control needed to be pinned to the bottom right of the screen, a great deal of measurement needed to happen to determine the necessary X and Y coordinates).

In WinForms and any coordinate system like that, the layout of controls is essentially delegated to the developer. You as the developer decide where you want controls to sit and must refine that location based on environmental changes like the window resizing. If no coordinate information is provided, the controls fall back to being positioned at location (0, 0), the top left corner. Arranging controls based on fixed pixel coordinates may work for a limited environment, but as soon as you want to use different screen resolutions or different font sizes, it will fail. The UWP provides a rich set of built-in layout panels that help you avoid common pitfalls.

Thankfully, HTML shifted away from this model, opting instead for flow layout as the default layout experience. In HTML, unless otherwise specified, controls are laid out from left to right until they reach the full width of the page. At this point, they are wrapped to the next line and continue moving from left to right. Simple and elegant. HTML also retains the ability to explicitly lay out controls based on X and Y coordinates among other coordinate systems.

The problem with the approach of baking the layout into a user interface framework is that it loses extensibility over time. As technology changes and the needs it fulfills shift, it is important that the frameworks used to deliver user experiences have the requisite flexibility to continue to deliver engaging UIs without the need to dramatically refactor. Encapsulating layout into controls not only allows for flexibility within the framework but also provides future developers the ability to add new layout engines to the UWP by building their own layout controls.

Understanding the Layout System

UWP layout, like HTML, is flow-based by default, and utilizes a recursive and iterative process to render content. At its simplest, layout describes the process of measuring and arranging the members of a container's children (stored in the container's `Children` property). UWP apps support resizing and repositioning of controls if the user changes screen resolution, or resizes the window containing controls, or adds or removes controls at runtime. As you will see in this chapter, this allows for UWP user interfaces to be resolution and size independent. Each time that a child `UIElement` changes its position, it has the potential to trigger a new pass by the layout system. The following describes the process that occurs when the layout system is invoked.

- A child `UIElement` begins the layout process by first having its core properties measured.
- Sizing properties defined on `FrameworkElement` are evaluated, such as `Width`, `Height`, and `Margin`.
- Panel-specific logic is applied, such as stacking orientation.
- Content is arranged after all children have been measured.
- The Children collection is drawn on the screen.

As you saw in all of the previous samples, UWP apps are predominantly navigation-based and as such rely heavily on Frames and Pages. You have seen that Pages, which are content elements, contain one child that will almost always be a layout control, commonly referred to as a container. (In the samples from previous chapters this has, thus far, been a Grid control.) All containers derive from the `Windows.UI.Xaml.Controls.Panel` class, a base class designed with the ability to contain control and, optionally, other containers.

Containers plug into the layout rendering system of the UWP, which makes two passes before drawing an element. In the Measure pass, the runtime queries each element to determine the element's size and location based on how the element was declared. In the Arrange pass, the runtime determines the actual size and position for each element based on modifications that have been made by its parent. The layout system determines the actual size of an element by taking into account the available screen space; the size of any constraints (such as maximum or minimum height or width); layout-specific properties such as alignment, margins, or padding; and the behavior of the element's parent container. Based on these factors, elements may or may not be sized and located where they requested. In fact, the layout system can shrink, grow, or move elements in a container. Take, for instance, an element at the bottom of a StackPanel that is itself within a ScrollViewer. Depending on the number of elements in that StackPanel, the element in question may not even be displayed.

Figure 4-1 illustrates this situation. In it, Child 3 and Child 4 are not displayed until they scroll into view. Until then, the layout engine ignores them. Although they are not displayed, they still possess the same attributes as Child 1 and Child 2. The difference is that they have been determined to be outside the visible area during the processing phases.

■ **Note** Keep in mind as you design your apps that with UWP, the entire layout process occurs each time the user resizes the window or your code adds or removes elements.

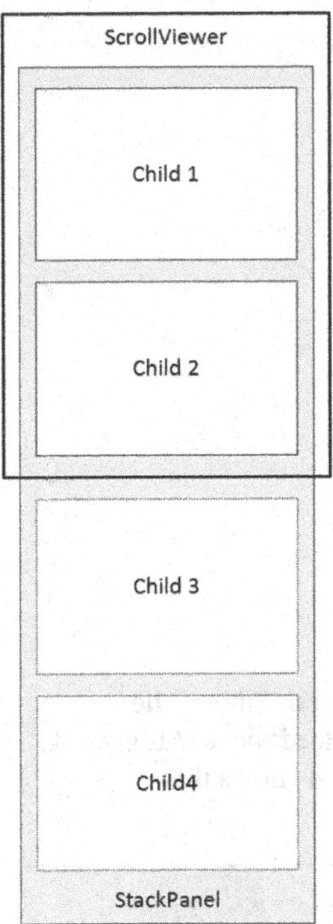

Figure 4-1. *Control layout in a ScrollViewer*

Alignment, Margins, and Padding

When being rendered, each element in the UWP is surrounded by a bounding box, as shown in Figure 4-2.

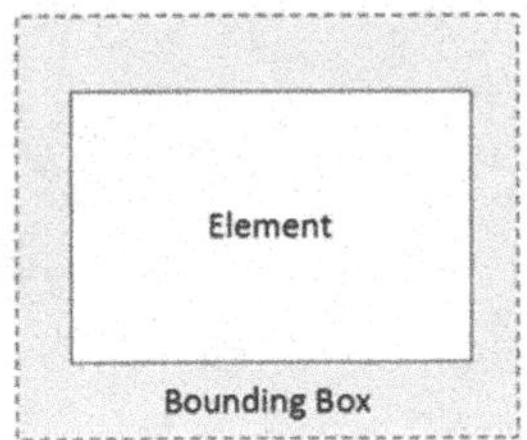

Figure 4-2. *A control's bounding box*

This represents the space allocated to an element within its parent. All elements have four properties that work in concert with this box to determine the final view of a given user interface element. These properties are `HorizontalAlignment`, `VerticalAlignment`, `Margin`, and `Padding`. You've been using alignment extensively to set the position of the controls you've been playing around with but have not properly explained it.

Alignment refers to how child elements should be positioned within a parent element's allocated layout space (the bounding box). The `HorizontalAlignment` property determines how an element is positioned horizontally within a container. The possible values for this property are `Left`, `Right`, `Center`, and `Stretch`. When this property is set to `Stretch`, which is the default, the control will expand to its maximum available width. Figure 4-3 shows a button in a grid with the alignment set to each of the four values.

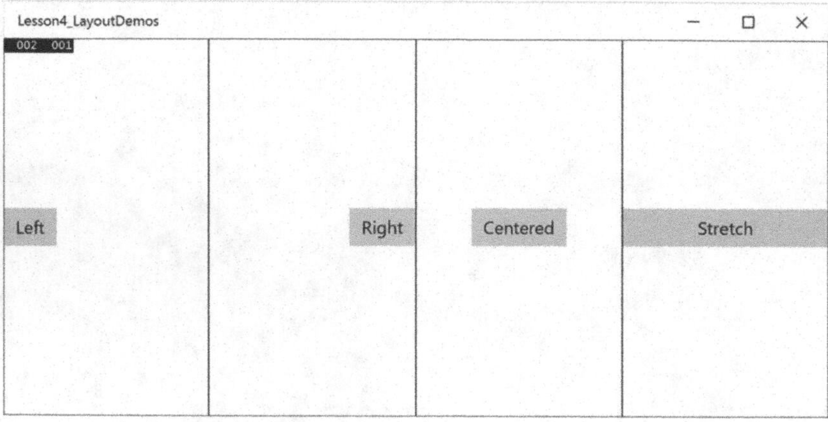

Figure 4-3. *HorizontalAlignment types*

`VerticalAlignment` determines how an element is positioned vertically within a container. The possible values for this property are `Top`, `Bottom`, `Center`, and `Stretch`. Just like with `HorizontalAlignment`, setting the value to `Stretch` expands it to take up all available vertical space. Figure 4-4 shows this.

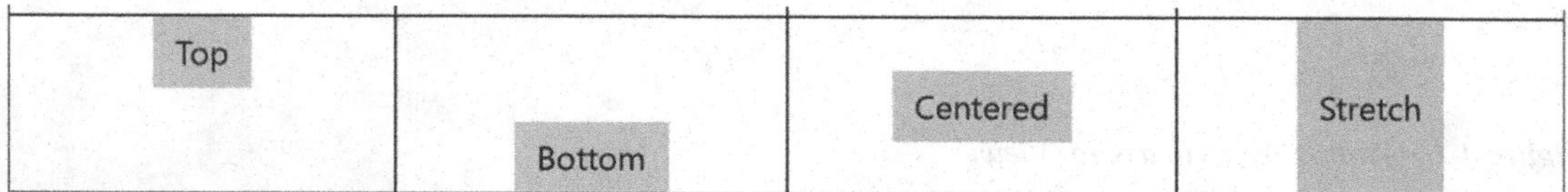

Figure 4-4. *VerticalAlignment types*

Listing 4-1 shows the XAML used to render the user interfaces from both Figure 4-2 and Figure 4-3.

Listing 4-1. Alignment in Action

```
<Grid Background="{ThemeResource ApplicationPageBackgroundThemeBrush}">
    <Grid.ColumnDefinitions>
        <ColumnDefinition />
        <ColumnDefinition />
        <ColumnDefinition />
        <ColumnDefinition />
    </Grid.ColumnDefinitions>
    <Grid.RowDefinitions>
        <RowDefinition />
        <RowDefinition />
        <RowDefinition />
        <RowDefinition />
    </Grid.RowDefinitions>

    <!-- horizontal alignment -->
    <Border BorderThickness=".5" BorderBrush="Black" Grid.Column="0">
        <Button Content="Left" HorizontalAlignment="Left" />
    </Border>
```

```
    <Border BorderThickness=".5" BorderBrush="Black" Grid.Column="1">
        <Button Content="Right" HorizontalAlignment="Right" Width="56" />
    </Border>
    <Border BorderThickness=".5" BorderBrush="Black" Grid.Column="2">
        <Button Content="Centered" HorizontalAlignment="Center" />
    </Border>
    <Border BorderThickness=".5" BorderBrush="Black" Grid.Column="3">
        <Button Content="Stretch" HorizontalAlignment="Stretch" />
    </Border>

    <!-- vertical alignment -->
    <Border BorderThickness=".5" BorderBrush="Black"
                        Grid.Column="0" Grid.Row="1">
        <Button Content="Top"
                HorizontalAlignment="Center" VerticalAlignment="Top" />
    </Border>
    <Border BorderThickness=".5" BorderBrush="Black"
                        Grid.Column="1" Grid.Row="1">
        <Button Content="Bottom" HorizontalAlignment="Center"
                        VerticalAlignment="Bottom" />
    </Border>
    <Border BorderThickness=".5" BorderBrush="Black"
                        Grid.Column="2" Grid.Row="1">
        <Button Content="Centered"
                HorizontalAlignment="Center" VerticalAlignment="Center" />
    </Border>
    <Border BorderThickness=".5" BorderBrush="Black"
                        Grid.Column="3" Grid.Row="1">
        <Button Content="Stretch" HorizontalAlignment="Center"
                VerticalAlignment="Stretch" />
    </Border>
</Grid>
```

The best way to describe the Margin property is as a value used to specify the offset distance between an element and its bounding box. This property consists of four parts: the left margin, the top margin, the right margin, and the bottom margin. Margin values are depicted in XAML as a comma-delimited string of decimal values. From left, these values are left margin, top margin, right margin, and bottom margin. Examine the following button definitions in Listing 4-2.

Listing 4-2. Using Margins

```
<Border BorderThickness=".5" BorderBrush="Black" Grid.Column="1" Grid.Row="2">
    <Button Margin="10,5,15,0" Content="Margin"
            HorizontalAlignment="Left" VerticalAlignment="Top" />
</Border>
<Border BorderThickness=".5" BorderBrush="Black" Grid.Column="0" Grid.Row="2">
    <Button Content="Margin"
            HorizontalAlignment="Left" VerticalAlignment="Top" />
</Border>
```

In Listing 4-2, the button that would normally be positioned at the top left corner of the border is now shifted to the left 10 pixels, from the top 5 pixels, from the right 15 pixels, and from the bottom 0 pixels. Figure 4-5 illustrates the difference applying a margin makes.

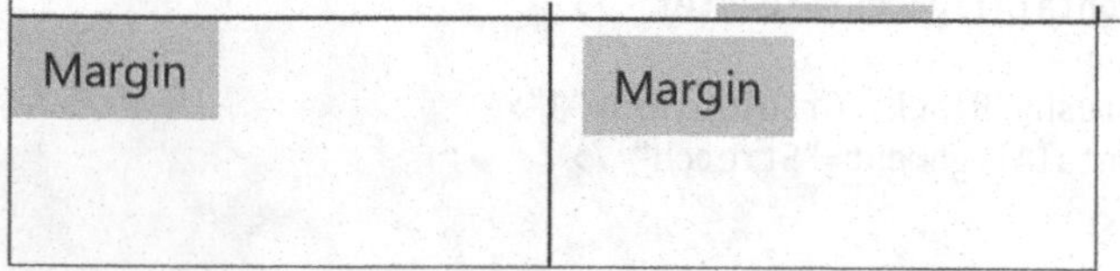

Figure 4-5. *Margins in action*

More specifically, the margins are applied against the element's bounding box in the manner depicted in Figure 4-6.

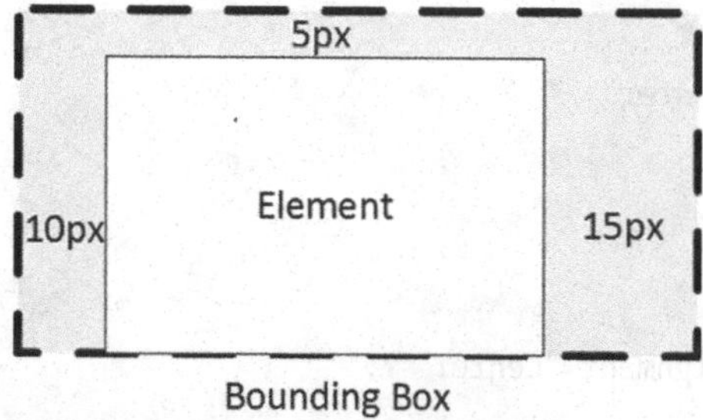

Figure 4-6. *Impact of a margin on a bounding box*

This is an important point to stress because your decisions when working with margins may have an effect on the visible area of the control you want displayed, especially if values like `Width` or `Height` are explicitly set. Remember that your controls can possess attributes that may be set but are not relevant to the issue of whether or not they display. And even if they do display, how much of their content area is visible? In Listing 4-2, you set a right margin of 15 pixels, and when you ran it, everything worked fine because at runtime there was plenty of space to the right of your button. Let's change things up a bit and see what happens. Start by modifying the second column definition element, as shown in Listing 4-3.

Listing 4-3. Specifying the Width of a Grid Column

```
<Grid.ColumnDefinitions>
    <ColumnDefinition />
    <ColumnDefinition Width="80" />
    <ColumnDefinition />
    <ColumnDefinition />
</Grid.ColumnDefinitions>
```

You've added a width to the column so that the particular column will now no longer take on all available space but will instead be fixed to that size. Run the app. See Figure 4-7. Notice that the button has now been clipped! Instead of presenting the full text margin, only a portion of it is displayed. This is because the button render area is being pushed back 15 pixels to account for the margin being set.

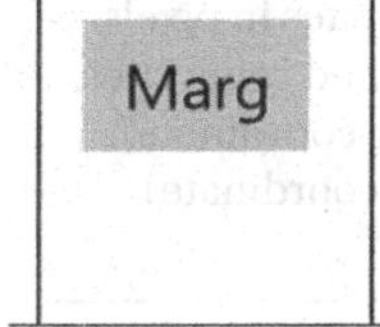

Figure 4-7. *Example of clipping that might occur when margin value is too high*

If you want the same margin on all four sides, you only need to specify one value. The following XAML sets the margin to 5 on all sides:

```
<Button Margin="5"...
```

If you want the same margin applied to top/bottom and left/right you can use just two values separated by a comma.

```
<Button Margin="9,3"...
```

This notation means that both left and right margins will be set to 9 pixels while both top and bottom margins will be set to 3 pixels.

Like the `Margin` property, padding is used to add offset space to the normal positioning of a control. Unlike `Margin`, padding is applied to the space between the inner edge of a given control and its content. Figure 4-8 illustrates.

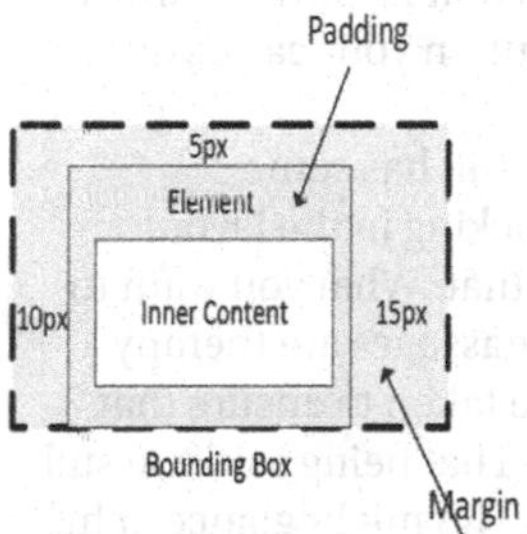

Figure 4-8. *Spatial structure of a XAML control*

Padding can only be applied on certain controls, including Border, Button, and TextBlock.

The Layout Controls

Now let's explore the various layout controls.

Canvas

The Canvas is a layout panel that supports absolute positioning of child elements relative to the top left corner of the canvas. It is the most efficient of the layout controls because it requires the least amount of special processing to evaluate the layout of its children.

You control the positioning of elements inside the Canvas by specifying X and Y coordinates in pixels. The X and Y coordinates are often specified by using the `Canvas.Left` and `Canvas.Top` attached properties. `Canvas.Left` specifies the object's distance from the left side of the containing Canvas (the x-coordinate), and `Canvas.Top` specifies the object's distance from the top of the containing Canvas (the y-coordinate).

■ **Note** Absolute positioning does not take into account the size of the app window, scaling, or other user-selected sizing. Using a container element that adapts to different orientations and screen settings, such as Grid or StackPanel, is often a better choice than using Canvas.

You can nest Canvas objects. When you nest objects, the coordinates used by each object are relative to its immediate containing Canvas.

Canvas is the host service class for several XAML attached properties. The purpose of these attached properties is to enable child elements in layout to report how they should be positioned in a Canvas parent.

These XAML attached properties are supported by Canvas:

- `Canvas.Left`
- `Canvas.Top`
- `Canvas.ZIndex`

There is almost always a better solution to using the Canvas as your layout control. It certainly makes little sense to do so now that an app is guaranteed to have multiple sizes during its run duration because there is no way to accurately predict positioning for the elements that have been placed in a Canvas.

You will be using Canvas for what it's good for: absolute positioning. This means that its purpose must be resolution- and size-dependent, which excludes using it for standard control layout. In your case, you will utilize the canvas as a surface for animating movement.

Control Corral, the project you started in Chapter 2 and continued in Chapter 3, still has some pieces missing from it. You've got most of the functionality in place but you are still lacking in the layout department. The controls we introduce and discuss later in this chapter will address that. What you want to do now is add some security to the platform to help protect the customer. Since the massages are therapy, they technically fall into the "medical" category. As such, proper precautions must be taken to ensure that when the app is open and not being used, the screen is disabled and cannot be read. That being said, we still want the app to look attractive and engaging for customers walking around your spa who might glance at it.

To accomplish this, you will build a screen-saver style screen that appears when the app has not been interacted with for 30 seconds. Let's get started.

Because the core functionality you are trying to implement affects every page in your app, you have two choices to make. You can either build it into every single page or expose some kind of application-level user interface that is always ready to be loaded. Fortunately, you designed the app with an app-wide page called RootHost that can serve this purpose. As a reminder, you added RootHost to host the app-wide Frame that normally is set to your Windows's content. At the time it might not have made sense, but building extensibility points into your app design is always a good thing because it minimizes the amount of refactoring you will have to do. You first implement the timer functionality in `RootHost.xaml.cs`. Listing 4-4 shows this.

Listing 4-4. Security Timer Enabled on RootHost

```
...
DispatcherTimer _security_timer;
public RootHost()
{
        this.InitializeComponent();
        SystemNavigationManager
                .GetForCurrentView()
                .AppViewBackButtonVisibility
                = AppViewBackButtonVisibility.Visible;
        SystemNavigationManager
                .GetForCurrentView()
                .BackRequested += RootHost_BackRequested;

        this.Loaded += RootHost_Loaded;
        _security_timer = new DispatcherTimer();
        _security_timer.Interval = TimeSpan.FromSeconds(30);
        _security_timer.Tick += async (a, b) =>
                {
                        _security_timer.Stop();
                        var msg = new MessageDialog("Secure", "Locked");
                        await msg.ShowAsync();
                        _security_timer.Start();
                };
}

private void RootHost_Loaded(object sender, RoutedEventArgs e)
{
        rootframe.Navigate(typeof(Dashboard));
        _security_timer.Start();
}
...
```

Listing 4-4 uses a DispatcherTimer object to trigger a message dialog every 30 seconds. You will next need to implement something to reset the timer so that it starts from scratch when a user interacts with it. Add the code in Listing 4-5 to do this.

Listing 4-5. Event Handlers for Handling User Input and Resetting the Timer

```
private void ResetTimer()
{
        _security_timer.Stop();
        _security_timer.Start();
}

protected override void OnKeyDown(KeyRoutedEventArgs e)
{
        base.OnKeyDown(e);
        ResetTimer();
}
```

```
protected override void OnPointerMoved(PointerRoutedEventArgs e)
{
        base.OnPointerMoved(e);
        ResetTimer();
}
```

Now the timer will be restarted whenever the user moves their finger or mouse, or presses a key on the keyboard. Run the app now to test this functionality. The final step is to implement the animation. Let's start by laying out the page. Listing 4-6 shows how the layout for RootHost should be set up.

Listing 4-6. New RootHost Page Layout

```
<Page
    x:Class="Lesson2_ControlCorral.RootHost"
    xmlns="http://schemas.microsoft.com/winfx/2006/xaml/presentation"
    xmlns:x="http://schemas.microsoft.com/winfx/2006/xaml"
    xmlns:local="using:Lesson2_ControlCorral"
    xmlns:d="http://schemas.microsoft.com/expression/blend/2008"
    xmlns:mc="http://schemas.openxmlformats.org/markup-compatibility/2006"
    mc:Ignorable="d">

    <Grid>
        <Frame x:Name="rootframe" />
        <Canvas x:Name="animation_root" Background="Black" Visibility="Collapsed"/>
    </Grid>

</Page>
```

At present, the canvas is collapsed. When the security timer runs out, it will be displayed. Refactor the code-behind so that it has the changes specified in bold in Listing 4-7.

Listing 4-7. Modifications to Display Animation When the Screen Times Out

```
...
public RootHost()
{
        this.InitializeComponent();
        SystemNavigationManager
                .GetForCurrentView()
                .AppViewBackButtonVisibility
                = AppViewBackButtonVisibility.Visible;
        SystemNavigationManager
                .GetForCurrentView()
                .BackRequested += RootHost_BackRequested;

        this.Loaded += RootHost_Loaded;
        _security_timer = new DispatcherTimer();
        _security_timer.Interval = TimeSpan.FromSeconds(30);
```

```
        _security_timer.Tick += (a, b) =>
                {
                        _security_timer.Stop();
                        animation_root.Visibility = Visibility.Visible;
                        _security_timer.Start();
                };
}

private void ResetTimer()
{
        _security_timer.Stop();
        _security_timer.Start();
        animation_root.Visibility = Visibility.Collapsed;
}
...
```

Run the code once again to test this new functionality. The final step is now to implement the animation logic. First, you implement the logic for displaying the circles. Listing 4-8 shows the code logic.

Listing 4-8. Animation Logic

```
private void DisplayCircle(Storyboard sb, DoubleAnimation motion_x, DoubleAnimation
motion_y,
                        DoubleAnimationUsingKeyFrames opacity,
                        int x, int y, int height, int width, Color color, bool fill,
                        double duration, int range_x, int range_y, Ellipse circle = null)
{
        if (circle == null)
        {
                circle = new Ellipse();
                animation_root.Children.Add(circle);
        }

        circle.Width = width;
        circle.Height = height;
        circle.SetValue(Canvas.LeftProperty, x);
        circle.SetValue(Canvas.TopProperty, y);
        circle.Stroke = new SolidColorBrush(color);
        if (fill)
                circle.Fill = new SolidColorBrush(color);
        circle.StrokeThickness = 1;
        circle.Opacity = 0;

        Storyboard.SetTarget(motion_x, circle);
        Storyboard.SetTarget(motion_y, circle);

        motion_x.To = range_x;
        motion_y.To = range_y;
        motion_x.Duration = new Duration(TimeSpan.FromSeconds(duration));
        motion_y.Duration = new Duration(TimeSpan.FromSeconds(duration));
```

```
Storyboard.SetTarget(opacity, circle);
Storyboard.SetTargetName(opacity, circle.Name);
Storyboard.SetTargetProperty(opacity, "Opacity");

opacity.Completed += (a, b) =>
{
        #region body
        Storyboard sb2 = new Storyboard();
        Random size_random = new Random();
        Random left_random = new Random();
        var bounds = Window.Current.Bounds;

        int size = size_random.Next(10, 500);
        int left = left_random.Next((int)bounds.Width);
        int top = left_random.Next((int)bounds.Height);
        int temp_range_x = left_random.Next((int)bounds.Width);
        int temp_range_y = left_random.Next((int)bounds.Height);
        int temp_duration = left_random.Next(5, 10);

        byte a2 = (byte)left_random.Next(0, 255);
        byte r2 = (byte)left_random.Next(0, 255);
        byte g2 = (byte)left_random.Next(0, 255);
        byte b2 = (byte)left_random.Next(0, 255);
        Color color2 = Color.FromArgb(a2, r2, g2, b2);

        DoubleAnimation motion_x2 = new DoubleAnimation();
        Storyboard.SetTargetProperty(motion_x2, "(Canvas.Left)");

        DoubleAnimation motion_y2 = new DoubleAnimation();
        Storyboard.SetTargetProperty(motion_y2, "(Canvas.Top)");

        DoubleAnimationUsingKeyFrames opacity2 =
                new DoubleAnimationUsingKeyFrames();
        LinearDoubleKeyFrame ld = new LinearDoubleKeyFrame();
        ld.KeyTime = KeyTime
                .FromTimeSpan(TimeSpan.FromSeconds(duration / 2.0));
        ld.Value = 1;
        LinearDoubleKeyFrame ld2 = new LinearDoubleKeyFrame();
        ld2.KeyTime = KeyTime
                .FromTimeSpan(TimeSpan.FromSeconds(duration));
        ld2.Value = 0;
        opacity2.KeyFrames.Add(ld);
        opacity2.KeyFrames.Add(ld2);

        DisplayCircle(sb2, motion_x2, motion_y2, opacity2, left, top,
        size, size, color2, fill, temp_duration,
        temp_range_x, temp_range_y, circle);

        sb2.Children.Add(motion_x2);
        sb2.Children.Add(motion_y2);
```

```
            sb2.Children.Add(opacity2);
            sb2.Begin();
            #endregion
        };
}
```

Listing 4-8 is used to create a circle of a certain size with a random fill color. Once created, it is used as the target of a storyboard animation. An event handler handles the Completed event for the animation associated with the circle's opacity. When the value hits zero (when the animation is finished), a new storyboard animation is spawned that recursively calls this method. We will discuss animations in more detail in Chapter 7. For now, you can just copy the code here verbatim.

Now create a new method called `StartScreenHider` where the logic to start hiding the control corral screen will be implemented. See Listing 4-9.

Listing 4-9. StartScreenHider Method

```
void StartScreenHider()
{
        animation_root.Visibility = Visibility.Visible;
        animation_root.Children.Clear();
        Random position_random = new Random();
        Color color = Colors.Gray;

        foreach (var i in Enumerable.Range(1, 50))
        {
            Storyboard sb = new Storyboard();

            #region code
            int size = position_random.Next(10, 500);
            int left = position_random.Next((int)this.ActualWidth);
            int top = position_random.Next((int)this.ActualHeight);
            int range_x = position_random.Next((int)this.ActualWidth);
            int range_y = position_random.Next((int)this.ActualHeight);

            int min_duration = 5, max_duration = 10;

            int duration = position_random.Next(min_duration, max_duration);

            byte a = (byte)position_random.Next(0, 255);
            byte r = (byte)position_random.Next(0, 255);
            byte g = (byte)position_random.Next(0, 255);
            byte b = (byte)position_random.Next(0, 255);

            DoubleAnimation motion_x = new DoubleAnimation();
            Storyboard.SetTargetProperty(motion_x, "(Canvas.Left)");

            DoubleAnimation motion_y = new DoubleAnimation();
            Storyboard.SetTargetProperty(motion_y, "(Canvas.Top)");

            DoubleAnimationUsingKeyFrames opacity =
                                    new DoubleAnimationUsingKeyFrames();
            LinearDoubleKeyFrame ld = new LinearDoubleKeyFrame();
```

```
            ld.KeyTime = KeyTime
                        .FromTimeSpan(TimeSpan.FromSeconds(duration / 2.0));
            ld.Value = 1;
            LinearDoubleKeyFrame ld2 = new LinearDoubleKeyFrame();
            ld2.KeyTime = KeyTime
                        .FromTimeSpan(TimeSpan.FromSeconds(duration));
            ld2.Value = 0;
            opacity.KeyFrames.Add(ld);
            opacity.KeyFrames.Add(ld2);

            DisplayCircle(sb, motion_x, motion_y, opacity,
                    left, top, size, size, color, true,
                    duration, range_x, range_y);

            sb.Children.Add(motion_x);
            sb.Children.Add(motion_y);
            sb.Children.Add(opacity);
            #endregion
            sb.Begin();

    }

}
```

Listing 4-9 is called whenever the security timer runs out. Once called, it instantiates a storyboard, creates the animations you need to run that storyboard, and then calls the DisplayCircle method, passing in all appropriate parameters. Finally, you change the security timer's tick event handler to call this method instead of just making the animation panel visible. Listing 4-10 illustrates.

Listing 4-10. Updated Tick Event Handler

```
_security_timer.Tick += (a, b) =>
{
        _security_timer.Stop();
        StartScreenHider();
        _security_timer.Start();
};
```

When this is run (and you wait around 30 seconds), you should see the security screen appear with the animations running. On my machine, this looks like Figure 4-9.

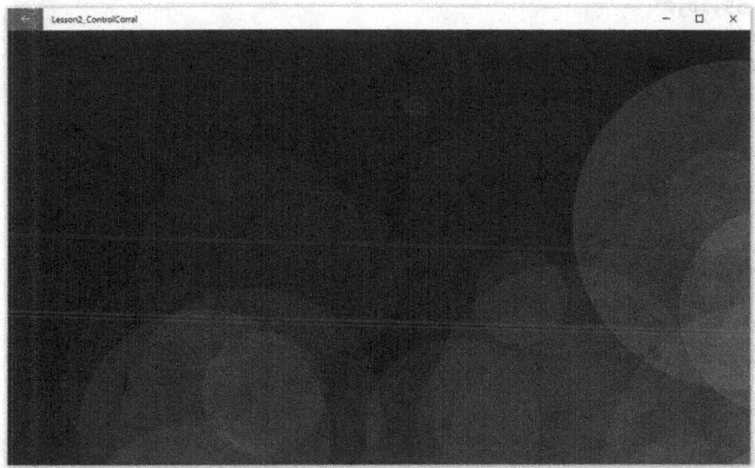

Figure 4-9. Animations running

StackPanel

The StackPanel is a layout panel that arranges child elements into a single line that can be oriented horizontally or vertically. StackPanel defines border attached properties: `StackPanel.BorderBrush`, `StackPanel.BorderThickness`, `StackPanel.CornerRadius`, and `StackPanel.Padding` to help with drawing a border around the StackPanel without using an additional Border element.

Now that you have a clearer understanding of StackPanels, let's modify some of your pages to utilize them. You will start with the Dashboard. Listing 4-11 illustrates; please note that portions of the code have been left out.

Listing 4-11. Using StackPanel

```
<Grid Background="White">
        <StackPanel Orientation="Vertical"
                    Background="SlateGray"
                    Width="100"
                    HorizontalAlignment="Left">
            <AppBarButton Icon="Calendar"
                          HorizontalAlignment="Center"
                          Label="New Reservation"
                          RequestedTheme="Dark"
                          Margin="5"
                          Click="OnReservation" />
            <AppBarButton Icon="List"
                          HorizontalAlignment="Center"
                          Label="List Reservations"
                          RequestedTheme="Dark"
                          Margin="5"
                          Click="ListReservations" />
        </StackPanel>
        <Grid Margin="110,0,0,0">
```

```
            <Border Margin="0,53,10,0"
                    Height="184"
                    BorderThickness="0,2,0,1"
                    BorderBrush="Gray"
                    VerticalAlignment="Top">
                ...
            </Border>
            ...

            <Border Margin="0,295,10,0"  Height="184"
                    BorderThickness="0,2,0,1"
                    BorderBrush="Gray"
                    VerticalAlignment="Top">

            ...
            </Border>
            ...

        </Grid>
    </Grid>
```

Running this sample produces the page shown in Figure 4-10.

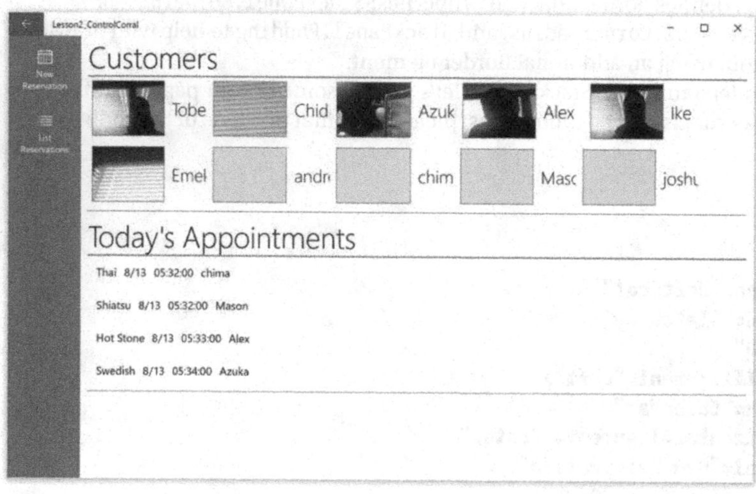

Figure 4-10. *StackPanel in action*

Grid

The Grid is a layout panel that supports arranging child elements in rows and columns. You typically define layout behavior for a Grid in XAML by providing one or more RowDefinition elements as the value of `Grid.RowDefinitions`, and one or more ColumnDefinition elements as the value of `Grid.ColumnDefinitions`. Then, you apply the `Grid.Row` and `Grid.Column` attached properties to each of the element children of the Grid, to indicate which row/column combination is used to position that element within the parent Grid. You saw this in Listing 4-2. The width of columns or height of rows can also be set using the `Width` property on a RowDefinition element or the `Height` property on a ColumnDefinition element. By default, a Grid contains one row and one column.

By default, each row or column divides layout space equally. Figure 4-11 shows the layout of two buttons when no sizing is provided.

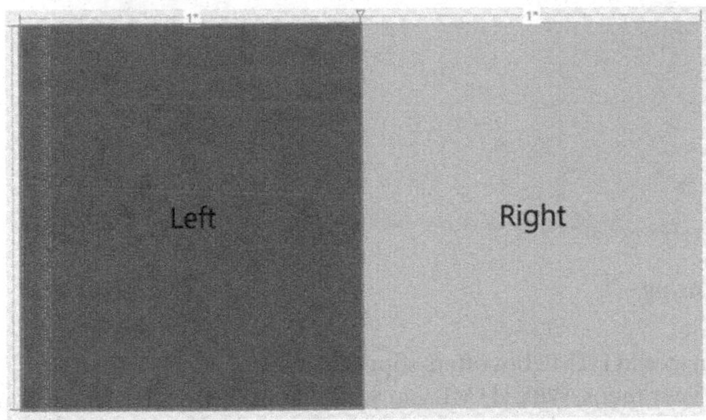

***Figure 4-11.** Grid with two columns*

You can change this behavior either by providing absolute pixel values, or by using Star sizing to divide the available space using a weighted factor. When the size of a row or column is defined explicitly, the other row/columns will once again fall back to dividing the remaining space evenly. In Figure 4-12, the left column has been modified to define a width of 50 pixels.

***Figure 4-12.** Grid with two columns, one set to a fixed width*

When Star sizing is used, ratios are applied to each of the columns/rows to produce the size for that row. For instance, if you want left to be twice as large as right, you specify left as 2* and right as 1* (not specifying a width value automatically means 1*, so in this case, it would not be necessary to specify the right column's width attribute). Figure 4-13 shows what this would look like.

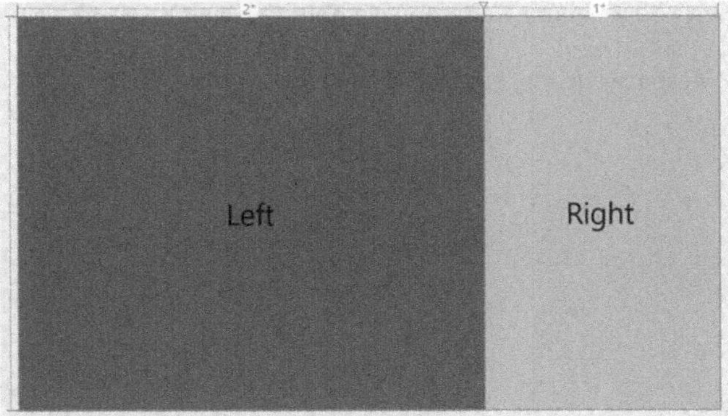

Figure 4-13. *Grid with two columns using star sizing*

Using star sizing is not unlike using percentages in HTML but offers superior functionality because you are not locked into a scale with which to define your ratios. With HTML you are always viewing sizes in terms of 100% and have to do your own calculations to determine the values specific rations might mean in terms of a percentage. With XAML star sizing, you can just specify the ratio.

To indicate that an element child should span multiple rows or multiple columns in the Grid, you can apply the `Grid.RowSpan` or `Grid.ColumnSpan` attached properties to child elements of a Grid.

As discussed earlier, you can precisely position child elements of a Grid by using a combination of the `Margin` property and alignment properties.

Now you'll use your newfound understanding of the Grid layout control to add a simple point-of-sale terminal to your application. In this sample, you will be using a new style of binding called *compiled binding*. In the three previous chapters, we introduced and used binding to help deliver the samples, so you should have a good understanding of how to use it to connect an underlying data model with what's being displayed on the screen. What is a point of concern with traditional binding is the lack of compile-time validation (each of the paths in the data binding expression are string literals). Combined with the fact that the data binding framework does not bubble up exceptions, it can be difficult to know when something has gone wrong with your code, and what that something is. Additionally, traditional binding can be quite expensive because of its reliance on reflection to pull values from. Compiled binding enhances the databinding experience by offering compile-time validation of binding paths. This means that the binding expression is statically linked to a specific type in the procedural part of a page.

In fact, for compiled bindings the DataContext is the object represented by the `x:Class` declaration in the XAML. To enable compiled binding, use the `x:Bind` markup extension. This markup extension effectively exposes the fields and properties of a code-behind class to the XAML. You can use `x:Bind` in any situation where traditional bindings are used, but in all cases `x:Bind` will require a code-behind file (as this is what is actually being bound to). This means that when you use `x:Bind` within a resource dictionary you must specify a code-behind for that resource dictionary (using `x:Class` notation). When `x:Bind` is used in template definitions, a type must be specified.

You start by adding a new page to your app called POS. Now navigate to your dashboard page and add a new AppBarButton to your navigation StackPanel. Use the calculator icon and label it POS. Set the click event to say OpenPOS, and then right-click and select Go To Definition to implement it. Your new app bar button should look like Listing 4-12.

Listing 4-12. POS Button Declaration

```
<AppBarButton Icon="Calculator"
                HorizontalAlignment="Center"
                Label="POS"
                RequestedTheme="Dark"
                Margin="5"
                Click="OpenPOS" />
```

In the code-behind method called `OpenPOS`, navigate to the POS page using the following code: `Frame.Navigate(typeof(POS))`. Run the sample and ensure that it is properly navigating to the desired page.

You will be using all the tricks of the trade from your Grid sample to implement the POS page. For now, it will use the column and row layout functionality that Grids provide to structure the user interface of the price entry panel. The POS page will also have a receipt panel that gives a real-time totaling (including taxes) of the items that have been purchased. In this implementation, no information about the purchase item will be presented. As you move through the various topics in this chapter, you will have an opportunity to revisit this feature and add more functionality to it; specifically, you will be adding support to pull the item being purchased directly from a catalog of potential items. Figure 4-14 shows the desired layout of the POS page.

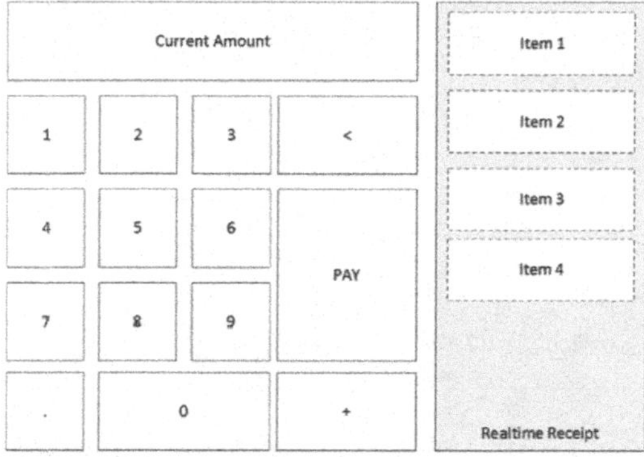

Figure 4-14. *Desired POS layout*

Based on the diagram in Figure 4-14, the POS page can be created with a five-column, five-row grid. Listing 4-13 shows the layout structure in XAML, with `ColumnSpan` values applied as needed to align the user interface with what you had in your sample file.

Listing 4-13. XAML to Layout POS

```
<Grid Background="{ThemeResource ApplicationPageBackgroundThemeBrush}">
    <Grid.ColumnDefinitions>
        <ColumnDefinition />
        <ColumnDefinition />
        <ColumnDefinition />
        <ColumnDefinition />
        <ColumnDefinition Width="350" />
    </Grid.ColumnDefinitions>
```

```
<Grid.RowDefinitions>
    <RowDefinition />
    <RowDefinition />
    <RowDefinition />
    <RowDefinition />
    <RowDefinition />
</Grid.RowDefinitions>
<Border BorderBrush="Gray" BorderThickness="1"
                Margin="5" Grid.ColumnSpan="4">
    <TextBlock x:Name="txt_currentamount" Text="0"
        FontFamily="segoe ui" FontWeight="ExtraBlack" FontSize="35"
        VerticalAlignment="Center" HorizontalAlignment="Right"/>
</Border>

    <Button Tag="1"
            Content="1"
            Click="NumberClicked"
            HorizontalAlignment="Stretch"
            VerticalAlignment="Stretch"
            Grid.Row="1"
            Grid.Column="0"
            Margin="5" />
    <Button Tag="2"
            Content="2"
            Click="NumberClicked"
            HorizontalAlignment="Stretch"
            VerticalAlignment="Stretch"
            Grid.Row="1"
            Grid.Column="1"
            Margin="5" />
    <Button Tag="3"
            Content="3"
            Click="NumberClicked"
            HorizontalAlignment="Stretch"
            VerticalAlignment="Stretch"
            Grid.Row="1"
            Grid.Column="2"
            Margin="5" />
    <Button Tag="4"
            Content="4"
            Click="NumberClicked"
            HorizontalAlignment="Stretch"
            VerticalAlignment="Stretch"
            Grid.Row="2"
            Grid.Column="0"
            Margin="5" />
    <Button Tag="5"
            Content="5"
            Click="NumberClicked"
            HorizontalAlignment="Stretch"
```

```
                VerticalAlignment="Stretch"
                Grid.Row="2"
                Grid.Column="1"
                Margin="5" />
        <Button Tag="6"
                Content="6"
                Click="NumberClicked"
                HorizontalAlignment="Stretch"
                VerticalAlignment="Stretch"
                Grid.Row="2"
                Grid.Column="2"
                Margin="5" />
        <Button Tag="7"
                Content="7"
                Click="NumberClicked"
                HorizontalAlignment="Stretch"
                VerticalAlignment="Stretch"
                Grid.Row="3"
                Grid.Column="0"
                Margin="5" />
        <Button Tag="8"
                Content="8"
                Click="NumberClicked"
                HorizontalAlignment="Stretch"
                VerticalAlignment="Stretch"
                Grid.Row="3"
                Grid.Column="1"
                Margin="5" />
        <Button Tag="9"
                Content="9"
                Click="NumberClicked"
                HorizontalAlignment="Stretch"
                VerticalAlignment="Stretch"
                Grid.Row="3"
                Grid.Column="2"
                Margin="5" />
        <Button Content="."
                Click="DotClicked"
                HorizontalAlignment="Stretch"
                VerticalAlignment="Stretch"
                Grid.Row="4"
                Grid.Column="0"
                Margin="5" />
        <Button Tag="0"
                Content="0"
                Click="NumberClicked"
                HorizontalAlignment="Stretch"
                VerticalAlignment="Stretch"
                Grid.Row="4"
```

```
            Grid.Column="1"
            Grid.ColumnSpan="2"
            Margin="5" />
    <Button Content="+"
            Click="AddItemClicked"
            HorizontalAlignment="Stretch"
            VerticalAlignment="Stretch"
            Grid.Row="2"
            Grid.Column="3"
            Margin="5" />
    <Button Content="PAY"
            Click="PayClicked"
            HorizontalAlignment="Stretch"
            VerticalAlignment="Stretch"
            Grid.Row="3"
            Grid.RowSpan="2"
            Grid.Column="3"
            Margin="5" />
    <Button Content="&lt;"
            Click="DeleteClicked"
            HorizontalAlignment="Stretch"
            VerticalAlignment="Stretch"
            Grid.Row="1"
            Grid.Column="3"
            Margin="5" />

    <StackPanel x:Name="reciept" BorderThickness="1" BorderBrush="Gray"
            HorizontalAlignment="Stretch"
            VerticalAlignment="Stretch"
      Grid.RowSpan="5" Grid.Row="0"
            Grid.Column="4" Margin="5">
    </StackPanel>
</Grid>
```

Listing 4-13 contains a layout that should be relatively straightforward to understand. Besides the TextBlock, which is named, there are no named elements here; instead you're using event handlers declared in XAML and expressed in the code-behind. The numbered buttons all define a `Tag` attribute, which you use to store the number they represent. They all also use the same event handler to handle their clicked event. The plan is to implement this as a catch-all handler that will apply that tag value to the display area when any of those buttons are clicked. The other three event handlers, `DeleteClicked`, `PayClicked`, and `DotClicked`, are used to handle those individual cases.

The XAML from Listing 4-13 will lay out in the design surface as shown in Figure 4-15.

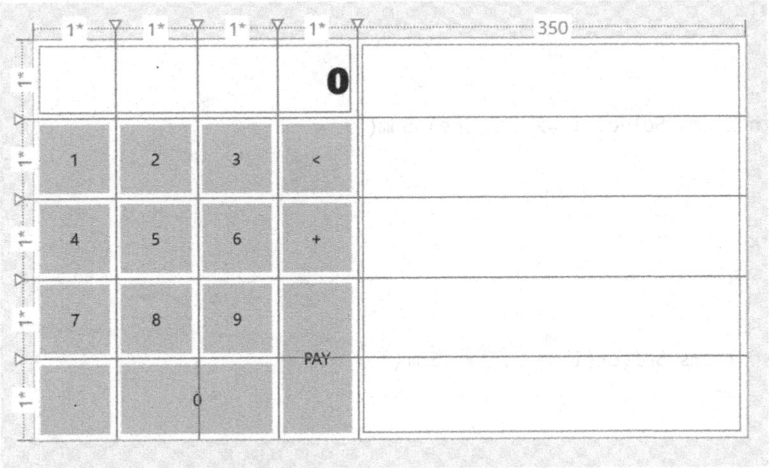

Figure 4-15. *POS layout in design window*

Before moving on with the next steps, let's add some classes to represent the activities involved in a point-of-sale interaction. You need a management class to use as the control class for interacting with the user interface. This class when instantiated will be the code version of the UI. You also need a class that represents each line item in a receipt. Every time a product is scanned or a price is typed in, a new entry is made to the receipt for that transaction; this class needs to encapsulate all the data stored in that entry. You will start with this class. Create a new class in your project called `ReceiptItem` and place the code in Listing 4-14 into it.

Listing 4-14. ReceiptItem Class Definition

```
public class ReceiptItem
{
        public Guid ItemID { get; set; }
        public string ItemName { get; set; }
        public double Price { get; set; }
        public double Tax { get; set; }
}
```

You next implement the management class we discussed earlier. Create another class in your project called `POSTransaction`. As stated previously, this class should encompass all activities necessary to perform your POS function. Listing 4-15 shows the code you should add to this class.

Listing 4-15. POSTransaction Class Definition

```
public class POSTransaction
{
        List<ReceiptItem> Items { get; } = new List<ReceiptItem>();

        public double DefaultTaxAmount { get; set; }
```

```
        public double SubTotal
        {
                get
                {
                        return Items.Select(i => i.Price).Sum();
                }
        }

        public double TotalTax
        {
                get
                {
                        return Items.Select(i => i.Tax).Sum();
                }
        }

        public void AddItemByPrice(double price)
        {
                var tax_amount = price * DefaultTaxAmount;
                Items.Add(
                new ReceiptItem
                {
                        ItemID = Guid.NewGuid(),
                        ItemName = "",
                        Price = price,
                        Tax = tax_amount,
                });
        }
        public void RemoveItem(ReceiptItem item)
        {
                Items.Remove(item);
        }

        public void ClearItems()
        {
                Items.Clear();
        }
}
```

POSTransaction will be used to track a given point-of-sale transaction. For the purposes of this case study, a transaction will start when the user clicks the POS button and is navigated to the POS page. A transaction ends when a sale is made or the transaction is cancelled by either navigating away or paying. AddItemByPrice is the primary method of interest here. Given a price, this method will calculate the appropriate tax and add it, along with a GUID to identify the specific line item, as well as an empty item name string, to the list of receipt items being tracked by this class. You can now wire up the code-behind file, POS.xaml.cs. Listing 4-16 shows all the methods that must be added to the POS class to enable the POS functionality.

Listing 4-16. Additions to POS Class

```
POSTransaction Transaction { get; set; } = new POSTransaction();

private void NumberClicked(object sender, RoutedEventArgs e)
{
        if (txt_currentamount.Text.Trim() == "0")
                txt_currentamount.Text = "";

        //test to see if two decimal places have already been specified
        var parts = txt_currentamount.Text.Split('.');
        if (parts.Length > 1)
        {
                if (parts[1].Length >= 2)
                        return;
        }
        Button target = sender as Button;
        var number = target.Tag as string;
        txt_currentamount.Text += number;
}

private void DotClicked(object sender, RoutedEventArgs e)
{
        if (txt_currentamount.Text.Contains(".") == false)
                txt_currentamount.Text += ".";
}

private void AddItemClicked(object sender, RoutedEventArgs e)
{
        Transaction.AddItemByPrice(double.Parse(txt_currentamount.Text));

        //add a reciept line item as a textblock
        TextBlock txt_item = new TextBlock();
        txt_item.Text = txt_currentamount.Text;
        reciept.Children.Insert(0, txt_item);

        txt_currentamount.Text = "0";
}

private void DeleteClicked(object sender, RoutedEventArgs e)
{
        if (txt_currentamount.Text.Length > 0)
                txt_currentamount.Text = txt_currentamount.Text
                                .Remove(txt_currentamount.Text.Length - 1);
        if (txt_currentamount.Text.Length == 0)
                txt_currentamount.Text = "0";
}

private void PayClicked(object sender, RoutedEventArgs e)
{

}
```

The first thing you need to do in Listing 4-16 is create a property that represents the transaction that will occur while on the POS page. The `Transaction` property represents this. You instantiate it for each new POS page that is created. You next implement the various event handlers needed to facilitate the POS functionality. In `NumberClicked`, you first do some cosmetic homework, removing the 0 that is automatically placed when no value is in the TextBlock. The next lines of code, outlined below, are there to prevent more than two decimal places being inputted into the POS console:

```
//test to see if two decimal places have already been specified
var parts = txt_currentamount.Text.Split('.');
if (parts.Length > 1)
{
        if (parts[1].Length >= 2)
                return;
}
```

You split the string by the dot (`DotClicked` ensures that there can only be one dot in the number string) and if the string to the right of the dot has two characters already ignore the entry. `AddItemClicked` takes the string value presently in the TextBlock, converts it to a double, and adds it to the transaction as a receipt line item. It then adds a TextBlock set to the display the value of the current entry to the receipt StackPanel. Note that you use `Children.Insert` as opposed to `Children.Add` here. You will be adding another control to this StackPanel to represent the total amount spent and you want this to always show at the bottom of the StackPanel. Using `Insert` allows you to place other controls above this control, so that the receipt user interface resembles that of a paper receipt. `DeleteClicked` deleted the last character inputted. If no characters are left, it shows a zero. Run the sample and ensure that it works.

Now let's add the code in Listing 4-17 into the StackPanel you are calling receipt. This TextBlock will be used to represent the sub-total value of the current transaction, which is the total cost without tax. In your POS transaction class, you have a property that maps to it called `SubTotal` so you `x:Bind` to it. Because compiled binding is always bound to the code-behind class, all you need to do here is specify the x-bind. There's no need to set DataContext.

Listing 4-17. Control to Display Total in Receipt StackPanel

```
<Border Margin="5" BorderThickness="0,1,0,0" BorderBrush="Black" Padding="5">
    <TextBlock Text="{x:Bind Path='Transaction.SubTotal', Mode=OneWay}" />
</Border>
```

Run this code and you will notice that although items are being added, the total amount is not being updated. We have deliberately left something out to help illustrate its value to the binding framework. When the page is first loaded, the binding mechanism is loaded, but it is never run automatically again. Given this, how does the binding framework know that values have changed so as to update the item being bound to? The answer can be found in the `INotifyPropertyChanged` interface. This interface serves two purposes. First, it serves as a marker to let the binding framework know that the object being bound is one that can change values during the runtime of the app. This is an important optimization technique. Second, it provides a `PropertyChanged` event that the runtime can subscribe to and use to update its bindings. You must modify `POSTransaction` to implement this interface if you want your TextBlock to be notified of the change when `SubTotal` is modified. Listing 4-18 shows the changes that need to be made, which are highlighted in bold.

Listing 4-18. Applying INotifyPropertyChanged to POSTransaction

```
public class POSTransaction : INotifyPropertyChanged
{
        public event PropertyChangedEventHandler PropertyChanged;

        ...

        public void AddItemByPrice(double price)
        {
                var tax_amount = price * DefaultTaxAmount;
                Items.Add(
                new ReceiptItem
                {
                        ItemID = Guid.NewGuid(),
                        ItemName = "",
                        Price = price,
                        Tax = tax_amount,
                });
                PropertyChanged?
                        .Invoke(this,
                        new PropertyChangedEventArgs("SubTotal"));
                PropertyChanged?
                        .Invoke(this,
                        new PropertyChangedEventArgs("TotalTax"));
        }

        ...
}
```

Run the sample now and you should see that the total TextBlock is updating properly.

RelativePanel

The RelativePanel is a layout container that is useful for creating UIs that do not have a clear linear pattern–that is, layouts that are not fundamentally stacked, wrapped, or tabular, where you might naturally use a StackPanel or Grid. It allows you to decide on the fly the spatial relationship that any two items within it share. If you want to define two StackPanels side by side, you might handle it as shown in Listing 4-19.

Listing 4-19. Laying Out Two Stack Panels Side by Side with Just a Grid

```
<Grid Background="{ThemeResource ApplicationPageBackgroundThemeBrush}">
    <Grid.ColumnDefinitions>
        <ColumnDefinition Width="Auto" />
        <ColumnDefinition Width="Auto" />
    </Grid.ColumnDefinitions>
    <StackPanel >
        <Button Content="1" />
        <Button Content="2" />
        <Button Content="3" />
    </StackPanel>
```

```
    <StackPanel Grid.Column="1">
        <Button Content="4" />
        <Button Content="5" />
        <Button Content="6" />
    </StackPanel>
</Grid>
```

This will produce a user interface like the one in Figure 4-16 when run (this figure is from the XAML designer).

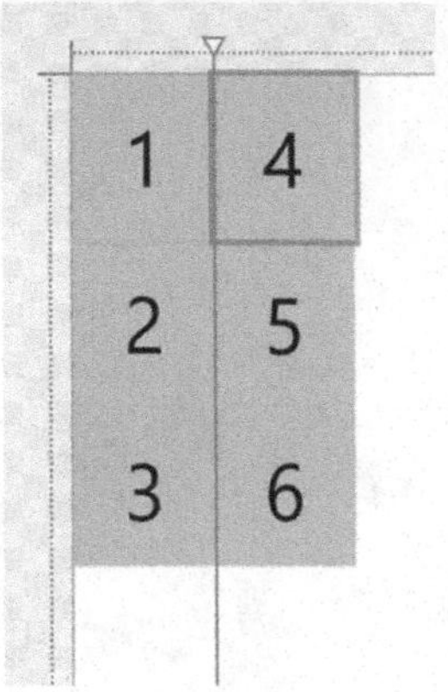

Figure 4-16. *Two StackPanels side by side (grid version)*

Using a StackPanel you might find this to be somewhat easier but you would lose the ability to predict the width of your content. Listing 4-20 illustrates.

Listing 4-20. Laying Out Two StackPanels Side by Side with Just a StackPanel

```
<StackPanel Orientation="Horizontal" >
    <StackPanel >
        <Button Content="1" />
        <Button Content="2" />
        <Button Content="3" />
    </StackPanel>
    <StackPanel >
        <Button Content="4" />
        <Button Content="5" />
        <Button Content="6" />
    </StackPanel>
</StackPanel>
```

This XAML would produce the same result as Figure 4-16 but at the cost of locking you into a layout structured around the StackPanel. The RelativePanel can be used to do things like this quickly (and without losing the flexibility to "fill" when needed). Listing 4-21 explains.

Listing 4-21. Laying Out Two StackPanels Side by Side with Just a RelativePanel

```
<RelativePanel >
    <StackPanel x:Name="stack_left" >
        <Button Content="1" />
        <Button Content="2" />
        <Button Content="3" />
    </StackPanel>
    <StackPanel  RelativePanel.RightOf="stack_left">
        <Button Content="4" />
        <Button Content="5" />
        <Button Content="6" />
    </StackPanel>
</RelativePanel>
```

Listing 4-21 will once again produce the same results as Figure 4-15, but with no commitments made on the future layout of the screen.

Now what if you tried to add another StackPanel to the right of these two controls, which takes up the remaining space? To do this with the Grid, you would have to add a new column, then add the StackPanel, then define it as being in that column. Tedious, but it can be done.

With the StackPanel solution, you could add the new column but because of the way the StackPanel works (your main StackPanel is oriented horizontally, and it will grow horizontally only based on the total width of elements it contains, so there is no way to make a StackPanel “fill” the remaining available space), it cannot be made to take up the remaining space.

Listing 4-22 shows how it would look with a RelativePanel.

Listing 4-22. Laying Out with Just a RelativePanel

```
<RelativePanel >
    <StackPanel x:Name="stack_left" Orientation="Vertical">
        <Button Content="1" />
        <Button Content="2" />
        <Button Content="3" />
    </StackPanel>
    <StackPanel x:Name="stack_right" RelativePanel.RightOf="stack_left">
        <Button Content="4" />
        <Button Content="5" />
        <Button Content="6" />
    </StackPanel>
    <StackPanel RelativePanel.RightOf="stack_right"
                        RelativePanel.AlignRightWithPanel="True">
        <Button Content="7" HorizontalAlignment="Stretch" />
        <Button Content="8" HorizontalAlignment="Stretch" />
        <Button Content="9" HorizontalAlignment="Stretch" />
    </StackPanel>
</RelativePanel>
```

Finally, what if you need to change the way these items lay out so that the last StackPanel you added was now underneath the other two StackPanels? And what if this needs to happen at runtime based on some user-driven event like the size of the windows changing? Although possible with the Grid, it would require so much code that it would be prohibitive. Listing 4-23 shows the code that would be needed to accomplish this.

Listing 4-23. Changing Layout in Code-Behind Using RelativePanel

```
stack_bottom.SetValue(RelativePanel.BelowProperty, stack_left);
stack_bottom.SetValue(RelativePanel.AlignLeftWithPanelProperty, true);
stack_bottom.SetValue(RelativePanel.AlignRightWithPanelProperty, true);
```

Like all the panels discussed thus far, RelativePanel defines attached properties that let you draw a border around the RelativePanel without using an additional Border element. The properties are `RelativePanel.BorderBrush`, `RelativePanel.BorderThickness`, `RelativePanel.CornerRadius`, and `RelativePanel.Padding`. In the next chapter, you will learn more about how the RelativePanel is used.

Let's update your POS sample to use a relative panel. Along the way, you will also make some improvements to it. First, let's add a `Total` property to your POSTransaction object to represent the total of the tax and subtotal. You will be binding to this property, so while you are modifying POSTransaction, you should also add the necessary event firing so that the binding system is aware each time the property value changes. Listing 4-24 provides the code.

Listing 4-24. POSTransaction.Total Property Definition

```
...
public double Total
{
        get
        {
                return SubTotal + TotalTax;
        }
}
...
public void AddItemByPrice(double price)
{
        var tax_amount = price * DefaultTaxAmount;
        Items.Add(
        new ReceiptItem
        {
                ItemID = Guid.NewGuid(),
                ItemName = "",
                Price = price,
                Tax = tax_amount,
        });
        PropertyChanged?
                .Invoke(this,
                new PropertyChangedEventArgs("SubTotal"));
        PropertyChanged?
                .Invoke(this,
                new PropertyChangedEventArgs("TotalTax"));
        PropertyChanged?
                .Invoke(this,
                new PropertyChangedEventArgs("Total"));
}
...
```

Next, you need to update the constructor for the code-behind file to set a value for POSTransaction's `DefaultTaxAmount` property. As you have seen from the definition of `AddItemByPrice`, this property is used to calculate the tax on each item that is added to the customer's transaction. In the previous section, you were not displaying the total amount taxed so it did not matter; now that you are, you should make sure there is a value assigned to this property. Listing 4-25 sets in the constructor for the POS code-behind class, the default amount taxed (the sales tax) to 15% of the product's value.

Listing 4-25. Setting DefaultTaxAmount

```
...
public POS()
{
        this.InitializeComponent();

        Transaction.DefaultTaxAmount = .15;
}
...
```

Finally, you modify the totals section of the receipt stack panel to include all the totals, not just the SubTotal. You do this using the RelativePanel to illustrate the power and flexibility of the layout control. No other layout control would allow you to do this without the need of other layout controls within it to help lay out each individual control. RelativePanel brings with it the power to function like every other control on a case by case basis. Replace the Border from Listing 4-17 with the code in Listing 4-26.

Listing 4-26. Totals Section Using RelativePanel

```
<Border Margin="5"
        BorderThickness="0,1,0,0"
        BorderBrush="Black"
        Padding="5">

    <RelativePanel>
        <TextBlock x:Name="txt_subtotal_label"
                   Text="Sub Total:" />
        <TextBlock x:Name="txt_tax_label"
                   Text="Tax Total:"
                   RelativePanel.Below="txt_subtotal" />
        <TextBlock x:Name="txt_total_label"
                   Text="Total:"
                   RelativePanel.Below="txt_tax_label" />
        <TextBlock x:Name="txt_subtotal"
                   Text="{x:Bind Path='Transaction.SubTotal', Mode=OneWay}"
                   RelativePanel.AlignRightWithPanel="True" />
        <TextBlock x:Name="txt_tax"
                   Text="{x:Bind Path='Transaction.TotalTax', Mode=OneWay}"
                   RelativePanel.Below="txt_subtotal"
                   RelativePanel.AlignRightWithPanel="True" />
        <TextBlock x:Name="txt_total"
                   Text="{x:Bind Path='Transaction.Total', Mode=OneWay}"
                   RelativePanel.Below="txt_tax"
                   RelativePanel.AlignRightWithPanel="True" />
    </RelativePanel>
</Border>
```

Figure 4-17 shows the new look of the POS interface when run.

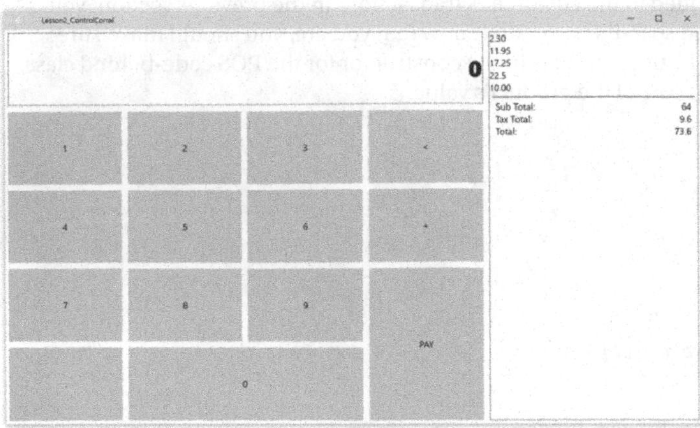

***Figure 4-17.** POS in action*

You will be revisiting this POS sample later on in this chapter when we discuss controls that you create yourself.

VariableSizedWrapGrid

The VariableSizedWrapGrid arranges elements in rows or columns just like Grid, but with this control, child elements will automatically wrap to a new row or column when the `MaximumRowsOrColumns` value is reached. The `Orientation` property specifies whether the grid adds its items in rows or columns before wrapping. When the value is `Vertical`, the grid adds items in columns from top to bottom, then wraps from left to right. When the value is `Horizontal`, the grid adds items in rows from left to right, then wraps from top to bottom. You can make items different sizes in the grid by making them span multiple rows and columns using the `VariableSizedWrapGrid.RowSpan` and `VariableSizedWrapGrid.ColumnSpan` attached properties.

SplitView

The SplitView control presents two areas of content: a Pane, which can exist in two possible widths (a narrow summary view, and a wider full view), and a Content area, which may also have two widths that it is presented in.

To open the Pane (to show it in its wider form), set the `IsPaneOpen` property. You can specify the length of the opened pane by setting the `OpenPaneLength` property. You can also specify whether you want to pane to appear on the left or right of the content area; to do so, use the `PanePlacement` property. Finally, you can change the default background color of the Pane by setting the `PaneBackground`.

By default, the Pane overlays the Content and disappears completely when closed. Setting the `DislayMode` on the SplitView allows you to specify one of several ways the Pane will behave when closed. The options are as follows:

- `Overlay`: The pane covers the content when it's open and does not take up space in the control layout. The pane closes when the user taps outside of it.
- `Inline`: The pane is shown side by side with the content and takes up space in the control layout. The pane does not close when the user taps outside of it.

- `CompactOverlay`: The amount of the pane defined by the `CompactPaneLength` property is shown side by side with the content and takes up space in the control layout. The remaining part of the pane covers the content when it's open and does not take up space in the control layout. The pane closes when the user taps outside of it.
- `CompactInline`: The amount of the pane defined by the `CompactPaneLength` property is shown side by side with the content and takes up space in the control layout. The remaining part of the pane pushes the content to the side when it's open and takes up space in the control layout. The pane does not close when the user taps outside of it.

■ **Note** For some bizarre reason, the SplitView does not include a built-in control for users to toggle the state of the Pane. All the samples from Microsoft use a "hamburger button" individually created for the scenario. No such button exists as part of the SplitView. You must provide this affordance and the code to toggle the `IsPaneOpen` property yourself!

The SplitView content area is always present and can contain a single child element (similar to Page, Border, or any other content control), which is typically a Panel-derived container that contains additional child elements.

The obvious choice for a location to place a SplitView control in your sample UWP app is the dashboard. You previously used a StackPanel pinned to the left edge of the page to control navigation. You will continue to use the StackPanel, but will wrap it as the Pane portion of a SplitView. Listing 4-27 shows the changes that need to be made to `Dashboard.xaml` to implement this.

Listing 4-27. Dashboard.xaml with SplitView

```
<Page x:Class="Lesson2_ControlCorral.Dashboard"
      xmlns="http://schemas.microsoft.com/winfx/2006/xaml/presentation"
      xmlns:x="http://schemas.microsoft.com/winfx/2006/xaml"
      xmlns:local="using:Lesson2_ControlCorral"
      xmlns:d="http://schemas.microsoft.com/expression/blend/2008"
      xmlns:mc="http://schemas.openxmlformats.org/markup-compatibility/2006"
      mc:Ignorable="d">

    <SplitView Background="White"
               PaneBackground="SlateGray"
               DisplayMode="Inline"
               IsPaneOpen="True"
               OpenPaneLength="100">
        <SplitView.Pane>
            <StackPanel Orientation="Vertical"
                        HorizontalAlignment="Center">

                <AppBarButton Icon="Calendar"
                              HorizontalAlignment="Center"
                              Label="New Reservation"
                              RequestedTheme="Dark"
                              Margin="5"
                              Click="OnReservation" />
```

```
            <AppBarButton Icon="List"
                          HorizontalAlignment="Center"
                          Label="List Reservations"
                          RequestedTheme="Dark"
                          Margin="5"
                          Click="ListReservations" />
            <AppBarButton Icon="Calculator"
                          HorizontalAlignment="Center"
                          Label="POS"
                          RequestedTheme="Dark"
                          Margin="5"
                          Click="OpenPOS" />

        </StackPanel>
    </SplitView.Pane>

    <Grid Margin="10,10">

    ...

    </Grid>
  </SplitView>
</Page>
```

In Listing 4-27, you replace the dashboard page's root Grid with a SplitView and move the StackPanel that was previously pinned to the left into the Pane element. Running the sample should produce the same basic layout as before. There is really no change to the UI, but switching to use the SplitView sets the foundation for future user interface optimizations. You will see many examples in the next chapter.

Building Your Own Controls

The UWP does a great job of providing many controls that can be used to perform the basic functions a developer might want. You saw many of them in the last two chapters and even more in this chapter. For many of you out there, what the UWP offers will be enough. To support scenarios where a developer needs to create their own controls, the platform provides two approaches. You can build templated controls or you can build user controls.

User Controls

User Controls are the easier of the two custom control technologies provided by the UWP. In scenarios where you need more logic and interactivity than a template can provide, where templating is not supported, or where the logic and layout of a particular interface must function together in unison to deliver a transportable functionality, User Controls are a safe bet. They are controls with a fixed template that are composed of other controls interacting together to provide functionality. They can be used anywhere a standard control is used, including as part of a template. A typical use of UserControls is to encapsulate functionality as described above for the purpose of consistency and transportability.

Many developers build User Control libraries that they then use from project to project and even sell on the open market. The great thing about them is that they come with designer support, so building a User Control is no different than building a Page.

In the POS example you have been working on, a User Control would be a great tool to spruce up the display shown to the user when a line item is added to the transaction. Presently you are dynamically adding a TextBlock to represent the cost of the item, but the amount taxed on that item should also be displayed. Doing this on the fly in code can be error-prone and time-consuming because there is now a design-time element in the process. You can alternatively use a template stored in a resource and wire up the interactivity yourself but it would be laborious to do so since you must account for elements in the template not being there. This kind of scenario is where User Controls really shine because they provide a means of encapsulating layout and behavior in one package.

Let's add this to your project and start using it. Add a new User Control to your project by right-clicking the project file and selecting Add ➤ New Item and then picking User Control from the Add New Item dialog. Call the control ReceiptLineItem. Replace the Grid within the User Control element with the code from Listing 4-28.

Listing 4-28. ReceiptLineItem Layout

```
<UserControl.Resources>
    <local:DoubleToCurrencyConverter x:Key="double_to_currency" />
</UserControl.Resources>
<RelativePanel Padding="10">
    <TextBlock x:Name="txt_amount"
               Text="{x:Bind Item.Price,Converter={StaticResource double_to_currency}}"
               RelativePanel.AlignBottomWithPanel="True"
               RelativePanel.AlignTopWithPanel="True"
               VerticalAlignment="Center" />
    <TextBlock Text=" tax-"
               RelativePanel.LeftOf="txt_tax" Margin="0,0,5,0"
               RelativePanel.AlignVerticalCenterWithPanel="True" />
    <TextBlock x:Name="txt_tax"
               Text="{x:Bind Item.Tax, Converter={StaticResource double_to_currency}}"
               VerticalAlignment="Center"
               RelativePanel.AlignRightWithPanel="True"
               RelativePanel.AlignBottomWithPanel="True"
               RelativePanel.AlignTopWithPanel="True" />
</RelativePanel>
```

Using the RelativePanel you have once again created a layout that would have required several controls nested together to create otherwise. The code layout is using compiled binding to connect to some properties on the code-behind class and even specifies a converter called `DoubleToCurrencyConverter`. Obviously at this point the code will not work, so let's create the converter first and then circle back and add all the appropriate code to `ReceiptLineItem.xaml.cs`. Create a new class in your project entitled `DoubleToCurrencyConverter` and populate it as shown in Listing 4-29.

Listing 4-29. DoubleToCurrencyConverter Class Definition

```
public class DoubleToCurrencyConverter : IValueConverter
{
        public object Convert(object value, Type targetType,
                object parameter, string language)
        {
                return $"{value:C}";
        }
```

```
    public object ConvertBack(object value, Type targetType,
        object parameter, string language)
    {
        throw new NotImplementedException();
    }
}
```

You've worked with converters before (in Chapter 1) so nothing here should be too surprising to you. In this case, all your converter is actually doing is formatting the double as currency. This is accomplished in the string formatting notation with a colon-C, as you see in the sample: `$"{value:C}";`

Now look at your ReceiptLineItem control in the code-behind. Open `ReceiptLineItem.xaml.cs` and add the code in bold to the `ReceiptLineItem` class definition. Listing 4-30 illustrates.

Listing 4-30. ReceiptLineItem Definition

```
public sealed partial class ReceiptLineItem : UserControl
{
        public ReceiptItem Item { get; private set; }

        public ReceiptLineItem()
        {
                this.InitializeComponent();
        }

        public void AddItem(ReceiptItem item)
        {
                Item = item;
        }
}
```

As you can see, there is not much to the code-behind file beyond specifying an `Item` property and setting its value when `AddItem` is called. To close out the loop, you must now modify the method `AddItemClicked` in `POSTransaction` to support using this control over TextBlock. Before you can do this, you need to modify your POS transaction class a bit. You see presently there is no easy way to retrieve the `ReceiptItem` object that is created when `AddItemByPrice` is called. In the new version of this method shown in Listing 4-31 it is now returning the created `ReceiptItem`.

Listing 4-31. New AddItemByPrice Definition

```
public ReceiptItem AddItemByPrice(double price)
{
        var tax_amount = price * DefaultTaxAmount;
        var item = new ReceiptItem
        {
                ItemID = Guid.NewGuid(),
                ItemName = "",
                Price = price,
                Tax = tax_amount,
        };
        Items.Add(item);
        PropertyChanged?
                .Invoke(this,
                new PropertyChangedEventArgs("SubTotal"));
```

```
        PropertyChanged?
                .Invoke(this,
                new PropertyChangedEventArgs("TotalTax"));
        PropertyChanged?
                .Invoke(this,
                new PropertyChangedEventArgs("Total"));
        return item;
}
```

You can now go back to POS.xaml.cs and redefine AddItemClicked as follows in Listing 4-32.

Listing 4-32. New AddItemClicked Definition

```
private void AddItemClicked(object sender, RoutedEventArgs e)
{
        var reciept_item = Transaction
                .AddItemByPrice(double.Parse(txt_currentamount.Text));

        //add a reciept line item as a ReceiptLineItem
        ReceiptLineItem line_item = new ReceiptLineItem();
        line_item.AddItem(reciept_item);

        reciept.Children.Insert(0, line_item);

        txt_currentamount.Text = "0";
}
```

As a final step, apply the DoubeToCurrencyConverter to the various bindings in the receipt StackPanel. Figure 4-18 illustrates how this page might now look when being used.

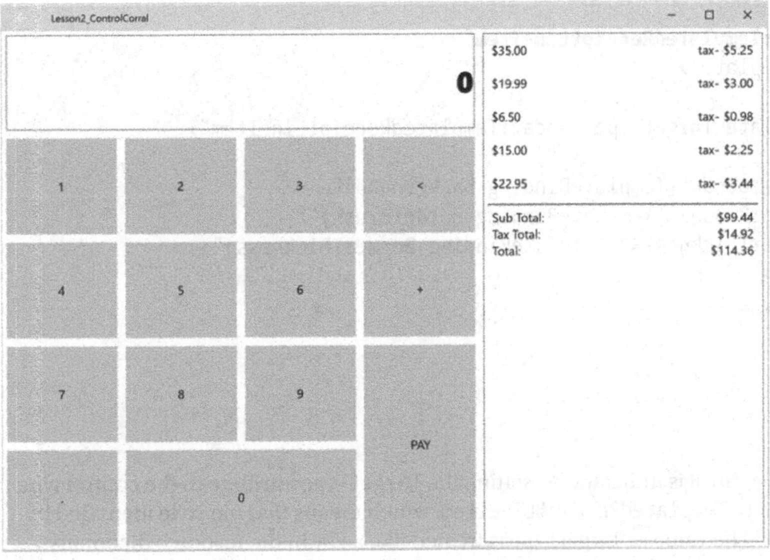

Figure 4-18. *POS in action*

Templated Controls

Templated controls are quite a bit more sophisticated than User Controls, but in return for your investment in time, they offer quite a bit more functionality than can be had from the basic User Control pattern. As with User Controls, they encapsulate functionality and user interface layout into a single package that can then be transported between projects. They come with the added benefit of downstream users being able to re-template them as needed (much like you do with the built-in controls).

Take your ReceiptLineItem control, for instance. In its present state, it works well, but if a different individual wanted to consume in a different layout (with the tax display showing directly below the price display), they would have to create a whole new control. With templated controls this is not the case. Let's create a new ReceiptLineItem templated control to illustrate how easy it is to do. Add a new templated control to the project by right clicking and selecting Add ➤ New Item ➤ Templated Control. Call the new control TemplatedReceiptLineItem.

■ **Note** You can do this all by yourself without the help of Visual Studio 2015. Templated controls are simply class files that inherit directly from Control.

Visual Studio 2015 will create a new folder called Themes and place a file called `Generic.xaml` into it. In a templated control, the user interface for the control is only loosely bound to the control itself. It is stored as a template in a special file called `generic.xaml`. Listing 4-33 shows the contents of `generic.xaml`; the parts relevant to your control are highlighted in bold.

Listing 4-33. TemplatedReceiptLineItem Initial Template in Generic.xaml

```
<ResourceDictionary
    xmlns="http://schemas.microsoft.com/winfx/2006/xaml/presentation"
    xmlns:x="http://schemas.microsoft.com/winfx/2006/xaml"
    xmlns:local="using:Lesson2_ControlCorral">

    <Style TargetType="local:TemplatedReceiptLineItem" >
        <Setter Property="Template">
            <Setter.Value>
                <ControlTemplate TargetType="local:TemplatedReceiptLineItem">
                    <Border
                        Background="{TemplateBinding Background}"
                        BorderBrush="{TemplateBinding BorderBrush}"
                        BorderThickness="{TemplateBinding BorderThickness}">
                    </Border>
                </ControlTemplate>
            </Setter.Value>
        </Setter>
    </Style>
</ResourceDictionary>
```

The user interface for a given control is indicated by setting the `TargetType` attribute to the control type. In this case, Visual Studio has set it to `TemplatedReceiptLineItem`, which means that the style identified by this key maps to your control class. The value of TargetType is treated like a key in the resource dictionary so only one style can be defined for a given type. Right now your user interface is just an empty border. Let's update it to look like the ReceiptLineItem control. Listing 4-34 shows the new structure.

Listing 4-34. TemplatedReceiptLineItem Template in generic.xaml

```
<Style TargetType="local:TemplatedReceiptLineItem">
    <Setter Property="Template">
        <Setter.Value>
            <ControlTemplate TargetType="local:TemplatedReceiptLineItem">
                <RelativePanel Padding="10">
                    <TextBlock x:Name="PART_Price"
                               RelativePanel.AlignBottomWithPanel="True"
                               RelativePanel.AlignTopWithPanel="True" />
                    <TextBlock x:Name="PART_Tax"
                               VerticalAlignment="Center"
                               RelativePanel.AlignRightWithPanel="True"
                               RelativePanel.AlignBottomWithPanel="True"
                               RelativePanel.AlignTopWithPanel="True" />
                </RelativePanel>
            </ControlTemplate>
        </Setter.Value>
    </Setter>
</Style>
```

In Listing 4-34, you remove the Border control and replace it instead with the same RelativePanel control you used in the ReceiptLineItem user control. You make some changes to it to support it being used in a template. First, you remove the `x-bind` statements and don't use the technique. X-binding is not supported in styles; it is supported in templates but requires a code-behind file to be added to the `generic.xaml` file, which is disruptive towards re-templating the control.

Note that you gave each TextBlock a name that starts with PART. This is a convention is used to identify the portions of a templated control's template that are required for the template to function properly. Because you use these two TextBlocks to store price and tax information, your code-behind expects them to be there with the specified names and to also be of the specified type. Finally, you remove the static TextBlock that simply served as a label for the tax TextBlock. You will be using the code-behind file to set these control's `Text` properties and can apply labeling directly to the strings you set these properties to, so there is no need for this TextBlock anymore. The code for TemplatedReceiptLineItem is in Listing 4-35.

Listing 4-35. TemplatedReceiptLineItem Definition

```
[
        TemplatePart(Name ="PART_Price",Type =typeof(TextBlock)),
        TemplatePart(Name = "PART_Tax", Type = typeof(TextBlock))
]
public sealed class TemplatedReceiptLineItem : Control
{
        TextBlock PART_Tax, PART_Price;
        public ReceiptItem Item { get; private set; }

        public TemplatedReceiptLineItem()
        {
                this.DefaultStyleKey = typeof(TemplatedReceiptLineItem);
        }
```

```
        protected override void OnApplyTemplate()
        {
                PART_Price = this.GetTemplateChild("PART_Price") as TextBlock;
                PART_Tax = this.GetTemplateChild("PART_Tax") as TextBlock;

                //set the values
                if (PART_Price != null && PART_Tax != null)
                {
                        PART_Price.Text = $"{Item.Price:C}";
                        PART_Tax.Text = $"tax - {Item.Tax:C}";
                }
        }

        public void AddItem(ReceiptItem item)
        {
                Item = item;
        }
}
```

In the constructor of Listing 4-35 you set the DefaultStyleKey property to the current type. This lets the framework know that this control supports templating and also identifies the key (the short name of the class) that will be used to find the user interface (style) for this control. You override OnApplyTemplate and in it use the GetTemplateChild helper method to retrieve the instantiated control represented by the name you specify. This maps to the names identified in the control's template. You make sure to test to see if GetTemplateChild returns null. Since the control template can be overwritten, there is no guarantee that these parts will be available with the same names. If they are there, you set the Text property on each of them to the appropriate value from the ReceiptItem object.

At the top of the class, two attributes help to declare to downstream users that the specified parts of the control's template are needed for proper operation. The TemplatePart attribute allows you to specify the name and type of any parts of your templated control that you expect to be available for the control to function properly. Finally, you simply need to update AddItemClicked in the POS page to use your new templated controls. Listing 4-36 does this.

Listing 4-36. AddItemClicked Modifications

```
private void AddItemClicked(object sender, RoutedEventArgs e)
{
        var reciept_item = Transaction
                .AddItemByPrice(double.Parse(txt_currentamount.Text));

        //add a reciept line item as a textblock
        TemplatedReceiptLineItem line_item = new TemplatedReceiptLineItem();
        line_item.AddItem(reciept_item);

        reciept.Children.Insert(0, line_item);

        txt_currentamount.Text = "0";
}
```

Running the sample now should result in a user interface like Figure 4-16.

Your Own Layout Controls

Building your own layout control is as simple as overriding the measure and arrange functions to lay your items out as you see fit. In this sample, you will be creating a CirclePanel control that will display its contents in a circular manner. See Listing 4-37.

Listing 4-37. CirclePanel Definition

```
public class CirclePanel : Panel
{
        public double Radius { get; set; }

        protected override Size MeasureOverride(Size availableSize)
        {
                Size s = base.MeasureOverride(availableSize);

                foreach (UIElement element in this.Children)
                        element.Measure(availableSize);

                return s;
        }
        protected override Size ArrangeOverride(Size finalSize)
        {
                // Clip to ensure items dont override container
                this.Clip =
                        new RectangleGeometry
                        { Rect = new Rect(0, 0, finalSize.Width, finalSize.Height) };

                // Size and position the child elements
                int i = 0;
                double degreesOffset = 360.0 / this.Children.Count;

                foreach (FrameworkElement element in this.Children)
                {
                        double centerX = element.DesiredSize.Width / 2.0;
                        double centerY = element.DesiredSize.Height / 2.0;

                        // calculate angle
                        double degreesAngle = degreesOffset * i++;

                        RotateTransform transform = new RotateTransform();
                        transform.CenterX = centerX;
                        transform.CenterY = centerY;

                        transform.Angle = degreesAngle;
                        element.RenderTransform = transform;

                        // calculate radian
                        var radianAngle = (Math.PI * degreesAngle) / 180.0;
```

```
                    // get x and y
                    double x = this.Radius * Math.Cos(radianAngle);
                    double y = this.Radius * Math.Sin(radianAngle);

                    // get real X and Y
                    var rectX = x + (finalSize.Width / 2.0) - centerX;
                    var rectY = y + (finalSize.Height / 2.0) - centerY;

                    // arrange element
                    element.Arrange(new
                            Rect(rectX, rectY,
                            element.DesiredSize.Width,
                            element.DesiredSize.Height));
            }
            return finalSize;
        }
}
```

Add this code to your project and try it out. In my project, I created a sample page and added the code in Listing 4-38 to it.

Listing 4-38. Using CirclePanel

```
<Grid Background="{ThemeResource ApplicationPageBackgroundThemeBrush}">
    <local:CirclePanel Radius="100"
                       Margin="20">
        <Button Content="Button1"
                HorizontalAlignment="Left"
                VerticalAlignment="Top" />
        <Button Content="Button2"
                HorizontalAlignment="Left"
                VerticalAlignment="Top" />
        <Button Content="Button3"
                HorizontalAlignment="Left"
                VerticalAlignment="Top" />
        <Button Content="Button4"
                HorizontalAlignment="Left"
                VerticalAlignment="Top" />
        <Button Content="Button5"
                HorizontalAlignment="Left"
                VerticalAlignment="Top" />
    </local:CirclePanel>
</Grid>
```

In the design surface, this layout displays as illustrated in Figure 4-19.

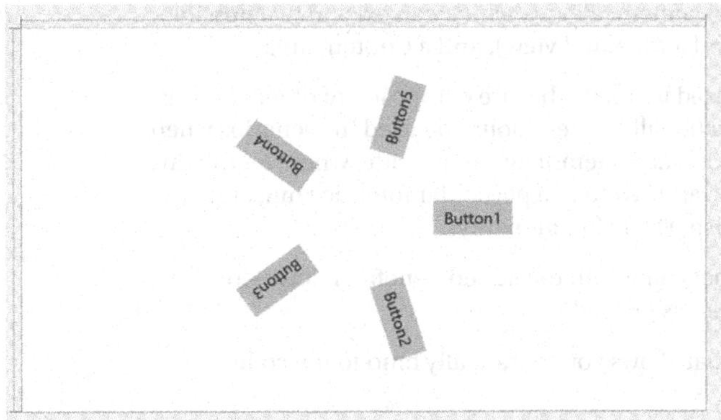

Figure 4-19. *CirclePanel in action*

Summary

Layout controls are a powerful way to encapsulate the manner in which the controls you use (or create) will be displayed on screen. In this chapter, you learned about how to use layout controls to structure the manner in which content is positioned and presented to a user. With this information on layout controls, you increase your ability to present powerful, flexible, and useable user interfaces to the user.

The layout system follows these specified steps to render content to the user:

- A child `UIElement` begins the layout process by first having its core properties measured.
- Sizing properties defined on `FrameworkElement` are evaluated, such as `Width`, `Height`, and `Margin`.
- Panel-specific logic is applied, such as stacking orientation.
- Content is arranged after all children have been measured.
- The Children collection is drawn on the screen.
- `Alignment`, `Margin`, and `Padding` can be used to shift a control's default position.
- The Canvas control supports absolute positioning of child elements relative to the top left corner of the canvas.
- The StackPanel arranges child elements into a single line that can be oriented horizontally or vertically.
- The Grid supports arranging child elements in rows and columns.
- The RelativePanel is useful for creating UIs that do not have a clear linear pattern.
- The VariableSizedWrapGrid arranges elements in rows or columns just like Grid, but with the added bonus that child elements will automatically wrap to a new row or column when the `MaximumRowsOrColumns` value is reached.

- The SplitView presents two areas of content: a Pane, which can exist in two possible widths (a narrow summary view and a wider full view), and a Content area.
- User Controls are controls with a fixed template that are composed of other controls interacting together to provide functionality. They should be used in scenarios where you need more logic and interactivity than a template can provide, where templating is not supported, or where the logic and layout of a particular interface must function together in unison to deliver a transportable functionality.
- Templated Controls are controls that come with the added benefit of downstream users being able to re-template them as needed.
- Compiled binding is a technique that allows you to statically bind to the code-behind class.

CHAPTER 5

Building an Adaptive Experience

Building with an adaptive user experience in mind is a critical tenet of Windows 10 development. In Chapter 1, you got a brief look at how Windows 10 was designed with multiple devices and form-factors in mind. The notion of writing code against a uniform API set that opaquely translates into executable code that can run on myriad device choices, technological capabilities, and resolution constraints is difficult to fathom without keeping adaptation in mind. Otherwise, how would a UWP app designed for the Surface Hub run on a mobile, how would an API call on the Xbox work when on a Raspberry Pi device, and how would a HoloLense app work when running on a laptop? The answer to these questions is through the adaptive experience mechanisms baked into Windows 10 programming with UWP. Given that the goal was to develop a Lord of the Rings-style operating system (one OS to rule them all), it makes sense that the programming interface exposed to developers extends this universality in both the programming model and layout for developers targeting the Windows 10 platform; this is in fact where the term "universal" comes from. In this chapter, you will be applying these adaptive layout techniques to your Control Corral sample so that your app runs smoothly on the various platform targets that Windows 10 supports. Here you go!

Note A common denominator among the various implementations of Windows 10 running on the many devices supported by the platform is the Windows 10 unified core. As part of the evolution of the programming paradigm of Windows 8/8.1, Microsoft has encapsulated the unified core into a programming interface that developers can leverage in a consistent manner, allowing them to target WinRT, Win32, and .NET APIs that are common across all devices. This means you can create a single app package that can be installed onto a wide range of devices. And, with that single app package, the Windows Store provides a unified distribution channel to reach all the device types upon which your app can run.

The POS page you created in the last chapter looked fine on a PC but if you were to view that same page on a mobile device, you would find that many parts of the user interface might not appear. Visual Studio provides the ability to view your apps in different resolutions and orientations so you can get a sense of how your user interface will lay out when run on certain screen configurations. Figure 5-1 illustrates.

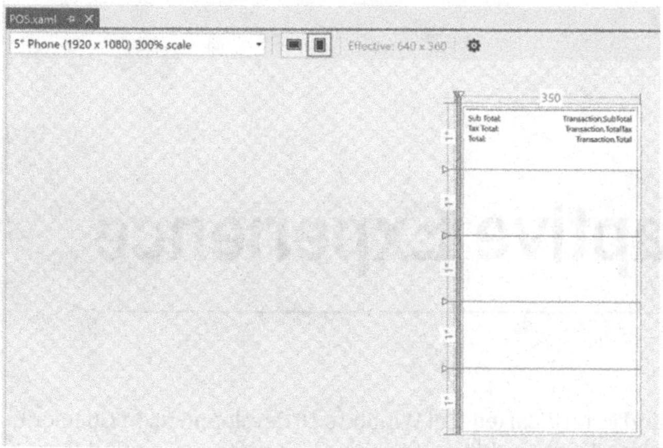

Figure 5-1. *Control Corral on small screen*

In Figure 5-1, you can see that several elements of the user interface do not show up when viewing the POS page on a small screen. The receipt area is the problem. To counteract this, you might be forced to design the page with the smallest screen in mind, such that the receipt area is navigated to only after the user pays; this way the basic POS functionality remains intact. The problem with this approach is that on a larger screen it makes the user interface look empty and disconnected. It also introduces an unnecessary navigation to view the receipt, since there is more than enough room to display the receipt on the main POS page when viewed on a larger screen. This is one example where building apps in an adaptive manner makes sense because it allows you to make the most use of available space.

Input optimization goes hand in hand with available space as another key reason to adapt a UWP app to the appropriate context it is being accessed through. It should be easy to see how a mobile device optimized for touch would have a different interaction pattern than the Raspberry Pi version, which users might only be able to interact with through the sensors on the device.

Finally, utilizing adaptation is a great idea when you need your UWP apps to take advantage of the devices' capabilities. Obviously, each device class and type offers its own set of unique features not found elsewhere. The approach to handling this in UWP allows developers to conditionally utilize APIs that make sense for their device families along with the APIs guaranteed to be available for all UWP apps.

We've written at length about adapting to various device types. Now we'll define the various types of devices and how they are classified in the UWP.

Device Families

A device family is a set of APIs collected together and given a name and a version number. It identifies the APIs, system characteristics, and behaviors that you can expect across devices within the device family, and it determines the set of devices on which your app can be installed from the Store. As of this writing, the available Windows 10 device families are

- Universal
- Desktop
- Mobile

- IoT
- IoT headless
- Surface Hub

■ **Note** Before you go any further, know that Windows doesn't provide a way for your app to detect the specific device your app is running on. It can tell you the device family (mobile, desktop, etc.) the app is running on, the effective resolution, and the amount of screen space available to the app (the size of the app's window), but it can't tell you if it is a Lumia 950 or Surface 3.

It is easy to see from the device family names that the device family maps to the device-specific version of Windows being used by that device type. Laptops and tablets use the desktop version of Windows so they map to the Desktop device family. Cell phones and some tablets use the mobile version of Windows so they map to the Mobile device family. See Figure 5-2.

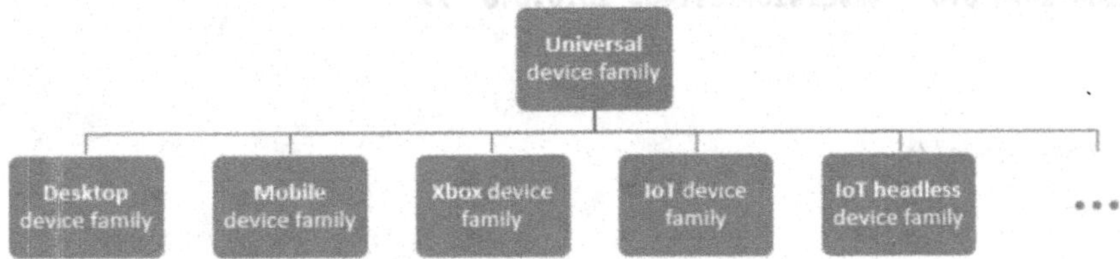

Figure 5-2. *Windows 10 device families*

If you have done object-oriented design using a CASE tool like Rational Rose, you will be very familiar with the relationships depicted in Figure 5-2. Like inheritance, each child inherits the set of APIs that the base (in this case, the Universal device family) has and then adds its own APIs to them. Unlike the other device families, the Universal device family is not directly mapped to any device type. It is instead mapped to the Windows Core, the portion of Windows 10 upon which every device-specific implementation of the OS is built. Since each of the other device families inherit APIs from Universal, the Universal device family APIs are guaranteed to be present in every OS and consequently on every device. The resulting union of APIs in any of the given child device families of Universal and OS-specific device family APIs is guaranteed to be present in the OS based on that device family, and consequently on every device running that OS.

By default, Microsoft Visual Studio 2015 specifies `Windows.Universal` as the target device family in the app package manifest file. To specify the device family or device families that your app is offered to from within the Store, manually configure the `TargetDeviceFamily` element in your `Package.appxmanifest` file. Listing 5-1 shows an app manifest for your app. In it, you tell the OS that this particular UWP is meant to run on only on the Windows desktop and Xbox. If you try to deploy this app on your phone or the Mobile Emulator, it will fail.

Listing 5-1. Specifying the Device Family

```
<?xml version="1.0" encoding="utf-8"?>

<Package
  xmlns="http://schemas.microsoft.com/appx/manifest/foundation/windows10"
  xmlns:mp="http://schemas.microsoft.com/appx/2014/phone/manifest"
  xmlns:uap="http://schemas.microsoft.com/appx/manifest/uap/windows10"
  IgnorableNamespaces="uap mp">
```

```
  <Identity
    Name="452940da-819a-4072-b3c9-04ac3093c6f4"
    Publisher="CN=Me"
    Version="1.0.0.0" />

  <mp:PhoneIdentity PhoneProductId="452940da-819a-4072-b3c9-04ac3093c6f4"
                PhonePublisherId="00000000-0000-0000-0000-000000000000"/>

  <Properties>
    <DisplayName>Lesson2_ControlCorral</DisplayName>
    <PublisherDisplayName>Me</PublisherDisplayName>
    <Logo>Assets\StoreLogo.png</Logo>
  </Properties>

  <Dependencies>
    <TargetDeviceFamily Name="Windows.Desktop"
            MinVersion="10.0.0.0" MaxVersionTested="10.0.0.0" />
    <TargetDeviceFamily Name="Windows.Xbox"
            MinVersion="10.0.0.0" MaxVersionTested="10.0.0.0" />
  </Dependencies>

  <Resources>
    <Resource Language="x-generate"/>
  </Resources>

  <Applications>
    <Application Id="App"
      Executable="$targetnametoken$.exe"
      EntryPoint="Lesson2_ControlCorral.App">
      <uap:VisualElements
        DisplayName="Lesson2_ControlCorral"
        Square150x150Logo="Assets\Square150x150Logo.png"
        Square44x44Logo="Assets\Square44x44Logo.png"
        Description="Lesson2_ControlCorral"
        BackgroundColor="transparent">
        <uap:DefaultTile Wide310x150Logo="Assets\Wide310x150Logo.png"/>
        <uap:SplashScreen Image="Assets\SplashScreen.png" />
      </uap:VisualElements>
    </Application>
  </Applications>

  <Capabilities>
    <Capability Name="internetClient" />
  </Capabilities>
</Package>
```

Adapting the User Interface

Windows 10 helps you target your UI to multiple devices with common input handling, adaptive scaling, and built-in controls that automatically adapt across device families and input modes. Common input handling allows you to receive input through touch, a pen, a mouse, a keyboard, or a controller such as a Microsoft Xbox controller; adaptive scaling adjusts to resolution and DPI differences across devices; and controls help to optimize your user interface for the device specific screen resolution your app might be in.

Triggered States

From the last chapter you learned that layout panels give size and position to their children, depending on available space. For example, in the POS sample you used a StackPanel to order receipt line items sequentially and vertically. You learned how to build layout panels by measuring the available space and then arranging the controls that need to be displayed based on these measurements. Layout panels share a similar set of problems and, consequently, solutions, as can be found when attempting to design with an adaptive UI in mind. In both cases, the available space needs to be measured, and the layout of the user interface (even the look and feel in some cases) is affected by the measurement result. The canonical way to build for an adaptive user interface is to figure out the dimensions of the window your content is in and make layout decisions based on the size of that window. Listing 5-2 contains a simple window with a StackPanel oriented horizontally.

Listing 5-2. Simple Window Layout with StackPanel

```
<Page x:Class="Lesson5_SimpleAdaptiveLayout.MainPage"
      xmlns="http://schemas.microsoft.com/winfx/2006/xaml/presentation"
      xmlns:x="http://schemas.microsoft.com/winfx/2006/xaml"
      xmlns:local="using:Lesson5_SimpleAdaptiveLayout"
      xmlns:d="http://schemas.microsoft.com/expression/blend/2008"
      xmlns:mc="http://schemas.openxmlformats.org/markup-compatibility/2006"
      mc:Ignorable="d">

<StackPanel x:Name="stack" BorderBrush="Black" BorderThickness="2"
            Background="{ThemeResource ApplicationPageBackgroundThemeBrush}"
            Orientation="Horizontal"
            HorizontalAlignment="Left">
    <Button Content="Button 1"
            Margin="5" />
    <Button Content="Button 2"
            Margin="5" />
    <Button Content="Button 3"
            Margin="5" />
    <Button Content="Button 4" />
    <Button Content="Button 5"
            Margin="5" />
    <Button Content="Button 6"
            Margin="5" />
    <Button Content="Button 7"
            Margin="5" />
    <Button Content="Button 8"
            Margin="5" />
```

```
    <Button Content="Button 9" />
    <Button Content="Button 10"
            Margin="5" />
</StackPanel>
</Page>
```

This StackPanel has 10 items in it. If you want to implement logic that will ensure that the panel is never clipped horizontally, you can use the code in Listing 5-3.

Listing 5-3. Adapting Layout Based on Screen Size

```
namespace Lesson5_SimpleAdaptiveLayout
{
        /// <summary>
        /// An empty page that can be used on its own or navigated to within a Frame.
        /// </summary>
        public sealed partial class MainPage : Page
        {
                public MainPage()
                {
                        this.InitializeComponent();
                        this.Loaded += MainPage_Loaded;
                }

                private void MainPage_Loaded(object sender, RoutedEventArgs e)
                {
                        if (stack.ActualWidth >= this.ActualWidth)
                        {
                                stack.Orientation = Orientation.Vertical;
                        }
                        else
                        {
                                stack.Orientation = Orientation.Horizontal;
                        }
                }

        }
}
```

The code sample is quite simple but illustrates the general pattern for adapting the visual state of your app based on how much space your app has to render. In the loaded event, you measure the page dimensions and, based on that, make your determination about what orientation the StackPanel should be placed in. Figure 5-3 shows how the app would look upon startup on a Windows desktop.

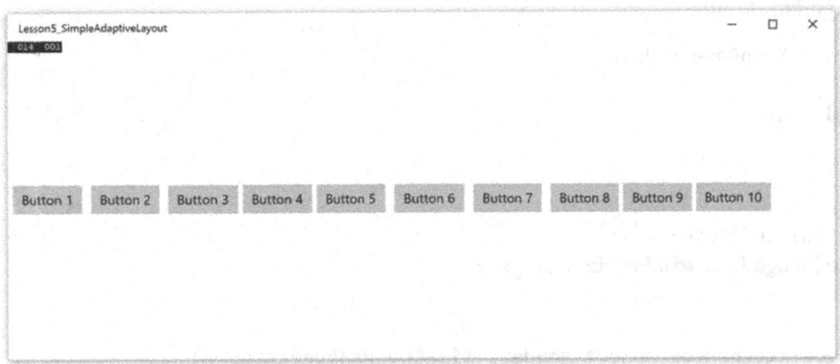

Figure 5-3. *App layout on a desktop*

Figure 5-4 shows how the app would look upon startup on a Windows Mobile Emulator. Note that the Windows Phone Emulator is not installed by default with Visual Studio 2015. You must explicitly select it as part of the installation process. To access it, set the processor type to ARM and then select one of the emulator choices from the Run menu.

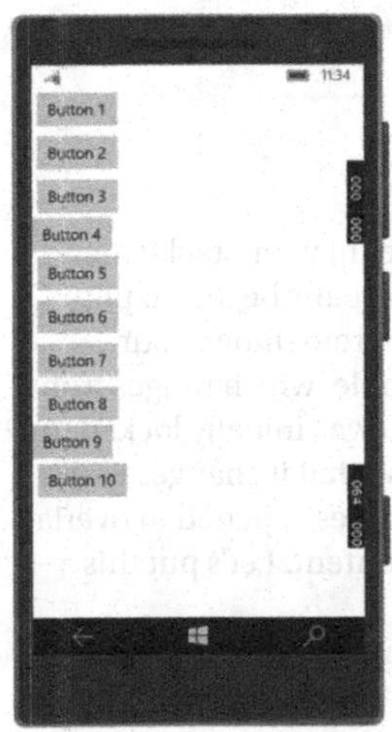

Figure 5-4. *App layout on the Mobile Emulator*

One problem with just setting this in one place is that it does not change when the app is resized. Apps may be resized based on numerous conditions.

Obviously, on a desktop the user can just manually change sizes, but pinning and orientation changes can also affect it; because of this, a much better approach is to handle the `SizeChanged` event. In fact, because the `SizeChanged` event is called once an app opens, you can completely remove the code in your `Loaded` event. Listing 5-4 illustrates.

Listing 5-4. Using SizeChanged to Handle

```
public sealed partial class MainPage : Page
{
        double _threshold = 0;

        public MainPage()
        {
                this.InitializeComponent();
                this.SizeChanged += WindowSizeChanged;
        }

        private void WindowSizeChanged(object sender, SizeChangedEventArgs e)
        {
                if (stack.ActualWidth >= e.NewSize.Width)
                {
                        stack.Orientation = Orientation.Vertical;
                        _threshold = e.NewSize.Width;
                }
                else
                {
                        if (e.NewSize.Width > _threshold)
                                stack.Orientation = Orientation.Horizontal;
                }
        }
}
```

When you run this sample, you will see the app resize once it hits the right border of your StackPanel.

The pattern of restructuring the layout of a page based on the size of the window really begins to pop when you use it in tandem with some of the more sophisticated layout controls. If you remember, your dashboard page used a SplitView to handle navigation. The `Pane` property in this sample, which ranges from not showing at all through to a compact size and then finally ending at the full layout, was initially locked to the `Compact` setting. Using the adaptation technique you just learned, let's modify it so that it changes width as the screen width gets bigger. On a small screen, you can set it to totally disappear unless opened in overlay mode with a button on the page. On a large screen, you can show it inline with the Content. Let's put this into play now and clean up the UI of the dashboard in process.

Open up the Control Corral project and open the Dashboard page. If the Document Outline window isn't open, then open it and right-click any one of the AppBarButtons in the Pane section of the page. Then select Edit Template ➤ Edit Copy. Figure 5-5 illustrates.

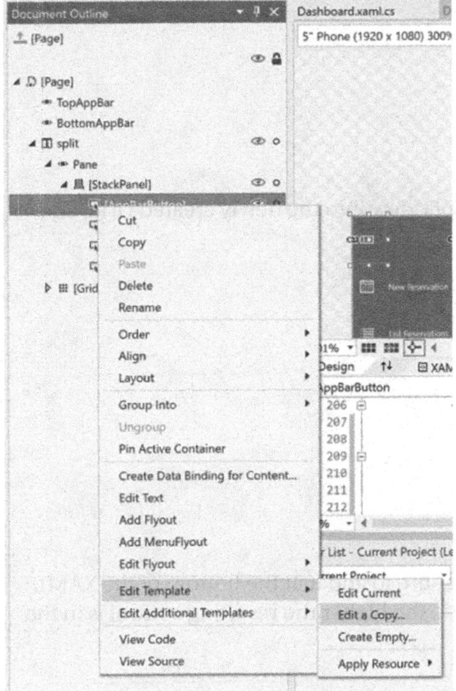

Figure 5-5. *Creating a copy of a control's template*

When the Create Style Resource dialog appears, set the name to PageNavButton and the "Define In" radio button to "This Document." The template is created as a page resource at the top of the XAML page. Replace the StackPanel named ContentRoot with the code from Listing 5-5.

Listing 5-5. Modifying AppBarButton Template

```
<RelativePanel x:Name="ContentRoot"
               Margin="10"
               HorizontalAlignment="Stretch"
               MinHeight="{ThemeResource AppBarThemeCompactHeight}">
    <ContentPresenter x:Name="Content"
                      RelativePanel.AlignLeftWithPanel="True"
                      AutomationProperties.AccessibilityView="Raw"
                      Content="{TemplateBinding Icon}"
                      Foreground="{TemplateBinding Foreground}"
                      HorizontalAlignment="Stretch"
                      Height="20"
                      Margin="0,14,0,4" />
    <TextBlock x:Name="TextLabel"
               RelativePanel.AlignVerticalCenterWithPanel="True"
               RelativePanel.AlignRightWithPanel="True"
               Foreground="{TemplateBinding Foreground}"
               FontSize="12"
               FontFamily="{TemplateBinding FontFamily}"
```

```
                   Margin="0,0,0,0"
                   TextAlignment="Left"
                   TextWrapping="NoWrap"
                   VerticalAlignment="Center"
                   Text="{TemplateBinding Label}" />
</RelativePanel>
```

Now create a new Grid underneath the SplitView, copy the SplitView into the newly created Grid, and change the SplitView definition to the code in Listing 5-6.

Listing 5-6. Changing SplitView Pane Properties

```
<SplitView x:Name="split"
           Background="White"
           PaneBackground="SlateGray"
           DisplayMode="CompactInline"
           IsPaneOpen="False"
           CompactPaneLength="48"
           OpenPaneLength="150">
```

Add a new AppBarButton directly to the new root Grid (make sure to add it at the bottom of the XAML page and not before the SplitView definition). The lower the XAML, the higher the resulting control is in the parent's z-index. See Listing 5-7.

Listing 5-7. Adding a Toggle Button to Open the SplitView Pane

```
<AppBarButton HorizontalAlignment="Left"
              Icon="DockLeft"
              Width="48"
              RequestedTheme="Light"
              Click="OnPaneOpened"
              Style="{StaticResource PageNavButton}" />
```

You now have a button at the top left corner of the screen so you need to move the TextBlocks used to label the two data controls you have on the page. Listing 5-8 illustrates.

Listing 5-8. Repositioning Dashboard Labels

```
...
<TextBlock Text="Customers"
           HorizontalAlignment="Right"
           FontSize="40"
           FontWeight="ExtraLight"
           VerticalAlignment="Top" />

...
<TextBlock Text="Today's Appointments"
           HorizontalAlignment="Right"
           FontSize="40"
           FontWeight="ExtraLight"
           VerticalAlignment="Top"
           Margin="0,242,0,0" />
...
```

You will also need to shift the navigation controls you have in the Pane section of the SplitView down a bit so that they do not overlap with the toggle button you just added. To make the area look cleaner, you also need to stretch the controls inside the Pane (presently they are all centered). Listing 5-9 illustrates.

Listing 5-9. Modifications to Navigation Pane Content

```
<StackPanel Orientation="Vertical"
            HorizontalAlignment="Stretch">

    <AppBarButton HorizontalAlignment="Stretch"
                  Icon="Calendar"
                  Margin="0,50,0,0"
                  Label="New Reservation"
                  RequestedTheme="Dark"
                  Click="OnReservation"
                  Style="{StaticResource PageNavButton}"
                  Width="Auto">

    </AppBarButton>
    <AppBarButton Icon="List"
                  HorizontalAlignment="Stretch"
                  Label="List Reservations"
                  RequestedTheme="Dark"
                  Width="Auto"
                  Style="{StaticResource PageNavButton}"
                  Click="ListReservations" />
    <AppBarButton Icon="Calculator"
                  HorizontalAlignment="Stretch"
                  Label="POS"
                  RequestedTheme="Dark"
                  Width="Auto"
                  Style="{StaticResource PageNavButton}"
                  Click="OpenPOS" />

</StackPanel>
```

In Listing 5-9, you apply a `Stretch HorizontalAlignment` to the StackPanel and all the controls within it. You have also added a margin of 50 to the first AppBarButton in the StackPanel. Since the StackPanel is oriented vertically, all controls underneath it will be shifted down as well.

Let's go to the definition for the AppBarButton you just created (the one for toggling the SplitView states) and implement the code in Listing 5-10 to toggle the Pane part of your SplitView showing.

Listing 5-10. Implementing SplitView Pane Toggling

```
private void OnPaneOpened(object sender, RoutedEventArgs e)
{
        if (split.IsPaneOpen)
                split.IsPaneOpen = false;
        else
                split.IsPaneOpen = true;
}
```

Now run the app and you should have something that looks like Figure 5-6 when normal.

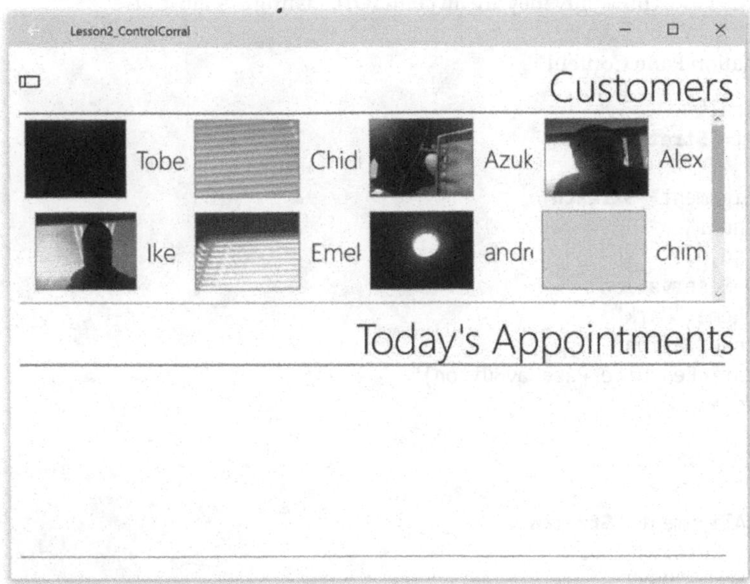

Figure 5-6. *Dashboard with collapsed pane toggle button*

It looks like Figure 5-7 when your button is clicked.

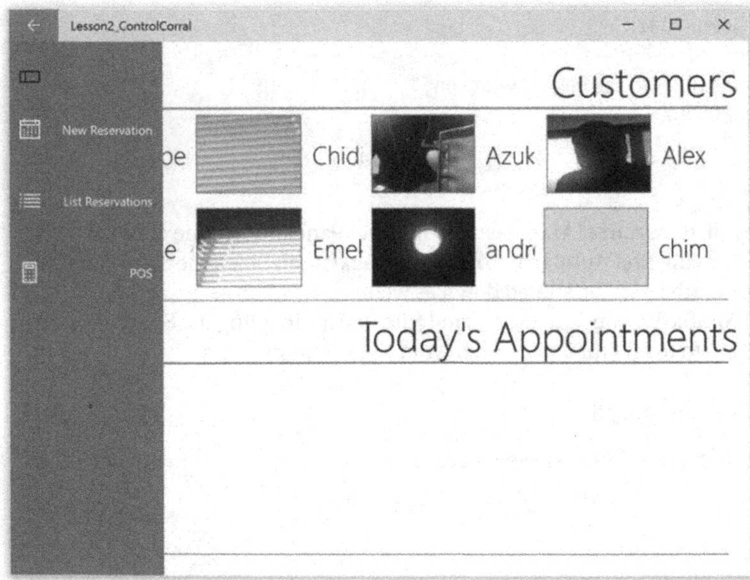

Figure 5-7. *Dashboard with pane activated via toggle button*

You can now sling some code to set up your adaptation pattern. Before you get started however, open RootHost and add the following line to the constructor of RootHost: `ApplicationView.GetForCurrentView().SetPreferredMinSize(new Size(300, 500));` This line is used to set the preferred minimum size of your windows. It is set on a page-by-page basis because each page may have its own minimums. You are adding it to RootHost so it affects all the pages in your app. Now let's go back to Dashboard and add the code from Listing 5-11.

Listing 5-11. Implementing an Adaptive UI with SplitView

```
public Dashboard()
{
        this.InitializeComponent();
        this.Loaded += Dashboard_Loaded;
        this.SizeChanged += Dashboard_SizeChanged;
}

private void Dashboard_SizeChanged(object sender, SizeChangedEventArgs e)
{
        if (e.NewSize.Width <= 320)
        {
                split.DisplayMode = SplitViewDisplayMode.Overlay;
                split.IsPaneOpen = false;
        }
        else if (e.NewSize.Width > 320 && e.NewSize.Width <= 720)
        {
                split.DisplayMode = SplitViewDisplayMode.CompactInline;
                split.IsPaneOpen = false;
        }
        else
        {
                split.DisplayMode = SplitViewDisplayMode.Inline;
                split.IsPaneOpen = true;
        }
}
```

Like the StackPanel example earlier, this code simply sets some properties based on the size of the page on a control (or set of controls) you target. When the page width is less than 320, it displays no visible pane; when it is between 320 and 720, it displays the compact pane; and for any other width, it is displayed in full. The running app should now look like Figure 5-8.

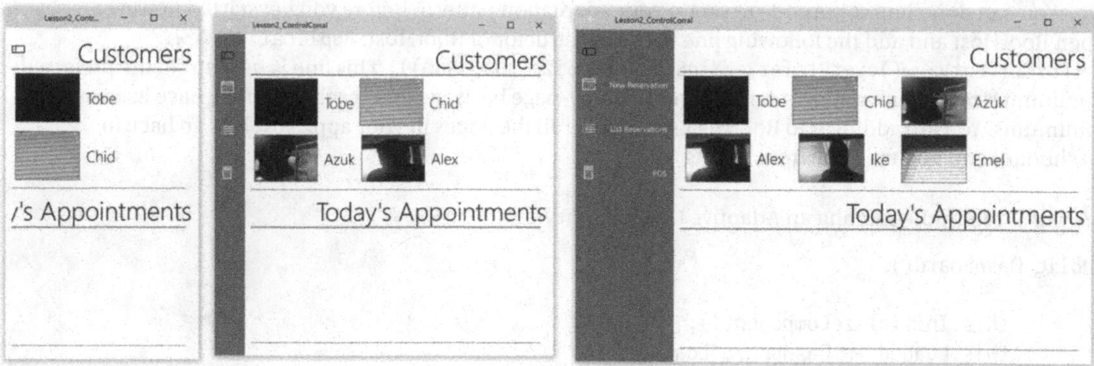

Figure 5-8. *SplitView in various states based on app width*

Let's retarget this for the Windows 10 Mobile Emulator and run it once again. To do this, select one of the mobile emulators from the run-target drop-down menu (Figure 5-9 illustrates). Note that when the app starts on mobile, it will be blank (meaning none of the data from before will be available here because it is reading data from a different source than your desktop). If you have not already done so, you will have to create some new appointments in order to see everything properly.

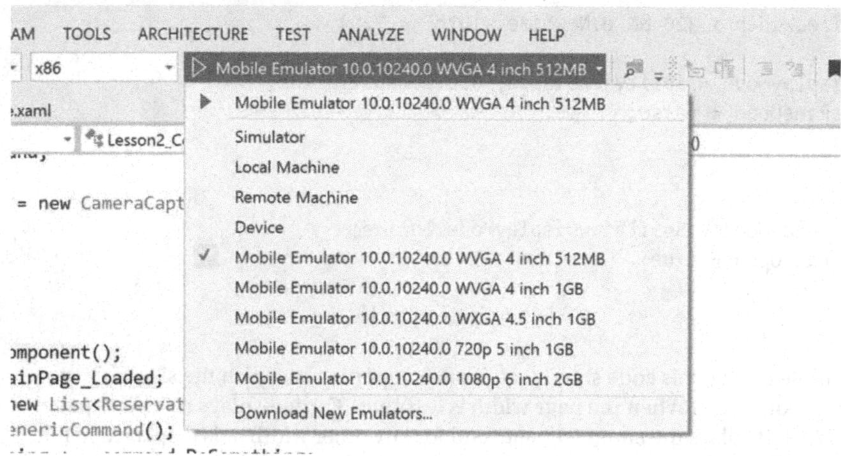

Figure 5-9. *Choices of where to deploy the app*

In this form factor, the app window is automatically laid out as less than 320 since you are on the Mobile Emulator. Figure 5-10 illustrates.

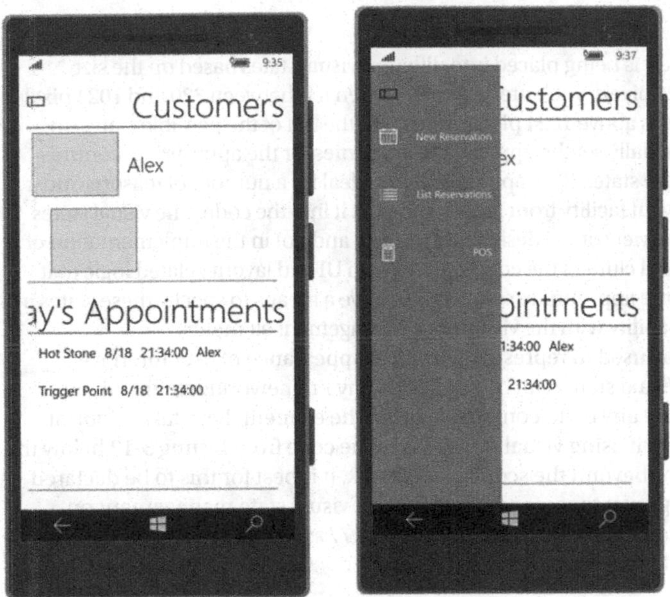

Figure 5-10. *Control Corral on mobile emulator*

Because your pattern is based on the window width and not the specific device, Figure 5-11 shows how the same app looks running on the 1080p emulator.

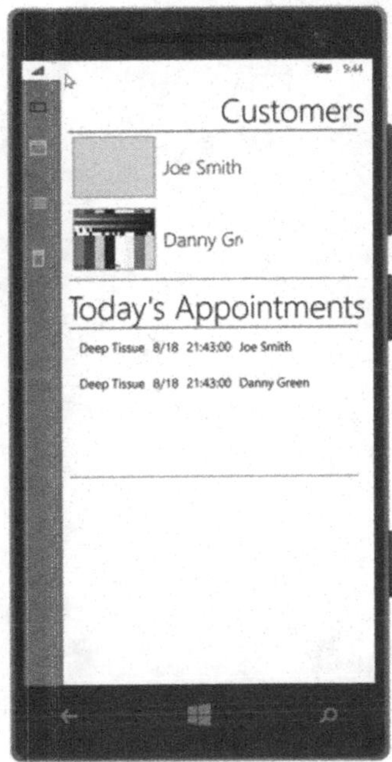

Figure 5-11. *Control Corral on larger screen mobile emulator*

Note that the Pane is showing in compact mode by default. Cool, right?

Visual States

From Figure 5-8 it can be seen that the app view is being placed into different visual states based on the size available to it. When the screen is less than 320 pixels, you enter one state; when it is between 320 and 1024 pixels, you are in another state; and finally when it goes above 1024 pixels, you are in the last of the possible states. In Listing 5-10, you used the code-behind to manually set the appropriate properties for the appropriate controls in order to create the appearance for each of the states. This approach is not ideal for a number of reasons, most notably because it removes the design and layout facility from XAML and puts it into the code. The visual states of the app should understandably be in the purview of the designer of the app and not in the implementation of its functionality. The approach you initially used clutters the code-behind with UI and layout-related logic that can grow exponentially as states change. A more appropriate solution is to have a means to specify these states in XAML. Fortunately, XAML provides this very ability with the visual state management elements.

The visual state element in XAML can be used to represent the visual appearance of user interface elements when they are in a specific state. Visual states can be applied to any FrameworkElement and are used to represent the state of the element or of any child contained within the element. Let's take a look at how the same sample from above would work if using visual states. Place the code from Listing 5-12 below the first element inside the root Grid. For reasons beyond the scope of this book, it is best for this to be declared under the first child of the root. We encourage you to research the details of visual state management on MSDN for more detailed information. You can find this on MSDN at `https://msdn.microsoft.com/library/windows/apps/windows.ui.xaml.visualstatemanager.aspx`.

Listing 5-12. Implementing VisualStateManager

```
<VisualStateManager.VisualStateGroups>
    <VisualStateGroup>
        <VisualState x:Name="Normal" />
        <VisualState x:Name="state_320">
            <VisualState.Setters>
                <Setter Target="split.DisplayMode"
                        Value="Overlay" />
                <Setter Target="split.IsPaneOpen"
                        Value="False" />
            </VisualState.Setters>
        </VisualState>
        <VisualState x:Name="state_btw_320_1024">
            <VisualState.Setters>
                <Setter Target="split.DisplayMode"
                        Value="CompactInline" />
                <Setter Target="split.IsPaneOpen"
                        Value="False" />
            </VisualState.Setters>
        </VisualState>
        <VisualState x:Name="state_gt_1024">
            <VisualState.Setters>
                <Setter Target="split.DisplayMode"
                        Value="Inline" />
                <Setter Target="split.IsPaneOpen"
                        Value="True" />
            </VisualState.Setters>
        </VisualState>
    </VisualStateGroup>
</VisualStateManager.VisualStateGroups>
```

This code simply takes the property setting logic out of the code-behind file and places into the XAML where it belongs. This way a XAML designer can change the appearance of each state without affecting the backed procedural code. To access states in the scope of a given control, use the static method call `VisualStateManager.GoToState(<control instance>, <state name>, <use transitions>)`. Rewrite the `SizeChanged` event handler to utilize your defined visual states, as shown in Listing 5-13.

Listing 5-13. Activating States Using VisualStateManager in Code-Behind

```
private void Dashboard_SizeChanged(object sender, SizeChangedEventArgs e)
{
        if (e.NewSize.Width <= 320)
        {
                VisualStateManager.GoToState(this, "state_320", false);
        }
        else if (e.NewSize.Width > 320 && e.NewSize.Width <= 1024)
        {
                VisualStateManager.GoToState(this, "state_btw_320_1024", false);
        }
        else
        {
                VisualStateManager.GoToState(this, "state_gt_1024", false);
        }
}
```

Run the app and you should see the same results as before. You've now used visual states to abstract away from code the details of what it means to be in a given state. It can be argued, though, that the adaptation of the app's appearance based on the size of the windows is also a designer-only concern and should be abstracted away from the code in the same manner. The visual state management framework provides the ability to enable given states based on triggers so that there is no need to programmatically call `VisualStateManager.GoToState`. In the case of responding to size changes, a trigger aptly called `AdaptiveTrigger` can be used. Let's modify the dashboard to use this. Start by removing all the adaptation code you have added. Get rid of the `SizeChanged` event hander and the handler subscription code in the constructor. You should have no trace of anything related to size changes in `Dashboard.xaml.cs` at this point. Now modify the visual state manager declaration as shown (new items in bold) in Listing 5-14.

Listing 5-14. Using AdaptiveTrigger with VisualStateManager

```
<VisualStateManager.VisualStateGroups>
    <VisualStateGroup>
        <VisualState x:Name="Normal" />
        <VisualState x:Name="state_320">
            <VisualState.StateTriggers>
                <AdaptiveTrigger MinWindowWidth="0" />
            </VisualState.StateTriggers>
            <VisualState.Setters>
                <Setter Target="split.DisplayMode"
                        Value="Overlay" />
                <Setter Target="split.IsPaneOpen"
                        Value="False" />
            </VisualState.Setters>
        </VisualState>
```

```
        <VisualState x:Name="state_btw_320_1024">
            <VisualState.StateTriggers>
                <AdaptiveTrigger MinWindowWidth="720" />
            </VisualState.StateTriggers>
            <VisualState.Setters>
                <Setter Target="split.DisplayMode"
                        Value="CompactInline" />
                <Setter Target="split.IsPaneOpen"
                        Value="False" />
            </VisualState.Setters>
        </VisualState>
        <VisualState x:Name="state_gt_1024">
            <VisualState.StateTriggers>
                <AdaptiveTrigger MinWindowWidth="1024" />
            </VisualState.StateTriggers>
            <VisualState.Setters>
                <Setter Target="split.DisplayMode"
                        Value="Inline" />
                <Setter Target="split.IsPaneOpen"
                        Value="True" />
            </VisualState.Setters>
        </VisualState>
    </VisualStateGroup>
</VisualStateManager.VisualStateGroups>
```

In Listing 5-14, the adaptive trigger defines a threshold at which the VisualState is activated. And as you saw in the previous samples, once activated, it sets the layout properties as appropriate. For adaptive triggers, that threshold is always identified by the minimum value for the state to remain active. This is why in the first state the minimum width is set to 0. Each subsequent state in the sample simply overrides the previous state. Running the app should once again yield the same result as Figure 5-7.

■ **Note** The number of device targets and screen sizes across the Windows 10 ecosystem is too great to worry about optimizing your UI for each one. Instead, we recommended designing for a few key widths (also called "breakpoints"): 320, 720, and 1024.

When designing for specific breakpoints, design for the amount of screen space available to your app (the app's window). When the app is running full-screen, the app window is the same size of the screen, but in other cases, it's smaller.

XAML Views

For most cases, shifting things around on screen to allow for them to fit nicely is a viable approach to dealing with the changing screen sizes and resolution problem. Sometimes, however, this kind of solution does not work. Sometimes a particular page, or the app as a whole, needs to be dramatically redesigned in order to make sense on a different device footprint rather than just because the screen is larger. A user interface might need to go from using a Grid to lay out the page on a desktop to using a Pivot or FlipView to lay out the page on a mobile device. This kind of change cannot be accommodated by the visual state system or by simply handling SizeChanged events because the requirements for the change might go beyond the size of the screen.

For instance, if you want the mobile version of your app to have a trimmed down "mobile experience" with some features not even visible, using the size of the screen to determine that your app is running on mobile will not work. As you saw in the previous sample, some mobile devices will have resolution requirements to appear as tablets or even desktops. Conversely, reducing the size of your app window when on a desktop should not remove functionality that makes sense on a desktop (as it would if you used size to judge device family). In these kinds of scenarios, device family-specific XAML views can be used.

Device family-specific views allow developers to define specific XAML views for specific device families while maintaining a single code-behind file. There are two primary ways to incorporate XAML views into your app. You can do it by adding a device family-specific folder into your project in the form *DeviceFamily-<type>* (where type is the name of the device family you are targeting). Within this folder, you add a XAML view with the same name as the XAML page you want to get a device-specific version. This approach is the most preferable because it allows you to organize your views into folders that clearly indicate their purpose. Alternatively, you can simply add a XAML view file with the same name as the XAML page you want a device-specific version of, but with the extension. *DeviceFamily-<Type>.xaml* where <Type> is the name of the device family you are targeting.

In the next sample, you will use a device-specific XAML view to override the appearance of your Create Reservation page. Presently, the page displays as a non-scrollable Grid on desktop devices. Let's first update the user interface so that at any size your user interface elements show properly. Open `MainPage.xaml` and modify it to add the code from Listing 5-15.

Listing 5-15. Using Scrollbar to Scroll Horizontally on a Small Screen

```
<ScrollViewer HorizontalScrollBarVisibility="Auto" HorizontalScrollMode="Auto">
        <Grid Background="{ThemeResource ApplicationPageBackgroundThemeBrush}">
                ...
        </Grid>
</ScrollViewer>
```

You now have a Create Reservation page that scrolls horizontally so that users can add pictures to a reservation as needed. Next, let's add a new folder to the project for the mobile device family. Name the folder `DeviceFamily-Mobile`.

You can add a new XAML view to this page by right-clicking the newly created folder and selecting Add ➤ New Item and picking XAML View from the Add New Item dialog that appears. In Visual Studio 2015 enterprise, XAML View is the first choice that appears in the list of possible project items (when Sort By is set to Default). Select this choice and specify the name MainPage.xaml, and then click Add to add it to your project. Note that `MainPage.xaml` is added to the project as a XAML file with no code-behind associated with it. This is because the code-behind for this particular instance of `MainPage.xaml` is the same for all instances. They all share the same code-behind, `MainPage.xaml.cs`. You should now have a project structure that looks like Figure 5-12.

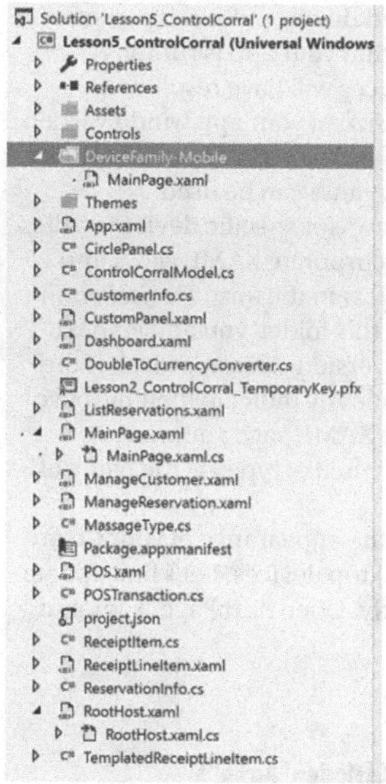

Figure 5-12. Device-specific folder added to project

As an experiment, target the Windows mobile emulator and run the app once more. Once the app starts, navigate to the Create New Reservation page. You should get an exception thrown by the app when you do this that looks like Figure 5-13.

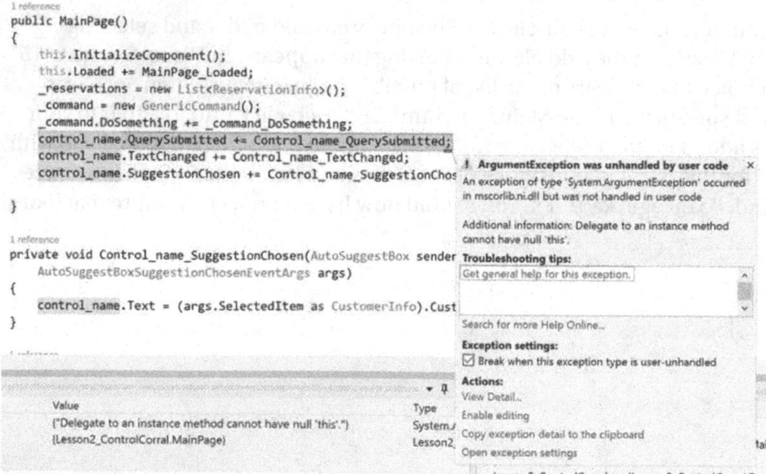

Figure 5-13. Exception thrown when using XAML view with none of the expected UI controls that the code-behind expects

You are getting this error because the mobile version of `MainPage.xaml` does not have any controls defined in it, but the code-behind is expecting a control called `control_name` (from the desktop version of the page) to be there. This highlights two things that are important to note. First, it emphasizes the fact that both copies of `MainPage.xaml` are using the same code-behind file. Second, it illustrates once again the perils of embedding user interface logic that relies on named elements in your code-behind file. `MainPage.xaml.cs` is littered with instances where this is happening. However, when working with XAML views, it is important that the separation between the XAML and the code-behind is maintained. To make the mobile version work, you need for all the controls named in the code-behind to be available in the XAML as well. You will add them in a moment; first let's set up the new layout you will be using for the mobile version of the page. Open the mobile version of MainPage.xaml and add a new Pivot to it, as shown in Listing 5-16.

Listing 5-16. Layout of MainPage Mobile XAML View

```
<Page
    x:Class="Lesson2_ControlCorral.MainPage"
    xmlns="http://schemas.microsoft.com/winfx/2006/xaml/presentation"
    xmlns:x="http://schemas.microsoft.com/winfx/2006/xaml"
    xmlns:local="using:Lesson2_ControlCorral"
    xmlns:d="http://schemas.microsoft.com/expression/blend/2008"
    xmlns:mc="http://schemas.openxmlformats.org/markup-compatibility/2006"
    mc:Ignorable="d">

    <Pivot Background="{ThemeResource ApplicationPageBackgroundThemeBrush}">
        <PivotItem Header="Customer">
            <StackPanel></StackPanel>
        </PivotItem>
        <PivotItem Header="Appointment">
            <StackPanel></StackPanel>
       </PivotItem>
    </Pivot>
</Page>
```

As you might have already guessed from this sample, you will be using the Pivot control to delineate the various controls that capture information necessary for you to make a reservation with your system. You can now open the other `MainPage.xaml` and copy the controls over that you are interested in. Note that the various PivotItems are using a StackPanel instead of a Grid as the root layout control. Now that you have a clearer understanding of the layout panels, it should be clear to you why this is a better choice in this scenario. Listing 5-17 shows the full layout of the mobile friendly `MainPage.xaml` page.

Listing 5-17. Full Layout of MainPage Mobile XAML View

```
<Page
    x:Class="Lesson2_ControlCorral.MainPage"
    xmlns="http://schemas.microsoft.com/winfx/2006/xaml/presentation"
    xmlns:x="http://schemas.microsoft.com/winfx/2006/xaml"
    xmlns:local="using:Lesson2_ControlCorral"
    xmlns:d="http://schemas.microsoft.com/expression/blend/2008"
    xmlns:mc="http://schemas.openxmlformats.org/markup-compatibility/2006"
    mc:Ignorable="d">
```

```
<Page.BottomAppBar>
    <CommandBar ClosedDisplayMode="Minimal"
                IsSticky="True">
        <AppBarButton Label="Reserve"
                      Icon="Calendar">
            <AppBarButton.Flyout>
                <MenuFlyout>
                    <MenuFlyoutItem Command="{Binding}"
                                    CommandParameter="make a reservation"
                                    Text="Pay Now" />
                    <MenuFlyoutItem Text="Pay Later"
                                    Command="{Binding}"
                                    CommandParameter="hold my spot" />
                </MenuFlyout>
            </AppBarButton.Flyout>
        </AppBarButton>
    </CommandBar>
</Page.BottomAppBar>
<Pivot Background="{ThemeResource ApplicationPageBackgroundThemeBrush}">
    <PivotItem Header="Customer">
        <StackPanel>
            <Button Click="ReplaceImage"
                    HorizontalAlignment="Stretch"
                    Height="166"
                    Margin="10,10,10,0"
                    VerticalAlignment="Top"
                    BorderThickness="1"
                    BorderBrush="Gray"
                    Background="Black">
                <Image x:Name="control_image"
                       Source="/alex.jpg" />
            </Button>
            <AutoSuggestBox x:Name="control_name"
                            HorizontalAlignment="Stretch"
                            Header="What's your name?"
                            Margin="10,10,10,0"
                            VerticalAlignment="Top"

                            QueryIcon="Find">
                <AutoSuggestBox.ItemTemplate>
                    <DataTemplate>
                        <StackPanel Orientation="Horizontal">
                            <Border HorizontalAlignment="Left"
                                    Height="75"
                                    Margin="5,5,10,5"
                                    Width="100"
                                    BorderThickness="1"
                                    BorderBrush="Gray"
                                    Background="Gainsboro">
```

```
                        <Image Stretch="Fill"
                               Loaded="CustomerImageLoaded" />
                    </Border>
                    <TextBlock Text="{Binding CustomerName}"
                               FontSize="24"
                               FontWeight="ExtraLight"
                               VerticalAlignment="Center" />
                </StackPanel>
            </DataTemplate>
        </AutoSuggestBox.ItemTemplate>
    </AutoSuggestBox>
    <DatePicker x:Name="control_dob"
                Header="When were you born?"
                HorizontalAlignment="Stretch"
                Margin="10,10,10,0"
                VerticalAlignment="Top" />
    <PasswordBox x:Name="txt_passphrase"
                 Header="Enter a passphrase"
                 HorizontalAlignment="Stretch"
                 Margin="10,10,10,0"
                 PlaceholderText="keep it a secret"
                 VerticalAlignment="Top"
                 />
</StackPanel>
    </PivotItem>
<PivotItem Header="Appointment">
    <StackPanel>
        <CalendarDatePicker x:Name="control_calendar"
                            HorizontalAlignment="Stretch"
                            Margin="10,10,10,0"
                            VerticalAlignment="Top"
                            PlaceholderText="What day works for you?"
                           />
        <TimePicker x:Name="control_time"
                    Header="What time works for you?"
                    Margin="10,10,10,0" HorizontalAlignment="Stretch"
                    VerticalAlignment="Top" />
        <ComboBox x:Name="control_procedure"
                  Header="Select a procedure"
                  HorizontalAlignment="Stretch"
                  Margin="10,10,10,0"
                  VerticalAlignment="Top"

                  ItemsSource="{Binding}"
                  DisplayMemberPath="Name" />
        <Slider x:Name="control_intensity"
                Header="Massage Intensity"
                HorizontalAlignment="Stretch"
                Minimum="20"
```

```
                        Maximum="100"
                        Margin="10,10,10,0"
                        VerticalAlignment="Top"
                        />
            </StackPanel>
        </PivotItem>
    </Pivot>
</Page>
```

Run this sample in the Mobile Emulator, navigate to the New Reservation page, and you should now see a user interface similar to Figure 5-13. Figure 5-14 shows the Control Corral desktop app running side by side with the mobile version.

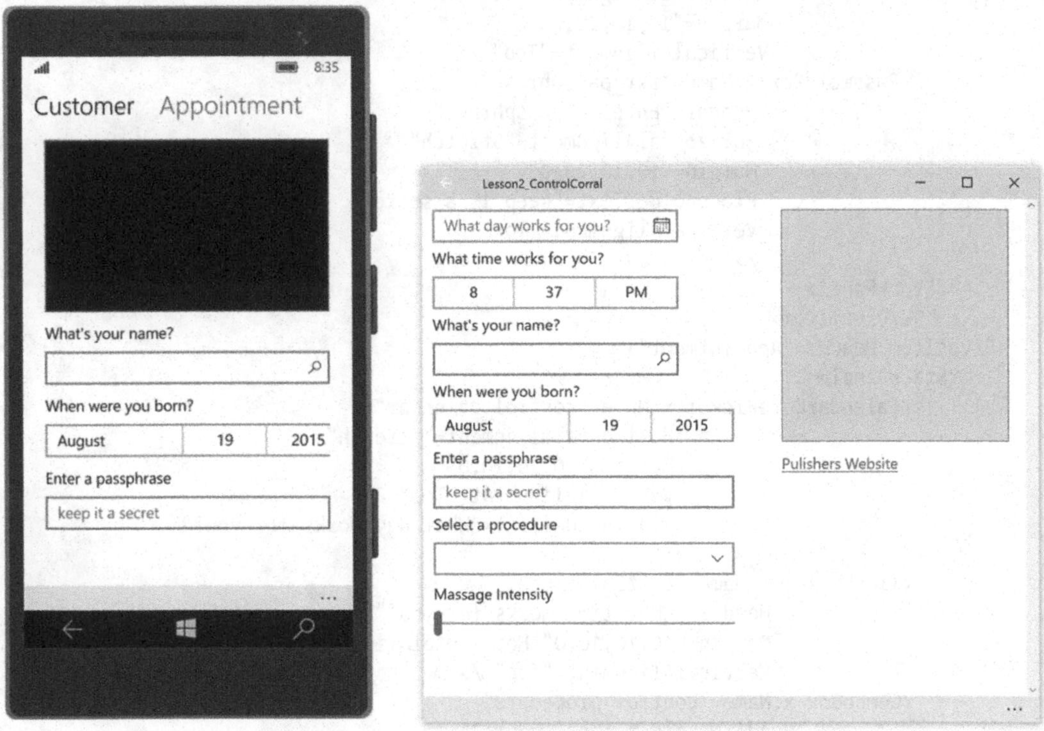

Figure 5-14. Control Corral dashboard running on the Mobile Emulator and the desktop

The following six rules are a good general practice to follow when designing UWP apps to be adaptive. They are borrowed from the rules for building responsive HTML pages.

1. Reposition: You can alter the location and position of app UI elements to get the most out of each device.
2. Resize: You can optimize the frame size by adjusting the margins and size of UI elements. This can allow you to augment the reading experience on a larger screen by simply growing the content frame.

3. Reflow: By changing the flow of UI elements based on device and orientation, your app can offer an optimal display of content.
4. Reveal: You can reveal UI based on screen real estate, or when the device supports additional functionality, specific situations, or preferred screen orientations.
5. Replace: This technique lets you switch the user interface for a specific device size class or orientation.
6. Re-architect: You can collapse or fork the architecture of your app to better target specific devices.

Adapting the Code

Much of the code written for UWP apps will be universal and as such will run the same way on all Windows devices. For code tailored to particular device families however, you have the option to use adaptive code.

As you would expect, whenever you want to call an API that is specific to a given device family, you need to know whether the API is implemented by the device family that your app is targeting. Be sure to use the API reference documentation found on `https://dev.windows.com/en-us/develop`. Figure 5-15 shows the typical requirements section for a UWP class, in this case the CalendarDatePicker. As you can see, the Device family is specified.

Requirements (Windows 10 device family)

Device family	Universal
API contract	Windows.Foundation.UniversalApiContract, introduced version 1.0
Namespace	Windows.UI.Xaml.Controls Windows::UI::Xaml::Controls [C++]
Metadata	Windows.Foundation.UniversalApiContract.winmd

Figure 5-15. *Requirements section of API documentation*

It is a good idea to further confirm that the class members that you want to call are also within your target, so you now know that the APIs are guaranteed to be present on every device that your app can be installed on.

■ **Note** Visual Studio's IntelliSense will not recognize APIs unless they are implemented by your app's target device family or any extension SDKs that you have referenced.

The ApiInformation Class

There are two steps to writing adaptive code. The first step is to make the APIs that you want to access available to your project. To do so, add a reference to the extension SDK that represents the device family that owns the APIs that you want to conditionally call. You can access the list of available extensions through the Add Reference dialog (right-click the Reference node in project and select Add Reference). In the Reference Manager dialog, select Universal Windows, and then select Extensions. If you have multiple versions of the UWP installed on your machine, you will see the same extensions listed multiple times, one for each version of the UWP you have installed. Figure 5-16 shows the list of extensions available on my machine.

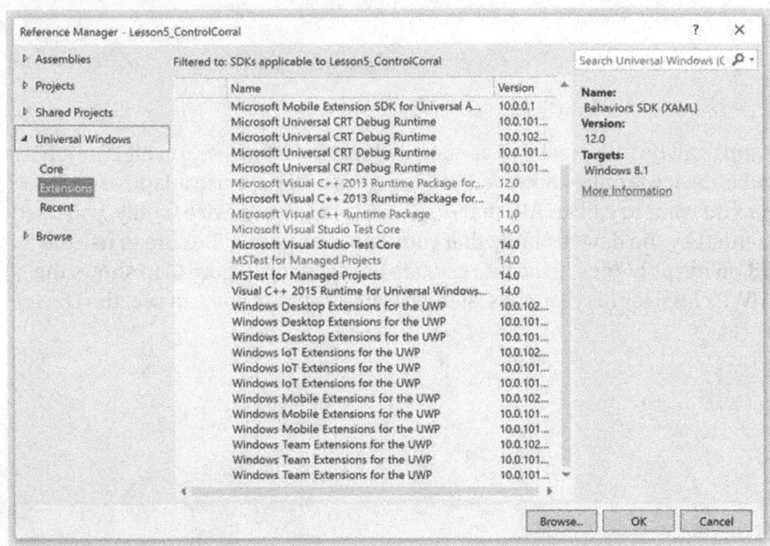

Figure 5-16. *Reference manager dialog for selecting extension SDKs*

The second step is to use the `Windows.Foundation.Metadata.ApiInformation` class in a condition in your code to test for the presence of the API you want to call. You can think of the evaluating `ApiInformation` like a runtime version of the `#define #if` pattern. The condition is evaluated wherever your app runs, but it evaluates to true only on devices where the API is present and therefore available to call. You can test out a typical usage scenario with yours Control Corral app. Suppose you want to let a user know that hitting the back button with no page left to navigate back to will close the application on phones. You can test for the back button `BackRequested` availability as follows in Listing 5-18. Add this code to `RootHost.xaml.cs` to see it at work.

Listing 5-18. Using APIs in an Adaptive Manner

```
public RootHost()
{

        ...

        if (ApiInformation.IsEventPresent(typeof(HardwareButtons).FullName, "BackPressed"))
                HardwareButtons.BackPressed += HardwareButtons_BackPressed;
}
```

```
async private void HardwareButtons_BackPressed(object sender, BackPressedEventArgs e)
{
        e.Handled = true;
        MessageDialog dialog =
                new MessageDialog("This action will close Control Corral", "Close
                Application?");

        dialog.Commands.Add(new UICommand("Yes"));
        dialog.Commands.Add(new UICommand("No"));
        var result = await dialog.ShowAsync();
        if (result.Label == "Yes")
                Application.Current.Exit();
}
```

Listing 5-18 will compile on all versions of Windows but will only run on Windows Mobile 10 devices (perhaps in the future on other devices that have a hardware back button). To even get this to show up as a real type in Visual Studio, you must add a reference to the Microsoft Mobile Extensions SDK.

You can alternatively use the `ApiInformation.IsTypePresent` method to check if an entire type is available; the problem with doing this is that it assumes that the presence of a type means the presence of all its members. This is not always the case. Established classes may have new members added to their definition over time. Doing these sorts of tests on a case by case basis will quickly get laborious. `ApiInformation` provides another method that can be used to test for the presence of a large number of APIs that all exist in the same version. Device families are further broken down into subdivisions known as API contracts which represent the full set of APIs that can be used to program against them. The `ApiInformation.IsApiContractPresent` method can be used to test for availability of an API set at that level. Changing the code from Listing 5-18 to Listing 5-19 will produce the same results as before.

Listing 5-19. Querying to See If an API Contract Is Available

```
if (ApiInformation.IsApiContractPresent("Windows.Phone.PhoneContract", 1))
        HardwareButtons.BackPressed += HardwareButtons_BackPressed;
```

There is no easy way to determine what contracts are available to you or what version numbers they are on at the time of this writing. The Object Explorer exposes contract as top level node on the tree (see Figure 5-17), and of course Microsoft documentation will have the list of contracts available to you.

Figure 5-17. *Using Object Explorer to determine API contract names and version numbers*

A Universal Windows app allows you to take advantage of the unique capabilities of the device on which it is running. Your app can make use of all of the power of a desktop device, the natural interaction of direct manipulation on a tablet (including touch and pen input), the portability and convenience of mobile devices, and the collaborative power of Surface Hub.

Good design is the process of deciding how users will interact with your app, as well as how it will look and function. User experience plays a huge part in determining how happy people will be with your app, so don't skimp on this step.

In addition to interaction on different devices, you should plan for your app to embrace the benefits of working across multiple devices. The following considerations should be taken into account when building a UWP app:

- Consider whether there are features of your app that don't make sense on a small mobile screen. There may also be areas that don't make sense on a stationary desktop machine and require a mobile device to light up.
- Consider how you'll accommodate multiple input modalities.
- Lay out your user interface for a specific window size, not for the available resolution.
- When the system scales your UI, it does so by multiples of 4. To ensure a crisp appearance, snap your designs to the 4x4 pixel grid: make margins, sizes, and positions of UI elements, and the position (but not the size because text can be any size) of text a multiple of 4 effective pixels. When your app runs on a Windows-powered device, the system uses an algorithm to normalize the way controls, fonts, and other UI elements display on the screen. This scaling algorithm takes into account viewing distance and screen density (pixels per inch) to optimize for perceived size (rather than physical size). The scaling algorithm ensures that a 24 pixel font on Surface Hub 10 feet away is just as legible to the user as a 24 pixel font on 5-inch phone that's a few inches away. The resulting pixel value is referred to as *effective pixels*.
- Design your workflow using navigation design basics in order to accommodate mobile, small-screen, and large-screen devices.
- You can ignore the pixel density and the actual screen resolution when designing. Instead, design for the effective resolution (the resolution in effective pixels) for a size class.

Summary

Universal app solutions produce one binary, an APPX package, that runs on any UWP device family it declaratively specifies. Since a UI that looks good on a mobile device probably won't look good on a 30-inch desktop monitor (and vice versa), it's incumbent upon you to learn how to write adaptive UIs. The notion of writing code against a uniform API set that opaquely translates into executable code that can run on the myriad of device choice, technological capabilities, and resolution constraints is difficult to fathom without keeping adaptation in mind. In this chapter, you learned the key features the UWP introduces to help develop adaptive user interfaces and applications. The key points to remember are as follows:

- There are presently five device families you can develop UWP apps for: Universal, Desktop, Mobile, IoT, and Surface Hub.
- Windows 10 helps you target your UI to multiple devices with common input handling, adaptive scaling, and built-in controls that automatically adapt across device families and input modes.

- The `SizeChanged` event can be used as means to modify the layout of a page to suit various resolutions.
- `ApplicationView.GetForCurrentView()` can be used to manage the starting dimensions of your windows (on a desktop).
- The visual state element in XAML can be used to represent the visual appearance of a user interface elements when they are in a specific state. Visual states can be applied to any FrameworkElement and used to represent the state of the element or of any child contained within the element.
- Adaptive triggers define a threshold at which the visual state is activated. They can be used to implement layout changes based on size in a declarative manner.
- Device family-specific views allow developers to define specific XAML views for specific device families while maintaining a single code-behind file.
- Apply the following six rules when building an adaptive user interface:
    - Reposition: You can alter the location and position of app UI elements to get the most out of each device.
    - Resize: You can optimize the frame size by adjusting the margins and size of UI elements. This can allow you to augment the reading experience on a larger screen by simply growing the content frame.
    - Reflow: By changing the flow of UI elements based on device and orientation, your app can offer an optimal display of content.
    - Reveal: You can reveal an UI based on screen real estate, or when the device supports additional functionality, specific situations, or preferred screen orientations.
    - Replace: This technique lets you switch the user interface for a specific device size-class or orientation.
    - Re-architect: You can collapse or fork the architecture of your app to better target specific devices.
- Effective pixels enable you to focus on the actual perceived size of a UI element without having to worry about the pixel density or viewing distance of different devices. For example, when you design a 1-inch by 1-inch element, that element will appear to be approximately 1 inches on all devices. On a very large screen with a high pixel density, the element might be 200 by 200 physical pixels, while on a smaller device like a phone, it might be 100 by 100 physical pixels.

CHAPTER 6

■ ■ ■

File IO

There are certain basic developer workflows to which you must become accustomed if you intend to build Windows 10 UWP apps, regardless of the technology stack you choose to use. At a fundamental level, having a good understanding of how to access the exposed file system is, if not critical, quite important to development in a given system. Indeed, the usefulness of your Control Corral samples would be limited if you did not provide a way to store information so that you could read it at a later time. This chapter introduces the various mechanisms the UWP provides for interacting with files and folders by exposing you to the APIs used to work with them. Detailed examples are provided to help you work through how these APIs function. By the end of this chapter, you should understand how to perform basic file access; how to use the built-in pickers to read and write to locations outside the isolated file system; how to configure your app to access user folders such as `Music`, `Pictures`, and `Videos`; how to access external storage; and how to expose files to other apps through shared storage, and customized pickers and choosers.

Developers who have built server-side style code or even desktop clients are probably very familiar with the general patterns of file access. If you've been building HTML user experiences, you might be at a slight disadvantage, but only a minor one. The truth is, we've all worked with files while working with computers, and we all certainly understand their nature. They can be opened, edited, closed, deleted, listed, searched, copied, and moved.

Although logically similar (if not the same), this discussion is broken into five core areas. First, the chapter talks about storage locations (meaning the places where files are stored). This conversation is important because it has a huge impact on how your app is built, delivered, and ultimately deployed to the Windows Store. You then get into the nitty-gritty of actually working with files. This is done second because the approach to accessing files through the UWP requires you to understand the meaning of storage locations first. Without that core understanding, you'll most likely be pulling your hair out wondering why a given piece of functionality seems to be inexplicably failing with completely useless and cryptic errors. Next, we discuss using dialogs to read and write files from and to protected locations. We then discuss two approaches of sharing: via shared storage and via your own custom pickers and choosers.

To help with this exercise, you will be creating a new project called Resume that is a resume management system. Resume will rely extensively on using the file system to store and manage a user's resume on their local machine.

Creating the ResumeManager Project

Let's start by setting up the ResumeManager project. You've done this several times so you should now be very comfortable with creating a blank UWP app. Use File > New > Project to create a one. Figure 6-1 illustrates.

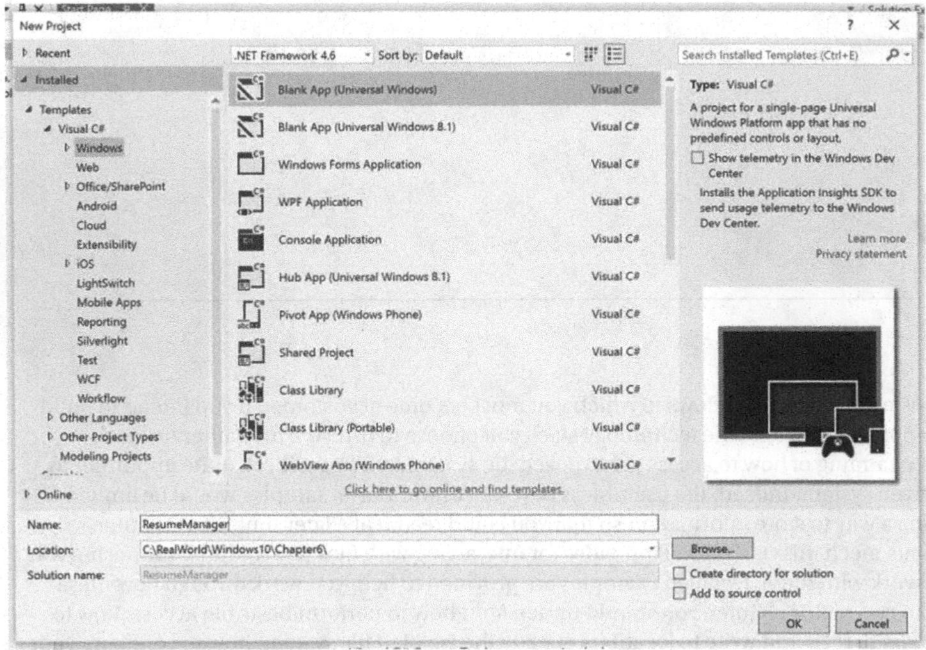

Figure 6-1. *New project dialog*

Your ResumeManager project will use the navigation pattern you established in the previous chapter: it will have a root page with a Frame in it which acts as the host for the entire application. Using a page like this allows you the freedom to utilize app-wide user experience constructs like overlays. For now, you will be using it as a basic replacement for the default Frame that the app uses. Add a new blank page to the project called ApplicationHost and configure your app to use it as the main content for your application window. Your app's `OnLaunched` event should look like the code in Listing 6-1.

Listing 6-1. OnLaunched Event

```
protected override void OnLaunched(LaunchActivatedEventArgs e)
{
        // Place the frame in the current Window
        Window.Current.Content = new ApplicationHost();

        // Ensure the current window is active
        Window.Current.Activate();
}
```

Delete `MainPage.xaml` and add a new page to the project called LandingPage. Your project file should now have three XAML pages: `App.xaml`, `LandingPage.xaml`, and of course your root application host page, `ApplicationHost.xaml`. Your project file should look Figure 6-2.

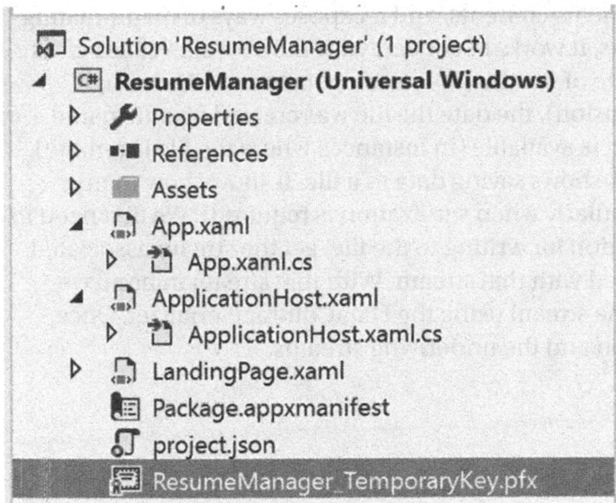

Figure 6-2. *ResumeManager project setup*

The final step to setting up your environment is to wire up ApplicationHost so that it points to `LandingPage.xaml` by default. Listing 6-2 illustrates.

Listing 6-2. ApplicationHost UI

```
<Page
    x:Class="ResumeManager.ApplicationHost"
    xmlns="http://schemas.microsoft.com/winfx/2006/xaml/presentation"
    xmlns:x="http://schemas.microsoft.com/winfx/2006/xaml"
    xmlns:local="using:ResumeManager"
    xmlns:d="http://schemas.microsoft.com/expression/blend/2008"
    xmlns:mc="http://schemas.openxmlformats.org/markup-compatibility/2006"
    mc:Ignorable="d">

    <Grid Background="{ThemeResource ApplicationPageBackgroundThemeBrush}">
        <Frame x:Name="root_frame" SourcePageType="local:LandingPage" />
    </Grid>
</Page>
```

In Listing 6-2, you add a root frame to ApplicationHost which is used to navigate to LandingPage. In previous examples, you typically performed the navigation using the code-behind file. In this example, you use the `SourcePageType` attribute on the Frame element in XAML rather than do anything in code. Both approaches result in the same thing, but doing it this way offers flexibility and separation between the code parts of your app and the layout and design parts.

Files

File access in Windows 10 is accomplished through a new set of APIs originally introduced in Windows 8. These APIs are all accessed through the symbolic representation of the file to the platform, the `StorageFile` class. In Windows 10 (and 8 as well), a file, regardless of where it exists, is represented through the Storage File infrastructure. Since files can be anywhere from a local machine to OneDrive, the complexity to access files changes when using the UWP infrastructure.

StorageFile provides information about a given file and its contents, and it exposes ways of manipulating the underlying file. As you've seen in the previous chapters, it works in concert with the `StorageFolder` class as a tool to create, modify, move, copy, or delete files. Some of the things you can get about a file through the `StorageFile` class are the content type, file type (extension), the date the file was created, the file name (without extension), the location of the file, and whether it is available (in instances where the file is remote). In Chapter 3, you saw how `StorageFile` works. Listing 6-3 shows saving data to a file. It shows how many steps are required to actually write content to a file (particularly when serilization is required). We first need to instantiate the serializer, then create a file, open a transaction for writing to the file, get the stream associated with that transaction, then get the OutputStream associated with that stream. With that stream in hand we can then write the object instance we need serialized to the stream using the DataContractSerializer. Once completed, we commit and dispose of both the transaction and the underlying streams.

```
using Windows.Storage;
using Windows.Storage.Streams;
using System.Threading.Tasks;
using System.Runtime.Serialization;
```

Listing 6-3. Implementing a Persistent Save Method

```
async public static Task SaveModelAsync()
{
        //serialize the model object to a memory stream
        DataContractSerializer dcs = new DataContractSerializer(Model.GetType());

        //write model string to file
        var file = await ApplicationData.Current
                                .LocalFolder
                                .CreateFileAsync("corralmodel.xml",
                                CreationCollisionOption.OpenIfExists);
        var transaction = await file.OpenTransactedWriteAsync();
        var opn = transaction.Stream;
        var ostream = opn.GetOutputStreamAt(0);
        var stream = ostream.AsStreamForWrite();
        dcs.WriteObject(stream, Model);
        stream.Flush();
        stream.Dispose();
        await transaction.CommitAsync();
        transaction.Dispose();
}
```

Listing 6-4 shows the convoluted process of reading a file.

Listing 6-4. LoadModelAsync Method

```
async public static Task<ControlCorralModel> LoadModelAsync()
{
        //read the target file's text
        try
        {
                var file = await ApplicationData
                        .Current
                        .LocalFolder.GetFileAsync("corralmodel.xml");
```

```
            var opn = await file
                    .OpenAsync(Windows.Storage.FileAccessMode.Read);
            var stream = opn.GetInputStreamAt(0);
            var reader = new DataReader(stream);
            var size = (await file
                    .GetBasicPropertiesAsync()).Size;
            await reader.LoadAsync((uint)size);
            var model_text = reader.ReadString((uint)size);

            //before attempting deserialize, ensure the string is valid
            if (string.IsNullOrWhiteSpace(model_text))
                    return null;

            //deserialize the text
            var ms = new MemoryStream(Encoding
                    .UTF8.GetBytes(model_text));
            var dsc =
                    new DataContractSerializer(typeof(ControlCorralModel));
            var ret_val = dsc.ReadObject(ms) as ControlCorralModel;
            return ret_val;
        }
        catch (Exception ex)
        {
            return null;
        }
}
```

The approach taken to read and write to a file can be quite convoluted for good reason. Unlike a local file that is always there and accessible, a "file" in Windows 10 can actually be just a placeholder. If you are not comfortable with the "safe" approach (as it accounts for where the file might be located) and you are sure that the files your app uses will always be local, you can opt for using the good, old fashioned `System.IO.File` static class for performing file IO. These APIs give free reign to the developer with regards to the location where files are created or read from, but be careful. Windows 10 restricts the locations where file access is allowed without user authorization. Later in this chapter, you will see how the `File` class can be used interchangeably with `StorageFile` to access files in an app's isolated storage. We don't recommend doing this ever, though.

A much better and much safer approach to accessing files is to use the `FileIO` static class. `FileIO` is great because it provides many of the same easy-to-use, straightforward, and quick methods as `File` but with the added benefit of being safe, asynchronous, and utilizing `StorageFile`. The connection of `FileIO` to `StorageFile` is so great in fact that it is hard to understand why its methods were not implemented as extension methods on `StorageFile`. Let's add a new class to your project called `StorageFileExtensions` and do just this.

Start by creating a new folder called `Library` and then within this folder add `StorageFileExtensions`. In the new class, change the namespace to `Windows.Storage` instead of `ResumeManager.Library`. Now modify the class definition so that it is a static class. Listing 6-5 shows the full contents of this class.

Listing 6-5. StorageFile Extension Methods

```
namespace Windows.Storage
{
	static class StorageFileExtensions
	{
		async public static Task AppendLinesAsync(this StorageFile file,
		IEnumerable<string> lines)
		{
			await FileIO.AppendLinesAsync(file, lines);
		}

		async public static Task AppendTextAsync(this StorageFile file, string
		contents)
		{
			await FileIO.AppendTextAsync(file, contents);
		}

		async public static Task<IBuffer> ReadBufferAsync(this StorageFile file)
		{
			return await FileIO.ReadBufferAsync(file);
		}

		async public static Task<IList<string>> ReadLinesAsync(this StorageFile file)
		{
			return await FileIO.ReadLinesAsync(file);
		}

		async public static Task<string> ReadTextAsync(this StorageFile file)
		{
			return await FileIO.ReadTextAsync(file);
		}

		async public static Task WriteBufferAsync(this StorageFile file, IBuffer
		buffer)
		{
			await FileIO.WriteBufferAsync(file, buffer);
		}

		async public static Task WriteBytesAsync(this StorageFile file, byte[] buffer)
		{
			await FileIO.WriteBytesAsync(file, buffer);
		}

		async public static Task WriteLinesAsync(this StorageFile file,
		IEnumerable<string> lines)
		{
			await FileIO.WriteLinesAsync(file, lines);
		}
```

```
            async public static Task WriteTextAsync(this StorageFile file, string
            contents)
            {
                    await FileIO.WriteTextAsync(file, contents);
            }

    }
}
```

In Listing 6-5, you simply take the default static methods on the FileIO class and created extension methods on StorageFile that pass the calls into these FileIO methods. The net result of this is that you can directly call these methods on any instance of StorageFile, which is a much faster and human readable approach than the alternative.

Storage Folders

A Windows 10 file can be resident in any number of places: on a physical machine, a thumb drive, a file share, or the cloud, just to name a few possible places. The StorageFolder class represents this general sense of a storage location. An application you develop has access to these locations either intrinsically or by declaring permissions in the UWP app's manifest. Some storage locations to which your app has intrinsic access include the app's package install location and the designated isolated storage area for the app. These storage locations are discussed in more detail in the following sections.

The Package Install Location

When your app is unpacked (installed) onto a user's machine, the package install location is the storage location where it is placed. It contains all the files and folders you created as part of your app project (any folders in your project that contain items that have a Build Action of "Content" will be created by Windows on a user's machine when the app is installed). Because this folder is completely deleted and recreated each time your app is installed (or updated), modifications made to the app's package install location are wiped away when a new update to your application is installed. You access this folder using the Windows.ApplicationModel.Package class. Package contains a property called InstalledLocation that returns a reference to a StorageFolder that represents the location on the end user's computer where the app was unpacked.

Given the volatility of this folder, one might be hard pressed to find a reason to use it. As a place to write information to, you would agree that there are better places to look (in fact, this is no longer allowed with Windows 10), but as a place to read data from, particularly initialization data, setup instructions, or data that simply needs to be copied from this location into the app's isolated storage, there is no better source.

This is because the Package Install location contains a kind of storage state that no other storage location exposed through the UWP has. It has storage state that originates at the app developer's UWP project. Let's illustrate this with a simple example of loading development-time data into your app. Add a new folder called Data in your project (the choice of name is not mandatory to UWP). In this folder, add a new text file and call it initData.txt. Your project file should now look like Figure 6-3.

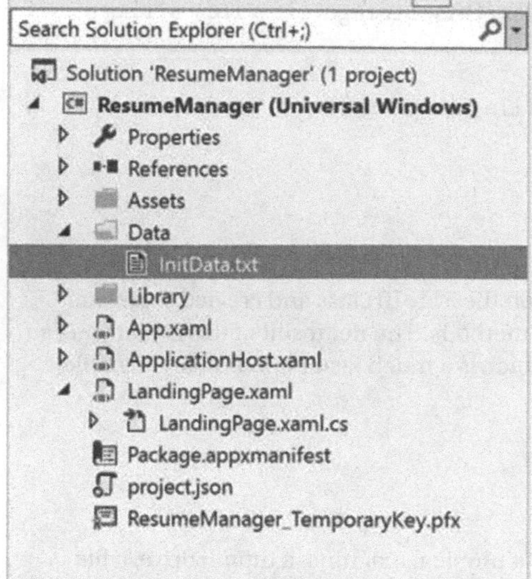

Figure 6-3. *Install directory data*

Open the `initData.txt` file and add some text to it. In my case, I added the following text "`this is a test of reading data from app init folder.`" Now modify LandingPage with the code in Listing 6-6.

Listing 6-6. Implementing INotifyPropertyChanged

```
public sealed partial class LandingPage : Page, INotifyPropertyChanged
{
        public event PropertyChangedEventHandler PropertyChanged;

        string InitialMessage { get; set; }

        public LandingPage()
        {
                this.InitializeComponent();
                this.Loaded += LandingPage_Loaded;
        }

        async private void LandingPage_Loaded(object sender, RoutedEventArgs e)
        {
                var file = await Windows.ApplicationModel.
                                        Package.Current.InstalledLocation
                                        .GetFileAsync(@"data\initdata.txt");
                var text = await file.ReadTextAsync();
                InitialMessage = text;
                PropertyChanged?.Invoke(this,
                                       new PropertyChangedEventArgs("InitialMessage"));
        }
}
```

In Listing 6-6, you change LandingPage so that it implements `INotifyPropertyChanged`. If you have been paying attention, you will know that this is because you plan to use it in binding in some way. As you saw from the previous chapter, code-behind files are used for databinding when compiled binding is being used (it is the only object supported). In the `Loaded` event, you are simply reading from the app's installed location and storing it to a variable that you can bind to in your XAML. Notice that the relative path to `initData.txt` matches the relative path (from project root) to `initData.txt` in your project. Place a breakpoint just after the file is retrieved and run the example. Figure 6-4 illustrates what you should see.

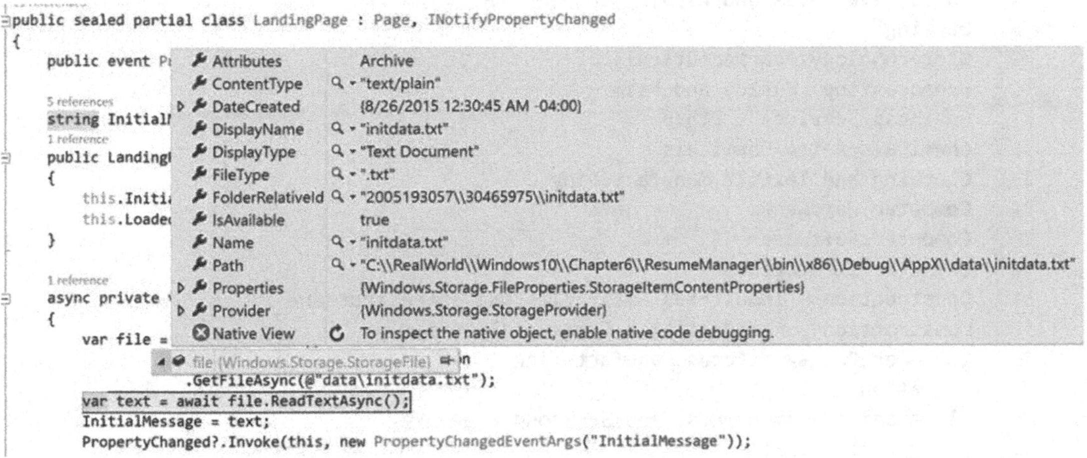

Figure 6-4. Relative path of install directory items

If you look at the `Path` property of the StorageFile instance you retrieved from your initial call to GetFile, you should see that the relative path to the file is maintained.

Listing 6-7 completes the example with the XAML layout used to render Landing. Replace the main grid in `LayoutPage.xaml` with this code.

Listing 6-7. LandingPage UI

```
...
<Grid Background="{ThemeResource ApplicationPageBackgroundThemeBrush}">
    <TextBlock x:Name="txt_message"
               HorizontalAlignment="Center"
               VerticalAlignment="Center"
               Text="{x:Bind InitialMessage, Mode=TwoWay}" />
</Grid>
...
```

As can be seen from the above code, binding is indeed used to separate the code-behind from the XAML layout. Because you are using compiled binding in this instance, you are forced to specify the mode of the binding (compiled bindings default to OneTime if no mode is explicitly specified).

A more practical use of the app install location is in carrying information that is static but used to classify things. In the Control Corral samples from the previous chapter, you maintained a list of massage types that was essentially hard coded into the app in one form or another. A more elegant approach would be to continue to read it from this folder location. The next sample expands on what you have created thus far. Start by deleting the `initData.txt` file and in its place add a file titled `Industries.txt`. In this folder, write out as many industries as you can think of (each industry in the same line). Figure 6-5 shows some of the industries I have listed.

```
Industries.txt
Accounting and Auditing Services
Advertising and PR Services
Aerospace and Defense
Agriculture/Forestry/Fishing
Architectural and Design Services
Automotive and Parts Mfg
Automotive Sales and Repair Services
Banking
Biotechnology/Pharmaceuticals
Broadcasting, Music, and Film
Business Services - Other
Chemicals/Petro-Chemicals
Clothing and Textile Manufacturing
Computer Hardware
Computer Software
Computer/IT Services
Construction - Industrial Facilities and Infrastructure
Construction - Residential & Commercial/Office
Consumer Packaged Goods Manufacturing
Education
Electronics, Components, and Semiconductor Mfg
Energy and Utilities
Engineering Services
Entertainment Venues and Theaters
Financial Services
Food and Beverage Production
Government and Military
```

Figure 6-5. *Install directory data loaded*

To test this, you must make some temporary modifications to your code base. First, you need to change the `InitialMessage` property to a list and also give it a name that is more appropriate to what it stores. You must also modify the name of the file being read and you must change the approach to reading the file to simply return a list of strings corresponding to each line of the document. Listing 6-8 illustrates.

Listing 6-8. Loading Data from Package Installed Location

```
List<string> IndustryList { get; set; }

async private void LandingPage_Loaded(object sender, RoutedEventArgs e)
{
        var file = await Windows.ApplicationModel.
                              Package.Current.InstalledLocation
                              .GetFileAsync(@"data\industries.txt");
        var industry_list = await file.ReadLinesAsync();
        IndustryList = industry_list.ToList();
        PropertyChanged?.Invoke(this, new PropertyChangedEventArgs("IndustryList"));

}
```

In your XAML, a ListBox would be a great way to present this information. Replace the TextBlock in `LandingPage.xaml` with the code in Listing 6-9.

Listing 6-9. ListBox Bound to IndustryList

```
<ListBox ItemsSource="{x:Bind IndustryList, Mode=OneWay}"
         HorizontalAlignment="Center"
         VerticalAlignment="Center" />
```

Running the app should produce the list of industries that was passed into it via the install folder. In the coming sections, you will be using this and other static data as part of ResumeManager. In XAML, you can access files in your package install location in a number of ways, some of which you have previously seen when pointing to images files in your package. One approach is to use the forward slash (/). The forward slash is used to refer to the package root. To access `Industries.txt` in XAML, you would use `/data/industries.txt`. You can also use the ms-appx protocol. Ms-appx is a protocol used to access items that are a part of your app package. It follows the format ms-appx://<package-name>/<resource-path>. You are allowed to omit the <package-name> part of the URI (but not the slash associated with it). So you can access a package resource as follows: `ms-appx:///<resource-path>` (`ms-appx:///data/industries.txt`).

The Isolated Storage Area

An app's *isolated storage area* is an unpublished location on the Windows 10 system partitioned specifically for the app. It serves as a cache for the app to read from and write to. Changes made to the isolated storage area through files being added or deleted, folders being created, and so on, are persisted across updates to your app. This is the principle difference between this area and the package install location discussed in the previous section.

You can access the isolated storage location for your using `ApplicationData.Current.LocalFolder` property. `ApplicationData` can be found in the `Windows.Storage` namespace. Like the Control Corral sample, your app will be using serialization (specifically the `DataContractSerializer` class) to convert an object model representation of a user's resume into XML. You will then store it directly in the app's isolated storage so you can use it as needed. Let's start by defining your resume in object terms. A resume is basically a list of work experiences that you define as follows. Create a new file in the `Library` folder named `ResumeInfo.cs` and add the contents of Listing 6-10. Note that since there is not a lot of complexity to the resume structure, you will use this file to place all the objects that make up your resume.

Listing 6-10. WorkExperience and Technology Class Definitions

```
public class WorkExperience
{
        public DateTime StartDate { get; set; }
        public DateTime? EndDate { get; set; }
        public string Company { get; set; }
        public string Title { get; set; }
        public List<Technology> TechnologiesUsed { get; set; }
}

public class Technology
{
        public string Name { get; set; }
}
```

A resume will typically also have information about an individual's education and any certifications or professional licenses they have. Add the two class definitions from Listing 6-11 to the resume file.

Listing 6-11. Certification and Education Class Definitions

```
public class Certification
{
        public string CertificationName { get; set; }

        public DateTime AcquisitionDate { get; set; }

        public string TechSponsor { get; set; }
}

public class Education
{
        public string SchoolName { get; set; }
        public string SchoolAddress { get; set; }
        public string Degree { get; set; }
        public DateTime StartDate { get; set; }
        public DateTime EndDate { get; set; }
        public string EducationLevel { get; set; }
}
```

Of course, you should also have an overarching resume object that contains these various work experiences. This object also needs the information to help present the resume. Listing 6-12 illustrates.

Listing 6-12. Resume Class Definition

```
public class Resume
{
        public string Name { get; set; }
        public DateTime CreateDate{get;set;}
        public DateTime LastUpdateDate{get;set;}
        public string EmailAddress { get; set; }
        public string PhoneNumber { get; set; }
        public string ProfileSummary { get; set; }

        public List<Certification> Certifications { get; set; }

        public List<Education> EductionHistory { get; set; }
        public List<WorkExperience> WorkHistory { get; set; }
}
```

Finally, you need a construct above this that does all the resume management for you. To reduce the memory impact on the system (particularly if a user ends up with lots of resumes), you won't use an object here. Instead you will maintain each resume object as its own file. Regardless of your approach, one key activity that needs to happen with the resume object is for it to be serialized to a string. Let's modify Resume to include this ability. Listing 6-13 illustrates. Add it to the definition of resume. `DataContractSerializer` requires the `System.Runtime.Serialization` namespace.

Listing 6-13. AsSerializedString Method

```
public string AsSerializedString()
{
        DataContractSerializer dcs = new DataContractSerializer(typeof(Resume));
        MemoryStream ms = new MemoryStream();
        dcs.WriteObject(ms, this);
        ms.Seek(0, SeekOrigin.Begin);
        byte[] buffer = new byte[ms.Length];
        ms.Read(buffer, 0, buffer.Length);
        string serialized_object = Encoding.ASCII.GetString(buffer);
        return serialized_object;
}
```

To come full circle, resume objects must also provide a means for reading and instantiating themselves from a serialized XML form. Listing 6-14 shows the implementation of this feature to also be added to the Resume class.

Listing 6-14. FromSerializedString Method

```
public static Resume FromSerializedString(string resume_string)
{
        try
        {
                var buffer = Encoding.ASCII.GetBytes(resume_string);
                MemoryStream ms = new MemoryStream(buffer);
                DataContractSerializer dcs = new DataContractSerializer(typeof(Resume));
                var retval = dcs.ReadObject(ms);
                return retval as Resume;
        }
        catch (Exception ex)
        {
                return null;
        }
}
```

Now that you have your object model and the means to serialize it, let's build in the facilities you need to store it in isolated storage. As mentioned above, all apps have access to this location through the `LocalFolder` property of ApplicationData. Rather than place your resumes in the root folder, however, you will create a new subfolder that you expect to be there called `resumes`. This can't be done anywhere but in the code because there is no mechanism available for structuring the isolated storage of downstream clients. Add a new file to your project (in the `Library` folder) called `AppStorageManager` and add the implementation code from Listing 6-15.

Listing 6-15. AppStorageManager Class Definition

```
public static class AppStorageManager
{
        async public static Task<StorageFolder> CreateOrOpenFolder(string folder_name)
        {
            if (!string.IsNullOrWhiteSpace(folder_name))
                return await ApplicationData.Current
```

```
                    .LocalFolder
                    .CreateFolderAsync(folder_name, CreationCollisionOption.OpenIfExists);

        return null;
    }

    async public static Task SaveResumeAsync(Resume resume)
    {
        await CreateOrOpenFolder("resumes");

        if (resume.Name != null)
        {
            //write model string to file
            var file = await ApplicationData.Current
                        .LocalFolder
                        .CreateFileAsync($"resumes\\{resume.Name}.xml",
                                         CreationCollisionOption.
                                         OpenIfExists);
            await file.WriteTextAsync(resume.AsSerializedString());
        }
        else
            throw new Exception("Resume objects require a name.");
    }

    async public static Task<Resume> LoadResumeAsync(string resume_name)
    {
        try
        {
            if (!string.IsNullOrWhiteSpace(resume_name))
            {
                var file = await ApplicationData.Current
                            .LocalFolder
                        .GetFileAsync($"resumes\\{resume_name}.xml");
                var resume_xml = await file.ReadTextAsync();
                var resume = Resume.FromSerializedString(resume_xml);
                return resume;
            }
        }
        catch (Exception ex)
        {

        }
        return null;
    }

    async public static Task<bool> DeleteResume(string resume_name)
    {
        try
        {
            var resume = await ApplicationData.Current
                            .LocalFolder
```

```
                                .GetFileAsync($"resumes\\{resume_name}.xml");
                await resume.DeleteAsync(StorageDeleteOption.PermanentDelete);
                return true;
            }
            catch (Exception ex)
            {
                return false;
            }
        }

        async public static Task<List<string>> ListResumes()
        {
            var folder = await CreateOrOpenFolder("resumes");
            var files = await folder.GetFilesAsync();
            return files.OrderByDescending(i => i.DateCreated).Select(i =>
            i.DisplayName).ToList();
        }
}
```

In Listing 6-15, the `CreateOrOpenFolder` method shows how to create a folder in isolated storage using the `Windows.Storage.ApplicationData.Current.LocalFolder.CreateFolder` function. The version of this function that you call expects two parameters: one that represents the folder name and one calls `Windows.Storage.CreationCollisionOption` to determine what to do when the folder you want created has the same name as a folder already present. There are two versions of this function: one expects a single parameter passed in (the folder name), and the other also expects the `CreationCollisionOption` to be included. When you use the first version, the `failIfExists CreationCollisionOption` is automatically used. `CreationCollisionOption` applies to both files and folders. In the function `SaveResumeAsync` you see it being used during the file creation process. Table 6-1 shows all the possible options of `Windows.Storage.CreationCollisionOption`.

Table 6-1. *`Windows.Storage.CreationCollisionOption` Members*

Member	Value	Description
GenerateUniqueName	0	Creates the new file or folder with the desired name, and automatically appends a number if a file or folder already exists with that name
ReplaceExisting	1	Creates the new file or folder with the desired name, and replaces any file or folder that already exists with that name
FailIfExists	2	Creates the new file or folder with the desired name, or returns an error if a file or folder already exists with that name
OpenIfExists	3	Creates the new file or folder with the desired name, or returns an existing item if a file or folder already exists with that name

`ListResumes` returns the list of files in the resumes folder while `LoadResumeAsync` reads the text from a given resume file and deserializes it into a `Resume` object. This method does this in three steps.

1. It generates a relative file path based on the name passed into it.
2. It opens the file and read the contents of it.
3. It deserializes the content using the `DataContractSerializer`.

Finally, in Listing 6-15, DeleteResume is used to remove the resume files from the user's Isolated Storage area. You can test how well this works by adding some test code anywhere in your project. In Listing 6-16, you add some code to test the file access and serialization functionality to your ApplicationHost's Loaded event.

Listing 6-16. ApplicationHost Loaded Event Handler

```
async private void ApplicationHost_Loaded(object sender, RoutedEventArgs e)
{

        await AppStorageManager.
                SaveResumeAsync(new Resume() { Name = "resume one" });
        await AppStorageManager.
                SaveResumeAsync(new Resume() { Name = "resume two" });
        var resume = await AppStorageManager.LoadResumeAsync("resume one");
        var resume_list = await AppStorageManager.ListResumes();
        foreach (var resume_name in resume_list)
        {
                await AppStorageManager.DeleteResume(resume_name);
        }
}
```

Listing 6-16 simply creates two resume objects and simultaneously saves them to isolated storage. You then list the resumes and, looping through each resume name retrieved, delete each one. If you put a breakpoint on the foreach statement, every time you run the app and it breaks there you should note that resume_list contains exactly two items. You can access files in this folder in XAML using the URI scheme ms-appdata:///local/<file-path>. The ms-appdata protocol is used to access files in your ApplicationData storage area.

■ **Note** To request that Windows index your app data for search, create a folder named Indexed under this folder and store the files that you want indexed there. Windows indexes the file content and metadata (properties) in this Indexed folder and all its subfolders.

RoamingFolder

The problem with your app so far is that each installed instance of it will have resume data that is tied to the specific machine that the app is installed on. Isolated storage works great in instances where a user will be using your app on one and only one device. However, you know from the first chapter of this book that this is far less of a reality with Windows 10 than ever before. Most likely a user will have access to your app on a wide range of devices, and you as the developer must tailored the experience of using the app to those device classes as needed. One of the main problems with having your product reach across multiple devices, though, is managing state. If the resume app was relying on a back-end service to store all the resume information, this would not be a problem. Regardless of the device a user is on, your app would simply connect to the back-end service (like Azure) and pull down all the appropriate information necessary to present a seamless experience to the user.

In your case, however, you are presently relying on files and folders to manager your user's resume information. Files and folders are located on the user's current machine and nowhere else. Remove the code to delete the resumes from ApplicationHost and run the app two more times, once using your location machine and the other using any one of the Windows 10 Mobile Emulators. If you place a breakpoint at the same place as you previously did, you will notice that although the code shows as having two resumes on your local machine, it shows as no resumes on the emulator. Roaming folders can be a possible solution for these kinds of scenarios (although the ideal approach is to use a service-based back end). They not only synchronize the files stored to it across Windows devices, they also associate those files to the presently logged-in user and not the machine. The great thing about this approach is that it allows users of your app to flow seamlessly across devices without you needing to explicitly synchronize their state back to a server. You simply store content in the folder, and let Windows 10 take care of the rest! You can access the folder location through the `RoamingFolder` property of ApplicationData. To access the contents of this folder through XAML, use the URI scheme `ms-appdata:///roaming/<file-path>`.

■ **Note** For files to properly roam, the files and folders you specify must also contain no leading white spaces.

There are restrictions on the total storage quota that can be roamed. You can use the `RoamingStorageQuota` property of ApplicationData to check to see how much space (measured in KB) is allotted to your app for roaming purposes. If the amount of data stored in your app's `RoamingFolder` location exceeds this value amount, synchronization will be paused until the value goes below the threshold.

In Listing 6-17, you make some changes to `AppStorageManager`. Since `RoamingFolder` behaves like a local folder when the total storage exceeds the allotted quota, you switch over to using it instead of `LocalFolder`. Your app will continue to work as normal and will roam the resume files until it hits the quota. At that point, you will notify your user that their quota has been hit and synchronization across devices has stopped. To accomplish this, you add a new method to `AppStorageManager` that measures the current size of the app's `Roaming` folder. You also modify the methods for saving and deleting resumes to check the current size of this folder and return an enum value that indicates whether the quota is in excess of its allotment. The new enum type `ResumeOperationResult` provides this flag. Listing 6-17 illustrates; changes are highlighted in bold.

Listing 6-17. AppStorageManager and ResumeOperationResult Definitions

```
public enum ResumeOperationResult
{
        Success,
        SuccessOverLimit,
        Failure,
}

public static class AppStorageManager
{
        async public static Task<StorageFolder> CreateOrOpenFolder(string folder_name)
        {
                if (!string.IsNullOrWhiteSpace(folder_name))
                        return await ApplicationData.Current
                                                        .RoamingFolder
                                                        .CreateFolderAsync(folder_name,
                                                        CreationCollisionOption.OpenIfExists);

                return null;
        }
```

```
async public static Task<ResumeOperationResult> SaveResumeAsync(Resume resume)
{
    await CreateOrOpenFolder("resumes");

    ResumeOperationResult result = ResumeOperationResult.Success;

    if (resume.Name != null)
    {
            //write model string to file
            var file = await ApplicationData.Current
                                    .RoamingFolder
                                    .CreateFileAsync($"resumes\\
                                    {resume.Name}.xml",
                                    CreationCollisionOption.OpenIfExists);
            await file.WriteTextAsync(resume.AsSerializedString());

            var total_storage = await AppStorageManager.GetTotalStorage();
            if (total_storage > ApplicationData.Current.RoamingStorageQuota)
            {
                    result = ResumeOperationResult.SuccessOverLimit;
            }
    }
    else
    {
            throw new Exception("Resume objects require a name.");
    }

    return result;
}

async public static Task<Resume> LoadResumeAsync(string resume_name)
{
    try
    {
            if (!string.IsNullOrWhiteSpace(resume_name))
            {
                    var file = await ApplicationData.Current
                                    .RoamingFolder
                                    .GetFileAsync($"resumes\\{resume_name}.xml");
                    var resume_xml = await file.ReadTextAsync();
                    var resume = Resume.FromSerializedString(resume_xml);
                    return resume;
            }
    }
    catch (Exception ex)
    {

    }
    return null;
}
```

```
async public static Task<ResumeOperationResult> DeleteResume(string resume_name)
{
        ResumeOperationResult result = ResumeOperationResult.Success;

        try
        {

                var resume = await ApplicationData.Current
                                                  .RoamingFolder
                                                  .GetFileAsync($"resumes\\{resume_name}.xml");
                await resume.DeleteAsync(StorageDeleteOption.PermanentDelete);

                var total_storage = await AppStorageManager.GetTotalStorage();
                if (total_storage > ApplicationData.Current.RoamingStorageQuota)
                {
                        result = ResumeOperationResult.SuccessOverLimit;
                }

        }
        catch (Exception ex)
        {
                result = ResumeOperationResult.Failure;
        }
        return result;
}

async public static Task<List<string>> ListResumes()
{
        var folder = await CreateOrOpenFolder("resumes");
        var files = await folder.GetFilesAsync();
        return files.OrderByDescending(i => i.DateCreated).Select(i =>
        i.DisplayName).ToList();
}

async public static Task<ulong> GetTotalStorage()
{
        var folder = await CreateOrOpenFolder("resumes");
        var files = await folder.GetFilesAsync();
        ulong accumulator = 0;
        foreach (var file in files)
        {
                accumulator += (await file.GetBasicPropertiesAsync()).Size;
        }
        return accumulator / 1024;
}

async public static Task<ResumeOperationResult> CheckStorage()
{
        ResumeOperationResult result = ResumeOperationResult.Success;
        var total_storage = await AppStorageManager.GetTotalStorage();
        if (total_storage > ApplicationData.Current.RoamingStorageQuota)
```

```
            {
                    result = ResumeOperationResult.SuccessOverLimit;
            }
            return result;
        }
}
```

To test this out, you will do some cleanup on ApplicationHost and LandingPage. In the code-behind for ApplicationHost, remove the `LocalFolder` test code you previously added. In LandingPage, remove the code you added to test your binding. Don't worry; you will be revisiting these subjects later in this chapter. For now you need a clean page to perform your tests so you don't get too confused with what is going on. ApplicationHost should now look like Listing 6-18.

Listing 6-18. ApplicationHost Class Definition

```
public sealed partial class ApplicationHost : Page
{
        public static ApplicationHost Current { get; private set; }
        public ApplicationHost()
        {
                this.InitializeComponent();
                Current = this;
        }

}
```

Replace the contents of `LandingPage.xaml` with the code in Listing 6-19.

Listing 6-19. LandingPage UI

```
<Grid Background="{ThemeResource ApplicationPageBackgroundThemeBrush}">
    <StackPanel HorizontalAlignment="Center"
                VerticalAlignment="Center">
        <Button Click="AddResume"
                HorizontalAlignment="Stretch"
                Margin="5"
                Content="Test Roaming Storage - Add" />
        <Button Click="RemoveResume"
                Margin="5"
                HorizontalAlignment="Stretch"
                Content="Test Roaming Storage - Remove" />
    </StackPanel>

</Grid>
```

Now change the code-behind for LandingPage so that it looks like Listing 6-20.

Listing 6-20. LandingPage Code-Behind

```
public sealed partial class LandingPage : Page
{

        int _count = 0;

        public LandingPage()
        {
                this.InitializeComponent();
                this.Loaded += LandingPage_Loaded;
        }

        async private void LandingPage_Loaded(object sender, RoutedEventArgs e)
        {
                var app_view = ApplicationView.GetForCurrentView();
                _count = (await AppStorageManager.ListResumes()).Count;
                app_view.Title = $"{_count} resumes, {(await AppStorageManager.
                GetTotalStorage())}↵
                                KB, QUOTA={ApplicationData.Current.RoamingStorageQuota} KB";
                if ((await AppStorageManager.CheckStorage()) ==
                        ResumeOperationResult.SuccessOverLimit)
                {
                        app_view.TitleBar.BackgroundColor = Windows.UI.Colors.Red;
                }
        }


        async private void RemoveResume(object sender, RoutedEventArgs e)
        {
                var app_view = ApplicationView.GetForCurrentView();
                var resume_list = await AppStorageManager.ListResumes();
                var oldest_resume = resume_list.LastOrDefault();

                var result = await AppStorageManager.
                        DeleteResume(oldest_resume);
                _count--;
                if (result == ResumeOperationResult.SuccessOverLimit)
                {
                        app_view.TitleBar.BackgroundColor = Windows.UI.Colors.Red;
                }
                else if (result == ResumeOperationResult.Success)
                        app_view.TitleBar.BackgroundColor = Windows.UI.Colors.Transparent;

                app_view.Title = $"{(await AppStorageManager.ListResumes()).Count} resumes, ↵
                                {(await AppStorageManager.GetTotalStorage())} KB, ↵
                                QUOTA={ApplicationData.Current.RoamingStorageQuota} KB";

        }
```

```
        async private void AddResume(object sender, RoutedEventArgs e)
        {
                var app_view = ApplicationView.GetForCurrentView();
                var result = await AppStorageManager.
                        SaveResumeAsync(new Resume() { Name = $"resume {_count}" });
                if (result == ResumeOperationResult.SuccessOverLimit)
                {
                        app_view.TitleBar.BackgroundColor = Windows.UI.Colors.Red;
                }
                var resume = await AppStorageManager.LoadResumeAsync($"resume {_count}");
                var resume_list = await AppStorageManager.ListResumes();
                app_view.Title = $"{resume_list.Count} resumes, {(await ➥
                                AppStorageManager.GetTotalStorage())} KB, ➥
                                QUOTA={ApplicationData.Current.RoamingStorageQuota} KB";
                _count++;
        }
}
```

In Listing 6-19 and Listing 6-20 you add two buttons to LandingPage, one for adding resumes and one for removing them. The Add button obviously adds resumes to your resume library (stored in the user's roaming storage folder) while the Delete button does the opposite. With each addition or removal you inspect the resulting `ResumeOperationResult` enum to see if the quota has been exceeded. If it has, you turn the title bar for the app red; otherwise, it remains null. You also check the size of your roaming storage using the `CheckStorage` method on page load. `CheckStorage` allows you to test for storage quota violations without performing any additions to or removals from the resume library. In each case, you display the app's quota and the current size (in KB) of storage in the roaming folder on the title bar. Figure 6-6 illustrates.

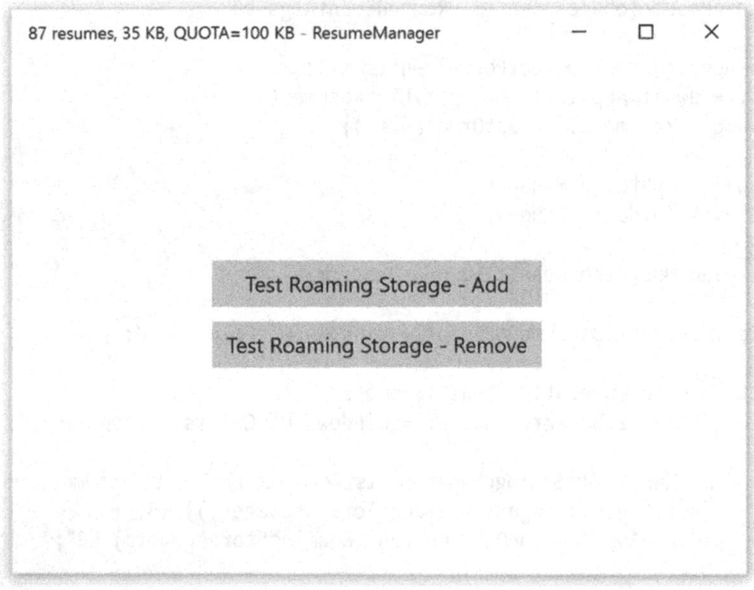

***Figure 6-6.** Reading roaming folder quota*

TemporaryFolder

The temporary store for your application is even more volatile than the package storage. Items stored in this location are only guaranteed to last as long as the currently running session of the app. Files here can be deleted by the system at any time and may even be manually removed by the user using the Disk Cleanup tool. Hence, the ideal usage of this location is as an in-application session cache, or not at all.

The User's Known Folders

Your app isn't limited to working with files in the application's isolated data store, package-install location, or the local/roaming/temporary locations just discussed. Apps built using the UWP can also access folders through the `Windows.Storage.KnownFolders` class. Table 6-2 lists some of the important `KnownFolders` properties exposed for accessing the underlying folders they represent. You can find the full list at `https://msdn.microsoft.com/library/windows/apps/windows.storage.knownfolders.aspx`.

Table 6-2. *`KnownFolders` Properties*

Property	Description
`DocumentsLibrary`	Gets the Documents library
`HomeGroup`	Gets the `HomeGroup` folder
`MediaServerDevices`	Gets the `Media Server Devices` (Digital Living Network Alliance [DLNA]) folder
`MusicLibrary`	Gets the Music library
`PicturesLibrary`	Gets the Pictures library
`RemovableDevices`	Gets the `Removable Devices` folder
`VideosLibrary`	Gets the Videos library

In order for an app to access these folders, it needs to ask the user by declaratively indicating that it intends to use a storage location other than the private ones automatically accessible to it, the app's isolated storage and package install location. In Windows 10, this is a two-step process. First, you enable the target Windows 10 library that you want access to as a *capability* your application is declaring that it uses. You can do this via the `Capabilities` section of the application manifest. In a standard UWP Windows 10 app, the app's manifest is located in the project's root folder with the name `package.appxmanifest` (see Figure 6-7).

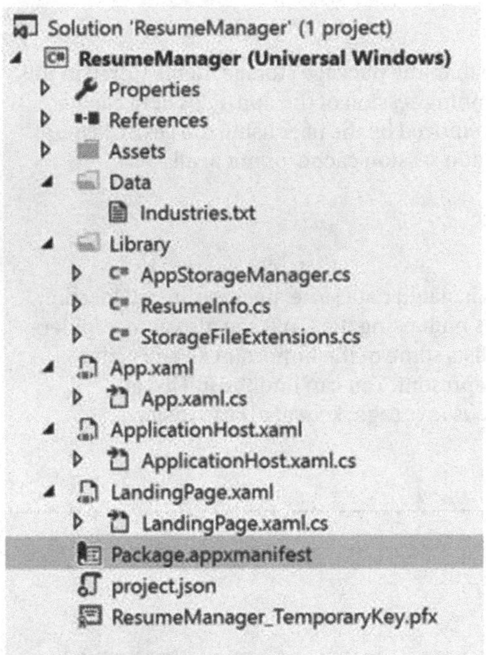

Figure 6-7. *Application manifest's location in the project structure*

When you open this file, you should see six tabs. Selecting the Capabilities tab opens the screen shown in Figure 6-8.

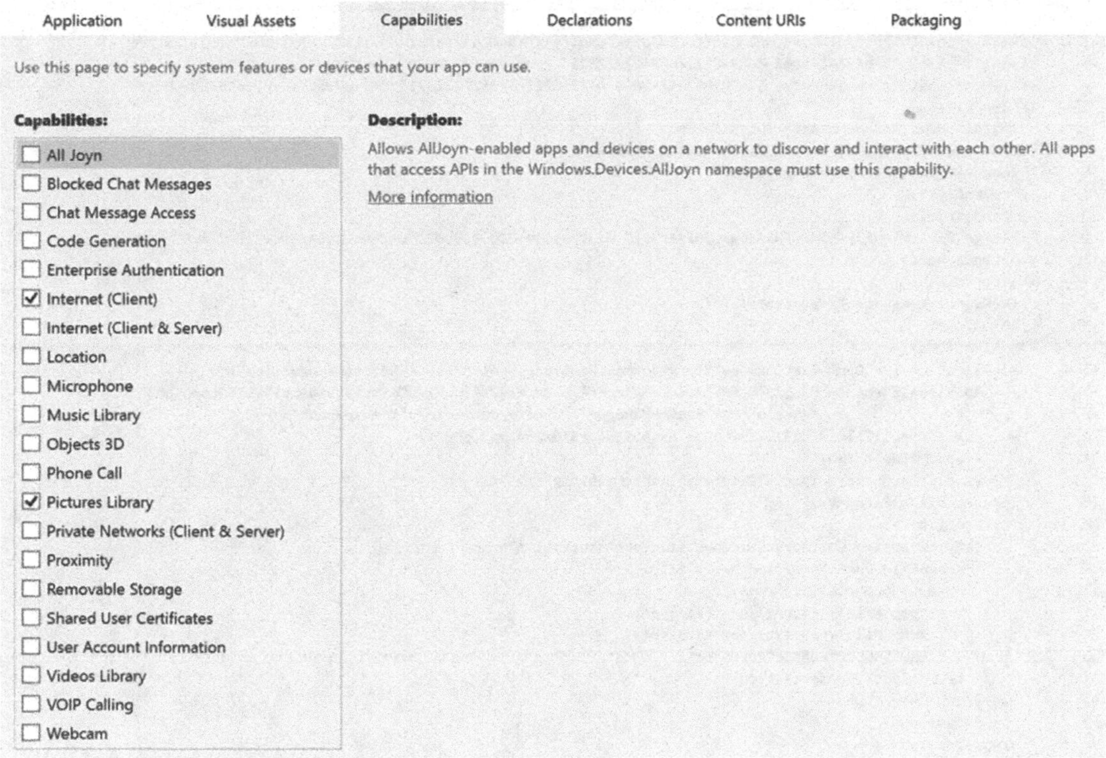

Application Visual Assets Capabilities Declarations Content URIs Packaging

Use this page to specify system features or devices that your app can use.

Capabilities:

- [ ] All Joyn
- [ ] Blocked Chat Messages
- [ ] Chat Message Access
- [ ] Code Generation
- [ ] Enterprise Authentication
- [x] Internet (Client)
- [ ] Internet (Client & Server)
- [ ] Location
- [ ] Microphone
- [ ] Music Library
- [ ] Objects 3D
- [ ] Phone Call
- [x] Pictures Library
- [ ] Private Networks (Client & Server)
- [ ] Proximity
- [ ] Removable Storage
- [ ] Shared User Certificates
- [ ] User Account Information
- [ ] Videos Library
- [ ] VOIP Calling
- [ ] Webcam

Description:

Allows AllJoyn-enabled apps and devices on a network to discover and interact with each other. All apps that access APIs in the Windows.Devices.AllJoyn namespace must use this capability.

More information

Figure 6-8. *Capabilities tab*

Selecting any one of the library capabilities (Music, Pictures, or Videos) enables access to the associated storage location through the appropriate `KnownFolder` property. The "External Known Folders" section discusses how to enable capabilities for the other three `KnownFolders` properties (`HomeGroup`, `MediaServerDevices`, and `RemovableDevices`).

■ **Note** `DocumentsLibrary` is a special capability that is actually available to you but is not listed through this user interface. To access it, right-click the `package.appxmanifest` file and select View Code. This should open up the file in its raw XML form. You can then manually add this capability to the capabilities section of the file. Although available, this capability is not meant for normal use. In most scenarios, a file picker will be ideal (and will provide a user with the choice of location where they want any app-generated files stored). Use the `DocumentsLibrary` capability to facilitate cross-platform, offline access to specific OneDrive content using valid OneDrive URLs or to save open files to the user's OneDrive automatically while offline. Figure 6-9 shows the XML for the `package.appxmanifest` and where to place the `DocumentsLibrary` capability for your app.

```
<?xml version="1.0" encoding="utf-8"?>
<Package xmlns="http://schemas.microsoft.com/appx/manifest/foundation/windows10" xmlns:mp="http://schem
  <Identity Name="0fb62a42-aa4d-4d89-8211-8b9f27222331" Publisher="CN=Me" Version="1.0.0.0" />
  <mp:PhoneIdentity PhoneProductId="0fb62a42-aa4d-4d89-8211-8b9f27222331" PhonePublisherId="00000000-00
  <Properties>
    <DisplayName>ResumeManager</DisplayName>
    <PublisherDisplayName>Me</PublisherDisplayName>
    <Logo>Assets\StoreLogo.png</Logo>
  </Properties>
  <Dependencies>
    <TargetDeviceFamily Name="Windows.Universal" MinVersion="10.0.0.0" MaxVersionTested="10.0.0.0" />
  </Dependencies>
  <Resources>
    <Resource Language="x-generate" />
  </Resources>
  <Applications>
    <Application Id="App" Executable="$targetnametoken$.exe" EntryPoint="ResumeManager.App">
      <uap:VisualElements DisplayName="ResumeManager" Square150x150Logo="Assets\Square150x150Logo.png"
                          Description="ResumeManager"   BackgroundColor="transparent">
        <uap:DefaultTile Wide310x150Logo="Assets\Wide310x150Logo.png">
        </uap:DefaultTile>
        <uap:SplashScreen Image="Assets\SplashScreen.png" />
      </uap:VisualElements>
      <Extensions>
        <uap:Extension Category="windows.fileTypeAssociation">
          <uap:FileTypeAssociation Name="files">
            <uap:SupportedFileTypes>
              <uap:FileType>.png</uap:FileType>
              <uap:FileType>.txt</uap:FileType>
            </uap:SupportedFileTypes>
          </uap:FileTypeAssociation>
        </uap:Extension>
      </Extensions>
    </Application>
  </Applications>
  <Capabilities>
    <Capability Name="internetClient" />
    <uap:Capability Name="picturesLibrary" />
    <uap:Capability Name="documentsLibrary"/>
  </Capabilities>
</Package>
```

Figure 6-9. *DocumentsLibrary capability*

Next, you must explicitly declare which file types your application reads from and writes to. You do so through the Declarations tab of the app's manifest (see Figure 6-10).

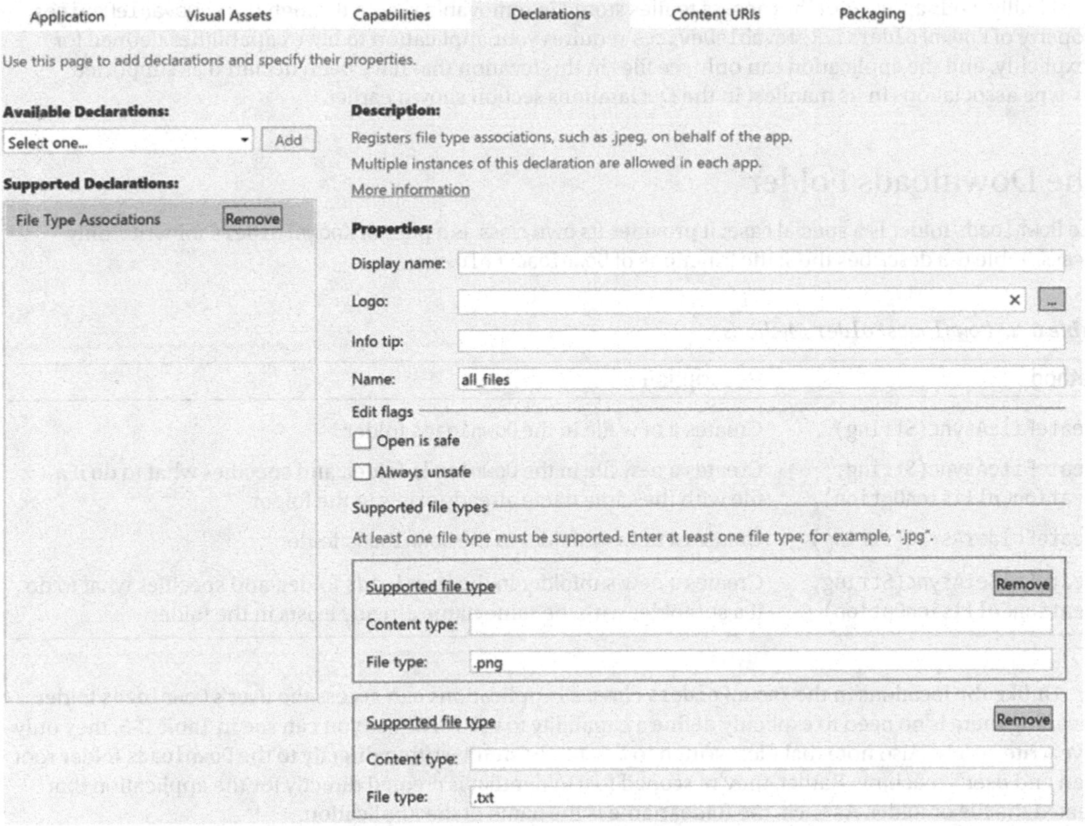

Figure 6-10. Declarations tab

You need to add a new file-type association to your app. An association must include the file extension (with the extension dot preceding it) and can optionally provide a MIME type. Additionally, the file-type association itself must have a name associated with it. Figure 6-10 shows adding a file association for text files (`.txt`) and image files (.png). You can read and write files of any kind that are associated to your application through this interface (as long as your application has access to that folder).

External Known Folders

If you request the Documents Library, Pictures Library, Music Library, or Videos Library, you can also access files on any connected media server as a storage location by using the `MediaServerDevices` property of `KnownFolders`. Note that the files you see on the device are scoped based on the capabilities you specify, meaning that if you only declare Music Library capabilities, you will see only music files on the media server to which you connect. Also note that, regardless of the capabilities you specify, you won't see documents in the Documents Library of the server you're connected to.

You can also treat your `HomeGroup` as a storage location. As with the results of `MediaServerDevices`, your app can only see the libraries declared in its manifest as capabilities. This also doesn't provide access to the HomeGroup Documents Library.

Finally, your application has access to files stored in removable media through the RemovableDevices property of KnownFolders. RemovableDevices requires your application to have capabilities defined for it explicitly, and the application can only see files in this location that have been declared as supported file-type associations in its manifest in the Declarations section shown earlier.

The Downloads Folder

The Downloads folder is a special case; it provides its own class as a peer of KnownFolders for write-only access. Table 6-3 describes the static functions of DownloadsFolder.

Table 6-3. *DownloadsFolder Methods*

Method	Description
CreateFileAsync(String)	Creates a new file in the Downloads folder
CreateFileAsync(String, CreationCollisionOption)	Creates a new file in the Downloads folder, and specifies what to do if a file with the same name already exists in the folder
CreateFolderAsync(String)	Creates a new subfolder in the Downloads folder
CreateFolderAsync(String, CreationCollisionOption)	Creates a new subfolder in the Downloads folder, and specifies what to do if a subfolder with the same name already exists in the folder

Unlike the locations in the KnownFolders class, all applications can access the user's Downloads folder (meaning there is no need to explicitly define a capability to use it), but as you can see in Table 2-5, they only have write access. Also note that files written to this folder aren't written directly to the Downloads folder root of an end user's machine. Rather, they're scoped to a folder that is created directly for the application that created the file or folder. As such, the folder name is the name of the application.

Let's take a look at the Downloads folder in action. Modify the contents of the root Grid in LandingPage.xaml so that it matches Listing 6-21.

Listing 6-21. LandingPage UI Modifications

```
<StackPanel HorizontalAlignment="Center"
            VerticalAlignment="Center">
    <ListView x:Name="list_resumes"
              ItemsSource="{x:Bind Resumes,Mode=OneWay}"
              HorizontalAlignment="Stretch"
              Height="200" />
    <Button Click="AddResume"
            HorizontalAlignment="Stretch"
            Margin="5"
            Content="Test Roaming Storage - Add" />
    <Button Click="RemoveResume"
            Margin="5"
            HorizontalAlignment="Stretch"
            Content="Test Roaming Storage - Remove" />
    <Button Click="DownloadResume"
            Margin="5"
            HorizontalAlignment="Stretch"
            Content="Download Resume" />
</StackPanel>
```

In this code, you add two new controls to the mix: a ListView that lists the resumes in your library and a button that you can use to download any selected resume. As you might imagine, the Download resume button uses the Downloads as a storage location to write the contents of the selected resume to. The code-behind adds a number of changes to LandingPage. First, you obviously need a list called Resumes (since it is the name used in the ListView declaration). Second, since you are once again utilizing databinding, you will apply the `INotifyPropertyChanged` interface. Finally, in the `Loaded` event you set the value of `Resumes` to the result of calling `ListResumes`. Listing 6-22 illustrates.

Listing 6-22. LandingPage Code-Behind Modifications

```
public sealed partial class LandingPage : Page, INotifyPropertyChanged
{
        ...
        List<string> Resumes { get; set; }
        public event PropertyChangedEventHandler PropertyChanged;

        ...
        async private void LandingPage_Loaded(object sender, RoutedEventArgs e)
        {
                Resumes = await AppStorageManager.ListResumes();
                ...
        }
        ...
        async private void DownloadResume(object sender, RoutedEventArgs e)
        {
                var selected_resume_name = list_resumes.SelectedItem as string;
                if (selected_resume_name != null)
                {
                        var resume = await AppStorageManager
                                .LoadResumeAsync(selected_resume_name);
                        var downloaded_file = await Windows.Storage.DownloadsFolder
                                .CreateFileAsync($"{selected_resume_name}.resume");
                        await downloaded_file.WriteTextAsync(resume.AsSerializedString());
                }
        }
        ...
}
```

Clicking the Download resume button when a resume named resume 87 is selected creates a file at the following location on my machine: `C:\Users\Edward Moemeka\Downloads\ResumeManager\resume 87.resume` (see Figure 6-11).

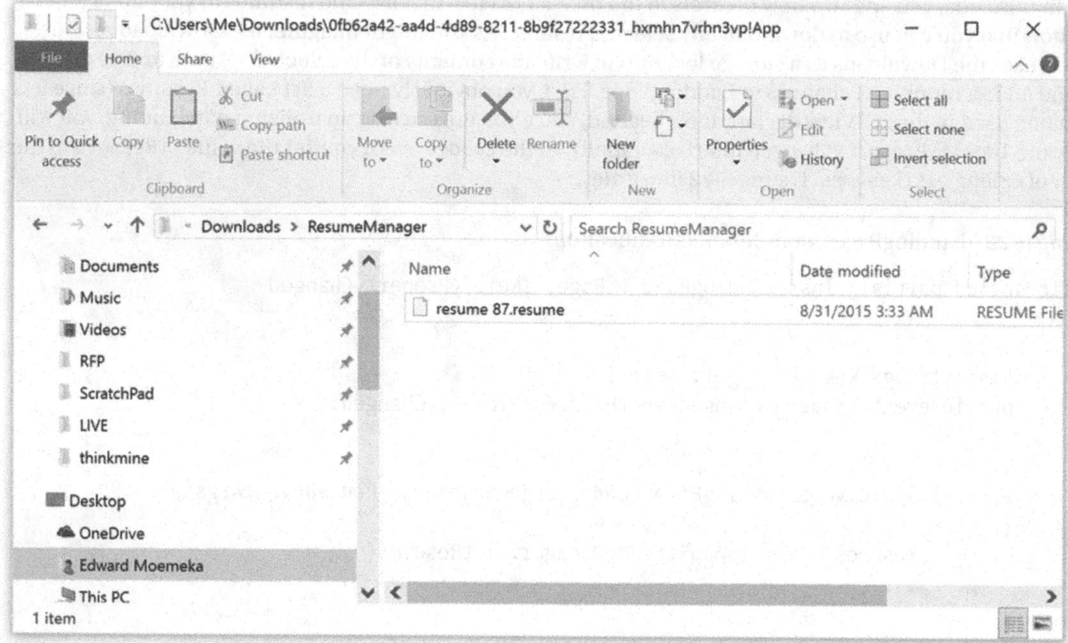

Figure 6-11. *`Downloads` folder root for the `ResumeManager` application*

■ **Note** The folder location `ResumeManager` is an alias for the actual folder name. You can see the actual folder path on the title bar of Windows Explorer above.

Final Thoughts on Storage via the ApplicationData Class

Regardless of what store you use for your file I/O functions, the `ApplicationData` object offers additional services that can help manage it. For instance, `ApplicationData.SetVersionAsync` allows you to change the application data format used in a future release of your app without causing compatibility problems with previous releases of the app.

You can also use `ApplicationData` to clear your Windows cache by calling `ApplicationData.ClearAsync()`. Note that this function clears the data from all storage locations associated with the application. An overloaded method exists for this function that targets a specified location.

Using Pickers

Dialogs are a mainstay in the pantheon of Windows applications. They provide a simple, elegant, yet powerful alternative to launching full-blown windows. Dialogs are typically used to prompt the user for some action, but in cases where you wish to save a file to or load a file from a user-defined location they are invaluable. The great thing about using dialogs in this way is that they allow you to access locations ordinarily impossible to reach using the UWP.

In the previous section, you used the user's Downloads folder to store a resume that they selected. There are certainly reasons why this might be the choice you make as an app developer but in general this would probably not be the best user experience when simply trying to provide the user with a way to access the content they have created through your app. You simply cannot expect your users to continually go to the Downloads folder in order to get documents exported from your app. A better is to provide them with a means to decide where they want the file stored and even what name they want to give the file.

Windows.Storage.Pickers.FileSavePicker provides this functionality in UWP apps. Like the SaveFileDialog of old, it allows the user to select the folder where they want a file saved, pick file types that will be allowed, and even provide a suggested name for the file. In Listing 6-23, you enhance your Download button to use FileSavePicker.

Listing 6-23. DownloadResume Event Handler

```
async private void DownloadResume(object sender, RoutedEventArgs e)
{
        var selected_resume_name = list_resumes.SelectedItem as string;
        if (selected_resume_name != null)
        {
                var resume = await AppStorageManager.
                                        LoadResumeAsync(selected_resume_name);

                FileSavePicker saver = new FileSavePicker();
                saver.DefaultFileExtension = ".resume";
                saver.SuggestedFileName = "my file";
                saver.FileTypeChoices.Add("ResumeManager File",
                                        new List<string>() { ".resume" });

                var new_file = await saver.PickSaveFileAsync();
                if (new_file != null)
                {
                        await new_file.WriteTextAsync(resume.AsSerializedString());
                }
        }
}
```

Conversely, the FileOpenPicker class (found in the same namespace as FileSavePicker) can be used to read files from locations your app would normally not have any access to. Like FileSavePicker, it is a user prompt. You will use this dialog to implement an Import Resume feature in your app. For this feature to work, it will need to

- Read the file being imported
- Attempt to deserialize it to a resume (if this fails let the user know (with a message dialog)
- Use the save resume functionality to save the item
- Refresh the Resumes list with the new list of resumes controlled by the app
- Once saved, notify the databinding framework of the change to the Resumes list

You start by adding a new button to LandingPage that users will use to trigger this functionality. The code in Listing 6-24 should be added to the Add Resume button.

Listing 6-24. ImportResume Button UI

```
<Button Click="ImportResume"
             Margin="5"
             HorizontalAlignment="Stretch"
             Content="Import Resume" />
```

The code-behind for this button is shown in Listing 6-25.

Listing 6-25. ImportResume Event Handler

```
async private void ImportResume(object sender, RoutedEventArgs e)
{
        var app_view = ApplicationView.GetForCurrentView();

        FileOpenPicker opener = new FileOpenPicker();
        opener.ViewMode = PickerViewMode.Thumbnail;
        opener.SuggestedStartLocation = PickerLocationId.Desktop;
        opener.CommitButtonText = "Import the resume";
        opener.FileTypeFilter.Add(".resume");
        var selected_file = await opener.PickSingleFileAsync();
        if (selected_file != null)
        {
                //read and deserialize resume
                var file_text = await selected_file.ReadTextAsync();
                var resume = Resume.FromSerializedString(file_text);

                if (resume == null)
                {
                        MessageDialog md = new MessageDialog("Cannot read resume data.");
                        await md.ShowAsync();
                        return;
                }

                //name resume
                int current_storage_count = (await AppStorageManager.ListResumes()).Count;
                resume.Name = $"resume [{Guid.NewGuid()}]";
                Resumes = await AppStorageManager.ListResumes();
                PropertyChanged?.Invoke(this, new PropertyChangedEventArgs("Resumes"));

                //now store the resume in AppData
                var result = await AppStorageManager.
                SaveResumeAsync(resume, CreationCollisionOption.GenerateUniqueName);
                if (result == ResumeOperationResult.SuccessOverLimit)
                {
                        app_view.TitleBar.BackgroundColor = Windows.UI.Colors.Red;
                }
                var resume_list = await AppStorageManager.ListResumes();
                app_view.Title = $"{resume_list.Count} resumes, {(await ↵
                                AppStorageManager.GetTotalStorage())} KB, ↵
                                QUOTA={ApplicationData.Current.RoamingStorageQuota} KB";
        }
}
```

Note that you also modify the SaveResume method to accept CreationCollisionOption as an optional parameter into the method. The new method definition is shown in Listing 6-26.

Listing 6-26. SaveResume Method Declaration Changes

```
async public static Task<ResumeOperationResult> SaveResumeAsync(Resume resume,
                        CreationCollisionOption creation_option = CreationCollisionOption.
                        OpenIfExists)
```

Finally, let's add the lines highlighted in Listing 6-26 to the other state-changing functions in AppStorageManager (the methods for saving and deleting resumes) so that the ListView always reflects an accurate list of resumes being managed by the app. The new add and remove event handlers are shown in Listing 6-27.

Listing 6-27. RemoveResume Event Handler

```
async private void RemoveResume(object sender, RoutedEventArgs e)
{
        var app_view = ApplicationView.GetForCurrentView();
        var resume_list = await AppStorageManager.ListResumes();
        var oldest_resume = resume_list.LastOrDefault();

        var result = await AppStorageManager.
                DeleteResume(oldest_resume);
        Resumes = await AppStorageManager.ListResumes();
        PropertyChanged?.Invoke(this, new PropertyChangedEventArgs("Resumes"));
        _count--;
        if (result == ResumeOperationResult.SuccessOverLimit)
        {
                app_view.TitleBar.BackgroundColor = Windows.UI.Colors.Red;
        }
        else if (result == ResumeOperationResult.Success)
                app_view.TitleBar.BackgroundColor = null;

        app_view.Title = $"{(await AppStorageManager.ListResumes()).Count} ↵
                        resumes, {(await AppStorageManager.GetTotalStorage())} KB, ↵
                        QUOTA={ApplicationData.Current.RoamingStorageQuota} KB";

}

async private void AddResume(object sender, RoutedEventArgs e)
{
        var app_view = ApplicationView.GetForCurrentView();
        var result = await AppStorageManager.
                SaveResumeAsync(new Resume() { Name = $"resume {_count}" });
        Resumes = await AppStorageManager.ListResumes();
        PropertyChanged?.Invoke(this, new PropertyChangedEventArgs("Resumes"));
        if (result == ResumeOperationResult.SuccessOverLimit)
        {
                app_view.TitleBar.BackgroundColor = Windows.UI.Colors.Red;
        }
        var resume = await AppStorageManager.LoadResumeAsync($"resume {_count}");
        var resume_list = await AppStorageManager.ListResumes();
```

```
                    app_view.Title = $"{resume_list.Count} resumes, ↵
                    {(await AppStorageManager.GetTotalStorage())} KB, ↵
                    QUOTA={ApplicationData.Current.RoamingStorageQuota} KB";
        _count++;
}
```

The UWP also allows you to select folders where you can store items using the `FolderPicker` class (in the same namespace). Given that these files and folders being exposed by the user to your app are not normally available to the user, the UWP provides a mechanism to allow you to access them directly without user prompting once a user has given the initial access (by selecting the storage item through the dialog system). Any storage item you need access to beyond the initial interaction provided through the pickers we discussed can be made available to you if you add them to the future access list. This list simply tells Windows that you will need to access the file/folder at a later time. As long as you have an instance of a storage file or storage folder, it can be added to this list using the following: `Windows.Storage.AccessCache.StorageApplicationPermissions.FutureAccessList`. The class also provides mechanisms to manage the list.

Sharing Files with Custom Pickers

Occasionally you might want to manage the manner in which files exposed by your app are accessed. It might not make sense to force a user to export items one by one to a certain location and might make less sense to simply copy your app contents away in an unmanaged manner. In such cases, your app might benefit from exposing itself as a picker, such that other apps will see a customized view of the contents in the app and be able to save or open content in a way that appears as native as the pickers you have been using thus far. The Windows 10 UWP introduces a means of doing this with the open and save file picker contracts. These constructs allow you to expose your internal file system to other apps on the system such that your app appears embedded in the standard Windows save and open dialogs, right alongside other folders and apps in the system. The one caveat to doing this is that it only works within the modern UWP app world. Native win32 apps are not exposed to this sharing feature inherently. In Chapter 11, we will talk more about communicating between apps.

In the following section, you will modify the code base you have created so far to allow for extending your local storage out to other apps on the system. As part of this exercise, you will clean up some of the classes you created. The first thing you need to do before that, however, is to declaratively notify the platform that your app will be providing a file save and file open dialog. You accomplish this through the app manifest.

Open up your project's app manifest and navigate to the Declarations tab. Use the Available Declarations drop-down to add File Open Picker and File Save Picker to the list of declarations your app makes. For each, ensure that the checkbox labeled "Supports any file type" is unchecked then add a new supported file type called ".resume". Figure 6-12 shows a portion of the declarations tab with a supported file type declared.

Available Declarations:
Select one... Add
Supported Declarations:
File Open Picker Remove
File Save Picker
File Type Associations
Description:
Registers the app as a file open picker, making the content in the app available to other Windows Store apps.
Only one instance of this declaration is allowed per app.
More information
Properties:
Supported file types
At least one file type must be supported. Either select "Supports any file type", or enter at least one specific file type; for example, ".jpg".
Supports any file type
Supported file type Remove
File type: .resume
Add New

Figure 6-12. File Open Picker declaration

You have been using the standard .xml file type to describe your resumes up to this point (mostly because the data contract serializer converts your resume object into an XML document). It is fine to continue to use XML as the underlying storage format but you need a way to distinguish your specific resume XML from just any old XML. This is very important when you start integrating yourself into an OS. You would not want to attempt to open and read just any XML; conversely, you would not want a program expecting XML to unpack and damage your well-defined resume format. For this reason, you will use a custom file format ".resume" as the file type (read file extension) for your resume files. While you are in the app manifest, add a file type association to the .resume file type as well. Once complete, your file type associations declaration should have the three items shown in Figure 6-13.

At least one file type must be supported. Enter at least one file type; for example, ".jpg".
Supported file type Remove
Content type:
File type: .png
Supported file type Remove
Content type:
File type: .txt
Supported file type Remove
Content type:
File type: .resume
Add New

Figure 6-13. ".resume" file type association

You are now done with configuring the app through the manifest and can focus on implementation. To that end, you now need to go back to your AppStorageManager class and ensure that it is storing all your resume objects with the .resume file extension. Before doing that, though, you have some tidying up to do in the Resume class. So far, you have been using the name of the resume to identify it. This can obviously become error prone so you will change it to use a unique identifier. In the interest of encapsulation and having clean code that is easy to read, you should also move some of the resume-specific file access functionality out of AppStorageManager and directly into the Resume class. Your app so far has been relying on the resume names for finding the resume; this will not always hold true. A better approach is to store a compact form of the resume, and when detailed information is needed, expand that smaller version into the full blown version you expect. At this juncture, you have not gotten to the point where you are even populating the resumes, so for now you can still get away with simply loading the entire resume into memory for each resume file. With that in mind, there are several changes you need to make to the class to accommodate the approach. Listing 6-28 shows the new ResumeInfo.cs with only the methods that have been modified in some way (or are new).

Listing 6-28. ResumeInfo.cs Changes

```
public class Resume
{
        public string ResumeID { get; set; } = Guid.NewGuid().ToString();
              StorageFile File { get; set; }
        ...

        public StorageFile GetFile()
        {
                return File;
        }

        async public Task DeleteAsync()
        {
                await File.DeleteAsync(StorageDeleteOption.PermanentDelete);
        }

        ...


        async public static Task<Resume> FromStorageFileAsync(StorageFile file)
        {
                var resume = FromSerializedString(await file.ReadTextAsync());
                resume.File = file;
                return resume;
        }
}
```

You haven't made much of a change, but the impact of the subtle shift from resume name to a uniquely identifiable id, allowing the resume to essentially delete itself, and allowing a resume to be created directly from a storage file will make a huge difference in readability.

Next, you move onto the AppStorageManager to modify it so it utilizes the changes you just implemented in Resume. The principal change here is the shift from having all state (except the resume name) read directly from the file system to using an in-memory store that is backed by the file system. Listing 6-29 highlights the new or modified pieces of AppStorageManager.

Listing 6-29. SaveResumeAsync Changes

```
async public static Task<ResumeOperationResult> SaveResumeAsync(Resume resume,
        CreationCollisionOption creation_option = CreationCollisionOption.OpenIfExists)
{
        await CreateOrOpenFolder("resumes");
        ResumeOperationResult result = ResumeOperationResult.Success;

        if (resume.Name != null)
        {
                //write model string to file
                var file = await ApplicationData.Current
                                    .RoamingFolder
                                        .CreateFileAsync ↵
                            ($"resumes\\{resume.ResumeID}.resume", ↵
                            creation_option);
                await file.WriteTextAsync(resume.AsSerializedString());

                var total_storage = await AppStorageManager.GetTotalStorage();
                if (total_storage > ApplicationData.Current.RoamingStorageQuota)
                {
                        result = ResumeOperationResult.SuccessOverLimit;
                }
        }
        else
        {
                throw new Exception("Resume objects require a name.");
        }
        return result;
}

async public static Task<Resume> LoadResumeAsync(string resume_id)
{
        try
        {
                if (!string.IsNullOrWhiteSpace(resume_id))
                {
                        var file = await ApplicationData.Current
                                            .RoamingFolder
                                                .GetFileAsync($"resumes\\{resume_id}.resume");
                        var resume_xml = await file.ReadTextAsync();
                        var resume = Resume.FromSerializedString(resume_xml);
                        return resume;
                }
        }
        catch (Exception ex)
        {

        }
        return null;
}
```

```
async public static Task<StorageFile> GetResumeFileAsync(string resume_id)
{
        try
        {
                if (!string.IsNullOrWhiteSpace(resume_id))
                {
                        var file = await ApplicationData.Current
                                                .RoamingFolder
                                                .GetFileAsync($"resumes\\{resume_id}.
                                                resume");
                        return file;
                }
        }
        catch (Exception ex)
        {

        }
        return null;
}

async public static Task<ResumeOperationResult> DeleteResume(Resume resume)
{
        ResumeOperationResult result = ResumeOperationResult.Success;
        try
        {
                await resume.DeleteAsync();
                var total_storage = await AppStorageManager.GetTotalStorage();
                if (total_storage > ApplicationData.Current.RoamingStorageQuota)
                {
                        result = ResumeOperationResult.SuccessOverLimit;
                }
        }
        catch (Exception ex)
        {
                result = ResumeOperationResult.Failure;
        }
        return result;
}

async public static Task<List<Resume>> ListResumes()
{
        var folder = await CreateOrOpenFolder("resumes");
        var files = await folder.GetFilesAsync();

        List<Resume> resumes = new List<Resume>();
        foreach (var file in files)
        {
                try
                {
                        var resume = await Resume.FromStorageFileAsync(file);
                        resumes.Add(resume);
                }
```

```
                catch { }
        }
        return resumes;
}

async public static Task ClearStorageAsync()
{
        var folder = await CreateOrOpenFolder("resumes");
        var files = await folder.GetFilesAsync();
        foreach (var file in files)
        {
                await file.DeleteAsync();
        }
}
```

Again, the changes here are quite minor. In most of the methods you have merely changed the file extension used for the resume files from .xml to .resume. In DeleteResume, you are now using the resume instance's DeleteAsync call instead of explicitly deleting the file within the method. Finally, to help with debugging and file management you have added a ClearStorageAsync method that does what the name implies.

The file dialogs work like controls in that they are embedded into another user interface rather than having their own windowing infrastructure. In Figure 6-14, you see the standard File Open dialog we all know and love. At the bottom there is a tree node for your UWP app, ResumeManager. When your app declares the File Open and File Save contracts, an icon for your app will be available to select from the file picker dialog, just like this.

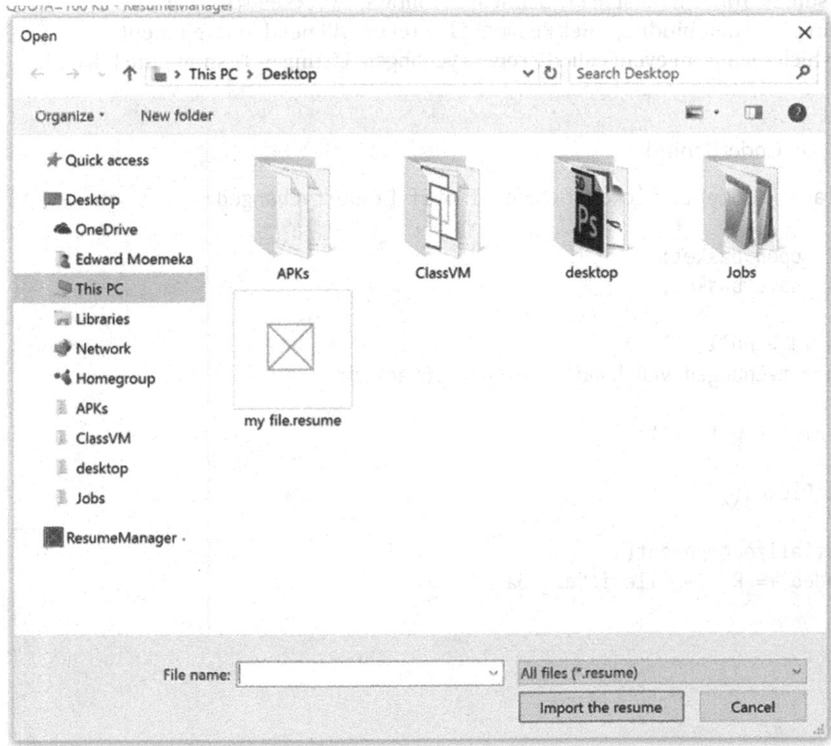

Figure 6-14. *File Open Picker with custom picker for ResumeManager*

When this item is clicked, the content area to the right of this navigation tree will be used to present the custom user interface you want to use for representing the files that the user can pick. This user interface must be rendered by the app that declared itself a custom picker. Let's create a user interface for your picker.

Start by adding a new page to the ResumeManager project called ResumeFilePicker and replace the contents of the XAML view associated with this class with the code from Listing 6-30.

Listing 6-30. ResumeFilePicker UI

```
<Grid>
    <ListView Margin="10,0"
                              DisplayMemberPath="Name"
            ItemsSource="{x:Bind Resumes, Mode=OneWay}"
            SelectionChanged="ResumeListSelectionChanged"
            SelectionMode="Single" />

</Grid>
```

Pretty simple, huh? But if you think about it a little, you will find that it makes very good sense. Open up Explorer and examine the content area; you will find a simple user interface designed specifically for selection and hierarchical navigation. It's perfect, so why spoil it? When you build custom pickers like this, you must bear in mind that users may not have a deep understanding of your specific app. Contracts such as this exist in the "public" area of a person's computer. Doing crazy things within your app is one thing, but behaving badly out there will get you uninstalled and ranked low very quickly!

The code-behind for `ResumeFilePicker` is where all the magic happens. As always, you need a place to store the data being databound through compiled binding. You should know by now from the XAML definition must be called Resumes. You will most likely define it as follows: `List<Resume> Resumes { get; set; }`. Again, as part of the databinding spiel, `ResumeFilePicker` will need to implement `INotifyPropertyChanged`, which means an event called `PropertyChanged`. Listing 6-31 shows the full code for `ResumeFilePicker`.

Listing 6-31. ResumeFilePicker Code-Behind

```
public sealed partial class ResumeFilePicker : Page, INotifyPropertyChanged
{
        FileOpenPickerUI _open_basket;
        FileSavePickerUI _save_basket;
        bool _saving;
        string _previous_id = null;
        public event PropertyChangedEventHandler PropertyChanged;

        List<Resume> Resumes { get; set; }

        public ResumeFilePicker()
        {
                this.InitializeComponent();
                this.Loaded += ResumeFilePicker_Loaded;

        }
```

```
async private void ResumeFilePicker_Loaded(object sender, RoutedEventArgs e)
{
        Resumes = await AppStorageManager.ListResumes();
        PropertyChanged?.Invoke(this, new PropertyChangedEventArgs("Resumes"));
}

public void Activate(FileOpenPickerActivatedEventArgs args)
{
        _saving = false;
        _open_basket = args.FileOpenPickerUI;
        Window.Current.Content = this;
        Window.Current.Activate();
}

public void Activate(FileSavePickerActivatedEventArgs args)
{
        _saving = true;
        _save_basket = args.FileSavePickerUI;
        _save_basket.TargetFileRequested += _save_basket_TargetFileRequested;
        Window.Current.Content = this;
        Window.Current.Activate();
}

async void _save_basket_TargetFileRequested(FileSavePickerUI sender,
                                TargetFileRequestedEventArgs args)
{
        var deferral = args.Request.GetDeferral();
        args.Request.TargetFile = await ApplicationData.Current
                                .RoamingFolder
                                    .CreateFileAsync ↵
                                ($"resumes\\{_save_basket.FileName}", ↵
                                CreationCollisionOption.GenerateUniqueName);
        deferral.Complete();
}

async private void ResumeListSelectionChanged(object sender,
SelectionChangedEventArgs e)
{
        if (!_saving)
        {
                var grid_view = sender as ListView;
                var resume = grid_view.SelectedItem as Resume;
                var resume_file = resume?.GetFile();
                if (resume_file != null)
                {
                        if (_previous_id != null)
                                _open_basket.RemoveFile(_previous_id);
```

```
                        _open_basket.AddFile(resume.ResumeID, resume_file);
                        _open_basket.Title = $"{resume.Name} selected";
                        _previous_id = resume.ResumeID;

                    }
                    else
                        await new MessageDialog("Resume is null").ShowAsync();
            }

        }

}
```

The logic here is one you will find used a lot for this kind of thing. In your case, you are using one class to serve as the user interface and controller for two distinct activities: saving a file and opening a file. The Boolean value `_saving` is used to delineate that distinction. When the file picker is activated, the argument passed into your app will determine which version of your `Activate` methods is executed. All the `Activate` method does is store an instance of the user interface object associated with the activation locally and then set `ResumeFilePicker` as the main content for the current window. This window is not the one we were previously discussing. You can think of this window as being essentially that content area to the right of your navigation menu from Figure 6-16. For file saving there's an additional event that you subscribe to that simply creates a file in your store and returns it to the calling app so it can use it to write content to your storage area. When an item in the ListView is selected, you retrieve the associated resume, get the file associated with that resume (through the GetFile function), and write that file back into the Open file dialog UI. A consuming app can then take that file and read its contents.

To enable the Activate methods to be called you must override some methods your app class. Open `App.xaml.cs` and add the code from Listing 6-32.

Listing 6-32. File Picker Activation Overrides in App.xaml.cs

```
protected override void OnFileOpenPickerActivated
                                        (FileOpenPickerActivatedEventArgs args)
{
        new ResumeFilePicker().Activate(args);
}

protected override void OnFileSavePickerActivated
                                        (FileSavePickerActivatedEventArgs args)
{
        new ResumeFilePicker().Activate(args);
}
```

When the icon for your app is pressed in the Open or Save dialog, the app does not start in a normal manner. It is not "launched;" it is "activated." Because of this, for these special cases `OnLaunched` is not called; rather (based on the type of activation that occurred), the appropriate override is called directly. Just as you do when launching the app as a whole, you must instantiate what will be the root user interface object for your app. In your case, you are using `ResumeFilePicker`.

At this point, you are basically done as far as implementing a file dialog. If you have any Modern apps on your system (apps based on WinRT/UWP) that have open file pickers, you should see the node for ResumeManager on your file picker user interface. Note that this will NOT show up for non-UWP apps at the time of this writing.

As a final step, you need to modify your landing page to utilize some of the changes you made to the object model of the app. Listing 6-33 shows the revised user interface for LandingPage.

Listing 6-33. LandingPage UI Changes

```
<Grid Background="{ThemeResource ApplicationPageBackgroundThemeBrush}">
    <ScrollViewer VerticalScrollBarVisibility="Auto"
                  VerticalScrollMode="Auto">
        <StackPanel HorizontalAlignment="Stretch"
                    VerticalAlignment="Center">
            <ListView x:Name="list_resumes"
                      ItemsSource="{x:Bind Resumes,Mode=OneWay}"
                      DisplayMemberPath="Name"
                      HorizontalAlignment="Stretch"
                      Height="300"
                      Margin="100,10,100,10" />
            <StackPanel Width="300">
                <Button Click="AddResume"
                        HorizontalAlignment="Stretch"
                        Margin="5"
                        Content="Test Roaming Storage - Add" />
                <Button Click="ImportResume"
                        Margin="5"
                        HorizontalAlignment="Stretch"
                        Content="Import Resume" />
                <Button Click="RemoveResume"
                        Margin="5"
                        HorizontalAlignment="Stretch"
                        Content="Test Roaming Storage - Remove" />
                <Button Click="ExportResume"
                        Margin="5"
                        HorizontalAlignment="Stretch"
                        Content="Save Resume" />
                <Button Click="ClearLibrary"
                        Margin="5"
                        HorizontalAlignment="Stretch"
                        Content="Clear Library" />
                <Button Click="SelectLibrary"
                        Margin="5,5,5,50"
                        HorizontalAlignment="Stretch"
                        Content="Select Library" />
            </StackPanel>

        </StackPanel>
    </ScrollViewer>

</Grid>
```

You've streamlined and cleaned up the code-behind with a tweak here and there to enhance readability. Listing 6-34 illustrates.

Listing 6-34. LandingPage Code-Behind Changes

```
public sealed partial class LandingPage : Page, INotifyPropertyChanged
{
        StorageFolder _library_folder;
        int _count = 0;
        List<Resume> Resumes { get; set; }

        public event PropertyChangedEventHandler PropertyChanged;

        public LandingPage()
        {
                this.InitializeComponent();
                this.Loaded += LandingPage_Loaded;
        }

        async private void LandingPage_Loaded(object sender, RoutedEventArgs e)
        {
                _count = (await AppStorageManager.ListResumes()).Count;
                await RefreshUIAsync();
        }

        async Task RefreshUIAsync(ResumeOperationResult? result = null)
        {
                var app_view = ApplicationView.GetForCurrentView();
                var resume_list = await AppStorageManager.ListResumes();
                app_view.Title = $"{resume_list.Count} resumes, {(await ➥
                                AppStorageManager.GetTotalStorage())} KB, ➥
                                QUOTA={ApplicationData.Current.RoamingStorageQuota} KB";
                Resumes = resume_list;
                PropertyChanged?.Invoke(this, new PropertyChangedEventArgs("Resumes"));

                if (result != null)
                {
                        if (result == ResumeOperationResult.SuccessOverLimit)
                        {
                                app_view.TitleBar.BackgroundColor = Windows.UI.Colors.Red;
                        }
                        else
                                app_view.TitleBar.BackgroundColor = null;
                }
        }

        async private void AddResume(object sender, RoutedEventArgs e)
        {
                var result = await AppStorageManager.
                        SaveResumeAsync(new Resume() { Name = $"Resume {_count}" });
                _count++;

                await RefreshUIAsync(result);
        }
```

```
async private void RemoveResume(object sender, RoutedEventArgs e)
{
        var resume_list = await AppStorageManager.ListResumes();
        var oldest_resume = resume_list.LastOrDefault();

        var result = await AppStorageManager.
                DeleteResume(oldest_resume);
        _count--;
        await RefreshUIAsync(result);
}

async private void ExportResume(object sender, RoutedEventArgs e)
{
        var app_view = ApplicationView.GetForCurrentView();
        var selected_resume = list_resumes.SelectedItem as Resume;
        if (selected_resume != null)
        {
                var resume = selected_resume;

                FileSavePicker saver = new FileSavePicker();
                saver.DefaultFileExtension = ".resume";
                saver.SuggestedFileName = "my file";
                saver.FileTypeChoices
                        .Add("ResumeManager File", new List<string>() { ".resume"
});

                var new_file = await saver.PickSaveFileAsync();
                if (new_file != null)
                {
                        var new_resume_id = Guid.NewGuid().ToString();
                        resume.Name = $"resume import [{new_resume_id}]";
                        resume.ResumeID = new_resume_id;
                        await new_file.WriteTextAsync(resume.AsSerializedString());
                        await RefreshUIAsync();
                }
        }
        else
        {
                await new MessageDialog("Select a resume first").ShowAsync();
        }
}

async private void ImportResume(object sender, RoutedEventArgs e)
{
        var app_view = ApplicationView.GetForCurrentView();

        FileOpenPicker opener = new FileOpenPicker();
        opener.ViewMode = PickerViewMode.Thumbnail;
        opener.SuggestedStartLocation = PickerLocationId.Desktop;
        opener.CommitButtonText = "Import the resume";
```

```
            opener.FileTypeFilter.Add(".resume");
            var selected_file = await opener.PickSingleFileAsync();
            if (selected_file != null)
            {
                    //read and deserialize resume
                    var resume = await Resume.FromStorageFileAsync(selected_file);

                    if (resume == null)
                    {
                            MessageDialog md = new MessageDialog("Cannot read resume
                            data.");
                            await md.ShowAsync();
                            return;
                    }

                    //name resume
                    var new_resume_id = Guid.NewGuid().ToString();
                            int current_storage_count = (await AppStorageManager.
                            ListResumes()).Count;
                    resume.Name = $"resume import [{new_resume_id}]";
                    resume.ResumeID = new_resume_id;

                    //now store the resume in AppData
                    var result = await AppStorageManager.
                    SaveResumeAsync(resume, CreationCollisionOption.GenerateUniqueName);
                    await RefreshUIAsync(result);
            }
    }

    async private void SelectLibrary(object sender, RoutedEventArgs e)
    {
            FolderPicker picker = new FolderPicker();
            picker.ViewMode = PickerViewMode.Thumbnail;
            picker.SuggestedStartLocation = PickerLocationId.Desktop;
            picker.CommitButtonText = "Select this location";
            picker.FileTypeFilter.Add(".resume");
            _library_folder = await picker.PickSingleFolderAsync();
            if (_library_folder != null)
            {
                    Windows.Storage.AccessCache
                            .StorageApplicationPermissions
                            .FutureAccessList.Add(_library_folder);
            }
    }

    async private void ClearLibrary(object sender, RoutedEventArgs e)
    {
            await AppStorageManager.ClearStorageAsync();
            await RefreshUIAsync();
    }
}
```

When this app is run (note that it cannot be run in debug mode) and you use the pickers to pick items, you should see windows in the open picker similar to Figures 6-15 and 6-16.

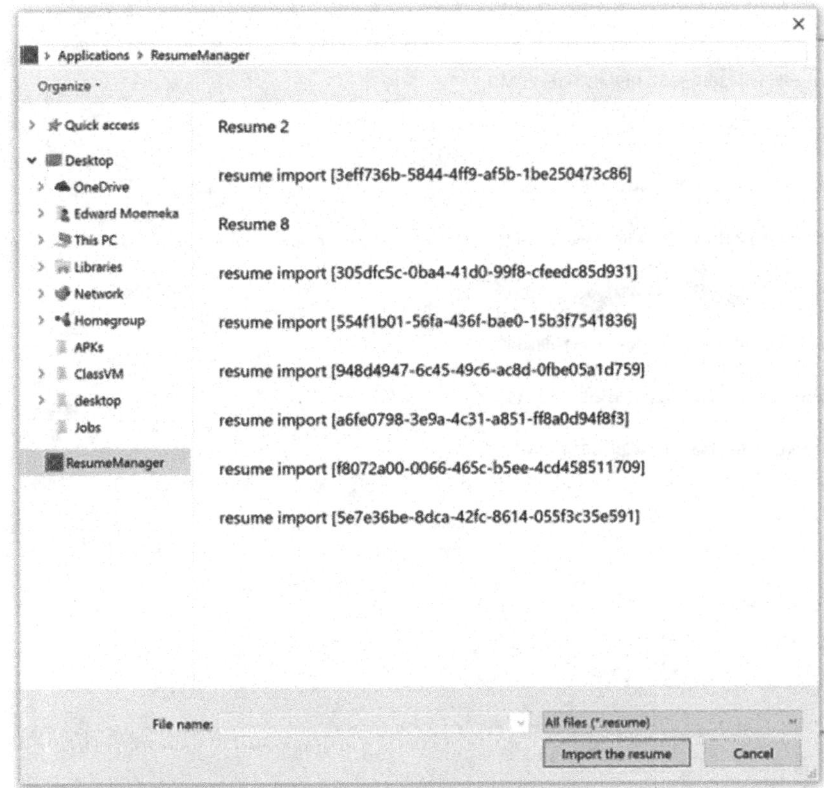

Figure 6-15. *Custom file open picker for ResumeManager*

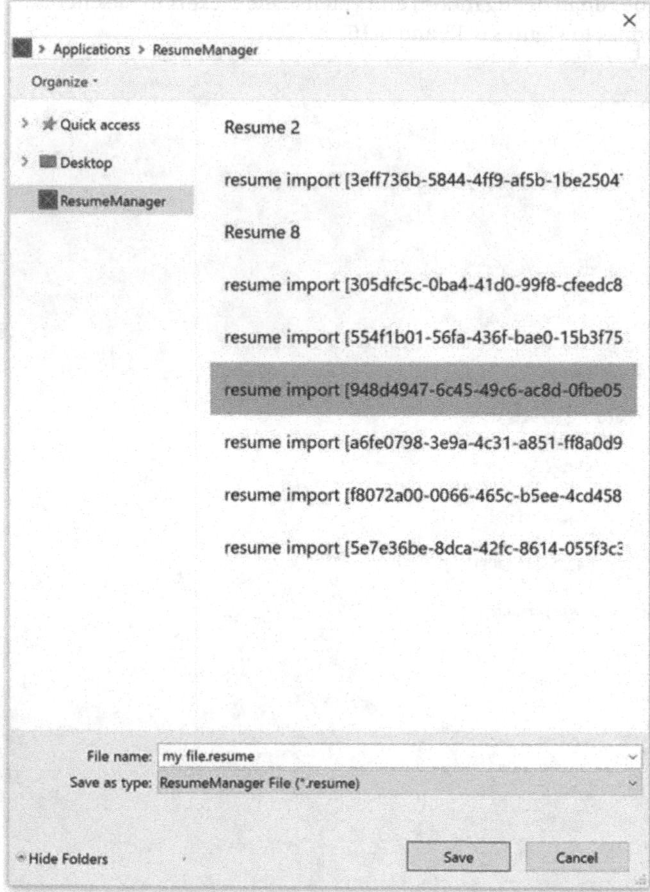

Figure 6-16. *Custom file save picker for ResumeManager*

Summary

This chapter went through some core IO workflows that a developer must master when developing Windows 10 apps. You should have gained an understanding of reading from and writing to the file system as well as what storage locations are. Here is an overview of what you learned in Chapter 6:

- The role of storage locations, and that certain locations are available to an application by default and other locations require you to explicitly declare capabilities through the application manifest.
- File pickers for saving files and opening files. You also learned the value of using pickers when you need to access locations normally unavailable to your app.
- Custom file picker dialogs, how they work in Windows 10, and when to use and not use such devices in your applications.
- Folder pickers and how to maintain access to a folder location that has been granted to you by the user.
- How to create a ResumeManager project.

CHAPTER 7

Working with Media

Media experiences have long been a weakness in Microsoft platforms, but not because those features aren't inherently available in the system. Windows provides a wide spectrum of built-in playback and management features. The area in which the platform has fallen short is in the exposing of media content-creation and -management facilities to the developers in an experience consistent with the programming paradigms they have marketed to us over the years. If you know DirectX or any of the low-level APIs, then you're good to go as far as this. But the reach of such technologies has traditionally not fallen far from organizations with the funding to hire resources with that knowledge.

Microsoft continues the strides introduced with Windows 8 with the release of Windows 10 through Windows Store apps, which have a programming interface that has been designed to ensure the delivery of modern, fast, and fluid applications. As a full-spectrum content-creation and -consumption platform, Windows 10 rises above the rest with its broad range of media support capabilities exposed to developers through the UWP. In this chapter, you will explore the many ways that you as a developer can incorporate media into your app. You will explore rendering and playing back media, and you'll be introduced to the numerous ways that media can be captured through your UWP app.

Creating a New Project

To help highlight the media features available to UWP developers, your next project will be for an entertainment company. Big Mountain Xochials (pronounced "socials") Theater Company is a small, traveling media and entertainment group focused on live entertainment experiences on the go. They feature comedians, stage acting, singers, poets, and live music. They are interested in generating interest in their performances by building a Windows 10 app that shows highlights of previous shows, gives users the ability to order full recorded shows, buy tickets to upcoming shows, view their calendar, and much more. They expect this app to provide a full multimedia experience to their end user.

Open Visual Studio 2015 and select File ➤ New ➤ Project. Select Blank App (Universal Windows) from the New Project dialog that appears. Call the project BigMountainX and click Ok. You are going to use this project in this chapter as a platform to explore the many things you can do with the various media-driven components of the UWP. You won't be implementing all the functionality at first, but over time you will start adding features to the app. Figure 7-1 shows the New Project dialog on my computer (it may appear different on yours based on the way you have configured the IDE).

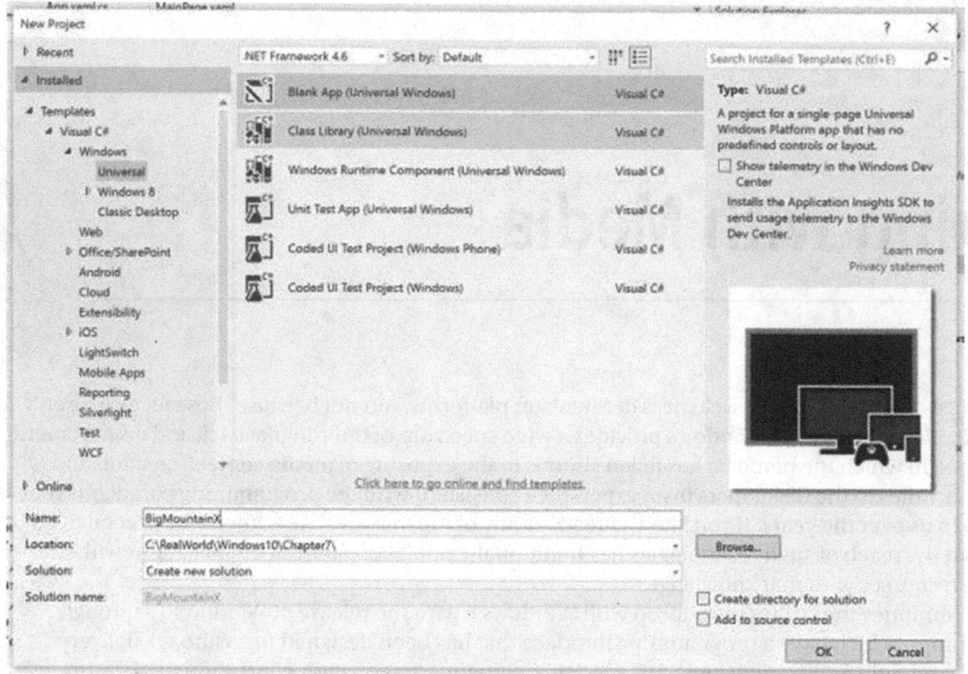

Figure 7-1. *New project dialog*

Once the project is created, delete `MainPage.xaml` and add a new XAML page to it called TestPage. You will use TestPage to do the testing and showcasing of the controls you utilize, and then add them to the solution as needed to fullfull the product requirements. Since MainPage was deleted, you need to open up the `App.xaml.cs` file and modify the initial page navigated to from MainPage to TestPage. Listing 7-1 shows new code for the `OnLaunched` event handler.

Listing 7-1. Default OnLaunched Event Handler

```
protected override void OnLaunched(LaunchActivatedEventArgs e)
{

#if DEBUG
    if (System.Diagnostics.Debugger.IsAttached)
    {
        this.DebugSettings.EnableFrameRateCounter = true;
    }
#endif

    Frame rootFrame = Window.Current.Content as Frame;

    // Do not repeat app initialization when the Window already has content,
    // just ensure that the window is active
    if (rootFrame == null)
```

```
    {
        // Create a Frame to act as the navigation context and navigate to the first page
        rootFrame = new Frame();

        rootFrame.NavigationFailed += OnNavigationFailed;

        if (e.PreviousExecutionState == ApplicationExecutionState.Terminated)
        {
            //TODO: Load state from previously suspended application
        }

        // Place the frame in the current Window
        Window.Current.Content = rootFrame;
    }

    if (rootFrame.Content == null)
    {
        // When the navigation stack isn't restored navigate to the first page,
        // configuring the new page by passing required information as a navigation
        // parameter
        rootFrame.Navigate(typeof(TestPage), e.Arguments);
    }
    // Ensure the current window is active
    Window.Current.Activate();
}
```

As you can see, the only change is modifying the page to which the window's root content, which in this case is a Frame, navigates. Your project should now look like Figure 7-2.

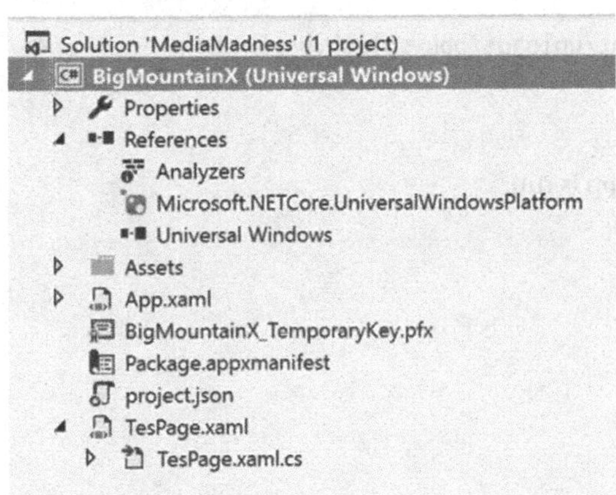

Figure 7-2. *Project structure*

Visualizing Media

It might be hard to comprehend in this modern world of real-time video communication and online gameplay on MMPGs like World of Warcraft, but there was a time not too long ago (and by that I mean the early 1990s, not 1800s) when seeing an image on screen was considered flashy. In the world you live in now, media content (especially in the form of images) is so prevalent that you may forget that images are in fact a type of media. UWP apps have a rich set of APIs for working with images locally and on the Web. You can even render your own images if you so desire. No matter how you get it, there are two places where an image will ultimately be displayed: the image control or an image brush.

Images

In Chapter 2, we introduced the image control and showed how it can be used to render an image coming from your app's package install location. Listing 7-2 shows how easy it is to add an image to a XAML page. Add it to the `TestPage.xaml`.

Listing 7-2. Adding an Image

```
<Image
                x:Name="control_image"
                Source="/assets/storelogo.png" />
```

As we mentioned back in Chapter 2, the notation used to specify the source attribute is based on the relative location of the image in the app package. Not surprisingly, images can also be rendered direct from the Web if you specify a URL instead. You will be targeting content located at `www.bigbuckbunny.org` for the remainder of this section on media visualization. In Listing 7-3, you display the image located at the following URL: `https://peach.blender.org/wp-content/uploads/bbb-splash.png`.

Listing 7-3. Image Source

```
<Image Source="https://peach.blender.org/wp-content/uploads/bbb-splash.png"
       HorizontalAlignment="Center"
       VerticalAlignment="Center" />
```

Figure 7-3 shows how this content renders when the app is run.

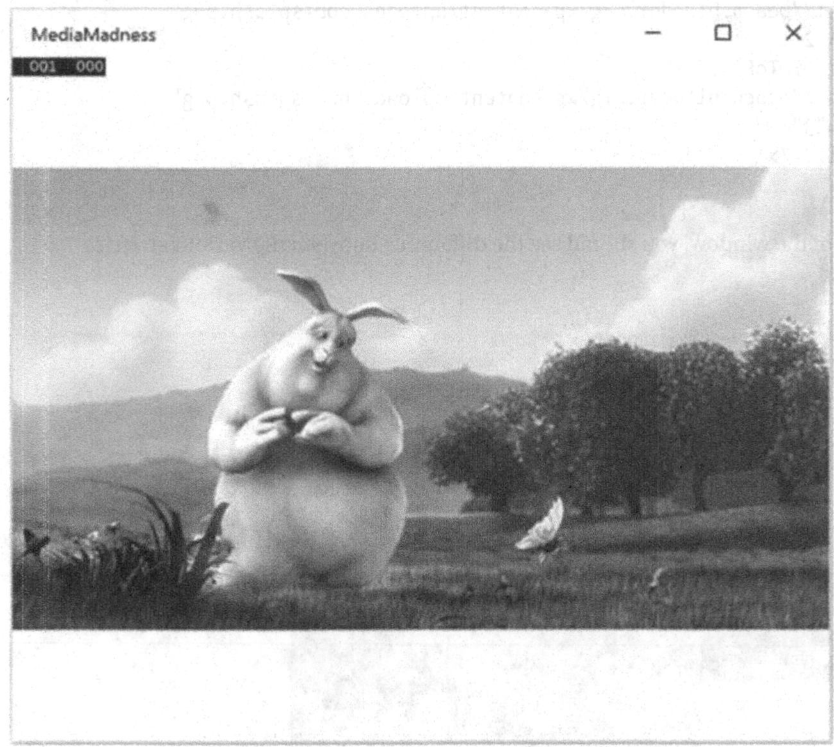

Figure 7-3. Image in action

Image contains a property, stretch, which can be used to determine the proportions the internal image will take in relation to the image control that renders it. With None, the image is shown in its full native size and aspect ratio. With Uniform and UniformToFill, the image will always maintain the native aspect ratio of the underlying image. UniformToFill will show as much of the image as is possible in as large a size as possible while still maintaining the proper aspect ratio, while Uniform will try to show the entire image in its largest possible size while still maintaining the correct aspect ratio. Fill will stretch to fill the available space (most likely distorting it in some way). Add the code from Listing 7-4 to TestPage and run the app.

Listing 7-4. Specifying Stretch Values

```
<Grid Background="{ThemeResource ApplicationPageBackgroundThemeBrush}">
    <Grid.ColumnDefinitions>
        <ColumnDefinition />
        <ColumnDefinition />
        <ColumnDefinition />
        <ColumnDefinition />
    </Grid.ColumnDefinitions>
    <Image Source="https://peach.blender.org/wp-content/uploads/bbb-splash.png"
            Stretch="None" />
    <Image Source="https://peach.blender.org/wp-content/uploads/bbb-splash.png"
            Grid.Column="1"
            Stretch="Uniform" />
```

```
    <Image Source="https://peach.blender.org/wp-content/uploads/bbb-splash.png"
           Grid.Column="2"
           Stretch="UniformToFill" />
    <Image Source="https://peach.blender.org/wp-content/uploads/bbb-splash.png"
           Grid.Column="3"
           Stretch="Fill" />
</Grid>
```

As you change the size of the window, you should see the difference between the various stretch settings. Figure 7-4 illustrates.

Figure 7-4. *Various Stretch values in action*

Updating the Project

Big Mountain events are social events that typically draw a crowd that includes the same people showing up over and over again, so the company would like to have their app reflect that social experience. One way to do this is to allow users to store a profile about themselves. The profile information need not be too sophisticated; it really only needs to store the user's basic identification information (like their first and last name) and information that can be used to contect them. Create a new folder called `Library` and in this folder add a class file called `BMXProfile`. Visual Studio 2015 treats items in subfolders as having their own namespace by default, and there seems to be no way of altering that default behavior. Be sure to remove the Library part of the new class' namespace declaration so that it remains in the BigMountainX namespace. Listing 7-5 shows the new class.

***Listing* 7-5.** BMXProfile Class

```
namespace BigMountainX
{

        public enum GenderCode
        {
            Male = 0,
            Female = 1,
        }

        public class BMXProfile
        {
                public string FirstName { get; set; }
                public string LastName { get; set; }
                public string Email { get; set; }
                public string ContactNumber { get; set; }
                public string ImageLocation{get;set;}
                public DateTime? DOB{get;set;}
                public GenderCode? Gender{get;set;}
        }
}
```

You also need a class to represent the app settings as a whole. The class will contain the user profile as well as other important information about the app. For now, this class will only have one property in it, the user's profile. Over time you will add other properties as they are needed. Add a new class to the `Library` folder called `AppState` and add the definition from Listing 7-6.

***Listing* 7-6.** AppState Class

```
namespace BigMountainX
{
        public class AppState
        {
                public BMXProfile UserProfile { get; set; }
        }
}
```

Using the same patterns you have utilized in the past, you must now create methods for serializing and deserializing this object so that it can be written to the file system and read from it as well. This ensures that state is maintained across multiple runs of the app. Add the coded from Listing 7-7 to `AppState`.

***Listing* 7-7.** Serialization Methods

```
public string AsSerializedString()
{
        DataContractSerializer dcs = new DataContractSerializer(typeof(AppState));
        MemoryStream ms = new MemoryStream();
        dcs.WriteObject(ms, this);
        ms.Seek(0, SeekOrigin.Begin);
        byte[] buffer = new byte[ms.Length];
        ms.Read(buffer, 0, buffer.Length);
```

```
        string serialized_object = Encoding.ASCII.GetString(buffer);
        return serialized_object;
}

async public Task ToStorageFileAsync(StorageFile file)
{
        var serialized = this.AsSerializedString();
        await file.WriteTextAsync(serialized);
}

public static AppState FromSerializedString(string resume_string)
{
        try
        {
                var buffer = Encoding.ASCII.GetBytes(resume_string);
                MemoryStream ms = new MemoryStream(buffer);
                DataContractSerializer dcs = new DataContractSerializer(typeof(AppState));
                var retval = dcs.ReadObject(ms);
                var app_state = retval as AppState;
                return app_state;
        }
        catch
        {
                return null;
        }
}

async public static Task<AppState> FromStorageFileAsync(StorageFile file)
{
        var app_state = FromSerializedString(await file.ReadTextAsync());
        return app_state;
}
```

Of course, because you are using the extension methods ReadTextAsync and WriteTextAsyc, which you created in Chapter 6, you need to add the file StorageFileExtensions.cs to this project. Right-click the Library folder of your project and select click Add ➤ Existing item. Now browse to the Library folder of your ResumeManager project, and select StorageFileExtensions.cs, and click Add. Figure 7-5 illustrates.

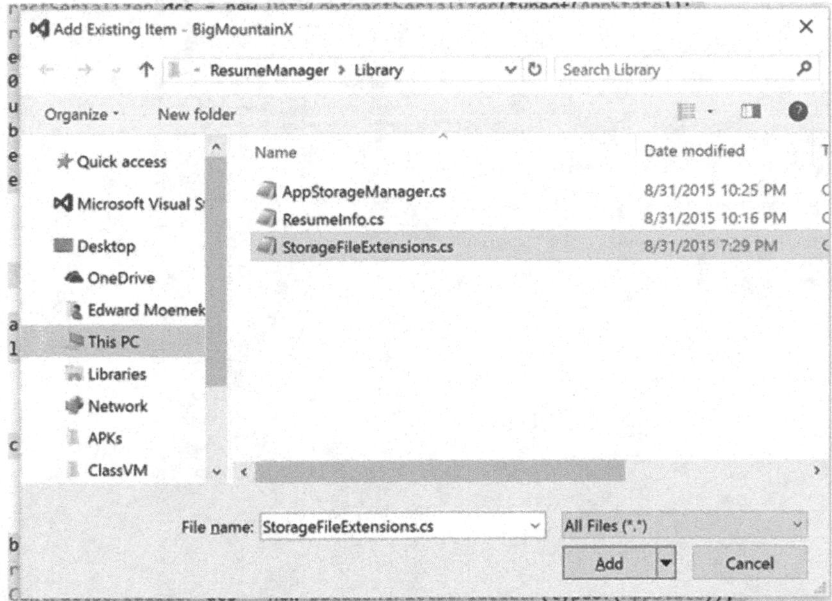

Figure 7-5. *Incorporating StorageFileExtensions*

Build the solution to ensure that everything is working as it should.

By now you might have noticed a recurring pattern in your samples. You typically use an object to store your application state, which at this point is read and written to a storage location in app storage. An ideal solution to prevent constant reuse by copying is to place this functionality into a base class that any state-aware classes can simply inherit from. For this approach to be transportable, you need to place it into a library that can then simply be referenced from any projects you chose.

Add a new library project (use the Universal Windows Class Library, not the standard class library project) to the solution called General.UWP.Library. This library will contain any general types that you expect to use across projects that you create. For now, you will be adding the base class for all app state management to the library such that you can redesign all your previous state management code to leverage this class by inheriting from it. The net result of this process should have no direct effect on app functionality because the actual code being executed has not changed. It is just for organizational purposes. Figure 7-6 shows the Add New Project dialog with the Class Library project template selected.

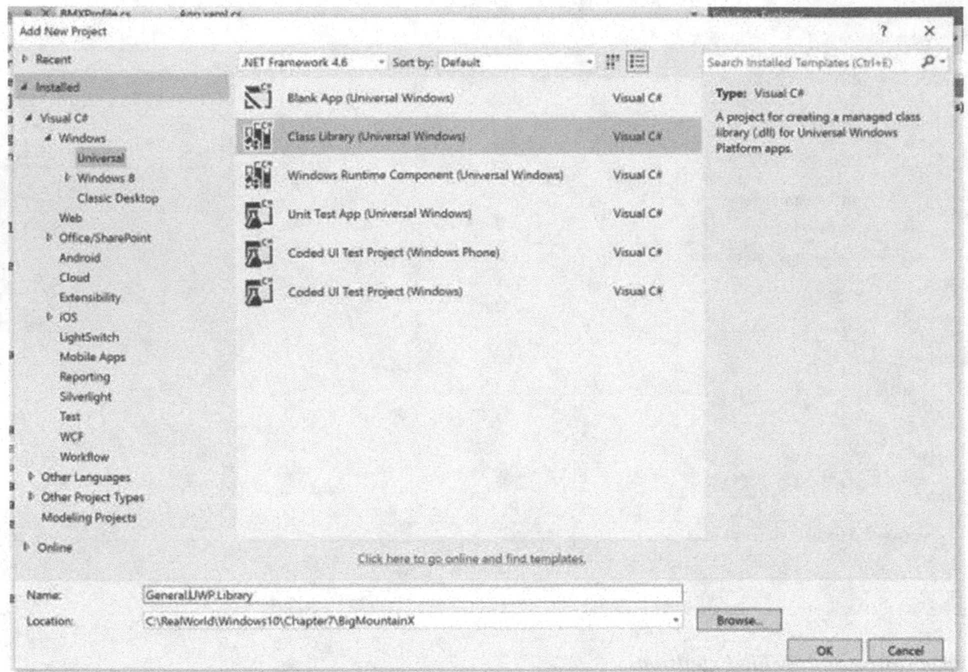

Figure 7-6. *The Add New Project dialog*

In the library project, delete `Class1` (the default class that is added by Visual Studio 2015 when a library project is created) and add a new class called `StateAwareObject`. Also, draw `StorageFileExtensions.cs` from the `Library` folder of BigMountainX to the root of General.UWP.Library. The library project should look like Figure 7-7.

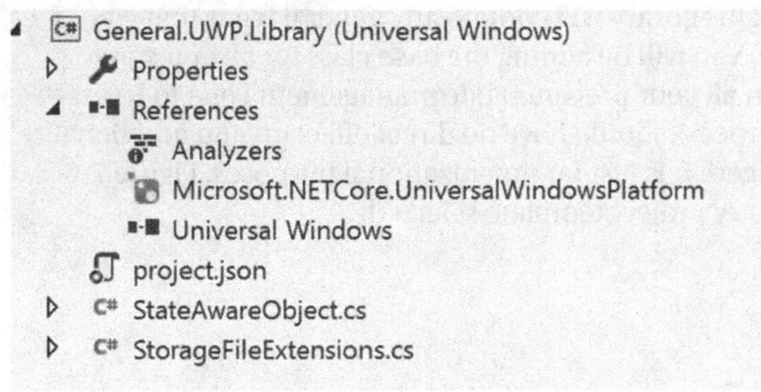

Figure 7-7. *General library project structure*

Open up `StateAwareObject`'s definition. You need to move all the state management code, the code from Listing 7-7, into this class so that future classes that inherit from this base class need not implement the same thing over and over again. Because the code uses serialization, however, it will not be as simple a process as simply copying the code over. You need to change the behavior of the serialization and deserialization methods such that the type you use for the process is generic, meaning parameterize the process of seriazation and de-serialization. Listing 7-8 illustrates.

Listing 7-8. StateAwareObject Class

```
public class StateAwareObject<T> where T : StateAwareObject<T>, new()
{
        StorageFolder _folder;
        StorageFile _file;
        string _file_name;

        public string AsSerializedString()
        {
                DataContractSerializer dcs = new DataContractSerializer(typeof(T));
                MemoryStream ms = new MemoryStream();
                dcs.WriteObject(ms, this);
                ms.Seek(0, SeekOrigin.Begin);
                byte[] buffer = new byte[ms.Length];
                ms.Read(buffer, 0, buffer.Length);
                string serialized_object = Encoding.ASCII.GetString(buffer);
                return serialized_object;
        }

        async public Task SaveAsync()
        {
                StorageFile file = _file;
                if (file == null)
                {
                        file = await _folder.CreateFileAsync(_file_name,
                                        CreationCollisionOption.ReplaceExisting);
                }

                var serialized = this.AsSerializedString();
                await file.WriteTextAsync(serialized);
        }

        async public Task DeleteAsync()
        {
                StorageFile file = _file;
                if (file != null)
                {
                        await file.DeleteAsync(StorageDeleteOption.PermanentDelete);
                }
        }
        public static T FromSerializedString(string resume_string)
        {
                try
                {
                        var buffer = Encoding.ASCII.GetBytes(resume_string);
                        MemoryStream ms = new MemoryStream(buffer);
                        DataContractSerializer dcs = new DataContractSerializer(typeof(T));
                        var retval = dcs.ReadObject(ms);
                        var app_state = retval as T;
                        return app_state;
                }
```

```
            catch
            {
                    return null;
            }
    }

    async public static Task<T> FromStorageFileAsync(StorageFile file)
    {
            var app_state = FromSerializedString(await file.ReadTextAsync());
            if (app_state == null)
                    app_state = new T();
            app_state._folder = await file.GetParentAsync();
            app_state._file = file;
            app_state._file_name = file.Name;
            return app_state;
    }

    async public static Task<T> FromStorageFileAsync(StorageFolder folder,
    string file_name)
    {
            var file = (await folder.TryGetItemAsync(file_name)) as StorageFile;
            if (file == null)
            {
                    var retval = new T();
                    retval._folder = folder;
                    retval._file_name = file_name;
                    return retval;
            }
            else
                    return await FromStorageFileAsync(file as StorageFile);
    }
}
```

In Listing 7-8, you construct `StateAwareObject` as a generic class expecting a type parameter T, which must be a reference type. T in the case represents the type of any state management class you create in the future that inherits from this base class. New overloads to `FromStorageFileAsync` and `StorageAsync` have been introduced to streamline the process of serialization. Other than this change, the flow of the code is essentially the same as before. Let's take a look at how `AppState` now changes to utilize this base class. To use this class, you must first add a reference to the General.UWP.Library project. Right-click the `References` folder of BigMountainX and select Add Reference. Select Projects from the tree on the left of the Reference Manager screen (this represents locations where libraries might exist). Select Solution, and then pick General.UWP.Library. Figure 7-8 illustrates.

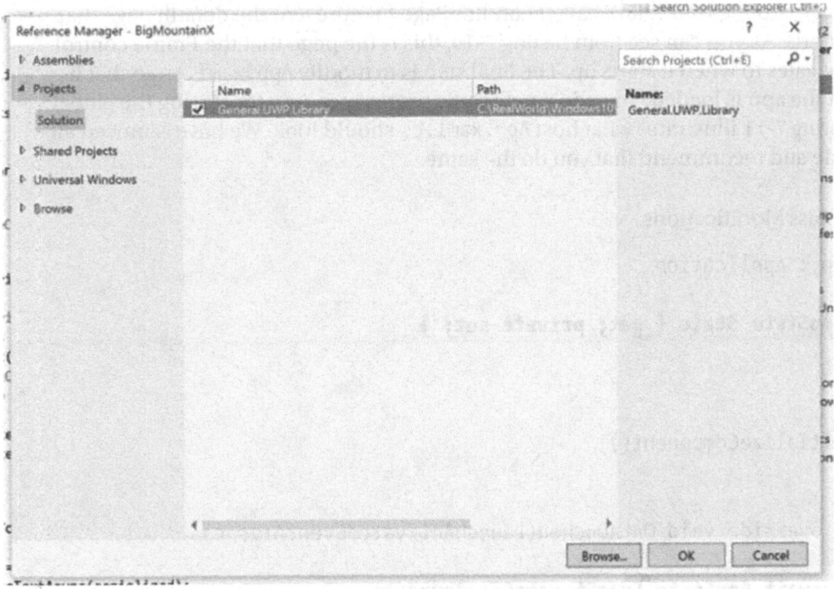

***Figure 7-8.** Referencing the general library*

With your library now in scope, you declare the namespace that contains your base class and add it as a base class to `AppState`, as shown in Listing 7-9.

Listing 7-9. AppState Modifications

```
public class AppState : StateAwareObject<AppState>
{
        public BMXProfile UserProfile { get; set; }
}
```

You now have your general state management in place. With any luck, you won't have to go through the process of creating a state management pattern anymore. Let's move on to the next task, which is building out the framework for navigation in your app. Presently, the app follows the default pattern of utilizing a frame as the root content for the app window. As you have done in previous chapters, you will augment this by wrapping that root frame in a Page, which gives you the flexibility to create overlays and also a place to host app-wide functionality that can impact the user UI. Add a new page to the BigMountainX project called ApplicationHostPage. Within this page add a Frame element. Add the code from Listing 7-10 to the `ApplicationHostPage.xaml` file.

Listing 7-10. ApplicationHostPage Modifications

```
<Grid Background="{ThemeResource ApplicationPageBackgroundThemeBrush}">
        <Frame x:Name="root_frame" SourcePageType="local:LandingPage" />
</Grid>
```

Now add another new page to BigMountainX called LandingPage to represent the default page that is displayed when the app starts. As you can see from Listing 7-10, this is the page that the Frame control in your application host navigates to when it starts up. The final step is to modify `App.xaml.cs` so that it attempts to load state when the app is loaded. You add a new static property to App for storing the global `AppState` object as well. Listing 7-11 illustrates what host `App.xaml.cs` should look. We have removed all extraneous code from the file and recommend that you do the same.

Listing 7-11. Application Class Modifications

```
sealed partial class App : Application
{
        public static AppState State { get; private set; }

        public App()
        {
                this.InitializeComponent();
        }

        async protected override void OnLaunched(LaunchActivatedEventArgs e)
        {
                State = await AppState.FromStorageFileAsync(↵
                                                ApplicationData.Current.RoamingFolder,↵
                                                "state.xml");

                Window.Current.Content = new ApplicationHostPage();

                Window.Current.Activate();
        }

}
```

Incorporating Image into BigMountainX

Your application will require two kinds of images to be rendered: static images that cannot be modified by the user (like app-related artwork and images of users you have no control over), and dynamic images that the user has the ability to modify by either selecting a file on their computer or using the device's camera (if available). For static images, the normal Image control will suffice. For dynamic images, you need to build in additional functionality to get the Image control to work as expected. This is a great scenario to build a UserControl and, given that it is a UserControl, an opportunity to add more functionality to your general UWP library.

Right-click the General.UWP.Library project and select Add ➤ New Item. From the Add New Item dialog, select User Control, and name the new control ImageViewerControl. Press the Enter key to add it to your project. Your new UserControl will need to do three primary things for the user: display an image, give the user the ability to select an image from their file system, and give the user the ability to take a picture using the device's camera and use it as the image to display. From this, it is plain to see that there are two interaction points for this control: browsing for and selecting pictures, and using the camera. You will use a MenuFlyout control to expose those two options so that when a user clicks on the image, they will be given two choices: browse or take a picture. In the next section when we discuss image capture, you will delve into the "take a picture" scenario, but for now you will focus on browsing for and displaying pictures from the user's device. Listing 7-12 shows the user interface layout for ImageViewerControl.

Listing 7-12. ImageViewerControl User Interface

```
<Grid Background="Gray"
        BorderBrush="Black"
        BorderThickness="1"
        PointerPressed="PointerPressedHandler">

    <Image x:Name="img_control"
            Stretch="Uniform"
            ImageOpened="OnImageOpened"
            HorizontalAlignment="Stretch"
            VerticalAlignment="Stretch">
        <FlyoutBase.AttachedFlyout>
            <MenuFlyout Placement="Bottom">
                <MenuFlyoutItem Text="Browse ..."
                                Click="BrowseImageClicked" />
                <MenuFlyoutItem Text="Take Picture"
                                Click="TakePictureClicked" />
            </MenuFlyout>
        </FlyoutBase.AttachedFlyout>
    </Image>
    <SymbolIcon x:Name="symbol_camera"
                Symbol="Camera"
                HorizontalAlignment="Center"
                VerticalAlignment="Center" />
</Grid>
```

Your UI consists of an image and a SymbolIcon inside a grid. The image has a flyout with two menu items than can be used to initiate either file search or the device's camera. Let's look at the code-behind for this control. Listing 7-13 shows the `ImageViewerControl` class.

Listing 7-13. ImageViewerControl Code-Behind

```
public sealed partial class ImageViewerControl : UserControl
{
        public event Action<ImageViewerControl> ImageSelected;
        public StorageFile ImageFile { get; set; }
        public ImageViewerControl()
        {
                this.InitializeComponent();

        }

        async public Task LoadImageAsync(StorageFolder folder, string image_file_path)
        {
                var image_file = await folder.GetFileAsync(image_file_path);
                await InternalLoadImageAsync(image_file);
        }
```

```
        private void TakePictureClicked(object sender, RoutedEventArgs e)
        {

        }

        async private void BrowseImageClicked(object sender, RoutedEventArgs e)
        {
                FileOpenPicker opener = new FileOpenPicker();
                opener.ViewMode = PickerViewMode.Thumbnail;
                opener.SuggestedStartLocation = PickerLocationId.PicturesLibrary;
                opener.CommitButtonText = "Select Picture";
                opener.FileTypeFilter.Add(".png");
                opener.FileTypeFilter.Add(".jpg");
                var selected_file = await opener.PickSingleFileAsync();
                if (selected_file != null)
                {
                        await InternalLoadImageAsync(selected_file);
                        ImageSelected?.Invoke(this);
                }
        }

        private async Task InternalLoadImageAsync(StorageFile selected_file)
        {
                ImageFile = selected_file;

                //display the image
                BitmapImage image = new BitmapImage();
                img_control.Source = image;
                var stream = await selected_file.OpenReadAsync();
                await image.SetSourceAsync(stream);
        }

        private void PointerPressedHandler(object sender, PointerRoutedEventArgs e)
        {
                FlyoutBase.ShowAttachedFlyout(img_control);
        }

        private void OnImageOpened(object sender, RoutedEventArgs e)
        {
                symbol_camera.Visibility = Visibility.Collapsed;
        }
}
```

In Listing 7-13, `LoadImageAsync` is called whenever a consumer of this control needs to display an image (from a storage folder somewhere). `TakePictureClicked` is deliberately left blank for now. `InternalLoadImageAsync` is a catch-all method for taking a storage file and rendering the image it represents. It is used throughout the class for this purpose. The main interactivity point, `BrowseImageClicked`, is called when the Browse button is clicked, and it simply opens a file picker to find and load the image file a user wanted to use. The Pointer Pressed handler is used to basically cause the flyout to display (only buttons display them by default). Finally, `OnImageOpened` (which is fired only if the image loaded successfully) is handled so that the `SymbolIcon` can be hidden if an image has successfully loaded.

Tying It All Together

You have your state management set up, and you have your profile class, and you even have an image control ready to go, but how do you tie all this loose functionality into a cohesive experience? Let's start with the profile; presumably many of the events a user will see will depend on who they are. Consequently, your app must know some things about the user before it is usable. Let's add some code to your application host to test to see if the user already has a profile defined. If this is the case, then you start the app by navigating to the landing page; otherwise, you navigate the user to the profile creation page. Before you get started, add a new page to the BigMountainX project entitled UserIntroPage. This will be the page where a user can enter their profile information in order to start the app.

Once completed, add the code from Listing 7-14 to `ApplicationHostPage.xaml.cs`.

Listing 7-14. ApplicationHostPage Modifications

```
public sealed partial class ApplicationHostPage : Page
{
        public ApplicationHostPage()
        {
                this.InitializeComponent();
                this.Loaded += ApplicationHostPage_Loaded;
        }

        private void ApplicationHostPage_Loaded(object sender, RoutedEventArgs e)
        {
                if (App.State.UserProfile == null)
                        root_frame.Navigate(typeof(UserIntroPage));
                else
                        root_frame.Navigate(typeof(LandingPage));
        }
}
```

The code in Listing 7-14 is straightforward. You basically check the `State` object to see if `UserProfile` is null (it will be null until a new `BMXProfile` instance is set to it). If null, you navigate to a page where the object can be filled in; otherwise, you start the app. `UserIntroPage` basically provides a UI for an uninitiated user to enter some profile information so you can build a profile for them. Listing 7-15 shows the layout for the page.

Listing 7-15. Incorporating ImageViewerControl

```
<ScrollViewer VerticalScrollBarVisibility="Auto"
                VerticalScrollMode="Auto">
    <StackPanel Orientation="Vertical">
        <lib:ImageViewerControl  HorizontalAlignment="Left"
                                  Margin="10"
                                  Height="200"
                                  Width="200"
                                  ImageSelected="OnImageSelected" />
```

```
        <StackPanel Width="400"
                    HorizontalAlignment="Left">
            <TextBox Header="First Name"
                        Margin="10"
                        Text="{x:Bind Profile.FirstName, Mode=TwoWay}" />
            <TextBox Header="Last Name"
                        Margin="10"
                        Text="{x:Bind Profile.LastName, Mode=TwoWay}" />
            <TextBox Header="Email Address"
                        Margin="10"
                        Text="{x:Bind Profile.Email, Mode=TwoWay}" />
            <TextBox Header="Contact Number"
                        Margin="10"
                        Text="{x:Bind Profile.ContactNumber, Mode=TwoWay}" />
        </StackPanel>

        <DatePicker x:Name="control_dob"
                    Header="When were you born?"
                    HorizontalAlignment="Left"
                    Margin="10"
                    DateChanged="OnDOBSelected"
                    VerticalAlignment="Top" />

        <ComboBox x:Name="control_procedure"
                    Header="Gender"
                    HorizontalAlignment="Left"
                    Margin="10"
                    SelectionChanged="OnGenderSelected"
                    VerticalAlignment="Top"
                    Width="296"
                    ItemsSource="{x:Bind Genders, Mode=OneWay}" />
        <Button Content="Continue"
                Click="OnContinue" Margin="10" />
    </StackPanel>

</ScrollViewer>
```

Note the element in bold, an ImageViewControl element. To incorporate this element properly, a XAML namespace declaration, `xmlns:lib="using:General.UWP.Library"`, must be added the page definition. The code-behind for Listing 7-15 is shown in Listing 7-16.

Listing 7-16. UserIntroPage Modifications

```
public sealed partial class UserIntroPage : Page, INotifyPropertyChanged
{
        public event PropertyChangedEventHandler PropertyChanged;

        BMXProfile Profile { get; set; }
        List<string> Genders { get; set; }
```

```
public UserIntroPage()
{
        this.InitializeComponent();
        Profile = new BMXProfile();
        this.Loaded += UserIntroPage_Loaded;
}

private void UserIntroPage_Loaded(object sender, RoutedEventArgs e)
{
        Genders = Enum.GetValues(typeof(GenderCode))
                .Cast<GenderCode>()
                .Select(i => i.ToString()).ToList();
        PropertyChanged?.Invoke(this, new PropertyChangedEventArgs("Genders"));

}

async private void OnContinue(object sender, RoutedEventArgs e)
{
        if (Profile.Gender != null
                && Profile.DOB != null
                && !string.IsNullOrWhiteSpace(Profile.FirstName)
                && !string.IsNullOrWhiteSpace(Profile.LastName)
                && !string.IsNullOrWhiteSpace(Profile.ContactNumber)
                && !string.IsNullOrWhiteSpace(Profile.Email)
                && !string.IsNullOrWhiteSpace(Profile.ImageLocation))
        {
                App.State.UserProfile = Profile;
                await App.State.SaveAsync();
                Frame.Navigate(typeof(LandingPage));
        }
        else
                await new MessageDialog("Please enter all fields").ShowAsync();
}

private void OnGenderSelected(object sender, SelectionChangedEventArgs e)
{
        ComboBox combo = sender as ComboBox;
        var selection = combo.SelectedItem as string;
        var gender_code = (GenderCode)Enum.Parse(typeof(GenderCode), selection);
        Profile.Gender = gender_code;
}

private void OnDOBSelected(object sender, DatePickerValueChangedEventArgs e)
{
        DatePicker date = sender as DatePicker;
        var selection = date.Date.Date;
        Profile.DOB = selection;
}
```

```
        async private void OnImageSelected(ImageViewerControl sender)
        {
                await sender.ImageFile.CopyAsync(ApplicationData.Current.LocalFolder);
                Profile.ImageLocation = sender.ImageFile.Name;
        }
}
```

Listing 7-16 starts by declaring some class-level properties that will be used for databinding purposes. Remember that you are using compiled bindings in your UI layout so these properties are made visible to the XAML. You don't directly connect to the global application state; instead you create an instance of the `BMXProfile` for use in this class. If the data entered passes all the criteria you specify, you copy it to the `App.State.UserProfile` property, but until then you keep it in the local `Profile` property. In the constructor, you instantiate `Profile` and also connect to the Page's `Loaded` event.

The `Loaded` event does two things. First, it enumerates the values of the `GenderCode` enum, converting them to string values in the process. It then fires the `PropertyChanged` event to notify the binding subsystem that the value of `Genders` property has changed. Like all the previous examples that rely on binding, `UserIntroPage` implements `INotifyPropertyChanged`, the event this is acquired from.

Two event handler methods, `OnGenderSelected` and `OnDOBSelected`, are used to pass the gender and date selection into `Profile`. `OnImageSelected` does the same with `ImageLocation`. It then copies the file over to the app's `LocalFolder`. You use the `LocalFolder` here instead of `RoamingFolder` because the quota for roaming folder is so low that it would never actually roam.

The final method, `OnContinue`, is fired when the Continue button is clicked. All this method does is ensure that none of the properties in `Profile` have a+ null or empty string value. If all values are valid, the `Profile` is saved to the global state and the global state is then saved. Otherwise, the user is prompted.

You will also be using your ImageViewerControl for viewing a user's profile image. On the landing page, let's add the control to the XAML. Listing 7-17 illustrates.

Listing 7-17. Declaring ImageViewerControl Event Handlers

```
<lib:ImageViewerControl  HorizontalAlignment="Left"
                         VerticalAlignment="Top"
                         Margin="10"
                         Height="200"
                         Width="200"
                         Loaded="OnImageViewerLoaded"
                         ImageSelected="OnImageSelected" />
```

This version of the image viewer will need to both render the image and provide a means to change the value of the image. In the code-behind of LandingPage, implement the methods from Listing 7-18 to fulfill this requirement.

Listing 7-18. Implementing Event Handlers

```
async private void OnImageViewerLoaded(object sender, RoutedEventArgs e)
{
        if (!string.IsNullOrWhiteSpace(App.State.UserProfile?.ImageLocation))
        {
                var image_viewer = sender as ImageViewerControl;
                await image_viewer
                        .LoadImageAsync(Windows.Storage.ApplicationData.Current.LocalFolder, ↵
                                        App.State.UserProfile?.ImageLocation);
        }
}
```

```
async private void OnImageSelected(ImageViewerControl sender)
{
        await sender.ImageFile.CopyAsync(Windows.Storage.ApplicationData.Current.LocalFolder);
        App.State.UserProfile.ImageLocation = sender.ImageFile.Name;
        await App.State.SaveAsync();
}
```

ImageBrush

In the previous section, you created a user control, ImageViewerControl, which was based on an underlying Image control. An Image control in UWP is used to display images. Although this works well in most cases, there are scenarios where utilizing an image might not be desired. One such case is in scenarios where an image needs to be rendered in a non-rectangular way. Typically, an image is basically displayed within the bounds of a rectangular shape, so if you wanted to place an image within a circle, using the Image control would obviously not be ideal. In such cases, use the `ImageBrush` feature to satisfy your requirement.

An `ImageBrush` is a type of `TileBrush` that defines its content as an image, which is specified by its `ImageSource` property. You can control how the image is stretched, aligned, and tiled, enabling you to produce patterns and other effects. An `ImageBrush` can paint shapes, controls, text, and more. If you define an `ImageBrush` using code, use the default constructor, and then set `ImageBrush.ImageSource`. This requires a `BitmapImage` (not a URI) in code. If your source is a stream, use the `SetSourceAsync` method to initialize the value. If your source is a URI, which includes content in your app that uses the `ms-appx` or `ms-resource` schemes, use the `BitmapImage` constructor that takes a URI. You might also consider handling the `ImageOpened` event if there are any timing issues with retrieving or decoding the image source where you might need alternate content to display until the image source is available.

The `Stretch` property is important for how the image is applied when used as a brush. Some images look good when stretched as applied to a particular `Brush` property with the `Fill` behavior, whereas other images do not stretch or scale well and might require a value of `None` or `Uniform` for `Stretch`. Also, some images are designed to tile whereas some are not. Experiment with different values for `Stretch` to see which behavior looks best when applied to the UI.

Open up `Landing.xaml` and add the XAML from Listing 7-19 right underneath your ImageViewControl definition.

Listing 7-19. Ellipse with ImageBrush

```
<Ellipse Width="722"
              Height="604"
              VerticalAlignment="Bottom"
              Margin="0,0,10,10">
    <Ellipse.Fill>
        <ImageBrush
        Stretch="Fill" ImageSource="https://peach.blender.org/wp-content/uploads/
        bbb-splash.png" />
    </Ellipse.Fill>
</Ellipse>
```

In Listing 7-19, you define an ellipse and, rather than give it a fill (background color) that is based on a solid color, you use an `ImageBrush` to fill the shape. The view in Visual Studio 2015 design should look like Figure 7-9.

Figure 7-9. *ImageBrush in action*

An ImageBrush can also be set programmatically. As with the Image control, it requires the use of an ImageSource (in this case a BitmapImage object). Listing 7-20 illustrates, so add it below your previous ellipse declaration.

Listing 7-20. Ellipse

```
<Ellipse HorizontalAlignment="Left"
         Width="489"
         Height="429"
         VerticalAlignment="Bottom"
         Margin="10,0,0,10"
         Loaded="LoadImageForEllipse">
</Ellipse>
```

The event handler for LoadImageForEllipse is shown in Listing 7-21.

Listing 7-21. Loading ImageBrush Programmatically

```
private void LoadImageForEllipse(object sender, RoutedEventArgs e)
{
        Ellipse ellipse = sender as Ellipse;
        BitmapImage img = new BitmapImage();
        img.UriSource = new Uri("https://peach.blender.org/wp-content/uploads/bbb-splash.png");
        ImageBrush brush = new ImageBrush();
        brush.ImageSource = img;
        ellipse.Fill = brush;
}
```

When the app is run, you should see something that looks like Figure 7-10. (Obviously your profile picture should be different.)

Figure 7-10. *Loading ImageBrush programmatically*

Let's apply this newfound ability to your Big Mountain X app. You will create a new, reusable control in your general library that you will then utilize on your landing page. Add a new UserControl to the General. UWP.Library project called ImageBannerControl. Once created, build the project, and then right-click the newly created file, `ImageBannerControl.xaml`, and selected "Design in Blend" from the context menu that appears. For many of the samples you will be working on, Visual Studio will be more than enough, but in this instance you will be creating something called a path, which is a shape type similar to ellipse and rectangle that defines a general shape to be drawn. You can use XAML to specify the data for a path you want drawn or you can explicitly draw the path, using a tool like Blend, and have the data for your drawing subsequently filled in for you. Figure 7-11 points out the menu item you will need to select in order to fire up Blend. As stated earlier, be sure to build the project first before attempting this connection. In most cases, Visual Studio 2015 and Blend play nicely together, but there are instances where they are not in sync.

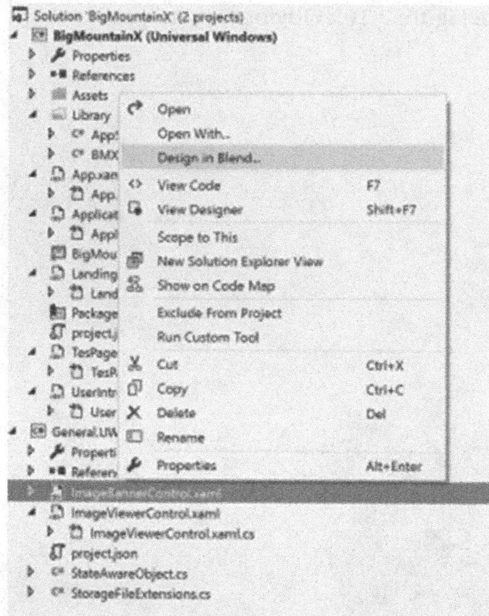

***Figure 7-11.** Designing in Blend*

In Blend, select the Pen tool, as indicated in Figure 7-12.

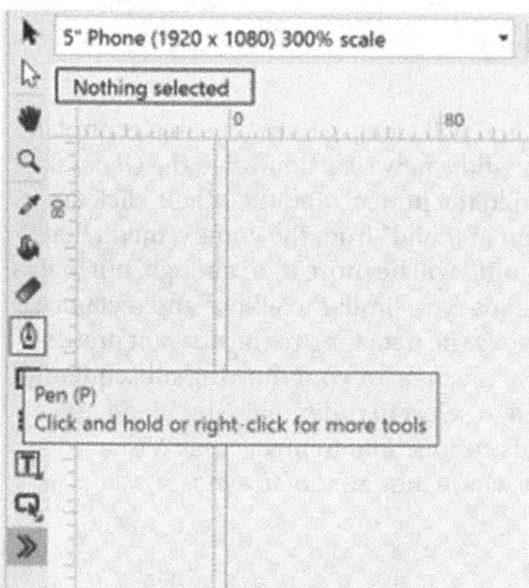

***Figure 7-12.** Blend's Pen tool*

Use the pen tool to draw a shape similar to the image in Figure 7-13. If you don't want to draw the image yourself, you can simply copy the code from Listing 7-22.

Figure 7-13. Pen-defined Path object

Listing 7-22. Path Data for Image Banner

```
<Path Data="M-19.1464,-17.9973 L420.5,-18.5 L420.5,248.5 L379.998,248.597 L359.834,231.537↵
L339.838,248.694 L-21.1464,248.503 z"
        Margin="-21.646,-19,-21,19.782"
        Stretch="Fill"
        Stroke="Black"
        UseLayoutRounding="False"
        d:LayoutOverrides="LeftPosition, RightPosition, TopPosition, BottomPosition" />
```

Specifying an image brush as the background for this path is as simple as applying the `ImageBrush` to the `Fill` property of the path. Listing 7-23 illustrates.

Listing 7-23. Applying ImageBrush to Path

```
<Path Data="M-19.1464,-17.9973 L420.5,-18.5 L420.5,248.5 L379.998,248.597 L359.834,231.537
L339.838,248.694 L-21.1464,248.503 z"
        Margin="-21.646,-19,-21,19.782"
        Stretch="Fill"
        Stroke="Black"
        UseLayoutRounding="False"
        d:LayoutOverrides="LeftPosition, RightPosition, TopPosition, BottomPosition">
    <Path.Fill>
        <ImageBrush x:Name="img_brush"
                    Stretch="UniformToFill" />
    </Path.Fill>
</Path>
```

Now add a new public method to the code-behind for this control. Listing 7-24 illustrates.

Listing 7-24. Generic SetImage Method

```
public void SetImage(string url)
{
        var image = new BitmapImage();
        image.UriSource = new Uri(url);
        img_brush.ImageSource = image;
}
```

Listing 7-24 simply creates a new bitmap image and sets its source to whatever is passed in by the caller of this method.

To complete the process, you now need to modify your landing page to use this control. Remember that the images you use here are sample images and not necessarily in the spirit of the app you are working on.

Add the new control just above the definition for your ImageViewerControl. Doing so ensures that the profile picture of the user is displayed above this banner. Listing 7-25 shows the code to be added.

Listing 7-25. ImageBannerControl

```
<lib:ImageBannerControl x:Name="img_banner"
                                  Margin="0,0,0,305" />
```

Now remove the previous ellipse controls you added to show how `ImageBrush` works. You must now modify the code behind for LandingPage as shown in Listing 7-26.

Listing 7-26. Implementing LandingPage Banner

```
public sealed partial class LandingPage : Page
{
        DispatcherTimer _timer;
        List<string> _images = new List<string>
        {
                "https://peach.blender.org/wp-content/uploads/bbb-splash.png",
                "https://peach.blender.org/wp-content/uploads/rodents.png",
                "https://peach.blender.org/wp-content/uploads/evil-frank.png",
                "https://peach.blender.org/wp-content/uploads/bunny-bow.png",
                "https://peach.blender.org/wp-content/uploads/rinkysplash.jpg",
                "https://peach.blender.org/wp-content/uploads/its-a-trap.png"
        };
        int _image_index = 0;
        public LandingPage()
        {
                this.InitializeComponent();
                this.Loaded += LandingPage_Loaded;
                _timer = new DispatcherTimer();
                _timer.Interval = TimeSpan.FromSeconds(5);
                _timer.Tick += _timer_Tick;
        }

        private void _timer_Tick(object sender, object e)
        {
                img_banner.SetImage(_images[_image_index]);
                _image_index++;
```

```
            if (_image_index >= _images.Count)
                _image_index = 0;
        }

        private void LandingPage_Loaded(object sender, RoutedEventArgs e)
        {
            _timer.Start();
            img_banner.SetImage(_images[_image_index]);
            _image_index++;
        }
        ...
}
```

In Listing 7-26, you start by defining a set of images you want to display with the banner. In this particular case, you want to make your banner scroll through images every 5 seconds, so you use a DispatcherTimer set to fire every 5 seconds to achieve this. You also need a numeric value to represent the index of the image (in the list of images) you are presently showing in your banner. When the page loads, you start the timer and display the first image in the list (the image at index 0), and then you increment the value of _image_index. Every 5 seconds you display the image at the new index and then increment the value once again. If the index value is ever larger than the number of items in the list of images, you cycle back to the beginning by setting the index back to 0 again. Figure 7-14 shows how the app looks when run.

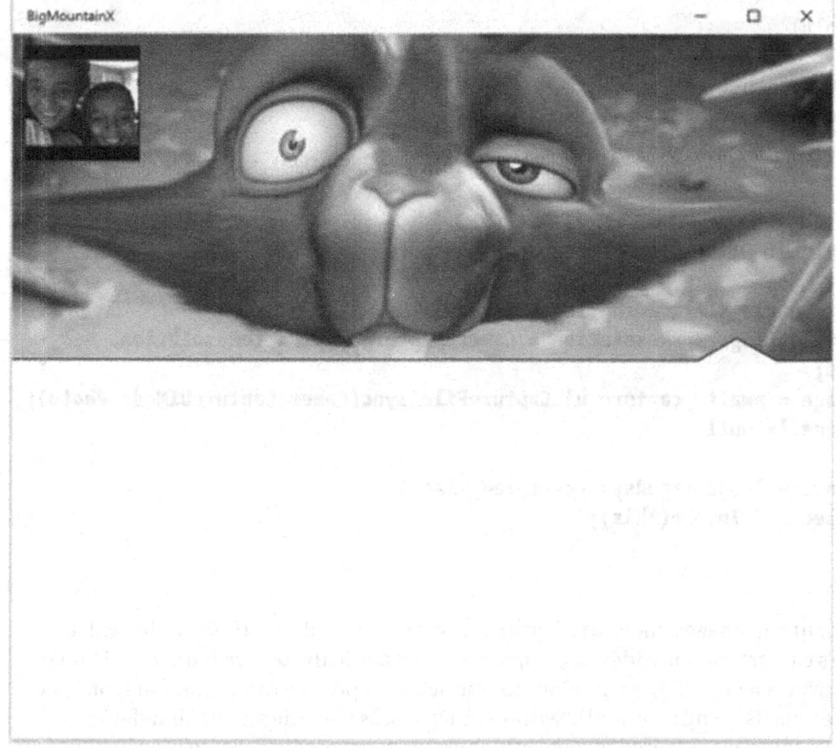

Figure 7-14. *Path with ImageBrush in action*

Capturing Images

In this section, you will use the image capturing APIs to complete the functionality of ImageViewerControl. If you remember, you used a flyout to represent the possible actions that can be taken on a dynamic image when the user clicks in one. In the last section, you implemented browsing for an image on the user's file system. In this section, we will show how to do the same thing via the camera capture mechanisms the UWP provides. Before you get started, be sure to add the appropriate permissions to your project for capture to work. In this case, and for video capture, you need the webcam and microphone capabilities enabled.

There are presently two main ways to capture images from one of the cameras attached to a user's device: using the `CameraCaptureUI` or using the `MediaCapture` class. `CameraCaptureUI`, the simpler of the two, provides a full window UI experience for capturing video and images. It provides controls for setting a time delay on photo captures, trimming video, and for adjusting the camera's settings such as video resolution, the audio device, brightness, and contrast. You have already seen `CameraCaptureUI` at work. You previously used it in the Control Corral sample from Chapter 2 to do the same sort of thing as you are doing with it now: capturing an image to be used as part of a user's profile. To launch the UI, call `CaptureFileAsync`, passing in a `CameraCaptureUIMode` value to indicate whether the user will be able to capture a picture, a video, or either a picture or video. This method returns a `StorageFile` object that represents the content captured. Listing 7-27 shows integrated camera capture into your ImageViewerControl.

Listing 7-27. CameraCaptureUI in Action

```
CameraCaptureUI _capture_ui;
...

public ImageViewerControl()
{
        this.InitializeComponent();
        _capture_ui = new CameraCaptureUI();
}

...

async private void TakePictureClicked(object sender, RoutedEventArgs e)
{
        _capture_ui.PhotoSettings.AllowCropping = true;
        _capture_ui.PhotoSettings.MaxResolution = CameraCaptureUIMaxPhotoResolution.
        HighestAvailable;
        var captured_image = await _capture_ui.CaptureFileAsync(CameraCaptureUIMode.Photo);
        if (captured_image != null)
        {
                await InternalLoadImageAsync(captured_image);
                ImageSelected?.Invoke(this);
        }
}
```

The other method of capturing images, the `MediaCapture` class, is also used to capture audio, video, and images from the device's camera, but provides more options to configure the device hardware. Unlike `CameraCaptureUI`, which provides a built-in user interface for the actual capturing of the content (complete with a preview surface to see what is being captured), `MediaCapture` works with the stream and devices alone. Consequently, any user interface required to convey to the user that a media capture is occurring must be created by you. To that end, an accompanying CaptureElement control is often used in conjunction with the media capture API. CaptureElement renders the UI portion of the stream being captured through the `MediaCapture` class. It is used to render the stream from the associated device.

To get started, you must call the InitializeAsync method, which initializes the capture device. InitializeAsync will launch a consent prompt to get the user's permission for the app to access the microphone or camera. In C# or C++ apps, the first use of the MediaCapture object to call InitializeAsync should be on something called an STA thread; it just so happens that the main UI of your app uses this thread. The recommendation is to call from there.

MediaCapture contains many options. For instance, it allows you to take single pictures or take pictures in burst mode. To do this, use the method PrepareLowLagPhotoSequenceCaptureAsync, which takes a rapid sequence of photos.

The VideoDeviceController property can be used to interact with the capture device when finer grained control is required. (You can use TorchControl and FlashControl properties to set the LED and flash on the device, for instance). The number of properties and features of this class are well beyond the scope of this book, so play around with them to see what they do. As you might imagine, the hardware associated with a particular feature might be available on one device and not another. Because of this, each control property provides a Supported property to determine if the device hardware supports it, so be sure to test against that property before using the feature.

To look at MediaCapture at work, you will modify the code for ImageViewerControl a bit. Listing 7-28 shows the changes you need to make to the layout, with the new additions in bold.

Listing 7-28. Using CaptureElement

```
<Grid Background="Gray"
      BorderBrush="Black"
      BorderThickness="1"
      PointerPressed="PointerPressedHandler">
    <Grid >
        <CaptureElement x:Name="capture_element" />
        <Button HorizontalAlignment="Right"
                VerticalAlignment="Bottom"
                Margin="10"
                Background="Gray"
                Content="Take Picture"
                Click="OnTakeMediaCapturePicture" />
    </Grid>

    <Image x:Name="img_control"
           Stretch="Uniform"
           ImageOpened="OnImageOpened"
           HorizontalAlignment="Stretch"
           VerticalAlignment="Stretch">
        <FlyoutBase.AttachedFlyout>
            <MenuFlyout Placement="Bottom">
                <MenuFlyoutItem Text="Browse ..."
                                Click="BrowseImageClicked" />
                <MenuFlyoutItem Text="Take Picture"
                                Click="TakePictureClicked" />
            </MenuFlyout>
        </FlyoutBase.AttachedFlyout>
    </Image>
```

```
    <SymbolIcon x:Name="symbol_camera"
                Symbol="Camera"
                HorizontalAlignment="Center"
                VerticalAlignment="Center" />
</Grid>
```

Because you are no longer using the default user interface provided by CameraCaptureUI, you need to build one out that contains both a viewfinder and a button for actually capturing your image. The grid specified here does just that. The idea here is that when the Take Picture menu item is selected, you hide the image currently being shown so that this user interface now appears. In OnTakeMediaCapturePicture, you will do all the MediaCapture stuff and then once again show the image. Listing 7-29 illustrates.

Listing 7-29. Using MediaCapture and CaptureElement

```
public sealed partial class ImageViewerControl : UserControl
{
        MediaCapture _capture;
        ...

        public ImageViewerControl()
        {
                this.InitializeComponent();
                _capture = new MediaCapture();
                this.Loaded += ImageViewerControl_Loaded;
        }

        async private void ImageViewerControl_Loaded(object sender, RoutedEventArgs e)
        {
                //initialize capture
                await _capture.InitializeAsync();
        }

        ...

        async private void TakePictureClicked(object sender, RoutedEventArgs e)
        {

                symbol_camera.Visibility = Visibility.Visible;
                img_control.Visibility = Visibility.Collapsed;

                //start previewing
                capture_element.Source = _capture;
                await _capture.StartPreviewAsync();
        }

        ...

        async private void OnTakeMediaCapturePicture(object sender, RoutedEventArgs e)
        {
                //set properties of image
                ImageEncodingProperties image_props = new ImageEncodingProperties();
                image_props.Height = (uint)this.ActualHeight;
```

```
            image_props.Width = (uint)this.ActualWidth;
            image_props.Subtype = "PNG";

            //specify where image will be stored
            var captured_image = await ApplicationData.Current.TemporaryFolder ↵
                                            .CreateFileAsync("temp.png", ↵
                                            CreationCollisionOption.GenerateUniqueName);

            //capture to file
            await _capture.CapturePhotoToStorageFileAsync(image_props, captured_image);
            img_control.Visibility = Visibility.Visible;
            await _capture.StopPreviewAsync();

            await InternalLoadImageAsync(captured_image);
            ImageSelected?.Invoke(this);
        }
}
```

The two important parts of Listing 7-29 are the TakePictureClicked and OnTakeMediaCapturePicture event handlers. In the first, you simply instantiate preview of the media capture using the CaptureElement control as the target where the stream should display. You can set what source you want to display in a CaptureElement using its Source property. In OnTakeMediaCapturePicture, you apply some specifications for the size and width of the picture you want taken using the ImageEncodingProperties class. You then create a location where you want the image stored (in this case you use the temp folder as the spot since this image will only be there for a very short time). Finally, you capture the image to the temp file and stop the CaptureElement's previewing. Since you now have a StorageFile that represents an image, you can use the same mechanisms as before to display the image on screen and notify all subscribers to the ImageSelected event.

Audio

Audio playback for UWP apps can be achieved in a number of ways. In this book, you will focus on two approaches: audio playback using the MediaElement control, and low-latency audio playback using the AudioGraph class. Later in the chapter, we will also discuss how another powerful control exposed to developers by the UWP, the WebView control, can be used to play audio located either on the Web or in your app package/isolated storage.

MediaElement

The easiest way to play audio in your UWP app is using the MediaElement control. You can use this control to play audio locally using any one of the ms- uris or point it to a location on the Web. To play media from the Web, set the Source property to the URI where the audio is stored. To play from your local repository, you can either set the URI to that local file (isolated storage or your app package) or use the programmatic approach of calling the SetSource method. Your app will play a sound in the background when the application starts, in this case the iconic windows "tada" sound.

Let's set up your project to do so. Start by creating a folder on the root of the project called Media and within that folder creating another folder called Audio. Within the Audio folder, right-click and select Add ➤ Existing Item, and then navigate to the location of tada.wav (on our machine, at C:\Windows\Media). Your project should now look like Figure 7-15.

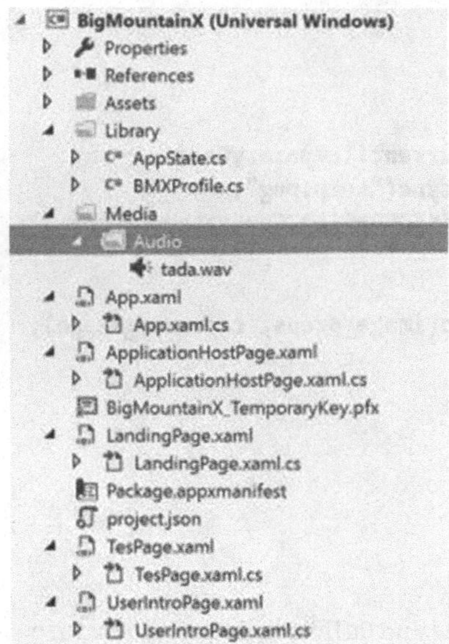

Figure 7-15. *Project structure*

In the LandingPage XAML layout, add the declaration from Listing 7-30 just above your ImageBannerControl declaration.

Listing 7-30. Audio-Only Media Element

```
<MediaElement x:Name="media" Source="ms-appx:///media/audio/tada.wav" AutoPlay="True" />
```

Run the app now. When it starts, the "tada" sound should play. Listing 7-31 shows the equivalent of this done programmatically in the Loaded event of LandingPage.

Listing 7-31. Loading Media from App Package

```
var file = await Windows.ApplicationModel.Package.Current.InstalledLocation ↵
                            .GetFileAsync("media\\audio\\tada.wav");
var raf_stream = await file.OpenReadAsync();
media.SetSource(raf_stream, "");
media.Play();
```

AudioGraph

MediaElement sits atop the stack of technologies that make up the Windows 10 audio features exposed to developers. This technology starts from the hardware, through the various drivers that interact with that hardware, through the audio engine that manipulates those drivers, and into the actual application-level APIs that utilize the audio engine. If you previously worked with Silverlight for Windows Phone, you might already be familiar with one of those APIs, the `SoundEffect` class. The `SoundEffect` class provided an easy way to play short audio clips by interacting directly with WASAPI, the low-level programming platform used to interact with the Windows Audio Engine. WASAPI, which stands for Windows Audio Session API, enables client applications to manage the flow of audio data between the application and an audio endpoint device. Within an app, WASAPI (and the MIDI control mechanisms) sit at the lowest level. Above that is the Windows Media Foundation, XAudio2 (a DirectX based audio technology), and finally a new API called the AudioGraph API. The following list described the two other low level technologies that interact with the WASAPI:

- XAudio2: Provides a signal processing and mixing foundation for games that is similar to its predecessors, DirectSound and XAudio.
- Windows Media Foundation: Underlying next-generation multimedia platform for Windows featuring enhanced robustness, quality, and interoperability.

Figure 7-16 illustrates the Windows 10 audio stack.

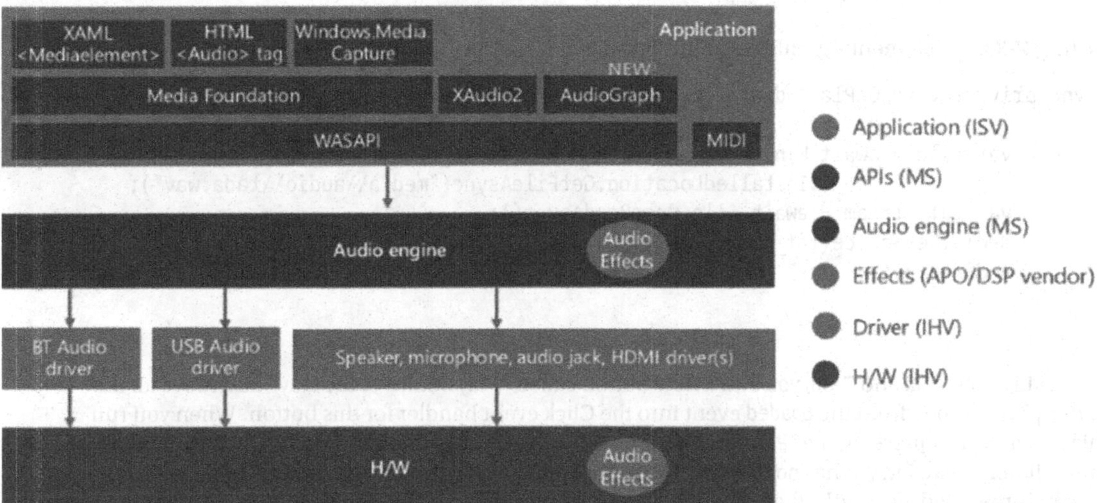

Figure 7-16. *Windows 10 audio stack*

To help process audio content in the appropriate manner, Windows 10 defines 10 categories for audio stream classification. You've already seen one of them in the previous section: using the MediaElement control you are working in what is tantamount to the Game Media category. It is designed to be played from start to finish and not to overlay itself of any other sound in the app.

Let's change the code in Listing 7-30 so that it tries to work more like a game effect that basic media. To do so, include a new button that you can click to start playing the "tada" sound. Listing 7-32 illustrates. Add the code in bold right before the ImageViewControl element.

Listing 7-32. The Play Sound of the Day Button

```
...
<MediaElement ...  />
...
<Button Content="Play Sound of the Day"
        Margin="10,0,0,10"
        Height="63"
        Width="203"
        Click="OnPlayAudioClicked"
        VerticalAlignment="Bottom" />
<lib:ImageViewerControl  HorizontalAlignment="Left"... />
...
```

The code behind for the `OnPlayAudioClicked` follows in Listing 7-33.

Listing 7-33. Implementing OnPlayAudioClicked Event Handler

```
async private void OnPlayAudioClicked(object sender, RoutedEventArgs e)
{
        var file = await Windows.ApplicationModel.Package.Current
                     .InstalledLocation.GetFileAsync("media\\audio\\tada.wav");
        var raf_stream = await file.OpenReadAsync();
        media.SetSource(raf_stream, "");
        media.Play();

}
```

In Listings 7-32 and 7-33, you add a new button called "Play Sound of the Day" and move all the audio-playing code from the `Loaded` event into the Click event handler for this button. When you run this app and start pressing the "Play Sound of the Day" button, the limitations of the media element are immediately clear. First, it has no fire-and-forget functionality. Each time the button is clicked, the audio stream is restarted. Secondly, there is a non-deterministic, unacceptable, audible clicking/popping sound that follows the ending of one tada sound and the beginning when the sound is not allowed to play till completion. When working with general purpose apps such as the Big Mountain X app, this might not be an issue, but if you were to develop a game, you would quickly find that the MediaElement control is an unacceptable approach playing game audio.

Let's change Listing 7-33 to use the `AudioGraph` class instead. The `AudioGraph` class encapsulates all the functionality of the Windows 10 Audio Graph feature set which, if you remember from Figure 7-16, lies beneath the layer where MediaElement is exposed. Listing 7-34 illustrates.

Listing 7-34. Modifying OnPlayAudioClicked to Use AudioGraph

```
async private void OnPlayAudioClicked(object sender, RoutedEventArgs e)
{
        var file = await Windows.ApplicationModel.Package.Current
                           .InstalledLocation.GetFileAsync("media\\audio\\tada.wav");

        AudioGraphSettings settings = new AudioGraphSettings(AudioRenderCategory.Media);
        var result = await AudioGraph.CreateAsync(settings);
```

```
        if (result.Status == AudioGraphCreationStatus.Success)
        {
            var graph = result.Graph;
            var output = await graph.CreateDeviceOutputNodeAsync();
            var input = await graph.CreateFileInputNodeAsync(file);
            input.FileInputNode.AddOutgoingConnection(output.DeviceOutputNode);
            graph.Start();
        }
        else
            await new MessageDialog("Not created").ShowAsync();
}
```

Run this app; now the audio is played each time the button is clicked regardless of whether it is already playing. The audio will in fact overlay any previously playing audio from the app. As easy to use as MediaElement is, it cannot fully satisfy the requirements of apps like games and audio mixers. AudioGraph introduces a mechanism to achieve this low latency (~10ms) goal, fire-and-forget audio playback. Table 7-1 shows the various audio stream categories exposed by Windows 10.

Table 7-1. *Audio Stream Categories*

Category	Description
Movie	**Replaces ForegroundOnlyMedia.** Movies, video with dialog
Media	**Replaces BackgroundCapableMedia.** Default category for media playback
Game chat	**New category.** In-game communication between users
Speech	**New category.** Speech input (e.g., personal assistant) and output (e.g., navigation apps)
Communications	VOIP, real-time chat
Alerts	Alarm, ringtone, notifications
Sound effects	Beeps, dings, etc.
Game media	In-game music
Game effects	Balls bouncing, car engine sounds, bullets, etc.
Other	Uncategorized streams

The audio graph is made up of input nodes (sources) and output nodes (sinks), and sub-mix nodes. An input or output node can represent either a pulse code modulation (PCM) buffer or an audio device, such as a capture device. There are no limits on the number of sources and sinks for an audio graph. The graph uses an audio connection that allows the same source node to provide output to different downstream nodes at different volumes. The entire audio graph must operate at the same sample rate. Sources can have different sample rates, but are resampled immediately. The most basic audio graph scenario consists of one input node, one output node, and playback. Effects can be added to any node in the graph. The graph processes them in the order in which they are added.

Audio Capture

Suppose you want to add a feature to the Big Mountain X app that allows users to send audio feedback to actors involved in each skit. How would you go about doing this? You've already seen how images can be captured using either the CameraCaptureUI or the MediaCapture class, so you should be somewhat familiar now with media capture in general. In addition to providing a mechanism for previewing and capturing images, the MediaCapture class also provides a way to capture audio to a file. To illustrate the audio capturing features of Windows 10, let's add a new toggle button called Audio Message that when toggled on will allow the user to record audio and when toggled off will store that audio in a new app data folder called AudioFeedback. Listing 7-35 shows the code. You make some modifications to the class (highlighted in bold) for readability and to encapsulate the audio playback functionality so it can be used to play any storage file passed into it.

Listing 7-35. Implementing Audio Feedback Using MediaCapture

```
MediaCapture _capture = null;
AudioGraph _graph_record;
StorageFile _target_file = null;

...

async private void OnPlayAudioClicked(object sender, RoutedEventArgs e)
{
        var file = await Windows.ApplicationModel.Package.Current
                .InstalledLocation.GetFileAsync("media\\audio\\tada.wav");
        await PlayAudio(file);
}

private static async Task PlayAudio(StorageFile file)
{
        AudioGraphSettings settings = new AudioGraphSettings(AudioRenderCategory.Media);
        var result = await AudioGraph.CreateAsync(settings);

        if (result.Status == AudioGraphCreationStatus.Success)
        {
                var graph = result.Graph;
                var output = await graph.CreateDeviceOutputNodeAsync();
                var input = await graph.CreateFileInputNodeAsync(file);
                input.FileInputNode.AddOutgoingConnection(output.DeviceOutputNode);
                graph.Start();

        }
        else
                await new MessageDialog("Not created").ShowAsync();
}

async private Task RecordAsync(ToggleButton btn_record_audio)
{
   MediaCaptureInitializationSettings settings = new MediaCaptureInitializationSettings();
   settings.StreamingCaptureMode = StreamingCaptureMode.Audio;
```

```
    _capture = new MediaCapture();
    await _capture.InitializeAsync(settings);
    var profile = MediaEncodingProfile.CreateMp3(AudioEncodingQuality.High);
    var local_folder =  ApplicationData.Current.LocalFolder;
    var feedback_folder = await local_folder.CreateFolderAsync("AudioFeedback" ↩
                                                          ,CreationCollisionOption.
                                                          OpenIfExists);

    _target_file = await feedback_folder.CreateFileAsync("audio message.mp3", ↩
                                                CreationCollisionOption.GenerateUniqueName);
    await _capture.StartRecordToStorageFileAsync(profile, _target_file);

}

async private Task StopRecordingAsync()
{
        await _capture.StopRecordAsync();
        await PlayAudio(_target_file);
}

async private void ToggleRecord(object sender, RoutedEventArgs e)
{
        var btn_record_audio = sender as ToggleButton;
        if (btn_record_audio.IsChecked == false)
        {
                await StopRecordingAsync();
        }
        else
        {
                await RecordAsync(btn_record_audio);
        }
}
```

In Listing 7-35, you start by initializing a new AudioGraphSettings object to Media. The value passed in here represents the class of audio being created for the AudioGraph. You went through the various media types in Table 7-1. Next, you create a new AudioGraph using the settings you specified. Then you test to see if this works and, if so, use it to create a DeviceOutputNode. As discussed earlier, you can think of an AudioGraph as a network of nodes working together to deliver the final audio that the user hears. Input nodes accept input from some source; this can be a file or an audio capture device. Output nodes send the audio stream that has passed through the graph out to some target. Again, this can be a device (like a speaker, midi, etc.), or it can be a file. In between this, submixing and effects may occur. In the case of this sample, your input node is the file you are planning to play and your output node is the audio device that will be playing the audio in the file. Once you have the graph fully connected, you use the Start method to execute it. This should play the file.

Next, modify the layout for your Landing page to add the new ToggleButton. Once again, the user interface has been cleaned up somewhat to allow for future modifications. Listing 7-36 shows the new layout.

Listing 7-36. UI Changes for Audio Capture

```
<Grid Background="{ThemeResource ApplicationPageBackgroundThemeBrush}">
...
<StackPanel Margin="10,0,0,10"
            VerticalAlignment="Bottom"
            HorizontalAlignment="Left"
            Orientation="Horizontal">
    <Button Content="Play Sound of the Day"
            Height="63"
            Width="203"
            Click="OnPlayAudioClicked"
            VerticalAlignment="Bottom"
            Margin="5" />
    <ToggleButton Content="Audio Message"
                  Height="63"
                  Width="203"
                  Click="ToggleRecord"
                  VerticalAlignment="Bottom"
                  Margin="5" />
</StackPanel>
<lib:ImageViewerControl  HorizontalAlignment="Left"
                                  VerticalAlignment="Top"
                                  Margin="10"
                                  Height="100"
                                  Width="100"
                                  Loaded="OnImageViewerLoaded"
                                  ImageSelected="OnImageSelected" />
</Grid>
```

In Listing 7-36, a new horizontally-oriented StackPanel has been added to the Landing page, and within it you add both buttons.

Audio can also be captured using the low latency APIs exposed through the AudioGraph class. As stated in the previous section, an audio graph is made up of input nodes and output nodes. Input nodes can be any PCM buffer but can also be an audio capture device (like the microphone). In Listing 7-37, you add a different event hander to the Audio Message function which uses the AudioGraph class to capture audio.

Listing 7-37. Using AudioGraph for Audio Capture

```
async private void ToggleRecord2(object sender, RoutedEventArgs e)
{
        var btn_record_audio = sender as ToggleButton;
        if (btn_record_audio.IsChecked == false)
        {
                _graph_record.Stop();
                _graph_record.Dispose();
                await PlayAudio(_target_file);
        }
        else
        {
```

```
            //initialize the audio graph for recording and then start recording
            AudioGraphSettings settings = new AudioGraphSettings(AudioRenderCategory.Media);
            settings.QuantumSizeSelectionMode = QuantumSizeSelectionMode.LowestLatency;

            CreateAudioGraphResult result = await AudioGraph.CreateAsync(settings);
            if (result.Status == AudioGraphCreationStatus.Success)
            {
                _graph_record = result.Graph;

                //setup the input
                var input_node = (await _graph_record↵
                .CreateDeviceInputNodeAsync(Windows.Media.Capture ↵
                .MediaCategory.Other)).DeviceInputNode;

                //setup the output (place where audio will be recorded to)
                var feedback_folder = await ApplicationData.Current.LocalFolder↵
                .CreateFolderAsync("AudioFeedback",
                                    CreationCollisionOption.OpenIfExists);
                _target_file = await feedback_folder.CreateFileAsync("audio
                message.mp3", CreationCollisionOption.GenerateUniqueName);

                var profile = MediaEncodingProfile.CreateMp3(AudioEncodingQuality.High);
                var file_output_node = (await _graph_record ↵
                                .CreateFileOutputNodeAsync(_target_file, profile))↵
                                                    .FileOutputNode;

                //direct the input to the output
                input_node.AddOutgoingConnection(file_output_node);
                _graph_record.Start();

            }
            else
                await new MessageDialog("Could not initialize recorder").ShowAsync();

        }
}
```

In Listing 7-37, you use the AudioGraph to capture audio from the default audio capture device on the user's computer. If the previous example and subsequent explanation did not make clear the power and flexibility of the AudioGraph class, this sample should. All you do here is reverse the direction of audio flow. In your AudioGraph-based audio playback example, you read from a file and published the data to an output device. In this example, you read from an audio input device and publish the stream data to a file. To utilize this code, change the Click event handler for the Audio Message ToggleButton from using ToggleRecord to using ToggleRecord2.

Video

Video playback for UWP apps works that same as audio playback; it follows the pattern of using the familiar MediaElement tag. As discussed in the Audio section, in UWP apps, media for playback can come from one of two places (in general): it can be local to the machine, or it can be streamed/progressively-downloaded from some remote source on the Web. Local media is placed in the project structure in the same manner as XAML content (and any other kind of content that needs to be referenced in your application); as such, the impact to your overall app deployment size is affected. Such content is accessed using the `ms-appx` notation but can also be access programmatically using the techniques outlined in Chapter 6.

You will be placing the video content you plan to play within your Big Mountain X project structure initially and you will also see how easy it is to stream that content using the MediaElement. You can directly download a copy of the recording from `http://download.blender.org/peach/bigbuckbunny_movies/BigBuckBunny_320x180.mp4`. Once downloaded, create a new folder in the `Media` subfolder of your project by right-clicking the `Media` folder and selecting Add ➤ New Folder. Call the new folder `Video`. Next, right-click the newly created folder and select Add ➤ Existing Item and add the downloaded media content to your project.

Now change your Landing page to show the MediaElement completely (in the sample you will also shift the position and size of the media element you use). Previously, it functioned as a control for enabling background audio; since you can use the `AudioGraph` to do this, you will repurpose it as a video preview area for the most recent event that the Big Mountain folks have put on. Change the definition of the MediaElement to that in Listing 7-38. Then move the MediaElement so that is the last element in the Grid (it should show up as the lowest element in the XAML for the Grid).

Listing 7-38. Simple MediaElement

```
<MediaElement x:Name="media"
              Visibility="Visible"
              Width="500"
              Height="400"
              Margin="0,109,22,0"
              AutoPlay="True"
              VerticalAlignment="Top"
        Source="media/video/BigBuckBunny_320x180.mp4"
              HorizontalAlignment="Right" />
```

When you run the app, the landing page should now look like Figure 7-17.

Figure 7-17. Landing Page user interface

As in the audio section, playback starts immediately here because the `AutoPlay` attribute is set to true. You can delegate playback control to the user by making the playback controls visible as shown in Listing 7-39.

Listing 7-39. Video Playback Controls

```
<MediaElement x:Name="media"
...
          AreTransportControlsEnabled="True"
 ...
 />
```

Of course, you can also control playback programmatically using the `Play`, `Pause`, and `Stop` methods.

In addition to `AutoPlay` and `AreTransportControlsEnabled`, you can apply various other attributes to the MediaElement tag. These include but are of course not limited to the following:

- `IsMuted`: Tells the video control to mute audio.
- `PosterSource`: Allows you to specify a URL that points to an image that is displayed while the video isn't playing. It can be quite useful for depicting the content of the video before the user decides to play it.
- `IsLooping`: Tells the video control to restart the video after it has completed.

Using the MediaElement tag, you can also play back media directly from a backend web server. For this to work, you have to add the *Internet Client* capabilities to your application manifest as described in Chapter 1. Internet Client grants a Windows 10 app permission to access the Internet. Without it, you can't connect to any cloud-based resource through any API. Fortunately, it is currently added by default by Visual Studio 2015.

Video Capture

Like audio capture, video capture uses the `MediaCapture` class to accomplish its task. As you saw earlier in the Images section, capturing using the `MediaCapture` class allows you to use a CaptureElement control to render a preview of the stream being presently captured. You can think of the CaptureElement control like a view finder on a camera (particularly when used for video capture). Listing 7-40 adds a video feedback button to the landing page for users who chose to leave video-based comments for the Big Mountain X crew.

Listing 7-40. Preparing UI for Video Capture

```
<StackPanel ...>
...
<Button Content="Video Message"
        Height="63"
        Width="203"
        Click="ToggleRecordVideo"
        VerticalAlignment="Bottom"
        Margin="5">
    <FlyoutBase.AttachedFlyout>
        <Flyout x:Name="flyout_videomessage"
                Placement="Top">
            <Grid Width="300"
                    Height="200"
                    Background="Yellow">
                <Grid.RowDefinitions>
                    <RowDefinition Height="80*" />
                    <RowDefinition Height="20*" />
                </Grid.RowDefinitions>

                <CaptureElement x:Name="capture_element"
                                Margin="2.5"
                                HorizontalAlignment="Stretch" />
                <Button x:Name="stop_recording"
                        Height="50"
                        Content="Stop Recording"
                        Margin="2.5"
                        HorizontalAlignment="Stretch"
                        Grid.Row="1"
                        Click="OnStopVideoCapture" />
                <MediaElement x:Name="media_message"
                                Grid.Row="0"
                                Grid.RowSpan="2"
                                Width="300"
                                AutoPlay="False"
```

```
                                            Height="200"
                                            Visibility="Visible"
                                            MediaOpened="OnVideoMessageRecordingReady"
                                            MediaEnded="OnVideoMessagePlaybackCompleted" />
                </Grid>
            </Flyout>
        </FlyoutBase.AttachedFlyout>
</Button>
</StackPanel>
```

The button from Listing 7-40 defines a flyout that contains the user interface for showing the recording preview as well as the actual recording that was made. When it is clicked, the flyout is displayed. When the Stop recording button is clicked, the video recording is stopped and played back to the user. At some point when the recording is completed, the flyout is forcibly closed. Listing 7-41 below shows the code-behind that enables this functionality. Add it to Landing to enable video messages be captured and stored to the user's app data folder.

Listing 7-41. Video Capture Using MediaCapture Class

```
async private void ToggleRecordVideo(object sender, RoutedEventArgs e)
{
        //initialize capture
        MediaCaptureInitializationSettings settings = new MediaCaptureInitializationSettings();
        settings.StreamingCaptureMode = StreamingCaptureMode.AudioAndVideo;
        _capture = new MediaCapture();
        await _capture.InitializeAsync(settings);

        //start preview
        capture_element.Source = _capture;
        await _capture.StartPreviewAsync();

        //start capturing media
        var profile = MediaEncodingProfile.CreateMp4(VideoEncodingQuality.Vga);
        var feedback_folder = await Windows.Storage.ApplicationData ↵
        .Current.LocalFolder.CreateFolderAsync("VideoFeedback", CreationCollisionOption.
        OpenIfExists);

        _target_file = await feedback_folder.CreateFileAsync("video message.mp4",↵
        CreationCollisionOption.GenerateUniqueName);
        await _capture.StartRecordToStorageFileAsync(profile, _target_file);

        //show the flyout menu
        media_message.Visibility = Visibility.Collapsed;
        media.Stop();  //stop playback since you are recording
        FlyoutBase.ShowAttachedFlyout(sender as FrameworkElement);
}
```

```
async private void OnStopVideoCapture(object sender, RoutedEventArgs e)
{
        await _capture.StopRecordAsync();
        await _capture.StopPreviewAsync();

        media_message.Visibility = Visibility.Visible;
        var raf_stream = await _target_file.OpenReadAsync();
        media_message.SetSource(raf_stream, "video/mp4");
}

private void OnVideoMessageRecordingReady(object sender, RoutedEventArgs e)
{
        media_message.Play();
}

private void OnVideoMessagePlaybackCompleted(object sender, RoutedEventArgs e)
{
        flyout_videomessage.Hide();
}
```

In Listing 7-41, ToggleRecordVideo uses the familiar `MediaCapture` class to enable the video capture functionality. The only real difference between the code here and the code used in the audio capture samples is that the encoding profile is mapped to a video file format (in this case mp4). This choice is also reflected in the file extension used.

Background Audio

The previous section started delving into the intricacies of MediaElement. You saw how it can be used to play audio data located on the user's machine or from a remote server. When these audio files play, however, they are designed by default to only play in the foreground. In the world of Windows 10, this means once you switch away from your app (minimize on the desktop), the sound stops. You can try this now with the app at this point. Start it and the Big Buck Bunny begins to play, minimize it (or navigate away from it on your Windows 10 mobile device/emulator) and the sound stops. Navigate back to the application, and the audio starts again. If you paid close attention to the playback time of the media when you navigated away, notice that it has increased in value from the point at which you navigated away (and also notice that the media is playing from a later position). This is because the audio has been playing while the app was shifted to the background. However, because audio configured in this manner can't be heard when the app hosting it is no longer visible to the user, you hear nothing when you switch to a different app.

Enabling background playback requires three steps. First, you need to declaratively tell Windows that the MediaElement is designed for background audio playback. You then need to inform Windows of your intent to have the application running in the background (for the purpose of playing the audio). Finally, you need to hook your application up to the background audio playback infrastructure so that a user can use the Windows media playback controls to control the background audio. Let's get started. Let's implement background media playback for the video playing when the app starts (your "most recent event" video).

In the MediaElement tag, you assign a value to the `AudioCategory` property. The system uses this property to identify and manage the performance and integration of audio. When the value is set to `BackgroundCapableMedia`, it earmarks audio being played through the MediaElement as available to the background audio player.

The next step is to add a new declaration in the Declarations tab of the project's package.appxmanifest configuration file. A background task must be implemented within a Windows Runtime Component, a kind of class library that can be interacted with from within any of the supported UWP languages. Right-click the Solution Explorer and add a new project to the solution entitled BMX.BackgroundTasks. Once created, remove the default class that is added (class1.cs) and add a new class called AudioPlayback. (Note that we will delve into background tasks in more detail in Chapter 9. For now you will mainly be working with the background audio piece of the much larger subject.) Add the class definition for the AudioPlayback class shown in Listing 7-42.

Listing 7-42. Implementing a Simple Background Audio Task

```
sealed public class AudioPlayback : IBackgroundTask
{
        private BackgroundTaskDeferral _deferral;
        public void Run(IBackgroundTaskInstance taskInstance)
        {
                _deferral = taskInstance.GetDeferral();
                taskInstance.Task.Completed += TaskCompleted;
        }

        void TaskCompleted(BackgroundTaskRegistration sender,
                                 BackgroundTaskCompletedEventArgs args)
        {
                _deferral.Complete();
        }
}
```

The important thing to note here is the use of the BackgroundTaskDefferal object. A deferral is used to prevent the closing of an activity; in this case once you have the deferral, the background task will be kept alive until you call complete. Build the solution and add the newly created library as a reference to your main BigMountainX app using the Add Reference feature.

You now need to register the class you created as being the background audio manager for your app. You add a new Background Task declaration that supports audio tasks and specify your newly created class as the entry point for the task. Open the package manifest and add a new background task declaration as Figure 7-18 illustrates.

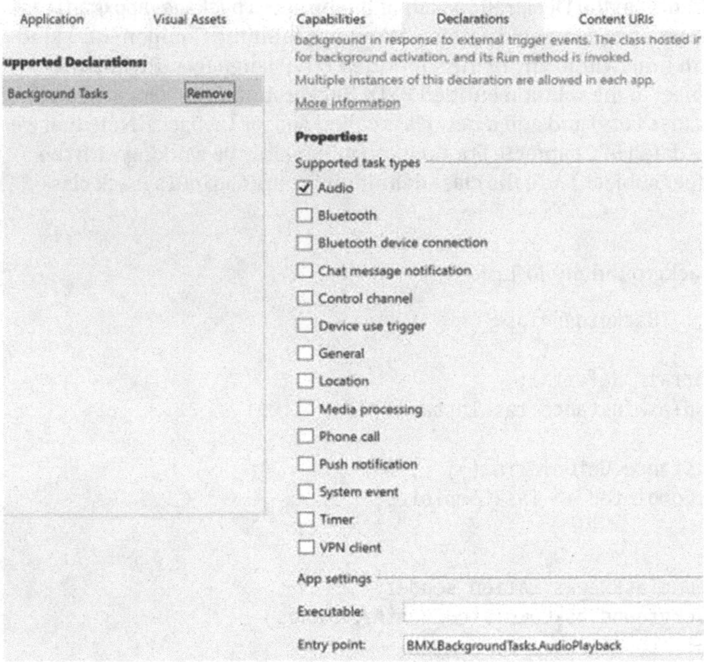

Figure 7-18. *Background audio declaration*

At this point you are basically ready to go, but when you run your app once again and minimize it, you should note that the audio for the movie is also lost. The reason for this is simple: although you have configured your background task, you have not started it.

The easiest way to start a background task such as this is to simply send a message to it. Doing so obviously causes it to be activated by the system, and since you have a deferral that keeps it from being closed until you are done with it, causes it to live until the foreground piece of your app exits. Add the code in Listing 7-43 to the `Loaded` event of LandingPage.

Listing 7-43. Starting Your Background Audio Task

```
await this.Dispatcher.RunAsync(CoreDispatcherPriority.Normal, () =>
{
        BackgroundMediaPlayer.SendMessageToBackground(new ValueSet());
});
```

Listing 7-43 uses the `BackgroundMediaPlayer` class to send a message to the background audio task associated with your app. A background audio task must be configured for this code to function properly. The runtime expects that a class that inherits from `IBackgroundTask` has been defined and that your manifest declares that class as being a background audio task. Run the app now and you will note that the audio for your Big Buck Bunny video continues to play even when minimized. In Chapter 9, when you get into more details on background tasks, you will revisit the background media player and learn how to create background playlists that an end user can skip through and even control using the system-wide media control buttons.

Using WebView to Display Render Media

So far, you have seen the many ways that media can be utilized in a UWP app. You walked through displaying and capturing images, audio, and video using not only the high-level controls and helper classes but also low-level APIs. As you went through the tutorial, we discussed the many media formats that are available to Windows 10 developers targeting UWP apps. But what if a media format is not available to you or you don't have direct access to the media files? In edge cases where no APIs are exposed to render or utilize a particular media format, embedding a web browser in your app might be the answer. In the following example, you will add a WebView to the app which points you to a video hosted on YouTube. YouTube video streams are notoriously difficult to access directly, but because WebView is essentially a web browser, it is possible to use it in this case like a media presentation control. Listing 7-44 illustrates.

Listing 7-44. Using WebView to Stream YouTube

```
...
<WebView x:Name="browser" HorizontalAlignment="Right" VerticalAlignment="Bottom"
         Margin="0,0,10,10"
         Source="http://www.youtube.com/embed/QKYuTuVqpWO?autoplay=1"
         Height="300" Width="400" />
<lib:ImageViewerControl ... />
```

When run, the app should now look like Figure 7-19.

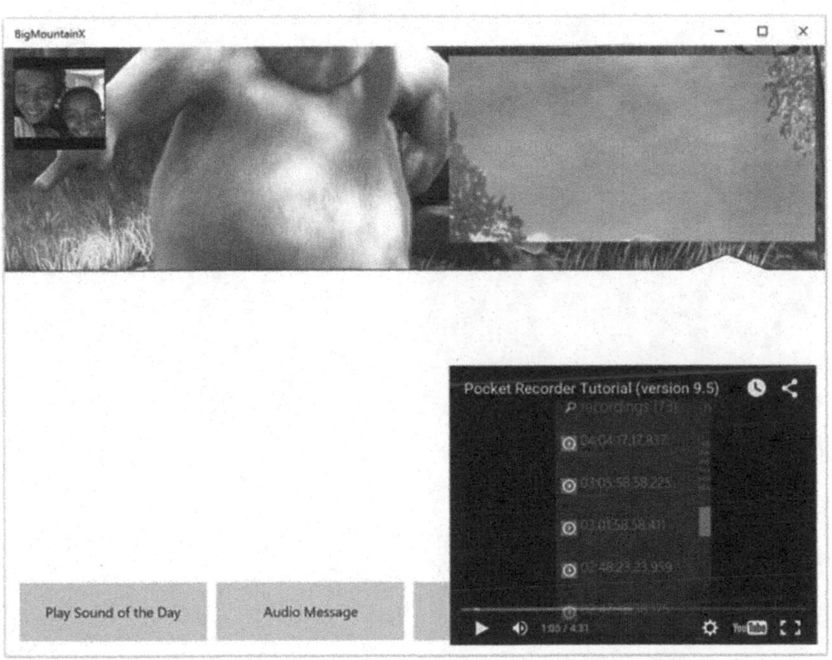

Figure 7-19. *WebView rendering YouTube video*

Summary

In this chapter, you learned about the many ways media can be used in your application. The findings in this chapter include the following:

- The integration of media playback into your app from local sources as well as remote websites
- Media capture and the many approaches you can take to facilitate it in your application, and the multitude of things you can do using the `CameraCaptureUI`
- The more powerful `MediaCapture` class, which provides functionality to capture audio and create custom viewfinders for capturing video
- Using the `MediaCapture` API in scenarios when it's important to stay in your application's user interface (and, of course, in advanced scenarios when you need lower-level refinement of the capture pipeline)
- Using the AudioGraph API in situations where low level access to audio streams with submixing is needed
- Using the WebView control as a fallback to access media that is not directly supported through the API set
- Background audio and how to implement a background audio task in your app so that when the app is minimized the audio continues to play

CHAPTER 8

Location and Mapping

In this chapter, you will examine the use of the device's location sensors to retrieve location data and enable UWP apps that are location aware. Location awareness is a component of an overarching technology set commonly referred to as *presence technology*, which is used to deliver information about a given device's physical location to apps that support reading this data. A device's location is usually determined by one of three methods: via GPS satellite tracking, cellular tower triangulation, or by the device's MAC address on a network. The accuracy of the location information depends on the source. The latitude and longitude may vary within the following ranges:

- GPS: Within approximately 10 meters (~33 feet)
- Wi-Fi: Between approximately 30 meters and 500 meters (between 98 and 1,640 feet)
- Cell towers: Between approximately 300 meters and 3,000 meters (between 984 feet and 2 miles)
- IP address: Between approximately 1,000 meters and 5,000 meters (between .5 and 3 miles)

The applications for this kind of telemetry information are endless. For instance, location-aware technology uses include the following:

1. Multi-factor security for ATM sign-in
2. GPS systems in vehicles
3. Auto-tagging of pictures with location data
4. Supply chain management

Mapping extends the power of location awareness by allowing you to place location data onto the map surface so as to give a visual representation of the location of the device. Additionally, because mapping data contains actual physical addresses, mapping can be used translate longitude/latitude information into more meaningful information like the city that encompasses the point and the address closest to the given point.

In this chapter, you will take an in-depth look at using these two technologies, mapping and location services, together to create engaging experiences for the user. You will extend the functionality currently present in your Big Mountain X app to now include the power of location awareness and mapping.

Location Awareness

Before a UWP app can access location data through the location-sensitive component on a user's device, location services must be enabled explicitly by the user on the device. To do this, open the Settings section and navigate to Privacy ➤ Location. On the details page, click the Change button under "Location for this device" and set the toggle button to On. As is explained on the page, setting this value to On enables each person who signs onto the device to change their own location settings. If the value is Off, then location is turned off for everyone who signs in.

Next, set the Location toggle button to On. Finally, check to see if the given app is listed in the section entitled "Choose apps that can use your location" and set the value for the app to On (if not already set). Doing this indicates to the system that the app is allowed to use location services.

This would be a laborious process if a user had to follow this process every time a new app that accessed locations was installed. Fortunately, there is a mechanism that can be used in-app to add an app to the list and set its location access value to true. We will be discussing the approach to building a location-aware app in the next section. Figure 8-1 shows the location privacy settings.

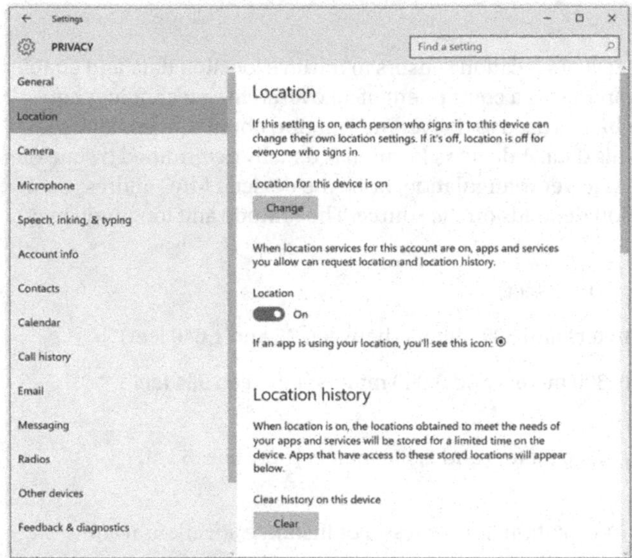

Figure 8-1. *Location setting screen*

Enabling Location Functionality

The approach identified above works in a situation where your app has been downloaded by an end user and the user wants to configure location awareness for it, but how do you as a developer declare that your app requires location services to begin with? The answer is to use the `package.appxmanifest` file.

Open the BigMountainX project that you started in Chapter 7. Once open, double-click `package.appxmanifest` in Solution Explorer to open the application manifest file. As with the other permissions discussed in previous chapters, enabling features requires declaring to the user that your app uses the corresponding UWP capability. You did this in Chapter 6 with the file permissions and you will be doing it in this chapter with location.

The UWP exposes one capability for enabling location services in your app, and that capability is the Location capability. Navigate to the Capabilities tab and check the Location checkbox in the list of capabilities. Figure 8-2 shows what your BigMountainX app manifest file should now look like with this capability enabled.

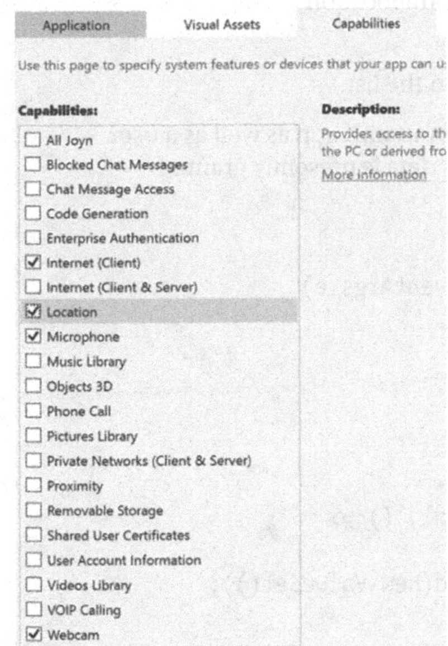

Figure 8-2. *Location capability in app manifest*

Now, create a new folder in the root of the BigMountainX project called `Data`. Next, download the project files for this chapter from this book's download site. Once downloaded, copy the file `cities.csv` (located in the same `Data` folder in the sample project) to your local project's `Data` folder.

Requesting Access to Location Data

Much of the functionality related to location services (all of the functionality we will discuss in this book) is encapsulated in the `Geolocator` class (found in the `Windows.Devices.Geolocation` namespace). The first step to using any of the location services APIs is to request access to the user's location using the `RequestAccessAsync` method of `Geolocator`. For `RequestAccessAsync` to work, the app from which it is called must be in the foreground and `RequestAccessAsync` must be called from the UI thread. This method prompts the user for permission to access their location once (per app). The result of this method is an entry into the list of apps that are a part of the Choose apps that can access your location section of the location privacy settings, as discussed earlier. If the user denies permission location, data cannot be accessed and the toggle button from this app is set to Off. If the user grants access, the toggle button is set to On (and of course location data can be accessed). `RequestAccessAsync` respects the settings defined in this list and uses them to determine the result of the method call going forward. This means that, after the very first call, you can freely call this method and it will always return with the present access permission granted by the user for location data.

To be clear, the process is as follows.

1. RequestAccessAsync is called.
2. The method checks to see if there is an entry in the list.
3. If there is an entry, it returns the result of that entry.

4. If there is no entry, the user is prompted to choose if they want location awareness enabled for that app.

5. The result of that user choice is used to create a new entry in the list.

In Listing 8-1, you add the location awareness request to the BigMountainX app as well as a user interface element to let the user know if the permission to read location data is presently granted.

Listing 8-1. Requesting Access to Location Information

```
async private void LandingPage_Loaded(object sender, RoutedEventArgs e)
{
        _timer.Start();
        img_banner.SetImage(_images[_image_index]);
        _image_index++;

        //initialize the background audio task
        this.Dispatcher.RunAsync(CoreDispatcherPriority.Normal, () =>
        {
                BackgroundMediaPlayer.SendMessageToBackground(new ValueSet());
        });

        var access_status = await Geolocator.RequestAccessAsync();
        switch (access_status)
        {
                case GeolocationAccessStatus.Allowed:
                        break;
                case GeolocationAccessStatus.Denied:
                        break;
                case GeolocationAccessStatus.Unspecified:
                        break;
        }
}
```

In Listing 8-1, you add the location access request to the `Loaded` event of the page so that it is one of the first things checked by the app. You set the result to a value that you then use as the condition of a switch statement. `RequestAccessAsync` returns an enum of type `GeolocationAccessStatus`, which at present can be of value `Allowed`, `Denied`, or `Unspecified`. Build and run this app, and you will be prompted once the app loads to allow BigMountainX to access your location. Figure 8-3 illustrates.

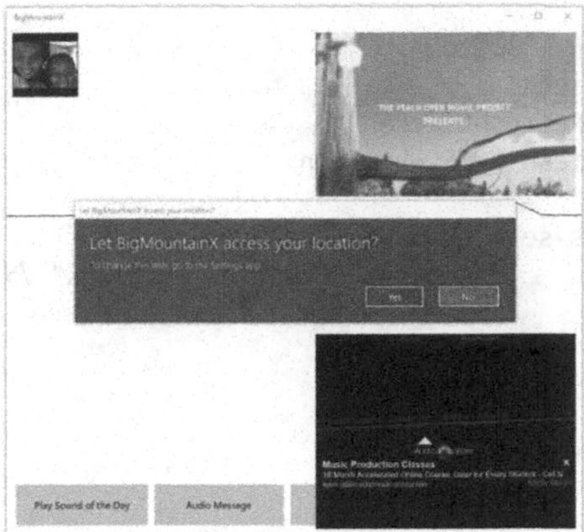

Figure 8-3. *Location access user prompt*

Make your choice (it does not have to be yes at the moment). Open Privacy ➤ Location and scroll down; you should now see your app present in the list with the selection you made. In our case, we selected No. Figure 8-4 shows the relevant section of the app location access list on our machine.

Choose apps that can use your location

App connector Off

BigMountainX Off

Camera On

Figure 8-4. *Location access toggle*

Run the app now and you will notice that you are no longer prompted.

Because all future permission must be granted using the settings page for location privacy, we recommend providing a link to this page so that the user can quickly navigate to that setting and toggle permissions as they see fit. Settings pages have specific URIs that can be used to access them, identified by the protocol *ms-settings*. For the location privacy settings page, the URI is `ms-settings:privacy-location`. For a full listing of the URIs to all the various settings, go to `https://msdn.microsoft.com/en-us/library/windows/apps/mt228342.aspx`.

In Listing 8-2, you add a new page, NoLocationPage, which you will configure to display when your app starts and location awareness has been disabled by the user.

Listing 8-2. NoLocationPage Page Definition

```
<Grid Background="{ThemeResource ApplicationPageBackgroundThemeBrush}">
        <Grid Height="105"
                        Width="400"
                        HorizontalAlignment="Center"
                        VerticalAlignment="Center">
                <TextBlock TextWrapping="WrapWholeWords"
                        Margin="0">Location services must be enabled for this app to
                        function propertly.  Use the link below to do so.
                </TextBlock>
```

```
            <StackPanel HorizontalAlignment="Right"
                              VerticalAlignment="Bottom">
                  <Button  HorizontalAlignment="Right"
                                    Click="RefreshClicked">
                        <SymbolIcon Symbol="Refresh"></SymbolIcon>
                  </Button>
                  <HyperlinkButton NavigateUri="ms-settings:privacy-location"
                                                      Content="Location Settings" />

            </StackPanel>

      </Grid>

</Grid>
```

Listing 8-2 configures your new page to display some basic text that tells the user that location services are needed. A link is provided which points the user to the location privacy settings page when clicked. A button is also present on the page with a click event handler. This button is used to requery the location infrastructure when clicked. The idea here is that the user first navigates to the settings page, changes the setting to enable location awareness, and then goes back into the app to click the button to once again test to see if location awareness has been enabled. If enabled, it navigates to your landing page. The code-behind in Listing 8-3 illustrates.

Listing 8-3. NoLocationPage Code-Behind

```
public sealed partial class NoLocationPage : Page
{
      public NoLocationPage()
      {
            this.InitializeComponent();
      }

      async private void RefreshClicked(object sender, RoutedEventArgs e)
      {
            var access_status = await Geolocator.RequestAccessAsync();
            switch (access_status)
            {
                  case GeolocationAccessStatus.Allowed:
                        Frame.Navigate(typeof(LandingPage));
                        break;
                  case GeolocationAccessStatus.Denied:

                        break;
                  case GeolocationAccessStatus.Unspecified:
                        break;
            }
      }
}
```

Although the landing page is a fine place to put the code, it is less than ideal. Presumably there might be calls to perform actions like data binding; there might even be external web services calls taking place in the landing page (some of the code might even execute outside of the loaded event). A better location for code like this is in the ApplicationHostPage, which is used to host the root frame that the app runs within. Modify ApplicationHostPage's loaded event as follows to enable the functionality. Listing 8-4 illustrates (new code is highlighted in bold).

Listing 8-4. Modifications to ApplicationHostPage's Loaded Event

```
async private void ApplicationHostPage_Loaded(object sender, RoutedEventArgs e)
{
        if (App.State.UserProfile == null)
                root_frame.Navigate(typeof(UserIntroPage));
        else
        {
                var access_status = await Geolocator.RequestAccessAsync();
                switch (access_status)
                {
                        case GeolocationAccessStatus.Allowed:
                                root_frame.Navigate(typeof(LandingPage));
                                break;
                        case GeolocationAccessStatus.Denied:
                                root_frame.Navigate(typeof(NoLocationPage));
                                break;
                        case GeolocationAccessStatus.Unspecified:
                                break;
                }

        }
}
```

To ensure that users cannot navigate to NoLocationPage (or any other page in the app) from LandingPage using the back-stack (by click the back button), add the following code to the loaded event of LandingPage:

```
Frame.BackStack.Clear();
```

Run the app and test the behavior based when location awareness in enabled and disabled.

Getting the Current Location

To access the user's position, use the `GetGeopositionAsync` method. `GetGeopositionAsync` performs a one-time reading of the current location. Unlike requesting access to the location data, `GetGeopositionAsync` requires an instance of the `Geolocation` object to be created. Listing 8-5 adds code to retrieve the location of the user's device and stores it in a global variable that can be accessed throughout the BigMountainX app. New code is highlighted in bold.

Listing 8-5. Modifications to ApplicationHostPage

```
Geolocator _geolocator;
public Geoposition CurrentLocation;
public static ApplicationHostPage Host { get; private set; }

public ApplicationHostPage()
{
        this.InitializeComponent();
        this.Loaded += ApplicationHostPage_Loaded;
        Host = this;
        _geolocator = new Geolocator();
}

async private void ApplicationHostPage_Loaded(object sender, RoutedEventArgs e)
{
        if (App.State.UserProfile == null)
                root_frame.Navigate(typeof(UserIntroPage));
        else
        {
                var access_status = await Geolocator.RequestAccessAsync();
                switch (access_status)
                {
                        case GeolocationAccessStatus.Allowed:

                                root_frame.Navigate(typeof(LandingPage));
                                CurrentLocation = await _geolocator.GetGeopositionAsync();

                                break;
                        case GeolocationAccessStatus.Denied:
                                root_frame.Navigate(typeof(NoLocationPage));
                                break;
                        case GeolocationAccessStatus.Unspecified:
                                break;
                }

        }
}
```

If you tried to use the value of `CurrentLocation` in LandingPage you might find that it is null at this point. This is understandable since the call to get the position is asynchronous. In Listing 8-6, you modify the code from Listing 8-5 to support reading the values in a safe manner. In Listing 8-6, the values are requested in ApplicationHostPage but used in the LandingPage.

Listing 8-6. Adding GetLocationChanged Event Handler

```
...

public event Action<Geopoint> GeoLocationChanged;
...
```

```
public ApplicationHostPage()
{
        ...
}

async private void ApplicationHostPage_Loaded(object sender, RoutedEventArgs e)
{
        if (App.State.UserProfile == null)
                root_frame.Navigate(typeof(UserIntroPage));
        else
        {
                var access_status = await Geolocator.RequestAccessAsync();
                switch (access_status)
                {
                        case GeolocationAccessStatus.Allowed:
                                root_frame.Navigate(typeof(LandingPage));
                                CurrentLocation = await _geolocator.GetGeopositionAsync();
                                GeoLocationChanged?.Invoke(CurrentLocation.Coordinate.
                                Point);

                                break;
                        case GeolocationAccessStatus.Denied:
                                root_frame.Navigate(typeof(NoLocationPage));
                                break;
                        case GeolocationAccessStatus.Unspecified:
                                break;
                }

        }
}
```

Now open LandingPage and add the code highlighted in bold in Listing 8-7 to the grid.

Listing 8-7. Adding txt_location TextBlock

```
...
<Grid>
        <Grid.RowDefinitions>
                <RowDefinition Height="40*" />
                <RowDefinition Height="60*" />
        </Grid.RowDefinitions>
        <lib:ImageBannerControl x:Name="img_banner" />
        <MediaElement x:Name="media"
                                        AudioCategory="BackgroundCapableMedia"
                                        Visibility="Visible"
                                        Stretch="Fill"
                                        Width="400"
                                        Margin="0,10,10,50"
                                        AutoPlay="True"
                                        AreTransportControlsEnabled="True"
                                        VerticalAlignment="Stretch"
                                        Source="media/video/BigBuckBunny_320x180.mp4"
                                        HorizontalAlignment="Right" />
```

```
        <TextBlock x:Name="txt_location"
                                Grid.Row="1"
                                HorizontalAlignment="Left"
                                VerticalAlignment="Top"
                                Margin="5"
                                Text="retrieving ..." />
</Grid>
...
```

In Listing 8-8, you modify LandingPage's code-behind to support it displaying the location information acquired from the location sensors.

Listing 8-8. Modifications to LandingPage

```
public LandingPage()
{
        this.InitializeComponent();
        this.Loaded += LandingPage_Loaded;
        _timer = new DispatcherTimer();
        _timer.Interval = TimeSpan.FromSeconds(5);
        _timer.Tick += _timer_Tick;
        _media_control = Windows.Media.SystemMediaTransportControls.GetForCurrentView();
        if (ApplicationHostPage.Host != null)
                ApplicationHostPage.Host.GeoLocationChanged += Host_GeoLocationChanged;
}

private void Host_GeoLocationChanged(Geopoint obj)
{
        var point = ApplicationHostPage.Host.CurrentLocation.Coordinate.Point;
        var location = $"LAT:{point.Position.Latitude}, ";
        location += $"LONG:{point.Position.Longitude}";
        txt_location.Text = location;
}
```

Run the sample now and you should note that the location is displayed on LandingPage once it is available to the app.

More on Permissions

In the "Requesting Access to Location Data" section, you learned how to use the `RequestAccessAsync` method to ask the user for permission to read location data. Using this method, you devised a technique to test to ensure location data was allowed and, if so, to present the user interface. If location data was not allowed for the app, you presented a page that notified the user of the app's dependency on location data (with a link to the settings where location could be enabled).

The pattern worked fine except for one thing: once the user made a change to the location privacy setting, she then had to navigate back to the app and click a refresh button to test for location data access once again (in this case, because the user had just changed the setting, it would work). Although this approach works, it can be jarring to a user to have to go back to the app to see if the setting change has been applied. A better approach is for the app to be notified of the change to the setting and refresh itself. `Geolocator` has a special event, `StatusChanged`, which does just that. Let's modify your app to use this feature.

First, you can remove the button and associated even handler from NoLocationPage. The new user interface should look like Listing 8-9.

Listing 8-9. Changes to NoLocationPage

```
<Grid Background="{ThemeResource ApplicationPageBackgroundThemeBrush}">
        <Grid Height="105"
                        Width="400"
                        HorizontalAlignment="Center"
                        VerticalAlignment="Center">
                <TextBlock TextWrapping="WrapWholeWords"
                                Margin="0">Location services must be enabled for
                                this app to function properly.  Use the link below
                                to do so.</TextBlock>

                <HyperlinkButton NavigateUri="ms-settings:privacy-location"
                                        Content="Location Settings"
                                        HorizontalAlignment="Right"
                                        VerticalAlignment="Bottom" />

        </Grid>
</Grid>
```

Next, modify ApplicationHostPage as shown in Listing 8-10 to include code that handles the StatusChanged event and performs all the navigation for all pages in the app when navigation is lost (or regained).

Listing 8-10. Modifications to ApplicationHostPage

```
Type _last_page_before_nav_lost = typeof(LandingPage);
...
public ApplicationHostPage()
{
        this.InitializeComponent();
        this.Loaded += ApplicationHostPage_Loaded;
        Host = this;
        _geolocator = new Geolocator();
        _geolocator.StatusChanged += _geolocator_StatusChanged;
}

async private void _geolocator_StatusChanged(Geolocator sender, StatusChangedEventArgs args)
{
     await this.Dispatcher.RunAsync(Windows.UI.Core.CoreDispatcherPriority.Normal, async () =>
    {
        var current_view = ApplicationView.GetForCurrentView();
        var status = args.Status;
        switch (status)
        {
                case PositionStatus.Disabled:
                        _last_page_before_nav_lost = root_frame.CurrentSourcePageType;
                        root_frame.Navigate(typeof(NoLocationPage));
                        break;
```

```
                case PositionStatus.Ready:
                        current_view.TitleBar.BackgroundColor = Colors.Transparent;
                        root_frame.Navigate(_last_page_before_nav_lost);
                        CurrentLocation = await _geolocator.GetGeopositionAsync();
                                GeoLocationChanged?.Invoke(CurrentLocation.
                                Coordinate.Point);
                        break;
                case PositionStatus.Initializing:
                        current_view.TitleBar.BackgroundColor = Colors.Yellow;
                        break;
                default:
                        current_view.TitleBar.BackgroundColor = Colors.Red;
                        break;
            }
        });
}
```

In Listing 8-10, you use the `StatusChanged` event to decide where to send the app's root frame. The `args.Status` property returns a `PositionStatus` enum that can be used to determine the status of location awareness. If location awareness is disabled, you store the current page being viewed and navigate to NoLocationPage. If it is ready (or turns ready), you navigate to the page type stored in `_last_page_before_nav_lost`. By default, this is LandingPage. You also use the `ApplicationView` class to set the background color of the title bar based on whether navigation is initializing or not. If location services are unavailable (but enabled by the user), it displays a red title bar.

Run the app and open up the location privacy settings page. Now toggle the switch for turning location awareness on or off in your app. Notice that the app automatically navigates to the appropriate page without any user input. This is the ideal approach to handling permission changes in UWP apps.

Responding to Location Updates

In most cases, location information will not be static, meaning that it will change either over time or as the user moves the device. `Geolocator` provides a `PositionChanged` event handler that apps can subscribe to. `PositionChanged` is triggered by either a change in position or at a pre-determined time interval. Triggering a change event based on movement is referred to as distance-based tracking. It is enabled by setting the `MovementThreshold` property on `Geolocator`. `MovementThreshold`, measured in meters, is the minimum distance from the previous registered position that the device must move in order to trigger `PositionChanged`. Conversely, triggering on based on time is called periodic-based tracking. It is enabled by setting the `ReportInterval`, the minimum amount of time between calls to trigger the `PositionChanged` event property on `Geolocator`. `ReportInterval` in measured in milliseconds.

Geofencing

For those of you that might not be familiar with the concept, geofencing is a feature in a software program that uses the global positioning system (GPS) or radio frequency identification (RFID) to define geographical boundaries. As such, a geofence is a virtual perimeter for a real-world geographic area. In general, a geofence can be dynamically generated, as in a radius around a store or point location, or it can be a predefined set of boundaries, like school attendance zones or neighborhood boundaries.

Setting Up a Geofence

For UWP apps, creating and monitoring geofences is managed through the `GeofenceMonitor` class. The code in Listing 8-11 uses this class to create a new geofence around a specific point. In this case, it is the location of the next Big Mountain Xocial event. Before you get started, let's add a new data class to your project for storing event information. In the `Library` folder, add a new class called `BMXEvent` with the definition from Listing 8-11. Be sure to set the class's namespace to `BigMountainX`.

Listing 8-11. BMXEvent Class Definition

```
public class BMXEvent
{
        public Guid EventID { get; set; }

        public string EventTitle { get; set; }

        public string Description { get; set; }

        public DateTime StartDateTime { get; set; }

        public TimeSpan Duration { get; set; }

        public string Address { get; set; }

        public double? Latitude { get; set; }

        public double? Longitude { get; set; }

        public DateTime CreateDate { get; set; }
}
```

You now need to modify your `AppState` class to include this property. Listing 8-12 illustrates.

Listing 8-12. Modification to AppState

```
public class AppState : StateAwareObject<AppState>
{
        public BMXProfile UserProfile { get; set; }

        public BMXEvent NextEvent { get; set; }

}
```

Next, you need to instantiate the `NextEvent` property with a new `BMXEvent` object. You do this in the `App.OnLaunched` event. Listing 8-13 illustrates with changes highlighted in bold.

Listing 8-13. Modifications to OnLaunched

```
async protected override void OnLaunched(LaunchActivatedEventArgs e)
{
        var roaming_folder = Windows.Storage.ApplicationData.Current.RoamingFolder;
            State = await AppState.FromStorageFileAsync(roaming_folder, "state.xml");
        if (State.NextEvent == null)
        {
                State.NextEvent = new BMXEvent
                {
                        EventID = Guid.NewGuid(),
                        Address = "350 5th Ave, New York, NY 10118",
                        Latitude = 40.7484,
                        Longitude = -73.9857,
                        CreateDate = DateTime.Now,
                        Description = "A night of wine and comedy",
                        EventTitle = "Comedy Night at the Empire State",
                        Duration = TimeSpan.FromHours(4),
                        StartDateTime = new DateTime(2015, 12, 1, 20, 0, 0),
                };
                await State.SaveAsync();
        }

        // Place the frame in the current Window
        Window.Current.Content = new ApplicationHostPage();

        Window.Current.Activate();
}
```

In Listing 8-13, you check to see if the instantiated AppState object has a value for NextEvent. If it does not have a value (which it won't the first time this app is run), you instantiate the property with a new BMXEvent that represents a party taking place at the Empire State Building at 8pm for 4 hours. You can now create a new Geofence object and add it to the list of geofences associated with the app. Modify the loaded event of ApplicationHostPage so that it follows Listing 8-14 (changes are highlighted in bold).

Listing 8-14. Changes to ApplicationHostPage Loaded Event Handler

```
async private void ApplicationHostPage_Loaded(object sender, RoutedEventArgs e)
{
    if (App.State.UserProfile == null)
        root_frame.Navigate(typeof(UserIntroPage));
    else
    {
        var access_status = await Geolocator.RequestAccessAsync();
        switch (access_status)
        {
            case GeolocationAccessStatus.Allowed:
                root_frame.Navigate(typeof(LandingPage));
                CurrentLocation = await _geolocator.GetGeopositionAsync();
                GeoLocationChanged?.Invoke(CurrentLocation.Coordinate.Point);
```

```
    var fence_id = App.State.NextEvent.EventID.ToString();
        var fences = GeofenceMonitor.Current.Geofences;
        var fence = fences.Where(i => i.Id == fence_id).FirstOrDefault();
        if (fence == null)
        {
            Geocircle event_radius = new Geocircle(new BasicGeoposition
            {
                Latitude = App.State.NextEvent.Latitude.Value,
                Longitude = App.State.NextEvent.Longitude.Value,
            }, 30); //30 represents the radius

            fence = new Geofence(fence_id, event_radius);

            //add a geofence
            GeofenceMonitor.Current.Geofences.Add(fence);
        }

        break;
    case GeolocationAccessStatus.Denied:
        root_frame.Navigate(typeof(NoLocationPage));
        break;
    case GeolocationAccessStatus.Unspecified:
        break;
    }

  }
}
```

In Listing 8-14, you start by setting the id for the Geofence you are about to create to the id of the BMXEvent stored in your app state's NextEvent property. The ID property of Geofence allows you to be able to identify one geofence from another. Because of this, geofences associated to an app must have IDs that are unique to them (within the given app). This is why in the next line you use LINQ to query the list of geofences presently associated with the app and attempt to return a fence with the ID you just assigned. If a fence with that ID does not exist, you create a new geofence using that ID and a geocircle that represents the area you are fencing. Once the fence is created, you assign it to the list of geofences stored in the app's GeofenceMonitor.

You can fine-tune a geofence further by using one of the other constructors. The following items can be passed into the Geofence constructor to help refine how the fence works:

- MonitoredStates: Indicates what geofence events you want to receive notifications for, such as entering the defined region, leaving the defined region, or removal of the geofence.
- SingleUse: Removes the geofence once all the states the geofence is being monitored for have been met.
- DwellTime: Indicates how long the user must be in or out of the defined area before the enter/exit events are triggered.
- StartTime: Indicates when to start monitoring the geofence.
- Duration: Specifies how long to monitor the geofence.

Foreground Notifications

A geofence would not be of much use if it just sat there in the ether doing nothing. The value of such an artifact is in comparing the location of a device relative to the geofences that have been defined for it. Once you have defined the area you are "fencing-in," you can then be notified when the user's device enters or leaves that area. The GeofenceState enum is used to indicate these states, as well as when the geofence itself is removed. Listening to these events can happen in two ways. You can listen for events directly from your app when it is running or register for a background task so that you receive a background notification when an event occurs (even if your app is not running). We will discuss background tasks in Chapter 9. For now, you will use the app itself to listen for events by subscribing to the GeofenceStateChange event.

■ **Note** Although geofence events can be handled in a background task, this only applies to the entered and left events. The background app is not activated for the removal event.

Big Mountain Theatre Company would like to determine when users who have their app (which serves as a VIP pass) arrive at an event location and when they leave. You can easily achieve this by creating a geofence around the event location and listening for the entered and exited events of the fence. In the previous section, you created a 30-meter geofence that surrounded the location of an event. Listing 8-15 continues the exercise by using the GeofenceStateChange event to listen for these events.

Listing 8-15. Modifications to ApplicationHostPage

```
...
public event Action<int> AttendanceChanged;
...
public ApplicationHostPage()
{
    this.InitializeComponent();
    this.Loaded += ApplicationHostPage_Loaded;
    Host = this;
    _geolocator = new Geolocator();
    _geolocator.StatusChanged += _geolocator_StatusChanged;

    GeofenceMonitor.Current.GeofenceStateChanged += Current_GeofenceStateChanged;
}

private void Current_GeofenceStateChanged(GeofenceMonitor sender, object args)
{
    var change_reports = sender.ReadReports();
    foreach (var change_report in change_reports)
    {
        var new_state = change_report.NewState;
        if (new_state == GeofenceState.Entered)
        {
            AttendanceChanged?.Invoke(1);
        }
```

```
        else if (new_state == GeofenceState.Exited)
        {
            AttendanceChanged?.Invoke(-1);
        }
    }
}
...
```

In Listing 8-15, you add a new event to the ApplicationHostPage class called AttendanceChanged. You also add a new entry to the class' constructor for handling the GeofenceStatusChanged event. The event handler for this event first makes a call to ReadReports. ReadReports retrieves a list of GeofenceChangeReport objects associated with the GeofenceMonitor that triggered the notification. Each report object is tied to one of the geofences that are stored in the triggering GeofenceMonitor. They can be used to retrieve the new state of their associated Geofence. For each of the reports you retrieve from the change report list, you get the new state of the associated Geofence; based on the state, you can invoke the AttendanceChanged event with either a 1 or a -1.

Run the app in the Mobile Emulator and use the Map section to change the location of the device, as shown in Figure 8-5. You should note that once you set the phone to a location within the range of your geofence, the event is fired. It is also fired when the location of the phone is moved outside the fence.

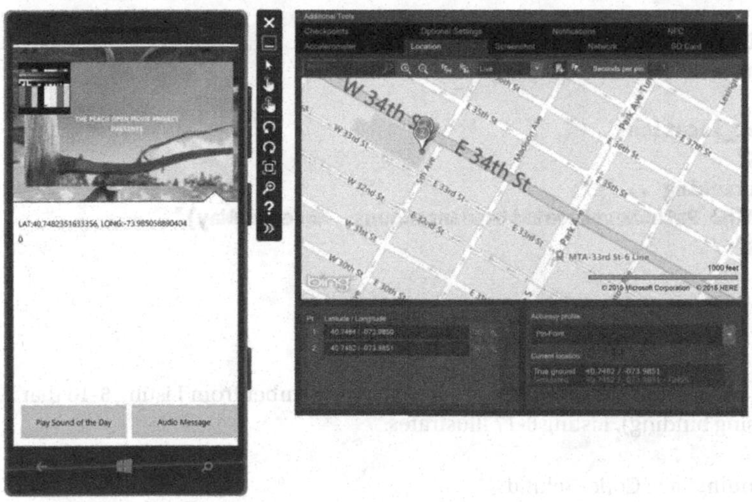

Figure 8-5. *Testing Geofencing using Windows 10 Mobile Emulator*

Let's close out the sample by modifying LandingPage such that it subscribes to the AttendanceChanged event and displays the count of users in attendance to the next Big Mountain Xocial event. Start the process by modifying the LandingPage UI slightly so that it has a place to store the count of attendees. Listing 8-16 illustrates. Modifications are highlighted in bold.

Listing 8-16. Modifications to LandingPage

```
...
<Grid>
    <Grid.RowDefinitions>
        <RowDefinition Height="40*" />
        <RowDefinition Height="60*" />
    </Grid.RowDefinitions>
    <lib:ImageBannerControl x:Name="img_banner" />
    <MediaElement x:Name="media"
                AudioCategory="BackgroundCapableMedia"
                Visibility="Visible"
                Stretch="Fill"
                Width="400"
                Margin="0,10,10,50"
                AutoPlay="True"
                AreTransportControlsEnabled="True"
                VerticalAlignment="Stretch"
                Source="media/video/BigBuckBunny_320x180.mp4"
                HorizontalAlignment="Right" />

    <StackPanel Grid.Row="1"
            HorizontalAlignment="Left"
            VerticalAlignment="Top"
            Margin="5">
        <TextBlock x:Name="txt_location"
                Margin="5"
                Text="retrieving ..." />
        <TextBlock Text="{x:Bind Path=NextEventAttendanceCount, Mode=OneWay}"
                Margin="5" />
    </StackPanel>
</Grid>
...
```

Next, in the code-behind you implement INotifyPropertyChanged (remember from Listing 8-16 that the new TextBlock you added is using binding). Listing 8-17 illustrates.

Listing 8-17. Modifications to LandingPage Code-Behind

```
public sealed partial class LandingPage : Page, INotifyPropertyChanged{
...
public event PropertyChangedEventHandler PropertyChanged;
public int NextEventAttendanceCount { get; private set; }
public LandingPage()
{
    this.InitializeComponent();
    this.Loaded += LandingPage_Loaded;
    _timer = new DispatcherTimer();
    _timer.Interval = TimeSpan.FromSeconds(5);
    _timer.Tick += _timer_Tick;
    _media_control = Windows.Media.SystemMediaTransportControls.GetForCurrentView();
```

```
    if (ApplicationHostPage.Host != null)
    {
        ApplicationHostPage.Host.GeoLocationChanged += Host_GeoLocationChanged;
        ApplicationHostPage.Host.AttendanceChanged += Host_AttendanceChanged;
    }
}

async private void Host_AttendanceChanged(int increment)
{
    //increment this value every time the next event changes
    NextEventAttendanceCount += increment;

    //tell the binding system
    await this.Dispatcher.RunAsync(Windows.UI.Core.CoreDispatcherPriority.Normal, () =>
    {
        PropertyChanged?.Invoke(this, new PropertyChangedEventArgs("NextEventAttendanceCount"));
    });
}
...
```

Run the app again in the emulator and try out the geofencing functionality. The attendance count should rise each time a user enters the geofence and drop each time they leave.

Mapping

Windows 10 offers a slew of new features for mapping, all of which are available to you as a developer for integration into your UWP apps. The following list highlights some of the new features:

- Offline maps: Starting with Windows 10, offline maps are available not just for phones but for desktops, laptops, tablets, etc. Users can visit the Settings window and download all necessary maps there. Once the maps are downloaded, the existing map control will use them by default.
- Unified platform: In the past, you had to go to various different services to accomplish different components of the mapping feature set (Here, Bing Maps, etc.). With Windows 10, all services are available under the same umbrella and can be used for any UWP applications.
- Adaptive interface: Works fine on all devices. You can use touch, pen, or mouse, and different screen sizes.
- 2D view with business and traffic information: Support for all common features for 2D maps like different views, traffic information (which you can turn on or off), information about business locations, and transit.
- Location: Integrates with location APIs.
- External elements: Developers can place their own icons, rectangles, polygons, and even XAML controls on maps. It allows for customization of existing maps and extends the number of possible scenarios.
- Routing: Developers can use Maps services to calculate routes to selected destinations. This feature now supports multiple modes of transportation (driving, walking, etc.).

- StreetSide: A very useful feature for users who want to know what a selected area looks like, StreetSide provides a street view of a location using images of the selected area.
- 3D views: Show maps not just in 2D but in 3D view modes.

There are two ways to implement mapping in a UWP app. You can leverage the existing Maps application by redirecting to it using either a HyperlinkButton or the `Launcher.LaunchUriAsync` method. Alternatively, you can directly embed the mapping functionality into your UWP app using MapControl, which is a new control for displaying and interacting with maps and locations.

Launching Maps via URI

The Maps application on a user's Windows 10 device has the protocols `bingmaps`, `ms-drive-to`, and `ms-walk-to` registered to it. Any URI on a Windows 10 system specified with this protocol will launch the Maps application. Opening Microsoft Edge and entering the URI bingmaps into the address bar will immediately launch the Maps application. This process is called *protocol activation* and it can be leveraged by any app built using the UWP. Using this mechanism, you can launch Maps from your UWP app. Of course, simply launching the Maps app will most likely not be enough; most apps will launch Maps for the purpose of displaying a map of something. The bingmaps URI scheme takes the form *bingmaps://?<query>* where query is a series of name/value pairs separated by an ampersand like the following: *param1=value1¶m2=value2*.

For the purposes of this exercise, you will use two parameters, `cp` and `where`. You can find the full list of possible parameters to pass at `https://msdn.microsoft.com/en-us/library/windows/apps/mt228341.aspx`.

The `cp` parameter, short for center point, is used to define the center point of the map displayed by the Maps app. It takes the format *cp=<lat>~<long>*. The following URI will open maps with New York City as the center point: `cp=40.726966~-74.006076`.

The `where` parameter works like a search applied to the map as a whole (like when you type in a search on the Bing maps website). When `where` is used, the value can be a location, landmark, or place. The following use of `where` will center the map on the White House: `bingmaps://?where=the white house`. Because the value passed into `where` is a search term, you may get a list of results back, in which case they will all be displayed on the map.

In the BigMountainX app, you are interested in using the Maps app to display the location of the next Big Mountain Xocial event, located at the Empire State Building, 350 5th Ave, New York, NY 10118. To do this, you have three choices: you can pass the geoposition (the latitude and longitude) of the event, pass the address for the Empire State Building, or just pass in the term "Empire State Building." Add a new button to LandingPage called Next Event Map. When this button is clicked, you will user the `Launcher` class to navigate to the following URI: `bingmaps://?where= 350 5th Ave, New York, NY 10118`. Listing 8-18 illustrates. This sample adds the Button control to the StackPanel created in Listing 8-16.

Listing 8-18. Modifications to LandingPage

```
...
<StackPanel Grid.Row="1"
            HorizontalAlignment="Left"
            VerticalAlignment="Top"
            Margin="5">
    <TextBlock x:Name="txt_location"
               Margin="5"
               Text="retrieving ..." />
```

```
    <TextBlock Text="{x:Bind Path=NextEventAttendanceCount, Mode=OneWay}"
               Margin="5" />
    <Button Content="Next Event Map" Click="OnClickNextEvent" Width="200" Margin="5" />
</StackPanel>
...
```

Listing 8-19 implements the event handler for this button. It uses the `Launcher.LaunchUriAsync` to carry out its function.

Listing 8-19. Implementing OnClickNextEvent Handler

```
async private void OnClickNextEvent(object sender, RoutedEventArgs e)
{
    var uri = new Uri($"bingmaps://?where={App.State.NextEvent.Address}");
    await Launcher.LaunchUriAsync(uri);
}
```

In Listing 8-19 you construct a URI based on the address of the next Big Mountain Xocial event. Once constructed, you pass it into the `LaunchUriAsync` method of the `Launcher` class. Clicking this link should launch the Maps app, as shown in Figure 8-6.

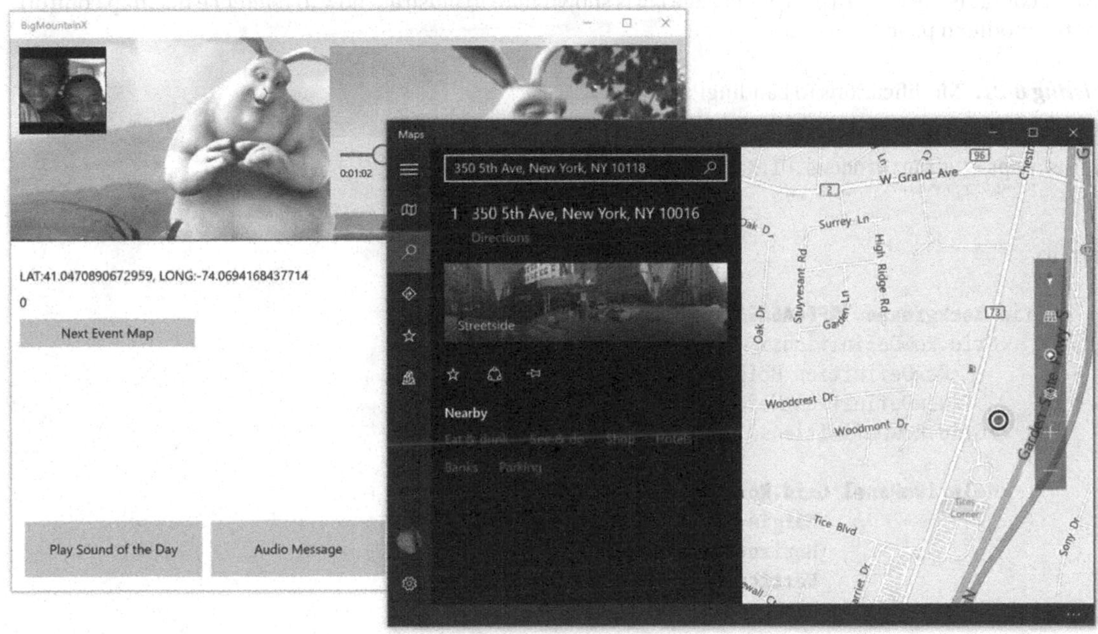

Figure 8-6. *Launching Maps from BigMountainX*

Adding Maps into Your App

For basic scenarios like locating a place on the map or providing directions, linking to and instrumenting the Maps application is more than adequate, the only non-ideal side-effect being that it opens the map in a different app. Whether or not this is an actual pitfall will depend on the app being developed. When your app needs just a quick view of the map to be displayed (without forcing the user to navigate to another app), customize the look and feel of the map, or just constrain the view of it in some way, using the Maps app starts to fall short. For those scenarios, the MapControl can be used. MapControl embeds the entirety of the map view into its control surface so that it can be placed into other UWP apps.

In the previous section, you provided a button that contained the address of the next event Big Mountain Theater Company is hosting. Clicking the link opened the Maps app and showed the location. This approach is not ideal for the BigMountainX app. What you want instead is to place the map where the button is so that the user can get a quick interactive view of the event location. MapControl is perfect for this type of scenario.

In order to start working with maps in your application you need to get an "access key" by visiting Maps Dev Center (`www.bingmapsportal.com/`). When an access key is not provided, you will see the message that MapServiceToken is not specified and you cannot publish your application without MapServiceToken. Listing 8-20 shows the key for mapping.

Listing 8-20. Sample of Application Key from `bingmapsportal.com`

```
xVw4m3LWqMqNhkkV6iTs~8xCzHMDnuTdugl7qS-7lQA~AgsDbT7TRxvrwzPA2TyPwbZnYKpauH3Ke4kgOl2W5M4VOs
IPXIF4Ir6oiAGjrNye
```

In Listing 8-21, you add a basic map control to LandingPage and configure it to display the zoom and tilt controls in addition to accepting touch inputs. The control uses the key you acquired from the Bing maps development portal. Let's take this opportunity to restyle LandingPage so it aligns more to a dark theme. The listing contains the XAML (part of the Page tag is shown here to illustrate how to reference the map control) for the modified page.

Listing 8-21. Modifications to LandingPage

```
<Page ...
xmlns:Maps="using:Windows.UI.Xaml.Controls.Maps"
...>

<Grid>

    <Grid Background="#FF6A6A6A">
        <Grid.RowDefinitions>
            <RowDefinition Height="40*" />
            <RowDefinition Height="60*" />
        </Grid.RowDefinitions>

        <RelativePanel Grid.Row="1"
                       Margin="0,-25,0,0" Width="500"
                       HorizontalAlignment="Left"
                       VerticalAlignment="Stretch"
                       Background="#FF444141">

            <Maps:MapControl x:Name="map"
                             Height="300"
                             Width="500"
                             Margin="0"
                             ZoomInteractionMode="GestureAndControl"
                             PanInteractionMode="Auto"
                             TiltInteractionMode="GestureAndControl"
                             MapServiceToken="abcd"
                             />
```

```
        <Button Content="More ..."
                Click="OnClickNextEvent"
                Width="200"
                Background="Gray"
                RelativePanel.Below="map"
                RelativePanel.AlignRightWithPanel="True"
                Margin="5" />

        <TextBlock x:Name="txt_location"
                   Margin="5"
                   Text="retrieving location..."
                   RelativePanel.AlignBottomWithPanel="True"/>
        <TextBlock Text="{x:Bind Mode=OneWay, Path=NextEventAttendanceCount}"
                   Margin="5"
                   HorizontalAlignment="Right"
                   RelativePanel.AlignRightWithPanel="True"
                   RelativePanel.AlignBottomWithPanel="True"
                   RelativePanel.RightOf="txt_location" />
    </RelativePanel>
 <StackPanel Grid.Row="1"
                Margin="10,0,0,10"
                VerticalAlignment="Top"
                HorizontalAlignment="Right"
                Orientation="Horizontal"
                Height="50">
        <Button Content="Play Sound of the Day"
                Width="180" Background="Gray"
                Click="OnPlayAudioClicked"
                Margin="2.5" />
        <ToggleButton Content="Audio Message"
                      Width="180"
                      Background="Gray"
                      Click="ToggleRecord"
                      Margin="2.5" />
        <Button Content="Video Message"
                Width="180"
                Background="Gray"
                Click="ToggleRecordVideo"
                Margin="2.5">
            ...
        </Button>
    </StackPanel>
...
    <lib:ImageBannerControl x:Name="img_banner" />
    <MediaElement x:Name="media"
                   AudioCategory="BackgroundCapableMedia"
                   Visibility="Visible"
                   Stretch="Fill"
                   Width="400"
                   Margin="0,10,10,50"
                   AutoPlay="True"
```

```
                        AreTransportControlsEnabled="True"
                        VerticalAlignment="Stretch"
                        Source="media/video/BigBuckBunny_320x180.mp4"
                        HorizontalAlignment="Right" />
    </Grid>

    <lib:ImageViewerControl  HorizontalAlignment="Left"
                             VerticalAlignment="Top"
                             Margin="10"
                             Height="100"
                             Width="100"
                             Loaded="OnImageViewerLoaded"
                             ImageSelected="OnImageSelected" />
</Grid>
</Page>
```

In Listing 8-21, you replace the StackPanel used for laying out the geo-location TextBlocks and Button with a RelativePanel. Also, the ImageBannerControl and the MediaElement are moved to the bottom of the Grid that contains them. This is so they will show above any other items in the Grid. Colors for all the controls have been modified to various shades of gray and the background for the buttons on the screen have been changed to gray. In the MapControl, you have explicitly set the `MapServiceToken` to the key you retrieved earlier from the Bing development portal. You have also set some properties on the MapControl to allow for using either gestures or controls on map itself to interact with it.

Listing 8-22 shows the changes to be made in the code-behind for LandingPage. Essentially you explicitly set the background color for the title bar of the app in the constructor.

Listing 8-22. Styling the Title Bar in LandingPage Code-Behind

```
public LandingPage()
{
    ...
    //set the application title bar look
    var current_view = ApplicationView.GetForCurrentView();
    var titlebar_color = Color.FromArgb(0xFF, 0x6A, 0x6A, 0x6A);
    current_view.TitleBar.BackgroundColor = titlebar_color; //Colors.DarkGray;
    current_view.TitleBar.InactiveBackgroundColor = titlebar_color;
    current_view.TitleBar.ButtonBackgroundColor = titlebar_color;
    current_view.TitleBar.ButtonInactiveBackgroundColor = titlebar_color;
}
```

To complete the transition to a dark them, open `App.xaml` and change the `RequestedTheme` attribute to Dark. Listing 8-23 illustrates.

Listing 8-23. Configuring the App to Expect a Dark Theme

```
<Application
    x:Class="BigMountainX.App"
    xmlns="http://schemas.microsoft.com/winfx/2006/xaml/presentation"
    xmlns:x="http://schemas.microsoft.com/winfx/2006/xaml"
    xmlns:local="using:BigMountainX"
    RequestedTheme="Dark">

</Application>
```

Modifying this attribute changes the text across the app to a light coloring (since the expectation is that your color choices for backgrounds will be darker). Finally, modify ImageBannerControl as shown in Listing 8-24.

Listing 8-24. Modifications to ImageBannerControl

```
<Path Data="M-19.1464,-17.9973 L420.5,-18.5 L420.5,248.5 L379.998,248.597 L359.834,231.537
L339.838,248.694 L-21.1464,248.503 z"
        Margin="-21.646,-19,-21,19.782"
        Stretch="Fill"
        StrokeThickness="5"
        UseLayoutRounding="False"
        d:LayoutOverrides="LeftPosition, RightPosition, TopPosition, BottomPosition">
    <Path.Fill>
        <ImageBrush x:Name="img_brush"
                    Stretch="UniformToFill" />
    </Path.Fill>
    <Path.Stroke>
        <SolidColorBrush Color="DarkGray" />
    </Path.Stroke>
</Path>
```

This change merely adds some thickness to the line that borders the path visual used in ImageBannerControl. When you run the app now, it should look like Figure 8-7.

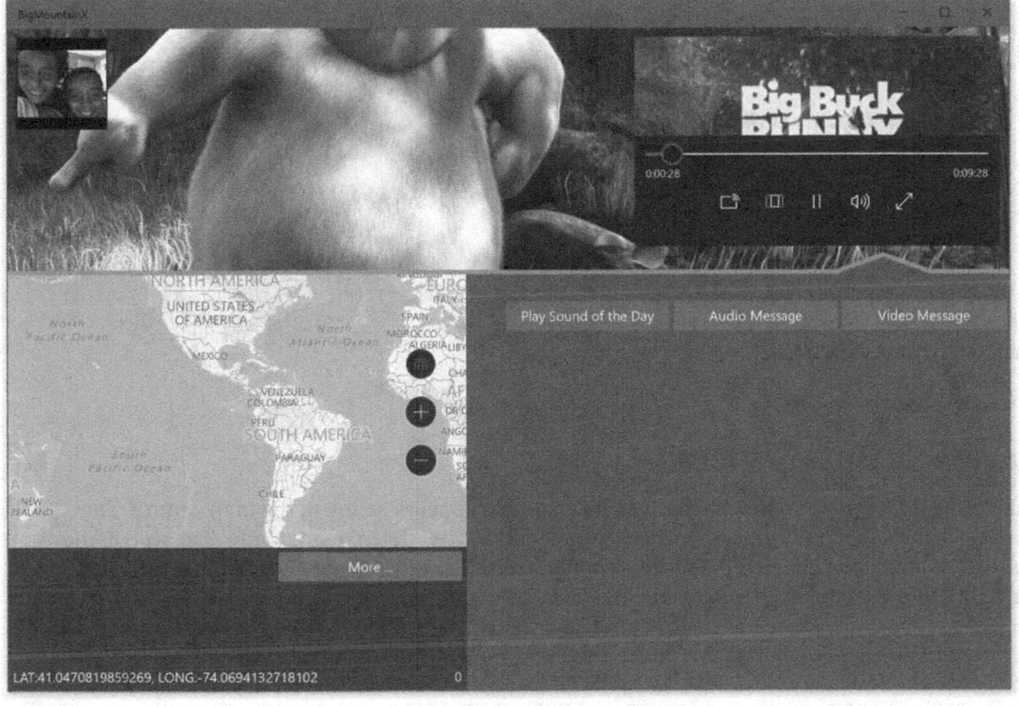

Figure 8-7. *New BigMountainX user interface*

The following properties can be used to further configure the appearance of the MapControl:

- Center: Sets a starting geographic position at the center of the map.
- ZoomLevel: Determines how zoomed in the map is. Set to a value between 1 and 20.
- Heading: Sets the rotation of the map where 0 or 360 degrees = North, 90 = East, 180 = South, and 270 = West.
- DesiredPitch: Sets the tilt of the map to a value between 0 and 65 degrees.
- MapStyle: Specifies the type of map, such as a road map or an aerial map.
- ColorScheme: Sets the color scheme of the map to either light or dark.
- LandmarksVisible: Displays buildings and landmarks on the map.
- PedestrianFeaturesVisible: Displays pedestrian features such as public stairs.
- TrafficFlowVisible: Displays traffic on the map.
- WatermarkMode: Specifies whether the watermark is displayed (the "Bing" label).

In Listing 8-25, you modify the loaded event of LandingPage by setting the Center property to start the MapControl at the location of the next event.

Listing 8-25. Modifications to LandingPage Loaded Event

```
async private void LandingPage_Loaded(object sender, RoutedEventArgs e)
{
    ...

    //set the starting point of the map
    map.Center = new Geopoint(new BasicGeoposition
    {
        Latitude = App.State.NextEvent.Latitude.Value,
        Longitude = App.State.NextEvent.Longitude.Value,
    });
    map.ZoomLevel = 17.5;

    //
    //clear the backstack so that you cannot navigate back from
    //this page
    Frame.BackStack.Clear();
}
```

Displaying Streetside Views

A streetside view is a street-level perspective of a location that appears on top of the map control. The experience once the user enters the Streetside view is separate from the map originally displayed in the map control. For instance, changing the location in the Streetside view has no effect on the location or appearance of the underlying map. After you close the Streetside view, the original map remains unchanged. Not all devices support the Streetside view feature. You can use the IsStreetsideSupported property on MapControl to determine whether it is currently supported. If supported, call FindNearbyAsync to create a StreetsidePanorama object near the specified location. To activate the view, you must assign an instance of StreetsideExperience to MapControl's CustomExperience property. The constructor of StreetsideExperience accepts a StreetsidePanorama object.

In Listing 8-26, you modify the More button in LandingPage by adding a flyout menu that can be used to accomplish a number of tasks related to the next event's location. You will add two menu items to the flyout, one for linking to the Maps application like before, and the other for enabling Streetside view on the MapControl.

Listing 8-26. Adding FlyoutMenu to the More button

```
<Button Content="More ..."
        Width="200"
        Background="Gray"
        RelativePanel.Below="map"
        RelativePanel.AlignRightWithPanel="True"
        Margin="5">
    <Button.Flyout>
        <MenuFlyout>
            <MenuFlyoutItem Click="OnShowStreetView"
                            Text="Show Streetview" />
            <MenuFlyoutItem Click="OnClickNextEvent"
                            Text="Open in Maps" />
        </MenuFlyout>
    </Button.Flyout>
</Button>
```

The code-behind for LandingPage now adds a new method, the event handler `OnShowStreetView`. Listing 8-27 illustrates.

Listing 8-27. Implementing OnShowStreetView

```
async private void OnShowStreetView(object sender, RoutedEventArgs e)
{
    if (map.IsStreetsideSupported)
    {
        var street_panorama = await StreetsidePanorama.FindNearbyAsync(map.Center);
        StreetsideExperience street_exp = new StreetsideExperience(street_panorama);
        map.CustomExperience = street_exp;
    }
}
```

Listing 8-27 implements the functionality of the Show Streetview menu item, which basically launches the street view of the map so that a user can explore how to get to the location of the next event.

Handling Events, User Interaction, and Changes

You can handle user input gestures on the map by handling the `MapTapped`, `MapDoubleTapped`, and `MapHolding` events of the MapControl. The `MapInputEventArgs` passed into the event handlers for these events has a `Location` and `Position` property that can be used to get information about the geographic location on the map and the physical position in the viewport where the gesture occurred.

The following events can be used to listen for when the user or the app changes the settings of the map. The event names are self-explanatory.

- CenterChanged
- HeadingChanged
- PitchChanged
- ZoomLevelChanged

Working with POIs (Points of Interest)

Another area where embedding MapControl into your app excels is when it comes to POIs. With the Maps application, POIs are already built in and cannot be altered from an external app. There is no way of adding new POIs that might be needed to illustrate some feature of the app. Using the MapControl, you can add pushpins, images, and shapes on the map by adding the MapIcon, MapPolygon, and MapPolyline objects to the MapElements collection using data binding or by adding the items programmatically. You also have the ability of embedding XAML control directly into the map, complete with any feature, animation, and built-in interactivity that they utilize.

Adding MapIcons

MapIcon is used to display an image such a pushpin, with optional text, on the map surface. MapIcon allows you to optionally set a title and image associated with the icon. When an image is not provided, a default image is used. In Listing 8-28, you place a MapIcon at the location of the next Big Mountain Xocial event. This allows it to be easily seen on the map.

Listing 8-28. Modifications to LandingPage Loaded Event Handler

```
async private void LandingPage_Loaded(object sender, RoutedEventArgs e)
{
    ...

    //set the starting point of the map
    map.Center = new Geopoint(new BasicGeoposition
    {
        Latitude = App.State.NextEvent.Latitude.Value,
        Longitude = App.State.NextEvent.Longitude.Value,
    });
    map.ZoomLevel = 17.5;
    MapIcon map_icon = new MapIcon();
    map_icon.Title = App.State.NextEvent.EventTitle;
    map_icon.Location = map.Center;
    map.MapElements.Add(map_icon);

    //
    //clear the backstack so that you cannot navigate back from
    //this page
    Frame.BackStack.Clear();
}
```

Figure 8-8 shows how the app looks when run.

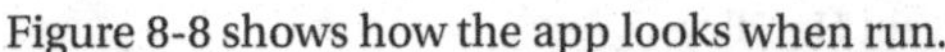

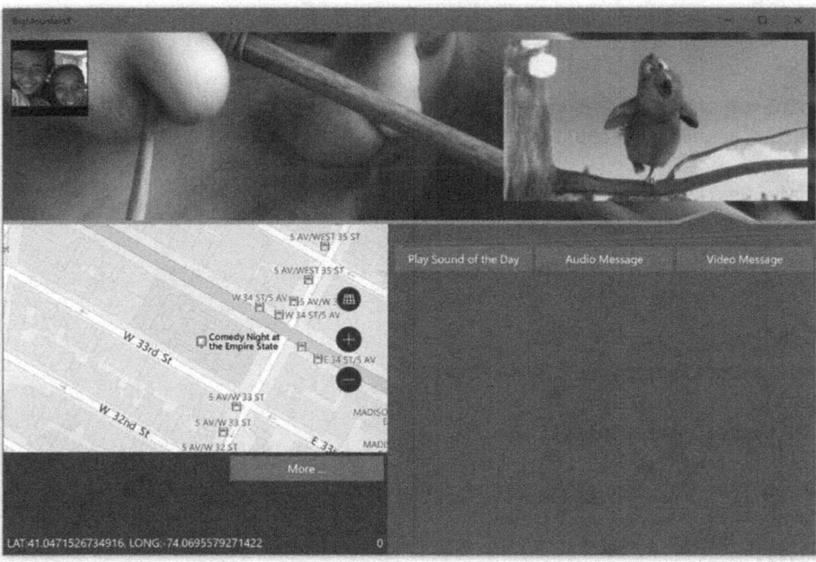

Figure 8-8. *Showing MapIcon on the map*

Keep the following considerations in mind when working with the `MapIcon` class:

- The `Image` property supports a maximum image size of 2048 x 2048 pixels.
- By default, the map icon's image is not guaranteed to be shown. It may be hidden when it obscures other elements or labels on the map. To keep it visible, set the map icon's `CollisionBehaviorDesired` property to `MapElementCollisionBehavior.RemainVisible`.
- The optional title of the `MapIcon` is not guaranteed to be shown. If you don't see the text, zoom out by decreasing the value of the `ZoomLevel` property of the MapControl.

Adding XAML Controls to Map

When a simple image is not enough, you can use XAML to display custom UI elements on the map. XAML controls are added to the map much the same way as they are added to any layout control, by adding an instance of the control to the Children collection of the map. MapControl requires an additional step to display the control properly, however. Once the control is added, call `SetLocation` to positon the XAML control geographically on the map surface. Listing 8-29 replaces the use of the `MapIcon` with a SymbolIcon XAML control.

Listing 8-29. Modifications to the LandingPage Loaded Event Handler

```
async private void LandingPage_Loaded(object sender, RoutedEventArgs e)
{
    ...

    //set the starting point of the map
    map.Center = new Geopoint(new BasicGeoposition
    {
        Latitude = App.State.NextEvent.Latitude.Value,
        Longitude = App.State.NextEvent.Longitude.Value,
    });
    map.ZoomLevel = 17.5;

    //add a XAML control to the map
    SymbolIcon symbol = new SymbolIcon(Symbol.Favorite);
    map.Children.Add(symbol);
    MapControl.SetLocation(symbol, map.Center);

    //clear the backstack so that you cannot navigate back from
    //this page
    Frame.BackStack.Clear();
}
```

Run the app and it should now look something like Figure 8-9.

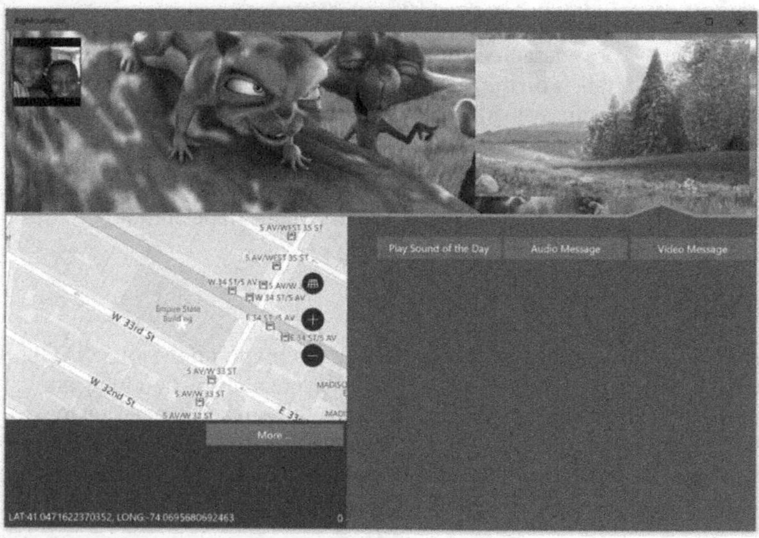

Figure 8-9. *Showing the XAML control on the map*

Geocoding

Using the Geocoding functionality built into the mapping APIs, it is easy to extend into UWP apps the ability to convert addresses to geographic locations (geocoding) and vice versa (reverse geocoding). Geocoding is achieved through the MapLocationFinder class in the Windows.Services.Maps namespace.

Reverse Geocoding: Getting an Address

MapLocationFinder finder contains a FindLocationsAtAsync method that can be used to convert a geographic location to an address (reverse geocoding). FindLocationsAtAsync returns a MapLocationFinderResult object that exposes a Locations property which represents the collection of matching MapLocation objects returned by the query. Each MapLocation contains an Address property of type MapAddress that represents the address matched to that location. In Listing 8-30, you replace the location text displayed in LandingPage with a string that displays the city and state the user accessing the app is in. You do this by performing a reverse geocode on the Geopoint passed into LandingPage's GeoLocationChanged event handler.

Listing 8-30. Modifications to GeoLocationChanged Event Handler

```
public LandingPage()
{
    ...
    if (ApplicationHostPage.Host != null)
    {
        ApplicationHostPage.Host.GeoLocationChanged += Host_GeoLocationChanged;
        ...
    }
...
}

async private void Host_GeoLocationChanged(Geopoint obj)
{
    await this.Dispatcher.RunAsync(Windows.UI.Core.CoreDispatcherPriority.Normal, async () =>
    {

        var point = obj;
        var location = $"LAT:{point.Position.Latitude}, ";
        location += $"LONG:{point.Position.Longitude}";

        txt_location.Text = "searching ... ";
        try
        {
            var location_results = await MapLocationFinder.FindLocationsAtAsync(point);

            //since we are only interested in city and state info
            //we only need the first item from the list
            var location_result = location_results.Locations.FirstOrDefault();
```

```
            if (location_result != null)
            {
                txt_location.Text = $"{location_result.Address.Town}, {location_result.
                Address.Region}";
            }
        }
        catch
        {
            txt_location.Text = "Location unknown";
        }

    });
}
```

Run the sample now and you should see that the textbox now displays the city and state where you are located instead of the latitude/longitude data.

Geocode: Getting a Location from an Address

You can alternatively convert an address or the name of a place to a geographic location (geocoding) using the `FindLocationsAsync` method of `MapLocationFinder`. `FindLocationsAsync` also returns a `MapLocationFinderResult` containing a collection of matching `MapLocation` objects that can be accessed through the `Locations` property. Another property of `MapLocation`, `Point`, can be used to get the Geopoint associated with the address/place that was searched for. Geocoding is ideal for converting addresses or point of interest inputted as text into locations on a map. It is the kind of thing that the Map application does when you type in "Empire State Building" or enter the address "350 5th Ave, New York, NY 10118" instead of entering the exact geocoordinates to that location.

Displaying Directions

Displaying directions can be achieved using the `MapRouteFinder` class. Calling either `GetDrivingRouteAsync` or `GetWalkingRouteAsync` can be used to retrieve a `MapRouteFinderResult` object that represents the route to the geoposition you specify. You can use the Legs collection to retrieve the list of legs tied to this route. Each leg, represented by a `MapRouteLeg` object, contains a `Maneuvers` property that is itself a collection of `MapRouteManeuver` objects. `MapRouteManeuver` contains an `InstructionText` property that provides the actual instruction in text format. For each route leg, you must iterate through the list of maneuvers associated with the leg, and for each of those, display the Instruction text it contains.

Add a new page to the BigMountainX project called DirectionsPage and populate its XAML as shown in Listing 8-31.

Listing 8-31. DirectionsPage Layout

```
<Page ...>
<Grid Background="{ThemeResource ApplicationPageBackgroundThemeBrush}">
    <ScrollViewer VerticalScrollBarVisibility="Auto"
                  VerticalScrollMode="Auto">
        <StackPanel x:Name="spanel_directions"
                    Orientation="Vertical"
                    Margin="10,50,10,50">

        </StackPanel>
    </ScrollViewer>
```

```
    <ProgressRing x:Name="progress"
                  IsActive="True"
                  Width="100"
                  Height="100" />
</Grid>
</Page>
```

In LandingPage, add a new `MenuFlyoutItem` to the More button as shown in Listing 8-32.

Listing 8-32. Adding a MenuFlyoutItem to the More Button

```
<Button Content="More ..."
        Width="200"
        Background="Gray"
        RelativePanel.Below="map"
        RelativePanel.AlignRightWithPanel="True"
        Margin="5">
    <Button.Flyout>
        <MenuFlyout>
            <MenuFlyoutItem Click="OnShowStreetView"
                            Text="Show Streetview" />
            <MenuFlyoutItem Click="OnClickNextEvent"
                            Text="Open in Maps" />
            <MenuFlyoutItem Click="OnDirectionsClicked"
                            Text="Directions" />

        </MenuFlyout>
    </Button.Flyout>
</Button>
```

In the code-behind for LandingPage, implement `OnDirectionsClicked` as shown in Listing 8-33.

Listing 8-33. Implementing the OnDirectionsClicked Event Handler

```
private void OnDirectionsClicked(object sender, RoutedEventArgs e)
{
    Frame.Navigate(typeof(DirectionsPage), map.Center);
}
```

All this method does is navigate to the DirectionsPage, passing in the center point of the map (which should be the location of the next event being held). Finally, in Listing 8-34, you implement the code-behind for DirectionsPage.

Listing 8-34. Implementing the DirectionsPage Code-Behind

```
public sealed partial class DirectionsPage : Page
{
    Geopoint _center;
    public DirectionsPage()
    {
        this.InitializeComponent();
        this.Loaded += DirectionsPage_Loaded;
    }
```

```
    async private void DirectionsPage_Loaded(object sender, RoutedEventArgs e)
    {
        var start = ApplicationHostPage.Host.CurrentLocation.Coordinate;
        var result = await MapRouteFinder.GetDrivingRouteAsync(start.Point,_center);
        progress.IsActive = false;
        progress.Visibility = Visibility.Collapsed;
        foreach (var leg in result.Route.Legs)
        {
            SymbolIcon leg_symbol = new SymbolIcon(Symbol.Refresh);
            leg_symbol.HorizontalAlignment = HorizontalAlignment.Center;
            leg_symbol.Margin = new Thickness(5);
            StackPanel stack_leg = new StackPanel();
            stack_leg.HorizontalAlignment = HorizontalAlignment.Center;
            foreach (var manuever in leg.Maneuvers)
            {
                TextBlock txt_instruction = new TextBlock();
                txt_instruction.Margin = new Thickness(5);
                txt_instruction.Text = manuever.InstructionText;
                stack_leg.Children.Add(txt_instruction);

            }

            spanel_directions.Children.Add(leg_symbol);
            spanel_directions.Children.Add(stack_leg);
        }
    }

    protected override void OnNavigatedTo(NavigationEventArgs e)
    {
        _center = e.Parameter as Geopoint;

        base.OnNavigatedTo(e);
    }
}
```

In Listing 8-34, you save the parameter passed in from LandingPage, the Geopoint corresponding to the location of the next Big Mountain Xocial event, to a field on the class after casting it back to its type. This point will serve as the end point to which you want your user to navigate. In the loaded event, you first retrieve the user's current location (this will serve as the start point for the driving directions). You then use it to call `GetDrivingRouteAsync`. Once that call returns (it may take a while), you deactivate and hide the ProgressRing control you use to let the user know that a long running activity is occurring. You then iterate through the various collections of the resulting objects, creating controls to represent each line item in the associated lists. At the end of it, all these controls are added to the Children collection of their parent. When you run BigMountainX now and click the Get Directions menu item, your app should look like Figure 8-10.

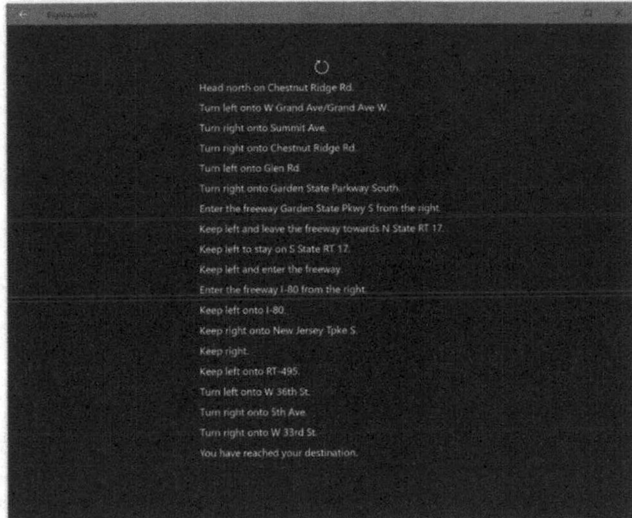

Figure 8-10. *DirectionsPage in action*

Displaying Routes

You can display the route returned from the call to get driving directions on the embedded MapControl using the `MapRouteView` class. A `MapRouteView` is constructed by passing in a `MapRoute` (the object you get as part of the driving directions query) into its constructor. MapControl exposes a list of routes that `MapRouteViews` can be added to. In Listing 8-35, you modify DirectionsPage to display a map on it. You also created a higher level StackPanel that contains both the MapControl and `spanel_directions`.

Listing 8-35. Modifying DirectionsPage

```
<Grid Background="{ThemeResource ApplicationPageBackgroundThemeBrush}">
    <ScrollViewer VerticalScrollBarVisibility="Auto"
                  VerticalScrollMode="Auto">
        <StackPanel>
            <Maps:MapControl x:Name="map"
                             Height="400"
                             Margin="0"
                             ZoomLevel="12"
                             HorizontalAlignment="Stretch"
                             ZoomInteractionMode="GestureAndControl"
                             PanInteractionMode="Auto"
                             TiltInteractionMode="GestureAndControl"
                             MapServiceToken="xVw4m3LWqMqNhkkV6iTs~8xCzHMDnu
                             Tdugl7qS-7lQA~AgsDbT7TRxvrwzPA2TyPwbZnYKpauH3Ke4kgOl2
                             W5M4VOsIPXIF4Ir6ofAGjrNye" />
            <StackPanel x:Name="spanel_directions"
                        Orientation="Vertical"
                        Margin="10,50,10,50">
            </StackPanel>
```

```
        </StackPanel>
    </ScrollViewer>
    <ProgressRing x:Name="progress"
                  IsActive="True"
                  Width="100"
                  Height="100" />
</Grid>
```

Listing 8-36 shows the modified loaded event for the DirectionsPage code-behind.

Listing 8-36. Modifications to DirectionsPage Loaded Event Handler

```
async private void DirectionsPage_Loaded(object sender, RoutedEventArgs e)
{
    var start = ApplicationHostPage.Host.CurrentLocation.Coordinate;
    var result = await MapRouteFinder.GetDrivingRouteAsync(start.Point, _center);

    progress.IsActive = false;
    map.Center = start.Point;

    SymbolIcon symbol_start = new SymbolIcon(Symbol.Favorite);
    map.Children.Add(symbol_start);
    MapControl.SetLocation(symbol_start, start.Point);

    SymbolIcon symbol_end = new SymbolIcon(Symbol.Favorite);
    map.Children.Add(symbol_end);
    MapControl.SetLocation(symbol_end, _center);

    MapRouteView route_view = new MapRouteView(result.Route);
    map.Routes.Add(route_view);
    await map.TrySetViewBoundsAsync(route_view.Route.BoundingBox,null,MapAnimationKind.Default);

    progress.Visibility = Visibility.Collapsed;
    foreach (var leg in result.Route.Legs)
    {
        SymbolIcon leg_symbol = new SymbolIcon(Symbol.Refresh);
        leg_symbol.HorizontalAlignment = HorizontalAlignment.Center;
        leg_symbol.Margin = new Thickness(5);
        StackPanel stack_leg = new StackPanel();
        stack_leg.HorizontalAlignment = HorizontalAlignment.Center;
        foreach (var manuever in leg.Maneuvers)
        {
            TextBlock txt_instruction = new TextBlock();
            txt_instruction.Margin = new Thickness(5);
            txt_instruction.Text = manuever.InstructionText;
            stack_leg.Children.Add(txt_instruction);

        }

        spanel_directions.Children.Add(leg_symbol);
        spanel_directions.Children.Add(stack_leg);
    }
}
```

In Listing 8-35, you see the use of the `MapRouteView` to encapsulate a `MapRoute` for the purpose of being displayed on the map. You also add two XAML controls to the map, one to indicate the start position of the route and the other to show where it ends. Finally, the call to `TrySetViewBoundsAsync` is used to center the map around the directions you have, so that both points can be seen clearly. Running the app and selecting Get Directions should show a page similar to Figure 8-11.

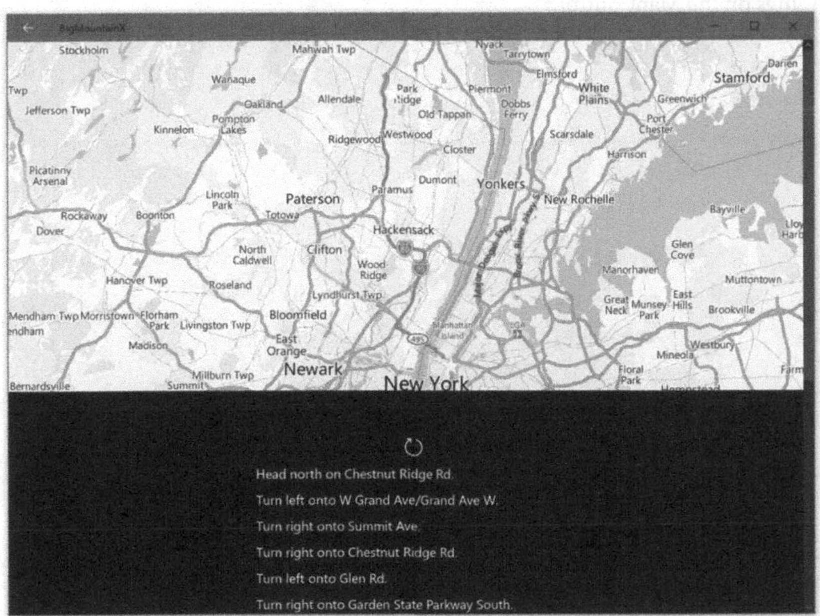

***Figure 8-11.** Modifications to DirectionsPage in action*

Summary

In this chapter, you learned the many ways that location and mapping can be used in your application. The findings in this chapter include the following:

- How to enable location functionality in a UWP app.
- How to gain access to location data, and how to react to access being changed.
- How to retrieve the current location of a device.
- How to navigate to the Settings application.
- How to handle location updates.
- How to implement geofencing in a UWP app and monitor for entering and exiting the fenced area from the foreground.
- How to launch the Maps application and instrument it to display specific locations, groups of locations, points of interests, and many more things.
- How to embed mapping into UWP apps using the MapControl.
- How to display a Streetside view for a point on the MapControl surface.

- How to add MapIcons to the MapControl map surface.
- How to add XAML controls to the MapControl map surface.
- How to geocode and reverse geocode.
- How to get driving directions based on a start and end point.
- How to display routes on the MapControl.

CHAPTER 9

Background Tasks

It should come as no surprise to anyone that the term *Windows* as defined, coined, and trademarked by Microsoft relates to the computing feature whereby the functioning area of an application can be partitioned to a corner of the screen, moved around, and maximized to take up the entire screen surface area. In short, Windows allows you a "window" into a running application. Through the years, that ability to display an application evolved into being able to run and use multiple applications, complete with window overlap, fast task switching, and many more delightful features we have all come to know, love, and expect from a self-respecting operating environment like Windows, Mac OS, and even from the Linux and Unix tree of products.

So we were all *completely* surprised when Windows 8 balked at all the beautiful innovations we've come to love. All the features that had naturally evolved over years and years of user feedback, trial and error, and functional adjustment were mostly tossed to the side in favor of a random and seemingly undercooked re-invention of the product. This chapter focuses on a tenet of Windows that has survived what we like to call the "great purge:" *background processing* in its many forms. In previous versions of Windows, applications ran in the background through a myriad of mechanisms. Simply switching away from one application to another essentially put the first app into the background (although in previous versions of Windows, it continued to run as though in the foreground). This provided the ultimate flexibility for both the user and developer but, as a downside, introduced incredible complexity into their work streams. As a user, it was difficult to know exactly what was running on your machine at any given time without breaking out all the super user tools. As a developer, it was nearly impossible to predict how other applications would react to and treat yours, and compatibility issues between your application and another were invariably tied to your application as bugs.

Because Windows 8 introduced a new approach to application behavior, one in which the app user interface always takes up the entire screen surface area, the foreground app is assumed to be the most important to the user. In this paradigm, the foreground application receives all the system resources, and apps that aren't visible to the user enter into a suspended state in which they are no longer executing. While Windows 10 has since reverted back to the line of thought that being able to do more than one thing at a time is generally good, many of the same rules related to app behavior still apply, the caveat being that the behaviors related to suspension will largely be dependent on the device family your app is running on. With Windows 10, now more than ever the question of maintaining consistent functionality across a vast set of hardware specifications and classifications falls not just to Microsoft but also to app developers targeting this platform. How else do you provide the same experience: application switching, background processing, windowing, and so on, while maintaining a new paradigm which allows Windows to run on anything from an ARM-based device (the type you might find on an iPhone) to the full-fledged Windows experience?

Let's get started.

Before You Begin

Before you get started with this chapter, let's take some time to clean up and optimize the code you have created thus far. Many of the things you have added to your app, although interesting in terms of showing you how the related functionality works, are really not needed and only add complexity to the mix. One such thing is the revolving background image used by the ImageBannerControl you have on LandingPage. Let's remove the code associated with it. Open the BigMountainX project and open LandingPage. Listing 9-1 shows all the code you need to get rid of in order to achieve this.

Listing 9-1. Code to Delete

```
//the image list
List<string> _images = new List<string>
{
        ...
};

//the image counter
int _image_index = 0;

//the timer used to determine when to switch images
_timer = new DispatcherTimer();
_timer.Interval = TimeSpan.FromSeconds(5);
_timer.Tick += _timer_Tick;

//the timer ticked event handler
private void _timer_Tick(object sender, object e)
{
    img_banner.SetImage(_images[_image_index]);
    _image_index++;
    if (_image_index >= _images.Count)
        _image_index = 0;
}

//the code to initialize the timer (inside Loaded event handler)
async private void LandingPage_Loaded(object sender, RoutedEventArgs e)
{
    _timer.Start();
    img_banner.SetImage(_images[_image_index]);
    _image_index++;
```

You will now set an image to the ImageBannerControl for the page. Rather than doing this in the Loaded event like you did previously, you will set the value during object construction. This prevents any lag that might occur while loading the image because it will already be loaded by the time the loaded event is triggered. Add the line from Listing 9-2 as the last line in LandingPage's constructor.

Listing 9-2. Setting the ImageBannerControl Image

```
img_banner.SetImage("ms-appx:///media/images/club1.jpg");
```

You have one more thing to do on LandingPage. In the XAML definition, wrap the MediaElement in a border and move that border (along with the MediaElement itself) into the Grid rpanel_right. Listing 9-3 shows the new layout for the Border.

Listing 9-3. New Layout of Border

```
...
<Border BorderThickness="1"
        Background="Black"
        Width="400"
        BorderBrush="LightGray"
        Height="250"
        Margin="10,10,0,0"
        VerticalAlignment="Top"
        HorizontalAlignment="Left">
    <MediaElement x:Name="media"
                  AudioCategory="BackgroundCapableMedia"
                  Visibility="Visible"
                  Stretch="Fill"
                  AutoPlay="True"
                  AreTransportControlsEnabled="True"
                  Source="media/video/black.mp4" />

</Border>
</Grid>
```

The MediaElement should now be position at the top left corner of your main content area, but when you run the app you will note that the video does not play. This is, of course, because you have not added it. Download the packet for this chapter and from it copy the video called `black.mp4` to the project folder `Media/Video`. Run it now and you should see the video of the Middle Eastern dancer playing.

Another piece of the app you don't need is the Sound of the Day button. Remove it and its associated event handler, and then move the StackPanel that contains the remaining buttons underneath the MediaElement, and then wrap the entire structure in a Border for good measure. Listing 9-4 shows how the Grid rpanel_right should now be laid out.

Listing 9-4. Grid rpanel_right Layout

```
<Grid  x:Name="rpanel_right"
        RelativePanel.AlignRightWithPanel="True"
        RelativePanel.RightOf="rpanel_left"
        RelativePanel.AlignTopWithPanel="True"
        RelativePanel.AlignBottomWithPanel="True">
    <Border Margin="10,10,30,0"
            BorderThickness="0,0,0,1"
            BorderBrush="LightGray"
            Padding="0,0,0,25"
            MaxHeight="400"
            VerticalAlignment="Top">
```

```
<Grid>
    <StackPanel Margin="0,250,0,0"
                VerticalAlignment="Top"
                HorizontalAlignment="Left"
                Orientation="Horizontal"
                Height="50">
        <ToggleButton Content="Audio Message"
                      Background="Gray"
                      Click="ToggleRecord"
                      Margin="0,2.5,2.5,2.5" />
        <Button Content="Video Message"
                Background="Gray"
                Click="ToggleRecordVideo"
                Margin="2.5">
            <FlyoutBase.AttachedFlyout>
                <Flyout x:Name="flyout_videomessage"
                        Placement="Top">
                    <Grid Width="300"
                          Height="200"
                          Background="Gray">
                        <Grid.RowDefinitions>
                            <RowDefinition Height="80*" />
                            <RowDefinition Height="20*" />
                        </Grid.RowDefinitions>

                        <CaptureElement x:Name="capture_element"
                                        Margin="2.5"
                                        HorizontalAlignment="Stretch" />
                        <Button x:Name="stop_recording"
                                Height="50"
                                Content="Stop Recording"
                                Margin="2.5"
                                HorizontalAlignment="Stretch"
                                Grid.Row="1"
                                Click="OnStopVideoCapture" />
                        <MediaElement x:Name="media_message"
                                      Grid.Row="0"
                                      Grid.RowSpan="2"
                                      Width="300"
                                      AutoPlay="False"
                                      Height="200"
                                      Visibility="Visible"
                                      MediaOpened="OnVideoMessageRecordingReady"
                                      MediaEnded="OnVideoMessagePlaybackCompleted" />

                    </Grid>
                </Flyout>
            </FlyoutBase.AttachedFlyout>
        </Button>
    </StackPanel>
```

```
            <Border BorderThickness="1"
                    Background="Black"
                    Width="400"
                    BorderBrush="LightGray"
                    Height="250"
                    VerticalAlignment="Top"
                    HorizontalAlignment="Left">
                <MediaElement x:Name="media"
                              AudioCategory="BackgroundCapableMedia"
                              Visibility="Visible"
                              Stretch="Fill"
                              AutoPlay="True"
                              AreTransportControlsEnabled="True"
                              Source="media/video/black.mp4" />

            </Border>
            <ScrollViewer Margin="405,0,0,0"
                          VerticalScrollBarVisibility="Auto"
                          VerticalScrollMode="Auto">
                <TextBlock FontFamily="verdana"
                           FontSize="12"
                           FontWeight="ExtraLight"
                           Text="{x:Bind Feature.BIO, Mode=OneWay}"
                           TextWrapping="Wrap" />
            </ScrollViewer>

        </Grid>
    </Border>
</Grid>
```

The code in Listing 9-4 has a TextBlock that uses binding to pull data from a field called BIO. This is part of some new types that you will be adding to the data model, so before you get into some more user interface changes, let's do that. For each event there will typically be a featured performer the Big Mountain group markets heavily in the weeks leading to the occasion. Let's create a new type to house the data for this individual. Create a new class in the `Library` folder called `BMXFeaturedPerformer` and add the contents from Listing 9-5 to it.

Listing 9-5. BMXFeaturedPerformer Class Definition

```
public class BMXFeaturedPerformer
{
    public string Name { get; set; }
    public string BIO { get; set; }
    public string VideoUri { get; set; }
    public string ImageUri { get; set; }
}
```

This class is attached to the data model through a property in the `BMXEvent` class called `Feature`. Add a new property to `BMXEvent` of type `BMXFeaturedPerformer` called `Feature`. Next, modify LandingPage to connect the changes to the data model. This will require adding a new property to the class called `Feature`. You set this property in the constructor for LandingPage so that you don't have to fire the `PropertyChanged` event. Listing 9-6 illustrates.

Listing 9-6. BMXFeaturedPerformer Class Definition

```
BMXFeaturedPerformer Feature { get; set; }
...
public LandingPage()
{
    this.InitializeComponent();
    this.Loaded += LandingPage_Loaded;

  ...
       Feature = App.State.NextEvent.Feature;
       ...
      }
      ...
```

The media packet for Chapter 9 should include a text file called `ArtistBio.txt`. Copy it into a new folder you add underneath the `Media` folder called `Text`. Now open `App.xaml.cs` and modify the `OnLaunched` event handler as shown in Listing 9-7.

Listing 9-7. Modified Application OnLaunched Event

```
async protected override void OnLaunched(LaunchActivatedEventArgs e)
{
    var bio_path = "media\\text\\artistbio.txt";
    var bio = await Package.Current.InstalledLocation.GetFileAsync(bio_path);
    var roaming_folder = ApplicationData.Current.RoamingFolder;
    State = await AppState.FromStorageFileAsync(roaming_folder, "state.xml");
    State.NextEvent = null;
    if (State.NextEvent == null)
    {
        State.NextEvent = new BMXEvent
        {
            EventID = Guid.NewGuid(),
            Address = "350 5th Ave, New York, NY 10118",
            Latitude = 40.7484,
            Longitude = -73.9857,
            CreateDate = DateTime.Now,
            Description = "A night of wine and comedy",
            EventTitle = "Comedy Night at the Empire State",
            Duration = TimeSpan.FromHours(4),
            StartDateTime = new DateTime(2015, 12, 1, 20, 0, 0),
            Feature = new BMXFeaturedPerformer
            {
                BIO = await bio.ReadTextAsync(),
            },
        };
        await State.SaveAsync();

    }
```

```
    // Place the frame in the current Window
    Window.Current.Content = new ApplicationHostPage();

    Window.Current.Activate();
}
```

Note that the line where you set NextEvent to null is only there so that you can generate a new BMXEvent which includes the new BMXFeaturedPerformer instance. Once you run the app once you can delete that line.

Continuing with the cleanup, move the title bar styling code from LandingPage into the ApplicationHostPage constructor (and add new color settings, as shown in Listing 9-8).

Listing 9-8. New Color Settings for Title Bar

```
//set the application titlebar look
Var titlebar_color = Color.FromArgb(OxFF, Ox6A, Ox6A, Ox6A);
current_view.TitleBar.BackgroundColor = titlebar_color; //Colors.DarkGray;
current_view.TitleBar.InactiveBackgroundColor = titlebar_color;
current_view.TitleBar.ButtonBackgroundColor = titlebar_color;
current_view.TitleBar.ButtonInactiveBackgroundColor = titlebar_color;
current_view.TitleBar.InactiveBackgroundColor = titlebar_color;
current_view.TitleBar.ForegroundColor = Colors.White;
current_view.TitleBar.InactiveForegroundColor = Colors.White;
current_view.TitleBar.ButtonForegroundColor = Colors.White;
current_view.TitleBar.ButtonInactiveForegroundColor = Colors.White;
```

Also, while working on the title bar, go to the _geolocator_StatusChanged event handler and, within that method, remove all instances where the title bar color is modified. You are almost done with your cleanup at this point.

Go to the XAML definition for ImageBannerControl (in the General.UWP.Library project) and change the stroke thickness for the Path object you use here to 2. Also modify the Stroke value (which indicated the stroke color) to "LightGray".

Finally, you need to modify the look and feel of UserIntroPage, the page that the user sees when a profile cannot be found for them, so that it is in line with your shift to using the dark theme. Presently, if you navigate to that page, the layout is aligned right and it is hard to see the controls on it. Let's clean it up a bit. Listing 9-9 shows the changes to make.

Listing 9-9. Changes Made to UserIntroPage Layout

```
<ScrollViewer VerticalScrollBarVisibility="Auto"
              VerticalScrollMode="Auto"
              Background="#FF6A6A6A">
    <StackPanel Orientation="Vertical"
              HorizontalAlignment="Center">
        ...
    </StackPanel>

</ScrollViewer>
```

To get this page to show, you may need to set State.UserProfile to null (as you did with NextEvent). Once you have tested it to your satisfaction, remove the line, and then build and run the app. Figure 9-1 shows how it looks on our machine.

Figure 9-1. New look for BigMountainX

You are now ready to move forward with applying background execution to BigMountainX. Let's get started.

Running in the Background

Windows 10 apps use background tasks to provide functionality that runs regardless of whether the underlying app is presently running. When registered, background tasks are initiated by external events called *triggers* and are allowed to start based on a number of criteria called *conditions*, all of which must be true in order for the background task to run. This is true even if the trigger event is fired. A triggering event for background tasks might be time, or some system event like the completion of a software installation or system update.

Because of the requirements around speed and fluidity, it is important that background tasks don't run rampant, slowing down the system without the user's knowledge. So tasks are executed through a resource-managed environment that provides only a limited amount of time to the background task to be used to run its arbitrary code. To that end, the following rules associated with processing are enforced by the system:

- Background tasks have no CPU time quota.
- Background tasks have a guarantee of only 10% of CPU.
- Background tasks have a wall clock quota of 25 second, plus 5 seconds for cancellation. The only exception to this rule is with long-running tasks.
- Background tasks have a memory quota for a minimum of 16MB (the ceiling on the actual amount is variable by device).
- As with memory, background tasks have a network quota which is also variable by device.

Given that Windows UWP 10 apps function in this manner, the question is what an app can do while not in the foreground. Windows 10 provides a number of features to give an app the opportunity to execute from a not-running state, execute from the background, or continue to execute when switched from the foreground. The execution mechanisms, even though they aren't in the foreground, are optimized for system performance and longer battery life. Some scenarios where Windows 10 allows this are as follows:

- To perform a task at a timed interval.
- To continue the background transferring of data after an app is closed.
- To continue the playback of audio after an app is closed (which you saw in Chapter 7)
- To perform a task when a system event occurs.

Before you can begin using a background task, you have to request permission from the user to do so. This step is similar to the one that you took in Chapter 8 before being allowed to access the user's location data. In that case, the concern was primarily privacy (but also battery life to a lesser extent). In this case, the concern is primarily device performance. As stated earlier, the choice of whether your app runs in the background is a choice that the user, not you, makes. To request access to create and run background tasks, use the `BackgroundExecutionManager` class. This class has a method `RequestAccessAsync` that is used to request permission from the user. This request must be made each time you need to start a task because the permission to do so may be disabled by the user at any point in time.

In the next example, you will create a generic method for requesting access to the background task engine and executing the task creation code. Using a pattern like this alleviates the effort of constantly calling `RequestAccessAsync` and testing for the results of that call. Open `ApplicationHostPage.cs` and modify it as shown in Listing 9-10. Changes are in bold.

Listing 9-10. Changes to ApplicationHostPage

```
async private void ApplicationHostPage_Loaded(object sender, RoutedEventArgs e)
{
    if (App.State.UserProfile == null)
        root_frame.Navigate(typeof(UserIntroPage));
    else
    {
        var access_status = await Geolocator.RequestAccessAsync();
        switch (access_status)
        {
            case GeolocationAccessStatus.Allowed:
                root_frame.Navigate(typeof(LandingPage));
                await InitializeApplication();
                break;
            case GeolocationAccessStatus.Denied:
                root_frame.Navigate(typeof(NoLocationPage));
                break;
            case GeolocationAccessStatus.Unspecified:
                break;
        }

    }
}
```

```
private async Task InitializeApplication()
{
    await InitializeLocation();
}
private async Task InitializeLocation()
{
    CurrentLocation = await _geolocator.GetGeopositionAsync();
    GeoLocationChanged?.Invoke(CurrentLocation.Coordinate.Point);
    var fence_id = App.State.NextEvent.EventID.ToString();
    var fences = GeofenceMonitor.Current.Geofences;
    var fence = fences.Where(i => i.Id == fence_id).FirstOrDefault();
    if (fence == null)
    {
        Geocircle event_radius = new Geocircle(new BasicGeoposition
        {
            Latitude = App.State.NextEvent.Latitude.Value,
            Longitude = App.State.NextEvent.Longitude.Value,
        }, 100);

        fence = new Geofence(fence_id, event_radius);

        //add a geofence
        GeofenceMonitor.Current.Geofences.Add(fence);

    }
}

public async Task StartBackgroundTaskAsync(Action create_task_action, string error_message)
{
    var status = await BackgroundExecutionManager.RequestAccessAsync();
    switch (status)
    {
        case BackgroundAccessStatus.AllowedMayUseActiveRealTimeConnectivity:
        case BackgroundAccessStatus.AllowedWithAlwaysOnRealTimeConnectivity:
            create_task_action();
            break;
        case BackgroundAccessStatus.Denied:
            await new MessageDialog(error_message).ShowAsync();
            break;
    }
}
```

In Listing 9-10, you extract the location activation code into its own method called `InitializeLocation` and call it from a new method you add to the class, `InitializeApplication`. You also modify the page loaded event to call `InitializeApplication` when location is available and the app is about to navigate to LandingPage. This is all cleanup stuff, though. The real change is in adding the method `StartBackgroudTaskAsync`, which accepts a delegate that represents the action that occurs if the background task is allowed to run. If background task execution is not allowed, a pop-up is presented to the user, letting them know the situation. The second argument of the method is an error message that is passed into this dialog.

Defining a Task to Run in the Background

In Chapter 7, you created a background task that you used to keep music playing in the background when your app was minimized. To do that, you had to create a new library called a Windows Runtime Component. For a quick refresher, see the section on playing audio in the background from that chapter.

In the BMX.BackgroundTasks project, right-click the project node in Solution Explorer and add a new class called `WallpaperSwitcherTask`. Modify the code in this class to match Listing 9-11.

Listing 9-11. WallpaperSwitcherTask Background Task Definition

```
sealed public class WallpaperSwitcherTask : IBackgroundTask
{
    public void Run(IBackgroundTaskInstance taskInstance)
    {

    }
}
```

Listing 9-11 represents the base amount of code that is needed to create a background task. All background tasks must be defined within a Windows Runtime Component library like BMX. BackgroundTasks and must implement the interface `IBackgroundTask`. This task defines a method, `Run`, which represents the method that is called when the background task is triggered. This is the method you use to do the work of the background task. When a background task is triggered to run, the system will create an instance of this task and an interface to this instance will be passed in as a parameter to the `Run` method. `IBackgroundTaskInstance` represents this interface. It defines a method, `GetDeferral`, which informs that system that the task might continue to perform work after the `Run` method ends. It also defines the following properties:

- `InstanceId`: Gets the instance ID of the background task instance.
- `Progress`: Gets or sets progress status for a background task instance.
- `SuspendedCount`: Gets the number of times the resource management policy caused the background task to be suspended.
- `Task`: Gets access to the registered background task for this background task instance.
- `TriggerDetails`: Gets additional information associated with a background task instance.

An important mindset to maintain while creating background tasks, particularly if you are targeting the Windows ecosystem at large, is that Windows may be operating on devices that have processing and memory constraints. Background tasks are not windows services or daemons that run in the background indefinitely. They are designed at present to come alive, do some work, and disappear. Four key issues should be examined, and addressed if necessary, in every background task you create:

- The cost to the system in memory usage and CPU time
- How task cancelation is handled
- Running in deferral
- Progress feedback

To identify the cost to the system of running a given background task, use the BackgroundWorkCost class. This class has a property named CurrentBackgroundWorkCost which returns an enum called BackgroundWorkCostValue. To report progress, you can use the Progress property on the supplied taskInstance object. For cancellation, the CancellationTokenSource object (part of System.Threading) can be utilized. Listing 9-12 adds code to your background task that utilizes these classes and properties.

Listing 9-12. Implementation of Wallpaper Switcher Background Task

```
sealed public class WallpaperSwitcherTask : IBackgroundTask
{
    public void Run(IBackgroundTaskInstance taskInstance)
    {
        //cost
        var cost = BackgroundWorkCost.CurrentBackgroundWorkCost;
        if (cost == BackgroundWorkCostValue.High)
            return;

        //handle cancelation if needed
        var cancel = new CancellationTokenSource();
        taskInstance.Canceled += (s, e) =>
            {
                cancel.Cancel();
                cancel.Dispose();
            };

        //progress
        taskInstance.Progress = 0;
    }
}
```

In Listing 9-12, you add some boilerplate code to handle cancelation, task progress, and to examine the system impact on the task running. For the use of deferrals in a background task, see the discussion on background audio from Chapter 7.

Registering a Background Task

Once you have a background task defined, registering it in your foreground app is relatively straightforward. Although it is not necessary for all background tasks (audio background tasks require it), it is a good idea to add the Windows Runtime Component library as a reference to your foreground app project. In your case, you have already added BMX.BackgroundTasks as a reference to the BigMountainX project, so there is no need to perform this step. The next step is to declare it in the app's manifest so that it is clear to the system that your app uses this kind of feature. This chapter began by talking about some of the disadvantages of traditional applications as they relate to the use of system resources. Again, given that legacy applications can run in the background without user notification or involvement (beyond starting them), the system as a whole may suffer from perceived laggy-ness. It's not that there is anything inherently wrong with running applications in the background, but the impact of such activity is scarcely communicated to the user. You would be surprised how many foreground applications on your system have one or more background tasks running, even when the app isn't running!

Following the overarching theme of Windows 10, decisions like this aren't left to the application developer but are delegated to the user. It's up to the user to pick which applications should run in the background. To help facilitate this, Modern Windows 10 apps seeking to use background tasks must explicitly declare themselves as such and specifically indicate which types of background tasks they expose.

Open BigMountainX's `package.appxmanifest` and in the Declarations tab add a new background task declaration. In the supported task types section, check Timer. Now set the entry point for this new declaration to the fully qualified type name of WallpaperSwitcherTask (`BMX.BackgroundTasks.WallpaperSwitcherTask`). Figure 9-2 shows the declaration.

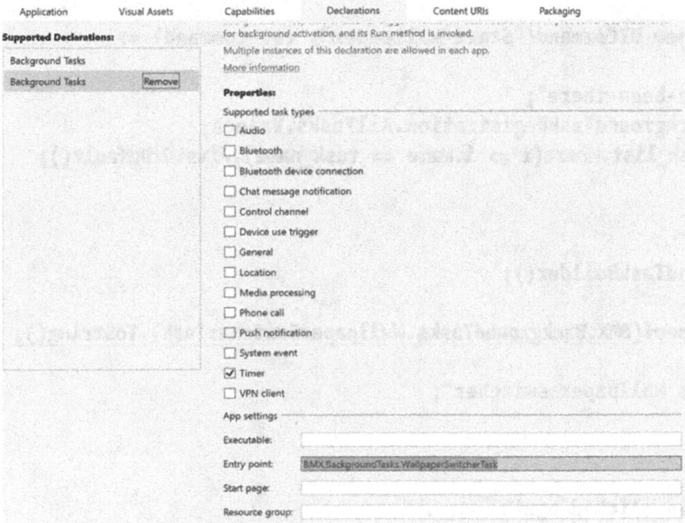

Figure 9-2. *Declaring wallpaper switcher as background task in app manifest*

In Figure 9-2, the entry point field represents the fully qualified type name of the class that contains an implementation of the background task. It should be used in scenarios where your background task has been developed using C# or C++/Cx. If the background task is defined in the hosting JavaScript application, the start page field should be populated with the path to the dedicated worker file. If you were to create the background task and attempt to register it without declaring it in this manner, the app would fail with an Access Denied error.

Now that you have the background task declared in the manifest and have the runtime component that contains your background task properly referenced, you can use the `BackgroundTaskBuilder` class to construct your background task. In the BigMountainX app, let's add a should-have-been-there feature that takes images of the fun people are having at Big Mountain Xocial events and sets them as the background on the user's desktop or phone every few minutes. This is a feature that Windows contains but has to date been completely missing from Windows Phone. To do this, you add a context menu to the ImageBannerControl instance on LandingPage with a menu item that, when clicked, initializes your `WallpaperSwitcherTask` class as a background task. Listing 9-13 illustrates. Changes are in bold.

Listing 9-13. Implementing a Context Menu on the ImageBannerControl Instance

```
...
PopupMenu image_banner_menu;

public LandingPage()
{
    ...

    image_banner_menu = new PopupMenu();

    image_banner_menu.Commands.Add(new UICommand("Start wallpaper", (ui_command) =>
    {
        var task_name = "should-have-been-there";
        var previous_task_list = BackgroundTaskRegistration.AllTasks.Values;
        var registered = previous_task_list.Where(i => i.Name == task_name).FirstOrDefault();

        if (registered == null)
        {
            var task = new BackgroundTaskBuilder();
            task.Name = task_name;
            task.TaskEntryPoint = typeof(BMX.BackgroundTasks.WallpaperSwitcherTask).ToString();
            task.Register();
            ui_command.Label = "Stop wallpaper switcher";
        }
        else
        {
            //unregister if button is clicked again
            registered.Unregister(true);
            ui_command.Label = "Start wallpaper";
        }
    }));
}

async private void Img_banner_PointerPressed(object sender, PointerRoutedEventArgs e)
{
    await image_banner_menu.ShowAsync(e.GetCurrentPoint(this).Position);
}
...
```

In Listing 9-13, you modify LandingPage by adding a PopupMenu field called image_banner_menu. This field is instantiated in the constructor for LandingPage and then a single command is added to it. Commands, of type UICommand, are essentially the menu items that are displayed when the pop-up menu shows. Each UICommand is made up of a label that displays when the pop-up is shown and a delegate that is fired when the associated label is clicked. In this case, the command "Start Wallpaper" is instantiated with a label of the same name and a delegate that represents attempts to define and register the background task.

To register the background task, you first query to see if a task by the specified name has already been defined; two tasks with the same name cannot be defined in a system. If the task has not been registered (if you do not find it in the list of registered tasks), you create a new one using the `BackgroundTaskBuilder` class. `BackgroundTaskBuilder` represents a background task to be registered with the system. In order for it to function properly, it expects two critical values to be set: a `Name` uniquely identifies the task in the system while `TaskEntryPoint` essentially indicates to the system which class will serve as the object to load and call Run on. It goes without saying that the fully qualified type name you specify here must point to a type that is in a Windows Runtime Component, and that implements IBackgroundTask. It will also need to be referenced for the background task to work.

Once the task is properly configured, you call the register method to register it and finally update the associated UICommand's label to indicate that the wallpaper switcher task has started and can now only be stopped. The alternative case is that the task has previously been registered, in which case you unregister it and update the label to the UICommand to indicate that the user can now start the wallpaper switcher.

Run the code now and you should note that the app crashes with an error when you click the menu item to start the wallpaper switcher. You may experience a situation where the context menu events are not being fired at certain areas of the ImageBannerControl. If you are having this issue, open ImageBannerControl's XAML layout and add a background color to the root Grid of the control. Use the color #FF6A6A6A so that the control continues to blend well with the page it is currently on (LandingPage). This is to be expected based on what you have done so far. In the next section, you will get into the missing piece the puzzle that, when left out, will cause this error–the last thing you need to add before registration of the background task will work.

Implementing Triggers

The background task processing system requires at least two bits of information in order to start a background task up and call the Run method on it. It needs to know the task that intends to run; the background task definition discussed in the previous section takes care of this bit. It also needs to have a triggering event associated with the background task specified so that when the targeted trigger is observed by the system, it in turn triggers the task. Triggers indicate when a task should run and provide a set of conditions that must be true for the task to run. When a trigger is fired, the underlying task infrastructure launches the class and calls the method associated with the trigger. This is done whether the app is presently running, suspended, or completely removed from memory. Without a trigger associated with the background task you created in the previous section, the task would never be run, hence the error message (rather than you pulling your hair out trying to figure out why the task in not firing). The complete list of triggers available to apply to a background task is beyond the scope of this book, but many of them can be found on MSDN at https://msdn.microsoft.com/en-us/library/windows/apps/br229871.aspx.

For the purposes of this example, you will be working with a trigger called TimeTrigger which, as you might image, triggers the associated background task once a redefined period of time has passed. TimeTrigger takes two arguments in its constructor. The first argument, freshnessTime, is a uint that defines the length of time (in minutes) between attempts to activate the task. For TimeTrigger this value can be no less than 15. The second argument, oneShot, tells the system if this particular task will be run just once (true) or indefinitely. Listing 9-14 rewrites the delegate definition from Listing 9-13 to include a TimeTrigger.

Listing 9-14. Adding TimeTrigger to the Background Task Definition

```
var task_name = "should-have-been-there";
var previous_task_list = BackgroundTaskRegistration.AllTasks.Values;
var registered = previous_task_list.Where(i => i.Name == task_name).FirstOrDefault();

if (registered == null)
{
    var task = new BackgroundTaskBuilder();
    task.Name = task_name;
    task.TaskEntryPoint = typeof(BMX.BackgroundTasks.WallpaperSwitcherTask).ToString();
    TimeTrigger timer = new TimeTrigger(20, false);
    task.SetTrigger(timer);
    task.Register();
    ui_command.Label = "Stop wallpaper switcher";
}
```

```
else
{
    //unregister if button is clicked again
    registered.Unregister(true);
    ui_command.Label = "Start wallpaper switcher";
}
```

In Listing 9-14, you add a new time trigger that is run every 20 minutes.

Implementing Wallpaper Switching

Your wallpaper changing functionality relies on the class `UserProfilePersonalizationSettings`, which can be used to either attempt to change a user's wallpaper or their lock screen image. Unlike many of the system-wide, user-impacting features available to UWP developers, this feature does not require user permissions to enable it; it does, however, need to be tested for because the feature set is not available on all Windows platforms. You won't add the wallpaper changing feature directly to the `WallpaperSwitcherTask` class; rather you will use this opportunity to highlight how both the foreground and background apps can access the same code base. You will do this by adding this code to your General.UWP.Library project and then referencing that project in `BMX.BackgroundTasks` so that both the app in the foreground and `WallpaperSwitcherTask` running in the background have the ability to change the wallpaper. Let's start by copying the images from your install location to the user's app data folder. Listing 9-15 illustrates by adding some new functionality to the `InitializeApplication` function of ApplicationHostPage.

Listing 9-15. Adding Functionality to InitializeApplication

```
private async Task InitializeApplication()
{
    //copy images to appdata
    var local_folder = Windows.Storage.ApplicationData.Current.LocalFolder;
    var install_path = Windows.ApplicationModel.Package.Current.InstalledLocation;
    var media_path = await install_path.GetFolderAsync("media\\images");
    var images = await media_path.GetFilesAsync();
    foreach (var image in images)
    {
        try
        {
            await local_folder.GetFileAsync(image.Name);
            continue;
        }
        catch { }
        await image.CopyAsync(local_folder, image.Name, ReplaceExisting);
    }

    //initialize location
    await InitializeLocation();
}
```

The new code simply reads all the image files in the `Media/Images` folder of your install location and writes them to the root of the user's local app data folder. The following namespace declaration must be added to the class for the use of `ReplaceExisting` to work:

```
using static Windows.Storage.NameCollisionOption;
```

Be sure to also change the Loaded event handler of this page so that InitializeApplication is now called before LandingPage is navigated to. Listing 9-16 illustrates.

Listing 9-16. Modifications to ApplicationHostPage Loaded Handler

```
async private void ApplicationHostPage_Loaded(object sender, RoutedEventArgs e)
{
    if (App.State.UserProfile == null)
        root_frame.Navigate(typeof(UserIntroPage));
    else
    {
        var access_status = await Geolocator.RequestAccessAsync();
        switch (access_status)
        {
            case GeolocationAccessStatus.Allowed:
                await InitializeApplication();
                var root_frame_type = root_frame.Content?.GetType();
                if (root_frame_type != typeof(LandingPage))
                        root_frame.Navigate(typeof(LandingPage));

                break;
            case GeolocationAccessStatus.Denied:
                root_frame.Navigate(typeof(NoLocationPage));
                break;
            case GeolocationAccessStatus.Unspecified:
                break;
        }

    }
}
```

The way the app is approached at this point will require that it is fully initialized before LandingPage is displayed to the user. This is because you are depending on files later in the app that only become available after InitializeApplication is completed.

Now you get to the good part. Add a new class to General.UWP.Library called UserSettings and implement it as shown in Listing 9-17.

Listing 9-17. UserSettings Class Definition

```
...
using static Windows.Storage.CreationCollisionOption;
using profile = Windows.System.UserProfile.UserProfilePersonalizationSettings;
public static class UserSettings
{
    async public static Task<uint> ChangeWallpaperAsync()
    {
        if (UserProfilePersonalizationSettings.IsSupported())
        {
            //open file
            var local_folder = Windows.Storage.ApplicationData.Current.LocalFolder;
            var file = await local_folder.CreateFileAsync("marker.txt", OpenIfExists);
```

```
            //read and convert value of file
            var value = await file.ReadTextAsync();
            var current_index = uint.Parse(value);

            //get file for index
            var image_path = $"ms-appdata:///local/club{current_index}.jpg";
            var image_uri = new Uri(image_path);
            var image_file = await StorageFile.GetFileFromApplicationUriAsync(image_uri);

            //display image file
            var was_set = await profile.Current.TrySetWallpaperImageAsync(image_file);

            if (was_set)
            {
                //increment index and store in file
                current_index++;
                if (current_index > 7)
                    current_index = 1;

                await file.WriteTextAsync(current_index.ToString());
            }
            return current_index;
        }
        return 0;
    }
}
```

Listing 9-17 defines the static class UserSettings, which at present defines a single static method ChangeWallpaper. ChangeWallpaper reads a numeric value from marker.txt (you will see more of this in a minute) and uses it to generate a file path that points to one of the seven images the app provides. (If you have not done this thus far, download the resource packet for this chapter. In it you will find the seven images we are discussing here, club1 through club7. Copy them to the folder Media/Images and you will be all set). From the file path you get the actual file using StorageFile.GetFileFromApplicationUirAsync; you then use that file to set the wallpaper on the next line. If the wallpaper sets correctly, you increment the index read from your marker text file and write the new value back to the file so that the next time you read the file it will provide that incremented value. If the value of current index is greater than seven, you simply restart the count by setting its value to one.

Now head over to the LandingPage constructor and modify the code to initialize the pop-up context menu as shown in Listing 9-18.

Listing 9-18. Modifications to LandingPage Constructor

```
//place in namespace declaration area
using static Windows.Storage.CreationCollisionOption;

//change to context menu
image_banner_menu.Commands.Add(new UICommand("Start wallpaper switcher", async (ui_command) =>
{

    var task_name = "should-have-been-there";
    var previous_task_list = BackgroundTaskRegistration.AllTasks.Values;
    var registered = previous_task_list.Where(i => i.Name == task_name).FirstOrDefault();
```

```
    if (registered == null)
    {
        var local_folder = Windows.Storage.ApplicationData.Current.LocalFolder;
        var file = await local_folder.CreateFileAsync("marker.txt", OpenIfExists);
        await file.WriteTextAsync("1");

        var task = new BackgroundTaskBuilder();
        task.Name = task_name;
        task.TaskEntryPoint = typeof(BMX.BackgroundTasks.WallpaperSwitcherTask).ToString();
        TimeTrigger timer = new TimeTrigger(20, false);
        task.SetTrigger(timer);
        task.Register();
        ui_command.Label = "Stop wallpaper switcher";
    }
    else
    {
         //unregister if button is clicked again
         registered.Unregister(true);
        ui_command.Label = "Start wallpaper switcher";
    }

}));

image_banner_menu.Commands.Add(new UICommand("Next Wallpaper", async (ui_command) =>
    {
        await UserSettings.ChangeWallpaperAsync();
    }));
```

In Listing 9-18, you add a new menu item to the ImageBanner's context menu. Now users of the app can explicitly change the wallpaper in real time. You also made a modification to the code that runs when the background wallpaper switcher is started. Now before starting the process of registering the task, you create the marker file and set its initial value to 1. `WallpaperSwitcherTask` uses `ChangeWallpaper` in much the same way. The difference in implementation here is that you set the response of the call, the value of the current index, as the value of `Progress`. Listing 9-19 illustrates.

Listing 9-19. Integrating ChangeWallpaperAsync

```
async public void Run(IBackgroundTaskInstance taskInstance)
{
    //cost
    var cost = BackgroundWorkCost.CurrentBackgroundWorkCost;
    if (cost == BackgroundWorkCostValue.High)
        return;

    //handle cancelation if needed
    var cancel = new CancellationTokenSource();
    taskInstance.Canceled += (s, e) =>
```

```
        {
            cancel.Cancel();
            cancel.Dispose();
        };

    //progress
    taskInstance.Progress = await UserSettings.ChangeWallpaperAsync();
}
```

Add a reference to General.UWP.Library to `BMX.BackgroundTasks` and then run and use the Next Wallpaper button. You should see your desktop wallpaper toggle between images, as shown in Figure 9-3.

***Figure 9-3.** The Next Wallpaper button in action*

Before you can finish this app, you still need to make one quick modification to the code base. If you run the app now and start the wallpaper switching, you might notice that the wallpaper never actually switches. This is not because you have a bug in your code or something has been done wrong; the problem on your system might be that the `Run` method exits before the `ChangeWallpaperAsync` method is done. To prevent this from happening (since it might take a moment to load up these large images), you apply the deferral pattern to the background task. Listing 9-20 shows the modifications to be made (highlighted in bold).

Listing 9-20. Applying Task Deferral to Wallpaper Switcher Background Task

```
private BackgroundTaskDeferral _deferral; // Used to keep task alive
async public void Run(IBackgroundTaskInstance taskInstance)
{

    //cost
    var cost = BackgroundWorkCost.CurrentBackgroundWorkCost;
    if (cost == BackgroundWorkCostValue.High)
        return;
```

```
        //handle cancelation if needed
        var cancel = new CancellationTokenSource();
        taskInstance.Canceled += (s, e) =>
            {
                cancel.Cancel();
                cancel.Dispose();
            };

        //get deferral
        _deferral = taskInstance.GetDeferral();

        try
        {
            //progress
            var result = await UserSettings.ChangeWallpaperAsync();
            taskInstance.Progress = result;
        }
        catch (Exception ex)
        {
            _deferral.Complete();
        }
}
```

In Listing 9-20, you simply make a call to the task instance's `GetDefferal` method. This lets the system know that the task should be kept running even after the `Run` method exits.

Reporting Progress

To report progress to the app (when the app is running in the foreground while the background task is executing), `BackgroundTaskRegistration` provides the `Progress` event handlers. `BackgroundTaskRegistration` also provides a `Completed` event that apps can use to be notified when the background task has completed. The completion status or any exception thrown while the task ran is passed to any completion handlers in the foreground app as an input parameter of the event handler. If the app is suspended when the task is completed, it receives the completion notification the next time it's resumed; however, in cases where the app is terminated, it doesn't receive the completion notification. In such cases, it's up to the app developer to persist any completion state information in a store that can also be accessed by the foreground app.

Because your background task for wallpaper changing is basically endless, you won't need the `Completed` event. You will, however, use the `Progress` event to indicate to the user which image is being displayed. In a real app, this would probably not be very relevant information; for us, though, it highlights the use of the `Progress` event to communicate information back to the foreground app. Listing 9-21 modifies the constructor for ApplicationHostPage to account for progress.

Listing 9-21. Adding Progress Checking to the Foreground App

```
var task_name = "should-have-been-there";
var previous_task_list = BackgroundTaskRegistration.AllTasks.Values;
var reg_task = previous_task_list.Where(i => i.Name == task_name).FirstOrDefault();
image_banner_menu.Commands.Add(new UICommand($"{(reg_task== null ? "Start" : "Stop")}
wallpaper switcher", async (ui_command) =>
```

```
{
    previous_task_list = BackgroundTaskRegistration.AllTasks.Values;
    var registered = previous_task_list.Where(i => i.Name == task_name).FirstOrDefault();
    if (registered == null)
    {
        var local_folder = Windows.Storage.ApplicationData.Current.LocalFolder;
        var file = await local_folder.CreateFileAsync("marker.txt", OpenIfExists);
        await file.WriteTextAsync("1");

        var task = new BackgroundTaskBuilder();

        task.Name = task_name;
        task.TaskEntryPoint = typeof(BMX.BackgroundTasks.WallpaperSwitcherTask).ToString();
        TimeTrigger timer = new TimeTrigger(20, false);
        task.SetTrigger(timer);
        registered = task.Register();
        registered.Progress += async (s, args) =>
        {
            await this.Dispatcher.RunAsync(CoreDispatcherPriority.Normal, () =>
                ApplicationView.GetForCurrentView().Title = $"Showing Image
                {args.Progress}");
        };

        ui_command.Label = "Stop wallpaper switcher";
    }
    else
    {
        //unregister if button is clicked again
        registered.Unregister(true);
        ui_command.Label = "Start wallpaper switcher";
    }
}));
```

Listing 9-21 starts moving the code to check for task registration, along with task naming, out of the UICommand delegate. The reason for this is that the use of Start or Stop in the menu item depends on the whether the background task is registered. Previously, when this was inside the delegate, the app always started with the menu item using the "Start" terminology. This was incorrect since when the app starts after a background task has been registered, the user should initially have the option to stop the task. The `Progress` event handler does not do much here. You only use it to display a string on the app's title bar indicating which image will be displayed next.

Now that you have all the pieces of the background task puzzle in place, the final step is to transition the code inside your `UICommand` event handler from not making the call to `RequestAccessAsync` to doing so. `RequestAccessAsync` must be called (in Windows 10) before the `TimeTrigger` will be allowed to trigger a background task. Listing 9-22 modifies this class to do this.

Listing 9-22. Applying Generic RequestAccessAsync Check

```
if (registered == null)
{
    var local_folder = Windows.Storage.ApplicationData.Current.LocalFolder;
    var file = await local_folder.CreateFileAsync("marker.txt", OpenIfExists);
    await file.WriteTextAsync("1");

    await ApplicationHostPage.Host.StartBackgroundTaskAsync(() =>
    {
        var task = new BackgroundTaskBuilder();

        task.Name = task_name;
        task.TaskEntryPoint = typeof(BMX.BackgroundTasks.WallpaperSwitcherTask).ToString();
        TimeTrigger timer = new TimeTrigger(20, false);
        task.SetTrigger(timer);
        registered = task.Register();
        registered.Progress += async (s, args) =>
        {
            await this.Dispatcher.RunAsync(CoreDispatcherPriority.Normal, () =>
                ApplicationView.GetForCurrentView().Title = $"Showing Image {args.Progress}");
        };

        ui_command.Label = "Stop wallpaper switcher";
    }, "Cant do this now");

}
else
{
    //unregister if button is clicked again
    registered.Unregister(true);
    ui_command.Label = "Start wallpaper switcher";
}
```

Conditions

Background tasks can also have conditions associated with them. You can add these using the `AddCondition` method of `BackgroundTaskBuilder`. Conditions applied to a background task must all evaluate to `true` for the task to execute. For example, if you want the background task from Listing 9-22 to execute only if an Internet connection is available, adding the snippet from Listing 9-23 after the call to `SetTrigger` activates the condition.

Listing 9-23. Adding Conditions to a Background Task

```
...
task.SetTrigger(timer);
task.AddCondition(new Background.SystemCondition ↵
    (Background.SystemConditionType.InternetAvailable));
...
```

Table 9-1 lists the possible condition types.

Table 9-1. *Conditions Types*

Member	Description
`UserPresent`	Specifies that the background task can only run when the user is present. If a background task with the `UserPresent` condition is triggered, and the user is away, the task won't run until the user is present.
`UserNotPresent`	Specifies that background task can only run when the user isn't present. If a background task with the `UserNotPresent` condition is triggered, and the user is present, the task won't run until the user becomes inactive.
`InternetAvailable`	Specifies that the background task can only run when the Internet is available. If a background task with the `InternetAvailable` condition is triggered, and the Internet isn't available, the task won't run until the Internet is available again.
`InternetNotAvailable`	Specifies that the background task can only run when the Internet isn't available. If a background task with the `InternetNotAvailable` condition is triggered, and the Internet is available, the task won't run until the Internet is unavailable.
`SessionConnected`	Specifies that the background task can only run when the user's session is connected. If a background task with the `SessionConnected` condition is triggered, and the user session isn't logged in, the task will run when the user logs in.
`SessionDisconnected`	Specifies that the background task can only run when the user's session is disconnected. If a background task with the `SessionDisconnected` condition is triggered, and the user is logged in, the task will run when the user logs out.

More on Triggers

As you can imagine, the timer-based background task isn't the only type of background task that an application can use. Like conditions, background tasks can be launched based on system events that occur during a user's session. Up to this point, you've been using the `TimeTrigger` class to trigger a background task; this trigger executes the background task at a given time interval. Table 9-2 provides a list of some of the possible triggers that can be used to initiate background tasks. Many trigger types follow a similar pattern, so this section focuses on common maintenance and system triggers.

Table 9-2. Background Task Trigger Types

Trigger Name	Description
Time trigger	`Windows.ApplicationModel.Background.TimeTrigger` represents a time event that triggers a background task to run.
System trigger	`Windows.ApplicationModel.Background.SystemTrigger` represents a system event that triggers a background task to run. Examples of system events are network loss, network access, and the user signing in or signing out.
Push notification trigger	`Windows.ApplicationModel.Background.PushNotificationTrigger` represents an object that invokes a background work item on the app in response to the receipt of a raw notification. Push notification is beyond the scope of this book; for more information on setting up push notification services for your Windows 10 app, go to the Windows 10 App Dev Center.
Maintenance trigger	`Windows.ApplicationModel.Background.MaintenanceTrigger` represents a maintenance trigger. Like `TimeTrigger`, `MaintenanceTrigger` is executed at the end of a time interval (it can be configured to execute only once), but the device must be connected to power for tasks that specify the trigger be valid.

For applications that require code to execute when a system event beyond the scope of time and AC power occurs, the `SystemTrigger` class is the catch-all alternative. `SystemTrigger` is instantiated with an enumeration that identifies which system event triggers the underlying background task. Listing 9-24 creates a system trigger that is fired when the device gains Internet connectivity.

Listing 9-24. System Trigger

```
var task = new Background.BackgroundTaskBuilder();
var internet_available = new Background.SystemTrigger(Background.SystemTriggerType.
InternetAvailable, false);

...
task.SetTrigger(internet_available);
background_task = task.Register();
```

Table 9-3 lists the available system trigger types.

Table 9-3. *Some System Trigger Types*

Trigger Type	Description
SmsReceived	The background task is triggered when a new SMS message is received by an installed mobile broadband device.
UserPresent	The background task is triggered when the user becomes present. Note: An app must be placed on the lock screen before it can successfully register background tasks using this trigger type.
UserAway	The background task is triggered when the user becomes absent. Note: An app must be placed on the lock screen before it can successfully register background tasks using this trigger type.
NetworkStateChange	The background task is triggered when a network change occurs, such as a change in cost or connectivity.
InternetAvailable	The background task is triggered when the Internet becomes available.
SessionConnected	The background task is triggered when the session is connected. Note: An app must be placed on the lock screen before it can successfully register background tasks using this trigger type.
ServicingComplete	The background task is triggered when the system has finished updating an app.
LockScreenApplicationAdded	The background task is triggered when a tile is added to the lock screen.
LockScreenApplicationRemoved	The background task is triggered when a tile is removed from the lock screen.
TimeZoneChange	The background task is triggered when the time zone changes on the device (for example, when the system adjusts the clock for Daylight Saving Time).
OnlineIdConnectedStateChange	The background task is triggered when the Microsoft account connected to the account changes.

Revisiting Background Audio

An app performing background playback consists of two processes. The first process is the main app, which contains the app UI and client logic, running in the foreground. The second process is the background playback task, which implements `IBackgroundTask` like all UWP app background tasks. The background task contains the audio playback logic and background services. The background task communicates with the system through the System Media Transport Controls.

The lifetime of an audio background task is closely tied to your app's current playback status. For example, when the user pauses audio playback, the system may terminate or cancel your app depending on the circumstances. After a period of time without audio playback, the system may automatically shut down the background task.

The `IBackgroundTask.Run` method is called the first time your app accesses either `BackgroundMediaPlayer.Current` from code running in the foreground app or when you register a handler for the `MessageReceivedFromBackground` event, whichever occurs first. Because there is no telling what will happen inside of `Run` (meaning the background task may attempt to notify the foreground once called), we recommended registering for the message received handler before calling `BackgroundMediaPlayer.Current` for the first time. You won't hit an error or anything, but you just might miss an important notification coming from the background audio task.

As discussed earlier in this chapter, a background task will run its course and end once control leaves the Run method, causing the Completed event to be raised. To keep the background task alive, your app must request a BackgroundTaskDeferral from within the Run method. Once the task instance completes or is cancelled, these tasks must call BackgroundTaskDeferral.Complete. In some cases, when your app gets the Canceled event, it can be also followed by the Completed event. Also, your task may receive a Canceled event while Run is executing, so be sure to manage this potential concurrence.

Let's modify the audio background task you created in Chapter 7 so that it now illustrates communication between the background and foreground of the app. For your Big Mountain X app, you will be adding transport controls to the task bar icon for the app so that a user can use those controls to control the playback of songs associated with the featured performer. When the user clicks one of these buttons, the video playback in the foreground app stops and the background audio task takes over by playing the audio in the background. All media audio playback in this sample happens in the background task even though all control events are handled in the foreground. Listing 9-25 shows the changes to LandingPage.

Listing 9-25. Adding Media Transport Control Handling to Foreground Media Player

```
SystemMediaTransportControls _media_control;
...
public LandingPage(){
...
    //initializes the background audio task
    BackgroundMediaPlayer.MessageReceivedFromBackground += BackgroundMessageRecieved;
    _media_control = SystemMediaTransportControls.GetForCurrentView();
    _media_control.ButtonPressed += _media_control_ButtonPressed;

    _media_control.IsPreviousEnabled = true;
    _media_control.IsNextEnabled = true;
}

async private void BackgroundMessageRecieved(object sender, MediaPlayerDataReceivedEventArgs e)
{
    await this.Dispatcher.RunAsync(Windows.UI.Core.CoreDispatcherPriority.Normal, () =>
    {
        media.Stop();
    });
}

private void _media_control_ButtonPressed(SystemMediaTransportControls sender,
                                          SystemMediaTransportControlsButtonPressedEventArgs args)
{
    //send the a message to the background to handle the action
    BackgroundMediaPlayer.SendMessageToBackground(new ValueSet
    {
        {"action",args.Button.ToString() }
    });
}
```

In Listing 9-25, you add a new SystemMediaTransportControls field to the LandingPage. You set the properties for the controls you want shown in task bar media transport controls list. As it stands, it will show the previous and next buttons with the play button greyed out. You can actually build and run the app at this point to see how it displays on the taskbar. Because this encompasses not just the buttons found here but also any hardware buttons on your device, and even media transport control buttons on an attached headset, this is a very powerful and versatile feature. Figure 9-4 illustrates how the controls look on the Windows 10 task bar.

Figure 9-4. *Task bar media transport controls in action*

The background task also handles two events, BackgroundMessageReceived and ButtonPressed. In order for the media transport controls to show in an enabled state (as you see in Figure 9-4), there must be an event hander associated with ButtonPressed. The other event handler, BackgroundMessageReceived, is a generic handler for any messages sent from the associated audio background task. In this case, the only things you want the app to do if it gets a message from the background task is to stop playing audio. It goes without saying that in the real world scenario you would most certainly be expecting the intent of a call from your audio background task to be for more than just one action. As this sample deals primarily with controlling background audio from the foreground, it is not necessary here. The real meat of the app is in the background task.

Open AudioPlayback.cs and modify the class definition as shown in Listing 9-26.

Listing 9-26. Implementing Background Audio Handling of Foreground Events

```
private BackgroundTaskDeferral _deferral; // Used to keep task alive
MediaPlayer _player;
public void Run(IBackgroundTaskInstance taskInstance)
{
    _deferral = taskInstance.GetDeferral();

    //declare controls for background task handling
    _player = BackgroundMediaPlayer.Current;
    _player.SystemMediaTransportControls.IsPreviousEnabled = true;
    _player.SystemMediaTransportControls.IsNextEnabled = true;

    //handle events
    BackgroundMediaPlayer.MessageReceivedFromForeground += ForegroundMessageReceived;
    _player.SystemMediaTransportControls.ButtonPressed += MediaButtonPressed;

    taskInstance.Task.Completed += (s, args) => _deferral.Complete();
}
```

```
async private void ForegroundMessageReceived(object sender, ReceivedArgs e)
{
    if (e.Data.ContainsKey("action"))
    {
        var button_string = e.Data["action"] as string;
        var button_type = typeof(MediaButton);
        var button = (MediaButton)Enum.Parse(button_type, button_string);
        await Play(button);
    }
}

async private void MediaButtonPressed(SystemMediaTransportControls sender, ButtonArgs args)
{
    await Play(args.Button);
}

async Task Play(MediaButton button)
{
    switch (button)
    {
        case MediaButton.Play:
            _player.Play();
            break;
        case MediaButton.Pause:
            _player.Pause();
            break;
        case MediaButton.Previous:
            {
                SendMessage("action", "stop");
                var file_path = "ms-appx:///media/video/zaharat.mp4";
                var file = await StorageFile.GetFileFromApplicationUriAsync(new
                Uri(file_path));
                _player.SetFileSource(file);
            }
            break;
        case MediaButton.Next:
            {
                SendMessage("action", "stop");
                var file_path = "ms-appx:///media/video/black.mp4";
                var file = await StorageFile.GetFileFromApplicationUriAsync(new
                Uri(file_path));
                _player.SetFileSource(file);
            }
            break;
    }
}
```

```
void SendMessage(string key, string value)
{
    BackgroundMediaPlayer.SendMessageToForeground(new ValueSet
    {
        { key,value}
    });
}
```

For the code above to run, the namespace declarations in Listing 9-27 must be added (to shorten the names of very long types).

Listing 9-27. Required Namespaces for Listing 9-26

```
using MediaButton = Windows.Media.SystemMediaTransportControlsButton;
using ButtonArgs = Windows.Media.SystemMediaTransportControlsButtonPressedEventArgs;
using ReceivedArgs = Windows.Media.Playback.MediaPlayerDataReceivedEventArgs;
```

Run the app now and test out the use of the transport controls to change the audio for your videos.

Monitoring the Contact Store

This final example will show the power and flexibility of background tasks in tandem with triggers and conditions. One thing the Big Mountain folks you've been working with are mindful of is their mailing list. It's a critical component of their business (and one of the principal ways they get the word out about their events). They would like to implement a feature that will give users of their app an opportunity to share contact information for any new contact that gets added to the user's machine with their app. In exchange for this, they are offering a free drink for each 10 users added.

This kind of system event triggering based on criteria is one of the cool things about background tasks. For this example, you will create a new background task that will handle each instance when a contact is added to the contact store (by adding a user to the People Hub). Once your background task is triggered, it will utilize a feature you will learn about in Chapter 10 to trigger a toast notification that will not only prompt the user to add the contact, but also stay present in the notification center. Let's get started by adding a new class to your BMX. BackgroundTasks project called `ContactsWatcher` and then define is as shown in Listing 9-28.

Listing 9-28. Implementing ContactsWatcher

```
private BackgroundTaskDeferral _deferral; // Used to keep task alive
public void Run(IBackgroundTaskInstance taskInstance)
{
    //cost
    var cost = BackgroundWorkCost.CurrentBackgroundWorkCost;
    if (cost == BackgroundWorkCostValue.High)
        return;

    _deferral = taskInstance.GetDeferral();
    Toast("Forward us that contact for a free drink!");
    _deferral.Complete();
}
```

```
void Toast(string toast_message)
{
    try
    {
        var xml = ToastNotificationManager.GetTemplateContent(ToastTemplateType.
        ToastImageAndText01);
        var texts = xml.DocumentElement.GetElementsByTagName("text");
        var text_node = texts.FirstOrDefault() as XmlElement;
        text_node.AppendChild(xml.CreateTextNode(toast_message));

        ToastNotification toast = new ToastNotification(toast_xml);
        var notifier = ToastNotificationManager.CreateToastNotifier();
        notifier.Show(toast);
    }
    catch (Exception ex)
    {

    }
}
```

The code in Listing 9-28 defines a `Toast` method that is called from the background task's `Run`. If you don't recognize any of the types defined here, it's because we haven't discussed them at all. In the Chapter 10, we will go into detail on how to create toast notifications. For now, just type it in.

The code to initialize the background task could probably be triggered by a checkbox in a user preferences page to prevent the app from becoming annoying (so that it can be toggled on and off as needed by the user), but for this demo you will keep it in ApplicationHostPage. As this is essentially a background watcher that requires little in the way of permissions, placing it here is fine. You'll tackle the other side of this when the user clicks the tile notification. Listing 9-29 adds the code to the `ApplicationInitialized` method of ApplicationHostPage.

Listing 9-29. Initializing ContactsWatcher

```
private async Task InitializeApplication()
{
    ...

    //initialize contacts watcher
    await StartBackgroundTaskAsync(() =>
    {
        var task_name = "contacts-watcher";
        var previous_task_list = BackgroundTaskRegistration.AllTasks.Values;
        var registered = previous_task_list.Where(i => i.Name == task_name).FirstOrDefault();
        registered?.Unregister(true);
        registered = null;
        if (registered == null)
        {
            BackgroundTaskBuilder task_builder = new BackgroundTaskBuilder();
            task_builder.Name = task_name;
            task_builder.TaskEntryPoint = typeof(ContactsWatcher).ToString();
            ContactStoreNotificationTrigger contact_trigger = new
            ContactStoreNotificationTrigger();
```

```
            task_builder.SetTrigger(contact_trigger);
            task_builder.Register();
        }
    });

    //initialize location
    await InitializeLocation();
}
```

In Listing 9-29, you create the new task with a trigger of type `ContactStoreNotificationTrigger`. This trigger is used to connect a background task to activities by the user that modifies the contact store. The final step to activating this background task is to declare it in the application's manifest. For tasks of this type you can use the General task type. Figure 9-5 shows how to configure `ContactsWatcher`.

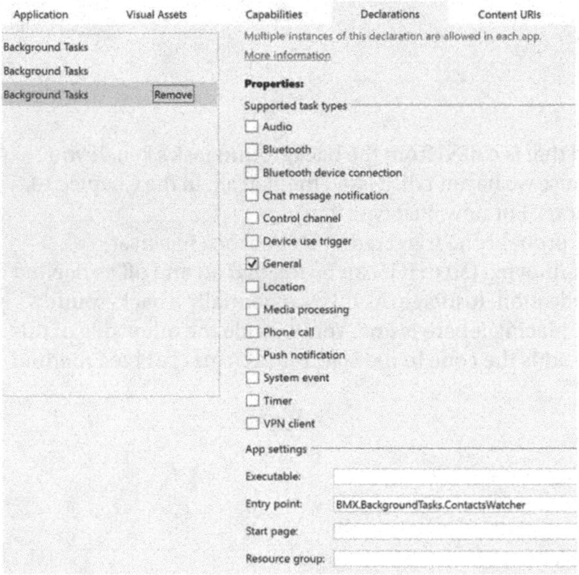

Figure 9-5. *Declaring ContactsWatcher*

Run the app and then close it immediately. Now fire up the People app and add a new contact. Figure 9-6 shows what you should see.

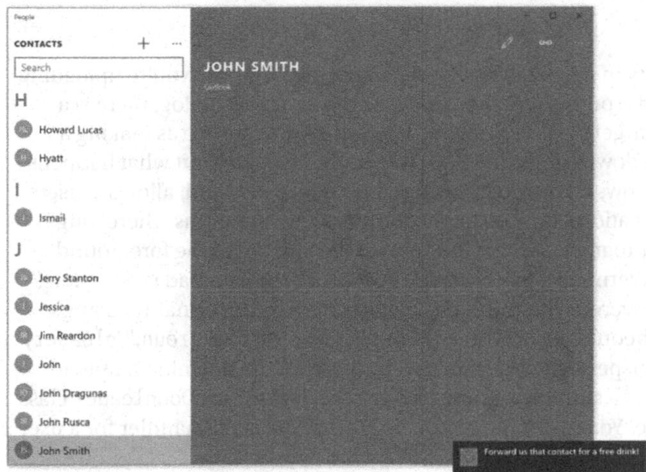

Figure 9-6. *ContactsWatcher in action*

That's not all, though. If you look at the tray menu icon for the Action Center, you will notice that it now has a solid white color (which indicates that there are unread notifications awaiting your evaluation). The great thing about toast notifications is that they not only give the user an immediate prompt but are also stored in the Action Center so that they can be evaluated at a later time.

Figure 9-7 shows the Action Center with the toasts you just received waiting to be evaluated.

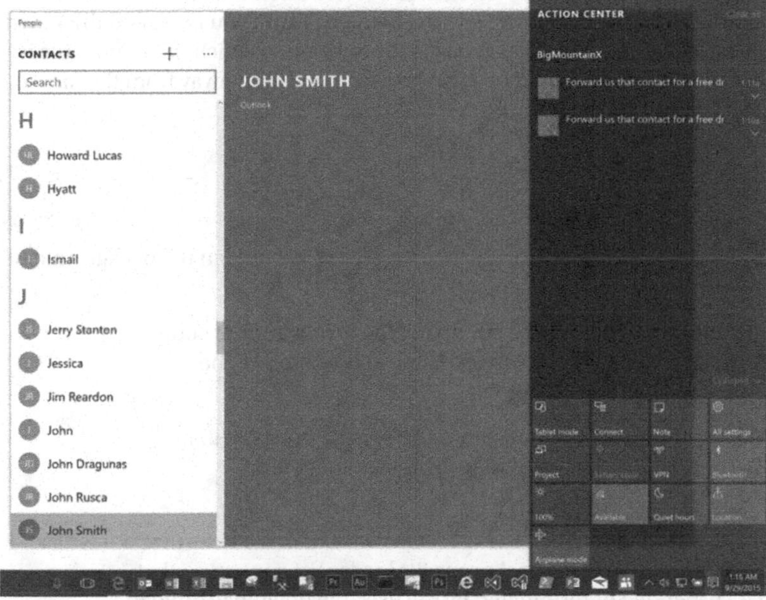

Figure 9-7. *Toast notifications in the Action Center*

Background Transfers

Moving files over a network is a common activity in this modern age of computing. Whether you're uploading video, audio, or images to a social networking site or downloading movies from a media catalog, there is a fundamental need for this functionality. If the target file is very small, this is usually as simple as making a connection to the content provider and pulling down (or pushing up) the desired content. But what happens when the content is very large? Given that Windows 10 has been designed to be fast and fluid, allowing users to quickly and seamlessly switch between applications, how do applications handle situations where long-running network data-transfer activities are in progress, and the user moves the app out of the foreground state? Surely the solution isn't to tell the user, "Warning: don't leave the app until the download is complete!"

The folks at Microsoft have this use case covered with the `BackgroundTransfer` functionality. Using `BackgroundDownloader`, an application can schedule the download (or upload, using `BackgroundUploader`) of content such that even if the application is suspended or terminated by the user, the download/upload continues in the background. Listing 9-30 shows a simple example of using the `BackgroundDownloader` class to pull down a large file from a remote resource. You might have code like this in the event handler for a user interaction control (like a button) to pull down a given file.

Listing 9-30. BackgroundDownloader at Work

```
var uri = "http://download.blender.org/peach/bigbuckbunny_movies/BigBuckBunny_320x180.mp4";
var result_file = await Windows.Storage.KnownFolders.VideosLibrary.
CreateFileAsync("bigbunny.wmv");

var downloader = new BackgroundDownloader();
await downloader.CreateDownload(new Uri(uri), result_file).StartAsync();
```

Listing 9-30 shows sample code that might run in the event handler for a button that, when clicked, initiates the download of a large file from a remote resource. For this example to run, you must add the Video Library capability to the target application's manifest, because that is the location to which the remote file is downloaded. Once the button is clicked and the download begins, the user can switch away from the target app or even stop it, and the download will still complete.

Summary

Now that you've completed your exploration of the ways in which to keep apps running in the background in the Windows 10 ethos, let's review some key points this chapter covered:

- You learned about the various types of triggers. For applications that require code to execute even when a system is beyond the scope of time and AC power, the `SystemTrigger` class is the catch-all alternative.
- Background tasks are meant to be quick-in-and-out, short-lived work units that consume very little system resources. CPU and network usage constraints apply to them.
- Using the `BackgroundTransfer` functionality, `BackgroundDownloader` is a class that can schedule a download (or upload, using `BackgroundUploader`) of content so that even if the application is suspended or terminated by the user, the download/upload will continue in the background.
- Background tasks execute in either a system-provided host executable or in the app process.

CHAPTER 10

Shell Integration

The discussion in the previous chapter ended with a sample that used a background task to send a toast notification to the user whenever a contact was added to the user's contacts store. Before you get into notifications, you will be looking at some lesser known integration points between UWP apps and the Windows System they reside on. Specifically, your focus in this chapter will be on the approach to windowing, working with title bars (which you used to style Big Mountain X in the last chapter), wallpapers and lock screens, and how UWP apps have the ability to modify the images they display. (You used the user profile APIs in the last chapter when you built a background task that was able to change the user's desktop wallpaper.)

Launch Conditions

You've been using the `Application` class since you started creating UWP samples. In essence, it encapsulates an app, providing it with unhandled exception detection, application scoped resources, lifetime management, and an entry point. Like the approach you take when creating pages, the `Application` object associated with a particular app is defined in two layers, XAML and an associated code-behind file that derives from a base `Application` class. Listing 10-1 shows the basic XAML for an application.

Listing 10-1. Basic XAML

```
<Application
    x:Class="BigMountainX.App"
    xmlns="http://schemas.microsoft.com/winfx/2006/xaml/presentation"
    xmlns:x="http://schemas.microsoft.com/winfx/2006/xaml"
    xmlns:local="using:BigMountainX"
    RequestedTheme="Dark">

</Application>
```

Like Page (and UserControl), the XAML for defining an application specifies the base class as the root element of the XAML document. In this case, you can assume that the actual class definition for the application will derive from `Application`. The XAML element for `Application` also defines an `x:Class` attribute that can be used to identify the object instance that will serve as the code-behind. Because of its position in the application model, code generation, and activation sequence, `Application` has some restrictions on its XAML usage:

- Other than the xmlns declarations, `RequestedTheme`, and `x:Class`, no other attributes can appear on the `Application` root tag.
- Don't attempt to change `x:Class` values that come from the project template `App.xaml` pages; there are additional dependencies on using that naming scheme that exist in the build actions.

- Don't wire the Application event handlers in XAML. All event wiring should be done in code (usually in the constructor). Also, you should generally use method overrides rather than event syntax for an event (for example, you override OnActivated to respond to that phase of the application life cycle.)
- The only allowed properties in an Application instance in XAML are the set of elements to populate the Application.Resources property, using a XAML property element usage.

The default project templates in Visual Studio generate an App class that derives from Application and provides an entry point where you can add initialization code. Using the default template, the code-behind subclass will always be named App (in Visual Studio 2015). The App class associates itself with the corresponding XAML by calling the generated InitializeComponent method in its constructor. You can add additional initialization code to the App constructor, but you will typically only add code to associate handlers to Application events. For other initialization code, you should override one or more initialization methods such as OnLaunched.

The system handles app lifetime by suspending your app whenever the user switches to another app or to the desktop, and resuming your app whenever the user switches back to it. However, the system can also terminate your app while it is suspended in order to free up resources. You should handle the Suspending event to save your app state in case of termination, and override the OnLaunched method to restore your app state. You should handle the Resuming event only if you need to refresh any displayed content that might have changed while the app is suspended. You do not need to restore other app state when the app resumes.

The application object doesn't just expose methods that are called by the system at various points through the lifecycle of the app; it also exposes data about the nature of the associated activation scenario. When an application is activated, the system notes the context under which it was launched. Using the Application object, you can override various methods to enable distinct behavior for those specific scenarios. It is this kind of targeted behavior based on activation context that is exploited in shell integration scenarios like file pickers, contact pickers, and protocol/file activation.

Let's look at a very simple example of this: protocol activation. If you remember, you saw this at work in Chapter 8 when you performed integration with the Maps app. If you recall, you were able to launch the Maps app by specifying a URI in Microsoft Edge that conformed to a protocol Maps supported: bingmaps://. With protocol activation, an app registers as the default hander for a particular protocol. Each time that protocol is used to open a resource, the system fires up the default handler for that protocol, passing it the URI to help handle the request.

Open the app manifest for BigMountainX and add a new declaration for specifying protocols. Figure 10-1 shows the declarations tab of the package.appxmanifest file of the project.

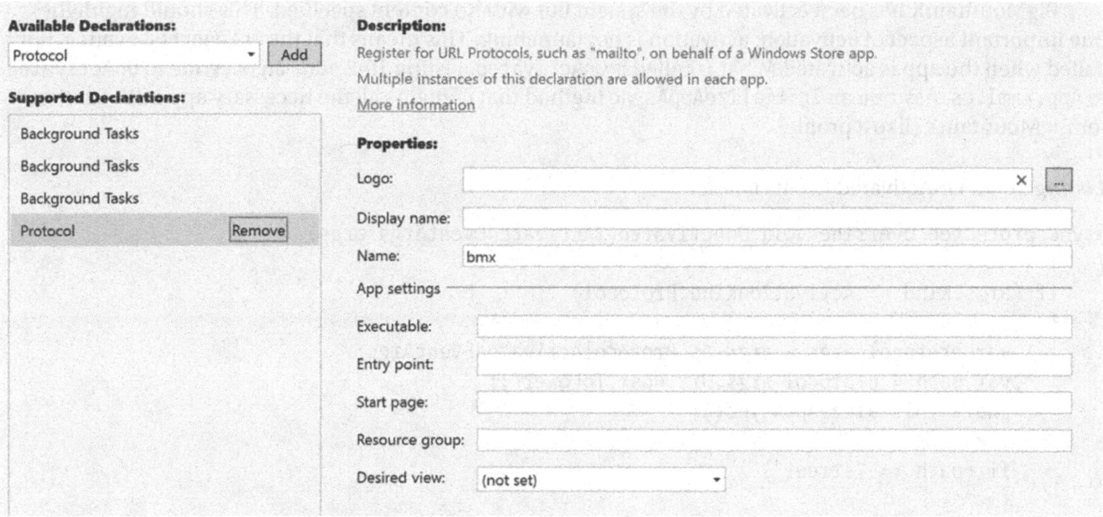

Figure 10-1. Protocol declaration in app manifest

The name specified will correspond to the protocol name (so to access a resource using this protocol, you would specify bmx://test/test or something of the sort). Build and deploy the app, and the open Edge and attempt to navigate to `bmx://hello world`. Figure 10-2 should be what you see.

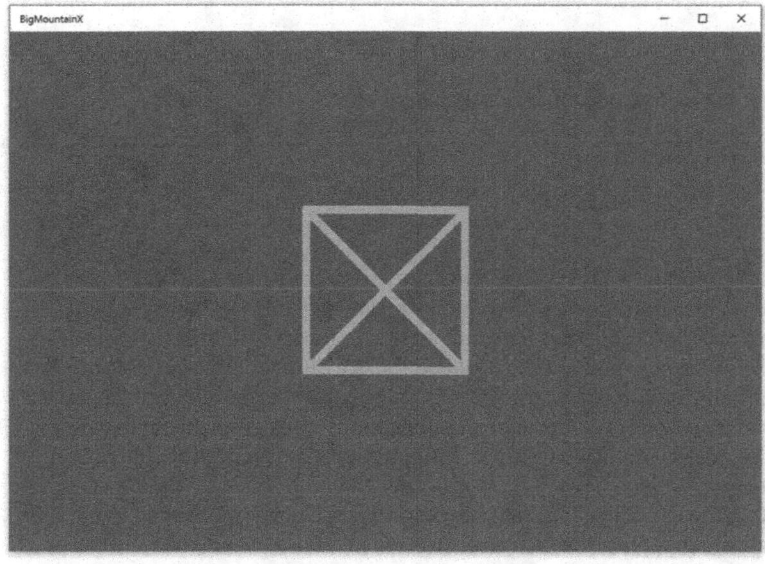

Figure 10-2. App window without content

BigMountainX has been activated by the system but with no content specified. This should highlight one important aspect of activation: activation is not launching. This means that the OnLaunched event is not called when the app is activated. What *is* called is OnActivated. Listing 10-2 adds an override to OnActivated to App.xaml.cs. Assume an InitializeAppAsync method that contains all the necessary app initialization for BigMountainX (like a profile).

Listing 10-2. OnActivated Event Handler

```
async protected override void OnActivated(IActivatedEventArgs args)
{
    if (args.Kind == ActivationKind.Protocol)
    {
        var protocol_args = args as ProtocolActivatedEventArgs;
        var path = protocol_args.Uri.Host.ToLower();
        await InitializeAppAsync();

        if (path == "street")
        {
            StreetSideViewPage street_view = new StreetSideViewPage();
            var center_point = new Geopoint(new BasicGeoposition
            {
                Latitude = App.State.NextEvent.Latitude.Value,
                Longitude = App.State.NextEvent.Longitude.Value,
            });
            await street_view.InitializeAsync(center_point);
            Window.Current.Content = street_view;
        }
        else
        {
            Window.Current.Content = new ApplicationHostPage();
        }
        Window.Current.Activate();
    }
}
```

In Listing 10-2, you use the Kind property of IActivateEventArgs to determine the kind of activation that has occurred. Based on that, you convert the interface instance back to its concrete type, ProtocolActivatedEventArgs. This class has properties that can be used to retrieve the URI that was used to activate the app. Based on the URI value, you pull out the host and make a decision on what user interface to present based on the value. If the value of host is the string "street", you display the StreetSide view map as the default content for the app; otherwise, you set an instance of ApplicationHostPage as the main window content. This is, of course, a very simplified view of what can be done with protocol activation, but it does hit all the main steps to utilizing the feature.

As can be seen from Listing 10-2, the use of the Application object for the purposes of shell integration comes to light when you begin to consider application activation beyond just normal launching. Many of the activation kinds have virtual methods that have been abstracted out of OnActivated. These convenience methods allow you to separate the code out for those specific scenarios without having to manage the control flow associated the scenario. If, for instance, you want to create a file picker, you can find method overrides for handling those particular launch conditions. Figure 10-3 shows what the app looks like when launched directly from the Microsoft Edge browser. You will add the page StreetsideViewPage to your app a little bit later on in the chapter, so hold tight. To get the app to compile and run for now, add a new page to the project entitled StreetSideViewPage with a function `IntializeAsync` that accepts a Geopoint as its parameter. The page does not need to do anything for now.

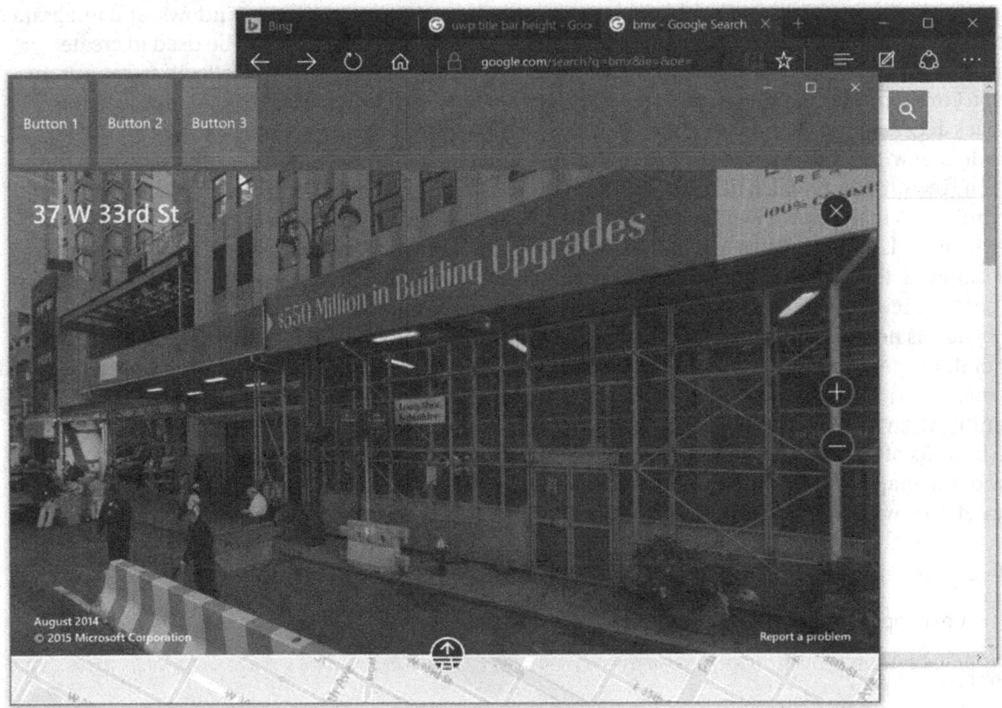

***Figure 10-3.** StreetSide view window protocol activated*

Windowing

This might come as a surprise to you, but windowing features, the cornerstone of what makes Windows "Windows," are new to the UWP platform. If you ever had the chance to work with a Windows 8 desktop, you will know why. With Windows 8, much was made of the intellectually sound choice to go back to single-page, full-screen apps that offered very little in the form of multitasking. Because of this, the normal windowing features you might be used to if you came from the world of WinForms or WPF did not exist. Although Windows 10 UWP apps targeting at the desktop offer this feature now, it must be with an air of caution. If you have been paying attention, you will remember that Windows 10 is a platform that can target anything from an IoT device like a low-level controller to a surface hub. Neither of these would seem like good targets for apps that utilizes windowing heavily. Because of this shift from the primarily desktop-oriented computing world to the new one where mobility is essential and devices encircle the user rather than the opposite, the approach to windowing has changed drastically in terms of the API.

Opening New Windows

To open new windows, and also to work with the initial window that is opened by the system, there are a number of important types that you will need to get comfortable with, the most important of which it the `CoreApplication` class. `CoreApplication` is the low-level representation of the running app. Created by the system as a singleton, this object enables apps to handle state changes, manage windows, and integrate with a variety of UI frameworks. By calling the `CreateNewView` function, this class can be used to create new application views (which correspond to a window if you are on a desktop). `CreateNewView` returns an instance of a `CoreApplicationView` that represents a window and its associated UI thread. Because this class provides access to the UI thread for the view, exposed via the `Dispatcher` property, you can use it to inject code that will run within the context of that particular user interface. Another critical class is the `ApplicationViewSwitcher`, which defines an important static method called `TryShowAsStandaloneAsync` for displaying views in their own window. `TryShowAsStándaloneAsync` takes as an argument the id of the view to be displayed. Acquiring this id can be somewhat tricky. We will get into the steps to do this in more detail in a moment. First, let's look at a third important class for enabling and managing application views, the `ApplicationView` class. An application view (window) is the displayed portion of a UWP app. The application view is not the same thing as the current page of the application. It is better thought of as the container of the pages. On Windows, a user's screen can have up to four windows of variable width displayed simultaneously.

Presently, when a user wants to see the street view of the map on LandingPage, it appears directly within the bounds of the MapControl on that page. You can improve usability by opening up the street view of the map in a new window. Open LandingPage and replace the code in the event handler `OnShowStreetView` with the code from Listing 10-3.

Listing 10-3. Creating an Application View

```
var view = CoreApplication.CreateNewView();
var view_id = 0;
var supported = true;
var center_point = map.Center;

await view.Dispatcher.RunAsync(Windows.UI.Core.CoreDispatcherPriority.Normal, async () =>
{
    view_id = ApplicationView.GetForCurrentView().Id;

    MapControl streetview_map = new MapControl();
    streetview_map.MapServiceToken = "<your map token>";
    streetview_map.PanInteractionMode = MapPanInteractionMode.Disabled;
    streetview_map.TiltInteractionMode = MapInteractionMode.Disabled;
    streetview_map.ZoomInteractionMode = MapInteractionMode.Disabled;
    streetview_map.CustomExperienceChanged += (s, args) =>
    {
        if (streetview_map.CustomExperience == null)
        {
            view.CoreWindow.Close();
        }
    };
```

```
        streetview_map.Center = center_point;
        if (streetview_map.IsStreetsideSupported)
        {
            var street_panorama = await StreetsidePanorama.FindNearbyAsync(streetview_map.Center);
            var street_exp = new StreetsideExperience(street_panorama);
            street_exp.OverviewMapVisible = true;
            streetview_map.CustomExperience = street_exp;

            Window.Current.Content = streetview_map;
            Window.Current.Activate();
        }
        else
        {
            supported = false;
        }

    });

    if (supported)
    {
        await ApplicationViewSwitcher.TryShowAsStandaloneAsync(view_id);
    }
    else
    {
        await new MessageDialog("StreetSide View is not supported.").ShowAsync();
    }
```

In Listing 10-3, you use `CoreApplication` to create a new view for the app. You then insert a delegate into that view's dispatcher (so that it will be run in the context of that view's thread/message pump). Within the delegate, you create a new MapControl that points to the same location as the one on LandingPage, set it to be in Streetside view by default, and then set it as the content to the view's primary Window. Note that in this case calling `Window.Current` does not map to the main window; instead it maps to the window that the system has created for this particular application view. Before doing this you capture the id of the current view you are working in. Remember, calls like `Window.Current` or `Application.GetForCurrentView()` as they are used here apply to the `CoreApplicationView` under which the code is running. When your app is created by the system, there is only one of these and you are automatically in it (I'm sure the code used by the system is somewhat similar to what you see here). In this case, you are creating a new `CoreApplicationView` along with its associated thread and then running this code within that thread. To help highlight the distinction between the contexts, add the code (highlighted in bold) in Listing 10-4 to the `OnShowStreetView` method.

Listing 10-4. Testing Dispatcher Hash Code Values

```
async private void OnShowStreetView(object sender, RoutedEventArgs e)
{
    var view = CoreApplication.CreateNewView();
    var view_id = 0;
    var supported = true;
    var center_point = map.Center;
```

```
        //access the base view context
        var disp1 = Window.Current.CoreWindow.Dispatcher.GetHashCode();
        var disp2 = CoreApplication.MainView.Dispatcher.GetHashCode();
        var disp3 = CoreWindow.GetForCurrentThread().Dispatcher.GetHashCode();
        var new_disp = view.Dispatcher.GetHashCode();
        await view.Dispatcher.RunAsync(Windows.UI.Core.CoreDispatcherPriority.Normal, async () =>
        {
            //within created view context
            var disp4 = Window.Current.CoreWindow.Dispatcher.GetHashCode();
            var disp5 = CoreWindow.GetForCurrentThread().Dispatcher.GetHashCode();

            if (disp1 != disp4 &&
            disp2 != new_disp &&
            disp3 != disp5)
            {
                //control logic should enter here
            }

           view_id = ApplicationView.GetForCurrentView().Id;  //place breakpoint here
           ...
        }
        ...
}
```

Once you have done this, place a breakpoint on the line that is indicated in the sample and run the app. When you invoke this page and mouse over the various disp values, you should note that disp1, disp2, and disp3 all have the same hash code, meaning that they are all pointing to the same instance, and that the value does not match with the value of new_disp. Two things should be clear from this first discovery. Firstly, it should be clear that regardless of how you access the dispatcher (whether through `CoreWindow` or through `CoreApplicationView`) you are accessing the same object. Secondly, it should be clear that the `CoreApplicationView` returned from calling `CoreApplication.CreateNewView()` has a different dispatcher associated with it.

When you mouse over disp4 and disp5, you should note that these two share the same value but that this value is different from the value of disp1, disp2, and disp3. You should also observe that this value is the same the value of new_disp, meaning that the dispatcher object created with the call to `CreateNewView` is the same object that is available for use within the delegate.

Continuing with the explanation of Listing 10-4, a new addition to the mix here is handling the `CustomExperienceChanged` event. You do this so you can test to see if there is a `CustomExperience` associated with the map. The purpose of the larger map is to display street view data; if the user closes StreetSide view, you want the entire window to close. The code here tests for this eventuality and closes the windows when it happens.

If you run the app at this point, you will notice two immediate issues with the sample. First, the window that is opened is quite large. While the purpose of the secondary windows is to give the user a larger size to browse with, making the window too large hides the actual app that launched it (or at least deters from it to an unacceptable extent). The second issue is that there is no test to see if the Streetside view window is already open before creating a new one. A more ideal approach is to test to see if the window is created and open; if neither is the case, then you create it. Otherwise, you simply hide and show the previously created window. Figure 10-4 illustrates the problem.

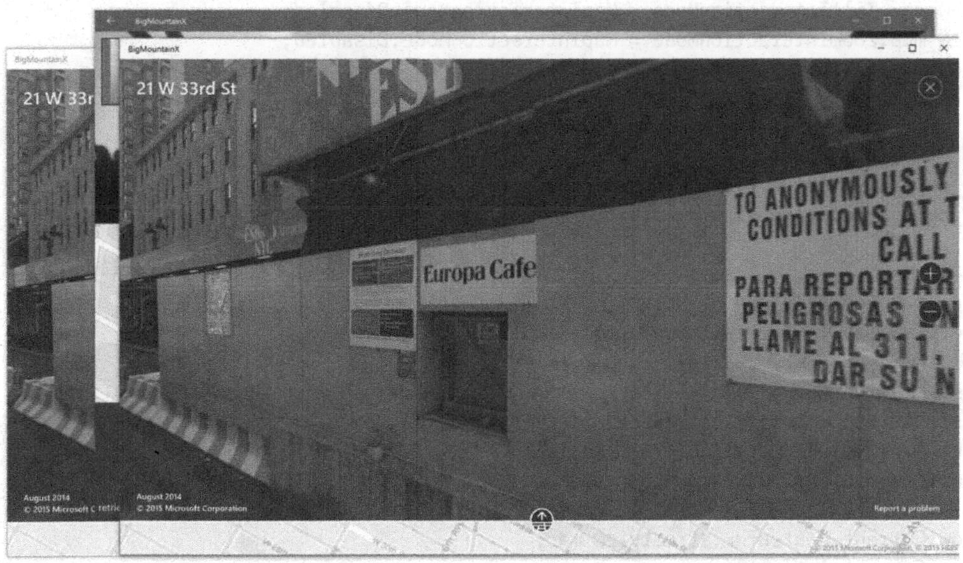

Figure 10-4. *Multiple windows being displayed*

You will solve the later of the problems in this section and save the former for the next section. Listing 10-5 shows the modified `OnShowStreetView` event handler code. Changes are highlighted in bold. Before you begin modifying this method, add the following as a class-level field:

```
CoreApplicationView _core_streetside_view;
```

Listing 10-5. Showing Streetside View One at a Time

```
var view_id = 0;
var supported = true;
var center_point = map.Center;

if (_core_streetside_view != null)
{
    await _core_streetside_view.Dispatcher.RunAsync(CoreDispatcherPriority.Normal, () =>
    {
        _core_streetside_view.CoreWindow.Close();
    });
}

_core_streetside_view = CoreApplication.CreateNewView();
await _core_streetside_view.Dispatcher.RunAsync(CoreDispatcherPriority.Normal, async () =>
{

    view_id = ApplicationView.GetForCurrentView().Id;

    MapControl streetview_map = new MapControl();
    streetview_map.MapServiceToken = "<map token>";
    streetview_map.PanInteractionMode = MapPanInteractionMode.Disabled;
```

```
    streetview_map.TiltInteractionMode = MapInteractionMode.Disabled;
    streetview_map.ZoomInteractionMode = MapInteractionMode.Disabled;
    streetview_map.CustomExperienceChanged += (s, args) =>
    {
        if (streetview_map.CustomExperience == null)
        {
            _core_streetside_view.CoreWindow.Close();
            _core_streetside_view = null;
        }
    };
    streetview_map.Center = center_point;
    if (streetview_map.IsStreetsideSupported)
    {
        var street_panorama = await StreetsidePanorama.FindNearbyAsync(streetview_map.Center);
        var street_exp = new StreetsideExperience(street_panorama);
        street_exp.OverviewMapVisible = true;
        streetview_map.CustomExperience = street_exp;

        Window.Current.Content = streetview_map;
        Window.Current.Activate();
    }
    else
    {
        supported = false;
    }
});

if (supported)
{
    await ApplicationViewSwitcher.TryShowAsStandaloneAsync(view_id);
}
else
{
    await new MessageDialog("StreetSide View is not supported.").ShowAsync();
}
```

In Listing 10-5, you move the variable used to store the newly created CoreApplicationView instance into class scope so that you can determine if a window has already been created. If the value is not null, meaning a view has been created and is presently showing, you close it and recreate a new one; otherwise, you just create it as you previously did. For this to work, you also need to add a new line to the CustomExperienceChanged event handler which sets the value of _core_streetside_view to null. Running the code now, you should note that only one Streetside view window is shown at a time. If a window is already open, it is closed first before a new window is created.

Sizing Windows

Whereas CoreApplicationView gives you access to the threading infrastructure in order to inject functionality into a new window, ApplicationView provides you with the means to manipulate that window. Using ApplicationView, you can set the initial size of a window, the minimum size of a window, and even try resizing a window. Listing 10-6 modifies BigMountainX to utilize this. Add the using declaration to enable the use of the window mode moniker. Then add the code in Listing 10-7.

Listing 10-6. Enabling Moniker

```
using windowmode = Windows.UI.ViewManagement.ApplicationViewWindowingMode;
```

Listing 10-7. Setting Size Preferences

```
...
await _core_streetside_view.Dispatcher.RunAsync(CoreDispatcherPriority.Normal, async () =>
{
    var app_view = ApplicationView.GetForCurrentView();
    view_id = app_view.Id;

    //size the window
    app_view.SetPreferredMinSize(new Size(500, 400));
    ApplicationView.PreferredLaunchWindowingMode = windowmode.PreferredLaunchViewSize;
    ApplicationView.PreferredLaunchViewSize = new Size(500, 400);
    app_view.Title = $"Help me find \"{App.State.NextEvent.EventTitle}\"";

    MapControl streetview_map = new MapControl();
    streetview_map.MapServiceToken = "<your token here>";
    streetview_map.PanInteractionMode = MapPanInteractionMode.Disabled;
    streetview_map.TiltInteractionMode = MapInteractionMode.Disabled;
    streetview_map.ZoomInteractionMode = MapInteractionMode.Disabled;
    streetview_map.CustomExperienceChanged += (s, args) =>
    {
        if (streetview_map.CustomExperience == null)
        {
            _core_streetside_view.CoreWindow.Close();
            _core_streetside_view = null;
        }
    };
    streetview_map.Center = center_point;
    if (streetview_map.IsStreetsideSupported)
    {
        var street_panorama = await StreetsidePanorama.FindNearbyAsync(streetview_map.Center);
        var street_exp = new StreetsideExperience(street_panorama);
        street_exp.OverviewMapVisible = true;
        streetview_map.CustomExperience = street_exp;

        Window.Current.Content = streetview_map;
        Window.Current.Activate();
    }
    else
    {
        supported = false;
    }
});
...
```

In Listing 10-7, you add code to set the preferred minimum size of the window. You also specify that you want the windows launched using the size value that comes from `PreferredLaunchViewSize`, a static property of the `ApplicationView` class, and then set the value of that property (`PreferredLaunchViewSize`) as well. You will find when you launch your app and access the Streetside view at least once that your entire app will now start launching at that size. This is because this particular property is application-wide. It was added here to illustrate the functionality but cannot simply be removed now. To get rid of the annoying behavior, delete the two lines associated with preferred size from the delegate and add the following line to the constructor of ApplicationHostPage (remember to add the `using` declaration for `windowmode`):

```
ApplicationView.PreferredLaunchWindowingMode = windowmode.Auto;
```

Another option is to use the `TryResize` method of an `ApplicationView` instance. This will work generally, but be wary of the fact that there is a bug in this current version of the UWP APIs (as of September 2015). If an activated window is not available to resize, it will resize the main window of the app.

TitleBar

In UWP, for the first time ever, Microsoft has exposed detailed programmability into the application title bar through the `ApplicationViewTitleBar` and `CoreApplicationViewTitleBar` classes. You've already seen the `ApplicationViewTitleBar` in action. In the Chapter 9, you modified the color scheme of the app's title bar to match the color scheme of the app. Using the `TitleBar` property of `ApplicationView`, you can set the foreground and background colors of any items that appear in the title bar. Using the `Title` property of the same class you can set the text that appears on the title bar. You saw this in Listing 10-7 where you used the line `app_view.Title = $"Help me find {App.State.NextEvent.EventTitle}";` to set the text that shows on your Streetside view window. `CoreApplicationViewTitleBar` provides some added functionality beyond basic styling; most notably it lets you extend the content of the view so that it overlays the title bar using the property `ExtendViewIntoTitleBar`. When the view is extended in this manner, the title bar functionality remains (meaning you can still use that area of the app to drag the application around). Add the code highlighted in bold in Listing 10-8 to your code.

Listing 10-8. Setting Title Bar Preferences

```
await _core_streetside_view.Dispatcher.RunAsync(CoreDispatcherPriority.Normal, async () =>
            {
                ...

                app_view.Title = $"Help me find \"{App.State.NextEvent.EventTitle}\"";
                app_view.TitleBar.ButtonBackgroundColor = Colors.Transparent;
                app_view.TitleBar.ButtonForegroundColor = Colors.White;
                _core_streetside_view.TitleBar.ExtendViewIntoTitleBar = true;
```

In Listing 10-8, you set the button background colors of the task bar to transparent and set their foreground color to white. You then use the `ExtendViewIntoTitleBar` to essentially make the title bar of the app transparent. This way the user sees only the content of the app window. Figure 10-5 shows how it looks. Using a technique such as this one, you can create what appears to the user to be custom task bars, but are really just sections of the app's view area that have been strategically placed such that they appear to be a customized title bar. If you open up Microsoft Edge, you can see an example of this kind of approach at work.

Figure 10-5. *Extending the title bar*

That area at the top of the Edge browser (Figure 10-6) might appear to be a customized title bar that allows for tabbed buttons to be added but it is most likely just a control strategically placed in that location.

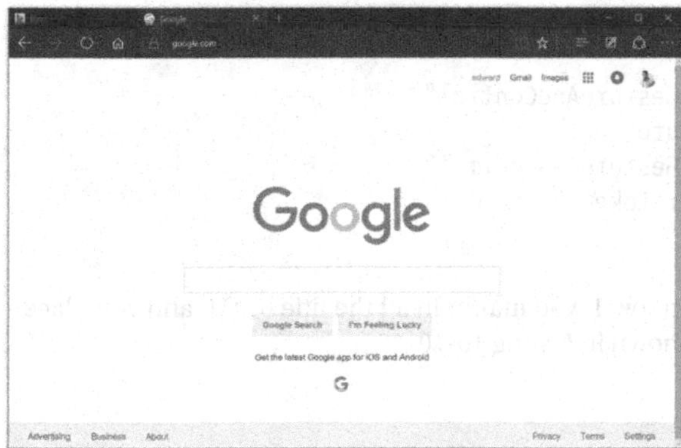

Figure 10-6. *Microsoft edge title bar*

To test this concept out, let's complete the definition for StreetSideViewPage. Listing 10-9 shows the layout for this new page.

Listing 10-9. StreetSideViewPage Layout

```
<Grid Background="{ThemeResource ApplicationPageBackgroundThemeBrush}">
    <Grid.RowDefinitions>
        <RowDefinition x:Name="row_titlebar"
                        Height="100" />
        <RowDefinition />
    </Grid.RowDefinitions>
    <Grid Grid.Row="0" HorizontalAlignment="Stretch" >
        <Rectangle x:Name="rect_titlebar" />
        <StackPanel  Orientation="Horizontal">
            <Button x:Name="btn_one"
                    Content="Button 1"
                    Margin="5"
                    VerticalAlignment="Stretch" />
            <Button x:Name="btn_two"
                    Margin="5"
                    Content="Button 2"
                    VerticalAlignment="Stretch" />
            <Button x:Name="btn_three"
                    Margin="5"
                    Content="Button 3"
                    VerticalAlignment="Stretch" />
        </StackPanel>
    </Grid>

    <Maps:MapControl x:Name="streetview_map"
                        Margin="0"
                        Grid.Row="1"
                        ZoomInteractionMode="GestureAndControl"
                        PanInteractionMode="Auto"
                        TiltInteractionMode="GestureAndControl"
                        MapServiceToken="<your token>" />
</Grid>
```

Listing 10-9 lays out the page in a two-row grid. In row 1, you maintain all the title bar UI and you place the map in row 2. The code-behind for this XAML is shown in Listing 10-10.

Listing 10-10. StreetSideViewPage Code-Behind

```
public event Action Close, NotSupported;
public Geopoint Center { get; private set; }
ApplicationView _appview;
CoreApplicationView _core_appview;
Color TitlebarColor { get; } = Color.FromArgb(0xFF, 0x6A, 0x6A, 0x6A);
public StreetSideViewPage()
{
    this.InitializeComponent();
    _appview = ApplicationView.GetForCurrentView();
    _core_appview = CoreApplication.GetCurrentView();
```

```
    this.Loaded += StreetSideViewPage_Loaded;
    streetview_map.CustomExperienceChanged += (s, args) =>
    {
        if (streetview_map.CustomExperience == null)
        {
            Close?.Invoke();
        }
    };
}

async public Task InitializeAsync(Geopoint center)
{
    Center = center;
    streetview_map.Center = Center;
    if (streetview_map.IsStreetsideSupported)
    {
        var street_panorama = await StreetsidePanorama.FindNearbyAsync(streetview_map.Center);
        var street_exp = new StreetsideExperience(street_panorama);
        street_exp.OverviewMapVisible = true;
        streetview_map.CustomExperience = street_exp;
    }
    else
    {
        NotSupported?.Invoke();
    }
    _core_appview.TitleBar.ExtendViewIntoTitleBar = true;

    //size the window
    _appview.SetPreferredMinSize(new Size(500, 400));

    //set background
    _appview.TitleBar.ButtonBackgroundColor = Colors.Transparent;
    _appview.TitleBar.ButtonForegroundColor = Colors.White;
    _appview.TitleBar.ButtonInactiveBackgroundColor = Colors.Transparent;
    _appview.TitleBar.ButtonInactiveForegroundColor = Colors.White;

    rect_titlebar.Fill = new SolidColorBrush(TitlebarColor);

}

private void StreetSideViewPage_Loaded(object sender, RoutedEventArgs e)
{

}
```

In Listing 10-10, you essentially take the functionality previously provided in the delegate you passed into your CoreApplicationView instance (from LandingPage) and move it here. This approach is far more standard than instantiating content on the fly. OnShowStreetView should now look like the following from Listing 10-11.

Listing 10-11. OnShowStreetView Modifications

```
var view_id = 0;
var supported = true;
var center_point = map.Center;

if (_core_streetside_view != null)
{
    await _core_streetside_view.Dispatcher.RunAsync(CoreDispatcherPriority.Normal, () =>
    {
        _core_streetside_view.CoreWindow.Close();
    });
}

_core_streetside_view = CoreApplication.CreateNewView();
await _core_streetside_view.Dispatcher.RunAsync(CoreDispatcherPriority.Normal, () =>
{
    var app_view = ApplicationView.GetForCurrentView();
    view_id = app_view.Id;

    StreetSideViewPage street_view = new StreetSideViewPage();
    await street_view.InitializeAsync(center_point);

    street_view.Close += () =>
    {
        _core_streetside_view.CoreWindow.Close();
        _core_streetside_view = null;
    };
    street_view.NotSupported += () => supported = false;

    Window.Current.Content = street_view;
    Window.Current.Activate();
});

if (supported)
{
    await ApplicationViewSwitcher.TryShowAsStandaloneAsync(view_id);
}
else
{
    await new MessageDialog("StreetSide View is not supported.").ShowAsync();
}
```

In Listing 10-11, you remove pretty much all the windowing code and now simply instantiate a new StreetSideViewPage object, call its InitializeAsync function, and then set it as the content for the current window. Run the app and activate the StreetSide view; you should see a window similar to Figure 10-7.

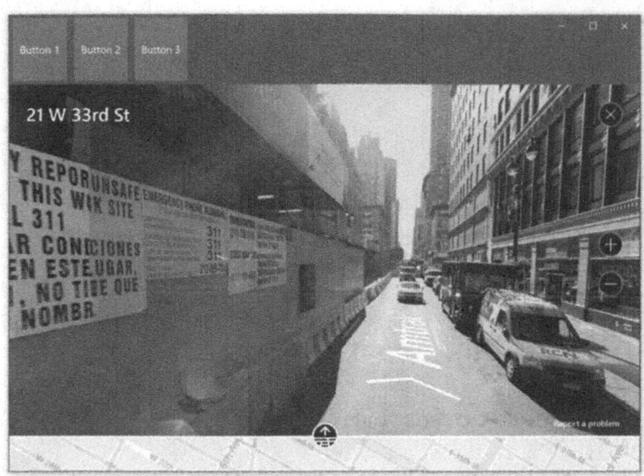

Figure 10-7. *StreetView page with custom title bar*

The problem with this approach will become instantly obvious to you once you start playing around with the example (especially if you try clicking the buttons). The problem is that the title bar, though transparent, is still very much present and as such continues to intercept user input. This is by design; there would, for example, be no way to move the map in your previous sample if the title bar were not still present in some form. As long as the area you are interacting with is below the bounds of the title bar, everything works as expected. However, once you cross into title bar vicinity, you immediately lose the ability to interact with any controls from your view. Another problem is that, in this sample, the title bar is 200 pixels tall. However, because the title bar is still set at its default height, the ability to drag the window is unavailable for any areas of your custom title bar not within those bounds.

You can address both of these issues using a method on the Window class. Add `Window.Current.SetTitleBar(rect_titlebar);` to the `InitializeAsync` method and the problem is solved. `SetTitleBar` allows you to define a `UIElement` to serve as the custom title bar for a window. In this case, you are specifying that the Rectangle within the Grid on the top row of your page will serve as the window's taskbar. This allows you to use any part of the surface of the Rectangle to move the window. The pattern you have utilized is also a key component of this working. The title bar itself will continue to have no interactivity built into it; however, because you have placed controls in front of the title bar, they will continue to have interactivity. Using this technique, you can build cool user interfaces like you see on Microsoft Edge or Word Mobile.

Lock Screen

In Chapter 9, you saw the APIs that can be used to modify a user's desktop wallpaper. The API for changing the lock screen is through the same class, `UserProfilePersonalizationSettings`. By calling `TrySetLockScreenImageAsync`, you can modify the background image of a lock screen. Listing 10-12 adds a new method to your `UserSettings` class (found in General.UWP.Library) for doing this.

Listing 10-12. Changing Lock Screen Background Image

```
async public static Task<uint> ChangeLockScreenAsync()
{
    if (UserProfilePersonalizationSettings.IsSupported())
    {
        //open file
        var local_folder = Windows.Storage.ApplicationData.Current.LocalFolder;
        var file = await local_folder.CreateFileAsync("marker_lock.txt", OpenIfExists);
        //read and convert value of file
        var value = await file.ReadTextAsync();
        var current_index = uint.Parse(value);

        //get file for index
        var image_path = $"ms-appdata:///local/club{current_index}.jpg";
        var image_uri = new Uri(image_path);
        var image_file = await StorageFile.GetFileFromApplicationUriAsync(image_uri);

        bool was_set = false;
        try
        {
            //display image file
            was_set = await profile.Current.TrySetLockScreenImageAsync(image_file);
        }
        catch (Exception ex)
        {
            was_set = false;
        }

        if (was_set)
        {
            //increment index and store in file
            current_index++;
            if (current_index > 7)
                current_index = 1;

            await file.WriteTextAsync(current_index.ToString());
        }
        return current_index;
    }
    return 0;
}
```

Like the ChangeWallpaperAsync, ChangeLockScreenAsync reads a numeric value from marker_lock.txt (you will see more of this in a minute) and uses it to generate a file path that points to one of the seven images the app provides. (If you have not done this thus far, download the resource packet for this chapter. In it you will find the seven images we are discussing here, club1 through club7. Copy them to the folder Media/Images and you will be all set). From the file path you get the actual file using StorageFile.GetFileFromApplicationUirAsync. You then use that file to set the lock screen image on the next line. If the lock screen image sets correctly, you increment the index read from your marker_lock text file and write the new value back to the file so that the next time you read the file it will provide you that incremented value. If the value of the current index is greater than seven, you simply restart the count by setting its value to one.

To ensure that there is a value to be read the first time a user wants to change the lock screen image, open `App.xaml.cs` and add the lines of code from Listing 10-13 just at the end of `InitializeAsync`.

Listing 10-13. Setting Initial Values for marker.txt and marker_lock.txt

```
//set the value of marker and marker lock
var local_folder = Windows.Storage.ApplicationData.Current.LocalFolder;
var file_marker = await local_folder.CreateFileAsync("marker.txt", OpenIfExists);
await file_marker.WriteTextAsync("1");
var file_marker_lock = await local_folder.CreateFileAsync("marker_lock.txt", OpenIfExists);
await file_marker_lock.WriteTextAsync("1");
```

All this code does is create/open the files indicated and set an initial value of 1 in each of them.

Next, you need to add a new context menu item to the ImageBannerControl context menu in LandingPage. Open LandingPage and add the menu item from Listing 10-14.

Listing 10-14. New Context Menu for ImageBannerControl

```
...
image_banner_menu.Commands.Add(new UICommand("Next Lock Screen", async (ui_command) =>
{
    await UserSettings.ChangeLockScreenAsync();
}));
...
```

Run the sample and test out switching the lock screen image. It should all work fine.

The Notification Process

Let's start by defining what notifications are in the context of Modern Windows 10 applications. A *notification* is a message that goes out to your app's end user and provides meaningful information about the use of your application. It could be letting the user know that their password is invalid, that they don't have access to certain content in your application, that they have been idle for some time and their session is about to time out, or that there was an error in the application.

This type of general-purpose notification isn't what this section discusses. Rather, you will focus on a class of notifications that previously had no official (and ubiquitous) representation in the API landscape of Windows development: notifications that occur while an application is out of focus.

Take Microsoft Office's Outlook mail client, for example. If you have toast notifications enabled in Outlook, a small borderless window appears above the system tray area every time you receive a new email message. Clicking this toast window immediately launches the full Outlook client and allows you to view the message. Sound great, but unfortunately a pattern like this isn't baked into legacy Windows application development as a whole. Each developer must create a distinct implementation of this functionality using hidden windows and system-tray icons. Most important, because the operating system doesn't provide any mechanisms to support it, any application wishing to use this mechanism must project the illusion of not running by either hiding itself when closed or having a separate executable (a *daemon*) that owns the notification process and also is in charge of launching the primary app when a user interacts with the toast window. Windows 10 takes the notion of notification and bakes it into the operating system so that all Windows 10 apps use the same mechanism, one that is instantly recognizable to all users and is uniform across all applications.

As a Windows 10 developer building applications that target the Modern app platform, you can use four key mechanisms to provide notifications to your users: toast notifications, tile notifications, badge notifications, and push notifications. Toast, tile, and badge notifications typically require the application to be running (if not in focus), whereas push notifications represent a new class of notification in which the app doesn't need to be running on the client.

As stated earlier, part of the problem statement of notifications that Windows 10 attempts to solve is that of uniformity. If every application had to create its own notification framework, as legacy applications do, it would be difficult for a user to easily ascertain not just whether a user interface element is a notification but also what type of notification it is and what interaction patterns it exposes. Internet Explorer 10, for example, uses notifications. When a download is complete, the taskbar icon flashes to notify the user. To a trained eye, this makes sense. But a novice user might not understand the implication, particularly because not every application functions this way. It was important when designing the Windows 10 API landscape to create a stronger sense of uniformity with regard to notifications. Toward that end, rather than just expose a user interface surface in which applications present their notifications, the Windows API designers chose to use a predefined set of templates. These templates ensure that all notifications follow a standardized presentation format that remains consistent across applications, preventing a fractured or inconsistent experience for the user. The following sections talk more about these templates during the discussion of the toast and tile notification types.

Toast Notifications

Toast notifications function similarly to the notifications discussed in the previous section. Whereas legacy Windows toast notifications are an interaction pattern that applications follow, the toast notification mechanism exposed to Modern Windows 10 apps is baked into the operating system and API surface area. This means all that Modern applications can use them through a common set of APIs and that the user is presented with an interaction pattern that is similar regardless of the notifier. This is consistent with the overarching Windows 10 paradigm: the primary differentiating factor between applications is the content. Of course, applications can differ in design, but generally speaking content is king and takes precedence over chrome in Modern Windows 10 applications.

Figure 10-8 shows how a toast notification looks when displayed while the user is on the Windows 10 Start screen. It appears, as you can see, in the lower-right corner of the screen.

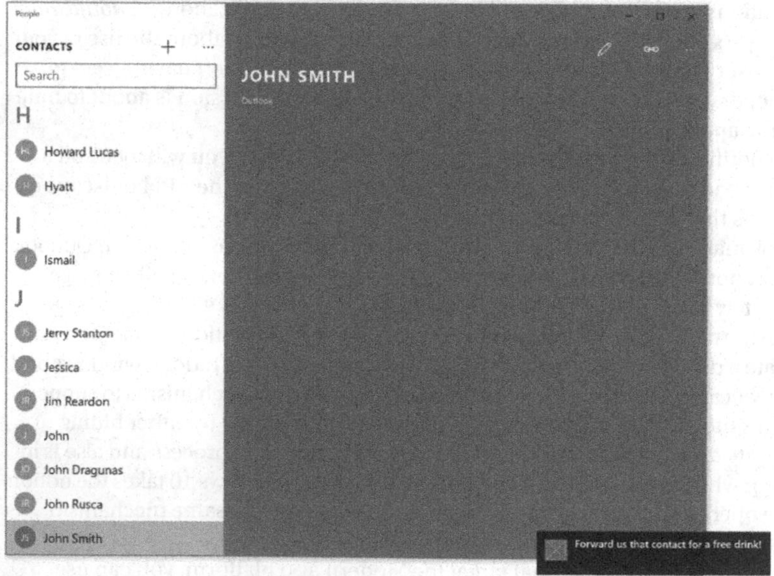

Figure 10-8. Example of a toast notification

No matter where you are or what you're doing in the operating system, a toast notification always appears in the lower-right corner and gradually fades when the user doesn't interact with it. Unlike in Windows 8 where multiple notifications where shown below one another, Windows 10 keeps only one notification visible at a time. Any other notifications coming from a given app are displayed in the Action Center. The Windows Action Center aggregates notifications across all the apps deployed to a Windows 10 system that utilize the notification framework to communicate with the user. Figure 10-9 shows how multiple toast notifications appear on a user's screen.

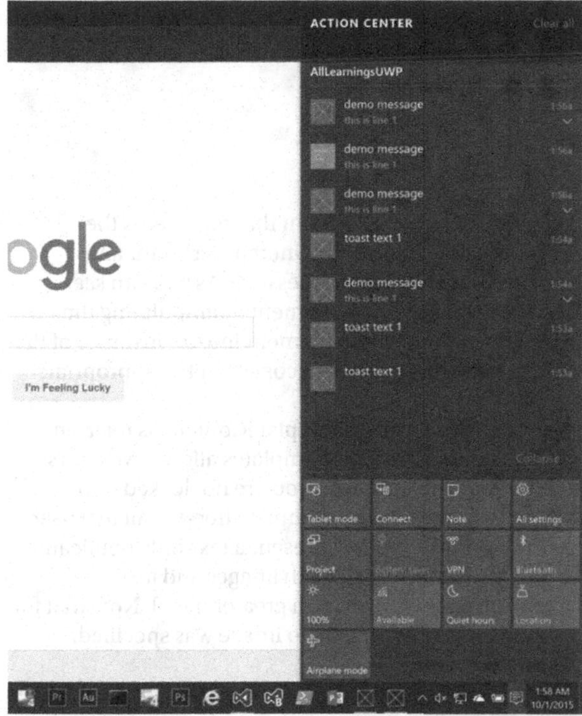

Figure 10-9. *Multiple toast notifications on screen*

Generating Toast Notifications

Toasts can be sent locally or via push notification. A user can select the toast by touching or clicking it in order to launch the associated app. Because these notifications are designed to be context aware, the context of the toast notification can be handled in the launched application such that it presents a detailed view of the notification content.

Listing 10-15 shows a very simple example of a local toast notification. The user clicks a button (`btn_toast`), and in the event handler you present a toast notification using a call to the `show` method.

Listing 10-15. Local Toast Notification

```
int _count = 0; //field level variable
void btn_toasttext01_Click(object sender, RoutedEventArgs e)
{
    XmlDocument toast_xml = ToastNotificationManager ↵
                                .GetTemplateContent(ToastTemplateType.ToastText01);
    var text_nodes = toast_xml.DocumentElement.GetElementsByTagName("text");
    var text_node = text_nodes.FirstOrDefault() as XmlElement;
    text_node.AppendChild(toast_xml.CreateTextNode($"toast number {_count++}"));

    ToastNotification toast = new ToastNotification(toast_xml);
    var notifier = ToastNotificationManager.CreateToastNotifier();
    notifier.Show(toast);
}
```

The example is relatively straightforward. First, you establish a variable count that represents the number of times the toast button is clicked. Each time `btn_toast` is clicked, you increment count and then generate a new toast notification that incorporates the new count into its message. As you can see from the listing, generating a toast is as simple as getting access to an XML document, manipulating the content in this document, and then passing the completed document as an argument into an instance of the `ToastNotificationManager` class. `ToastNotificationManager` then uses this to construct the appropriate `ToastNotifier`.

The XML document used to start the process, the one returned from GetTemplateContent, is referred to as a *template* and is exposed through the enumeration `ToastTemplateType`. Templates allow developers to present toast notifications in a variety of predetermined ways. With templates you are not locked into presenting in just one way no matter the circumstance but it is also not such a complete free-for-all that users find it hard to recognize notifications as notifications. In this example, you will present a text-only notification. Windows 10 provides eight templates: four that are text-only and four that use both images and text.

The following section walks through the various toast notification formats in greater detail. Note that for all instances, overrun text is trimmed and invalid images are treated as though no image was specified.

ToastText01

ToastText01 is the most basic form of text toast. This template presents a single string wrapped across a maximum of three lines of text. Listing 10-2 shows the XML for this template type. The node in bold represents the area to be targeted based on the pattern illustrated in Listing 10-16.

Listing 10-16. ToastText01 Template Definition

```
<toast>
    <visual>
        <binding template="ToastText01">
            <text id="1">bodyText</text>
        </binding>
    </visual>
</toast>
```

ToastText02

The ToastText02 template presents one string in bold text on the first line and one string of regular text wrapped across the second and third lines. Listing 10-17 shows the XML for this template type. The node in bold represents the area to be targeted based on the pattern illustrated in Listing 10-15. Note that in Listing 10-15 you targeted one node by using `FirstOrDefault`. In this case, the call to `GetElementsByTagName` will return two entries, so using `FirstOrDefault` will not fully populate the toast. For these scenarios, use standard XML parsing techniques such as the following pattern:

```
var text_nodes = toast_xml.DocumentElement.GetElementsByTagName("text");
text_nodes[0].AppendChild(toast_xml.CreateTextNode("this is the headline text"));
text_nodes[1].AppendChild(toast_xml.CreateTextNode("this is the body text"));
```

Listing 10-17. ToastText02 Template Definition

```
<toast>
    <visual>
        <binding template="ToastText02">
            <text id="1">headlineText</text>
            <text id="2">bodyText</text>
        </binding>
    </visual>
</toast>
```

ToastText03

A variation of the design from ToastText02, the ToastText03 template presents one string in bold text across the first and second lines with one string of regular text on the third line. Listing 10-18 shows the XML for this template type. Notice that the only distinction between this and Listing 10-3 is the template name. The node in bold represents the area to be targeted.

Listing 10-18. ToastText03 Template Definition

```
<toast>
    <visual>
        <binding template="ToastText03">
            <text id="1">headlineText</text>
            <text id="2">bodyText</text>
        </binding>
    </visual>
</toast>
```

ToastText04

The ToastText04 template presents one string in bold text on the first line and one string of regular text on each subsequent line (note that there is no wrapping; each line has its own unique string). Listing 10-19 shows the XML for this template type. The node in bold represents the area to be targeted based on the pattern illustrated in Listing 10-19.

Listing 10-19. ToastText04 Template Definition

```
<toast>
    <visual>
        <binding template="ToastText04">
            <text id="1">headlineText</text>
            <text id="2">bodyText1</text>
            <text id="3">bodyText2</text>
        </binding>
    </visual>
</toast>
```

Adding Images to Toasts

Toast notifications may also include images. Figure 10-10 shows the modified toast notification, now programmed to support an image.

Figure 10-10. *Toast notification with an image*

To accomplish this, you only need to change the template being used and insert the appropriate content into the appropriate node of the underlying document. Listing 10-20 shows the code used to generate the toast notification in Figure 10-10.

Listing 10-20. Toast Notification with an Image

```
XmlDocument toast_xml = ToastNotificationManager ↩
                            .GetTemplateContent(ToastTemplateType.ToastImageAndText03);

var text_nodes = toast_xml.DocumentElement.GetElementsByTagName("text");
text_nodes[0].AppendChild(toast_xml.CreateTextNode("demo message"));
text_nodes[1].AppendChild(toast_xml.CreateTextNode($"toast number {_count++}"));

//image MUST be smaller than 800x800 and less than 256kb
//app data can be reached with ms-appdata:/// protocol (this is isolated storage for the
most part)
var image_node = toast_xml.DocumentElement.GetElementsByTagName("image")[0] as XmlElement;
image_node.SetAttribute("src", "ms-appx:///assets/tile-square.png");

ToastNotification toast = new ToastNotification(toast_xml);
var notifier = ToastNotificationManager.CreateToastNotifier();
notifier.Show(toast);
```

Notice the use of the protocol `ms-appx` when specifying the source of the image to use. You can use this protocol to retrieve content from the application's deployment package. The API also supports `http/https` to retrieve web-based images and `ms-appdata:///local/` to pull images from local storage.

Listing 10-21 shows all the document template types exposed for toast notifications with images. They mirror the same documents exposed for plain-text toast notifications (with the exception of the added image element), so there is no need for further explanation.

Listing 10-21. Image-Based Toast Notification Document Types

```
<toast>
    <visual>
        <binding template="ToastImageAndText01">
            <image id="1" src="image1" alt="image1"/>
            <text id="1">bodyText</text>
        </binding>
    </visual>
</toast>

<toast>
    <visual>
        <binding template="ToastImageAndText02">
            <image id="1" src="image1" alt="image1"/>
            <text id="1">headlineText</text>
            <text id="2">bodyText</text>
        </binding>
    </visual>
</toast>

<toast>
    <visual>
        <binding template="ToastImageAndText03">
            <image id="1" src="image1" alt="image1"/>
            <text id="1">headlineText</text>
            <text id="2">bodyText</text>
        </binding>
    </visual>
</toast>

<toast>
    <visual>
        <binding template="ToastImageAndText04">
            <image id="1" src="image1" alt="image1"/>
            <text id="1">headlineText</text>
            <text id="2">bodyText1</text>
            <text id="3">bodyText2</text>
        </binding>
    </visual>
</toast>
```

Adding Sound to Toasts

Toast notifications may also have sounds associated with them. Imagine a scenario in which a VoIP-style application like Skype is receiving an incoming call. Just popping up a notification might not be enough (particularly if the user isn't presently working on the computer!). In this area, the API designers again chose uniformity over ultimate flexibility by allowing only a prescribed set of sounds to be used in concert with toast notifications. Windows 10 provides eight sounds in all: four that can be looped (like a phone call sound) and four that can't. Additionally, you can specify that a toast notification be silent. Listing 10-22 shows the audio node in full.

Listing 10-22. Audio Node

```
<audio src="ms-winsoundevent:Notification.Mail" loop="false" silent="false"/>
```

You can add toast notification audio to any of the aforementioned templates by adding the `audio` tag as a direct child of the top-level toast element. (Remember that everything else you've looked at thus far has been tied to the visual representation of the toast. It wouldn't make much sense for the `audio` element to be a child of the `visual` node.) In Listing 10-23, you add a looping sound to the existing example.

Listing 10-23. Toast Notification with Audio

```
XmlDocument toast_xml = ToastNotificationManager ↵
                              .GetTemplateContent(ToastTemplateType.ToastText01);
var text_node = toast_xml.DocumentElement.GetElementsByTagName("text") ↵
                                              .FirstOrDefault() as XmlElement;
text_node.AppendChild(toast_xml.CreateTextNode("custom sound notification"));

//add a custom audio sound to the notification (in this case it is the new mail sound)
/**
    * it can also be:
    * ms-winsoundevent:Notification.Default
    * ms-winsoundevent:Notification.SMS
    * ms-winsoundevent:Notification.IM
    * ms-winsoundevent:Notification.Reminder
    * Silent
    *
    * */
var audio_node = toast_xml.CreateElement("audio");
audio_node.SetAttribute("src", "ms-winsoundevent:Notification.Looping.IM");
audio_node.SetAttribute("loop", "true");
IXmlNode toastNode = toast_xml.SelectSingleNode("/toast");
toastNode.AppendChild(audio_node);

ToastNotification toast = new ToastNotification(toast_xml);
var notifier = ToastNotificationManager.CreateToastNotifier();
notifier.Show(toast);
```

As you can see, to add sound to a toast notification you create the audio node, populate the appropriate attributes, and add it to the XML document the template represents, and you're done.

Your top-level element may add a `duration` attribute, which can be set to `long`. This can be used in all toast notifications to create persistent toasts. Persistent toasts remain visible longer. For a full list of sounds that can be played in a notification, go to `https://msdn.microsoft.com/en-us/library/windows/apps/br230842.aspx`. To explore the schema hierarchy for toast notifications go to `https://msdn.microsoft.com/en-us/library/windows/apps/br230846.aspx`.

Scheduling Toasts

In certain scenarios, it might be more appropriate to schedule a toast to happen at some point in the future (or perhaps happen in a recurring manner) than to have the notification fired off as soon as the command to show it is executed. In such scenarios, you can use a specialized class called `ScheduledToastNotification`. `ScheduledToastNotification` provides a constructor that accepts not only the XML template for the notification but also a date when the notification should be displayed, a sleep time for the notification (in scenarios where the notification repeats over a period of time), and a number that indicates the maximum number of times the notification will sleep before finally terminating. Listing 10-24 shows the use of this type of toast notification. When the user clicks the toast button, you schedule a notification for ten seconds into the future and repreated every minute (repeated 5 times in all).

Listing 10-24. Toasting the End of the World

```
XmlDocument toast_xml = ToastNotificationManager ↵
                                            .GetTemplateContent(ToastTemplateType.ToastText01);
var text_node = toast_xml.DocumentElement.GetElementsByTagName("text")↵
                                                    .FirstOrDefault() as XmlElement;
text_node.AppendChild(toast_xml.CreateTextNode("scheduled toast!"));

ToastNotification toast = new ToastNotification(toast_xml);

ScheduledToastNotification stoast = new ScheduledToastNotification(toast_xml,
    DateTime.Now.AddSeconds(10),
    TimeSpan.FromMinutes(1), 5);

stoast.Id = "hello";
var notifier = ToastNotificationManager.CreateToastNotifier();
notifier.AddToSchedule(stoast);
```

Note the use of `AddToSchedule` instead of `Show`. As the name implies, `AddToSchedule` will queue the toast notification request and, at the point when the date specified is hit, display the toast.

Responding to Toast Notification Events

Earlier, you learned that one of the cool things about toast notifications—something that makes them different from the other types of notifications discussed in this chapter—is that they're context aware. This means your application can react in unique and context-specific ways to toast notifications activated or dismissed by the user. UWP exposes events on the `ToastNotification` class to handle this scenario. See Listing 10-25.

Listing 10-25. Using the Events of the ToastNotification Class

```
XmlDocument toast_xml = ToastNotificationManager ↵
.GetTemplateContent(ToastTemplateType.ToastImageAndText03);

var text_nodes = toast_xml.DocumentElement.GetElementsByTagName("text");
text_nodes[0].AppendChild(toast_xml.CreateTextNode("demo message"));
text_nodes[1].AppendChild(toast_xml.CreateTextNode($"toast number {_count++}"));
```

```
//image MUST be smaller than 800x800 and less than 256kb
//app data can be reached with ms-appdata:/// protocol (this is isolated storage for the
most part)
var image_node = toast_xml.DocumentElement.GetElementsByTagName("image")[0] as XmlElement;
image_node.SetAttribute("src", "ms-appx:///assets/tile-square.png");

var audio_node = toast_xml.CreateElement("audio");
audio_node.SetAttribute("src", "ms-winsoundevent:Notification.IM");
audio_node.SetAttribute("loop", "true");
IXmlNode toastNode = toast_xml.SelectSingleNode("/toast");
toastNode.AppendChild(audio_node);

ToastNotification toast = new ToastNotification(toast_xml);
toast.Failed += async (a, b) =>
{
    if (b.ErrorCode != null)
    {
        await new MessageDialog("Failed!").ShowAsync();
    }
};
toast.Activated += async delegate (ToastNotification n, object s)
{
    await Dispatcher.RunAsync(Windows.UI.Core.CoreDispatcherPriority.Normal, async () =>
    {
        await new MessageDialog("Activated!").ShowAsync();
    });

};
toast.Dismissed += async delegate (ToastNotification a, ToastDismissedEventArgs b)
{
    await Dispatcher.RunAsync(Windows.UI.Core.CoreDispatcherPriority.Normal, async () =>
    {
        await new MessageDialog("Dismissed!").ShowAsync();
    });
};
var notifier = ToastNotificationManager.CreateToastNotifier();
notifier.Show(toast);
```

In this example, you use a MessageDialog to display the disposition of your toast notifications by the user. If the user activates a toast by clicking or tapping, you display the message "Activated!"; if the user cancels it, you display the message "Dismissed!".

You've tried the code from the various samples in TestPage. Figure 10-11 shows the app in action after a toast notification is used to active it.

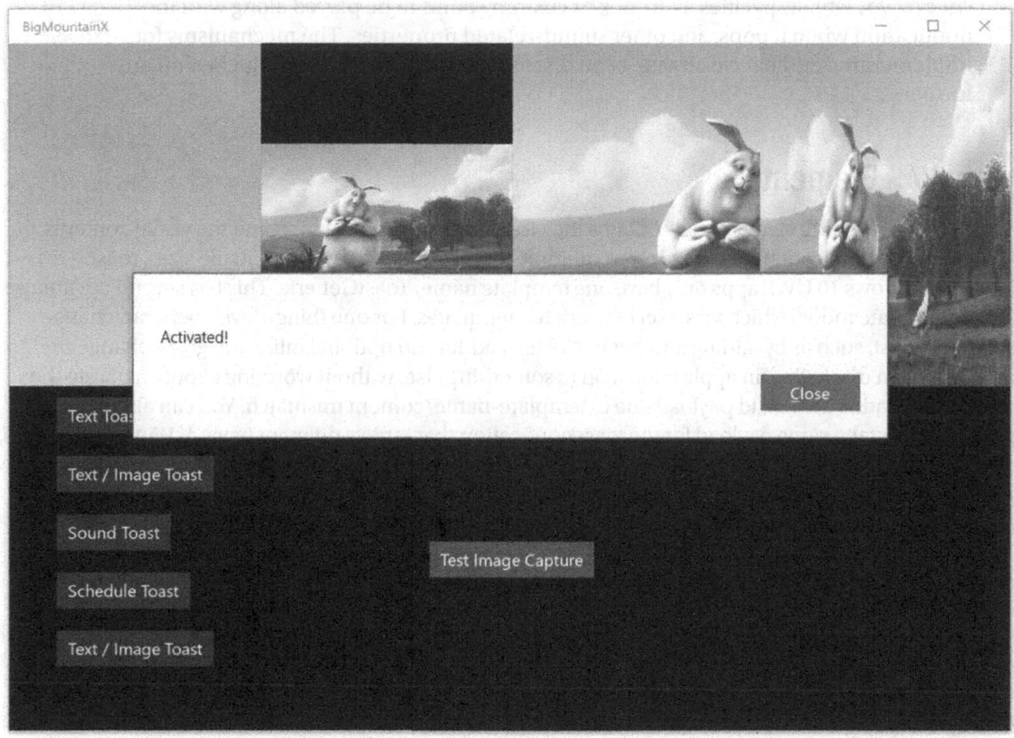

***Figure 10-11.** Toast notification handling events*

Adaptive Toasts

Windows 10 introduces another way of presenting toast notification to the user: adaptive toasts. Adaptive and interactive toast notifications are a new feature in Windows 10. They allow you to

- Create flexible toast notifications with more content and optional inline images without being limited to the existing restricted "toast template catalog."
- Create actionable toast notifications that enable user interaction.

Uisng this new paradigm you now have the ability to

- Be creative for specific scenarios, including alarm, reminder, and incoming call.
- Providing three different activation types for the main toast notification and for each action.
- Include custom actions and system actions in the payload.

In Windows 10, developers construct a toast notification using XML, which should typically contain the following key elements:

- `<visual />`, which covers the content available for the users to visually see, including text and images.
- `<actions />`, which contains the custom interactions the developer wants to add inside the notification.

- <audio />, which specifies an in-box or custom sound to be played along with the notification when it pops, and other sound-related properties. The mechanisms for implementing audio have already been discussed, so they will not be touched on any further.

The <visual /> Element

It is required to have a binding element that contains the visual template information and the visual contents of the toast. Unlike tile notifications, which support multiple templates based on different tile sizes, toast notifications for Windows 10 UWP apps only have one template name, ToastGeneric. This has several advantages over the legacy template model which was a set of restricted templates. For one thing, developers can change the content of the toast, such as by adding another line of text, adding an optional inline image, or change the thumbnail image from displaying an application icon to something else, without worrying about changing the entire template or creating an invalid payload due to template-name/content mismatch. You can also use the same code to construct the same payload for the toast notification that targets different types of Windows devices, such as phone, tablet, desktop PC, or even Xbox; the different devices will accept the notification, and display it to the user under their own UI policies with appropriate visual affordance and interaction model.

The <action /> Element

In Windows 10 UWP apps, developers can add custom interactions to their toast notification to empower the users to do more outside the app. There are two types of elements you can specify: action elements and input elements. You can specify up to three custom or system actions inside a toast notification using action. With input, you can enable users to provide input to an app via a toast notification.

When an action is taken by the user, you can choose to do one of the following by specifying the `activationType` attribute inside of `<action />`:

- Activate the app in the foreground, with an action-specific argument that can be used to navigate to a specific page/context.
- Activate the app's background task without affecting the user.
- Activate another app via protocol.
- Specify a system action to perform. The current available system actions are snoozing and dismissing scheduled alarm/reminder, which will be further explained in a section below.

The other big distinction between the legacy method of defining toast templates and the new adaptive model is that tile content can be read from any source that can be accessed via URI. This allows the developer to modify the content of the template as needed without having to rely on XML documents. Add a new XML document to the project under the `Data` folder called AdaptiveToast and copy the content from Listing 10-26 into it.

Listing 10-26. Adaptivetoast XML Definition

```
<?xml version="1.0" encoding="utf-8" ?>
<toast version="3">
  <visual>
    <binding template="ToastGeneric">
      <text hint-style="body">Big Mountain X</text>
      <text hint-wrap="true" hint-style="captionsubtle">Want a free drink?</text>
```

```
      <text hint-wrap="true" hint-style="captionsubtle">Enter the email address of a contact
      to get a free drink at your next event.</text>
      <image placement="AppLogoOverride" src="ms-appx:///assets/tile-square.png" />
    </binding>
  </visual>
</toast>
```

Listing 10-26 shows a basic adaptive tile notification. The template can be used in your app using the code in Listing 10-27.

Listing 10-27. Using adaptivetoast XML

```
var uri = new Uri("ms-appx:///data/adaptivetoast.xml");
var adaptive_template = await StorageFile.GetFileFromApplicationUriAsync(uri);

XmlDocument tile_xml:doc = await XmlDocument.LoadFromFileAsync(adaptive_template);
var toast = new ToastNotification(tile_xml:doc);
var toast_notifier = ToastNotificationManager.CreateToastNotifier();
toast_notifier.Show(toast);
```

Using this new paradigm, you will extend the contact store notification sample you created in the last chapter with an interactive toast notification that updates the application without ever opening it. You start by modifying the AppState class so that it now has a property for storing emails associated with the app's mailing list. Listing 10-28 illustrates.

Listing 10-28. AppState Modifications

```
public class AppState : StateAwareObject<AppState>
{
    public BMXProfile UserProfile { get; set; }

    public BMXEvent NextEvent { get; set; }

    public List<string> MailingList { get; set; } = new List<string>();

}
```

Next, you must modify the content of your adaptive template. Listing 10-29 adds some actions to the mix.

Listing 10-29. AdaptiveToast Modifications (Adding Interactivity)

```
<?xml version="1.0" encoding="utf-8" ?>
<toast version="3">
    <visual>
        <binding template="ToastGeneric">
            <text hint-style="body">Big Mountain X</text>
            <text hint-wrap="true" hint-style="captionsubtle">Want a free drink?</text>
            <text hint-wrap="true" hint-style="captionsubtle">Enter the email address of a
            contact to get a free drink at your next event.</text>
            <image placement="AppLogoOverride" src="ms-appx:///assets/tile-square.png" />
        </binding>
    </visual>
```

```
    <actions>
        <input title="Enter contact email" id="txt_email" type="text" />
        <action activationType="background" arguments="test background" content="Add
        Contact" />
    </actions>
</toast>
```

In Listing 10-29, you add two actions to the toast notification template. One is an input that allows the user to enter some information; the other is a button that when clicked will send the user data to a background task associated with the app to process. All this happens without the app starting in the foreground.

You must next open `ContactsWatcher` and modify it to use this new template you defined. Listing 10-30 shows the modifications to the code in bold.

Listing 10-30. ContactsWatcher Modifications

```
private BackgroundTaskDeferral _deferral; // Used to keep task alive
async public void Run(IBackgroundTaskInstance taskInstance)
{
    //cost
    var cost = BackgroundWorkCost.CurrentBackgroundWorkCost;
    if (cost == BackgroundWorkCostValue.High)
        return;
    _deferral = taskInstance.GetDeferral();
    await ToastAsync("Forward us that contact for a free drink!");
    _deferral.Complete();
}

async Task ToastAsync(string toast_message)
{
    try
    {
        var uri = new Uri("ms-appx:///data/adaptivetoast.xml");
        var adaptive_template = await StorageFile.GetFileFromApplicationUriAsync(uri);

        XmlDocument tile_xml:doc = await XmlDocument.LoadFromFileAsync(adaptive_template);
        var toast = new ToastNotification(tile_xml:doc);
        var toast_notifier = ToastNotificationManager.CreateToastNotifier();
        toast_notifier.Show(toast);
    }
    catch (Exception ex)
    {

    }
}
```

The major change here is the need to load the template file from a storage lcoation. Because you are using file access (which is awaitable), you must now extend the async nature out to all calling methods. Hence `Toast` is now `ToastAsync` and the `Run` method is now classified as async. Figure 10-12 shows what happens when a new contact is added now.

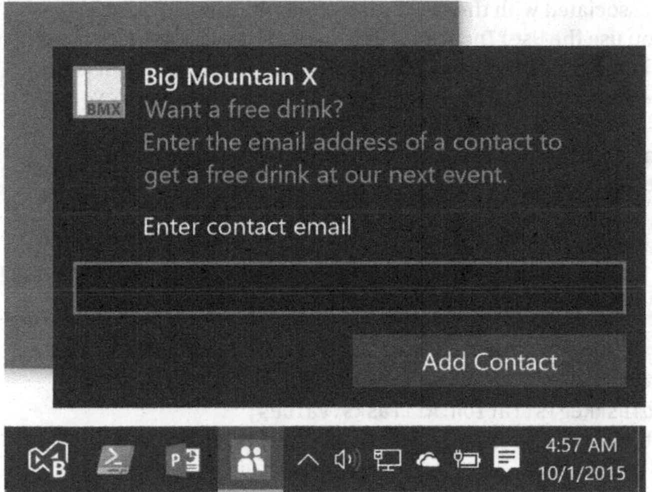

Figure 10-12. *New contact watch notification*

Since you would like this toast notification to not open up your app while processing the user's input, you need to create a new background task that will handle reading input from the user and storing it. Create a new class in the BMX.BackgroundTasks project called `ActionableToastServer`. Add the code from Listing 10-31 to it. To get this to work, you need to move the `Library` folder from your BigMountainX project into General.UWP.Library. This way the code for reading the `AppState` object can be accessed within your background task library.

Listing 10-31. ActionableToastServer Implementation

```
async public void Run(IBackgroundTaskInstance taskInstance)
{
    var deferral = taskInstance.GetDeferral();
    var details = taskInstance.TriggerDetails as ToastNotificationActionTriggerDetail;
    if (details != null)
    {
        var roaming_folder = ApplicationData.Current.RoamingFolder;
        var state = await AppState.FromStorageFileAsync(roaming_folder, "state.xml");

        object value;
        details.UserInput.TryGetValue("txt_email", out value);
        if (value != null)
        {
            state.MailingList.Add(value as string);
            await state.SaveAsync();
        }

    }
    deferral.Complete();
}
```

Listing 10-31 converts the trigger details associated with the task into its concrete type, in this case `ToastNotificationActionTriggerDetail`. You use the `UserInput` property to read the value entered by the user. Note the name queried for in the call to `TryGetValue`. The name specified here is "txt_email". It is not coincidence that this value is the same as is used in the template; naming the input element allows you to read the value from them at a latter point.

The final step is to register the background task with the system. Open ApplicationHostPage and add the code from Listing 10-32 to the `InitializeApplication` method.

Listing 10-32. Registering ActionableToastServer Background Task

```
//initialize actionable toast server
await StartBackgroundTaskAsync(() =>
{
    var task_name = "contacts-toast-server";
    var previous_task_list = BackgroundTaskRegistration.AllTasks.Values;
    var registered = previous_task_list.Where(i => i.Name == task_name).FirstOrDefault();
    registered?.Unregister(true);
    registered = null;
    if (registered == null)
    {
        BackgroundTaskBuilder task_builder = new BackgroundTaskBuilder();
        task_builder.Name = task_name;
        task_builder.TaskEntryPoint = typeof(ActionableToastServer).ToString();
        ToastNotificationActionTrigger toast_trigger = new ToastNotificationActionTrigger();
        task_builder.SetTrigger(toast_trigger);
        task_builder.Register();
    }
});
```

You should be fairly familiar with what is going on in Listing 10-32. To complete the process, add a new background task decalration to your app manifest. The task types should be specified as system event and the entry point should be the type `BMX.BackgroundTasks.ActionableToastServer`. To enable the background task, you must also run the app at least once. Now your app is ready to process actions generated from the toast that pops up every time a new contact is added to your contact store. You can test this out by using the People app. Add a new contact and the toast notification should pop up. Once it does, enter a value for the email address and click the Add Contact button.

To see if any modifications have been made, open the app and put a breakpoint in the `IntializeAppAsync` method. Run the app and, once it breaks at your breakpoint, advance the break step by step until you have the value of State read into memory. Inspect that value to determine if the contacts you entered are now stored. Figure 10-13 illustrates.

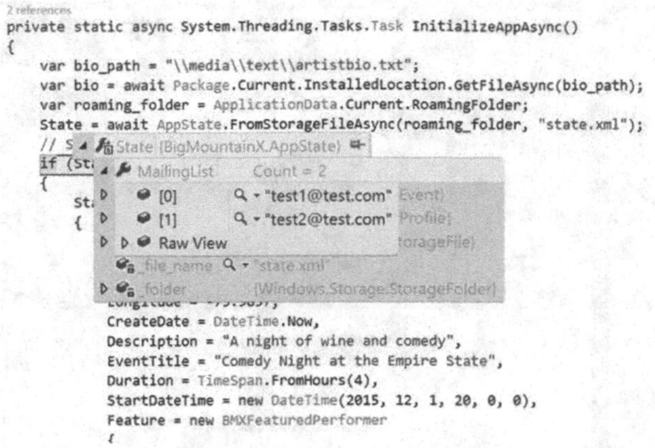

```
2 references
private static async System.Threading.Tasks.Task InitializeAppAsync()
{
    var bio_path = "\\media\\text\\artistbio.txt";
    var bio = await Package.Current.InstalledLocation.GetFileAsync(bio_path);
    var roaming_folder = ApplicationData.Current.RoamingFolder;
    State = await AppState.FromStorageFileAsync(roaming_folder, "state.xml");
    // S  State {BigMountainX.AppState}
    if (St   MailingList     Count = 2
    {
        St      [0]     "test1@test.com"  Event}
        {       [1]     "test2@test.com"  Profile}
                Raw View                  torageFile}
             _file_name   "state.xml"
             _folder      {Windows.Storage.StorageFolder}
            CreateDate = DateTime.Now,
            Description = "A night of wine and comedy",
            EventTitle = "Comedy Night at the Empire State",
            Duration = TimeSpan.FromHours(4),
            StartDateTime = new DateTime(2015, 12, 1, 20, 0, 0),
            Feature = new BMXFeaturedPerformer
            {
```

Figure 10-13. *Checking for changes from ActionableToastServer*

Tile Notifications

Remember the overview discussion of Windows 10 from Chapter 1? It talked about the rectangular shapes on the Start menu that combine the functionality of the quick launch area with an application's launch shortcut, with the representation of an application on the taskbar. As mentioned in Chapter 1, these rectangular shapes are known as *live tiles*. The great thing about their "live-ness" is that it turns these tiles into yet another surface upon which applications can present notifications to users. Tile notifications differ from toast notifications in many ways.

First, they're really a pattern of application behavior layered on top of the notion of live tiles. You could argue that they aren't notifications at all. Many applications, such as Travel, employ the live-tile functionality without informing the user of anything. (Travel shows pictures of different places in the world, which is markedly different than the Mail app's use of tiles.) Second, because this style of notification uses a given application's tile, it can be limited in a number of ways. For one thing, if the tile isn't on the Windows Start screen, there is no notification (and no indication from the application that a notification hasn't happened). Yet another problem is that this type of notification is localized to the Windows Start screen; depending on where the tile sits on a user's Start screen, it may not be visible. Finally, and most important, the application's live tile is primarily designed for non-intrusive glance-and-go information. It isn't meant to be a dialog or message box; it's meant to present quick tidbits of information to the user that might entice them to click the tile and get more information.

Keep this functionality in perspective as you work through this section. Because the use of the term *notification* here is somewhat misleading (particularly when juxtaposed against its counterparts in this section), you might be tempted to limit your use of live tiles to presenting messages to the user. Doing so would grossly underuse the power of this technology. Figure 10-14 shows the live tiles of a number of popular Windows 10 apps.

***Figure 10-14.** Live tiles for some Modern Windows 10 apps*

Tile notifications can be text only, text with an image, all image, or a combination of images, or they can encompass another class of notifications called *badge notifications*. Unlike toast notifications, which as mentioned earlier should mainly be used to alert the user about actions or information they need to act on relatively quickly, tile notifications focus on presenting notification content that is more persistent and less intrusive. Think of the distinction between toast notifications and tile notifications (as far as the content they should present) in this way: live tiles present content and represent events the user *could* be interested in, whereas toast notifications present content and represent events the user *should* be interested in.

Leaving aside what a powerful notification mechanism an app's live tile is, there are benefits to using the live-tile infrastructure to present notifications to the user. For one thing, because a live tile is about enticing the user, it can be used as an alert or update—something to grab the user's attention. You can find a comprehensive list of all tile templates, complete with images of the final tile layout, on the Microsoft MSDN site at `http://msdn.microsoft.com/en-us/library/windows/apps/hh761491.aspx`. This can be used as a reference to get a sense of what you can and can't do with live tiles.

Generating Tile Notifications

Like toast notifications, tile notifications can be sent locally or via push notification. Unlike toasts, there is no separate interaction pattern for the notifications that target an application's tile. They're simply presented on the tile, and it's left to the user to decide whether to launch the application or not. Listing 10-33 shows a very simple example of local tile notification.

Listing 10-33. Simple Tile Notification

```
var tile_xml = TileUpdateManager.GetTemplateContent(TileTemplateType.TileWide310x150Text04);

var text_nodes = tile_xml.DocumentElement.GetElementsByTagName("text");
text_nodes[0].AppendChild(tile_xml.CreateTextNode("simple demo message"));

var tile = new TileNotification(tile_xml);

var tile_updater = TileUpdateManager.CreateTileUpdaterForApplication();
tile_updater.Update(tile);
```

If you read the entire previous section, then you should notice something here. The development pattern for creating tile notifications is similar to the approach used for creating toast notifications. It starts with selecting an appropriate template (which maps to an XML document). Once you retrieve the template, you find the sections of the document in which you need to place content. You then place content in those elements/attributes, use the created document to generate the appropriate tile-notification object, and pass the object to the `TileUpdateManager`. It's the job of the `TileUpdateManager` to update the actual tile. What you can surmise from this is that once again, Microsoft has chosen uniformity and a template-driven approach to provide a surface on which developers can place one-off presentations of application-specific notifications. The example in Listing 10-33 produces the result shown in Figure 10-15 when the associated button is clicked.

Figure 10-15. *Updated live tile*

Because tile presentation is significantly more complex than the simple examples you saw when working with toast notifications, it follows that the templates exposed to tiles are also different and varied. In all, there are 79 templates to choose from! They range from simple text, as shown in Figure 10-15, to arrays of images with no text. The templates also encompass the two possible tile types available to Modern Windows 10 applications: square tiles and wide (rectangular) tiles. Square tiles come in varing sizes (small, medium, and large). You saw rectangular tiles in Figures 10-14 and 10-15. Square tiles function in a similar manner but take up less space on the Windows 10 Start screen.

In general, tile templates take six forms: text only, image only, image and text, peeking images and text, peeking images, and peeking image collection. You might have seen the peeking phenomena on your Windows Start screen with the People app. The tile update appears from the bottom of the tile as if peeking and then slides back down. Within a few seconds, it slides up and overlays the previous tile content.

This discussion focuses exclusively on wide tile templates. The development and interaction patterns for both are the same, so it should be no trouble to apply the concepts outlined in the following sections to square app tiles. Also, rather than discuss all the wide template types, this chapter focuses on a few interesting ones that you may find helpful in presenting content to the user.

Presenting Text Content with a Heading

TileWide310x150Text09 is the mainstay for presenting simple text content to the user. It uses the first text element as the header and a second element wrapped across the remaining four lines as text content. Listing 10-34 shows the template definition for this template type.

Listing 10-34. TileWide310x150Text09 Template Definition

```
<tile>
  <visual>
    <binding template="TileWide310x150Text09">
      <text id="1">Message : 1</text>
      <text id="2">1 quick brown fox jumped over a lazy dog!</text>
    </binding>
  </visual>
</tile>
```

This is a great template for presenting text because it allows you to wrap the content area across multiple lines. Almost all the other template types require you to enter text into each line separately, which forces you to monitor the length of your notification strings. If you don't need line breaks in your content area, this approach is recommended. Figure 10-16 illustrates.

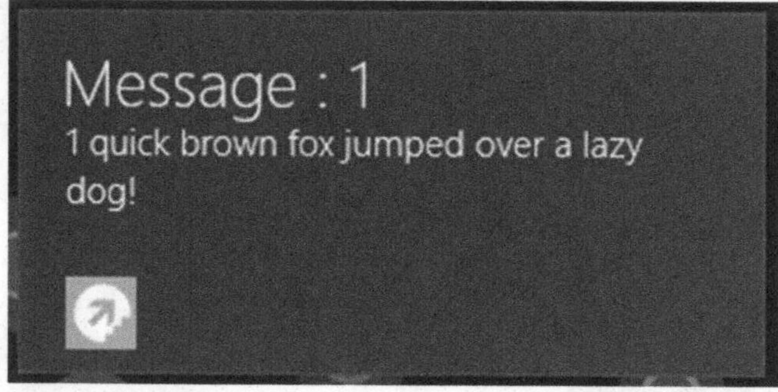

Figure 10-16. *View of a tile template*

Text-Only Content

In situations when you need to present text-only content with no heading (for instance, headlines for news-type applications), TileWide310x150Text04 is a great template. It removes the heading and gives the application one line of text wrapped across all five lines of the tile. Listing 10-35 shows the template definition for this template.

Listing 10-35. Template Definition for TileWide310x150Text04

```
<tile>
  <visual>
    <binding template="TileWide310x150Text04">
      <text id="1">Text Field 1</text>
    </binding>
  </visual>
</tile>
```

Templates for Summaries

Finally, if an application needs to present summary information in a text-only list format, `TileWide310x150Text02` and `TileWide310x150Text01` are good templates to use. Listing 10-12 used `TileWide310x150Text01` to present some simple text on screen. It lists text lines individually with a header above them, as you saw in Figure 10-6. `TileWideText02` follows this same format, with one key distinction: the text is displays in two columns, each containing four rows of text. Listing 10-36 shows the template definition for `TileWide310x150Text02`.

Listing 10-36. Template Definition for TileWide310x150Text02

```
<tile>
  <visual>
    <binding template="TileWide310x150Text02">
      <text id="1">Text Header Field 1</text>
      <text id="2">Text Field 2</text>
      <text id="3">Text Field 3</text>
      <text id="4">Text Field 4</text>
      <text id="5">Text Field 5</text>
      <text id="6">Text Field 6</text>
      <text id="7">Text Field 7</text>
      <text id="8">Text Field 8</text>
      <text id="9">Text Field 9</text>
    </binding>
  </visual>
</tile>
```

When this application runs and the user clicks, the tile looks like Figure 10-17.

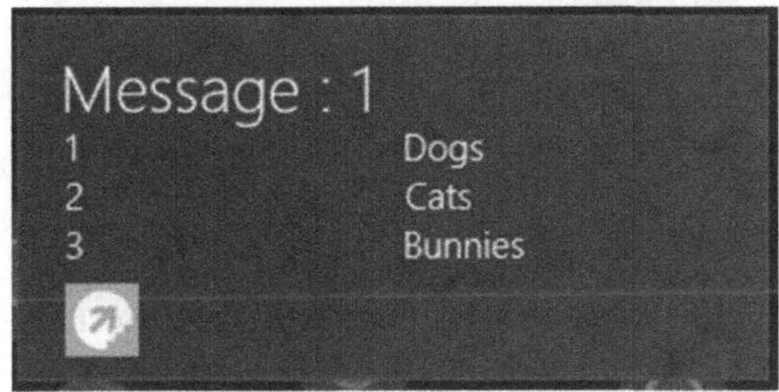

Figure 10-17. *Using TileWide310x150Text02*

Creating a Cleaner Template

`TileWide310x150Text02` does a good job but suffers from a disjointed aesthetic in my opinion. If the notification's look and feel are of paramount importance, then you can use a cleaner template like `TileWide310x150BlockAndText01`. This template renders as four strings of unwrapped text on the left and a large block of text over a single short string of bold text on the right. You lose the columns but can use the free text on the left to display both numbers and text, as shown in Figure 10-18.

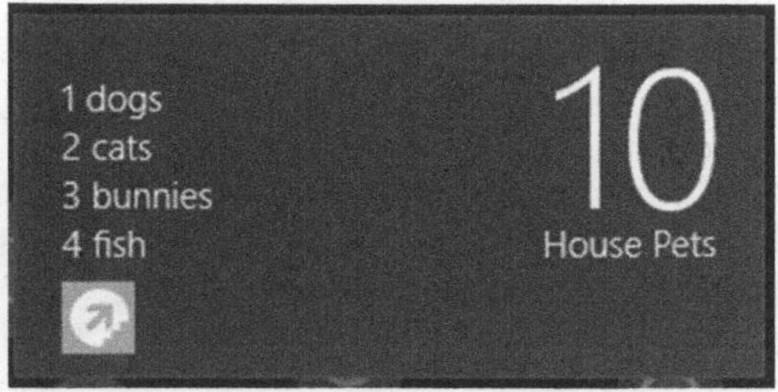

***Figure 10-18.** Using TileWide310x150BlockAndText01*

This notification was achieved by applying the template definition outlined in Listing 10-37.

Listing 10-37. TileWide310x150BlockAndText01 Template Definition

```
<tile>
  <visual>
    <binding template="TileWide310x150BlockAndText01">
      <text id="1">1 dogs</text>
      <text id="2">2 cats</text>
      <text id="3">3 bunnies</text>
      <text id="4">4 fish</text>
      <text id="5">10</text>
      <text id="6">House Pets</text>
    </binding>
  </visual>
</tile>
```

Adding Images to Tile Notifications

As with toast notifications, images can be applied to tile notifications to improve the overall aesthetic of the tile. In extreme scenarios when you're unsatisfied with any of the 45 possible template types provided by Microsoft, you can use one of the image-only notification templates and generate your own notification layout through dynamic image generation. At present, UWP doesn't provide a means to create images from user interface elements, but in future releases this may become a possibility. Also, nothing prevents you from doing this through a web service call. The various forms of tile notifications as they relate to images are too many and too similar in utilization to go into further in this book.

Scheduling Tile Notifications

Like toast notifications, tile notifications can be scheduled to run at a predetermined time. As stated previously, in certain scenarios it's more appropriate to schedule a tile update to happen at some point in the future rather than have the notification fired off as soon as the command to do so is executed. In such scenarios, you can use `ScheduledTileNotification`. Its constructor accepts not only the XML template for the notification but also a date when the notification should be displayed.

Summary

I hope you've found this thorough explanation of toast and tile notifications informative and beneficial for your future app development. To review, the discussion included generating toast and tile notifications, adding images and sound, scheduling, and responding to notifications. With the rules and forms covered in this chapter, Windows 10 again creates uniformity for the user, in this case, through notifications. As a Windows 10 developer, you now have the tools and real-world examples to use these notifications for tile design and lock-screen interaction. The following are some points to remember from this chapter:

- Launch conditions
- Windowing
- Lock screen background changing
- Toast and tile notifications can be sent locally.
- Toast notifications are context aware. An application can react uniquely and in a contextually specific manner to toast notifications that are activated or dismissed by the user.
- Tile notifications are essentially a pattern above the notion of live tiles. If a tile isn't on the Windows Start screen, there is no notification.
- Tile notifications can be text-only, text with images, all images, or a combination of images. Toast notifications can be text-only or text with images.
- Toast and tile notifications can serve as dynamic tools for grabbing the user's attention in a variety of ways.

CHAPTER 11

Communicating Between Apps

You've already seen a number of ways that apps can communicate with each other. In Chapter 6, you used `FileOpenPicker` and `FileSavePicker` to share resume data between UWP apps. In Chapters 8 and 10, you used the URI launcher to launch a completely separate application. In the case of the Maps app from Chapter 8 you learned how parameters can be passed from the calling app and utilized in the receiving app. This chapter continues the notion of app-to-app communication by introducing a number of new ways in which apps can communicate with one another. You will also be revisiting the aforementioned approaches. The primary ways that data can be shared between apps are

- URI launching with custom parameters
- File launching where the file being launched contains the data that will be used by the receiving app
- Through the Open file dialog
- Through the Save file dialog
- Through share contracts
- Through shared files
- Through a special kind of background task called app services

Using any number of these technologies together you can create sophisticated applications in such a way that, even local to the user's desktop, they become an ecosystem of publishers and subscribers that can be used to accomplish much more than each member app ever intended. We call it *windows app synergy*.

Before You Get Started

Before you get started with the lessons of this chapter, let's unify some of the apps you have been creating thus far under one umbrella. If you recall your samples from Chapters 1 and 2, you worked on an app that could be used by bouncers to track how many users entered and exited an event. An app like this would work quite well as an alternative to the geofencing technique introduced in Chapter 8. While geofencing works well for users who have Windows devices that are mobile enough to carry around, users with iPhone- or Android-based devices are left to the wind in the current implementation. For those patrons of Big Mountain events, the people counter features of your initial app work well.

You also worked on a customer management app for a health spa. This app had three primary parts to it:

- A scheduling system that was used to schedule massages for customer
- A customer management system that was used to manage the various customers of the business
- A point-of-sale system for handing retail transactions

The point-of-sale and customer management systems can most likely be transferred without much modification, as the needs they address translate quite nicely to the Big Mountain X app. The scheduling piece will need to be modified slightly.

One part of the Big Mountain Xocial events we have not discussed so far is the format of the show. During every event they throw, one hour is spent showcasing local talent in an all-out open mic. The winner of this contest is incorporated into the show as a "special guest" and gets a couple of free drinks to boot! Doing something like this in real-time while the show is going on can be a disjointed experience with unpredictability built in. Although the segment of the show is open mic, the Big Mountain guys still want some measure of curation in place so as not to bore their patrons. Because of this, they would like potential performers to use their app to submit a request to perform. This request would, of course, require the potential performers to include a video, image, and contact information. Those chosen are also notified through the app. Despite the difference in data captured, these two screens are essentially the same. They can be used to input events into an underlying schedule. So you will add a new Open Mic Signup page, which will use the Massage Appointment creation page as a foundation to build from. Let's get started by modifying the object model to account for these changes.

Changing the Object Model

Add a new class in the `Library` folder of General.UWP.Library called `BMXOccasion`. This class is a copy of the `Occasion` class you created in Chapter 1, with some additions to fit into the current app. Listing 11-1 illustrates. The namespace for this class should be `BigMountainX`.

Listing 11-1. BMXOccasion Class Definition

```
[DataContract]
public class BMXOccasion
{
    public Guid OccasionID { get; private set; }
    public int AttendanceCount { get; private set; }

    public BMXOccasion(BMXEvent bmx_event)
    {
        OccasionID = bmx_event.EventID;
    }

    public void Enter()
    {
        AttendanceCount++;
    }
```

```
    public void Leave()
    {
        if (AttendanceCount > 0)
            AttendanceCount--;
    }
}
```

In Listing 11-1, you add an OccasionID property and a constructor that accepts a BMXEvent object and sets the OccasionID for the BMXOccasion to the EventID of the BMXEvent. This way you are always able to get the event that served as the baseline for a given occasion. Why not just store the attendance information in the BMXEvent object? Event and Occasion have a classification/instance relationship. An occasion is an instance of an event. There might be multiple instances of the same event and you will need to track the attendance of each instance individually. To connect this class to the overarching object model, add the following line to BMXEvent:

```
public List<BMXOccasion> Occasions {get; set;}
```

Add another class to the Library folder called BMXCustomerInfo and use the content in Listing 11-2 to populate it.

Listing 11-2. BMXCustomerInfo Class Definition

```
public class BMXCustomerInfo
{
    public Guid CustomerID { get; set; }
    public string CustomerName { get; set; }
    public byte[] CustomerImage { get; set; }
    public string Email { get; set; }
    public DateTime DOB { get; set; }
}
```

This class maps directly to the CustomerInfo class from Chapter 5 with two modifications: you add a way to identify the customer (CustomerID) and an email address field as well.

You've got some more stuff to add. Create another class in the General.UWP.Library's Library folder called ReceiptItem. In it, place the code outlined in Listing 11-3.

Listing 11-3. ReceiptItem Class Definition

```
public class ReceiptItem
{
    public Guid ItemID { get; set; }    public string ItemName { get; set; }
    public double Price { get; set; }
    public double Tax { get; set; }
}
```

In the same project folder location, also add an item called POSTransaction. This will be a direct representation of the POSTransaction class from Chapter 5. Listing 11-4 illustrates.

Listing 11-4. POSTransaction Class Definition

```
public class POSTransaction : INotifyPropertyChanged
{
    public event PropertyChangedEventHandler PropertyChanged;

    List<ReceiptItem> Items { get; } = new List<ReceiptItem>();
    public double DefaultTaxAmount { get; set; }
    public double SubTotal
    {
        get
        {
            var total = Items.Select(i => i.Price).Sum();
            return total;
        }
    }
    public double TotalTax
    {
        get
        {
            return Items.Select(i => i.Tax).Sum();
        }
    }

    public double Total
    {
        get
        {
            return SubTotal + TotalTax;
        }
    }

    public ReceiptItem AddItemByPrice(double price)
    {
        var tax_amount = price * DefaultTaxAmount;
        var item = new ReceiptItem
        {
            ItemID = Guid.NewGuid(),
            ItemName = "",
            Price = price,
            Tax = tax_amount,
        };
        Items.Add(item);
        PropertyChanged?
            .Invoke(this,
            new PropertyChangedEventArgs("SubTotal"));
        PropertyChanged?
            .Invoke(this,
            new PropertyChangedEventArgs("TotalTax"));
```

```
        PropertyChanged?
            .Invoke(this,
            new PropertyChangedEventArgs("Total"));
        return item;
    }
    public void RemoveItem(ReceiptItem item)
    {
        Items.Remove(item);
    }

    public void ClearItems()
    {
        Items.Clear();
    }
}
```

Point-of-sale transactions will be tracked by occasion so you need to open BMXOccasion and add a link to this class as follows:

```
public List<POSTransaction> Transactions { get; set; }
```

The final change that needs to be made to the object model involves converting the ReservationInfo class from Chapter 5 (the one that was used to store information about the reservation a customer made) to an OpenMicRequest class, used to store reservations the customers make to compete in the open mic challenge. Add a class by that name to the general library's Library folder (as with the other types you have been adding) and implement it as shown in Listing 11-5.

Listing 11-5. OpenMicRequest Class Definition

```
public class OpenMicRequest
{
    public string AdditionalInfo { get; set; }
    public BMXCustomerInfo Customer { get; set; }
}
```

You've reduced the properties in the class quite a bit. You now only care about the person that made the request and any additional information they might have that would be relevant to the Big Mountain folks. Because this does not apply directly to the customer or even to an event, you need to create a top-level property AppState to store it as follows:

```
public List<OpenMicRequest> OpenMicRequests { get; set; }
```

There is one more thing to do. So far your app has been working based on an object model that has now been modified quite drastically. You need to clear the contents of your appdata folder by calling the ClearAsync method on the ApplicationData object right before you attempt to retrieve the app state from your AppState object. While you are at it, let's also switch from using the roaming folder to using the local one. Your app data is now far too large for it to ever get synced across devices. Listing 11-6 shows the modifications that must be made to InitializeAppAsync with changes in bold.

Listing 11-6. InitializeAppAsync Modifications

```
private static async Task InitializeAppAsync()
{
    var bio_path = "\\media\\text\\artistbio.txt";
    var bio = await Package.Current.InstalledLocation.GetFileAsync(bio_path);
    var appdata_folder = ApplicationData.Current.LocalFolder;
    await ApplicationData.Current.ClearAsync();
    State = await AppState.FromStorageFileAsync(appdata_folder, "state.xml");
   ...
}
```

The second line in bold is temporary. After running the app once, be sure to comment it out. Not doing so would consistently clear all your local content, effectively removing any changes you made while running the app.

One more item you need in your object model is a converter that will present an occasion in text form (as a string that indicates how many patrons have entered a given event). You created this converter in Chapter 1; it was called `OccasionConverter`. Create a new class in the General.UWP.Library project called `BMXOccasionConverter`, which contains the definition highlighted in Listing 11-7.

Listing 11-7. BMXOccasionConverter Class Definition

```
public class BMXOccasionConverter : IValueConverter
{
    public object Convert(object value,
        Type targetType,
        object parameter,
        string language)
    {
        if (value is BMXOccasion)
        {
            var occasion = value as BMXOccasion;
            var ui_command = parameter as string;
            if (ui_command == "number of attendants")
                return $"{occasion.AttendanceCount} attendants";
        }
        return "Unknown number of attendants";
    }

    public object ConvertBack(object value,
        Type targetType,
        object parameter,
        string language)
    {
        throw new NotImplementedException();
    }
}
```

As was shown in Chapter 1, this class simply displays a text string that represents a given occasion.

Applying SplitView to ApplicationHostPage

Now that your object model has been modified to support all the changes coming to BigMountainX, you can start modifying the user interface to reflect some of those changes. You can start by adding a SplitView to the root application page so that users can easily navigate between the customer-facing view of the page and some of the employee-centric views (like the point-of-sale and patron counters). Listing 11-8 illustrates.

Listing 11-8. ApplicationHostPage Layout Modifications

```
<Grid Background="#FF6A6A6A">

    <Rectangle x:Name="rect_titlebar"
               Height="50"
               Fill="#FF6A6A6A"
               VerticalAlignment="Top" />
    <SplitView x:Name="panel_splitter"
               IsPaneOpen="False"
               DisplayMode="CompactInline"
               CompactPaneLength="40"
               OpenPaneLength="200"
               Margin="0">
        <SplitView.Pane>

            <Grid Background="#AA6A6A6A">
                <StackPanel Orientation="Vertical"
                            Margin="0,50,0,0"
                            VerticalAlignment="Top"
                            HorizontalAlignment="Stretch">
                    <Button HorizontalAlignment="Stretch"
                            HorizontalContentAlignment="Left"
                            Margin="0,5,0,0"
                            Click="OnDashboardClicked"
                            Background="Transparent">
                        <StackPanel Orientation="Horizontal">
                            <SymbolIcon Symbol="GoToStart"
                                        Margin="0,0,20,0" />
                            <TextBlock Text="Dashboard" />
                        </StackPanel>
                    </Button>
                    <Button HorizontalAlignment="Stretch"
                            HorizontalContentAlignment="Left"
                            Margin="0,5,0,0"
                            Click="OnManageProfileClicked"
                            Background="Transparent">
                        <StackPanel Orientation="Horizontal">
                            <SymbolIcon Symbol="Contact2"
                                        Margin="0,0,20,0" />
                            <TextBlock Text="Manage Profile" />
                        </StackPanel>
                    </Button>
```

```
            <Button HorizontalAlignment="Stretch"
                    HorizontalContentAlignment="Left"
                    Margin="0,5,0,0"
                    Click="OnOpenMicClicked"
                    Background="Transparent">
                <StackPanel Orientation="Horizontal">
                    <SymbolIcon Symbol="Calendar"
                                Margin="0,0,20,0" />
                    <TextBlock Text="Schedule Open Mic" />
                </StackPanel>
            </Button>

        </StackPanel>
        <StackPanel Orientation="Vertical"
                    HorizontalAlignment="Stretch"
                    VerticalAlignment="Bottom"
                    Margin="0,0,0,20">
    <Button HorizontalAlignment="Stretch"
            HorizontalContentAlignment="Left"
            Margin="0,5,0,0"
            Click="OnPatronCounterClicked"
            Background="Transparent">
        <StackPanel Orientation="Horizontal">
            <SymbolIcon Symbol="AddFriend"
                        Margin="0,0,20,0" />
            <TextBlock Text="Patron Counter" />
        </StackPanel>
    </Button>
            <Button HorizontalAlignment="Stretch"
                    HorizontalContentAlignment="Left"
                    Margin="0,5,0,0"
                    Click="OnManageContactsClicked"
                    Background="Transparent">
                <StackPanel Orientation="Horizontal">
                    <SymbolIcon Symbol="ContactInfo"
                                Margin="0,0,20,0" />
                    <TextBlock Text="Manage Contacts" />
                </StackPanel>
            </Button>
            <Button HorizontalAlignment="Stretch"
                    HorizontalContentAlignment="Left"
                    Margin="0,5,0,0"
                    Click="OnPOS"
                    Background="Transparent">
                <StackPanel Orientation="Horizontal">
                    <SymbolIcon Symbol="Calculator"
                                Margin="0,0,20,0" />
                    <TextBlock Text="POS" />
                </StackPanel>
            </Button>
        </StackPanel>
```

```
            </Grid>
        </SplitView.Pane>
        <Grid>
            <Frame x:Name="root_frame"
                   Margin="0,50,0,0"
                   SourcePageType="local:LandingPage" />
        </Grid>
    </SplitView>
    <StackPanel Width="40"
                Orientation="Vertical"
                HorizontalAlignment="Left"
                VerticalAlignment="Top">
        <Button Height="50"
                Background="Transparent"
                Click="OnPaneOpened">
            <SymbolIcon Symbol="DockLeft" />
        </Button>
        <Rectangle Stroke="Gray"
                   StrokeThickness=".5"
                   Margin="5,0,5,0"
                   Height=".5"
                   HorizontalAlignment="Stretch" />
    </StackPanel>

</Grid>
```

In Listing 11-8, you employ the SplitView control to partition the ApplicationHostPage into an area where the content is displayed and one where the user can navigate between content areas. To complete this step, modify the constructor for ApplicationHostPage as indicated in Listing 11-9.

Listing 11-9. ApplicationHostPage Code Modifications

```
public ApplicationHostPage()
{
    ...

    CoreApplication.GetCurrentView().TitleBar.ExtendViewIntoTitleBar = true;
    Window.Current.SetTitleBar(rect_titlebar);
}
...
private void OnPaneOpened(object sender, RoutedEventArgs e)
{
    panel_splitter.IsPaneOpen = !panel_splitter.IsPaneOpen;
}
```

If you try to compile the code now, you should receive an error. This is because each of the buttons shown in the compact view needs to have their event handler implemented. If you haven't done so yet, take the time to right-click each of the button's Click attributes and select "Go to Definition" from the context menu that appears. This action creates a stub of the event handler to which you can add code. Now add a new page to the project called PatronCounter and add the XAML from Listing 11-10 to it.

Listing 11-10. PatronCounter Layout

```
<Page.Resources>
    <local:BMXOccasionConverter x:Key="attendant_ext" />
</Page.Resources>
<Grid>
    <StackPanel Orientation="Vertical"
                HorizontalAlignment="Center"
                VerticalAlignment="Center">
        <TextBlock x:Name="txt_attendants"
                   HorizontalAlignment="Center"
                   Text="{Binding Converter={StaticResource attendant_ext},
                                 ConverterParameter='number of attendants'}"
                   FontSize="42"
                   FontFamily="Segoe UI"
                   FontWeight="ExtraLight" />
        <StackPanel Orientation="Horizontal"
                    Margin="0,20,0,0"
                    HorizontalAlignment="Center">
            <Button x:Name="btn_reset"
                    Width="200"
                    Height="100"
                    Margin="5"
                    Click="ResetToZero">
                <Button.Content>
                    <Border Padding="20"
                            BorderThickness="0,0,0,5"
                            BorderBrush="Red">
                        <TextBlock Text="Reset Attendants"
                                   HorizontalAlignment="Left"
                                   VerticalAlignment="Center" />
                    </Border>
                </Button.Content>
            </Button>
            <Button x:Name="btn_remove"
                    Width="200"
                    Height="100"
                    Margin="5"
                    Click="RemoveAttendant">
                <Button.Content>
                    <Border Padding="20"
                            BorderThickness="0,0,0,5"
                            BorderBrush="Yellow">
                        <TextBlock Text="Remove Attendant"
                                   HorizontalAlignment="Left"
                                   VerticalAlignment="Center" />
                    </Border>
                </Button.Content>
            </Button>
        </StackPanel>
```

```
        <Button x:Name="btn_add"
                Width="410"
                Height="100"
                Margin="5,50,5,5">
            <Button.Content>
                <Border Padding="100,20,100,20"
                        BorderThickness="0,0,0,5"
                        BorderBrush="Green">
                    <TextBlock Text="Add Attendant" />
                </Border>
            </Button.Content>
        </Button>
    </StackPanel>
</Grid>
```

The XAML here is a copy from the example in Chapter 1 and serves the same function. The code-behind for this XAML is shown in Listing 11-11.

Listing 11-11. Patron Counter Code

```
public sealed partial class PatronCounter : Page
{
    BMXOccasion _occasion;
    BMXEvent _event;
    public PatronCounter()
    {
        this.InitializeComponent();
        this.Loaded += PatronCounter_Loaded;
        _event = new BMXEvent();
        _occasion = new BMXOccasion(_event);

        btn_add.Click += Btn_add_Click;
    }

    private void PatronCounter_Loaded(object sender, RoutedEventArgs e)
    {
        DisplayAttendants();
    }

    private void MainPage_Loaded(object sender, RoutedEventArgs e)
    {

    }

    void UseProgrammaticallyCreatedTextblocl()
    {
        TextBlock txt_attendants_prog = new TextBlock();
        txt_attendants_prog.HorizontalAlignment = HorizontalAlignment.Center;
        txt_attendants_prog.Text = "0 attendants";
        txt_attendants_prog.FontFamily = new FontFamily("Segoe UI");
        txt_attendants_prog.FontSize = 42;
        txt_attendants_prog.FontWeight = Windows.UI.Text.FontWeights.ExtraLight;
    }
```

```
    private void DisplayAttendants()
    {
        txt_attendants.DataContext = null;
        txt_attendants.DataContext = _occasion;
    }

    private void Btn_add_Click(object sender, RoutedEventArgs e)
    {
        _occasion.Enter();
        DisplayAttendants();
    }

    private void RemoveAttendant(object sender, RoutedEventArgs e)
    {
        _occasion.Leave();
        DisplayAttendants();
    }

    private void ResetToZero(object sender, RoutedEventArgs e)
    {
        _occasion = new BMXOccasion(_event);
        DisplayAttendants();
    }
}
```

The only change to the example is to change the name of the class `Occasion` to the class `BMXOccasion`. Other than that, the code functions the same.

Your next step is to create a Sign in page for the portions of the app that are admin/employee-centric. Add a new page to the project called EmployeeSignIn and place the XAML in Listing 11-12 into it.

Listing 11-12. EmployeeSignIn Layout

```
<Grid Background="{ThemeResource ApplicationPageBackgroundThemeBrush}">
    <StackPanel Width="300"
                HorizontalAlignment="Center"
                VerticalAlignment="Center">

        <PasswordBox x:Name="txt_employeecode"
                        Header="Enter Passcode" />
        <Button Content="Sign In"
                Margin="0,10,0,0"
                Click="OnSignInRequested"
                HorizontalAlignment="Right" />
    </StackPanel>
</Grid>
```

Now implement the code-behind for this page as shown in Listing 11-13.

Listing 11-13. EmployeeSignIn Code

```
public sealed partial class EmployeeSignIn : Page
{
    Type _target_type;
    public EmployeeSignIn()
    {
        this.InitializeComponent();
    }

    private void OnSignInRequested(object sender, RoutedEventArgs e)
    {
        if (txt_employeecode.Password == "employee")
            Frame.Navigate(_target_type);
    }

    protected override void OnNavigatedTo(NavigationEventArgs e)
    {
        _target_type = e.Parameter as Type;
        base.OnNavigatedTo(e);
    }
}
```

In Listing 11-13, the sign-in page expects a parameter passed into it that represents the page to which the user expects to be navigated. Once the sign-in occurs, this value is used to navigate the user as expected. Once you have created the appropriate pages, you will be able to use this page to perform the necessary authentication before navigating the current user to them. Now open up ApplicationHostPage and modify the definition of `OnPatronCounterClicked` to the following from Listing 11-14.

Listing 11-14. Event Handler

```
private void OnPatronCounterClicked(object sender, RoutedEventArgs e)
{
    root_frame.Navigate(typeof(EmployeeSignIn),typeof(PatronCounter));
}
```

This completes the process of calling any one of the admin pages. In the example, you navigate to `EmployeeSignIn`, passing as a parameter to that page the type of the page you really want to navigate to, `PatronCounter`. From Listing 11-14, you should know what happens next. Run the example now and test the code. The user interface of Big Mountain X should now look like Figure 11-1. If you don't get this view, immediately reset the profile by calling await `ApplicationData.Current.ClearAsync()` before the call to `InitializeAppAsync` (in the `OnLaunched` event handler of `app.xaml.cs`).

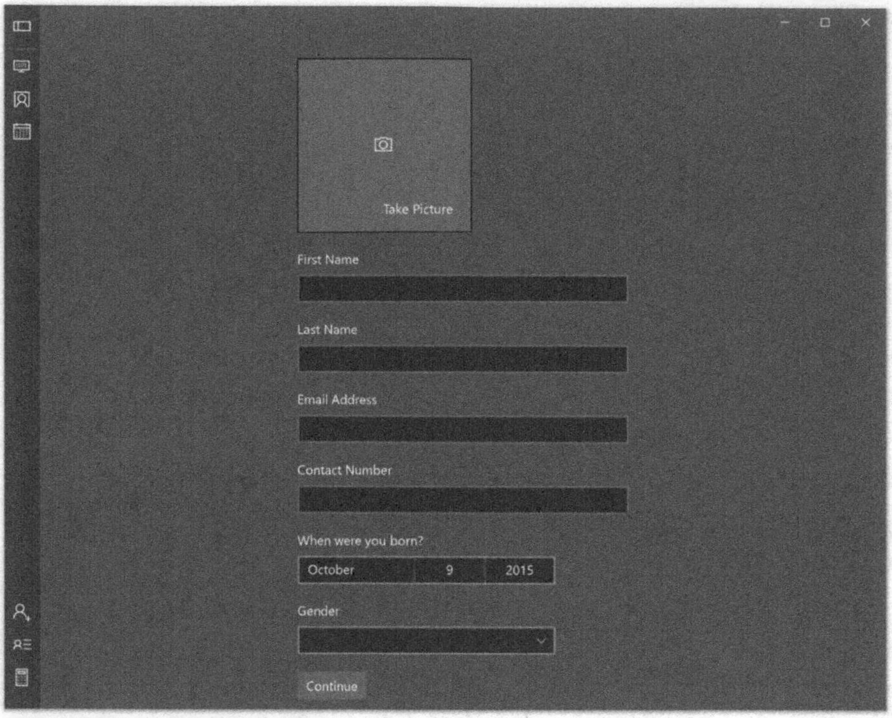

Figure 11-1. *New Big Mountain X UI*

The image shows the app as it is when it is first opened (with no profile associated with it yet). This is because you completely clear the profile as one of the first actions the app takes in the `Launching` event. If you have successfully run the app at least one time in this manner, switch back to the code and remove the line `await ApplicationData.Current.ClearAsync();` from the `InitializeAppAsync` method of your application class. You can find this method in `App.xaml.cs`.

Let's take the time to implement some measure of functionality for the other buttons you have in the navigation area. Although you do not have pages defined for them yet, you can create a page that serves as an indication to the user that those pages are not available (so they know that the buttons work properly). First, you must create a page to convey this message to the user. Add a new page to the BigMountainX project titled PageNotFound and implement the XAML within this page as follows from Listing 11-15.

Listing 11-15. XAML Layout

```
<Grid>
    <Border HorizontalAlignment="Center"
            Width="500" Padding="50" Background="Gray"
            VerticalAlignment="Center">

        <TextBlock TextWrapping="Wrap"
                   FontSize="40" Foreground="White"
                   Height="213">
```

```
            <Run Text="The functionality you are requesting is not available yet. Please try
            again later." />
            </TextBlock>
        </Border>
</Grid>
```

Continue the process by adding code to handle the events raised by the buttons on ApplicationHostPage. Listing 11-16 adds this code.

Listing 11-16. Event Handlers

```
...
private void OnDashboardClicked(object sender, RoutedEventArgs e)
{
    root_frame.Navigate(typeof(EmployeeSignIn), typeof(PageNotFound));
}

private void OnPOS(object sender, RoutedEventArgs e)
{
    root_frame.Navigate(typeof(EmployeeSignIn), typeof(PageNotFound));
}

private void OnManageContactsClicked(object sender, RoutedEventArgs e)
{
    root_frame.Navigate(typeof(EmployeeSignIn), typeof(PageNotFound));
}

private void OnOpenMicClicked(object sender, RoutedEventArgs e)
{
    root_frame.Navigate(typeof(EmployeeSignIn), typeof(PageNotFound));
}

private void OnManageProfileClicked(object sender, RoutedEventArgs e)
{
    root_frame.Navigate(typeof(EmployeeSignIn), typeof(PageNotFound));
}
...
```

Finally, create a new project in the solution called TestHarnessApp. In the MainPage for this app, add the code from Listing 11-17.

Listing 11-17. XAML Layout

```
<Grid Background="{ThemeResource ApplicationPageBackgroundThemeBrush}">
    <StackPanel Orientation="Vertical"
                HorizontalAlignment="Center"
                VerticalAlignment="Center"
                Width="400">

    </StackPanel>
</Grid>
```

Now that you have all the pieces you need, let's go through each of the ways that apps can communicate with each other and apply the principles of each approach to BigMountainX. There are various cross-functional classes of communication that can occur between UWP apps. For example, some communication methods follow a publish/subscribe model. In this type of data transfer, the app that is sending the information is unaware of who will receive the data or how the data will be used. Also, the choice of what app will be used, or of whether an app exists on the system in the first place, may not fall on the user, and may be an inadvertent one. An example of this already exists in Windows systems today. When you double-click a file to open it, a program on your system is used to do so. If that program were to be deleted, any attempt to open the file now brings up a dialog saying that you must select a program to use. The Windows 10 UWP supports this as well as the ability to target specific apps. Let's explore this further.

Communicating Through URI Launching

You saw this type of communication in Chapter 8 and 10. With URI launching, you basically use the `Launcher` class to launch a URI, causing any app that can handle that URI to be launched. When using URI launching, note that the entire URI is sent to the app and handled through the `OnActivated` event handler. The URI used must be a valid URI and, in order to pass parameters in a manner that the URI object understands, should use the question mark character before the parameter section of the string begins. As an example, to pass the name of john as a parameter, you use `bmx:?name=john`. The system will activate your app based on the URI you entered, passing it a `ProtocolActivatedEventArgs` object instance through an `IActivatedEventArgs` interface. Within `OnActivated`, you must convert this back into a strongly typed instance so that you can operate on it in a meaningful manner. For URI activation you need it to be converted to this type so you can get access to the URI that was used to activate your app. In Listing 11-18, you create a new type called `QueryReader` that can be used to read values out of a well-formed query string (that uses commas as the delimiter). Add this to General.UWP.Library.

Listing 11-18. QueryReader Definition

```
public class QueryReader
{
    Dictionary<string, string> _values;

    public string this[string name]
    {
        get
        {
            if (_values.ContainsKey(name))
                return _values[name];
            else
                return null;
        }
    }
    public static QueryReader Load(string query_string)
    {
        var reader = new QueryReader();
        reader._values = new Dictionary<string, string>();
        if (query_string.StartsWith("?"))
        {
            query_string = query_string.TrimStart('?');
            var parts = query_string.ToLower().Split(',');
            foreach (var query_item in parts)
```

```
            {
                var key_value = query_item.Split('=');
                if (key_value.Length == 2)
                    reader._values.Add(key_value[0], key_value[1]);
            }
        }
        return reader;
    }
}
```

Now that you have this, you can use it to read parameters that are passed into your activation target easily. Listing 11-19 modifies your `OnActivated` event to open either `TestPage`, `PatronCounter`, or `PageNotFound` based on the parameters passed in.

Listing 11-19. OnActivated Method

```
async protected override void OnActivated(IActivatedEventArgs args)
{
    if (args.Kind == ActivationKind.Protocol)
    {
        var protocol_args = args as ProtocolActivatedEventArgs;
        var query = protocol_args.Uri.Query.ToLower();
        var reader = QueryReader.Load(query);

        await InitializeAppAsync();

        var target_page = reader["page"];

        if (target_page == "street")
        {
            StreetSideViewPage street_view = new StreetSideViewPage();
            var center_point = new Geopoint(new BasicGeoposition
            {
                Latitude = App.State.NextEvent.Latitude.Value,
                Longitude = App.State.NextEvent.Longitude.Value,
            });
            await street_view.InitializeAsync(center_point);
            Window.Current.Content = street_view;
        }
        else if (target_page == "main")
        {
            Window.Current.Content = new ApplicationHostPage();
        }
        else if (target_page == "counter")
        {
            Window.Current.Content = new PatronCounter();
        }
        else if (target_page == "test")
        {
            Window.Current.Content = new TestPage();
        }
```

```
        else
        {
            Window.Current.Content = new PageNotFound();
        }
        Window.Current.Activate();
    }
}
```

In Chapter 10 you added URI launching to BigMountainX so you won't have to do any declaration in the app manifest of the project. Based on that chapter's use of URI launching you should be able to test this out using Microsoft Edge by placing an address that starts with `bmx:` into it. Let's test this out more formally through the TestHarnessApp project. To get started, right-click it and set it as the start project for the solution. This targets a particular project as the target to be started and debugged. Next, open the XAML for MainPage and modify it as indicated in Listing 11-20. Changes are in bold.

Listing 11-20. MainPage Layout Modifications

```
<Grid Backound="{ThemeResource ApplicationPageBackgroundThemeBrush}">
    <StackPanel Orientation="Vertical"
                HorizontalAlignment="Center"
                VerticalAlignment="Center"
                Width="400">
        <StackPanel Orientation="Horizontal">
            <TextBox x:Name="txt_page"
                     Width="200"
                     Margin="5" />
            <Button Content="Launch a Uri"
                    Margin="5"
                    HorizontalAlignment="Stretch"
                    Click="TestUriLaunch1" />
        </StackPanel>
    </StackPanel>
</Grid>
```

There is not much to write home about in Listing 11-20. You add a TextBox and Button to the main StackPanel of the test harness app. The code-behind for this is where all the fun happens; in it you use the `Launcher` class to start BigMountainX. Listing 11-21 illustrates.

Listing 11-21. TestUriLaunch1

```
async private void TestUriLaunch1(object sender, RoutedEventArgs e)
{
    await Launcher.LaunchUriAsync(new Uri($"bmx:?page={txt_page.Text}"));
}
```

Listing 11-21 is quite straightforward in what it does. You basically attempt to launch the specified URI, which is dynamically created to include the value of text the user enters as the page parameter. Run the app and test it by typing in values that correspond to the values expected at the other end by BigMountainX. Be sure to use Visual Studio 2015 to deploy BigMountainX first (using the project context menu). You should note that all the appropriate pages are launching as expected. Also, try launching the `using` values that BigMountainX is not expecting; the PageNotFound screen should be displayed. Figure 11-2 shows what you would see if "street" were typed in.

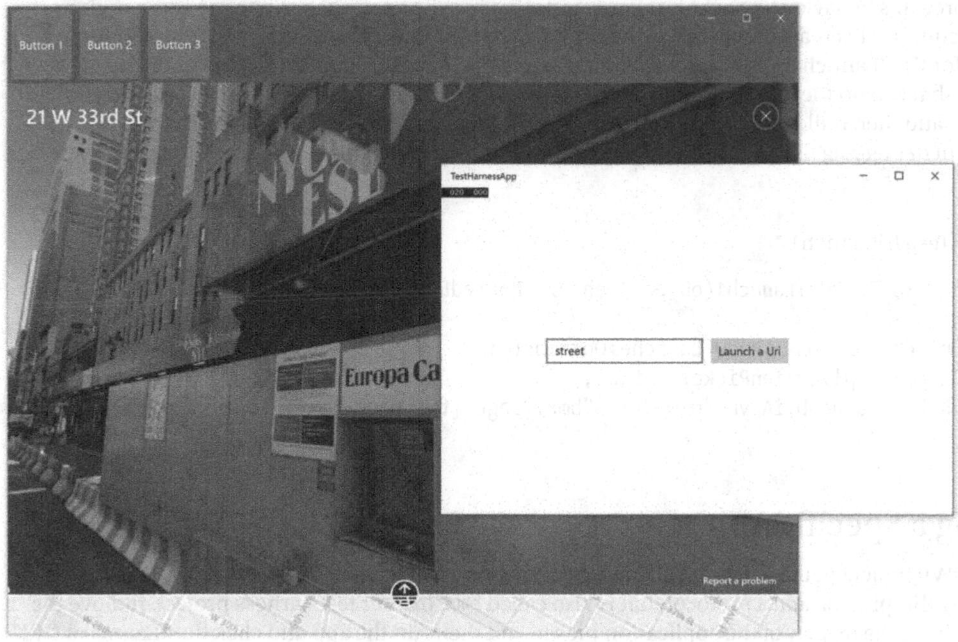

Figure 11-2. *Protocol activation direct to StreetView*

When no app exists in the system to handle the user interface, the app picker dialog typically pops up. Open the app manifest of BigMountainX and remove the protocol declaration, and then run the test harness app again. This time you should see something like Figure 11-3.

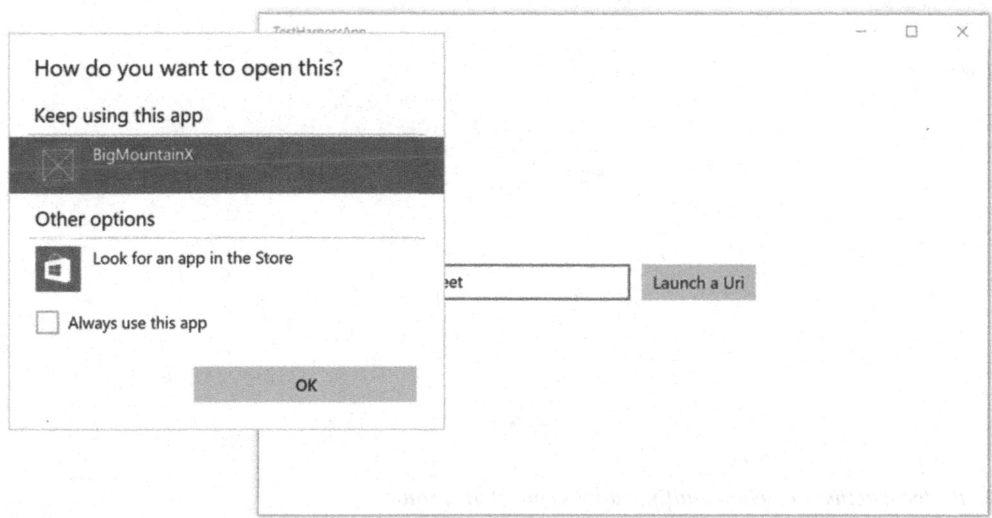

Figure 11-3. *Protocol activation prompt when an app exists to handle a protocol*

You can force this behavior even when an app exists that has the protocol by applying some options to the launch request. This is accomplished using the LauncherOptions class. Listing 11-22 modifies the event handler for the "Launch a URI" button so that it explicitly forces the application picker dialog even if an app exists that can do the job. To test this properly, re-declare the protocol that you just erased (in BigMountainX), and then build and deploy it. It is important that you remember to deploy in this case, since you are not debugging this particular project at this time, so your changes will not automatically be deployed.

Listing 11-22. TestUriLaunch1

```
async private void TestUriLaunch1(object sender, RoutedEventArgs e)
{
    LauncherOptions options = new LauncherOptions();
    options.DisplayApplicationPicker = true;
    await Launcher.LaunchUriAsync(new Uri($"bmx:?page={txt_page.Text}"), options);
}
```

Launching a Specific App

Create a new UWP project in the solution you have been working with called CompetingBMXApp. In the app manifest for this project, add a protocol that is also called bmx. In your test harness project, remove the line where you force the display of the application picker, and then run the app and click the "Launch a URI" button. You should now see something like Figure 11-4.

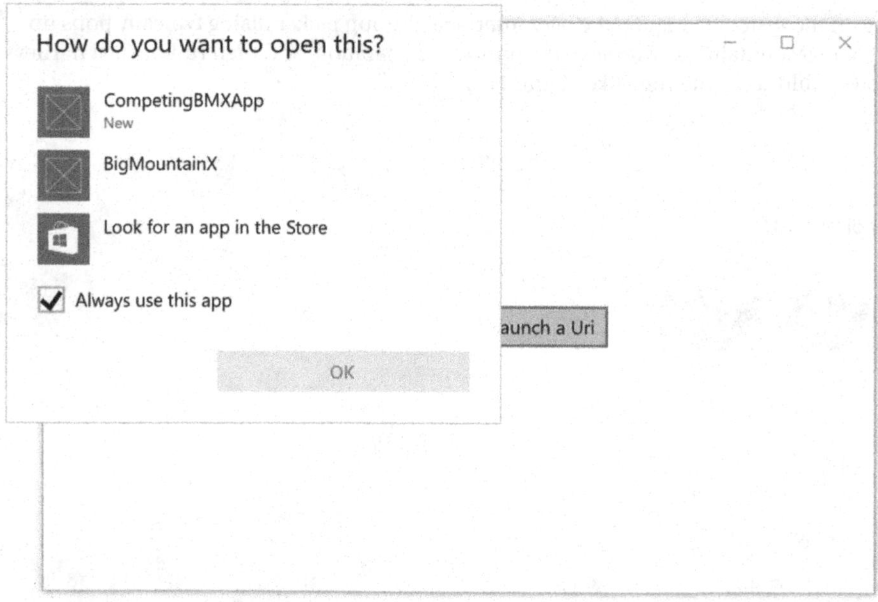

Figure 11-4. *Protocol activation when multiple apps support the protocol*

Because you now have two apps that share this protocol, the system has no idea which of the two apps it should launch, so it delegates the resolution of this problem to the user. The problem with this is that the user may not know the intentions of the developer and how those intentions (and the expectations they depend on) are realized in the inner workings of the app. If the user picks CompetingBMXApp here, none of the functionality you expect to be presented to the user will occur, since that app does not have the behavior you are expecting it to have. To make matters worse, it might have a completely different behavior altogether! Up to this point the apps that are receiving the data you are sending are unknown to you at development time. As you just saw, if another app exists on the system that can handle the URI scheme you have specified, the user is given the choice to pick which app they want to use. But what if the requirement is to have a specific app handle it? Using the `LauncherOptions`, you can also use this functionality to launch specific apps on the system. To do this, however, you must know the package family name of the app you are targeting. Listing 11-23 shows how you can use the `TargetApplicationFamilyName` of `LauncherOptions` to achieve this.

Listing 11-23. TestUriLaunch1

```
async private void TestUriLaunch1(object sender, RoutedEventArgs e)
{
    LauncherOptions options = new LauncherOptions();
    options.TargetApplicationPackageFamilyName = "<package family name>";
    await Launcher.LaunchUriAsync(new Uri($"bmx:?page={txt_page.Text}"), options);
}
```

In Listing 11-23, you explicitly identify the app you would like to use to handle the launch request by specifying the package family name for that app. The package family name for an app is private to the developer of the target app and must be acquired from them. For debugging purposes only, you can find it in the Packaging section of your app manifest, as shown in Figure 11-5.

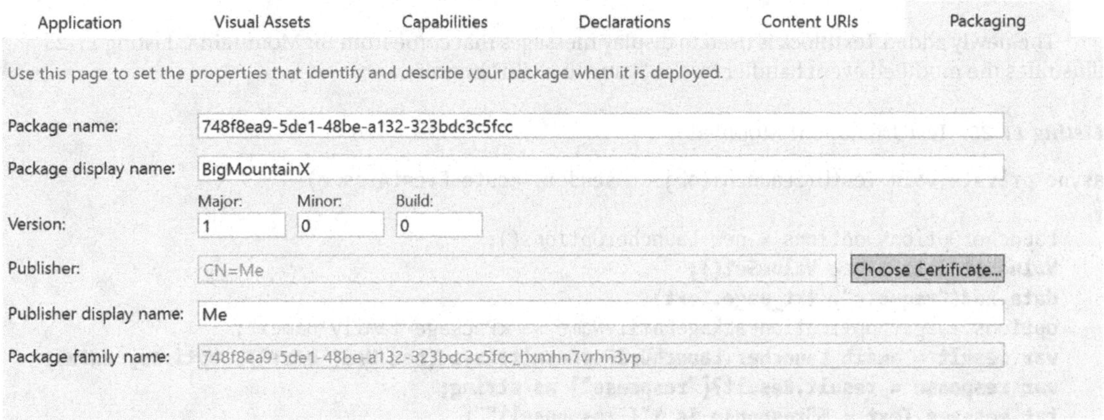

Figure 11-5. *Package family name location*

Launching a URI and Waiting for Results

In certain cases, you will want to get a response back from launching an app (assuming the app has been written with this in mind). To do this, use the LaunchUriForResults method. In the following example, you utilize LaunchUriForResults to send messages between BigMountainX and TestHarnessApp. You start by modifying the MainPage XAML of TestHarnessApp as follows in Listing 11-24.

Listing 11-24. MainPage Modifications

```
<Grid Background="{ThemeResource ApplicationPageBackgroundThemeBrush}">
    <StackPanel Orientation="Vertical"
            HorizontalAlignment="Center"
            VerticalAlignment="Center"
            Width="400">
        <Border Background="Gray">
            <TextBlock x:Name="txt_message"
                       Height="30" />
        </Border>
        <StackPanel Orientation="Horizontal">
            <TextBox x:Name="txt_page"
                       Width="200"
                       Margin="5" />
            <Button Content="Launch a Uri"
                    Margin="5"
                    HorizontalAlignment="Stretch"
                    Click="TestUriLaunch1" />
        </StackPanel>
    </StackPanel>
</Grid>
```

The newly added TextBlock is used to display messages that come from BigMountainX. Listing 11-25 illustrates the modified event handler for the "Launch a URI" button.

Listing 11-25. TestUriLaunch1 Modified

```
async private void TestUriLaunch1(object sender, RoutedEventArgs e)
{
    LauncherOptions options = new LauncherOptions();
    ValueSet data = new ValueSet();
    data.Add("request", txt_page.Text);
    options.TargetApplicationPackageFamilyName = "<Package family name>";
    var result = await Launcher.LaunchUriForResultsAsync(new Uri("bmx:"), options, data);
    var response = result.Result?["response"] as string;
    txt_message.Text = $"response is \"{ response}\"";
}
```

In Listing 11-25, you store the value of txt_page in a ValueSet object (a kind of key value pair) that you then pass into a call to LaunchUriForResultsAsyc. This method treats the launched app like a model dialog that will take additional information from the user, perform some action, and then return some result set back to the calling app. You might imagine an app like PayPal being used in this manner to check out. For this and all the other aforementioned reasons (predictability, consistency), you cannot perform a launch for the results type operation without knowing the app that will be returning the results to you.

Hence TargetApplicationPackageFamilyName must be set before the launch request is made. When the request returns, you read the value of a key value pair in it (response) and display it in the TextBlock you just added to the XAML. Note from the code that you have removed the URI parameters from the call to launch BigMountainX. URI parameters are needed in the generic use of protocol activation; in this more advanced version where the app is known and you are passing in parameters through the ValueSet data container, there is no need to pass values as query string parameters.

To facilitate this functionality in BigMountainX, you create a new page to represent the app in a modal dialog state. Add a new page to the BigMountainX project called LaunchResponsePage and define its XAML as follows from Listing 11-26.

Listing 11-26. LaunchResponsePage

```
<Grid Background="#FF6A6A6A">
    <StackPanel Orientation="Vertical"
                HorizontalAlignment="Center"
                VerticalAlignment="Center"
                Width="500">
        <Border Background="Gray">
            <TextBlock x:Name="txt_message"
                       Height="30" />
        </Border>
        <StackPanel Orientation="Horizontal">
            <TextBox x:Name="txt_page"
                     Width="250"
                     Margin="5" />
            <Button Content="Respond"
                    Margin="5"
                    Width="150"
                    HorizontalAlignment="Stretch"
                    Click="ResponseClicked" />
        </StackPanel>
    </StackPanel>
</Grid>
```

The layout of this page should be familiar to you; it is the same exact layout as that of the MainPage from TestHarnessApp. Define the code-behind for this page as shown in Listing 11-27.

Listing 11-27. LaunchResponsePage Code-Behind

```
public sealed partial class LaunchResponsePage : Page
{
    ProtocolForResultsActivatedEventArgs _args;

    public LaunchResponsePage(ProtocolForResultsActivatedEventArgs args)
    {
        this.InitializeComponent();
        _args = args;
        var request = _args.Data["request"] as string;
        txt_message.Text = $"request is \"{ request}\"";
    }
```

```
    private void ResponseClicked(object sender, RoutedEventArgs e)
    {
        ValueSet response_data = new ValueSet();
        response_data.Add("response", txt_page.Text);
        _args.ProtocolForResultsOperation.ReportCompleted(response_data);
    }
}
```

This page is created when a ProtocolForResultsActivatedEventArgs object is passed into it. It stores in it a class field and then reads the value of "request" from its Data property and sets it to the text of the TextBlock txt_message. The "request" value read here is the same value that you passed in in Listing 11-25. This is how values can be passed to the target of a launch operation. In the event handler for the Respond button, ResponseClicked, you create a new ValueSet and store a value in a "response" key-value pair that will be sent back to the caller. To close the called app and return the value back to the caller, you use the instruction _args.ProtocolForResultsOperation.ReportCompleted(response_data);. This method requires a ValueSet.

The final step to enabling this functionality must be done in BigMountainX's App.xaml.cs file. When an app in launched in this manner, it is treated by the system as a different kind of activation. So far, you have worked with the generic Protocol activation. When you use LaunchUriForResultsAsyc, your activation type will be ProtocolForResults. Listing 11-28 shows the modified OnActivated event handler.

Listing 11-28. OnActivated Event Handler

```
async protected override void OnActivated(IActivatedEventArgs args)
{
    await InitializeAppAsync();
    if (args.Kind == ActivationKind.Protocol)
    {

        ...

    }
    else if (args.Kind == ActivationKind.ProtocolForResults)
    {
        var protocol_args = args as ProtocolForResultsActivatedEventArgs;
        Window.Current.Content = new LaunchResponsePage(protocol_args);
    }
    Window.Current.Activate();
}
```

As in the use of standard protocol activation, you first convert the generic args parameter into its concrete type (so that you can operate on it as needed). Once you have the type, you pass it as an argument into the constructor for your LaunchResponsePage class, all the while setting it as the root content for the app. Build and run the app now, and test out sending messages between the two apps. The user interface should look like Figure 11-6.

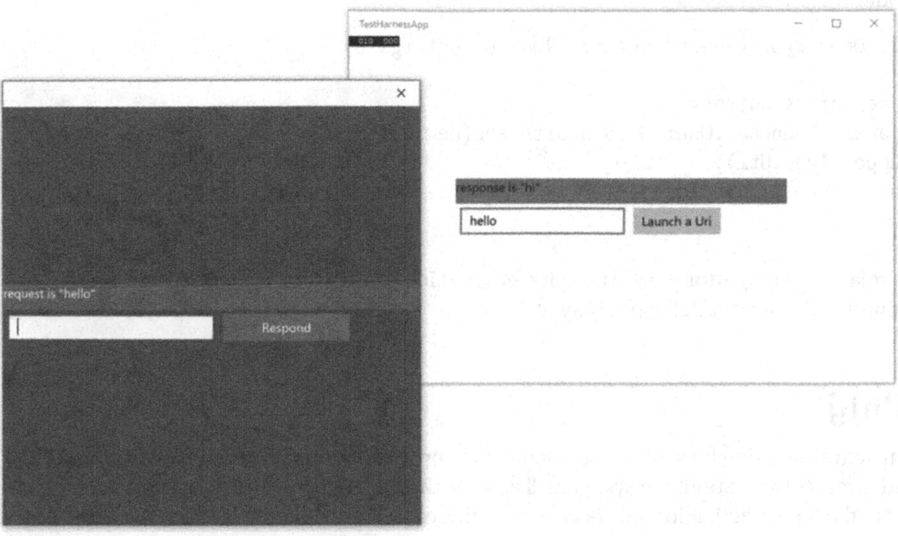

Figure 11-6. *Sharing data between apps*

Querying URI Support

It is a good idea to check to see if the system supports a given URI before blasting out a message to handle it. And in scenarios where you need a specific app to be available, it is also a good idea to be able to check for that app in the process. The `QueryUriSupportAsync` method allows you to do this. Add the code from Listing 11-29 to MainPage. It should be added as the last item to the main StackPanel on the page.

Listing 11-29. MainPage Modifications

```
...
  <StackPanel Orientation="Horizontal">
    <TextBox x:Name="txt_uri"
             Width="200"
             Margin="5" />
    <Button Content="Query Uri"
            Margin="5"
            HorizontalAlignment="Stretch"
            Click="OnQueryUri" />
  </StackPanel>
 </StackPanel>
</Grid>
```

Implement the `OnQueryUri` event handler as shown in Listing 11-30.

Listing 11-30. OnQueryUri Event Handler

```
async private void OnQueryUri(object sender, RoutedEventArgs e)
{
    var button = sender as Button;
    var result = await Launcher.QueryUriSupportAsync(new Uri($"{txt_uri.Text}:"),
    LaunchQuerySupportType.Uri);
    button.Content = result.ToString();
}
```

The example is relatively straightforward. The value entered into the textbox is used to check for protocol support using a call to `QueryUriSupportAsync`.

File Launching

You can also perform activation using files. A file is passed to the app and handled through the `OnActivated` event handler. As with protocol activation, the system will activate the targeted app and pass it an event args object that is specific to the type of activation that occurred–in this case, file activation. Within `OnActivated` you must convert the event args back into a strongly typed instance so that you can operate on it in that manner.

For file activation to work, a file association must be declared in the target app's manifest. Like protocols, file associations can be used to determine which apps have the ability to handle the appropriate files. You will start the example for this project by adding a new file association to the BigMountainX project. Figure 11-7 illustrates the process once again.

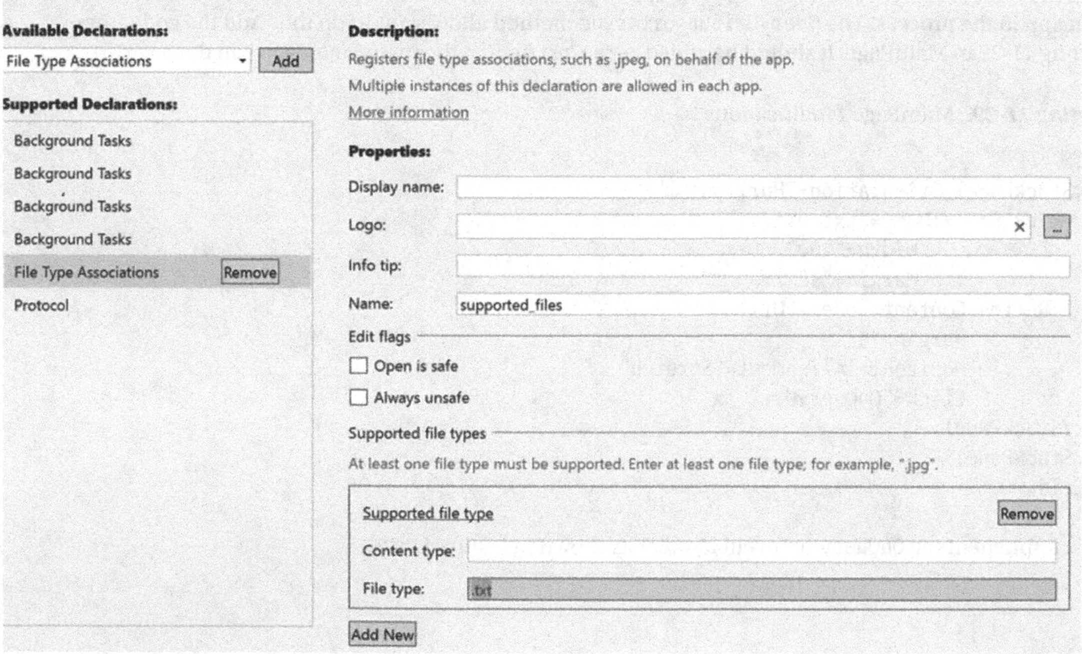

Figure 11-7. *File type association declaration*

Deploy the project once you are done. Now that BigMountainX has been configured to handle this file type, you should notice a few things. First, if you right-click any text file in the system and select "Open with" from the context menu, BigMountainX should now be one of the apps that shows up. Second, you should be able to open any text file in the system using this app by double-clicking it. Let's test this out by creating a text file with the contents from Listing 11-31 in it.

Listing 11-31. Query String

```
?page=counter
```

Save this file wherever you would like it to be saved and call it whatever name makes sense to you (make sure it has the .txt file extension, however). Now open BigMountainX's `App.xaml.cs` file and implement the `OnFileActivated` handler as shown in Listing 11-32.

Listing 11-32. OnFileActivated

```
async protected override void OnFileActivated(FileActivatedEventArgs args)
{
    var target_file = args.Files.FirstOrDefault() as StorageFile;
    var query = await target_file.ReadTextAsync();
    var reader = QueryReader.Load(query);
    var target_page = reader["page"];
    if (target_page == "street")
    {
        StreetSideViewPage street_view = new StreetSideViewPage();
        var center_point = new Geopoint(new BasicGeoposition
        {
            Latitude = App.State.NextEvent.Latitude.Value,
            Longitude = App.State.NextEvent.Longitude.Value,
        });
        await street_view.InitializeAsync(center_point);
        Window.Current.Content = street_view;
    }
    else if (target_page == "main")
    {
        Window.Current.Content = new ApplicationHostPage();
    }
    else if (target_page == "counter")
    {
        Window.Current.Content = new PatronCounter();
    }
    else if (target_page == "test")
    {
        Window.Current.Content = new TestPage();
    }
    else
    {
        Window.Current.Content = new PageNotFound();
    }
    Window.Current.Activate();
}
```

Listing 11-32 simply reuses the same logic as the basic URI activation example you worked on earlier in the chapter. The only difference between the two is that this version reads the parameters from a file while the other reads them from a query string. Right-click the text file you previously created and selection Open with ➤ BigMountainX from the context menu. Figure 11-8 shows what you should see when the app opens.

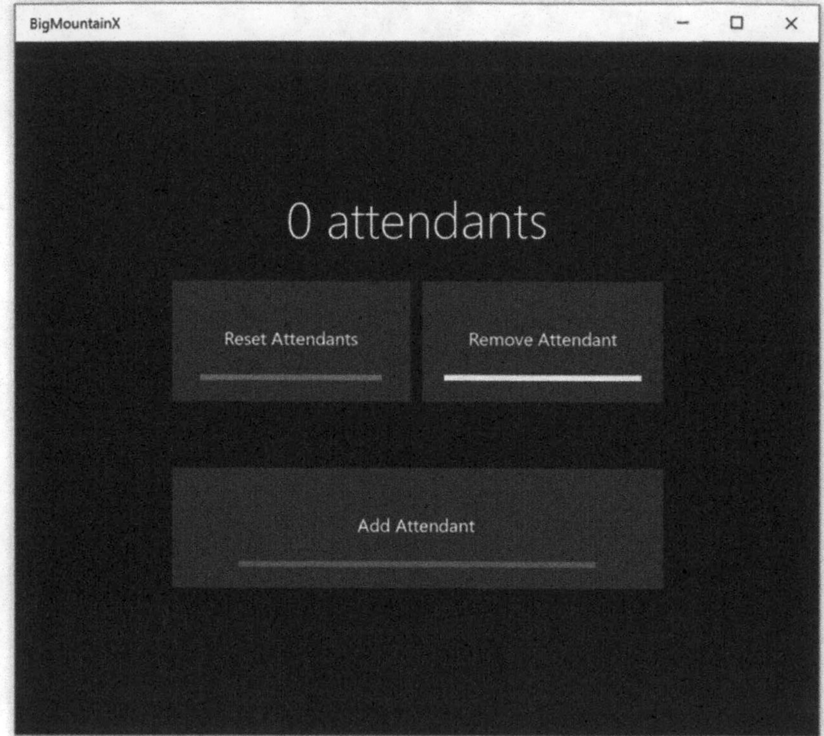

Figure 11-8. *Attendee Counter UI*

Now that you have established the file activation algorithm, you can implement the sharing of data from TestHarnessApp. Start by adding a new button to the bottom of the main stack panel as shown in Listing 11-33.

Listing 11-33. MainPage Modifications

```
<Button Content="File Activate"
        Margin="5"
        HorizontalAlignment="Stretch"
        Click="OnFileActivate" />
```

Now implement OnFileActivate as shown in Listing 11-34.

Listing 11-34. OnFileActivate

```
async private void OnFileActivate(object sender, RoutedEventArgs e)
{
    var folder = ApplicationData.Current.LocalFolder;
    var file = await folder.CreateFileAsync("test.txt", CreationCollisionOption.
OpenIfExists);
    await file.AppendTextAsync("?page=street");
    await Launcher.LaunchFileAsync(file);
}
```

The code in Listing 11-34 does essentially the same thing as you did manually with the text file. It dynamically creates a file and populates it with the parameters you want sent to BigMountainX. It then uses the function LauncFileAsync to launch the file. Figure 11-9 shows what happens if you build and run this app now.

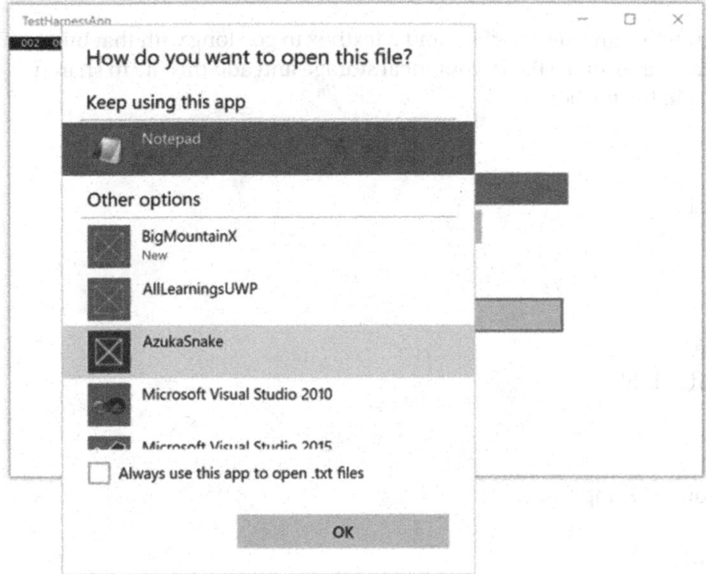

Figure 11-9. *App Picker UI*

With files more than anything you will find that numerous apps will intrinsically have the ability to handle the file types you declare. There is simply no telling what app might be out there that is built to handle files that end with a certain file extension. Because of this, when using file launching to communicate, it is imperative that you explicitly target the app you are communicating with using LaunchOptions and the package family name, just as you did with URI launching.

Communicating Through Sharing Files (Shared Storage)

All the approaches you explored so far have required both apps to be up and running at the same time, meaning you have, for the most part, needed to launch the app you were sending information into and pass it the parameters needed at launch time. The solutions you have specified up to this point have also actively sent data between the two participating apps (at least in concept). Another alternative, shared storage, accomplishes the same task by simply exposing a file such that another app in the system can operate on it. This is a stark departure from one of the primary tenets of UWP development, complete app isolation. To help reconcile this, access to the file is not directly granted; rather a token is generated that can then be shared between participating apps and used to access the file in order to operate on it. Step-wise, the process is as follows:

- Add the file to the shared storage. This process uses the class `SharedStorageAccessManager` and returns a token that represents the permission to access that file.
- Send the token to another application. This can use any of the methods utilized but does not have to.
- From the other app, use the token to retrieve the file using a call to `RedeemTokenForFileAsync`.

In Listing 11-35, you add a new button to your user interface and a textbox to go along with that button. When the button is clicked, you generate a new storage file in your local storage and add this file to shared storage. You then display the token string in the textbox.

Listing 11-35. MainPage Modifications

```
<StackPanel Orientation="Horizontal">
    <TextBox x:Name="txt_token”
             Width="200"
             Margin="5" />
    <Button Content="Shared File"
            Margin="5"
            HorizontalAlignment="Stretch"
            Click="OnShareFile />
</StackPanel>
```

And the event handler for this button in Listing 11-36.

Listing 11-36. OnShareFile Event Handler

```
async private void OnShareFile(object sender, RoutedEventArgs e)
{
    //create or replace the file
    var folder = ApplicationData.Current.LocalFolder;
    var file = await folder.CreateFileAsync("customer.xml", CreationCollisionOption.
    ReplaceExisting);

    //write the message
    var xml = @"<customer>
                <name>john</name>
                    <dob>10/19/1990</dob>
                    <email>john@test.com</email>
                </customer>";
    await file.AppendTextAsync(xml);
```

```
    //share the file
    var token = SharedStorageAccessManager.AddFile(file);
    txt_token.Text = token;
}
```

In the BigMountainX project, create a new page called ManageCustomer with a layout as shown in Listing 11-37.

Listing 11-37. ManageCustomer Layout

```
<Grid Background="#FF6A6A6A">
    <ScrollViewer>
        <StackPanel Margin="20"
                    Orientation="Vertical">
            <Button Click="ReplaceImage"
                    HorizontalAlignment="Left"
                    Height="227"
                    Margin="10"
                    VerticalAlignment="Top"
                    Width="225"
                    BorderThickness="1"
                    BorderBrush="Gray"
                    Background="Gainsboro">
                <Image x:Name="control_image"
                        Source="/alex.jpg" />
            </Button>
            <TextBox x:Name="txt_name"
                        Header="Name"
                        Margin="10"
                        Width="225"
                        HorizontalAlignment="Left" />
            <TextBox x:Name="txt_email"
                        Header="Email Address"
                        Margin="10"
                        Width="225"
                        HorizontalAlignment="Left" />
            <DatePicker Margin="10"
                        x:Name="control_dob"
                        Header="When were you born?"
                        HorizontalAlignment="Left"
                        VerticalAlignment="Top" />
            <StackPanel Orientation="Horizontal">
                <Button Margin="10"
                        Content="Save"
                        Width="100"
                        Click="SaveCustomer" />
                <Button Margin="10"
                        Width="100"
                        Content="Cancel"
                        Click="CancelCustomer" />
            </StackPanel>
        </StackPanel>
    </ScrollViewer>
```

```
    <Grid x:Name="grid_overlay" Background="Gray">
        <StackPanel HorizontalAlignment="Center" VerticalAlignment="Center">
            <TextBox x:Name="txt_token"
                        Header="Token ID"
                        Margin="10"
                        Width="225"
                        HorizontalAlignment="Left" />
            <Button Margin="10"
                    Content="Load Customer"
                    Width="150"
                    Click="LoadToken" />
            <Button Margin="10"
                    Content="New Customer"
                    Width="150"
                    Click="CreateNew" />
        </StackPanel>
    </Grid>
</Grid>
```

You will be populating the controls on this page with the content that was created in TestHarnessApp. The most interesting aspects of this code used to run this page can be found in the LoadToken event handler in Listing 11-38.

Listing 11-38. LoadToken Event Handler

```
async private void LoadToken(object sender, RoutedEventArgs e)
    {
        var token = txt_token.Text;
        var file = await SharedStorageAccessManager.RedeemTokenForFileAsync(token);
        if (file != null)
        {
            //initialize customer
            _customer = new BMXCustomerInfo
            {
                CustomerID = Guid.NewGuid(),
            };

            //load xml
            var xml:text = await file.ReadTextAsync();
            var xml = XElement.Parse(xml:text);

            //red xml into local values
            var customer_name = xml.Element("name").Value;
            var customer_email = xml.Element("email").Value;
            var customer_dob = xml.Element("dob").Value;
            var dob = DateTime.Parse(customer_dob);

            //set values of controls
            txt_name.Text = customer_name;
            txt_email.Text = customer_email;
            control_dob.Date = dob;
```

```
        //hide overlay
        grid_overlay.Visibility = Visibility.Collapsed;
    }
```

Here you see the other end of SharedStorageAccessManager. Calling RedeeemTokenForFileAsync here and passing the token you generated from the TestHarnessApp project should retrieve the XML file you created there. Once you have this shared file, you simply read its values and use those values to populate the controls on the page. The full code-behind for ManageCustomer is shown in Listing 11-39. You will need to add the following property to your AppState class:

```
public List<BMXCustomerInfo> Customers { get; set; } = new List<BMXCustomerInfo>();
```

Listing 11-39. ManageCustomer Code-Behind

```
public sealed partial class ManageCustomer : Page
{
    CameraCaptureUI ccui = new CameraCaptureUI();
    BMXCustomerInfo _customer;

    public ManageCustomer()
    {
        this.InitializeComponent();
    }

    async private void ReplaceImage(object sender, RoutedEventArgs e)
    {
        BitmapImage image = new BitmapImage();
        control_image.Source = image;

        ccui.PhotoSettings.AllowCropping = true;
        ccui.PhotoSettings.MaxResolution =
            CameraCaptureUIMaxPhotoResolution.HighestAvailable;
        var result = await ccui.CaptureFileAsync(CameraCaptureUIMode.Photo);
        if (result != null)
        {
            var stream = await result.OpenReadAsync();
            await image.SetSourceAsync(stream);

            //get the image data and store it
            stream.Seek(0);
            BinaryReader reader =
                new BinaryReader(stream.AsStreamForRead());
            _customer.CustomerImage = new byte[stream.Size];
            reader.Read(_customer.CustomerImage, 0,_customer.CustomerImage.Length);
        }
    }

    private void CancelCustomer(object sender, RoutedEventArgs e)
    {
        Frame.GoBack();
    }
```

```
    async private void SaveCustomer(object sender, RoutedEventArgs e)
    {
        _customer.CustomerName = txt_name.Text;
        _customer.Email = txt_email.Text;
        _customer.DOB = control_dob.Date.Date;
        App.State.Customers.Add(_customer);
        await App.State.SaveAsync();
        Frame.GoBack();
    }

    private void CreateNew(object sender, RoutedEventArgs e)
    {
        grid_overlay.Visibility = Visibility.Collapsed;
        _customer = new BMXCustomerInfo
        {
            CustomerID = Guid.NewGuid(),
        };
    }

    async private void LoadToken(object sender, RoutedEventArgs e)
    {
        var token = txt_token.Text;
        var file = await SharedStorageAccessManager.RedeemTokenForFileAsync(token);
        if (file != null)
        {
            //initialize customer
            _customer = new BMXCustomerInfo
            {
                CustomerID = Guid.NewGuid(),
            };

            //load xml
            var xml:text = await file.ReadTextAsync();
            var xml = XElement.Parse(xml:text);

            //red xml into local values
            var customer_name = xml.Element("name").Value;
            var customer_email = xml.Element("email").Value;
            var customer_dob = xml.Element("dob").Value;
            var dob = DateTime.Parse(customer_dob);

            //set values of controls
            txt_name.Text = customer_name;
            txt_email.Text = customer_email;
            control_dob.Date = dob;

            //hide overlay
            grid_overlay.Visibility = Visibility.Collapsed;
        }
    }
}
```

Finally, open ApplicationHostPage and connect this page to the navigation structure by modifying `OnManageContactsClicked` as shown in Listing 11-40.

Listing 11-40. Modifying OnManageContactsClicked

```
private void OnManageContactsClicked(object sender, RoutedEventArgs e)
{
    root_frame.Navigate(typeof(EmployeeSignIn), typeof(ManageCustomer));
}
```

Application Services

In the previous section, you saw sharing between two apps in a manner in which the receiving app was not necessarily aware of the intention to share until much later (when it came time to retrieve the file that it needed). This is a departure from the approach to sharing you have practiced up to this point. For the most part, all the other forms of sharing we have discussed have actively forced the app being shared with to open. You saw this with both forms of URI launching and with the file launcher.

In contrast to this approach, application services extend the notion of sharing in a manner that does not require the other participant to be opened. Application services allow you to do this by exposing a background task to any apps that want to send data directly to it. In this case, the data is passed to the background task and would ideally be stored in a location that allows the foreground app to load it when it starts. You will use this method to improve on the design of the ManageCustomer example from the previous section.

The process starts with the TestHarnessApp project. In it, you need to add a new button to the button of MainPage's primary StackPanel as you have been doing thus far. Listing 11-41 illustrates.

Listing 11-41. MainPage Modifications

```
<Button Content="App Service Shared File"
        Margin="5"
        HorizontalAlignment="Stretch"
        Click="OnAppServiceShareFile" />
```

Now you must implement the handler `OnAppServiceShareFile`. This handler will function the same as `OnShareFile` in that it will use the `SharedStorageAccessManager` class to add a file to shared storage. The change here is in what happens to the token that is returned from this call. Previously, you stored the token in a TextBox, with the expectation that the user would copy that token into a participating app whenever it needed to retrieve the created file. You will do things differently here. With the token in hand, you will send it as a message to the application service of an app you expect to be running on the system. Because application services run in the background, the message will be delivered without the app opening. Listing 11-42 illustrates the handler for `OnAppServiceShareFile`.

Listing 11-42. OnAppServiceShareFile

```
int _name_count = 0;
async private void OnAppServiceShareFile(object sender, RoutedEventArgs e)
{
    //used to randomize names
    _name_count++;
```

```
    //create or replace the file
    var folder = ApplicationData.Current.LocalFolder;
    var file = await folder.CreateFileAsync("customer.xml", CreationCollisionOption.
    ReplaceExisting);

    //write the message
    var xml = $"<customer><name>john_{_name_count}</name>"
                + @"<dob>10/19/1990</dob>
                <email>john@test.com</email>
            </customer>";
    await file.AppendTextAsync(xml);

    //share the file
    var token = SharedStorageAccessManager.AddFile(file);

    AppServiceConnection connection = new AppServiceConnection();
    connection.AppServiceName = "bmx-service";
    connection.PackageFamilyName = "<package family>";

    AppServiceConnectionStatus status = await connection.OpenAsync();
    if (status == AppServiceConnectionStatus.Success)
    {
        //Send data to the service _
        var message = new ValueSet();
        message.Add("command", "customer-file-share");
        message.Add("token", token);

        //Send message and wait for response _
        AppServiceResponse response = await connection.SendMessageAsync(message);
        if (response.Status == AppServiceResponseStatus.Success)
        {
            await new MessageDialog("sent").ShowAsync();
        }
        else
            await new MessageDialog("Failed when sending message to app").ShowAsync();
    }
    else
    {
        await new MessageDialog(status.ToString()).ShowAsync();
    }
    connection.Dispose();
}
```

In Listing 11-42, you create, populate, and eventually store the customer XML file in shared storage and then attempt to send the token to an application service associated with the Big Mountain X app. Application services utilize the `AppServiceConnection` object to identify the service being requested, open a connection to that service, and then ultimately send messages to it (using the `ValueSet` object). To begin sending messages, you must first call `OpenAsync` on the `AppServiceConnection` object. This tells you whether the service is available or not. If the result returns as a success, you proceed with sending the messages using the `SendMessageAsync` method. If it fails, you prompt the user with the status of the connection and then dispose of the connection. Run the app now and click the associated button; you should get the error prompt shown in Figure 11-10.

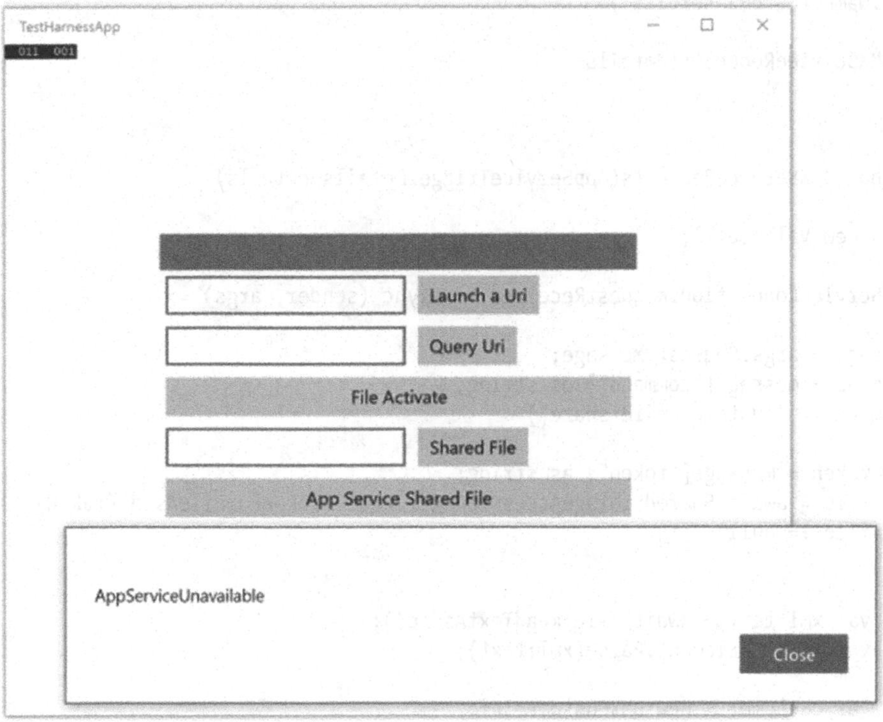

Figure 11-10. *Application service-based sharing error*

The service is failing at present because you have obviously not created it. To do so, you must add a new background task to Big Mountain X and then register that task in the manifest.

To get going, add a new class to the BMX.BackgroundTasks called `BMXAppServices`. This class will be used to encapsulate all the application services that the BMX app exposes. In app service, add code to read the token values passed into it, retrieve the associated file from shared storage, and copy that file to a location within the Big Mountain X app so that it can be used locally the next time the app is run. Listing 11-43 illustrates.

Listing 11-43. BMXAppServices Class Definition

```
sealed public class BMXAppServices : IBackgroundTask
{
    AppState State { get; set; }
    BackgroundTaskDeferral _deferral;

    async public void Run(IBackgroundTaskInstance taskInstance)
    {
        _deferral = taskInstance.GetDeferral();
        var local = ApplicationData.Current.LocalFolder;
        State = await AppState.FromStorageFileAsync(local, "state.xml");
        var details = taskInstance.TriggerDetails as AppServiceTriggerDetails;
```

```
        if (details.Name == "bmx-service")
        {
            HandleBMXServiceRequests(details);
        }
    }

    private void HandleBMXServiceRequests(AppServiceTriggerDetails details)
    {
        var retval = new ValueSet();

        details.AppServiceConnection.RequestReceived += async (sender, args) =>
        {
            var message = args.Request.Message;
            var command = message["command"] as string;
            if (command == "customer-file-share")
            {
                var token = message["token"] as string;
                var file = await SharedStorageAccessManager.RedeemTokenForFileAsync(token);
                if (file != null)
                {

                    var xml:text = await file.ReadTextAsync();
                    var xml = XElement.Parse(xml:text);

                    var customer = new BMXCustomerInfo
                    {
                        CustomerID = Guid.NewGuid(),
                        CustomerName = xml.Element("name").Value,
                        Email = xml.Element("email").Value,
                        DOB = DateTime.Parse(xml.Element("dob").Value)
                    };

                    State.Customers.Add(customer);
                    await State.SaveAsync();

                    retval.Add("result", "File was copied");
                }
                else
                {
                    retval.Add("result", "Could not retrieve file");
                }
                await args.Request.SendResponseAsync(retval);
            }
            _deferral.Complete();
        };
    }
}
```

Listing 11-43 defines a new background task that will serve as the application service that receives the message from TestHarnessApp. In the Run method for this class, you first get a deferral and then you load the AppState object into memory. AppState is the global application state you have been using in the foreground portion of BigMountainX so far. Because you are dynamically loading customers into your data store, you need this object. Next, you convert the trigger details object into the concrete type `AppServiceTriggerDetails` so that you can work with it as an app service trigger, and gain access to the functionality defined for those kinds of background tasks. Once you have this instance, you use it to filter functionality to the name of the service being requested. One app service class may handle multiple app service declarations (each with its own set of functionality). Testing for the service being called ensures that the app service is doing what it is supposed to do. You then call `HandeBMXServiceRequests`, the request handler you have defined for handling requests for any request for an app service named `bmx-service` (the kind `TestHarnessApp` requests). In this method you listen for the `details.AppServiceConnection.RequestReceived` event to be fired and handle it as needed. The critical thing you are doing here is reading the shared file and using it to create an XML document that you can then populate a customer object with. Once you have created an instance of `BMXCustomerInfo` from the data you received, you add that instance to the Customers list of your `AppState` object and then call `SaveAsync` to save it. You then notify the caller that the load was successful (or not if it failed). Figure 11-11 shows how this must be set up in the app manifest for the service to work. Once you have it properly configured, publish BigMountainX.

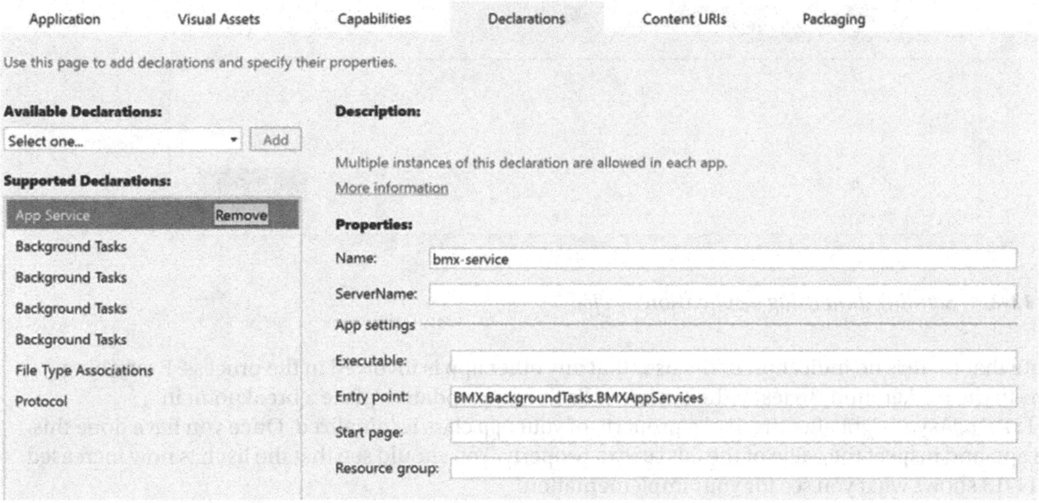

Figure 11-11. *Configuring application service*

You can now run TestHarnessApp and use the App Service Shared File button to send many customer files to BigMountainX. Figure 11-12 illustrates.

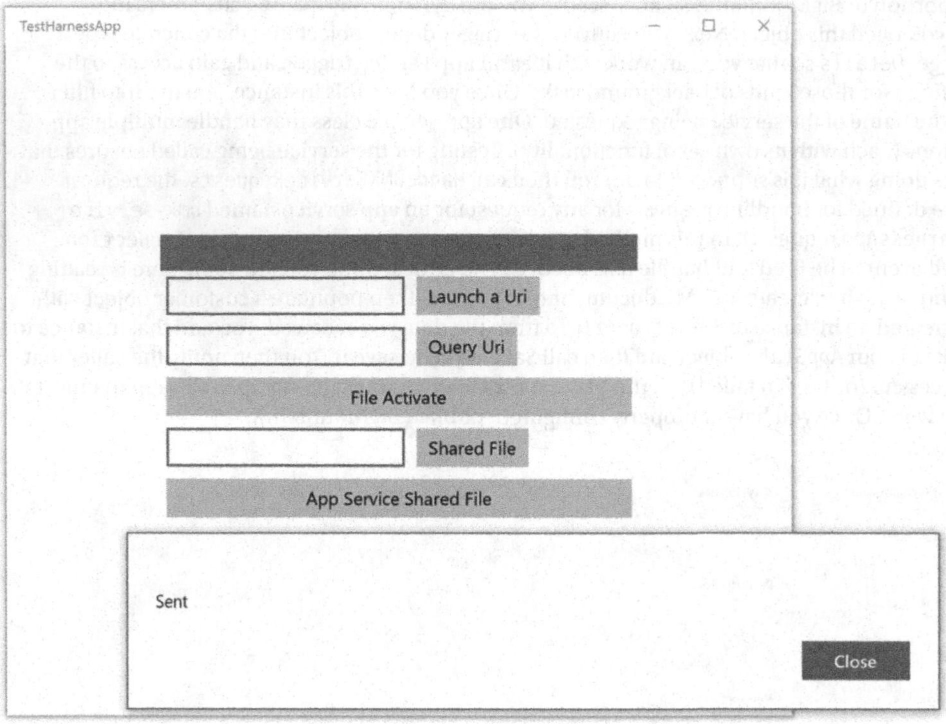

Figure 11-12. *Sending data using application service*

Note that there is no indication to the user that any other app is involved in the process. Everything happens in the background. To test if the customer list is being updated, place a breakpoint in `InitializeAppAsync` right after the `State` property of your `App` class is initialized. Once you have done this, run the app and inspect the value of the `Customers` property. You should see that the list has now increased. Figure 11-13 shows what you see for your implementation.

```
2 references
private static async Task InitializeAppAsync()
{
    var bio_path = "\\media\\text\\artistbio.txt";
    var bio = await Package.Current.InstalledLocation.GetFileAsync(bio_path);
    var roaming_folder = ApplicationData.Current.LocalFolder;
    //await ApplicationData.Current.ClearAsync();
    State = await AppState.FromStorageFileAsync(roaming_folder, "state.xml");
    // St  State {BigMountainX.AppState}
    if (Sta  Customers          Count = 12
    {          [0]      {BigMountainX.BMXCustomerInfo}
        Sta          CustomerID      {f56b2092-9890-44fb-ac15-fc03e0dc5a00}
        {            CustomerImage   null
                     CustomerName    "john_1"
                     DOB             {10/19/1990 12:00:00 AM}
                     Email           "john@test.com"
               [6]      {BigMountainX.BMXCustomerInfo} eFolder)
            D  [7]      {BigMountainX.BMXCustomerInfo}
            E  [8]      {BigMountainX.BMXCustomerInfo} ate",
            D  [9]      {BigMountainX.BMXCustomerInfo}
            S  [10]     {BigMountainX.BMXCustomerInfo} ), 0, 0),
            F  [11]     {BigMountainX.BMXCustomerInfo}
            {  Raw View
            },
        };
        await State.SaveAsync();
    }
```

Figure 11-13. *Testing customer creation*

Sharing Data Between the Apps You Created

Another way of communicating between apps (in scenarios where you published each app) is to simply use some predefined shared storage location. In Windows 10 UWP, it is possible for apps from the same publisher to share a common storage area using publisher cache functionality. This allows you to maintain some measure of continuity across the suite of products you utilize. You can store the EULA (end user license agreement) text for all your apps in this location for instance, or perhaps any suite-wide logos and logo text. If you expect your applications to work together, this might also be a great place to get that done quickly. `ApplicationData` exposes two methods for working with the publisher cache: `GetPublisherCacheFolder` can be used to retrieve the folders you have specified as a publisher cache folder while `ClearPublisherCacheFolderAsync` can be used to clear the contents of the publisher cache folder you specify. As with many of the features exposed through the UWP, the process of enabling publisher cache folders starts in the app's manifest file. Unfortunately, there is presently no user interface to modify this, so you will have to open the manifest by right-clicking and selecting View Code.

For this feature to work across your apps, each app that you want to have access to this cache must explicitly declare access to the folder. Access to this folder means access to any subfolders of it as well. You do this in both BigMountainX and TestHarnessApp by adding the XML from Listing 11-44 to the app manifest, at the package level.

Listing 11-44. Adding Publisher Cache Folder Support to the App Manifest

```
<Package ...>
...
<Extensions>
    <Extension Category="windows.publisherCacheFolders">
        <PublisherCacheFolders>
            <Folder Name="bmx_shared_state"/>
        </PublisherCacheFolders>
    </Extension>
</Extensions>
</Package>
```

It is important to note that although this is an extension, it is an extension applied to the package and not any of the applications within the package (like the other extensions you have been working with). Since you have the manifest open in its XML form, take the time to look through and note the distinction. The `PublisherCacheFolders` node can contain multiple Folder elements, each corresponding to a folder that will be provided by the system.

Next, you add another button to MainPage in the same manner as you have been doing. Listing 11-45 shows the XAML for the button.

Listing 11-45. New Button in MainPage

```
<Button Content="Write to Publisher Cache"
        Margin="5"
        HorizontalAlignment="Stretch"
        Click="OnWriteToPublisherCache" />
```

And finally you implement the `OnWriteToPublisherCache` method as shown in Listing 11-46.

Listing 11-46. OnWriteToPublicherCache

```
async private void OnWriteToPublisherCache(object sender, RoutedEventArgs e)
{
    var folder = ApplicationData.Current.GetPublisherCacheFolder("bmx_shared_state");
    var file = await folder.CreateFileAsync("customer.xml", CreationCollisionOption.
ReplaceExisting);

    //write the message
    var xml = $"<customer><name>james_{_name_count}</name>"
        + @"<dob>10/19/1990</dob>
        <email>john@test.com</email>
    </customer>";
    await file.AppendTextAsync(xml);
}
```

In Listing 11-46, you use the publisher cache folder you declared in the manifest to store a customer XML file. When you call `GetPublisherCacheFolder`, the name specified must match a name declared in the manifest for one of the publisher cache folders. Once you have the storage folder corresponding to this location, it is business as usual as far as interacting with it.

To test this functionality, in BigMountainX open the ManageCustomer XAML and add the following button to the StackPanel inside `grid_overlay`. Listing 11-47 illustrates.

Listing 11-47. New button in MainPage

```
<Button Margin="10"
        Content="Load Cached Customer"
        Width="150"
        Click="OnLoadCachedCustomer" />
```

Implement `OnLoadCachedCustomer` as follows (Listing 11-48).

Listing 11-48. OnLoadCachedCustomer

```
async private void OnLoadCachedCustomer(object sender, RoutedEventArgs e)
{
    var folder = ApplicationData.Current.GetPublisherCacheFolder("bxm_shared_state");
    var file = await folder.GetFileAsync("customer.xml");
    //initialize customer
    _customer = new BMXCustomerInfo
    {
        CustomerID = Guid.NewGuid(),
    };

    //load xml
    var xml:text = await file.ReadTextAsync();
    var xml = XElement.Parse(xml:text);

    //red xml into local values
    var customer_name = xml.Element("name").Value;
    var customer_email = xml.Flement("email").Value;
    var customer_dob = xml.Element("dob").Value;
    var dob = DateTime.Parse(customer_dob);

    //set values of controls
    txt_name.Text = customer_name;
    txt_email.Text = customer_email;
    control_dob.Date = dob;

    //hide overlay
    grid_overlay.Visibility = Visibility.Collapsed;
}
```

In Listing 11-48, you get the `customer.xml` file that was created in your publisher cache folder and use it to populate the fields of this page. Run this example and note that you are able to create and read files in your publisher cache as easily as anywhere else. For collaborating apps, publisher cache is a powerful was of sharing state.

Sharing Contracts

Sharing using contracts is the most prominent means of sharing between apps. It's specifically designed for such functionality and in that way is the resident first-class inter-app communication mechanism for Windows 10. When an application subscribes to the sharing experience, it can send and receive content in various forms ranging from plain text and HTML content to complex structures.

Sharing follows a pattern similar to protocols, file type association, pickers, and all the other declaration types when it comes to permissions. In the case of sharing, the Share Target declaration is required. As with other declarations, when a declaration is required for an app to run, it is surfaced as a permission that the user is aware of before install. When deciding whether to download and install your apps, the declarations you require will undoubtedly have an impact. Should they miss this out of sheer excitement, they need only use the various settings app to access the same list of permissions required for a given app to run.

Sharing supports two types of contracts: essentially, one for giving content and one for receiving content. Because the giving side of the equation can only ever be activated by the end user through performing some interactive action on the app, there is no requirement to explicitly define anything to get it going. We will discuss this approach first.

Sharing as a Source

As far as a UWP app is concerned, it can always share content that it deems meaningful to share. However, like protocol and file activation, the type of content being shared is an important part of what apps on your system will be available to share with. The process of sharing begins when a call to DataTransferManager.ShowShareUI() is made. Calling this method triggers the system to ask your app for the type of content being shared. This is surfaced in your app as the DataRequested event of DataTransferManager. If this event goes unhandled, the system will share a screenshot of your app. Depending on what data you chose to share when handling the event, the system will determine the appropriate apps that have the ability to handle that content type. These apps will be listed in the Sharing Pane (which appears as a slide-out on the right of the user's screen). To get access to an instance of DataTransferManager, call the static method GetForCurrentView. In the next example, you modify MainPage of TestHarnessApp to use sharing to publish the customer XML you have been generating and storing to a file. You will be sharing it as text. To start, you must add a new button to your page (within the StackPanel you have been placing them in). Listing 11-49 illustrates.

Listing 11-49. New Button in MainPage

```
<Button Content="Share Customer"
        Margin="5"
        HorizontalAlignment="Stretch"
        Click="OnShareCustomer" />
```

Next, in the code-behind you must modify the constructor to specify a handler for the DataRequested event and also implement OnShareCustomer. Listing 11-50 illustrates.

Listing 11-50. Changes to MainPage

```
public sealed partial class MainPage : Page
{
    int _name_count = 0;
    public MainPage()
    {
        this.InitializeComponent();
        DataTransferManager.GetForCurrentView().DataRequested += MainPage_DataRequested;
    }
    ...
    private void OnShareCustomer(object sender, RoutedEventArgs e)
    {
        DataTransferManager.ShowShareUI();
    }
```

```
    private void MainPage_DataRequested(DataTransferManager sender,
    DataRequestedEventArgs args)
    {
        _name_count++;
        var xml = $"<customer><name>james_{_name_count}</name>"
            + @"<dob>10/19/1990</dob>
    <email>john@test.com</email>
    </customer>";
        args.Request.Data.Properties.Title = "New Customer";
        args.Request.Data.Properties.Description = "Create a new Customer";
        args.Request.Data.SetText(xml);
    }
}
```

In Listing 11-50, you specify two methods: `OnShareCustomer` simply invokes the Sharing pane while `MainPage_DataRequested` handles the `DataRequested` event. In this event handler, you create the customer XML and publish it to the sharing framework as text. You also set a title and description to the data you are sharing (so the user has some context they can use in making the choice of which app to use). Run this app now and click the Share Customer button and you should see a share pane similar to Figure 11-14. Please note that the apps that appear will differ based on the system this code is run on.

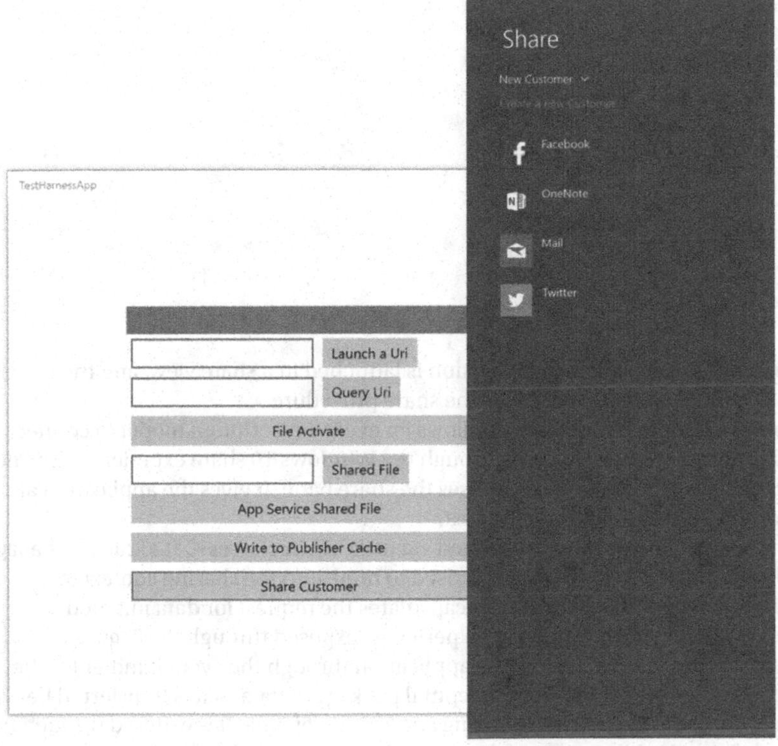

***Figure 11-14.** Sharing pane*

Note that the title and description show that based on the content type, four apps are available to share (on your system). Clicking any of these apps will take the user to a secondary screen where they can visualize the data to be shared between the apps. Figure 11-15 shows the next screen that appears when OneNote is the app selected.

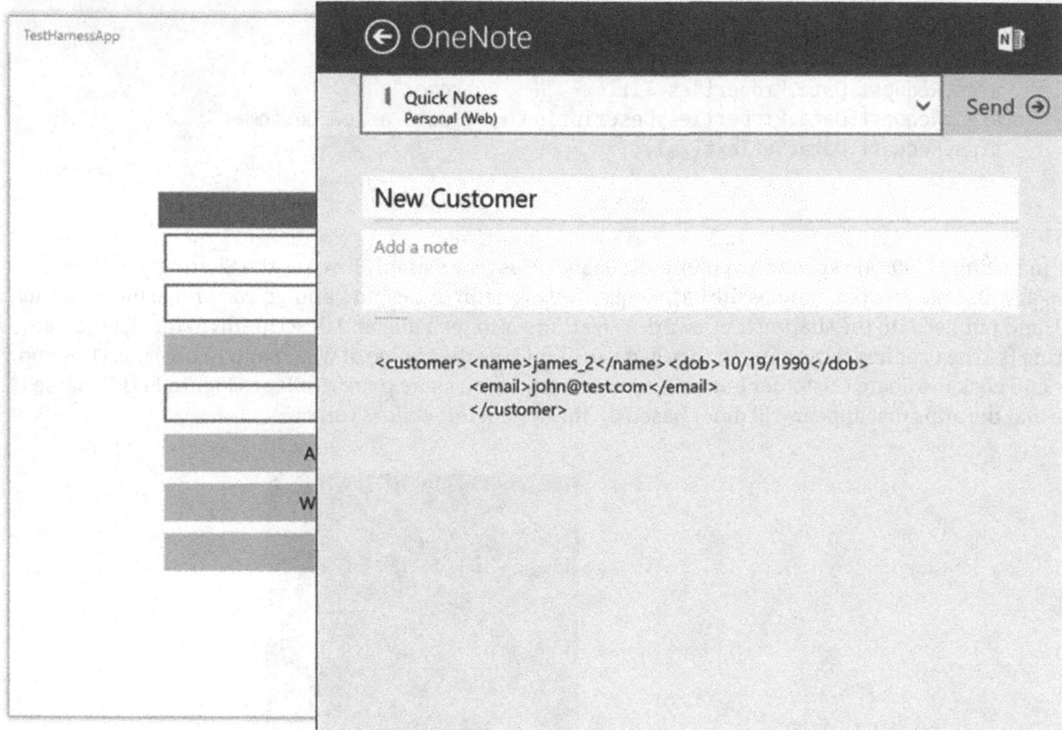

Figure 11-15. *Sharing view*

When one of the applications is selected, that application is launched in a share view, and the user is given the option to make last-minute edits and complete the share procedure.

What you can see from this example is that sharing follows an event subscription model to connect. This is because, as stated, sharing happens exclusively through the Windows 10 share experience. The event handler `OnDataRequested` is called any time the user exposes the share pane. It gives the application an opportunity to load any information into the sharing context.

The giving end of the share relationship is accomplished via three main classes: `DataTransferManager`, `DataRequest`, and `DataPackage`. `DataTransferManager` is used to hook into the sharing context to listen for the launching of the Share pane. `DataRequest` encapsulates the request for data initiated by Windows 10 in response to the user starting the share experience, exposed through the `Request` property of `DataRequestedEventArgs`. It's passed into the application through the event handler for the `OnDataRequested` event. `DataPackage` represents the conceptual package of data that is transferred between the sharing applications; hence it controls the actual reading and writing of data. It is exposed through the `Data` property of `DataRequest`. Table 11-1 lists some of the methods of the `DataPackage` class.

Table 11-1. *DataPackage Methods*

Name	Description
GetView	Returns a DataPackageView object. This object is a read-only copy of the DataPackage object.
SetBitmap	Sets the bitmap image contained in the DataPackage.
SetData	Sets the data contained in the DataPackage in a RandomAccessStream format.
SetDataProvider	Sets a delegate to handle requests from the target app.
SetHtmlFormat	Adds HTML content to the DataPackage.
SetRtf	Sets the Rich Text Format (RTF) content that is contained in a DataPackage.
SetStorageItems (IIterable(IStorageItem))	Sets the files and folders contained in a DataPackage.
SetStorageItems(IIterable (IStorageItem), Boolean)	Adds files and folders to a DataPackage.
SetText	Sets the text that a DataPackage contains.
SetUri	Sets the Uniform Resource Identifier (URI) that is contained in the DataPackage.

DataPackage also exposes a property of type DataPackagePropertySet through its properties property, which you can use to apply metadata to the content being shared. It contains Title and Description properties but is also a property bag that can be used to store additional properties in name/value format.

Listing 11-50 sends data between applications using one of the standard formats provided through the data package classes: Text. As you saw from Table 11-1, in addition to this you can also send images, RTF content, HTML content, and even raw data (using SetData) across applications.

Sharing as a Target

Each application has a set of content types that it supports (some public and some private). The Windows Mail application, for instance, can accept HTML for use in rendering a message being generated from a "giving" application. For the content to render properly, the message must follow a specific format (controlled by Microsoft, in this case). The moral of the story is that content format is less of a concern than specific application requirements as defined by documentation received directly from the application authors.

Receiving content through the share contract is far more involved than sending. For starters, unlike sending content to other applications, receiving content requires an application to be registered as a target for the type of content being shared. This makes sense because you wouldn't want every application that can possible share presented in the listing of share targets when the user wishes to transfer content that is unrelated to many of them. Instead, Windows 10 filters the list of applications that appear when the user clicks the Share button to include only those applications that can consume content in the format being shared. It isn't difficult to see why applications that want to register as share targets need to declare the type of content they can handle.

Not surprisingly, the pattern for doing this is similar to the manner in which background tasks, pickers, and protocols are registered and processed. First, you must add the Share Target capability to the application's manifest. Open BigMountainX and add the Share Target declaration, specifying that the app can receive text content. Figure 11-16 illustrates.

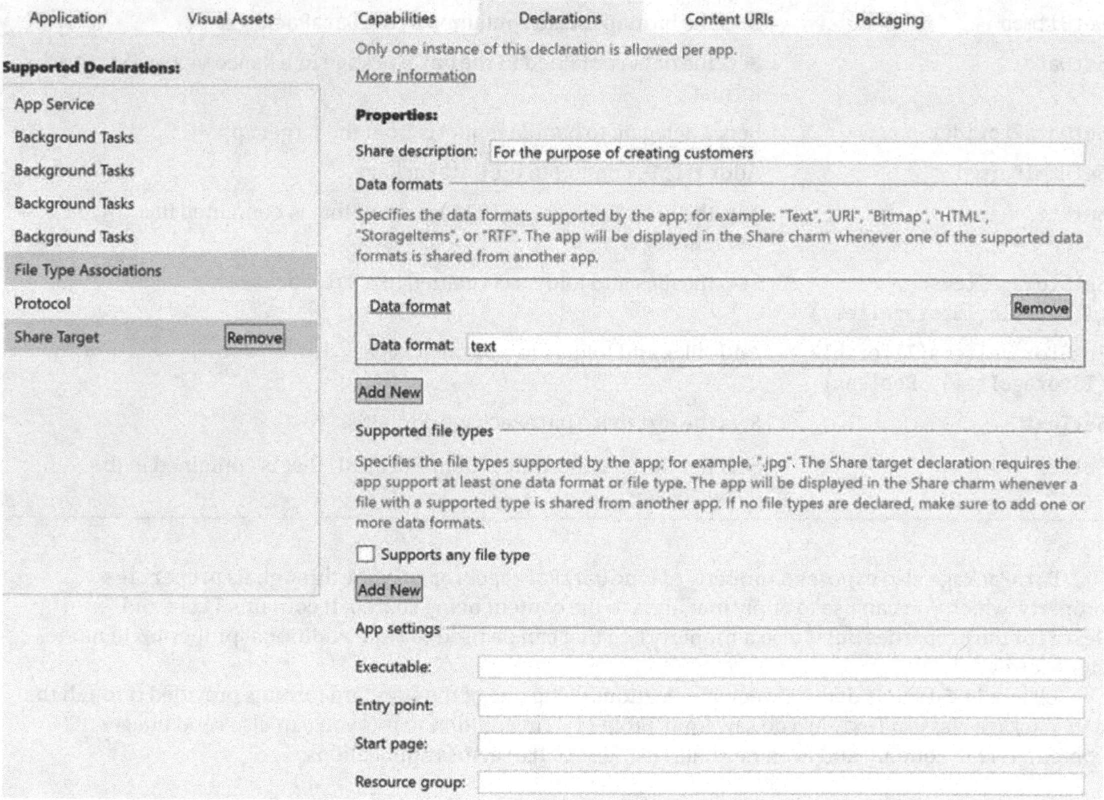

Figure 11-16. *Configuring a share target*

In the image, the text data format has been added as the primary format that the application supports. You add data formats by specifying the format moniker for the format type. In this case, the application can handle text of any kind. You can also use file-type associations to enable sharing. Doing so allows the application to use nonstandard formats to share data through the `StorageItems` property of `DataPackage`. If a file format is used that matches the data formats specified, it's treated as such; otherwise, the share source must use the `args.Request.Data.SetStorageItems` method to add the nonstandard format (as a storage file) to the sharing context.

Once you have declared the app as being a share target, you must do two things. First, you must override the `OnShareTargetActivated` method of the `App` class in order to handle when the app is activated in this manner. Listing 11-51 shows how it should be implemented for BigMountainX.

Listing 11-51. OnShareTargetActivated

```
async protected override void OnShareTargetActivated(ShareTargetActivatedEventArgs args)
{
    await InitializeAppAsync();
    ManageCustomer cust = new ManageCustomer();
    await cust.Activated(args);
}
```

The second thing that needs to happen is that a user interface needs to be created to display in the Share pane when your app is selected. You saw this UI in your share source example when you selected OneNote. In this exercise, you will be using `ManageCustomer` as the user interface (you might have figured this out based on the last code listing). You probably noticed the red squiggly underneath the call to `Activated`. The `OnShareTargetActivated` method makes a call to an `Activated` method on `ManageCustomer` that presently does not exist. Listing 11-52 shows the modifications to `ManageCustomer` to add this method and also to enable it to function as a share target.

Listing 11-52. Modifications to ManageCustomer

```
public sealed partial class ManageCustomer : Page
{
    ...
    bool _share_activated = false;
    ShareOperation _share;

    public ManageCustomer()
    {
        ...
    }

    async public Task Activated(ShareTargetActivatedEventArgs args)
    {
        _share = args.ShareOperation;
        var xml:text = await args.ShareOperation.Data.GetTextAsync();
        var xml = XElement.Parse(xml:text);

        _customer = new BMXCustomerInfo
        {
            CustomerID = Guid.NewGuid(),
        };

        //red xml into local values
        var customer_name = xml.Element("name").Value;
        var customer_email = xml.Element("email").Value;
        var customer_dob = xml.Element("dob").Value;
        var dob = DateTime.Parse(customer_dob);

        //set values of controls
        txt_name.Text = customer_name;
        txt_email.Text = customer_email;
        control_dob.Date = dob;
        grid_overlay.Visibility = Visibility.Collapsed;
```

```
        _share_activated = true;
        //set this as the window
        Window.Current.Content = this;
        Window.Current.Activate();
    }

  ...

    async private void SaveCustomer(object sender, RoutedEventArgs e)
    {
        _customer.CustomerName = txt_name.Text;
        _customer.Email = txt_email.Text;
        _customer.DOB = control_dob.Date.Date;
        App.State.Customers.Add(_customer);
        await App.State.SaveAsync();

        if (_share_activated)
            _share.ReportCompleted();
        else
            Frame.GoBack();
    }
    ...
}
```

In Listing 11-52, you first retrieve the share-specific object instance from the args object and save it to the field variable _share. Next, you use the appropriate method to retrieve the shared content (in this case, GetTextAsync). Finally, you use this text to load an XML document which you then read values from and use to populate the fields on the page, as you have been doing all chapter long. Figure 11-17 shows how the app looks when selected from the sharing pane.

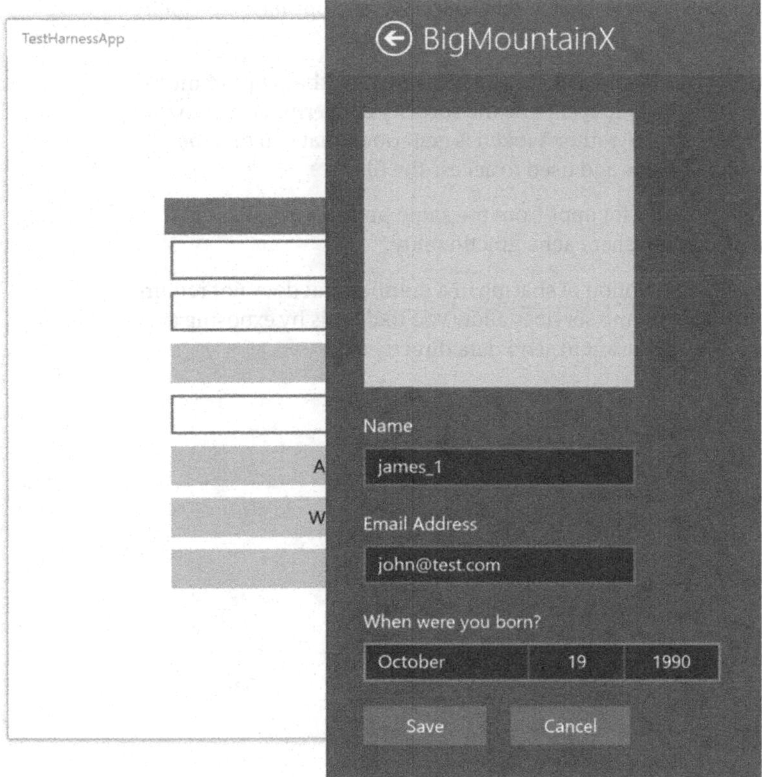

Figure 11-17. *BigMountainX sharing view*

One thing to note is that share targets don't have the same width as normal applications. The layout of the share view must account for this, or the user experience suffers. Navigating the user to a standard page with normal dimensions (which is pixel or margin positioned) may make sharing impossible for the user.

Summary

You just completed a meaty chapter with a comprehensive and in-depth investigation into incorporating communication and data exchange between apps. With the close of this chapter, you should feel well on your way toward gaining more in-depth knowledge of the Windows 10 ethos and environment to serve you as you forge ahead into development for the platform. Through the use of contracts, interoperability between applications can be enhanced further. The following are some key points:

- Share contract is the most prominent means of sharing between applications. When an application subscribes to the sharing experience, it can send and receive content in various forms ranging from simple to complex structures.
- Protocol activation uses the `Launcher` class to launch a URI, causing any app that can handle that URI to be launched. It can be used to launch apps generally, launch specific apps, and even to launch apps for the purpose of returning results.
- `QueryUriSupportAsync` allow you to check to see if the system supports a given URI before blasting out a message to handle it.

- File activation, like protocols, can be used to determine which apps have the ability to handle appropriate files.
- `SharedStorageAccessManager` exposes files in such a way that other apps in the system can operate on them. To help reconcile the security concerns, access to the exposed file is not directly granted; rather a token is generated that can then be shared between participating apps and used to access the file.
- In Windows 10 UWP, it is possible for apps from the same publisher to share a common storage area using publisher cache functionality.
- Application services extend the notion of sharing in a manner that does not require the other participant to be open. App services allow you to do this by exposing a background task to any apps that want to send data directly to it.

CHAPTER 12

Leveraging Cortana and Speech

In light of the developments we have seen in the world of mobile computing with regard to personal assistant software, it would not be hyperbole to say that speech will be a major part of the future of computing. The truth is that more and more, natural user interfaces will take computing further and further away from the ones and zeros of the digital age to a more user-centric, service-oriented world where intention masks the underlying technology used to create a digital experience. For Microsoft, products like Kinect and HoloLense exemplify this shift in interaction patterns from the old guard of mouse and keyboard to new natural ones. Search, speech, and to a greater extent Cortana sit at the center of this drive towards alternative ways of interacting with your PCs. Cortana has the following advantages:

- The world's most personal digital assistant helps you get things done throughout the day.
- A whole new natural, way of interacting with your PC.
- Available to millions of users across Windows 10 PCs, tablets, and phones.
- Integrated search across device, the Web, and personal and professional clouds.

As it is a built-in part of the search and "assistant" functionality in every Windows 10 installation, integrating into this feature set, and exposing aspects of your app through it, represents a powerful way of surfacing your apps to the user. If you are considering supporting speech interactions in your app, here are some things to consider:

- What actions can be taken through speech? Can a user navigate between pages, invoke commands, or enter data as text fields, brief notes, or long messages?
- Is speech input a good option for completing a task?
- How does a user know when speech input is available?
- Is the app always listening, or does the user need to take an action for the app to enter listening mode?
- What phrases initiate an action or behavior? Do the phrases and actions need to be enumerated on screen?
- Are prompt, confirmation, and disambiguation screens or TTS (text-to-speech) required?
- What is the interaction dialog between app and user?
- Is a custom or constrained vocabulary required (such as medicine, science, or locale) for the context of your app?
- Is network connectivity required?

In this chapter, you will learn how you can use Cortana within your apps and how you can extend the services Cortana provides through your app. Finally, you will learn how users can interact with your app through the Cortana interface without your app even running. Let's get started.

Making Your Program Speak

Text-to-speech, commonly referred to as TTS, uses a speech synthesis engine (voice) to convert a text string into spoken words. The simplest form of this takes as input the text you actually want the engine to utter. A more complex approach uses Speech Synthesis Markup Language (SSML). SSML provides a standard way to control characteristics of speech output, such as pronunciation, volume, pitch, rate or speed, and emphasis. To enable TTS in your apps, use the `SpeechSynthesizer` class. Speech requires at a minimum a MediaElement to use for playing the audio stream generated by the speech synthesizing engine. In Listing 12-1, you use TTS to add a measure of security to the employee sign-in page of Big Mountain X. Presently a passphrase is required to enter the system in this mode. You will accompany this by requiring the user to type in the text for a random phrase generated by this page, thus eliminating automated brute force attacks on the system. You start by opening `EmployeeSignIn` and modifying the XAML layout as follows.

Listing 12-1. Employee Sign-In XAML

```
<Grid Background="#FF6A6A6A">
    <MediaElement x:Name="speech_player" />
    <StackPanel Width="300"
                HorizontalAlignment="Center"
                VerticalAlignment="Center">

        <StackPanel Margin="0,0,0,5" BorderThickness="0,0,0,1" BorderBrush="Gray">
            <TextBox x:Name="txt_passphrase"
                PlaceholderText="Click speak and enter the text you hear"
                Header="Passphrase"  />
            <Button Content="Speak" Margin="0,5,0,10" Click="OnPlayPassphrase" />
        </StackPanel>

        <PasswordBox x:Name="txt_employeecode"
                     Header="Enter Passcode" />
        <Button Content="Sign In"
                Margin="0,10,0,0"
                Click="OnSignInRequested"
                HorizontalAlignment="Right" />
    </StackPanel>
</Grid>
```

The code-behind for `EmployeeSignIn` is as shown in Listing 12-2.

Listing 12-2. Employee Sign-In Code-Behind

```
public sealed partial class EmployeeSignIn : Page
{
    List<string> passphrases = new List<string>
    {
        "the quick brown fox jumped over the lazy dogs",
        "it's not you its me",
```

```
        "be the spoon",
        "don't worry be happy"
    };
    string _passphrase;
    Type _target_type;
    public EmployeeSignIn()
    {
        this.InitializeComponent();
    }

    async private void OnSignInRequested(object sender, RoutedEventArgs e)
    {
        bool failed_signin = true;
        if (!string.IsNullOrWhiteSpace(_passphrase)
            && !string.IsNullOrWhiteSpace(txt_passphrase.Text))
        {
            if (txt_employeecode.Password == "employee"
                && txt_passphrase.Text.ToLower() == _passphrase.ToLower())
            {
                failed_signin = false;
                Frame.Navigate(_target_type);
            }
        }

        if (failed_signin)
        {
            await new MessageDialog("Login Failed").ShowAsync();
        }
    }

    protected override void OnNavigatedTo(NavigationEventArgs e)
    {
        _target_type = e.Parameter as Type;
        base.OnNavigatedTo(e);
    }

    async private void OnPlayPassphrase(object sender, RoutedEventArgs e)
    {
        //select a random item
        Random random = new Random();
        int seed_value = random.Next(0, 1000);
        int selection = seed_value % 4;
        _passphrase = passphrases[selection];

        //initalize the synthesizer
        var speech = new SpeechSynthesizer();

        //create an audio stream of the text
        var speech_stream = await speech.SynthesizeTextToStreamAsync(_passphrase);
```

```
        //set the stream
        speech_player.SetSource(speech_stream, speech_stream.ContentType);
    }
}
```

In Listing 12-2, you first add two new fields to the class, one that contains the list of possible passphrases that the sign-in screen uses to prompt employees and the other a variable for storing the currently active prompt. When the Play button is clicked, you generate a random number and use it to pick which of the phrases will be used for validation. You then generate a stream of the synthesized audio for that text using `SynthesizeTextToStreamAsync` and then play it in the MediaElement using the `SetSource` function of the control. Finally, you modify the sign-in handler to ensure that the text entered into the passphrase field matches the currently selected passphrase. If so, the user is signed in.

Using SSML

For straightforward situations like the scenario just described, passing a text string directly into the speech synthesizer works fine. But what if you want to apply emphasis to certain words, or pause between saying one word and another? SSML can be used to describe the manner in which you want a speech synthesis engine to read text that is inputted into it. The structure of SSML documents is beyond the scope of this text but you can find out about it at `www.w3.org/TR/speech-synthesis/`. In the following example, you will use four different SSML documents to present the same content as you did before. From this you should begin to get a sense of the power of utilizing this technique. You start by defining the markup for the speaking, create four XML documents in the `Media/Audio` folder called `phrase1`, `phrase2`, `phrase3`, and `phrase4` and define each as shown in Listing 12-3.

Listing 12-3. SSML File

```
Phrase 1
<speak version="1.0" xmlns="http://www.w3.org/2001/10/synthesis" xml:lang="en-us">

    The quick brown fox jumped over the

    <prosody duration="1000ms"  contour="(0%,+20Hz) (10%,+30%) (40%,+10Hz)">Lazy</prosody>
    dogs.

</speak>

Phrase 2
<speak version="1.0" xmlns="http://www.w3.org/2001/10/synthesis" xml:lang="en-us">
  It's not you
    <break time="1000ms" />
    It's me
</speak>

Phrase 3
<speak version="1.0" xmlns="http://www.w3.org/2001/10/synthesis" xml:lang="en-us">
    <prosody contour="(0%,+80Hz) (10%,+80%) (40%,+80Hz)">Be the spoon</prosody>
</speak>
```

```
Phrase 4
<speak version="1.0" xmlns="http://www.w3.org/2001/10/synthesis" xml:lang="en-us">
    Dont worry
    <break time="500ms" />
   be happy
</speak>
```

With these files defined, you must now modify the code base for EmployeeSignIn to allow for them to be used. When synthesizing speech using unadorned text, you used the function SynthesizeTextToStreamAsync. For synthesizing speech based on an SSML file, you use SynthesizeSsmlToStreamAsync. Listing 12-4 shows the changes to be made.

Listing 12-4. Employee Sign-In

```
public sealed partial class EmployeeSignIn : Page
{
    List<dynamic> passphrases = new List<dynamic>
    {
            new {Phrase= "the quick brown fox jumped over the lazy dogs",File="phrase1.xml" },
            new { Phrase="it's not you its me",File="phrase2.xml" },
            new  { Phrase="be the spoon",File="phrase3.xml" },
            new  { Phrase="don't worry be happy",File="phrase4.xml" }
    };

    string _passphrase;
    Type _target_type;
    public EmployeeSignIn()
    {
        this.InitializeComponent();
    }

    async private void OnSignInRequested(object sender, RoutedEventArgs e)
    {
        bool failed_signin = true;
        if (!string.IsNullOrWhiteSpace(_passphrase)
            && !string.IsNullOrWhiteSpace(txt_passphrase.Text))
        {
            if (txt_employeecode.Password == "employee"
                && txt_passphrase.Text.ToLower() == _passphrase.ToLower())
            {
                failed_signin = false;
                Frame.Navigate(_target_type);
            }
        }

        if (failed_signin)
        {
            await new MessageDialog("Login Failed").ShowAsync();
        }
    }
```

```
    protected override void OnNavigatedTo(NavigationEventArgs e)
    {
        _target_type = e.Parameter as Type;
        base.OnNavigatedTo(e);
    }

    async private void OnPlayPassphrase(object sender, RoutedEventArgs e)
    {
        //select a random item
        Random random = new Random();
        int seed_value = random.Next(0, 1000);
        int selection = seed_value % 4;
        var tuple = passphrases[selection];

        _passphrase = tuple.Phrase;

        var ssml_path = $"ms-appx:///media/audio/{tuple.File}";
        var ssml_uri = new Uri(ssml_path);
        var ssml_file = await StorageFile.GetFileFromApplicationUriAsync(ssml_uri);
        var ssml_string = await ssml_file.ReadTextAsync();

        //initalize the synthesizer
        var speech = new SpeechSynthesizer();

        //create an audio stream of the text
        var speech_stream = await speech.SynthesizeSsmlToStreamAsync(ssml_string);

        //set the stream
        speech_player.SetSource(speech_stream, speech_stream.ContentType);
    }
}
```

In Listing 12-4, you modify the code-behind for EmployeeSignIn such that it uses an SSML file instead of unadorned text to present an audio prompt to the user. The key change in the code base is modifying the list of passphrases from being a list of strings to a list of dynamic objects that have a Phrase and File property. Phrase continues to represent the passphrase while File points to the location where the SSML for that passphrase is stored. When an item is selected from the list, you use the Phrase portion of the item to store the value you will eventually use to test against the user's input. You use the other value, File, to generate a path to the SSML file bearing that name. You then read the file and use the adorned string that is returned to call SynthesizeSsmlToStreamAsync.

Be mindful of the user experience when designing your apps to use speech synthesis. You should have a clear sense of the use cases where speech provides an additive element to the experience, such as reading a text message out to the user. You should consider whether you should read long strings of text. It's one thing to listen to a text message, but quite another to listen to a long list of search results that are difficult to remember. Also, try to design prompts that are polite and encouraging. If you believe the audio might be on the long side, you should provide media controls to let users pause, or stop, TTS. You should listen to all TTS strings to ensure they are intelligible and sound natural. Stringing together an unusual sequence of words or speaking part numbers or punctuation might cause a phrase to become unintelligible.

Recognizing Speech

Speech recognition does the exact opposite of what speech synthesizing does. It converts words spoken by the user into text, which ultimately can be used for form input, for text dictation, to specify an action or command, and to accomplish tasks. In Windows 10, both predefined grammars for free-text dictation and web search, and custom grammars authored using Speech Recognition Grammar Specification (SRGS) are supported.

Speech recognition is made up of a speech runtime, recognition APIs for programming the runtime, ready-to-use grammars for dictation and web search, and a default system UI that helps users discover and use speech recognition features. Speech for text input can range from short form (single word or phrase) to long form (continuous dictation). Short form input must be less than 10 seconds in length, while long form input session can be up to two minutes in length. (Long form input can be restarted without user intervention to give the impression of continuous dictation.) Take note of the following guidelines when implementing speech recognition in your apps:

- Always provide a visual cue to indicate that speech recognition is supported and available to the user and whether the user needs to turn it on.
- Provide ongoing recognition feedback to minimize any apparent lack of response while recognition is being performed.
- Let users revise recognition text using keyboard input, disambiguation prompts, suggestions, or additional speech recognition.
- Stop recognition if input is detected from a device other than speech recognition, such as touch or keyboard. This probably indicates that the user has moved onto another task, such as correcting the recognition text or interacting with other form fields.
- Specify the length of time for which no speech input indicates that recognition is over. Do not automatically restart recognition after this period of time because it typically indicates the user has stopped engaging with your app.
- Disable all continuous recognition UI and terminate the recognition session if a network connection is not available. Continuous recognition requires a network connection.

In the example to follow, you will be using speech recognition as an alternative authentication mechanism on the `EmployeeSignIn` page. If the user does not want to type in the text that they are prompted with, they can alternatively speak a written prompt in order to gain access to the employee portal area of the app. To get started, be sure to add the Microphone capability to the app (it should already be added from your work in Chapter 7). In Listing 12-5, you modify the layout of `EmployeeSignIn` to include the section for using a verbal phrase to authenticate.

Listing 12-5. Modified Employee SignIn

```
<Grid Background="#FF6A6A6A">
    <MediaElement x:Name="speech_player" />
    <StackPanel Width="300"
                HorizontalAlignment="Center"
                VerticalAlignment="Center">

        <StackPanel Margin="0,0,0,5"
                    BorderThickness="0,0,0,1"
                    BorderBrush="Gray">
```

```
            <PasswordBox x:Name="txt_employeecode2"
                         PlaceholderText="Enter passcode"
                         Header="Voice Authentication" />
            <Button  Content="Voice Sign In"
                     HorizontalAlignment="Right"
                     Margin="0,5,0,10"
                     Click="OnSayPrompt" />
        </StackPanel>
        <StackPanel Margin="0,0,0,5"
                    BorderThickness="0,0,0,1"
                    BorderBrush="Gray">
            <TextBox x:Name="txt_passphrase"
                     PlaceholderText="Click speak and enter the text you hear"
                     Header="Listen Authentication" />
            <Button Content="Listen"
                    Margin="0,5,0,10"
                    Click="OnPlayPassphrase" />
        </StackPanel>

        <PasswordBox x:Name="txt_employeecode"
                     PlaceholderText="Enter passcode"
                     Header="Just enter passcode" />
        <Button Content="Sign In"
                Margin="0,10,0,0"
                Click="OnSignInRequested"
                HorizontalAlignment="Right" />
    </StackPanel>
</Grid>
```

In Listing 12-5 you add a new StackPanel that contains a PasswordBox/Button combo. This time, instead of simply testing the value entered into the PasswordBox, you also test to ensure that the user utters a certain passphrase. If there is no match between what is said and what is expected, the sign-in will not occur. Listing 12-6 shows the code-behind.

Listing 12-6. Employee SignIn Code-Behind

```
public sealed partial class EmployeeSignIn : Page
{
    List<dynamic> passphrases = new List<dynamic>
    {
            new {Phrase= "the quick brown fox jumped over the lazy dogs",File="phrase1.xml" },
            new { Phrase="it's not you it's me",File="phrase2.xml" },
            new  { Phrase="be the spoon",File="phrase3.xml" },
            new  { Phrase="don't worry be happy",File="phrase4.xml" }
    };

    string _passphrase;
    Type _target_type;

    ...
```

```
async private void OnSayPrompt(object sender, RoutedEventArgs e)
{
    try
    {
        var button = sender as Button;
        button.Content = "…";
        bool failed_signin = true;
        Random random = new Random();
        int seed_value = random.Next(0, 1000);
        int selection = seed_value % 4;
        var tuple = passphrases[selection];

        var prompt = (string)tuple.Phrase;

        //general dictation
        var recognizer = new SpeechRecognizer();

        recognizer.UIOptions.ExampleText = $"Repeat the phrase '{prompt}'";
        await recognizer.CompileConstraintsAsync();
        var result = await recognizer.RecognizeWithUIAsync();
        if (result.Status == SpeechRecognitionResultStatus.Success)
        {
            if (result.Text.ToLower() == prompt.ToLower())
            {
                if (txt_employeecode2.Password == "employee")
                {
                    failed_signin = false;
                    Frame.Navigate(_target_type);
                }
            }

        }

        if (failed_signin)
        {
            button.Content = "Failed connection";
        }
    }
    catch (Exception ex)
    {
        await new MessageDialog(ex.Message).ShowAsync();
    }
}

}
```

Listing 12-6 uses the `SpeechRecognizer` class to call the function `RecorgnizeWithUIAsync`. This function displays a modal dialog that indicates to the user that speech recognition is happening. Figure 12-1 shows how the app looks when run and speech recognition is enabled through the “Voice Sign In” button.

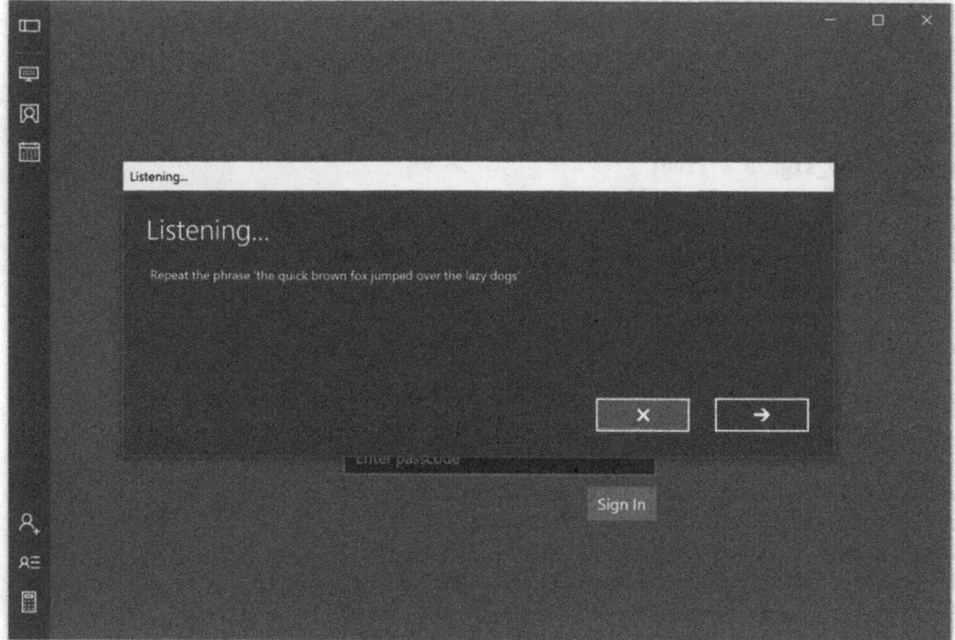

Figure 12-1. *Voice command pop-up UI*

With the passcode entered, pressing this button opens up the system-wide voice recognition dialog. In your example, you present the user with the term you want them to say within this dialog. You can also set a number of other values regarding the way the dialog appear (or even if it appears at all) through the many properties of this class.

Constraints and Grammars

By default, when nothing more is done with the `SpeechRecognizer` instance beyond initializing it, compiling its constraints, and begin recognizing, the framework is in dictation mode. In this mode, it will listen to whatever is said by the user and try it's best to translate that to text verbatim. If this basic functionality is less than ideal for your scenario, then you can use constraints to extend what the recognizer listens for. A constraint defines the words and phrases (vocabulary) that an app recognizes in speech input. They are at the core of speech recognition and give your app great influence over the accuracy of speech recognition. Constraints are applied using predefined grammars, which provide speech recognition for your app without requiring you to author a grammar. When using these grammars, speech recognition is performed by a remote web service and the results are returned to the device. (A grammar can be thought of as a list of words indexed by the words that map to them.)

Because predefined dictation and web-search grammars can be large, and because they are online (not on the device), performance might not be as fast as with a custom grammar installed on the device. They can be used to recognize up to 10 seconds of speech input and require no authoring effort on your part. However, they do require connection to a network.

As stated, the default free-text dictation grammar can recognize most words and phrases that a user can say in a particular language, and is optimized to recognize short phrases. The predefined dictation grammar is used if you don't specify any constraints for your `SpeechRecognizer` object. Free-text dictation is useful when you don't want to limit the kinds of things a user can say. You use this in your example.

SpeechRecognitionListConstraint

Programmatic list constraints provide a lightweight approach to creating simple grammars using a list of words or phrases. A list constraint works well for recognizing short, distinct phrases. Explicitly specifying all words in a grammar also improves recognition accuracy because the speech recognition engine must only process speech to confirm a match. The list can also be programmatically updated. List constraints consist of an array of strings that represents speech input that your app will accept for a recognition operation. You can create a list constraint in your app by creating a speech-recognition list-constraint object and passing an array of strings. Then add that object to the constraints collection of the recognizer. Recognition is successful when the speech recognizer recognizes any one of the strings in the array. In Listing 12-7, you change your example to use a list constraint instead of the generic grammar.

Listing 12-7. OnSayPrompt Method

```
async private void OnSayPrompt(object sender, RoutedEventArgs e)
{
    try
    {
        var button = sender as Button;
        button.Content = "...";
        bool failed_signin = true;
        Random random = new Random();
        int seed_value = random.Next(0, 1000);
        int selection = seed_value % 4;
        var tuple = passphrases[selection];

        var prompt = (string)tuple.Phrase;
        //general dictation
        var recognizer = new SpeechRecognizer();
        var phrases = passphrases.Select(i => (string)i.Phrase).ToList();

        var list_constraint = new SpeechRecognitionListConstraint(phrases);
        recognizer.Constraints.Add(list_constraint);

        recognizer.UIOptions.ExampleText = $"Repeat the phrase '{prompt}'";
        await recognizer.CompileConstraintsAsync();
        var result = await recognizer.RecognizeWithUIAsync();
        if (result.Status == SpeechRecognitionResultStatus.Success)
        {
            if (result.Text.ToLower() == prompt.ToLower())
            {
                if (txt_employeecode2.Password == "employee")
                {
                    failed_signin = false;
                    Frame.Navigate(_target_type);
                }
            }

        }
```

```
        if (failed_signin)
        {
            button.Content = "Failed connection";
        }
    }
    catch (Exception ex)
    {
        await new MessageDialog(ex.Message).ShowAsync();
    }
}
```

The only change needed to implement this approach is creating the constraint and adding it to the list of constraints available to the recognizer. To get the list of phrases your recognizer supports, you use a LINQ expression to extract just the phrase part of your phrase list into a list of strings. Using this approach, you should notice that the process of recognizing is much faster. This is because there is no need to go out to the Internet. The recognizer waits until it hears the targeted words in the prescribed order and only marks the input text as recognized when this happens.

You can perform voice recognition without the user interface altogether, and even perform continuous speech recognition if needed. Listing 12-8 shows how continuous integration in an app might work. When using continuous recognition, be sure to stop recognizing when done.

Listing 12-8. OnContinuousRecognize Method

```
async private void OnContinuousRecognize(object sender, RoutedEventArgs e)
{
    var recognizer = new SpeechRecognizer();
    await recognizer.CompileConstraintsAsync();
    recognizer.ContinuousRecognitionSession.ResultGenerated += async (s, args) =>
    {
        await txt_dictation.Dispatcher.RunAsync(CoreDispatcherPriority.Normal, () =>
            {
                txt_dictation.Text += args.Result.Text;
            });
    };
    await recognizer.ContinuousRecognitionSession.StartAsync(SpeechContinuousRecognitionMo
de.Default);
}
```

The code in Listing 12-9 shows some of the properties that can be set on the recognizer user interface to customize it to your liking.

Listing 12-9. SpeechRecognizer Properties

```
var recognizer = new SpeechRecognizer();
recognizer.UIOptions.ExampleText = "You can say 'Something'";
recognizer.UIOptions.AudiblePrompt = "Say something I'm giving up on you.";
recognizer.UIOptions.IsReadBackEnabled = true;
recognizer.UIOptions.ShowConfirmation = true;
```

Listing 12-10 shows how recognition can be done without launching the default recognition dialog. This can be useful in scenarios where the developer would like to use their own user interface.

Listing 12-10. Using SpeechRecognizer

```
var recognizer = new SpeechRecognizer();
var topic = new SpeechRecognitionTopicConstraint(SpeechRecognitionScenario.WebSearch,
"webSearch");
recognizer.Constraints.Add(topic);
await recognizer.CompileConstraintsAsync();
var result = await recognizer.RecognizeAsync();
txt_dictation.Text = result.Text;
```

Using Cortana

The easiest way to use Cortana is to click the Cortana button on your system task bar. Your system settings may have Cortana set up in its mini form, as the full text box on the taskbar, or not showing at all. Additionally, you may be able to access Cortana by simply saying "Hey, Cortana." This particular form of activating Cortana only works when you have configured it to be activated in this manner. Figure 12-2 shows the basic user interface for the feature.

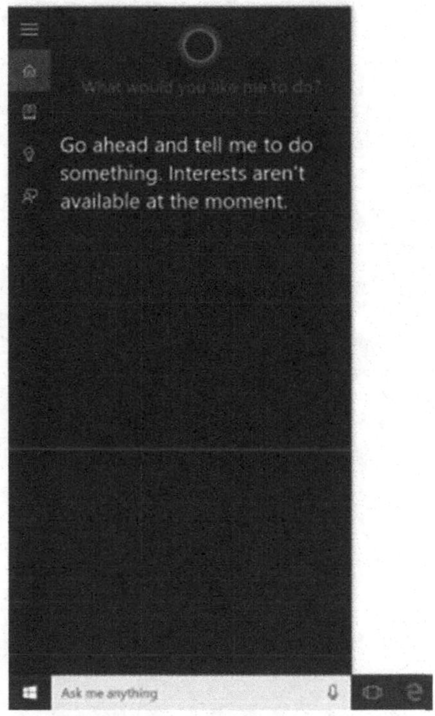

Figure 12-2. *Cortana UI*

Figure 12-3 shows the settings pane for Cortana. Unlike the other settings on Windows 10 systems, the Cortana settings area shows up within the Cortana interface rather than the settings app. You can still use the Settings app to activate that view directly.

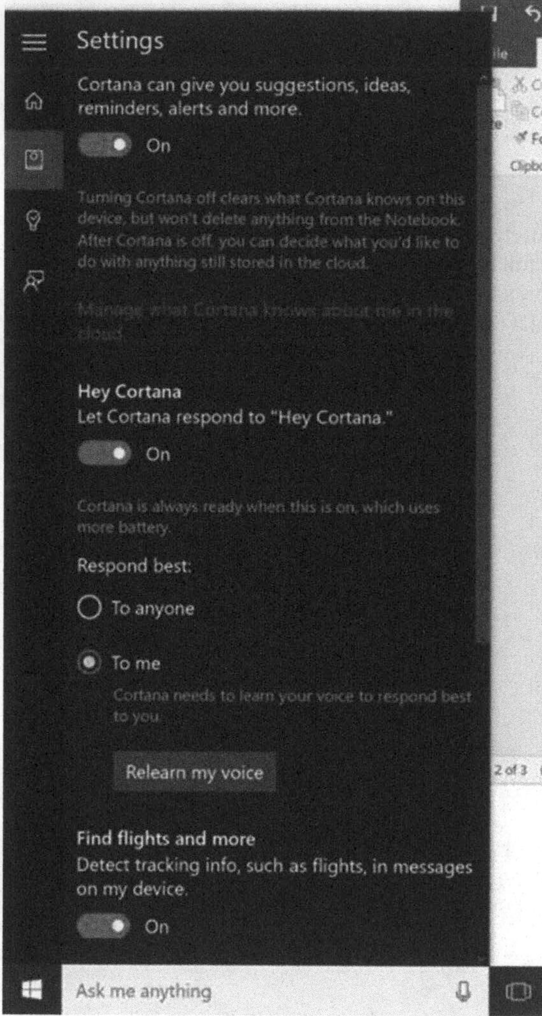

Figure 12-3. *Cortana settings UI*

Setting Up for Cortana

Incorporating sound into your app is a great way to introduce voice interactivity for your users. With the voice interactivity you have examined thus far, your app must be running in order for it to be utilized. With Cortana integration, this is does not have to be the case. The UWP allows for you to use Cortana to launch your UWP apps as though they were commands intrinsically built into the tool. The user's voice input is interpreted and then used to start the app that corresponds to the alias provided by the user. It is passed into the app as a parameter of the `OnActivated` method. Apps launched in this manner are launched into the foreground, meaning that the app takes focus and Cortana is dismissed. In general, this type of interactivity is best for commands that require additional context or user input.

In the following example, you will be adding some functionality to Cortana that enables the user to find the upcoming events that the Big Mountain Theater company is putting on. To get the processing going, however, you will need to add a few new pages to the mix. The first page will be for creating events; you will need this so you can populate the system with events. The second will be an events list page which you will use to list events that fit a given search criterion (by default this page will return all appointments). You start the process with a bit of homework in the `AppState` object. Add a new property to represent the list of events available at a given time. Listing 12-11 illustrates.

Listing 12-11. Events List

```
public List<BMXEvent> Events { get; set; } = new List<BMXEvent>();
```

Now open ApplicationHostPage and add a new button to the SplitView for accessing the event management functionality. Add this to the “Manage Contacts” button as shown in Listing 12-12.

Listing 12-12. Manage Events Button

```
...
<Button HorizontalAlignment="Stretch"
        HorizontalContentAlignment="Left"
        Margin="0,5,0,0"
        Click="OnPatronCounterClicked"
        Background="Transparent">
    <StackPanel Orientation="Horizontal">
        <SymbolIcon Symbol="AddFriend"
                    Margin="0,0,20,0" />
        <TextBlock Text="Patron Counter" />
    </StackPanel>
</Button>
<Button HorizontalAlignment="Stretch"
        HorizontalContentAlignment="Left"
        Margin="0,5,0,0"
        Click="OnManageEventsClicked"
        Background="Transparent">
    <StackPanel Orientation="Horizontal">
        <SymbolIcon Symbol="CalendarDay"
                    Margin="0,0,20,0" />
        <TextBlock Text="Manage Events" />
    </StackPanel>
</Button>
    <Button HorizontalAlignment="Stretch"
            HorizontalContentAlignment="Left"
            Margin="0,5,0,0"
            Click="OnManageContactsClicked"
            Background="Transparent">
        <StackPanel Orientation="Horizontal">
            <SymbolIcon Symbol="ContactInfo"
                        Margin="0,0,20,0" />
            <TextBlock Text="Manage Contacts" />
        </StackPanel>
    </Button>
...
```

Before moving forward, add a new page to the project called ManageEventsPage with the default layout provided by Visual Studio. You'll get to it in a moment; for now, create an `OnManageEventsClicked` event handler to match the event exposed by the Manage Events button in ApplicationHostPage. Implement is as shown in Listing 12-13.

Listing 12-13. Manage Events Handler

```
private void OnManageEventsClicked(object sender, RoutedEventArgs e)
{
    root_frame.Navigate(typeof(EmployeeSignIn), typeof(ManageEventsPage));
}
```

As with all the other employee-facing screens in the app, clicking Manage Events navigates the user to EmployeeSignIn where they must enter credentials in one of the ways you have previously specified.

The next step is to implement the code for actually creating events. For good measure, you will also add a page for listing all events currently planned. This is the page where the command to create a new event will reside. Listing 12-14 shows the modified XAML layout for the page ManageEventsPage. Add it as shown.

Listing 12-14. ManageEventPage XAML

```
<Grid Background="#FF6A6A6A">
    <ListView x:Name="gridview_events"
              SelectionMode="Single"
              ItemsSource="{x:Bind Events, Mode=OneWay}"
              IsItemClickEnabled="True"
              ItemClick="EventSelected">
        <ListView.ItemTemplate>
            <DataTemplate>
                <StackPanel Orientation="Vertical">
                    <Border HorizontalAlignment="Stretch"
                            Height="15"
                            Margin="5,5,10,5"
                            Width="Auto"
                            BorderThickness="0"
                            BorderBrush="Gray"
                            Background="Gainsboro">

                    </Border>
                    <TextBlock Text="{Binding EventTitle}"
                               FontSize="24"
                               FontWeight="ExtraLight"
                               VerticalAlignment="Center" />
                    <TextBlock Text="{Binding StartDateTime.Date}"
                               FontSize="24"
                               FontWeight="ExtraLight"
                               VerticalAlignment="Center" />
                    <TextBlock Text="{Binding StartDateTime.TimeOfDay}"
                               FontSize="24"
                               FontWeight="ExtraLight"
                               VerticalAlignment="Center" />
                    <TextBlock Text="{Binding Address}"
                               FontSize="12" TextWrapping="Wrap"
```

```
                                FontWeight="ExtraLight"
                                VerticalAlignment="Center" />
                </StackPanel>
            </DataTemplate>
        </ListView.ItemTemplate>
    </ListView>
</Grid>
```

ManageEventsPage uses the familiar compiled binding pattern you have been utilizing since its introduction. The OneNewEventClicked event opens a new page called CreateEventPage. (Take the time to add a new page to the project with this name.) Implement the code-behind for ManageEventsPage as shown in Listing 12-15.

Listing 12-15. ManageEventsPage Code-Behind

```
public sealed partial class ManageEventsPage : Page, INotifyPropertyChanged
{
    public event PropertyChangedEventHandler PropertyChanged;
    List<BMXEvent> Events { get; set; }

    public ManageEventsPage()
    {
        this.InitializeComponent();
        this.Loaded += ManageEventsPage_Loaded;
    }

    private void ManageEventsPage_Loaded(object sender, RoutedEventArgs e)
    {
        Events = App.State.Events;
        PropertyChanged?.Invoke(this, new PropertyChangedEventArgs("Events"));
    }

    private void OnNewEventClicked(object sender, RoutedEventArgs e)
    {
        Frame.Navigate(typeof(CreateEventPage),null);
    }

    private void EventSelected(object sender, ItemClickEventArgs e)
    {
        Frame.Navigate(typeof(CreateEventPage), e.ClickedItem);
    }
}
```

The interesting thing about this page is that when CreateEventPage is navigated to it passes either a null (for a new event being created), or an event instance selected from the list being displayed on the page. Now add the CreateEventPage to the project and implement its XAML layout as shown in Listing 12-16.

Listing 12-16. CreateEventPage XAML

```
<ScrollViewer HorizontalScrollBarVisibility="Auto"
              HorizontalScrollMode="Auto">
    <StackPanel Orientation="Vertical"
                Width="350"
                Background="#FF6A6A6A"
                HorizontalAlignment="Center">
        <TextBox x:Name="txt_eventtitle"
                 Header="Event Title"
                 Margin="10"
                 HorizontalAlignment="Stretch" />
        <TextBox x:Name="txt_eventdescription"
                 Header="Event Description"
                 Margin="10"
                 AcceptsReturn="True"
                 Height="200"
                 HorizontalAlignment="Stretch" />
        <TextBox x:Name="txt_address"
                 Header="Event Address"
                 Margin="10"
                 HorizontalAlignment="Stretch" />
        <CalendarDatePicker x:Name="control_calendar"
                            HorizontalAlignment="Stretch"
                            Margin="10"
                            Header="Event Day"
                            VerticalAlignment="Top"
                            PlaceholderText="What day will it be held?"
                                />
        <TimePicker x:Name="control_time"
                    Header="What time will it be held?"
                    Margin="10"
                    HorizontalAlignment="Stretch"
                    VerticalAlignment="Top" />
        <Slider x:Name="slider_duration"
                Header="Event Duration"
                HorizontalAlignment="Stretch"
                Minimum="1"
                Maximum="24"
                Margin="10"
                VerticalAlignment="Top" />
        <StackPanel Orientation="Horizontal">
            <Button Margin="10"
                    Content="Save"
                    Width="100"
                    Click="SaveEvent" />
```

```
            <Button Margin="10"
                    Width="100"
                    Content="Cancel"
                    Click="CancelEvent" />
        </StackPanel>
    </StackPanel>

</ScrollViewer>
```

In Listing 12-16, the user interface elements on the page are meant to basically capture the fields of the BMXEvent class so that you can either create a new one, or edit one that has already been created and passed in. Listing 12-17 shows the code-behind for this page.

Listing 12-17. CreateEventPage Code-Behind

```
public sealed partial class CreateEventPage : Page
{
    BMXEvent CurrentEvent;

    public CreateEventPage()
    {
        this.InitializeComponent();
    }

    async private void SaveEvent(object sender, RoutedEventArgs e)
    {
        var default_position = new BasicGeoposition
        {
            Latitude = 40.7484,
            Longitude = -73.9857,
        };
        Geopoint point = new Geopoint(default_position);
        var lat = default_position.Latitude;
        var lon = default_position.Longitude;

        if (CurrentEvent == null)
        {
            CurrentEvent = new BMXEvent
            {
                EventID = Guid.NewGuid(),
                EventTitle = txt_eventtitle.Text,
                Description = txt_eventdescription.Text,
                Address = txt_address.Text,
                Longitude = lon,
                Latitude = lat,
                CreateDate = DateTime.Now,
                Duration = TimeSpan.FromHours(slider_duration.Value),
                StartDateTime = control_calendar.Date.Value.Date.Add(control_time.Time),
            };
        }
```

```
        else
        {
            CurrentEvent.EventTitle = txt_eventtitle.Text;
            CurrentEvent.Description = txt_eventdescription.Text;
            CurrentEvent.Address = txt_address.Text;
            CurrentEvent.Longitude = lon;
            CurrentEvent.Latitude = lat;
            CurrentEvent.CreateDate = DateTime.Now;
            CurrentEvent.Duration = TimeSpan.FromHours(slider_duration.Value);
            CurrentEvent.StartDateTime = control_calendar.Date.Value.Date.Add
            (control_time.Time);
        }

        App.State.Events.Add(CurrentEvent);
        await App.State.SaveAsync();
        Frame.GoBack();
    }

    private void CancelEvent(object sender, RoutedEventArgs e)
    {
        Frame.GoBack();
    }

    protected override void OnNavigatedTo(NavigationEventArgs e)
    {
        if (e.Parameter != null)
        {
            CurrentEvent = e.Parameter as BMXEvent;

            //brute force populate fields
            txt_eventtitle.Text = CurrentEvent.EventTitle;
            txt_eventdescription.Text = CurrentEvent.Description;
            txt_address.Text = CurrentEvent.Address;
            control_calendar.Date = CurrentEvent.StartDateTime;
            slider_duration.Value = CurrentEvent.Duration.Hours;
        }

    }
}
```

Let's start the examination of Listing 12-17 with the OnNavigatedTo handler. In it, you test the Parameter property to see if it is null. If there is a value passed in through this property, you use its state to initialize all the fields on the page.

When the Save button is clicked, SaveEvent is called to handle it. For the purposes of this example, we have set up this page so that every event will be geographically located at the Empire State Building, regardless of the actual address. When you implement this yourself, you may want to use MapLocationFinder.FindLocationsAsync to retrieve a meaningful geoposition based on the address the user enters. After the first part of the function does this, you test to see if CurrentEvent has a value associated with it. If it does, you can skip any initialization code; just set the values of the object based on the values specified in fields. Otherwise, you initialize the object first, and then set its values. Run the code and add a good number of events into the system. You should have enough events with varying start times, durations, and addresses to allow for meaningful queries to be performed on the data you provide.

Be sure to have different values in each of the fields from entry to entry. It won't break your code to ignore this request but it will make it harder to identify the different events you have created.

In the next part of this section, you will write search methods that can be used to query and retrieve the list of events based on the criteria you have outlines here. Figure 12-4 shows how ManageEventPage looks on your machine. Note that a ListView is used here and not a GridView so the items appear vertically from top to bottom.

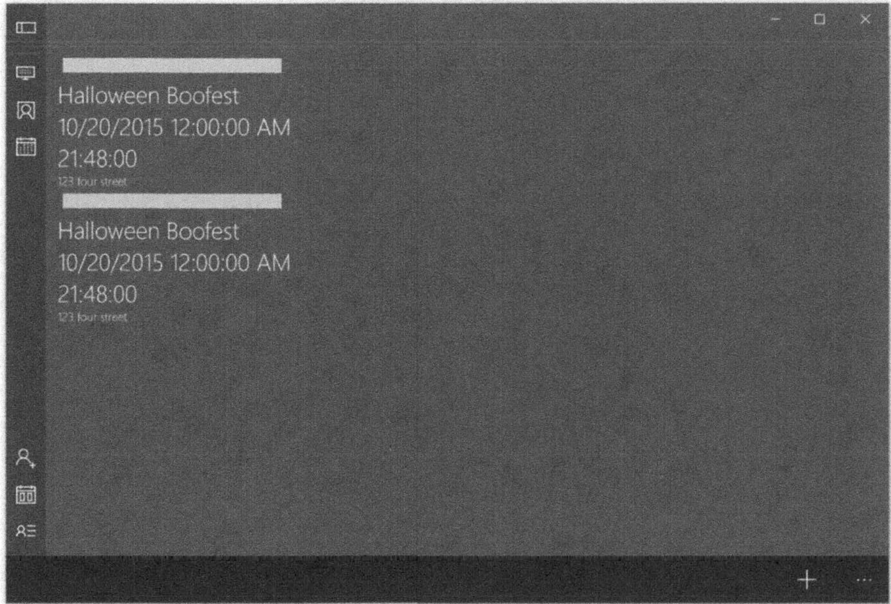

Figure 12-4. *Manage events view*

When the plus button at the bottom right of the page is clicked, the CreateEventPage will be initialized. That page should look like Figure 12-5.

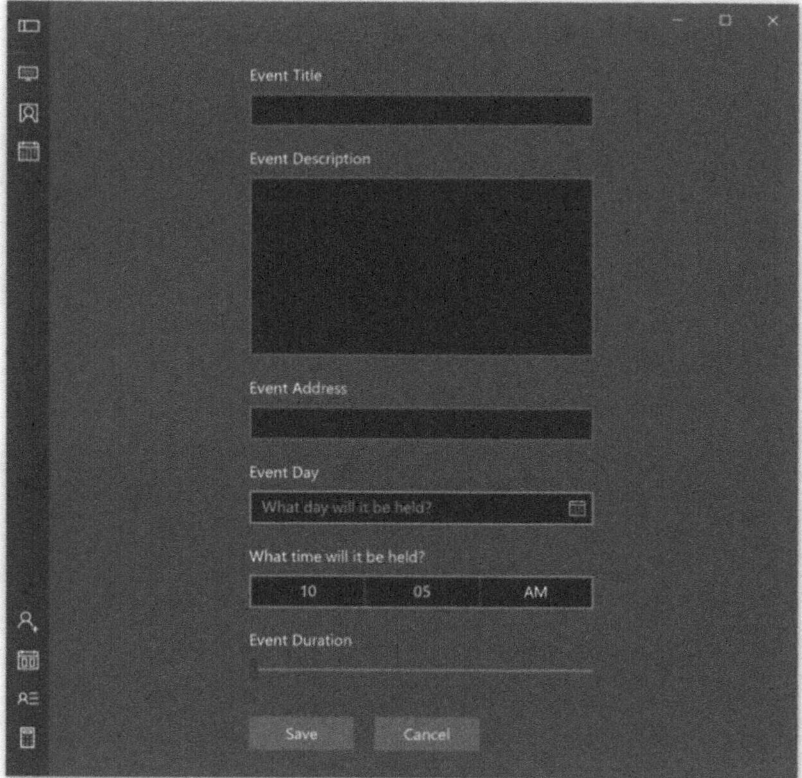

Figure 12-5. *Create Events view*

If you use the edit functionality you will notice that there is a little surprise "bug" in the mix to help with quickly populating events. In case you didn't catch it, the `App.State.Events.Add(CurrentEvent)` should only be called when a new BMXEvent is created; right now it is being called regardless of whether an item is created or edited. I used this technique to quickly create copies of the same basic event with different locations. Once you feel you have enough, be sure to move that line to the right location.

There are two more steps you need to take before you begin your Cortana integration example. First, you need to create a new page, ListEventsPage that essentially mirrors ManageEventsPage in XAML layout with one exception. This page will use a GridView instead of a ListView control. Add the page and implement it as shown in Listing 12-18.

Listing 12-18. ListEventsPage XAML

```
<Grid Background="#FF6A6A6A">
    <GridView x:Name="gridview_events"
              SelectionMode="Single"
              Margin="0,0,0,50"
              ItemsSource="{x:Bind Events, Mode=OneWay}"
              IsItemClickEnabled="True"
              ItemClick="EventSelected">
        <GridView.ItemTemplate>
            <DataTemplate>
```

```
                <StackPanel Orientation="Vertical">
                    <Border HorizontalAlignment="Stretch"
                            Height="15"
                            Margin="5,5,10,5"
                            Width="Auto"
                            BorderThickness="0"
                            BorderBrush="Gray"
                            Background="Gainsboro">
                    </Border>
                    <TextBlock Text="{Binding EventTitle}"
                               FontSize="24"
                               FontWeight="ExtraLight"
                               VerticalAlignment="Center" />
                    <TextBlock Text="{Binding StartDateTime.Date}"
                               FontSize="24"
                               FontWeight="ExtraLight"
                               VerticalAlignment="Center" />
                    <TextBlock Text="{Binding StartDateTime.TimeOfDay}"
                               FontSize="24"
                               FontWeight="ExtraLight"
                               VerticalAlignment="Center" />
                    <TextBlock Text="{Binding Address}"
                               FontSize="12"
                               TextWrapping="Wrap"
                               FontWeight="ExtraLight"
                               VerticalAlignment="Center" />
                </StackPanel>
            </DataTemplate>
        </GridView.ItemTemplate>
    </GridView>
    <Button Margin="5" HorizontalAlignment="Left" VerticalAlignment="Bottom"
            Content="Done"
            Width="100"
            Click="CompletedEvent" />
</Grid>
```

Besides changing the root data control that will present the list of events to the user, this page also removes the Add button from the button right corner of the page and replaces it with a Done button. Later in this section, when you add the code-behind for this class, you will see the significance of this button.

You also need to add a new page for displaying event information. This page defers from the CreateEventPage in that it is a read-only view of event information. Add a new page to the project called ViewEventPage and implement the layout for this page as shown in Listing 12-19.

Listing 12-19. ViewEventPage XAML

```
<ScrollViewer HorizontalScrollBarVisibility="Auto"
              HorizontalScrollMode="Auto" >
    <StackPanel Orientation="Vertical"
              Width="350"
              Background="#FF6A6A6A"
              HorizontalAlignment="Center">
```

```
        <TextBox x:Name="txt_eventtitle"
                 Header="Event Title"
                 Margin="10" IsReadOnly="True"
                 HorizontalAlignment="Stretch" />
        <TextBox x:Name="txt_eventdescription"
                 Header="Event Description"
                 Margin="10"
                 IsReadOnly="True"
                 AcceptsReturn="True"
                 Height="200"
                 HorizontalAlignment="Stretch" />
        <TextBox x:Name="txt_address"
                 IsReadOnly="True"
                 Header="Event Address"
                 Margin="10"
                 HorizontalAlignment="Stretch" />
        <CalendarDatePicker x:Name="control_calendar"
                            HorizontalAlignment="Stretch"
                            Margin="10"
                            IsEnabled="False"
                            Header="Event Day"
                            VerticalAlignment="Top"
                            PlaceholderText="What day will it be held?" />
        <TimePicker x:Name="control_time"
                    Header="What time will it be held?"
                    Margin="10" IsEnabled="True"
                    HorizontalAlignment="Stretch"
                    VerticalAlignment="Top" />
        <Slider x:Name="slider_duration" IsEnabled="False"
                Header="Event Duration"
                HorizontalAlignment="Stretch"
                Minimum="1"
                Maximum="24"
                Margin="10"
                VerticalAlignment="Top" />
        <StackPanel Orientation="Horizontal">

            <Button Margin="10"
                    Width="100"
                    Content="Done"
                    Click="CompletedEvent" />
        </StackPanel>
    </StackPanel>

</ScrollViewer>
```

Take a look at Listing 12-19 and you will notice that the controls on the page are either disabled or set as read-only. Unlike its counterpart, this page is the designed to display information, not edit it.

You now go back to ListEventsPage and show the implementation of its code-behind. Listing 12-20 illustrates.

Listing 12-20. ListEventsPage Code

```
public sealed partial class ListEventsPage : Page
{
    List<BMXEvent> Events { get; set; }

    public ListEventsPage(List<BMXEvent> events)
    {
        Events = events;
        this.InitializeComponent();
    }

    private void EventSelected(object sender, ItemClickEventArgs e)
    {
        Window.Current.Content = new ViewEventPage(Events, e.ClickedItem as BMXEvent);
    }

    private void CompletedEvent(object sender, RoutedEventArgs e)
    {
        Window.Current.Content = new ApplicationHostPage();
    }
}
```

In Listing 12-20, you implement the EventSelected handler and in it navigated the user to the ViewEventPage, passing in the item that was selected and the entire search result list. You also implement the `CompletedEvent` handler, which also navigates to ApplicationHostPage in the same manner (by switching the primary content of the window). This should give you a clue as to the nature of this page. If it is a peer to ApplicationHostPage, then it is itself a top level page of the app. Notice also that the `Loaded` event handler of ManageEventsPage is missing here; instead the content for the page, a list of events, is loaded through the page's constructor. Because the page data is loaded in this manner you will not need to use the `INotifyPropertyChanged` pattern you have been utilizing up to this point. Listing 12-21 shows the implementation of ViewEventPage.

Listing 12-21. ViewEventPage Code

```
public sealed partial class ViewEventPage : Page
{
    BMXEvent CurrentEvent { get; set; }
    List<BMXEvent> Events { get; set; }

    public ViewEventPage(List<BMXEvent> events, BMXEvent current_event)
    {
        this.InitializeComponent();

        Events = events;
        CurrentEvent = current_event;
        txt_eventtitle.Text = CurrentEvent.EventTitle;
        txt_eventdescription.Text = CurrentEvent.Description;
        txt_address.Text = CurrentEvent.Address;
        control_calendar.Date = CurrentEvent.StartDateTime;
        slider_duration.Value = CurrentEvent.Duration.Hours;
    }
```

```
    private void CompletedEvent(object sender, RoutedEventArgs e)
    {
        Window.Current.Content = new ListEventsPage(Events);
    }
}
```

Like its counterpart, Listing 12-21 takes an event object and uses it to populate the state of its fields. You should be all set to implement the speech integration now. Now that you have an adequate list of events, you can see how your app can be used to extend the feature set Cortana offer.

Launching Your App in the Foreground with Cortana

In addition to using voice commands within Cortana to access search, personal assistant, and system features, you can also extend Cortana with features and functionality from any app that supports it. This is done using voice commands that specify an action or command to execute within the app. A voice command is a single utterance with a specific intent, defined in a Voice Command Definition (VCD) file, and directed at an installed app through Cortana. A voice command definition can vary in complexity. It can support anything from a single, constrained utterance to a collection of more flexible, natural language utterances, all denoting the same intent. VCD files define one or more of these voice commands, each with a unique intent. The steps to enabling this functionality are as follows.

1. Create a VCD file. This is an XML document that defines all the spoken commands that the user can say to initiate actions or invoke commands when activating your app.
2. Register the command sets in the VCD file when the app is launched.
3. Handle the foreground activation of the app through the `OnActivated` handler. As part of the launch parameters you will have access to the command that was triggered by Cortana and the text of the words that were uttered.

The owners of Big Mountain X want to apply these features to their app so that their users will have the ability to interact with their app in this compelling manner. The following list highlights the functionality they would like enabled:

- Tell users what is happening today
- Tell users what is happening tomorrow
- Tell users what is happening this week
- Tell users what is happening this month
- Buy tickets

Using the approach outlined earlier, the first thing you need to do in order to enable this kind of interaction is create a VCD file. Create a new file in your `Media/Audio` folder called `VoiceCommands_1.xml` and add the markup from Listing 12-22; the contents should work for all the items in your requirements list.

Listing 12-22. VCD File

```
<?xml version="1.0" encoding="utf-8"?>
<VoiceCommands xmlns="http://schemas.microsoft.com/voicecommands/1.1">
    <CommandSet xml:lang="en-us" Name="en-us-CommandSet">
        <CommandPrefix>Big Mountain,</CommandPrefix>
        <Example> Show me what's happening /Example>
```

```
        <Command Name="show-events-today">
            <Example>what's happening today in New York</Example>
            <ListenFor>what's happening today in {location}</ListenFor>
            <Feedback> here is what's happening today in {location}</Feedback>
            <Navigate/>
        </Command>
        <Command Name="show-events-tomorrow">
            <Example>what's happening tomorrow in New York</Example>
            <ListenFor>what's happening tomorrow in {location}</ListenFor>
            <Feedback> here is what's happening tomorrow in {location}</Feedback>
            <Navigate/>
        </Command>
        <Command Name="show-events-thisweek">
            <Example>find me upcoming shows in New York this week</Example>
            <ListenFor>find me upcoming shows in {location} this week</ListenFor>
            <Feedback>Finding this week's shows in {location}</Feedback>
            <Navigate/>
        </Command>
        <Command Name="show-events-thismonth">
            <Example>find me this weekend's shows in New York</Example>
            <ListenFor>find me this weekend's shows in {location}</ListenFor>
            <Feedback>Finding shows for this weekend in {location}</Feedback>
            <Navigate/>
        </Command>
        <PhraseList Label="location">
            <Item>Miami</Item>
            <Item>Boston</Item>
            <Item>New York</Item>
            <Item>Chicago</Item>
        </PhraseList>
    </CommandSet>
</VoiceCommands>
```

What follows is by no means an exhaustive exploration of what VCD files have to offer but should give you a good foundation of what is going on in order to enable basic app launching through Cortana. At the highest level of a VCD file (after the XML declaration of course) is the VoiceCommands node. This basically encapsulates a set of Command specifications that represent the commands Cortana listens to for a match. Within each Command node is a Name attribute to uniquely identify that command (this will come into play later when it is time to figure out which command activated the control). Within the command node are four children:

- Example: A hint to the user on the kind of phrase Cortana will understand.
- ListenFor: The phrase that Cortana is listening for in that context. When this phrase is heard, the associated command will be sent as part of the startup arguments for the targeted app.
- Feedback: The message that Cortana sends to the user.
- Navigate: This tells Cortana to navigate to the app that registered the command.

Within the nodes ListenFor and Feedback you might have noticed the use of a wild-card label "location" as shown:

```
<ListenFor>find me this weekend's shows in {location}</ListenFor>.
```

The wild-card part of the phrase Cortana listens for must map to one of the values identified in the PhraseList node. This allows some variability to what the user says while still letting it match to a specific command. For instance, based on the VCD defined the following phrases will all match to the same command "show-events-today":

```
"what's happening today in Miami"
"what's happening today in Boston"
"what's happening today in Chicago"
```

The following phrase will not match:

```
"what's happening today in Detroit"
```

As you might imagine, this can raise concerns when you start thinking about matching large data sets. For instance, if you want Big Mountain X to match against every city in the United States, the file could become very large. In a little while we will show you how easy it is to resolve this issue. For now, let's take the next step in the process outlined earlier and register the VCD when the app is launched. Open up `App.xaml.cs` and add the code from Listing 12-23 to the bottom of `InitializeAppAsync`.

Listing 12-23. InitializeAppAsync Changes

```
private static async Task InitializeAppAsync()
{
    ...

    //launch cortana integration (foreground)
    var vcd_path = "ms-appx:///media/audio/voicecommands_1.xml";
    var vcd_uri = new Uri(vcd_path);
    var vcd_file = await StorageFile.GetFileFromApplicationUriAsync(vcd_uri);
    await VoiceCommandDefinitionManager.InstallCommandDefinitionsFromStorageFileAsync
    (vcd_file);
}
```

In Listing 12-23, you load the VCD file and, once loaded, call `VoiceCommandDefinitionManager.InstallCommandDefinitionsFromStorageFileAsync` to register it with the system. Believe it or not, that's all it takes to get Cortana integration going. Build and run the app now and say any one of the legal phrases (start by saying "Big Mountain" to identify your app as the target of the query). The app should launch and display a screen like Figure 12-6.

Figure 12-6. *Window with no content*

It should be obvious to you that this is not ideal. The app is launching but it is doing so in a manner that implies the main content has not been set for the window. This highlights one of the important realizations you must come to when working with UWP apps: `OnLaunched` is not connected to `OnActivated`. In fact, when explicitly available to the developer, each entry point into a Windows 10 app is solely meant for the activation pattern it is designed for. The only exception to this is `OnActivated` but only for activation types with no explicit handler override. Files will be activated only through `OnFileActivated`, share contracts only through their activation hander, and so on.

Because your `OnActivated` event has only been designed up to this point to listen for URI-based activation, the content for the window is never set. Let's add logic into the method to enable Cortana scenarios. Add another `else-if` clause to the giant `if` statement in this function. Listing 12-24 makes the adjustment.

Listing 12-24. Voice Command URI Activation

```
else if (args.Kind == ActivationKind.VoiceCommand)
{
    var command_args = args as VoiceCommandActivatedEventArgs;
    if (command_args != null)
    {
        var rule_path = command_args.Result.RulePath[0];
        var location = command_args.Result.SemanticInterpretation.Properties["location"][0].
        ToLower();

        var events = App.State.Events;

        switch (rule_path)
        {
            case "show-events-today":
                {
                    var today = DateTime.Now.Date;
                    events = (from evt in events
```

```
                                 where evt.StartDateTime.Date == today
                                 && evt.Address.ToLower().Contains(location)
                                 select evt).ToList();

                }
                break;
            case "show-events-tomorrow":
                {
                    var tomorrow = DateTime.Now.Date.Add(TimeSpan.FromDays(1));
                    events = (from evt in events
                                 where evt.StartDateTime.Date == tomorrow
                                 && evt.Address.ToLower().Contains(location)
                                 select evt).ToList();
                }
                break;
            case "show-events-thisweek":
                {
                    var today = DateTime.Now.Date;
                    var week_starting = today.Subtract(TimeSpan.FromDays((int)today.DayOfWeek));
                    var week = Math.Floor(week_starting.DayOfYear / 7.0);

                    events = (from evt in events
                                 let evt_day = evt.StartDateTime
                                 let evt_dow = (int)evt_day.DayOfWeek
                                 let days_to_subtract = TimeSpan.FromDays(evt_dow)
                                 let evt_week_starting = evt_day.Subtract(days_to_subtract)
                                 let evt_week = Math.Floor(evt_week_starting.DayOfYear / 7.0)
                                 where week == evt_week
                                 && evt.Address.ToLower().Contains(location)
                                 select evt).ToList();
                }
                break;
            case "show-events-thismonth":
                {
                    var today = DateTime.Now;
                    events = (from evt in events
                                 where evt.StartDateTime.Month == today.Month
                                 && evt.Address.ToLower().Contains(location)
                                 select evt).ToList();
                }
                break;
        }
        Window.Current.Content = new ListEventsPage(events);
    }
}
```

Create some events that start at different points times within the current month you are in. Have some start on the same day, others the next day, and others within the same week. Finally, add a few events that map to the month you are in. Run the example and test this result. Figure 12-7 shows what I get when I ask Cortana to "find me this month's shows in Boston."

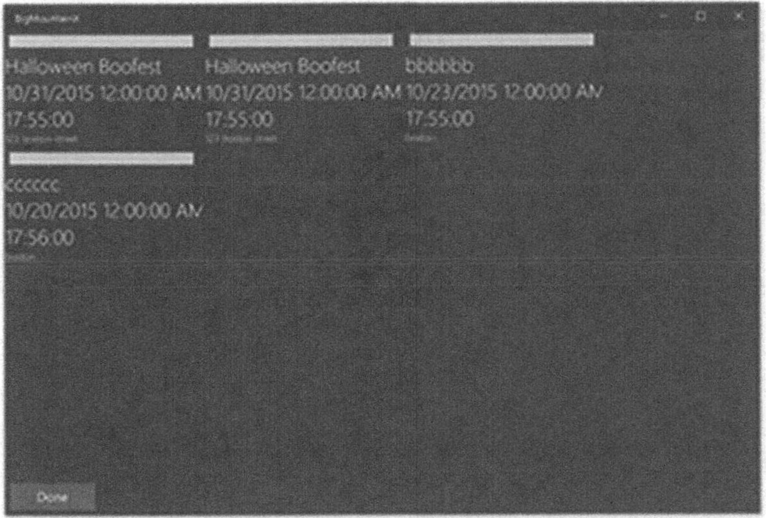

Figure 12-7. *List Events view*

As discussed earlier, the use of the PhraseList can be limiting. In the scenario shown, if the user were to ask for San Antonio, the command would not be recognized. This is because the list of phrases is defined ahead of time in the VCD XML. This does not need to be the case, however. You can use the `InstalledCommandDefinitions` indexer of `VoiceCommandDefinitionManager` to gain access to the command definitions you have specified in your VCD and then set the Phrase List you want associated with that phrase list. For this to work, you must have at least an empty phrase list with a name specified on it in the VCD. From code, you can then set what you want that phrase list to be. Be careful, though; you cannot add to the phrase list. You can only set it, which means that if you set a phrase list in the VCD file and then use `SetPhraseList` in your code, the VCD phrase list will be overwritten. In Listing 12-25, you modify the phrase list you previously created to just be empty.

Listing 12-25. Location Phrase List

```
<PhraseList Label="location" />
```

You can then use `InitializeAsync` as shown in Listing 12-26.

Listing 12-26. InitializeAsync Changes

```
...
//set the value of marker and marker lock
var local_folder = Windows.Storage.ApplicationData.Current.LocalFolder;
var file_marker = await local_folder.CreateFileAsync("marker_.txt", OpenIfExists);
await file_marker.WriteTextAsync("1");
var file_marker_lock = await local_folder.CreateFileAsync("marker_lock.txt", OpenIfExists);
await file_marker_lock.WriteTextAsync("1");

//launch cortana integration (foreground)
var vcd_path = "ms-appx:///media/audio/voicecommands_1.xml";
var vcd_uri = new Uri(vcd_path);
var vcd_file = await StorageFile.GetFileFromApplicationUriAsync(vcd_uri);
await VoiceCommandDefinitionManager.InstallCommandDefinitionsFromStorageFileAsync(vcd_file);
```

```
//modifying phrase list programmatically (for more dynamic interactions)
VoiceCommandDefinition command_set = VoiceCommandDefinitionManager.
InstalledCommandDefinitions["en-us-CommandSet"];
await command_set.SetPhraseListAsync("location", new string[]
                                                   { "London",
                                                       "Dallas",
                                                       "Maine",
                                                       "Phoenix",
                                                       "Miami",
                                                       "Boston",
                                                       "Chicago",
                                                       "New York"
                                                   });
...
```

One can imagine pulling the values for a phrase list from a database or external service. Remember that the phrase is just that, a phrase. This means that it does not have to be limited to just a word. Try it out: add a new location term "my regular spot."

Launching Your App in the Background with Cortana

The power of what you have accomplished up to this point goes without saying. Being able to surface your app's functionality via Cortana is not only wonderful from the perspective of app visibility, it also allows users to interact with your app without having to go searching for it. With functionality like this, all a user needs do is ask Cortana the right question and your app can answer it. But what if you want even tighter integration than that? From the previous example the user is able to use Cortana to launch your app and navigate to context-specific pages, (and for a lot of use cases this makes perfect sense), but what if you want that same flexibility of Cortana but without the burden of launching your app explicitly?

With UWP apps running on Windows 10, you can also extend Cortana with features and functionality from a background app using voice commands that specify an action or command to execute within the app. The added benefit here is that when an app handles a voice command in the background, it can display feedback on the Cortana canvas and communicate with the user using the Cortana voice. This means that basically the user will truly see your app as an extension of Cortana!

Using Cortana in the background requires the same VCD file as the foreground app, but in the background usage scenario you are using a background task, in this case an app service, rather than your full foreground app. In general, when little or no interaction (other than the user's voice) is required, this approach of interacting with Cortana through an app service is ideal. In situations where more interactivity is required (like the need to view complex data or interact with the app interface in a sophisticated way), launching the app in the foreground is preferable.

The basic steps to add voice-command functionality and extend Cortana with background functionality from your app using speech or keyboard input are as follows.

1. Create a VCD file. This is an XML document that defines all the spoken commands that the user can say to initiate actions or invoke commands when activating your app. See VCD elements and attributes v1.2.

2. Create an app service (see `Windows.ApplicationModel.AppService`) that Cortana invokes in the background. See Chapter 11 for more details on the subject.

3. Register the command sets in the VCD file when the app is launched.

4. Handle the background activation of the app service and the execution of the voice command.

5. Display and/or speak the appropriate feedback to the voice command within Cortana.

The first step in this case is to create a VCD. Note that with background integration the system requires version 1.2 of the specification (you used version 1.1 for the last example). Add a new file to the `Media/Audio` folder called `VoiceCommands_2.xml` and populate it with the code from Listing 12-27.

Listing 12-27. VCD File VoiceCommands_2.xml

```
<?xml version="1.0" encoding="utf-8"?>
<VoiceCommands xmlns="http://schemas.microsoft.com/voicecommands/1.2">
    <CommandSet xml:lang="en-us" Name="en-us-CommandSet">
        <CommandPrefix>Big Mountain,</CommandPrefix>
        <Example> Show me what's hapenning </Example>
        <Command Name="change-desktop-wallpaper">
            <Example>change my wallpaper</Example>
            <ListenFor>change my wallpaper</ListenFor>
            <Feedback>okay</Feedback>
            <VoiceCommandService Target="bmx-cortana-service"/>
        </Command>
        <Command Name="joke-knock-knock">
            <Example>tell me a joke</Example>
            <ListenFor>tell me a joke</ListenFor>
            <Feedback>okay</Feedback>
            <VoiceCommandService Target="bmx-cortana-service"/>
        </Command>
        <Command Name="joke-whos-there">
            <Example>tell me a joke</Example>
            <ListenFor>who's there</ListenFor>
            <Feedback>it's</Feedback>
            <VoiceCommandService Target="bmx-cortana-service"/>
        </Command>
        <Command Name="joke-punchline">
            <Example>tell me a joke</Example>
            <ListenFor>{joke_name} who</ListenFor>
            <Feedback>okay</Feedback>
            <VoiceCommandService Target="bmx-cortana-service"/>
        </Command>
        <Command Name="buy-tickets">
            <Example>Get me tickets to the next evening show in Miami</Example>
            <ListenFor>Get me tickets to the next {event_type} in {location}</ListenFor>
            <Feedback>Getting tickets to {event_type} in {location}</Feedback>
            <VoiceCommandService Target="bmx-cortana-service"/>
        </Command>
        <Command Name="make-suggestions">
            <Example>Give me some fun suggestions</Example>
            <ListenFor>Give me some fun suggestions in {location}</ListenFor>
            <Feedback>here are some fun suggestions in {location}</Feedback>
            <VoiceCommandService Target="bmx-cortana-service"/>
        </Command>
```

```
        <Command Name="count">
            <Example>give me the count</Example>
            <ListenFor>give me the count</ListenFor>
            <Feedback>okay</Feedback>
            <VoiceCommandService Target="bmx-cortana-service"/>
        </Command>
        <PhraseList Label="location" />
        <PhraseList Label="joke_name" >
            <Item>amos</Item>
            <Item>who</Item>
            <Item>honey bee</Item>
            <Item>letuce</Item>
            <Item>double</Item>
        </PhraseList>
        <PhraseList Label="event_type" >
            <Item>morning show</Item>
            <Item>afternoon show</Item>
            <Item>evening show</Item>
            <Item>night show</Item>
        </PhraseList>
    </CommandSet>
</VoiceCommands>
```

From the VCD in Listing 12-27 you can tell that you will be building a new background app service for handling buying tickets, changing the computer's wallpaper, getting suggested places to go to, and even telling jokes. You also have an extra command for getting a count. This extra command is meant to be used to highlight the manner in which state is managed across multiple requests into a background task like this; it is not meant to be part of the overall app being built. The key difference between this VCD and the one used for foreground apps is the introduction of the `VoiceCommandService` element. This service maps a given voice command to an application service used to service the voice command request. Ordinarily we would be telling you to open up your app manifest and start adding declarations right now, but with Cortana app services you do not need to do this…just kidding! You do. Open up your app manifest and add a new declaration for an app service. Give the new service the same name as your VCD file is expecting (from the VoiceCommandService node of the VCD element). Call it **bmx-cortana-service**. Figure 12-8 shows how the configuration should look.

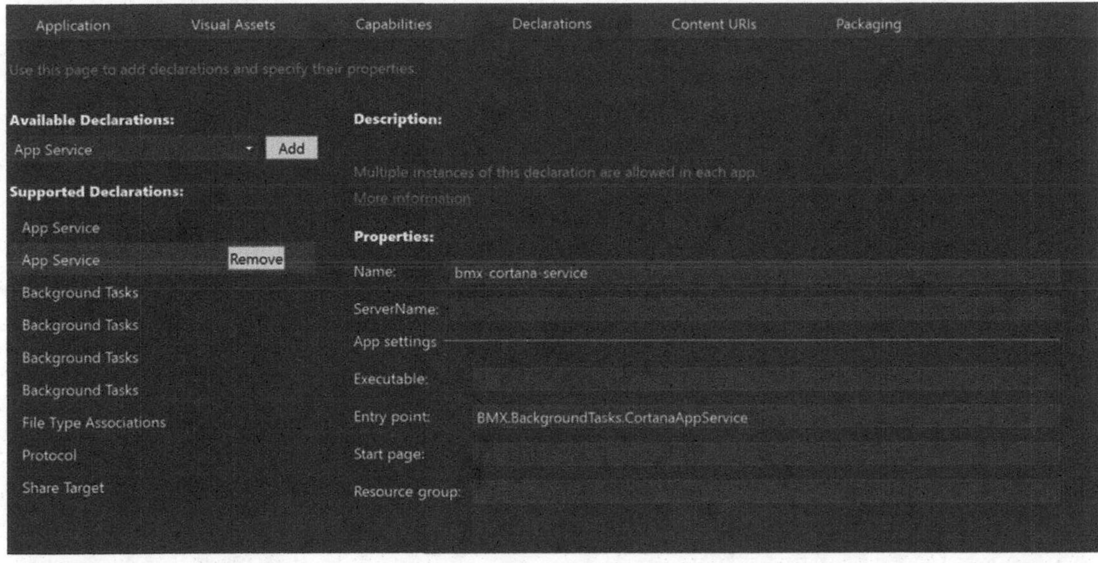

Figure 12-8. *Declarations tab*

Add a new class file to your BMX.BackgroundTasks project called `CortanaAppService` (to match the entry point type you identified in your manifest. The `Run` method for this class should be defined as shown in Listing 12-28.

Listing 12-28. Cortana App Service Run Method

```
async public void Run(IBackgroundTaskInstance taskInstance)
{
    _deferral = taskInstance.GetDeferral();

    var local = ApplicationData.Current.LocalFolder;
    State = await AppState.FromStorageFileAsync(local,"state.xml");

    var app_service = taskInstance.TriggerDetails as AppServiceTriggerDetails;
    var connection = VoiceCommandServiceConnection.FromAppServiceTriggerDetails(app_service);

    //get the voice command
    var command = await connection.GetVoiceCommandAsync();
    var rule_path = command.SpeechRecognitionResult.RulePath[0];

    VoiceCommandUserMessage user_message = new VoiceCommandUserMessage();
    if (rule_path == "change-desktop-wallpaper")
    {
        //await HandleChangeWallpaper(connection, user_message);
    }
    else if (rule_path == "make-suggestions")
    {
        //await HandleMakeSuggestions(connection, command, user_message);
    }
```

```
    else if (rule_path == "buy-tickets")
    {
        //await HandleBuyTickets(connection, command, user_message);
    }
    else if (rule_path == "count")
    {
        count++;
        user_message.SpokenMessage = $"the current count is {count}";
        user_message.DisplayMessage = user_message.SpokenMessage;
        var response = VoiceCommandResponse.CreateResponse(user_message);
        await connection.ReportSuccessAsync(response);
    }
    else if (rule_path == "joke-knock-knock")
    {
        //await HandleTellJoke(connection, user_message);
    }
    else if (rule_path == "joke-whos-there")
    {
        //await HandleWhosThere(connection, user_message);
    }
    else if (rule_path == "joke-punchline")
    {
        //await HandlePunchline(connection, command, user_message);
    }

    _deferral.Complete();
}
```

As with every other background task you have worked on, you start by getting a deferral. You then initialize the app state so that you have access to the `AppState` object instance used by the foreground app. You then pull the trigger details out from the task instance and use the `VoiceCommandServiceConnection` to generate an appropriate connection to the voice command interaction through the method `VoiceCommandServiceConnection.FromAppServiceTriggerDetails(app_service)`. With this class instance you can gain access to what was said and also interact back with the user through the Cortana interface. In your case, you next call `GetVoiceCommand`, which gives you access to the command that triggered the background task. The rest of the code follows a pattern you should be familiar with from your previous examples. `command.SpeechRecognitionResult.RulePath[0]` gives you the command that Cortana believes the user's request maps to; the value should map to one of the Command node's `Name` attribute from the VCD file you registered. With this value in hand, you use it to decide which of the helper methods you want to call to handle that specific request. For each one of the helper commands, you pass in a `VoiceCommandUserMessage` object instance, the connection object, and optionally the VoiceCommand itself. The `VoiceCommandUserMessage` object is used to send messages back to the user in TTS form. It basically allows you to talk to the user through Cortana.

State Management

Add a static global int to the class called `count` to enable the *count* scenario. Compile and run the app. Then try using the command "Big Mountain give me the count". You will note that regardless of how many times this command is made, the result is always the same: the count is always shown as 1. It is important to clearly understand why this is happening. Basically, the background task used to handle this request is always being recreated. With each request an entirely new app domain containing the CortanaAppService is instantiated so that even when a static variable is used, its value restarts at zero.

Long story short, you must use some other external source to handle state management. In the examples that follow, you utilize the file system for this purpose; however, there is nothing that prevents you from using the application settings or even external services to get this done. Figure 12-9 shows what the Cortana interface looks like when the result is displayed.

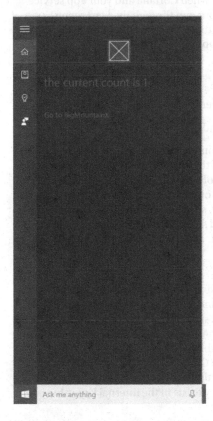

***Figure 12-9.** Cortana display message*

Note from the image that the result is also displayed on the Cortana interface. Users may be interacting with Cortana through the text interface as well as the speech one, so be sure to include responses for both cases. The `DisplayMessage` property of `VoiceCommandUserMessage` is used to set this value. For a voice command to be successful it must pass the created `VoiceCommandResponse` object into a call to `ReportSuccessAsync` on the `VoiceCommandServiceConnection` object. This class has a number of other overrides that you can explore when building your own Cortana integration. You will be looking at a few of them as you work through this example.

Deep Linking

You can provide deep links from the background app service in Cortana to launch the app to the foreground in a specific state or context. A deep link is displayed by default on the Cortana completion screen, but you can display deep links on various other screens. Deep linking is useful when Cortana and your app service are a gateway to the full app (instead of requiring the user to launch your app through the Start menu), or for providing access to richer detail and functionality within your app that is not possible through Cortana. Deep linking is another way to increase usability and access to your app.

There are three ways to provide deep links:

- A "Go to <app>" link on various Cortana screens
- A link embedded in a content tile on various Cortana screens
- The app service programmatically launches the foreground app

Cortana can expose a "Go to *<app>*" deep link to the content tile on various screens. You can provide a launch argument for this link to open your app with similar context as the app service. If you don't provide a launch argument, the app is launched to the main screen. Regardless of whether you provide an app launch argument or not, you need to add a declaration to the app manifest in order for it to be launched by Cortana. This declaration has no user interface associated with it unfortunately, so you must open the manifest to its XML view and add it there. Right-click your project's app manifest and selected View Code from the context menu that appears. In the Extensions node of the Application element, add the following declaration:

```
<uap:Extension Category="windows.personalAssistantLaunch"/>
```

Your app is launched to the foreground through URI activation using a Protocol contract. As with any protocol contract, your app must override its `OnActivated` event and check for an ActivationKind of Protocol. When your app is launched in this manner, the resulting URL sent to it is "windows.personalassistantlaunch:?LaunchContext=*<AppLaunchArgument>*", where `AppLaunchArgument` is the value of the property `AppLaunchArgument` of the `VoiceCommandResponse` object returned to the user. Let's extend your app to support launching directly into the All events page when opened from Cortana. The process starts with you extending the functionality of your `QueryReader` class. Add a new function called `Contains` as shown in Listing 12-29. As the name implies, this app basically tests to see if a key exists in the internal key-value pair of the object.

Listing 12-29. QueryReader Contains Method

```
public bool Contains(string key)
{
    return _values.ContainsKey(key);
}
```

With this added feature you can now organize the protocol activation piece of `OnActivated` more readily. Listing 12-30 illustrates.

Listing 12-30. OnActivated Changes

```
if (args.Kind == ActivationKind.Protocol)
{
    var protocol_args = args as ProtocolActivatedEventArgs;
    var query = protocol_args.Uri.Query.ToLower();
    var reader = QueryReader.Load(query);
```

```
        if (reader.Contains("launchcontext"))
        {
            var context = reader["launchcontext"];
                        if (context == "all_events")
                            Window.Current.Content = new ListEventsPage(App.State.Events);
        }
        else if (reader.Contains("page"))
        {
            var target_page = reader["page"];

            if (target_page == "street")
            {
                StreetSideViewPage street_view = new StreetSideViewPage();
                var center_point = new Geopoint(new BasicGeoposition
                {
                    Latitude = App.State.NextEvent.Latitude.Value,
                    Longitude = App.State.NextEvent.Longitude.Value,
                });
                await street_view.InitializeAsync(center_point);
                Window.Current.Content = street_view;
            }
            else if (target_page == "main")
            {
                Window.Current.Content = new ApplicationHostPage();
            }
            else if (target_page == "counter")
            {
                Window.Current.Content = new PatronCounter();
            }
            else if (target_page == "test")
            {
                Window.Current.Content = new TestPage();
            }
            else
            {
                Window.Current.Content = new PageNotFound();
            }
        }
    }
```

In Listing 12-30, you use your newly created `Contains` method to test to see if certain URI parameters exist in the activation URI. Based on their existence you are making a finer grained determination on the purpose of the launch. In this situation, you first test for a launch with the parameter `launchcontext` and then within that you test the value of that parameter. If it is `all_events`, you launch the ListEventsPage with no filter on the events listed.

Besides the "Go to <your app>" link that appears in the Cortana interface you can also create custom ones called content tiles by adding `VoiceCommandContentTile` objects to the `VoiceCommandResponse` you respond to the user with. `VoiceCommandResponse` can be created with a list of these content tiles, each representing a link into the app. Each of these tiles has their own `AppLaunchArgument` property that can be used to set the launch parameters under which the app will launch. In Listing 12-31, you implement the `HandleMakeSuggestions` method and uncomment the section of `Run` that calls it.

Listing 12-31. HandleMakeSuggestions Method

```
private async Task HandleMakeSuggestions(VoiceCommandServiceConnection connection,
VoiceCommand command, VoiceCommandUserMessage user_message)
{
    var tiles = new List<VoiceCommandContentTile>();
    var location = command.SpeechRecognitionResult.SemanticInterpretation.
Properties["location"][0].ToLower();

    //find events
    var events = State.Events;
    events = (from evt in events
              where evt.Address.ToLower().Contains(location)
              select evt).ToList();

    //create tiles
    foreach (var evt in events)
    {
        tiles.Add(new VoiceCommandContentTile
        {
            ContentTileType = VoiceCommandContentTileType.TitleWithText,
            AppLaunchArgument = $"event,event_id={evt.EventID}",
            Title = evt.EventTitle,
            TextLine1 = evt.Description,
        });
    }

    //respond
    var response = VoiceCommandResponse.CreateResponse(user_message, tiles);

    response.AppLaunchArgument = "all_events";

    await connection.ReportSuccessAsync(response);
}
```

Listing 12-31 basically reads the location value specified by the user and uses this to filter the BMXEvents to just those that contain the value. So if the user says "Give me some fun suggestions in Boston," only Boston-based events will be displayed. For each of the events in the filtered list you then build a `VoiceCommandContentTile` that will represent that event. Note that you have set the value of `AppLaunchArgument` for the content tile to include the event id and the value event; "event" will be the value set to `launchcontext`. Further down the code base you create a new `VoiceCommandResponse` object using the `CreateResponse` method but in this case use an override that also accepts a list of `VoiceCommandContentTile` objects; you pass in the list you previously created. Finally, you provide the `AppLaunchArgument` for the response as a whole, in this case setting it to `all_events`. When Cortana is invoked, it will show the list of specific events you have provided and at the bottom it will have a link to launch the app. When this link is clicked, it will launch the app as though it were launched via protocol activation (the content tiles do the same).

You must now modify the `OnActivated` handler to expect the new URIs introduced by the content tiles. As stated earlier, they add a new potential value for `launchcontext`, event. When `launchcontext` has this value you will expect to see an `event_id` parameter that you can use to filter the events available in the system. Listing 12-32 shows the changes made to the `launchcontext` section of the `if` statement. Changes are in bold.

Listing 12-32. OnActivated Handler

```
...
var protocol_args = args as ProtocolActivatedEventArgs;
var query = WebUtility.UrlDecode(protocol_args.Uri.Query.ToLower());
var reader = QueryReader.Load(query);

if (reader.Contains("launchcontext"))
{
    var context = reader["launchcontext"];
    if (context == "all_events")
        Window.Current.Content = new ListEventsPage(App.State.Events);
    else if (context == "event")
    {
        var event_id = Guid.Parse(reader["event_id"]);
        var event_list = App.State.Events.Where(i => i.EventID == event_id).ToList();
        Window.Current.Content = new ListEventsPage(event_list);
    }
}
...
```

Be sure to use the WebUtility to decode the query coming into the app; it is encoded by Windows before being used (because it is expected to be an argument and not a list of parameters) so you will lose any delimiting character like comma and the equal sign.

Figure 12-10 shows how the Cortana looks when the user requests fun suggestions in Boston (based on events created on your machine).

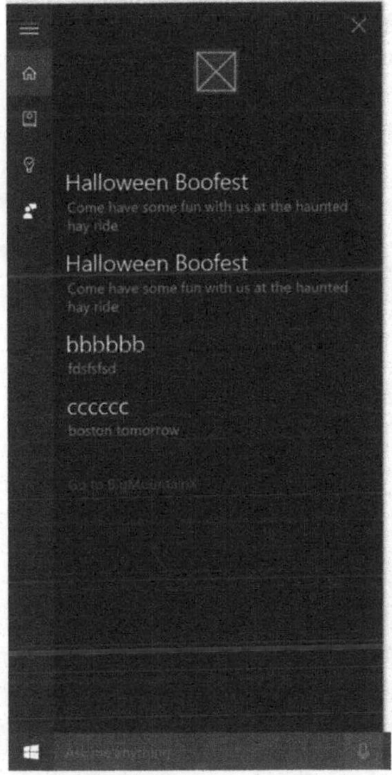

Figure 12-10. *Content tiles on Cortana UI*

From this screen, clicking "Go to BigMountainX" will launch the app through the protocol activation mechanisms described. In this case, it will be launched with the parameter `all_events`. Figure 12-11 shows how the app looks when launched (this is based on events you have created on your machine).

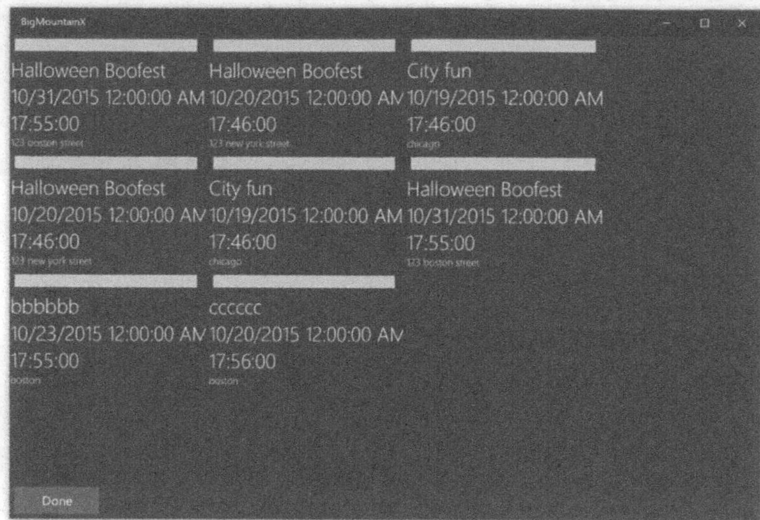

Figure 12-11. *Search results page*

Try using Cortana again with the same statement. This time, instead of clicking the link "Go to BigMountainX," click one of the content tiles provided. Depending on whether or not you exploited your little "copy" trick when creating these events, you should see something like Figure 12-12.

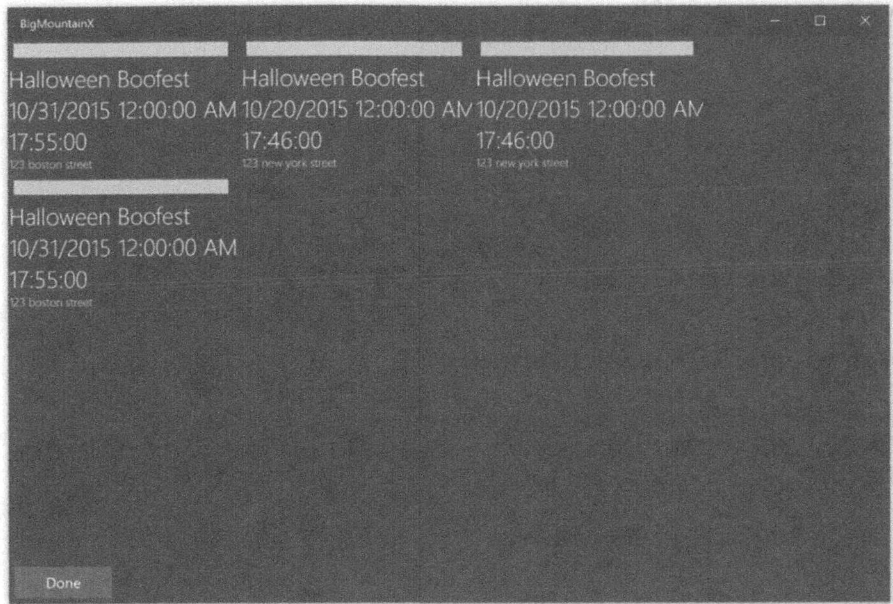

Figure 12-12. *View event page*

Your eyes are not deceiving you; there should be only one event showing but the app is displaying four. This is because all the events shown here have the same event id, a side effect of the approach you used to quickly create tons of events.

Prompting the User

In certain scenarios it may be necessary to ask the user for a confirmation before proceeding with an action through the background app service. For this kind of situation, the method `CreateResponseForPrompt` of the class `VoiceCommandResponse` can be used. When `CreateResponseForPrompt` is used, the resulting voice command response must be used with the `RequestConfirmationAsync` method of the `VoiceCommandServiceConnection`. In Listing 12-33, you use this technique to ask the user if they want to also change their lock screen image once you are done changing their desktop wallpaper. Don't forget to uncomment the call to `HandleChangeWallpaper` within the `Run` method before testing it.

Listing 12-33. HandleChageWallpaper Method

```
private async Task HandleChangeWallpaper(VoiceCommandServiceConnection connection,
VoiceCommandUserMessage user_message)
{
    //copy images to appdata
    var local_folder = ApplicationData.Current.LocalFolder;
    var install_path = Package.Current.InstalledLocation;
    var media_path = await install_path.GetFolderAsync("media\\images");
```

```
    var images = await media_path.GetFilesAsync();
    foreach (var image in images)
    {
        try
        {
            await local_folder.GetFileAsync(image.Name);
            continue;
        }
        catch { }
        await image.CopyAsync(local_folder, image.Name, ReplaceExisting);
    }

    //change wallpaper and prepare response back to user

    var result = await UserSettings.ChangeWallpaperAsync();
    user_message.SpokenMessage = "Your wallpaper was modified, do you want me to change the
                                  lock screen as well?";

    var backup_message = new VoiceCommandUserMessage
    {
        SpokenMessage = "Change your lock screen",
    };

    var response = VoiceCommandResponse.CreateResponseForPrompt(user_message, backup_message);
    var confirm_result = await connection.RequestConfirmationAsync(response);

    if (confirm_result.Confirmed)
    {
        await UserSettings.ChangeLockScreenAsync();
        user_message.SpokenMessage = "Your lock screen was also modified.";
        response = VoiceCommandResponse.CreateResponse(user_message);
        await connection.ReportSuccessAsync(response);
    }
    else
    {
        user_message.SpokenMessage = "okay, you're all set then";
        response = VoiceCommandResponse.CreateResponse(user_message);
        await connection.ReportSuccessAsync(response);
    }
}
```

In Listing 12-33, you define a method that will be dedicated to handling the case where Cortana evaluates what the user has said as "change my wallpaper." Because you will be toggling between images (and counting in the process), you will need to maintain some measure of state between calls to for this command. This functionality is built into the use of `ChangeWallpaperAsync` on the class `UserSettings`. Before doing this, though, you must try to copy all the images from the app package to local storage (this is a condition of the programming logic you have chosen to utilize and not a requirement of changing wallpapers or Cortana). Once the wallpaper is changed, you use the `CreateResponseForPrompt` and `RequestConfirmationAsync` to send a prompt to the user for information on whether they want the lock screen image changed as well. If they chose to, you modify it; otherwise, you end the conversation. Figure 12-13 shows how the prompt UI looks within Cortana.

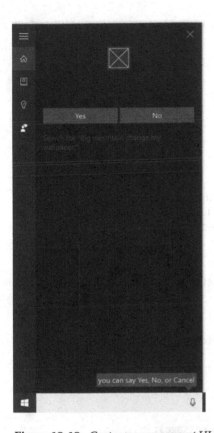

Figure 12-13. *Cortana user prompt UI*

Multi-Command Interactions

In the previous section, we secretly introduced the notion of multi-command interactions when you used the file-system to store the index of the image that was last displayed (see the implementation of `ChangeWallpaper` for details on how this is implemented). To summarize, `ChangeWallpaper` stores a number in a file that it reads every time it is called. Once called, it gets that number, increments it, gets the image associated with the new number, sets the wallpaper for that image, and finally stores the new number back to the file. Consequently, each time you ask Cortana to change your wallpaper, a fresh image is used. In the context of Cortana, doing this is a multi-command interaction because it maintains state across individual commands. In the following example, you will be utilizing the same approach to enable the joke telling functionality of the app. You will be implementing your joke command as a "knock-knock" joke which, as you might know, has three parts:

- The "knock-knock" part
- The "who's there?" part
- The punchline

With each section the user will of course have to re-initialize Cortana and include the command prefix in the statement. A normal interaction would be as follows:

1. User: "big mountain tell me a joke"
2. Cortana: "knock-knock"
3. User: "big mountain who's there?"
4. Cortana: "amos"
5. User: "amos who?"
6. Cortana: "amosquito!"

To accomplish this, you must implement a command for each of the statements you expect the user to make. You start with the first: asking Cortana to tell you a joke. Listing 12-34 implements the `HandleTellJoke` method. Be sure to uncomment the call to this method in `Run`.

Listing 12-34. HandleTellJoke Method

```
private static async Task HandleTellJoke(VoiceCommandServiceConnection connection,
VoiceCommandUserMessage user_message)
{
    var local_folder = ApplicationData.Current.LocalFolder;
    var file = await local_folder.CreateFileAsync("joke_state.txt", CreationCollisionOption.
ReplaceExisting);
    await file.WriteTextAsync("knock knock");

    user_message.SpokenMessage = "knock knock";
    user_message.DisplayMessage = "knock knock!";
    var response = VoiceCommandResponse.CreateResponse(user_message);
    await connection.ReportSuccessAsync(response);
}
```

In Listing 12-34, you start by creating a file in local storage where you will store state about the location of the user within the joke dialogue. The StorageFile is created as `ReplaceExisting` because asking for a joke will always restart the process. Beyond that, all this method does is respond back with the statement "knock-knock."

The next part of the conversation starts with you listening for the "who's there" from the user. Listing 12-35 implements the method `HandleWhosThere`. Be sure to uncomment the call to this method in `Run`.

Listing 12-35. HandleWhosThere Method

```
private static async Task HandleWhosThere(VoiceCommandServiceConnection connection,
VoiceCommandUserMessage user_message)
{
    var local_folder = ApplicationData.Current.LocalFolder;
    var file = await local_folder.CreateFileAsync("joke_state.txt", CreationCollisionOption.
    OpenIfExists);
    var text = await file.ReadTextAsync();
    if (text == "knock knock")
    {
        await file.WriteTextAsync("joke");
        Random random = new Random();
```

```
        var next = random.Next(100);
        var index = next % 5;

        var jokes = new string[] {
                "amos",
                "who",
                "honey bee",
                "lettuce",
                "double"
            };

        var joke = jokes[index];

        user_message.SpokenMessage = joke;
        user_message.DisplayMessage = user_message.SpokenMessage;
        var response = VoiceCommandResponse.CreateResponse(user_message);
        await connection.ReportSuccessAsync(response);
    }
    else
    {
        user_message.SpokenMessage = "first ask me to tell you a joke";
        var response = VoiceCommandResponse.CreateResponse(user_message);
        await connection.ReportSuccessAsync(response);
    }
}
```

In Listing 12-35, you start by opening the StorageFile `joke_state.txt` that was created as part of the initializing conversation (saying "big mountain, tell me a joke"). Once open, you test to see if the text "knock-knock" is in the file. The previous method, `HandleTellJoke`, created this file and added that text; this method will only work as the second step in the process, the step where you ask Cortana "who's there?" If the text in the file is correct, you overwrite it to now say "joke" and then insert a list of supported knock-knock joke setups into an array. Next, you generate a random number and use that number to determine which of the joke intros you want to use for this interaction. Whichever joke intro is randomly selected is then used to respond back to the user.

The final step in the process is for the background service to say the punchline when the user invokes the `"{joke_name} who"` command (As you know, `joke_name` is a label connected to the phrase list of possible knock-knock joke setups you have). Listing 12-36 implements the method `HandlePunchline`, which says the punchline for the joke based on the setup phrase used. Be sure to uncomment the place where this is called in the `Run` method.

Listing 12-36. HandlePunchline Method

```
async Task HandlePunchline(VoiceCommandServiceConnection connection, VoiceCommand command,
VoiceCommandUserMessage user_message)
{
    var local_folder = ApplicationData.Current.LocalFolder;
    var file = await local_folder.CreateFileAsync("joke_state.txt", CreationCollisionOption.
    OpenIfExists);
    var text = await file.ReadTextAsync();
    if (text != "joke")
    {
        user_message.SpokenMessage = "first ask me to tell you a joke";
```

```
        var response = VoiceCommandResponse.CreateResponse(user_message);
        await connection.ReportSuccessAsync(response);
        return;
    }
    var name = command.SpeechRecognitionResult.SemanticInterpretation.Properties["joke_name"]
    [0].ToLower();
    switch (name)
    {
        case "amos":
            {
                user_message.SpokenMessage = "a mosquito";
                user_message.DisplayMessage = user_message.SpokenMessage;
                var response = VoiceCommandResponse.CreateResponse(user_message);
                await connection.ReportSuccessAsync(response);
            }
            break;
        case "who":
            {
                user_message.SpokenMessage = "that's what an owl says";
                user_message.DisplayMessage = user_message.SpokenMessage;
                var response = VoiceCommandResponse.CreateResponse(user_message);
                await connection.ReportSuccessAsync(response);
            }
            break;
        case "honey bee":
            {
                user_message.SpokenMessage = "honey bee a dear and get me some juice";
                user_message.DisplayMessage = user_message.SpokenMessage;
                var response = VoiceCommandResponse.CreateResponse(user_message);
                await connection.ReportSuccessAsync(response);
            }
            break;
        case "lettuce":
            {
                user_message.SpokenMessage = "lettuce in it's cold out here";
                user_message.DisplayMessage = user_message.SpokenMessage;
                var response = VoiceCommandResponse.CreateResponse(user_message);
                await connection.ReportSuccessAsync(response);
            }
            break;
        case "double":
            {
                user_message.SpokenMessage = "double u";
                user_message.DisplayMessage = user_message.SpokenMessage;
                var response = VoiceCommandResponse.CreateResponse(user_message);
                await connection.ReportSuccessAsync(response);
            }
            break;
    }
```

```
    //the joke has now been told, reset
    await file.DeleteAsync(StorageDeleteOption.PermanentDelete);
}
```

Although Listing 12-36 is long, the code is relatively straightforward and should be easy for you to dissect. First, you open and read the text in `joke_state` to ensure that the previous interaction was the "who's there?" part of the knock-knock joke. If this is the case, you read the value of "joke_name" from the voice command and use it to determine which response to send back to the user. Each response in this switch statement corresponds to the appropriate punchline.

The Final Command

The final command that you have not implemented is the "buy tickets" command. Listing 12-37 shows the implementation for `HandleBuyTickets`. Be sure to uncomment the call to this method in the `Run` method.

Listing 12-37. HandleBuyTickets Method

```
private async Task HandleBuyTickets(VoiceCommandServiceConnection connection, VoiceCommand
command, VoiceCommandUserMessage user_message)
{
    var location = command.SpeechRecognitionResult.SemanticInterpretation.
Properties["location"][0].ToLower();
    var event_type = command.SpeechRecognitionResult.SemanticInterpretation.
Properties["event_type"][0].ToLower();

    var events = State.Events;
    var target_event = (from evt in events
                        where evt.Address.ToLower().Contains(location)
                        select evt).FirstOrDefault();
    user_message.SpokenMessage = $"I got your tickets to {target_event.EventTitle}";
    var response = VoiceCommandResponse.CreateResponse(user_message);
    await connection.ReportSuccessAsync(response);
}
```

Based on what you have worked on thus far, the meaning of the implementation for this method should be easily gleaned. You get the values for `location` and `event_type`, two phrase list parameters that are passed in by the user's request. You simply query your event list to find an event at the given location provided by the user and respond to the user if you find the event. You should have all you need to complete the exercise: add functionality that responds with a different message when the event is not found. Also, try modifying the query to include the `event_type` parameter that is passed in.

Summary

You just completed a meaty chapter with a comprehensive and in-depth investigation into incorporating speech and Cortana integration in your app. Through the use of VCD files, text to speech, and integration between Cortana and your app in foreground and background scenarios, you should be able to develop rich and powerful applications that provide alternative interaction patterns to the user. The following are some key points:

- Text-to-speech uses a speech synthesis engine (voice) to convert a text string into spoken words. The simplest form of this takes as input the text you actually want the engine to utter.
- SSML provides a standard way to control characteristics of speech output, such as pronunciation, volume, pitch, rate or speed, and emphasis.
- Constraints define the words and phrases (vocabulary) that an app recognizes in speech input. They are at the core of speech recognition and give your app great influence over the accuracy of speech recognition. Constraints are applied using predefined grammars, which provide speech recognition for your app without requiring you to author a grammar.
- A voice command is a single utterance with a specific intent, defined in a Voice Command Definition (VCD) file, and directed at an installed app through Cortana. A voice command definition can vary in complexity. It can support anything from a single, constrained utterance to a collection of more flexible, natural language utterances, all denoting the same intent.
- VCD files define one or more voice commands, each with a unique intent.
- Cortana integration comes in two flavors:
  - Foreground causes the app to be launched then uses the app to process the voice commands.
  - Background integration targets a background task associated with the app and uses it to process voice commands.

CHAPTER 13

App Monetization

When all is said and done, most developers aren't in it just for the sake of creative expression. In most cases, you want some financial gain from the work you've done—even if it's only enough to cover the expenses of building an app. And to be sure, building and maintaining apps can get very expensive very quickly. For one thing, because of the sandboxed nature of Windows 10 apps, many features aren't available in the Windows 10 app world. Windows 10 apps are sandboxed for a reason—to minimize the damage a misbehaving app can do to a device—but the side effect of these well-deserved limitations is a need for apps to generally include a cloud component. This cloud resident part of the app functions like a traditional application with full access to the cloud server's environment. Hosting such a solution quickly turns your fixed-cost app (the sweat equity used to build the app has a one-time price tied to it) into a recurring-cost app.

The market adds to this problem. Consumers of apps are generally accustomed to the ease and frequency with which apps can be installed and are updated. This means an underlying expectation of ongoing development is extended to any app in the marketplace, whether it is created by a billion-dollar organization like Facebook or by you. When you publish an app out to the market, you must also consider the cost of the time required to support it.

For these and many more reasons, digital marketplaces such as the Windows Store, Windows Phone Store, and Google Play all let you monetize apps through direct sales, with the marketplaces acting as merchants. Using this marketplace mode, prospective Windows 10 users can discover and purchase apps from the Windows Store. A percentage of the profits go to the developer who built the target app, and the rest goes to Microsoft to help offset the cost of maintaining the Windows Store. Figure 13-1 shows the landing screen of the Windows Store.

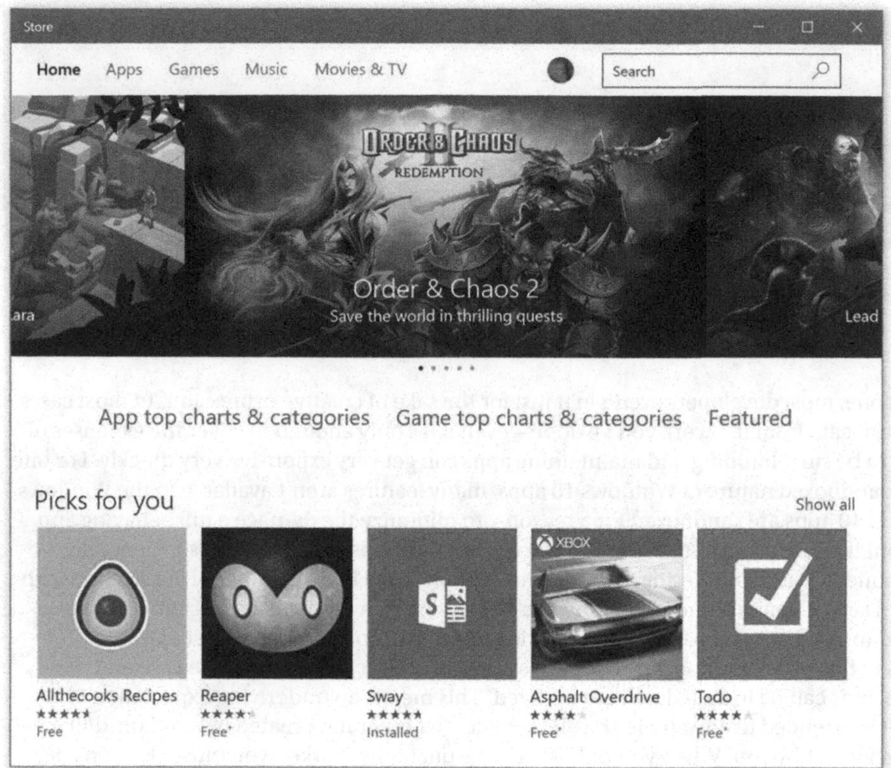

Figure 13-1. Windows Store landing page

This chapter discusses two common ways to make money through your app: selling the app and selling within the app. Many apps also generate revenue through in-app advertising, but the nuances of that approach are outside of the scope of this book.

Selling Your App

If you've had the opportunity to own an iPhone and walk through Apple's App Store purchasing process, you might have noticed that many non-free/for-cost apps have two versions: a free "demo" version that is used to show what the app can do, and an accompanying full-featured version. The demo version either has limited functionality or is totally open but ad supported. The accompanying full-featured version typically isn't ad supported. Users can get used to a convention like this, but on the development side it can lead to headaches because features must essentially be managed across two code bases: one for the demo version of the app and one for the full version (technically the same code base can be used with different deployment parameters applied during the build process).

Microsoft's Windows Store helps resolve this issue by letting you publish paid apps as trials. This allows developers to maintain one version of an app to serve as both the trial version and the full version-and specify the conditions under which the app can be migrated from one version to the other. From the standpoint of the Windows Store, this prevents needless repetition. From the perspective of the end user, it provides a simple and easy way to try an app and purchase it if you like it. Figure 13-2 shows a Windows Store paid app page with a trial mode available for the user.

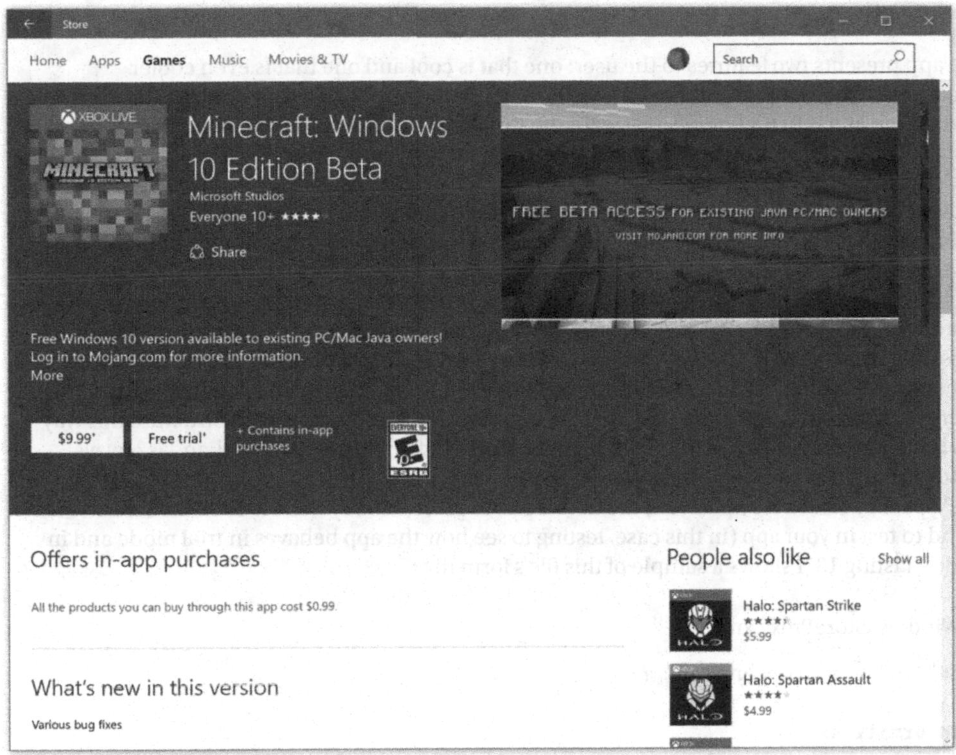

Figure 13-2. *App with trial mode*

From the developer's perspective, the workflow for building an app that will be for sale but includes a trial component is relatively straightforward:

1. Build the app as a full-featured app without worrying about which pieces of functionality are trial bits and which aren't.
2. After the app is built and tested, and you're sure everything works as intended, determine which features you want available to trial-version users and which bits you want to make visible only to paid-version users.
3. Use the Microsoft-provided classes to gate the sections of the app that a trial user can't access.

Each app has its own means of gating trial users. For some apps, such as games, you might want to show everything the app can do, but time-restrict the advanced features (or usage of the app as a whole). The idea of the trial isn't just to give a test drive of the app; it's also to market the app's goodies. When you're building apps for the purpose of monetization, keep this core concept in mind: upsell, upsell, upsell!

Next, let's look at sample trial app.

App Trial Mode

The trial-mode app presents two features to the user: one that is cool and one that is even cooler. Presumably, you want to allow users of this app to be able to use the cool feature but only see the even cooler feature. Also, when the app is in trial mode, you want the Buy App button to be visible, but after the app has been purchased, you want the button to disappear; otherwise the user may become confused and think their purchase wasn't registered or that the app is defective.

For Windows 10 apps, purchases are managed through the Windows Store APIs available via the `Windows.ApplicationModel.Store` namespace. This is your entry point to all relevant information about whether the user is using a trial version and, if so, how much time is left in that trial. Unfortunately, these classes work solely against the actual production Windows Store data, meaning they expect that your app is in the store and live. This poses a problem, because an unpublished app has no information available, making it impossible to test the trial-mode workflow. To help with this quagmire, the Windows Store API includes a simulator API-set that mimics the live functionality but works against an XML file that you provide. Working on a Windows Store app that uses the Windows Store commerce infrastructure this way requires you to build and manage this XML file, which is called `WindowsStoreProxy.xml` and is always located in the `%userprofile%\appdata\local\packages\<package-moniker>\localstate\microsoft\Windows Store\Apidata` folder. It's up to you, the developer, to place/modify this file to fit the scenario in which you intend to test in your app (in this case, testing to see how the app behaves in trial mode and in purchased mode). Listing 13-1 shows a sample of this file's format.

Listing 13-1. WindowsStoreProxy.xml

```
<?xml version="1.0" encoding="utf-16" ?>
<CurrentApp>
    <ListingInformation>
        <App>
            <AppId>2B14D306-D8F8-4066-A45B-0FB3464C67F2</AppId>
            <LinkUri>http://apps.microsoft.com/app/2B14D306-D8F8-4066-A45B-0FB3464C67F2
            </LinkUri>
            <CurrentMarket>en-us</CurrentMarket>
            <AgeRating>12</AgeRating>
            <MarketData xml:lang="en-us">
                <Name>Trial management full license</Name>
                <Description>Sample app for demonstrating trial license management
                </Description>
                <Price>4.99</Price>
                <CurrencySymbol>$</CurrencySymbol>
            </MarketData>
        </App>
        <Product ProductId="bmx_ticket">
            <MarketData xml:lang="en-us">
                <Name>Buy Ticket</Name>
                <Price>49.99</Price>
                <CurrencySymbol>$</CurrencySymbol>
            </MarketData>
        </Product>
        <Product ProductId="bmx_table">
            <MarketData xml:lang="en-us">
                <Name>Register for Open Mic</Name>
                <Price>150.00</Price>
                <CurrencySymbol>$</CurrencySymbol>
```

```
            </MarketData>
        </Product>
        <Product ProductId="bmx_openmic">
            <MarketData xml:lang="en-us">
                <Name>Buy Table</Name>
                <Price>19.99</Price>
                <CurrencySymbol>$</CurrencySymbol>
            </MarketData>
        </Product>
    </ListingInformation>
    <LicenseInformation>
        <App>
            <IsActive>true</IsActive>
            <IsTrial>true</IsTrial>
            <ExpirationDate>2016-01-01T00:00:00.00Z</ExpirationDate>
        </App>
        <Product ProductId="bmx_ticket">
            <IsActive>true</IsActive>

        </Product>
        <Product ProductId="bmx_table">
            <IsActive>false</IsActive>
        </Product>
        <Product ProductId="bmx_openmic">
            <IsActive>false</IsActive>
            <ExpirationDate>2016-01-01T00:00:00.00Z</ExpirationDate>
        </Product>
    </LicenseInformation>
</CurrentApp>
```

An exciting marketing feature available for Windows is transparency into the origin of your app's downloads. This feature, called campaign tracking, allows you to track the referral source of customers who visited your app product description page in the Windows Store.

Licensing Your App (Trial Mode)

The next section goes into more detail about the various elements of the WindowsStoreProxy.xml file. For now, let's focus on the LicenseInformation section, with an emphasis on the IsTrial node, which in this document is set to true.

You interact with the Windows Store primarily through one class: CurrentApp. (Due to the aforementioned reasons, in this example you will use another class, the one that uses WindowsStoreProxy.xml, called CurrentAppSimulator. It mimics the API surface area of CurrentApp.) CurrentApp exposes a LicenseInformation property of type LicenseInformation which you can use to read the license data associated with an app. The bolded section of the WindowsStoreProxy.xml file in Listing 13-2 corresponds to this section. LicenseInformation provides properties like IsActive, IsTrial, and ExpirationDate. In normal circumstances (when your app has been published to the Windows Store and is public), calling Windows.ApplicationModel.Store.CurrentApp.LicenseInformation returns the LicenseInformation instance for the app. In this case, because your app isn't published yet, you have to use CurrentAppSimulator, which expects the WindowsStoreProxy.xml file to be in the previously discussed location when the property is invoked; otherwise an error occurs. Rather than digging through the Windows Store folders looking for the location where this file should be placed and manually editing it there, you might consider creating a temporary version of the file in your app package. This way the file can be edited as needed, and then, each time the app is started, published to the appropriate folder location.

In the BigMountainX project, add the `StoreProxy` folder; within it, add the file `TrialManagement.xml`, which is a copy of the `WindowsStoreProxy.xml` file you created in Listing 13-1. In Listing 13-2, you modify `App.xaml.cs` to load this proxy XML file.

Listing 13-2. Code for InitializeLicencingAsync

```
public static LicenseInformation License { get; set; }
public static ListingInformation ListingInfo { get; set; }
private static async Task InitializeAppAsync()
{
    ...

    await InitializeLicensingAsync();
}

async static Task InitializeLicensingAsync()
{
    var local = ApplicationData.Current.LocalFolder;
    var install_location = Windows.ApplicationModel.Package.Current.InstalledLocation;
    var proxyFolder = await local.CreateFolderAsync("Microsoft\\Windows Store\\ApiData", ↵
CreationCollisionOption.OpenIfExists);
    var installLocation = await install_location.GetFolderAsync("samples\\inapppayment\\
    licensedata");
    // open the proxy file
    StorageFile proxyFile = await installLocation.GetFileAsync("trialmanagement.xml");

    // create proxy file in application data
    var simulator_settings = await proxyFolder.CreateFileAsync("WindowsStoreProxy.xml", ↵
CreationCollisionOption.ReplaceExisting);

    // replace the contents
    await proxyFile.CopyAndReplaceAsync(simulator_settings);

    //load the listing information read from the file.  The currentproductsimulator seems
    //to expect a file in the location where i put it.  It reads it and uses it as if it is
    //coming from the marketplace.
    License = CurrentAppSimulator.LicenseInformation;
    ListingInfo = await CurrentAppSimulator.LoadListingInformationAsync();

}
```

Listing 13-2 starts by specifying the properties that store both the licensing and listing information for the app. The licensing information is self-explanatory; the listing information represents the data that would ideally show up in the Windows Store when the product is listing. Regardless of whether you're using a proxy file or going to the Windows Store for information about the app's license, it makes sense to store these values in a global area where they can easily be accessed throughout your app. After all, you use this information to determine what functionality to expose to the user and what functionality to hide. As the final step of the InitializeAppAsync function you make a call to InitializeLicenseAsync, the method that will do all the licensing initialization for the app.

InitializeLicensingAsync is fairly straightforward; you open or create the target folder where the proxy file should be, create the official proxy file there, and then copy the contents of your temporary proxy file (the one you work with and modify) to the official WindowsStoreProxy.xml file. At the end of the async chain you read the LicenseInformation. Again, because you're using CurrentAppSimulator, this reads from your WindowsStoreProxy.xml file and not the actual Windows Store.

To implement this functionality, you must first add a new page to the app dedicated to handling purchasing of tickets; the functionality you will be using highlights the purchasing features of Windows 10. For the purposes of this sample, BigMountainX will not allow users to purchase tickets unless they have purchased the app. This means that in trial mode you should see the options to buy things (and even get a prompt that allows the user to buy the item), but the user should not be able to make a purchase. Add a new page to the project called TicketingPage and apply the XAML shown in Listing 13-3 to it.

Listing 13-3. TicketingPage XAML

```
<Grid Background="#FF6A6A6A ">
    <StackPanel HorizontalAlignment="Center"
                VerticalAlignment="Center">
        <Button Content="Buy Standard Ticket"
                Margin="5"
                Click="OnStandardTicket"
                HorizontalAlignment="Stretch" />
        <Button Content="Buy Table (VIP Ticket)"
                Margin="5"
                Click="OnVIPTicket"
                HorizontalAlignment="Stretch" />
        <Button Content="Buy Open Mic Ticket"
                Margin="5"
                Click="OnOpenMicTicket"
                HorizontalAlignment="Stretch" />
    </StackPanel>
</Grid>
```

You must also modify ApplicationHostPage to connect to this page. Listing 13-4 shows the changes to the ApplicationHostPage XAML layout. Place this XAML directly underneath the layout for the Schedule Open Mic button.

Listing 13-4. Modifications to ApplicationHostPage

```
<Button HorizontalAlignment="Stretch"
        HorizontalContentAlignment="Left"
        Margin="0,5,0,0"
        Click="OnGetTicketsClicked"
        Background="Transparent">
    <StackPanel Orientation="Horizontal">
        <SymbolIcon Symbol="Calendar"
                    Margin="0,0,20,0" />
        <TextBlock Text="Get Tickets" />
    </StackPanel>
</Button>
```

Finally, you need to change the handlers for both this button and the Schedule Open Mic button to point to your newly created page. Listing 13-5 illustrates.

Listing 13-5. Modifications to ApplicationHostPage

```
...
private void OnOpenMicClicked(object sender, RoutedEventArgs e)
{
    root_frame.Navigate(typeof(TicketingPage));
}

private void OnGetTicketsClicked(object sender, RoutedEventArgs e)
{
    root_frame.Navigate(typeof(TicketingPage));
}
...
```

Listing 13-5 simply calls your new page, TicketingPage, whenever the Schedule Open Mic or Buy Tickets button is clicked. As stated earlier, the implementation you will initially be going with prevents any of the functionality found on this page if the app has not been previously purchased. The user can see the potential functionality but they can't use it. Listing 13-6 shows the code behind for TicketingPage.

Listing 13-6. TicketingPage Code

```
public sealed partial class TicketingPage : Page
{
    public TicketingPage()
    {
        this.InitializeComponent();
    }

    async void BuyApp(IUICommand c)
    {
        await CurrentAppSimulator.RequestAppPurchaseAsync(true);
    }

    async private void OnStandardTicket(object sender, RoutedEventArgs e)
    {
        if (App.License.IsTrial)
        {

            MessageDialog dlg = new MessageDialog(string.Format("{1}: I cost {0}", ➥
App.ListingInfo.FormattedPrice, App.ListingInfo.Description), "app is trial, why not buy it?");
            dlg.Commands.Add(new UICommand("Buy It", BuyApp));
            dlg.Commands.Add(new UICommand("No thanks", cmd =>
            {

            }));
```

```
            dlg.DefaultCommandIndex = 1;
            await dlg.ShowAsync();
        }
        else
        {
            MessageDialog dlg = new MessageDialog("Standard Ticket was purchased?");
            await dlg.ShowAsync();
        }
    }

    async private void OnVIPTicket(object sender, RoutedEventArgs e)
    {
        if (App.License.IsTrial)
        {

            MessageDialog dlg = new MessageDialog(string.Format("{1}: I cost {0}", ↵
App.ListingInfo.FormattedPrice, App.ListingInfo.Description), "app is trial, why not buy it?");
            dlg.Commands.Add(new UICommand("Buy It", BuyApp));
            dlg.Commands.Add(new UICommand("No thanks", cmd =>
            {

            }));
            dlg.DefaultCommandIndex = 1;
            await dlg.ShowAsync();
        }
        else
        {
            MessageDialog dlg = new MessageDialog("VIP Ticket was purchased?");
            await dlg.ShowAsync();
        }
    }

    async private void OnOpenMicTicket(object sender, DragEventArgs e)
    {
        if (App.License.IsTrial)
        {

            MessageDialog dlg = new MessageDialog(string.Format("{1}: I cost {0}", ↵
App.ListingInfo.FormattedPrice, App.ListingInfo.Description), "app is trial, why not buy it?");
            dlg.Commands.Add(new UICommand("Buy It", BuyApp));
            dlg.Commands.Add(new UICommand("No thanks", cmd =>
            {

            }));
```

```
            dlg.DefaultCommandIndex = 1;
            await dlg.ShowAsync();
        }
        else
        {
            MessageDialog dlg = new MessageDialog("Open Mic was purchased?");
            await dlg.ShowAsync();
        }
    }
}
```

Now that you have the details of the app's license, you can begin showing and hiding functionality as needed. As shown in Listing 13-6, all you need to do is read the value of `IsTrial` and, based on that, decide whether or not to allow the user to move forward.

Build and run the app, and then try to purchase a ticket. Figure 13-3 shows the look and feel of the app at this point.

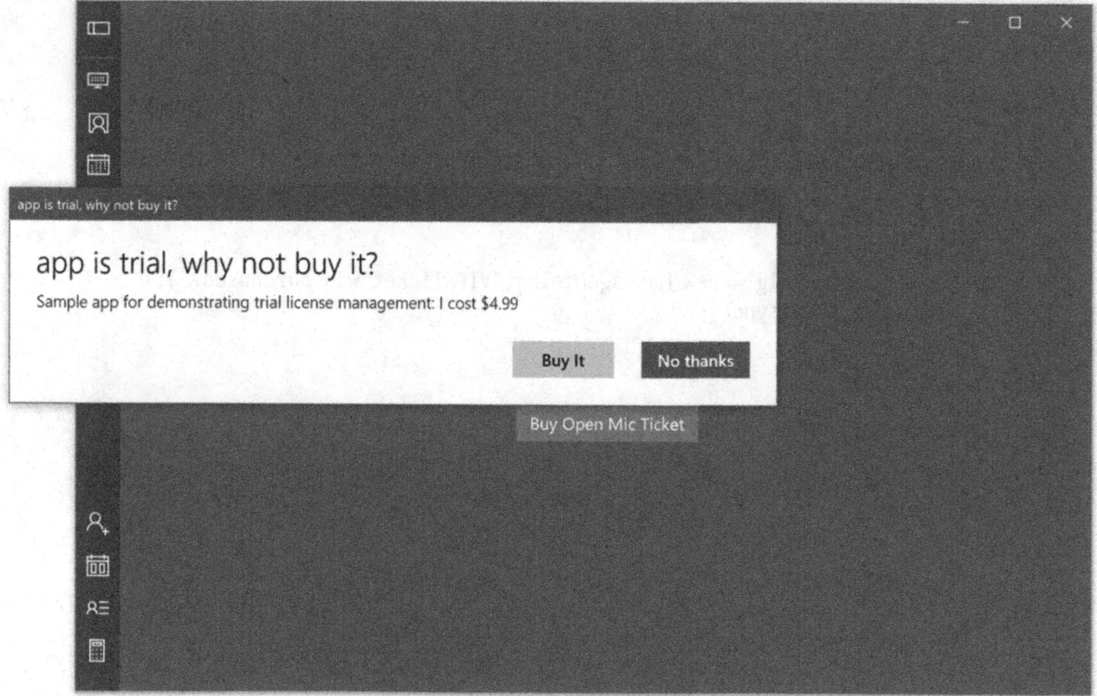

Figure 13-3. *Trial mode sample app*

To test the alternative scenario, update the license file with the value highlighted in Listing 13-7.

Listing 13-7. Updating the License File

```
<LicenseInformation>
    <App>
        <IsActive>true</IsActive>
        <IsTrial>false</IsTrial>
        <ExpirationDate>2016-01-01T00:00:00.00Z</ExpirationDate>
    </App>
    <Product ProductId="bmx_ticket">
        <IsActive>true</IsActive>

    </Product>
    <Product ProductId="bmx_table">
        <IsActive>false</IsActive>
    </Product>
    <Product ProductId="bmx_openmic">
        <IsActive>false</IsActive>
        <ExpirationDate>2016-01-01T00:00:00.00Z</ExpirationDate>
    </Product>
</LicenseInformation>
```

You can use the `IsTrial` value set here to toggle between testing the app as a trial and testing it as a full app. Alternatively, you can test by actually clicking the Buy It button. Figure 13-4 shows what is displayed in this case.

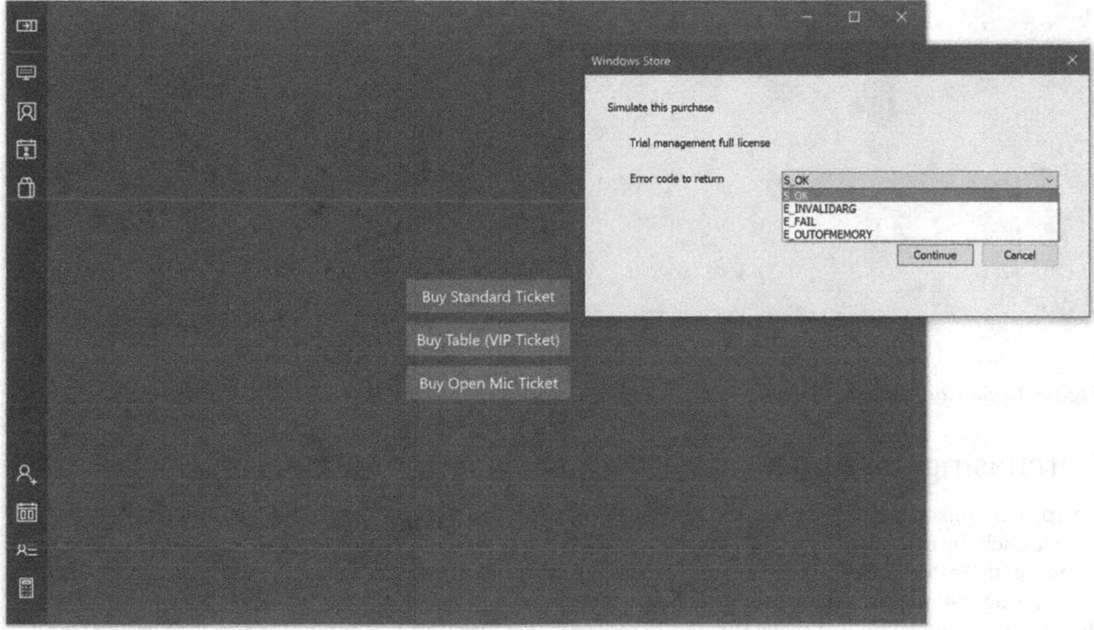

Figure 13-4. *App Simulator purchase dialogue*

This system-generated user interface allows you to test for the various situations that can occur during the purchasing process so that your app behaves appropriately in each case. If you proceed with the S_OK value, as shown in Figure 13-4, the app is shifted to a "purchased" state and all subsequent calls to this function treat it as such. The contextual meaning of each of these arguments in beyond the scope of this book. The important thing to keep track of is not blindly expecting any call to purchase an app to succeed when in trial mode. The Windows Store is not local to a user's machine; this means that at any point in time the network connection to it may fail, leaving the app unable to implement any change requested. As the developer, you must account for this scenario and provide a meaningful user interface to the user so that they have some idea of what is going on. The worst thing anyone can get from a user experience perspective is a cryptic, meaningless message. One of the key things that separates the top tier app developer from the run-of-the-mill app dev shop is the time that is taken on support and user messaging, specifically in scenarios where errors have occurred. Figure 13-5 shows the purchased screen.

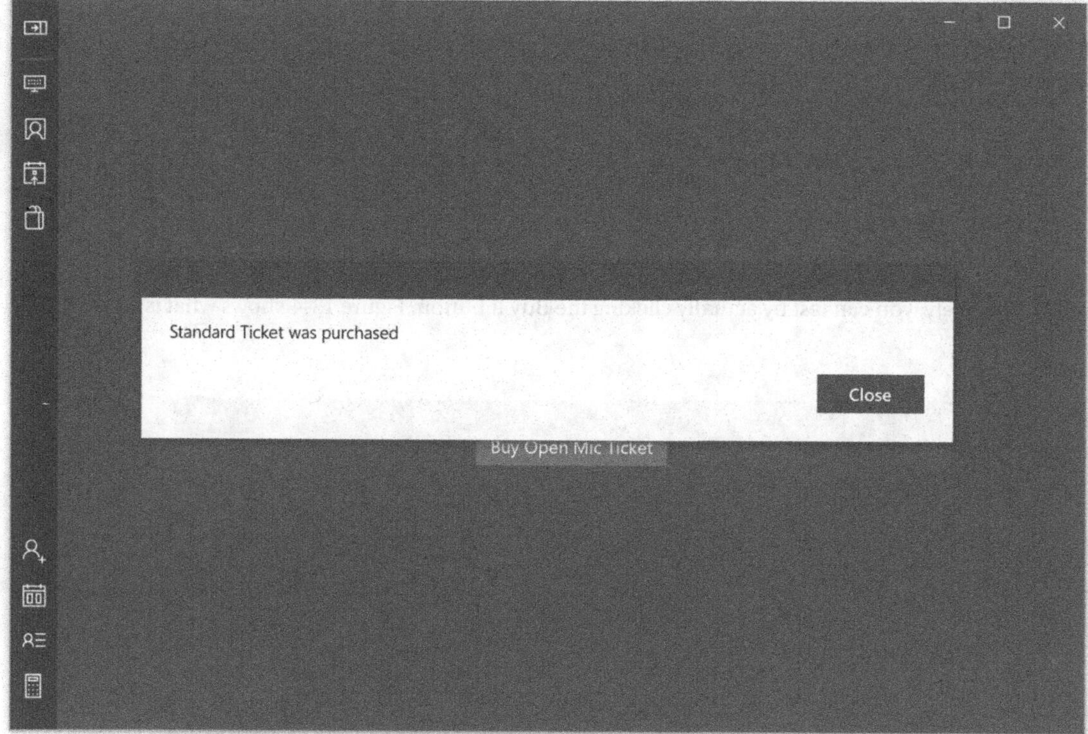

Figure 13-5. *Confirmation screen*

Purchasing the App

An app can make a purchase request on behalf of the user (this must be done via a user-driven event like a mouse click) by invoking the `RequestAppPurchaseAsync` method of `CurrentApp` or `CurrentAppSimulator`. Although the API is the same, the actions that follow differ based on which class is used. `CurrentApp` invokes the Windows Store purchasing user interface, whereas `CurrentAppSimulator` launches a legacy Windows dialog box in which you can select the type of response you want the simulator to return to your app (the same dialog box used earlier for purchasing the app). You can use this functionality to simulate various use cases beyond the happy path. Figure 13-8 (shown later in the chapter) offers a close-up look at the resulting dialog box when the Buy App button is clicked.

Your code should be able to handle these scenarios so your app doesn't crash. The value selected in the dialog in Figure 13-6 is passed as a parameter into the error event handler. You can use this value to present an appropriate message to the user.

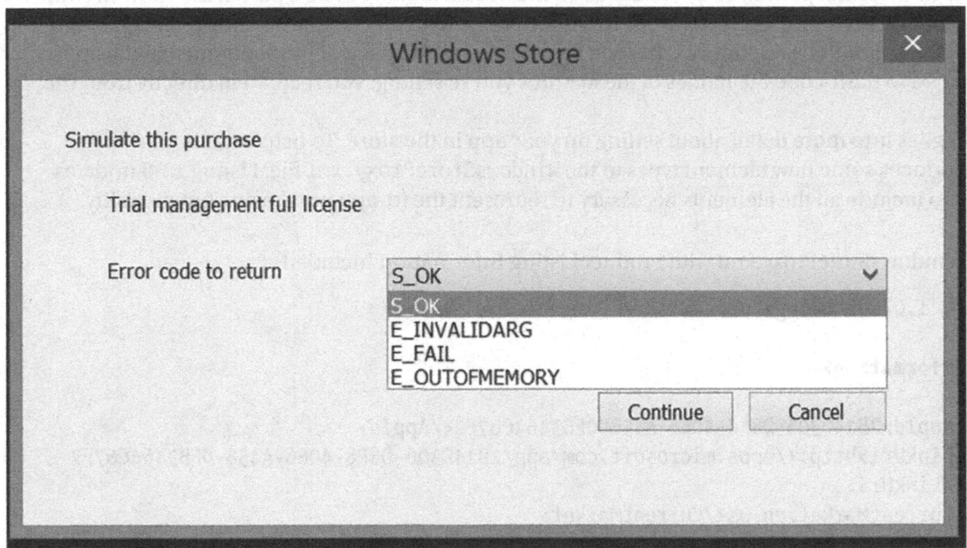

Figure 13-6. *CurrentAppSimulator purchasing dialog for testing purchasing scenarios*

Selling Within an App

You've looked at how to build out an app so it supports trials. This approach is predicated on publishing your app as a paid app. Paid apps represent the principle way of monetizing your app through the Windows Store but only scratch the surface of the overarching model.

Offering a trial is a good way to get potential customers to download your app and give it a dry run before committing to the cost, but this approach suffers from some distinct disadvantages when it comes to competing with the free counterparts. Statistics show beyond a reasonable doubt (and across all major app stores) that free apps are downloaded far more than paid apps and also have more activity and dialogue tied to them. Although a trial app is technically free, it is still listed in the Windows Store within the paid category, making discovery of your app an issue. Furthermore, as you saw from the previous example, the paid/trial model has limited flexibility. What we mean by this is that, as a developer, you really have only two products that you are presenting to the end user: the free version of the app and the full version of the app. The binary nature of the implementation restricts the opportunities for commerce that naturally exist within the app. For instance, suppose you created another cool piece of functionality that you valued at an extra dollar amount. That would raise the cost of the app to $5.99 (based on the `WindowsStoreProxy.xml` file, the product presently costs $4.99). Not only might the high price point be hard to digest, but it also removes the option of the user just paying for that one feature for the dollar. With in-app purchases, you can shift the pressure of purchasing away from the app as a whole and into specific features within the app. This kills two birds with one stone. On one hand, you shift your app to the higher-traffic free side of the world, making it easier to discover. On the other hand, you continue to monetize your app, this time with finer-grained control over which pieces of the app you provide for free.

A category of app that stands out in regard to in-app purchasing is gaming. Users often stumble on free games, which they are quick to download due to the nonexistent price tag. Once engaged (*addicted* is a common term), users are more apt to pay for additional features.

Adding In-App Purchasing to an App

Let's modify the example app to use in-app purchasing. So far you have an app that allows the user to purchase tickets as a normal patron, as a VIP, and as an individual looking to be a part of the show in some fashion (the Open Mic scenario). As you will see in a moment, you do this to take advantage of one of the benefits of using in-app purchases: the fact that you can define your catalog of products outside the app. You no longer need to hard-code the names of the features you're selling; you read them directly from the Windows Store.

Chapter 15 goes into more detail about setting up your app in the store. To help with this, in-app purchasing introduces some new element types to the `WindowsStoreProxy.xml` file. Listing 13-8 updates your local copy to include all the elements necessary to represent the in-app purchasing functionality.

Listing 13-8. WindowsStoreProxy.xml with Product Listing Information Included

```
<?xml version="1.0" encoding="utf-16" ?>
<CurrentApp>
    <ListingInformation>
        <App>
            <AppId>2B14D306-D8F8-4066-A45B-0FB3464C67F2</AppId>
            <LinkUri>http://apps.microsoft.com/app/2B14D306-D8F8-4066-A45B-0FB3464C67F2
            </LinkUri>
            <CurrentMarket>en-us</CurrentMarket>
            <AgeRating>12</AgeRating>

            <MarketData xml:lang="en-us">
                <Name>Trial management full license</Name>
                <Description>Sample app for demonstrating trial license management
                </Description>
                <Price>4.99</Price>
                <CurrencySymbol>$</CurrencySymbol>
            </MarketData>
        </App>
        <Product ProductId="bmx_ticket">
            <MarketData xml:lang="en-us">
                <Name>Buy Ticket</Name>
                <Price>49.99</Price>
                <CurrencySymbol>$</CurrencySymbol>
            </MarketData>
        </Product>
        <Product ProductId="bmx_table">
            <MarketData xml:lang="en-us">
                <Name>Register for Open Mic</Name>
                <Price>150.00</Price>
                <CurrencySymbol>$</CurrencySymbol>
            </MarketData>
        </Product>
        <Product ProductId="bmx_openmic">
            <MarketData xml:lang="en-us">
                <Name>Buy Table</Name>
                <Price>19.99</Price>
                <CurrencySymbol>$</CurrencySymbol>
            </MarketData>
```

```
        </Product>
    </ListingInformation>
    <LicenseInformation>
        <App>
            <IsActive>true</IsActive>
            <IsTrial>true</IsTrial>
            <ExpirationDate>2014-01-01T00:00:00.00Z</ExpirationDate>
        </App>
        <Product ProductId="bmx_ticket">
            <IsActive>true</IsActive>

        </Product>
        <Product ProductId="bmx_table">
            <IsActive>false</IsActive>
        </Product>
        <Product ProductId="bmx_openmic">
            <IsActive>false</IsActive>
            <ExpirationDate>2011-01-01T00:00:00.00Z</ExpirationDate>
        </Product>
    </LicenseInformation>
</CurrentApp>
```

Implementing In-App Purchasing

Implementing in-app purchasing changes an app in numerous ways. In the previous approach, you let the user click any of the purchasing buttons and they are immediately prompted with a message stating that they must purchase the app in order to use the feature. Now that you are transitioning the app to a commerce-style app, you should provide the user up front with information to help them make a purchase decision. To that end, you need to access product-listing information to identify the name of each feature and how much the feature costs. To start, you will need to add identifiable names to the buttons you previously created in TicketingPage. Listing 13-9 illustrates.

Listing 13-9. Modifications to TicketingPage XAML

```
<StackPanel HorizontalAlignment="Center"
            VerticalAlignment="Center">
    <Button x:Name="btn_ticket"
            Content="Buy Standard Ticket"
            Margin="5"
            Click="OnStandardTicket"
            HorizontalAlignment="Stretch" />
    <Button x:Name="btn_vipticket"
            Content="Buy Table (VIP Ticket)"
            Margin="5"
            Click="OnVIPTicket"
            HorizontalAlignment="Stretch" />
    <Button x:Name="btn_openmic"
            Content="Buy Open Mic Ticket"
            Margin="5"
            Click="OnOpenMicTicket"
            HorizontalAlignment="Stretch" />
</StackPanel>
```

Next, you modify TicketingPage to use the values from the `ListingInfo` object (the listing object you load up when the app starts). Listing 13-10 illustrates.

Listing 13-10. Modifications to TicketingPage Code

```
public TicketingPage()
{
    this.InitializeComponent();
    this.Loaded += TicketingPage_Loaded;
}

private void TicketingPage_Loaded(object sender, RoutedEventArgs e)
{
    SetButtonLabel("bmx_openmic", btn_openmic);
    SetButtonLabel("bmx_ticket", btn_ticket);
    SetButtonLabel("bmx_table", btn_vipticket);
}

public void SetButtonLabel(string key, Button button)
{
    var product_name = App.ListingInfo.ProductListings[key].Name;
    var product_price = App.ListingInfo.ProductListings[key].FormattedPrice;
    button.Content = $"{product_name} - {product_price}";
}
```

When you run the app at this point and navigate to the ticketing page, you should see something like Figure 13-7.

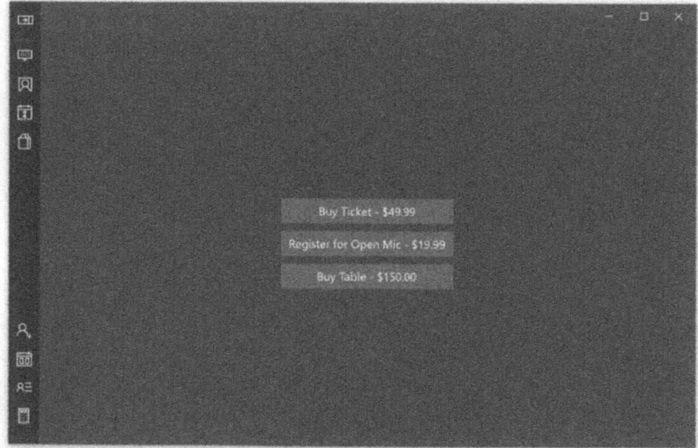

Figure 13-7. *User interface elements populated from the Windows Store listing*

Based on the sample so far, the user should be allowed to purchase one of the features highlighted in Figure 13-7 once they have bought the app. Listing 13-11 implements the necessary code to achieve the purchasing part of the functionality.

Listing 13-11. The PurchaseFeatureAsync Method

```
async Task PurchaseFeatureAsync(string feature_name)
{
    var feature = App.License.ProductLicenses[feature_name];
    if (App.ListingInfo.ProductListings.ContainsKey(feature_name))
    {
        var feature_listinginfo = App.ListingInfo.ProductListings[feature_name];
        if (feature.IsActive)
        {
            MessageDialog dlg = new MessageDialog($"You already have
            {feature_listinginfo.Name}");
            await dlg.ShowAsync();
        }
        else
        {
            MessageDialog dlg = new MessageDialog($"{feature_listinginfo.FormattedPrice}
            costs {feature_listinginfo.Name}", $"Buy {feature_listinginfo.Name}?");
            dlg.Commands.Add(new UICommand($"Buy {feature_listinginfo.Name}",
            async delegate (IUICommand c)
            {
                await CurrentAppSimulator.RequestProductPurchaseAsync(feature.ProductId);
                //CurrentAppSimulator.
            }));
            dlg.Commands.Add(new UICommand("No thanks", cmd =>
            {

            }));
            await dlg.ShowAsync();
        }
    }
    else
    {
        MessageDialog dlg = new MessageDialog($"{feature_name} does not exist in this
        application");
        await dlg.ShowAsync();
    }
}
```

In Listing 13-11, you use the `License` and `LicenseInfo` objects to determine which license is being requested for purchasing. Once identified, you call `RequestProductPurchaseAsync` on `CurrentAppSimulator` to purchase it. The logic is simple: when the user clicks either button, you check to see if the product feature has an active license. If it does, the feature functionality is invoked. If it doesn't, a request to purchase the feature is initiated with the store. As with app purchasing, `CurrentAppSimulator` presents the dialog in Figure 13-8.

The code in Listing 13-12 contains the modifications that need to be made to the TicketingPage page to enable using this functionality.

Listing 13-12. Modifications to TicketingPage to Support In-App Purchasing

```
async private void OnStandardTicket(object sender, RoutedEventArgs e)
{
    if (App.License.IsTrial)
    {

        MessageDialog dlg = new MessageDialog(string.Format("{1}: I cost {0}",
        App.ListingInfo.FormattedPrice, App.ListingInfo.Description), "app is trial,
        why not buy it?");
        dlg.Commands.Add(new UICommand("Buy It", BuyApp));
        dlg.Commands.Add(new UICommand("No thanks", cmd =>
        {

        }));
        dlg.DefaultCommandIndex = 1;
        await dlg.ShowAsync();
    }
    else
    {
        await PurchaseFeatureAsync("bmx_ticket");
    }
}

async private void OnVIPTicket(object sender, RoutedEventArgs e)
{
    if (App.License.IsTrial)
    {

        MessageDialog dlg = new MessageDialog(string.Format("{1}: I cost {0}",
        App.ListingInfo.FormattedPrice, App.ListingInfo.Description), "app is trial,
        why not buy it?");
        dlg.Commands.Add(new UICommand("Buy It", BuyApp));
        dlg.Commands.Add(new UICommand("No thanks", cmd =>
        {

        }));
        dlg.DefaultCommandIndex = 1;
        await dlg.ShowAsync();
    }
    else
    {
        await PurchaseFeatureAsync("bmx_table");
    }
}
```

```
async private void OnOpenMicTicket(object sender, RoutedEventArgs e)
{
    if (App.License.IsTrial)
    {

        MessageDialog dlg = new MessageDialog(string.Format("{1}: I cost {0}",
        App.ListingInfo.FormattedPrice, App.ListingInfo.Description), "app is trial,
        why not buy it?");
        dlg.Commands.Add(new UICommand("Buy It", BuyApp));
        dlg.Commands.Add(new UICommand("No thanks", cmd =>
        {

        }));
        dlg.DefaultCommandIndex = 1;
        await dlg.ShowAsync();
    }
    else
    {
        await PurchaseFeatureAsync("bmx_openmic");
    }
}
```

Running the sample here should function similar to the flow of purchasing the app. Figure 13-8 shows the UI when the user attempts to buy the "Register for Open Mic" feature.

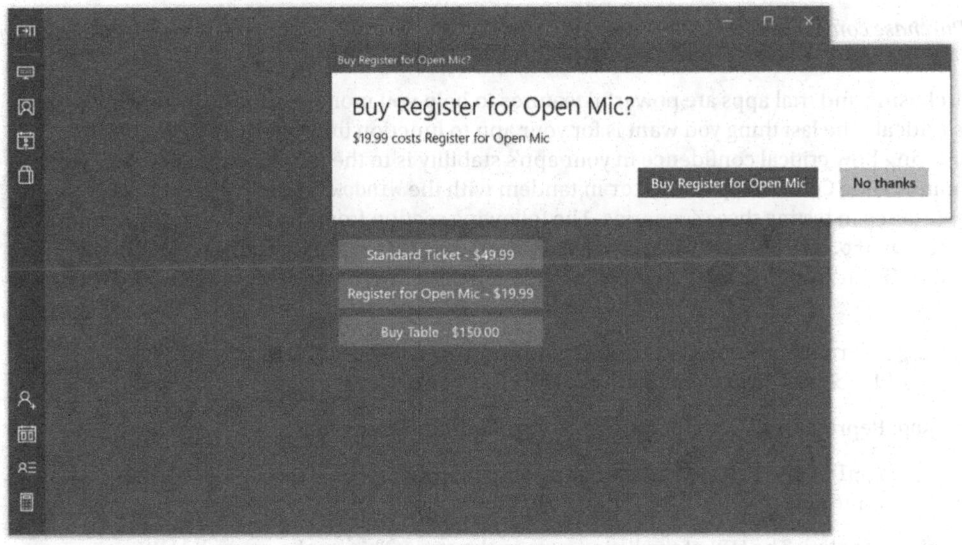

***Figure 13-8.** Prompt populated from the Windows Store listing*

Once you have purchased the item, each subsequent call to purchase will notify the user that they already own it. Another approach that might be taken is to simply remove the ability to attempt purchasing items that the user has already purchased by either disabling the button or removing it outright. Figure 13-9 shows the prompt the user gets if they attempt to purchase "Register Open Mic" again.

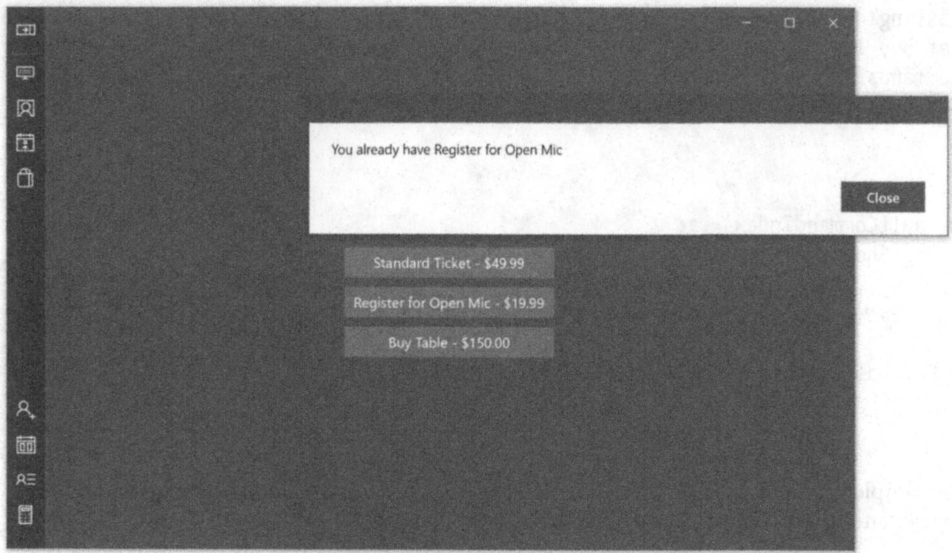

***Figure 13-9.** Purchase confirmation*

In-app purchasing and trial apps are powerful features to help you monetize apps, so ensuring proper functionality is critical. The last thing you want is for your app to function improperly in a purchasing scenario, considering how critical confidence in your app's stability is to the purchasing experience from a user's standpoint. Using `CurrentAppSimulator` in tandem with the `WindowsStoreProxy.xml` file is of paramount importance in testing these scenarios. The following section from the MSDN documentation (`http://msdn.microsoft.com/en-us/library/windows/apps/hh779766.aspx`) outlines in detail this file's various nodes. If you're interested in monetizing your app, be sure you understand how each of these nodes work.

1. `ListingInformation`: Represents data that would normally be found in the app's listing and includes these elements:

   a. `App`: Represents data about the app and contains these elements:

      i. `AppId`: The GUID that identifies the app in the store. This can be any GUID for testing.

      ii. `LinkUri`: The URI of the listing page in the store. This can be any valid URI for testing.

      iii. `AgeRating`: An integer that represents the minimum age rating of the app. This is the same value you specify in the Dashboard when you submit the app. The values used by the Windows Store are 3, 7, 12, and 16.

iv. CurrentMarket: The customer's country/region. For each country/region in which the app is listed, there must be a MarketData element:

1. MarketData: Info about the app for this country/region. Requires the xml:lang attribute, which specifies the country/region for which this info applies:

a. Name: The name of the app in this country/region.

b. Description: The description of the app for this country/region.

c. Price: The price of the app in this country/region.

d. CurrencySymbol: The currency symbol used in this country/region.

b. Product: Describes a product or a feature in this app that is enabled when the customer makes an in-app purchase. Requires the ProductId attribute, which contains the string used by the app to identify the product or feature. Requires the LicenseDuration attribute, which contains the number of days the license will be valid after the purchase. The expiration date of the new license created by a product purchase is the purchase date plus the license duration:

i. MarketData: Info about the product or feature for this country/region. Requires the xml:lang attribute, which specifies the country/region for which this information applies:

a. Name: The name of the product or feature in this country/region.

b. Price: The price of the product or feature in this country/region.

c. CurrencySymbol: The currency symbol used in this country/region.

d. CurrencyCode: The currency code used in this country/region.

2. LicenseInformation: Represents data that describes the licenses available for this app and includes the following elements:

a. App: Describes the app's license:

i. IsActive: Describes the current license state of this app. true indicates the license is valid. Normally this value is true, whether the app has a trial mode or not. false indicates an invalid license. Set this value to false to test how your app behaves when it has an invalid license.

ii. IsTrial: Describes the current trial state of this app. true indicates the app is being used during the trial period. false indicates the app isn't in a trial, either because the app has been purchased or because the trial period has expired.

iii. ExpirationDate: The date the trial period for this app expires. The date must be express as yyyy-mm-ddThh:mm:ss.ssZ. For example, 05:00 on January 19, 2012 is specified as 2012-01-19T05:00:00.00Z. This element is required when IsTrial is true. Otherwise, it isn't required.

iv. `DefaultResponse`: Describes the default error code returned by a given method. The `MethodName` attribute allows you to specify one of these methods: `RequestAppPurchaseAsync_GetResult`, `RequestProductPurchaseAsync_GetResult`, or `LoadListingInformationAsync_GetResult`. The `HResult` attribute allows you to specify the error code.

b. `Product`: Describes the license status of a product or feature in the app:

i. `IsActive`: Describes the current license state of this product or feature. `true` indicates the product or feature can be used. `false` indicates the product or feature can't be used or has not been purchased.

ii. `ExpirationDate`: The date the product or feature expires. The date must be express as yyyy-mm-ddThh:mm:ss.ssZ. For example, 05:00 on January 19, 2012 is specified as `2012-01-19T05:00:00.00Z`. If this element is present, the product or feature has an expiration date. If this element isn't present, the product or feature doesn't expire.

Summary

Whether taking steps to monetize your app is a necessary evil or the icing on the cake, it's something you should know about and can benefit from in real-world app development. This chapter provided the steps to follow, as well as some useful insight into how to effectively monetize your app. Key points covered in this chapter include the following:

- The Microsoft Windows Store can publish paid apps as trials, allowing you to create and maintain both a trial (free) and a full-functionality (paid) version of a single app, and to specify the conditions under which your app can be migrated from one version to the other.
- Implementing both trial and full-functionality versions of a single app is instrumental to upselling your app.
- It's important to use `CurrentAppSimulator` in tandem with the `WindowsStoreProxy.xml` file in testing scenarios.
- Monetizing your app via selling it is different than monetizing the app via selling within it.
- There are potential pros and cons to offering your app free, as a paid app, or as a paid app with a free trial option.
- Implementing in-app purchasing is a powerful methodology for monetizing the app.

CHAPTER 14

Leveraging Existing Code

If you're like us and you have been using Microsoft-based technologies to build user interfaces, you will likely be quite skeptical about the UWP and Windows 10 app development in general. It's been a long hard road for us. .NET was introduced on February 2002 and with it came WinForms, a replacement for Visual Basic 6 and MFC. Three years later (2005), WinForms was essentially supplanted (at least in the minds of Microsoft) by the paradigm-shifting Windows Presentation Foundation (WPF). Two years later (2007), Silverlight was introduced as an alternative to the heavy WPF for line of business applications, and it was awesome!

No sooner had we begun accepting this as the framework on which to build our legacies then the ground was pulled from under us, and WinRT was introduced as the "actual" future. This was 2012. If you consider that Visual Basic and MFC came out roughly in 1992/1992, it means that in the time that it took for Microsoft to go from those technologies to WinForms (10 years), Microsoft launched and re-launched three different paradigm-shifting user interface frameworks upon which we have had to create and recreate our apps.

It is no wonder the Windows Store is devoid of apps. Many think it is primarily because of lack of adoption tied to a lack of interest. The truth is it is a lack of adaption due to fear. Many app developers are simply in a wait-and-see mode when it comes to the constantly rebooting (no pun intended) frameworks introduced. I certainly cannot recommend ANY firm that I work with to adopt any such technology without at least waiting four years to see if it will stick.

The moral of the story is that the frameworks can and most certainly will change. Because of this, to get the most out of your work and save yourself a ton of rework, it is imperative that you build solutions that are composable, flexible, and transferable. In some cases, this might mean exploring technologies that allow you to leverage the code that you presently have within UWP apps. In this case, the approach to your legacy code will most likely not be affected by your introduction of WinRT to your portfolio. Others cases might mean utilizing code that is shared in some manner between your UWP app and your legacy code. In this case, there are a number of techniques that can be used.

In this chapter, you will explore several approaches to leveraging existing code from legacy applications. You will focus primarily on the following techniques:

- Portable class libraries
- Shared projects
- Localhost communication

Bear in mind that your choice of approach may have an impact on the deployment footprint of your app. If, for instance, you utilize a technique that allows you to make calls to the Win32 API, don't expect to run on anything but the Windows 10 desktop experience.

Sharing Code

In the old days, when you wanted to share code between multiple Visual Studio projects (and didn't want to get yelled at by the architect for copying the same class multiple times), you would use the trusty Add as Link context menu item on the Add Existing Item dialog. Figure 14-1 illustrates.

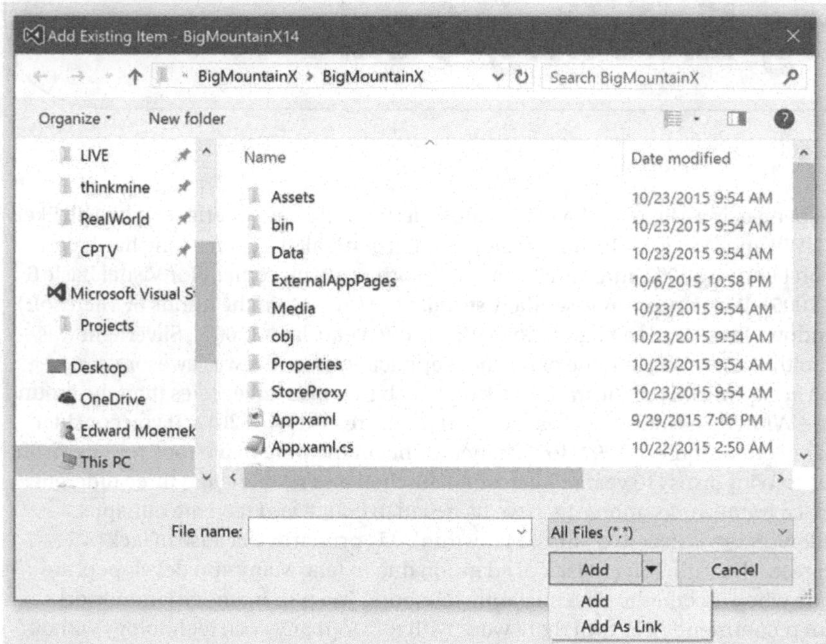

***Figure 14-1.** Adding a file as a link*

But this approach, while usable, was clunky since each separate source file had to be selected individually. With the move to supporting multiple disparate platforms (iOS, Android, etc.), Microsoft has finally innovated on this and decided to make it easier to share source between projects by adding the concept of a shared project. Shared projects provide a way of linking files in the manner described above at the project level. With shared projects, the files are consolidated into a project structure that can then be linked as a whole to other projects.

Unlike a class library, which is compiled and the unit of reuse is the output assembly, the unit of reuse for a shared project is the source code, and the shared code is incorporated into each assembly that references the shared project. This is quite useful when there is a need to create separate assemblies that target specific platforms but still have code that should be shared among them. The following example will illustrate how powerful shared projects are in helping you maintain a core set of functionality that can be transported across your projects, regardless of the technologies they utilize. For the purposes of this lesson, let's pretend that the sample you will be creating here came first. This will typically be the case for UWP apps as they are too young to have amassed the kind of library of work we see from legacy WinForms (or older apps). In this case, you will be creating a profile generation command line utility that can be quickly used to create and test profiles.

The common problem here is that you do not want to re-create all the types associated with your application state in this app. Using shared projects, you won't have to.

Start by adding a new console application to your project entitled ProfileGenerator. Figure 14-2 illustrates a created console application.

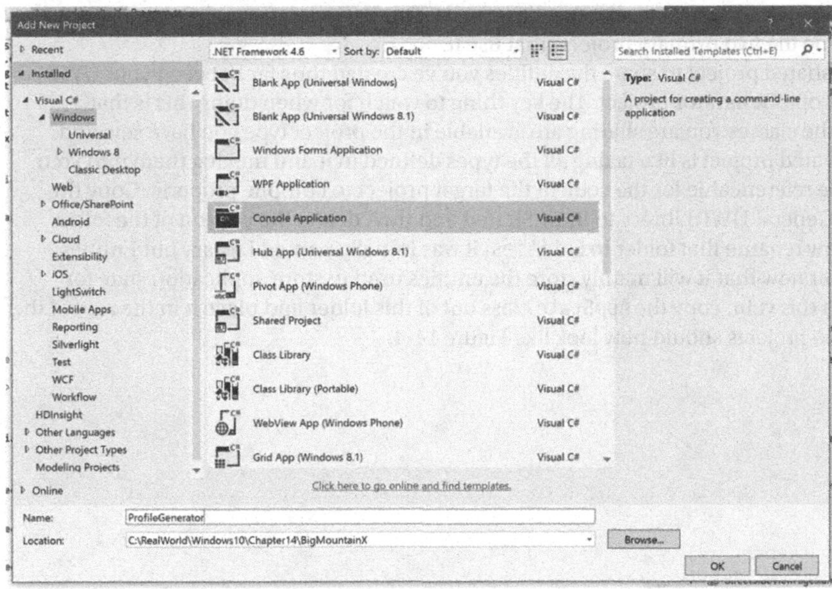

Figure 14-2. *Creating a console application*

Next, add a reference to the `System.Runtime.Serialization` assembly to this project.

Follow this up be adding another new project to the solution. This time select the Shared Project template and call it BMX.Shared. Figure 14-3 illustrates.

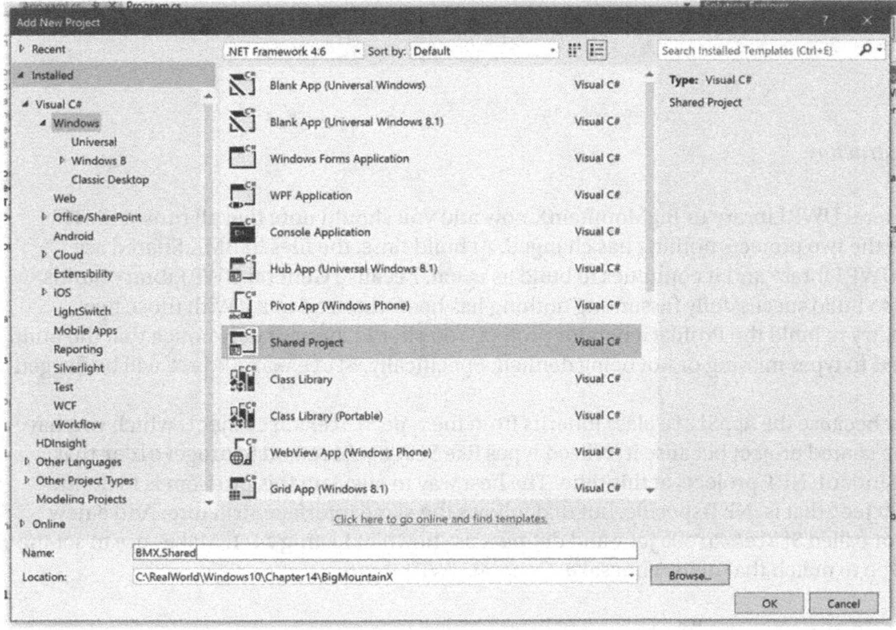

Figure 14-3. *Creating a shared project*

The next step is to add a BMX.Shared as a reference to both the ProfileGenerator and General.UWP.Library projects. These will be the two primary projects that use it.

You will be using your shared project to share the entities you've created thus far between your UWP app and your .NET-based ProfileGenerator project. The key thing to watch for when doing this is that the types exposed through the classes you are sharing are available in the project type you have selected. Remember, referencing a shared project is like taking all the types defined in it and moving them into your project. Those types must be referencable for the code in the target project to compile properly. Copy the entire `Library` folder from General.UWP.Library to BMX.Shared and then delete the version of the folder in General.UWP.Library. Now rename that folder to `Entities`; it was initially named Library but Entities is a better name for the folder now that it will mainly store the entities used to store application state for BigMountainX. Following in this vein, copy the `AppState` class out of this folder and place it in the root of the project. The layout of the two projects should now look like Figure 14-4.

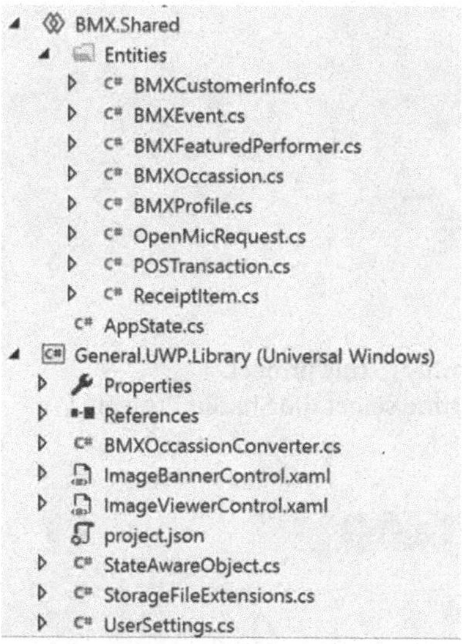

BMX.Shared
Entities
BMXCustomerInfo.cs
BMXEvent.cs
BMXFeaturedPerformer.cs
BMXOccassion.cs
BMXProfile.cs
OpenMicRequest.cs
POSTransaction.cs
ReceiptItem.cs
AppState.cs
General.UWP.Library (Universal Windows)
Properties
References
BMXOccassionConverter.cs
ImageBannerControl.xaml
ImageViewerControl.xaml
project.json
StateAwareObject.cs
StorageFileExtensions.cs
UserSettings.cs

Figure 14-4. *Project structure*

Try building General.UWP.Library or BigMountainX now and you should note that all runs well. This is because in terms of the two projects nothing has changed. At build time, the files in BMX.Shared are copied into General.UWP.Library and it continues to build as usual. Because General.UWP.Library builds, BigMountainX will also build successfully (assuming nothing has been changed in it). With those two projects building fine, try to build the ProfileGenerator project. You should immediately notice that the build fails with errors related to types missing or not being defined. Specifically, `StateAwareObject` will be flagged as unavailable.

You get this error because the `AppState` class inherits from the type `StateAwareObject`, which you have not carried over to the shared project because it utilized types like `StorageFile` and `StorageFolder` that are not available to standard .NET projects at this time. The best way to alleviate this problem is to define another `StateAwareObject` that is .NET-specific, but that follows the same interface structure. Add a new file to ProfileGenerator called `StateAwareObject` and define it as shown in Listing 14-1. Make sure to set the namespace for this type to match that of its namesake: General.UWP.Library.

Listing 14-1. Alternate StateAwareObject Class Definition

```
public class StateAwareObject<T> where T : StateAwareObject<T>, new()
{
    string _file_path;

    public string AsSerializedString()
    {
        DataContractSerializer dcs = new DataContractSerializer(typeof(T));
        MemoryStream ms = new MemoryStream();
        dcs.WriteObject(ms, this);
        ms.Seek(0, SeekOrigin.Begin);
        byte[] buffer = new byte[ms.Length];
        ms.Read(buffer, 0, buffer.Length);
        string serialized_object = Encoding.ASCII.GetString(buffer);
        return serialized_object;
    }

    public void Save()
    {
        var f = File.CreateText(_file_path);
        var serialized = this.AsSerializedString();
        f.Write(serialized);
        f.Flush();
        f.Close();
    }

    public void Delete()
    {
        File.Delete(_file_path);
    }

    public static T FromSerializedString(string resume_string)
    {
        try
        {
            var buffer = Encoding.ASCII.GetBytes(resume_string);
            MemoryStream ms = new MemoryStream(buffer);
            DataContractSerializer dcs = new DataContractSerializer(typeof(T));
            var retval = dcs.ReadObject(ms);
            var app_state = retval as T;
            return app_state;
        }
        catch
        {
            return null;
        }
    }
```

```
    public static T FromFileAsync(string file_path)
    {
        T app_state = null;
        if (File.Exists(file_path))
        {
            var serialized = File.ReadAllText(file_path);
            app_state = FromSerializedString(serialized);

        }

        if (app_state == null)
            app_state = new T();
        app_state._file_path = file_path;

        return app_state;
    }
}
```

In Listing 14-1, you have defined a new StateAwareObject with file access that is tailored to the full .NET Framework. Notice that both serialization methods remain unchanged. Build this and note that ProfileGenerator now contains no errors.

With the entities and state management shared between both projects, you can now implement the profile generation functionality in your console application. Listing 14-2 shows the implementation for the static method GenerateProfile on the Program class. This class does the actual profile generation.

Listing 14-2. GenerateProfile Method

```
private static bool GenerateProfile(int number_of_records)
{

    // State.UserProfile = null;
    if (State == null)
    {
        WriteLine("call load first.");
        return false;
    }

    //create sample customers
    int dob_years = (number_of_records % 20); //keep it to a max of 20 years
    foreach (var item_id in Enumerable.Range(0, number_of_records))
    {
        State.Customers.Add(new BMXCustomerInfo
        {
            CustomerID = Guid.NewGuid(),
            CustomerName = $"John Smith {item_id}",
            DOB = DateTime.Now.Subtract(TimeSpan.FromDays(365 * dob_years)),
            Email = $"test{item_id}@test.com",
        });
    }
```

```
    //create sample events
    foreach (var item_id in Enumerable.Range(0, number_of_records))
    {
        State.Events.Add(new BMXEvent
        {
            Address = $"{item_id} test street",
            Latitude = 40.7484,
            Longitude = -73.9857,
            CreateDate = DateTime.Now,
            Duration = TimeSpan.FromHours(item_id % 5), //keep it to a max of 5 hours
            EventID = Guid.NewGuid(),
            Description = $"A night of wine and comedy-{item_id}",
            EventTitle = $"Comedy Night at the Empire State-{item_id}",
            StartDateTime = DateTime.Now.AddDays(item_id),
            Feature = new BMXFeaturedPerformer
            {
                BIO = File.ReadAllText("../../artistbio.txt"),
            },
        });
    }
    //next event
    State.NextEvent = State.Events.OrderBy(i => i.StartDateTime).FirstOrDefault();

    //create sample mailing list data
    foreach (var item_id in Enumerable.Range(0, number_of_records))
    {
        State.MailingList.Add($"patron{item_id}@test.com");
    }

    State.Save();
    return true;
}
```

Given an AppState instance and a count, Listing 14-2 simply iterates through the count and adds some profile artifacts to the AppState object. Once completed, the AppState is then saved. The remainder of the class is implemented as shown in Listing 14-3.

Listing 14-3. ProfileGenerator REPL Loop

```
static AppState State { get; set; }
static void Main(string[] args)
{
    while (true)
    {
        Write(">");
        var input = ReadLine().Trim().ToLower();
        if (string.IsNullOrWhiteSpace(input))
            break;
```

```
        if (input == "load")
        {
            Write("File name>");
            input = ReadLine().Trim().ToLower();
            string bio_path = $"../../{input}.xml";

            State = AppState.FromFileAsync(bio_path);
            WriteLine($"Loaded {input}.xml");
        }
        else if (input == "end")
            break;
        else if (input == "clear")
       {
           State.Delete();

        }
        else if (input == "generate")
        {
            Write("Number of records>");
            input = ReadLine().Trim().ToLower();
            int count;
            if (int.TryParse(input, out count))
            {
                GenerateProfile(count);
                WriteLine("Generated");
            }
            else
            {
                WriteLine($"I dont understand '{input}'.");
                WriteLine("Enter 'end' or a number.\n");
            }
        }
        else
        {
            WriteLine($"I dont understand '{input}'.");
        }
    }
}
```

In Listing 14-3, you see that ProfileGenerator is a simple REPL (Read-Eval-Print) loop used to manage the population of arbitrary `AppState` files. The entire application is wrapped in a while loop that only ends when the user types "end" into the prompt. Typing "load" allows the user to load any arbitrary `AppState` file; if a file does not exist, an empty `AppState` object is used (as per the rules of `StateAwareObject`). Typing "clear" deletes the `AppState` (using the Delete function), and typing "generate" uses the next value inputted (a number) to generate the profile objects. Figure 14-5 shows a sample usage of the application.

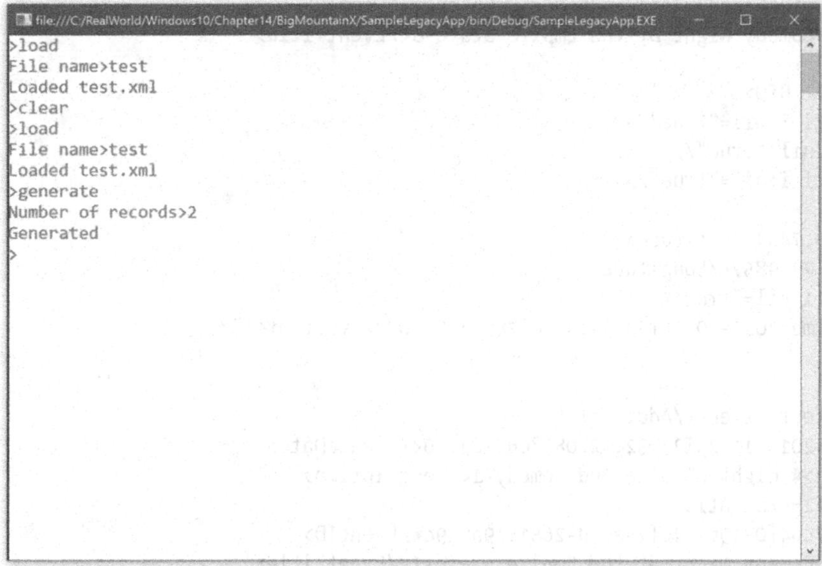

Figure 14-5. *ProfileGenerator interaction*

The commands shown in Figure 14-5 will generate the AppState XML in Listing 14-4 (the BIO section has been excluded to reduce length).

Listing 14-4. Generated AppState File

```
<AppState xmlns="http://schemas.datacontract.org/2004/07/BigMountainX"
xmlns:i="http://www.w3.org/2001/XMLSchema-instance">
    <Customers>
        <BMXCustomerInfo>
            <CustomerID>97670f39-1235-4732-a37f-93e33936e99e</CustomerID>
            <CustomerImage i:nil="true"/>
            <CustomerName>John Smith 0</CustomerName>
            <DOB>2013-10-25T23:32:32.0878067-04:00</DOB>
            <Email>test0@test.com</Email>
        </BMXCustomerInfo>
        <BMXCustomerInfo>
            <CustomerID>baa2e9c3-6c4c-407b-86db-90fa69263372</CustomerID>
            <CustomerImage i:nil="true"/>
            <CustomerName>John Smith 1</CustomerName>
            <DOB>2013-10-25T23:32:32.0878067-04:00</DOB>
            <Email>test1@test.com</Email>
        </BMXCustomerInfo>
    </Customers>
    <Events>
        <BMXEvent>
            <Address>0 test street</Address>
            <CreateDate>2015-10-25T23:32:32.0878067-04:00</CreateDate>
            <Description>A night of wine and comedy-0</Description>
            <Duration>PT0S</Duration>
```

```
            <EventID>c88b1d46-6e47-4ea1-ba23-96460a9bbcb2</EventID>
            <EventTitle>Comedy Night at the Empire State-0</EventTitle>
            <Feature>
                <BIO>...</BIO>
                <ImageUri i:nil="true"/>
                <Name i:nil="true"/>
                <VideoUri i:nil="true"/>
            </Feature>
            <Latitude>40.7484</Latitude>
            <Longitude>-73.9857</Longitude>
            <Occassions i:nil="true"/>
            <StartDateTime>2015-10-25T23:32:32.0878067-04:00</StartDateTime>
        </BMXEvent>
        <BMXEvent>
            <Address>1 test street</Address>
            <CreateDate>2015-10-25T23:32:32.0878067-04:00</CreateDate>
            <Description>A night of wine and comedy-1</Description>
            <Duration>PT1H</Duration>
            <EventID>017c04f0-19e5-4cf2-ae5d-26518c9a6a9c</EventID>
            <EventTitle>Comedy Night at the Empire State-1</EventTitle>
            <Feature>
                <BIO>...</BIO>
                <ImageUri i:nil="true"/>
                <Name i:nil="true"/>
                <VideoUri i:nil="true"/>
            </Feature>
            <Latitude>40.7484</Latitude>
            <Longitude>-73.9857</Longitude>
            <Occassions i:nil="true"/>
            <StartDateTime>2015-10-26T23:32:32.0878067-04:00</StartDateTime>
        </BMXEvent>
    </Events>
    <MailingList xmlns:a="http://schemas.microsoft.com/2003/10/Serialization/Arrays">
        <a:string>patron0@test.com</a:string>
        <a:string>patron1@test.com</a:string>
    </MailingList>
    <NextEvent>
        <Address>0 test street</Address>
        <CreateDate>2015-10-25T23:32:32.0878067-04:00</CreateDate>
        <Description>A night of wine and comedy-0</Description>
        <Duration>PT0S</Duration>
        <EventID>c88b1d46-6e47-4ea1-ba23-96460a9bbcb2</EventID>
        <EventTitle>Comedy Night at the Empire State-0</EventTitle>
        <Feature>
            <BIO>...</BIO>
            <ImageUri i:nil="true"/>
            <Name i:nil="true"/>
            <VideoUri i:nil="true"/>
        </Feature>
```

```
        <Latitude>40.7484</Latitude>
        <Longitude>-73.9857</Longitude>
        <Occassions i:nil="true"/>
        <StartDateTime>2015-10-25T23:32:32.0878067-04:00</StartDateTime>
    </NextEvent>
    <OpenMicRequests i:nil="true"/>
    <UserProfile i:nil="true"/>
</AppState>
```

Portable Class Libraries (PCL)

The good thing about shared projects is unfortunately the bad thing about them. Shared projects are ultimately a file-linking technology, which means that at compile time any referenced shared projects must have types within it that the referencing project understands. You saw this in the previous section when you tried to add `AppState` and found that because it inherits from `StateAwareObject` your console application would not compile. Because shared projects are a pre-compile linking technology, there are no framework compatibility issues associated with it. As you saw in the previous sample, if you are able to resolve any missing types (for instance, if you took the time to create a `StorageFile` and `StorageFolder` class in your console application, you would have been able to add both the `AppState` and `StateAwareObject` classes to `GenerateProfile`. Portable class libraries are a post compile-time technology that allow .Net IL code to be shared amongst participating platforms. They can help reduce the time and costs of developing and testing code. The types and members that are available in Portable Class Library projects are constrained by several compatibility factors:

- They must be shared across the targets you selected.
- They must behave similarly across those targets.
- They must not be candidates for deprecation.
- They must make sense in a portable environment, especially when supporting members are not portable. As an example, a Portable Class Library may contain UI-related types only when you target two platforms that support compatible UI-related functionality: Windows 10, Windows Phone Silverlight 8.1, and Windows Phone 8.1, for instance.

Creating a PCL

Add a new project to the solution called BMX.Portable, as shown in Figure 14-6.

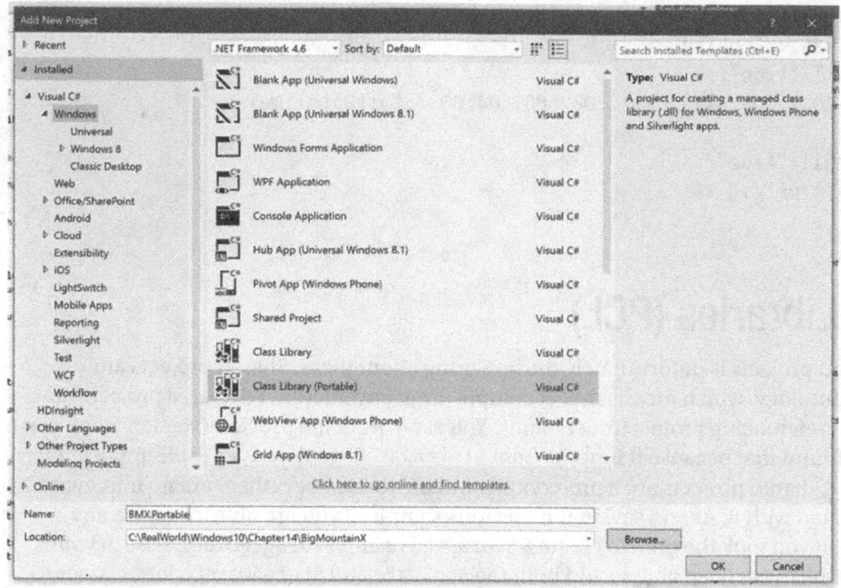

Figure 14-6. *Creating a Portable Class Library (PCL)*

Once you have clicked okay, you will be prompted to select the targets you want to have the ability to reference this portable library. Figure 14-7 illustrates.

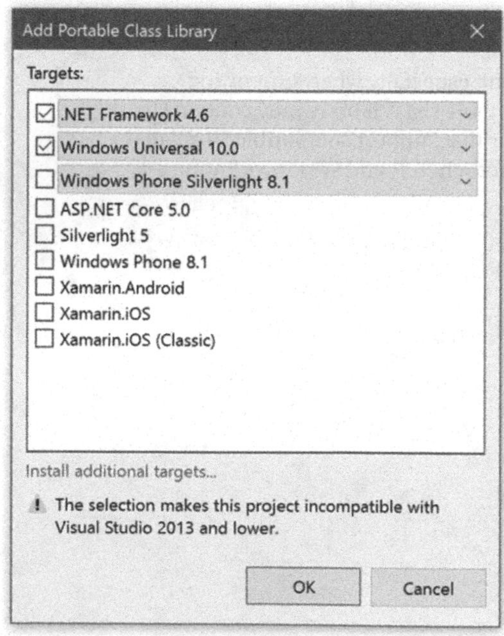

Figure 14-7. *Managing PCL targets*

In this case, you are saying that you want this library to be compatible with the .NET Framework and Windows Universal SDK 10 (UWP). As can be seen from the figure, you can also select to have the file compatible with Silverlight, Xamarin apps, and Windows Phone if needed. Don't be afraid of the choices made here. At any point in time they can be changed through the project properties page, as shown in Figure 14-8.

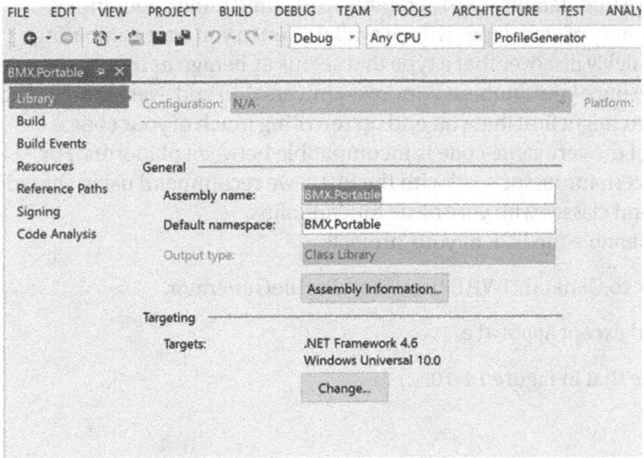

Figure 14-8. *Managing PCL targets*

Let's change the projects in your solution so they use this Portable Library instead of a shared project. You start the process by removing the reference to BMX.Shared from both ProfileGenerator and General. UWP.Library. To both of these projects, add the BigMountainX project and add a reference to the BMX. Portable library. Next, copy all the files from BMX.Shared to BMX.Portable. Also copy the file `QueryReader.cs` from General.UWP.Library to the portable class library (be sure to remove the original from General.UWP. Library). Because you have removed the reference to the BMX.Shared project, there is no need to delete the files from this project. Figure 14-9 shows what the project structure should look like at this point.

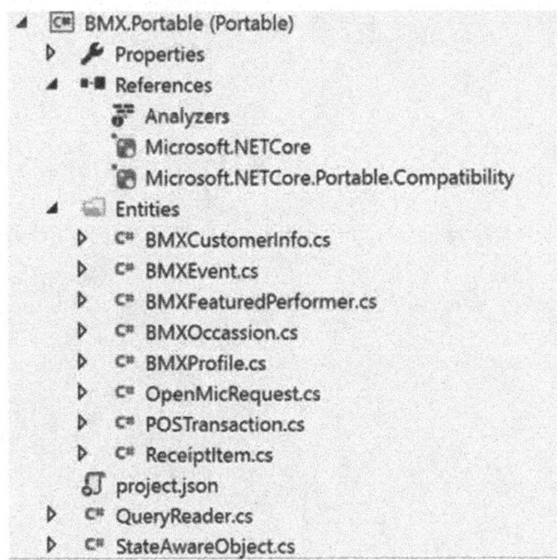

Figure 14-9. *Project structure*

You should immediately notice errors popping up all over the place. Because this is a standard library referencing pattern and not the linking strategy that shared projects employ, the approach you took in the last section will not apply. Creating an alternate version of `StateAwareObject` would mean that `AppState` would have to be aware of types in the project that references, something that would result in a circular reference if it were allowed. To employ Portable Class Libraries for your solution, a major redesign of `StateAwareObject` will be required. This redesign will need to take into account the fact that these types will be shared between platforms with varying technology implementations. The incredibly frustrating thing about this technique to leverage existing code is in the mystery of what types will be available once you start combining platforms. In your case, for instance, you will quickly discover that a type that seems as benign as the `DataContractSerializer` is no longer available once you combine Windows Universal 10 and .Net Framework. Based on the technologies you have utilized, you might find that you end up rewriting much of your code verbatim simply because the implementation of the very same code is incompatible between platforms. For this and the aforementioned high degree of uncertainty associated with the PCLs, we recommend using shared projects on anything other than entity classes and classes with very basic functionality.

Modify the project structure as follows to enable the PCL in your projects.

1. Add a BMX.Shared reference back to General.UWP.Library and ProfileGenerator.
2. Delete every file from BMX.Shared except `AppState`.

You project structure should now look like that in Figure 14-10.

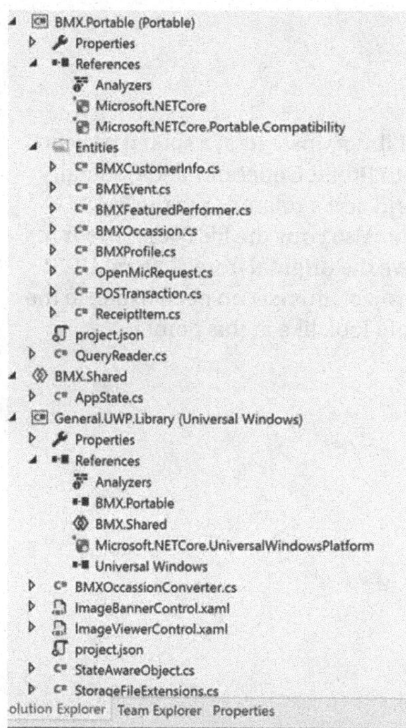

Figure 14-10. *Project structure*

Be sure to also comment out the `DataContractAttribute` decorating BMXOccassion. You will have a problem with serialization when you do this. This is because BMXOccassion does not have a public parameterless constructor (the constructor expects a BMXEvent instance). The best way to resolve this is to add this default parameterless constructor and then make the EventID setter public (it is presently private).

With the entities referenced in this manner they can easily be reused in your other apps, whether those apps run on WinRT, the UWP, or some future framework.

Localhost Access

When all else fails and there is simply no easy way to get your existing code over to the UWP world, some integration techniques exist that can be utilized to leverage the legacy code as is. The primary approach to accomplish this is through localhost access. Localhost allows you to communicate between your app and the local computer the code is running on through the networking stack. Programs running on the user's desktop (acquired through other means) can then be accessed from your UWP through this networking interface.

In the example to follow, you will be utilizing Windows Communication Framework (WCF for short) to accomplish this. WCF was released in 2005 alongside WPF, so it is a quite mature communication framework; it allows API-style interaction between disparate components through a varying number of supported protocols. In the example to follow, you will be utilized the TCP/IP stack to send the mailing list you generate via WCF to BigMountainX. To start the process, add a new interface to BMX.Shared called `IProfileGenerator`. Figure 14-11 illustrates.

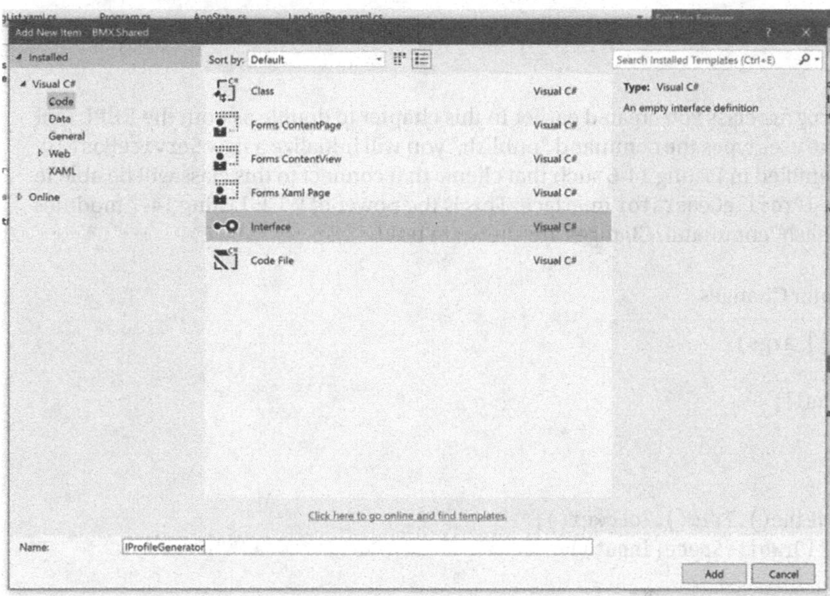

Figure 14-11. *Adding an interface to the project*

The code for IProfileGenerator is shown in Listing 14-5.

Listing 14-5. IProfileGenerator Interface

```
[ServiceContract]
public interface IProfileGenerator
{
    [OperationContract]
    List<string> GetMailingList(string file_name);
}
```

IProfileGenerator, shown in Listing 14-5, is a basic WCF interface, declared as such with the ServiceContract and OperationContract attributes used to decorate it. It exposes a single method called GetMailingList that returns a list of strings. In Listing 14-6, you modify the Program file from ProfileGenerator to implement this interface.

Listing 14-6. IProfileGenerator Implementation

```
class Program : IProfileGenerator
{
    static AppState State { get; set; }

    public List<string> GetMailingList(string file_name)
    {
        WriteLine("Retrieving...");
        string profile_path = $"../../{file_name}.xml";
        var app_state = AppState.FromFileAsync(profile_path);
        WriteLine($"{app_state.MailingList.Count} items found.");
        return app_state.MailingList;
    }
    ...
}
```

You will be using the Program class you created earlier in this chapter to double as both the REPL tool and a WCF service. When the user types the command "publish," you will initialize a new ServiceHost that exposes the method identified in Listing 14-6 such that clients that connect to this class will be able to call the method through the IProfileGenerator interface. This is the power of WCF. Listing 14-7 modifies Program to support the "publish" command. Changes are shown in bold.

Listing 14-7. ProfileGenerator Changes

```
static void Main(string[] args)
{
    ServiceHost host = null;
    while (true)
    {
        Write(">");
        var input = ReadLine().Trim().ToLower();
        if (string.IsNullOrWhiteSpace(input))
            break;
        if (input == "load")
        {
            Write("File name>");
            input = ReadLine().Trim().ToLower();
            string bio_path = $"../../{input}.xml";

            State = AppState.FromFileAsync(bio_path);
            WriteLine($"Loaded {input}.xml");
        }
        else if (input == "end")
            break;
```

```
        else if (input == "clear")
        {
            State.Delete();
        }
        else if (input == "generate")
        {
            Write("Number of records>");
            input = ReadLine().Trim().ToLower();
            int count;
            if (int.TryParse(input, out count))
            {
                GenerateProfile(count);
                WriteLine("Generated");
            }
            else
            {
                WriteLine($"I dont understand '{input}'.");
                WriteLine("Enter 'end' or a number.\n");
            }
        }
        else if (input == "publish")
        {
            if (host == null)
            {
                    host = new ServiceHost(typeof(Program));
                    NetTcpBinding tcp_binding = new NetTcpBinding(SecurityMode.None);
                    var address = "net.tcp://localhost:9999/profile-generator";
                    host.AddServiceEndpoint(typeof(IProfileGenerator), tcp_binding, address);
                    host.Open();
            }
        }
        else
        {
            WriteLine($"I dont understand '{input}'.");
        }
    }
}
```

That's it for the backed code. You are now able to listen to calls into your ProfileGenerator console application through WCF. Let's next turn our attention to the user interface for BigMountainX. Add a new page to the project called ManageMailList and implement the layout, as shown in Listing 14-8.

Listing 14-8. MainMailingList XAML Layout

```
<Page.BottomAppBar>
    <CommandBar>
        <AppBarButton Icon="ImportAll"
                          Label="Import All"
                          Click="OnImportAllClicked" />
    </CommandBar>
</Page.BottomAppBar>
```

```
<Grid Background="#FF6A6A6A">
    <ListView x:Name="gridview_events"
              SelectionMode="Single"
              ItemsSource="{x:Bind MailingList, Mode=OneWay}"
              >

    </ListView>
</Grid>
```

This view does nothing other than show a list of email address (strings from the mail list) returned from your call to ProfileGenerator through the localhost integration. Implement the code-behind class as shown in Listing 14-9.

Listing 14-9. ManageMailList Code-Behind

```
public sealed partial class ManageMailingList : Page, INotifyPropertyChanged
{
    public event PropertyChangedEventHandler PropertyChanged;
    List<string> MailingList { get; set; }
    public ManageMailingList()
    {
        this.InitializeComponent();
    }

    private void OnImportAllClicked(object sender, RoutedEventArgs e)
    {
        NetTcpBinding tcp_binding_client = new NetTcpBinding(SecurityMode.None);
        EndpointAddress address = new EndpointAddress("net.tcp://localhost:9999/
        profile-generator");
        ChannelFactory<IProfileGenerator> channel = new ChannelFactory
        <IProfileGenerator>(tcp_binding_client, address);
        var profile_gnerator = channel.CreateChannel();
        var list = profile_gnerator.GetMailingList("live");
        MailingList = list;
        PropertyChanged?.Invoke(this, new PropertyChangedEventArgs("MailingList"));
    }
}
```

In Listing 14-9, `OnImportAllClicked` creates a new WCF connection to the service running in ProfileGenerator. This is done via the Uri specified in the initialization of the `EndpointAddress` class. Once the class is created, you pass it into the call to create a new `ChannelFactory` (along with a `NetTcpBinding` object). Note that, at the time of this writing, security has not yet been implemented for this connection. Once you have the channel factory instantiated, you use it to create a channel to the remote object (`Program`) and then call `GetMailingList`, passing in the value "live". (For this to work, you must have created a new `AppState` file with the name "live".) When you get the results back, you store them in the local property your UI ListView is bound to (through compiled binding) and then invoke the `PropertyChanged` event, so that the binding framework is aware that `MailingList` has modified. The final step in the process is to modify ApplicaitonHostPage so that you can navigate to this page. Add the XAML from Listing 14-10 to below the "Manage Contacts" button.

Listing 14-10. ApplicationHostPage Modifications

```
<Button HorizontalAlignment="Stretch"
        HorizontalContentAlignment="Left"
        Margin="0,5,0,0"
        Click="OnManageMailingListClicked"
        Background="Transparent">
    <StackPanel Orientation="Horizontal">
        <SymbolIcon Symbol="List"
                    Margin="0,0,20,0" />
        <TextBlock Text="Manage Mailing List" />
    </StackPanel>
</Button>
```

Next implement OnManageMailingListClicked, as shown in Listing 14-11.

Listing 14-11. OnManageMailingListClicked Method

```
private void OnManageMailingListClicked(object sender, RoutedEventArgs e)
{
    root_frame.Navigate(typeof(EmployeeSignIn), typeof(ManageMailingList));
}
```

To test the connection, first create a new AppState file called "live" that you load with some records. Next, use the "publish" command to publish the WCF endpoint associated with ProfileGenerator. Finally, run BigMountainX. Figure 14-12 shows how ProfileGenerator looks when servicing requests from BigMountainX.

Figure 14-12. *The ProfileGenerator WCF interface in action*

Figure 14-13 shows how the BigMountainX ManageMailList page looks when the call to ProfileGenerator succeeds.

Figure 14-13. *BigMountainX ManageMailingList interface*

Summary

To put as simply and bluntly as possible, if you are building client-side applications that utilize Microsoft-based technology, be sure to separate the parts of your application that are technology agnostic from those parts that are not. This way, when Microsoft inevitable change strides yet again, you can minimize the amount of work you have to do to adopt the latest whim. Too many developers have suffered frustrating losses for this to be left to chance! To be successful and agile with the platform, your ability to leverage existing code will be critical. Using the approaches outlined in this chapter you will be on your way to building stable, transportable products. Key points covered in this chapter include the following:

- Using localhost integration to leverage application functionality from legacy apps through WCF.
- Using shared projects to abstract away program functionality that can easily be transportable. With shared projects, code files are consolidated into a project structure that can then be linked as a whole to other projects.
- Portable Class Libraries offer an alternate, albeit volatile, approach to sharing code between your projects.

- Portable Class Libraries must be shared across the targets you select.
- Portable Class Libraries must behave similarly across all selected targets.
- Portable Class Libraries must not include candidates for deprecation.
- Portable Class Libraries must make sense in a portable environment, especially when supporting members are not portable. As an example, a Portable Class Library may contain UI-related types only when you target two platforms that support compatible UI related functionality: Windows 10, Windows Phone Silverlight 8.1, and Windows Phone 8.1, for instance.

CHAPTER 15

Distributing Universal Apps

In Chapter 13, we dove into the monetization of your apps. We discussed, among other things, approaches to selling content through your app, and even selling your apps directly to the user. One part of the discussion was on enabling the app commerce functionality through the use of the `CurrentAppSimulator` class. We used this class because the primary class for app-based commerce, `CurrentApp`, connects directly to the Windows Store.

Using `CurrentAppSimulator` requires setting up an XML file to represent the state of the app in the store. You can use it to test out the behavior of your app based on the user's purchasing choices. In the real world, however, this XML file is not used. In real world scenarios, you must use the Windows Store app submission interface to configure and manage the purchasing requirements for your app, among other factors.

Pay close attention to the nuances of deploying apps into the Windows Store.

As a developer, getting your app on the Windows Store may be the most tedious part of the journey. But rest assured that adherence to the guidelines set forth in previous chapters will make getting your app accepted for publication as seamless as possible. Some administrative duties await that mustn't be ignored in order for you to get your app published in the Windows Store. This chapter discusses setting up a developer account, app submission, app tracking, and app management. You will learn about post-publication features including tools that provide a view of your sales data, downloads, activations, and telemetry. Hang on tight: you're almost there. You are now completing the final step toward sharing your Windows 10 app with the world!

Registering with the Dev Center

Windows 10 app submission starts and ends with the Windows Store Developer Portal (Dev Center) found at `http://dev.windows.com`. You will need a Microsoft account registered to this site in order to sign in. Figure 15-1 shows the landing page once you have signed in.

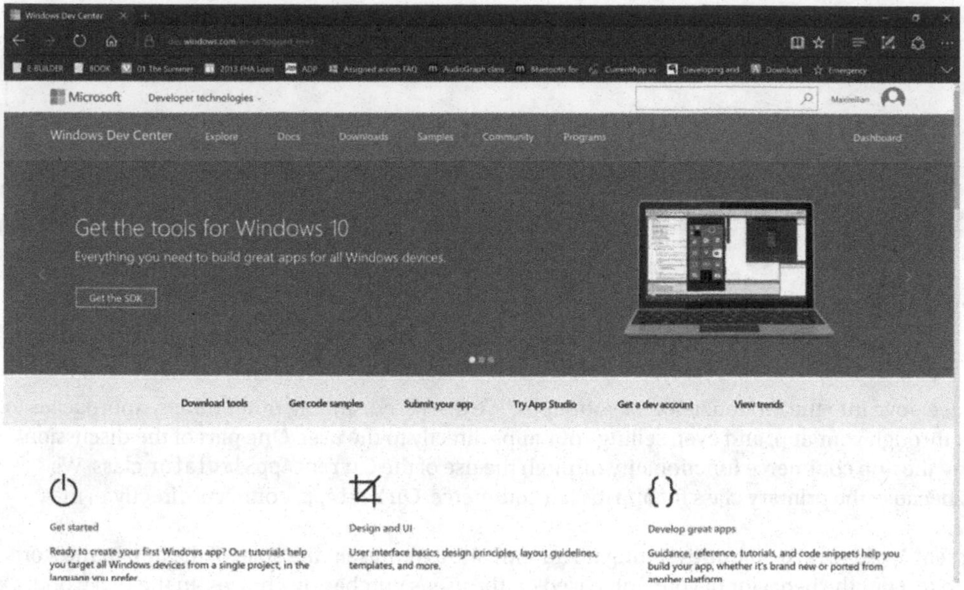

Figure 15-1. *Windows Dev Center landing page*

Clicking the Dashboard link at the top right of the page (just below your profile decal) will take you to the page shown in Figure 15-2 (cropped to reduce size).

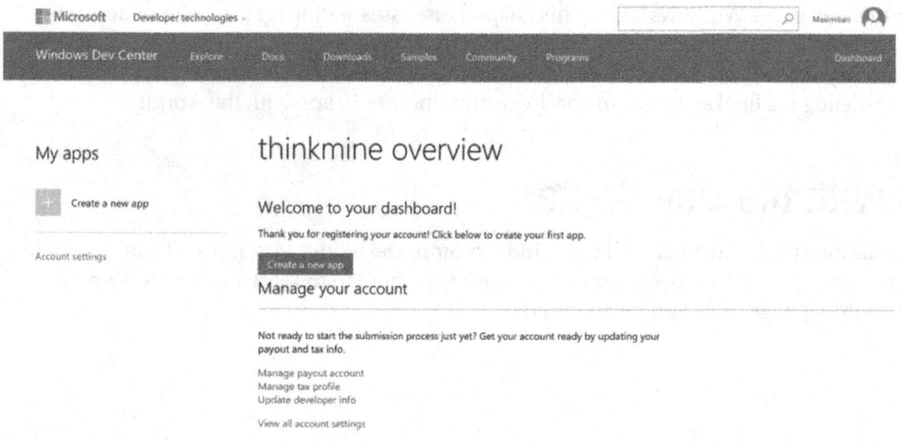

Figure 15-2. *Developer dashboard*

The dashboard is capable of providing detailed telemetry about your app's adoption metrics, which are too numerous to outline here. If you can imagine what a top level product manager might be interested in knowing to help craft adaption, the tools you might come up with will likely be on par with what is available through this dashboard. This information is tracked individually and across all your apps. The dashboard view in Figure 15-3 shows how the apps shown have fared in the past 30 days.

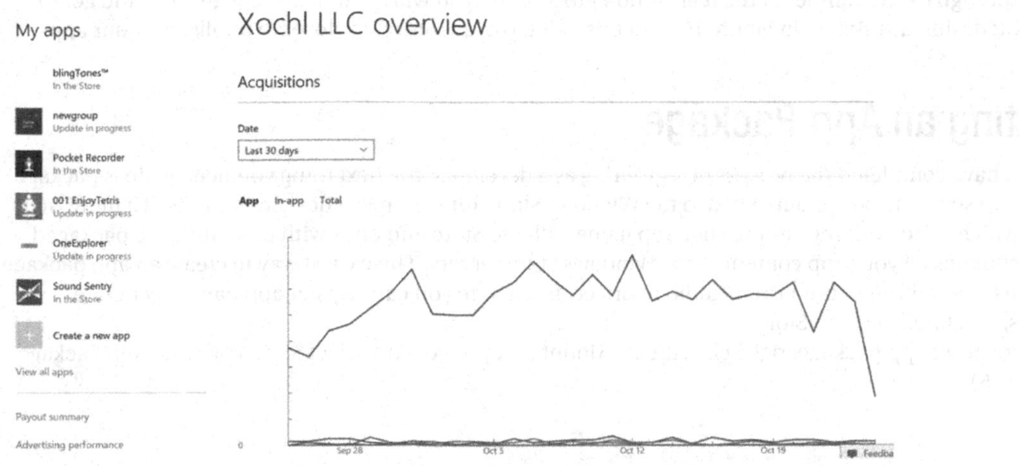

Figure 15-3. *Populated developer dashboard*

If you haven't already done so, go through the process of creating a new developer account by signing into the Dev Center with a valid Microsoft account. Once signed in, click the dashboard link as described above to start the process of registering to be a Windows 10 app developer. The process is relatively straightforward but may require you to pay a registration fee to get started. Additionally, if you are a business, you will have to go through a more detailed registration process. This chapter will only cover the "Individual" use case. To find out more about the "Business" use case, look to the Dev Center.

Figure 15-4 shows the top half of the registration page you are presented with once you sign in with your Microsoft account. This will, of course, only be presented to you if you have not previously registered as a Microsoft developer.

Figure 15-4. *Developer registration process*

Go through the remainder of the registration process and you will eventually be registered and get to the default dashboard shown in Figure 15-3. At this point, you are one step closer to publishing your apps.

Creating an App Package

Once you have completed the process of registering as a developer, the next thing you need to do is package your app up so that it can be published to the Windows Store. Interestingly enough, this is itself a multi-step process which starts with registering your app name with the Store and ends with uploading the packaged file that contains all your app content to the Windows Store servers. The easiest way to create an app package for submission is through the Visual Studio interface. From here you can register app names, generate packages, and publish to the Store.

To create an app package, right-click the BigMountainX project and select Store ➤ Create App Package (Figure 15-5).

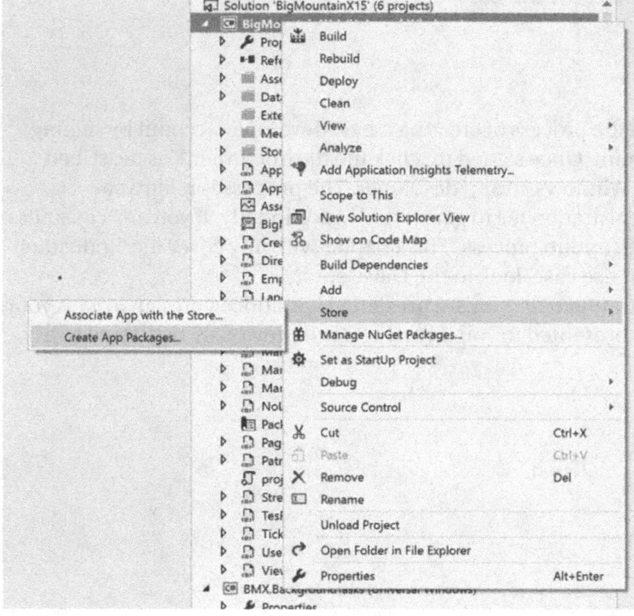

Figure 15-5. *Visual Studio's Submit App drop-down menu and submenu selections*

On the next screen, you will be prompted to select whether you want to build the app package for the Windows Store or not. Apps that are not built for the Windows Store publish the app package to a local directory. Apps that are meant for the Windows Store obviously are published there. Figure 15-6 shows the screen in question.

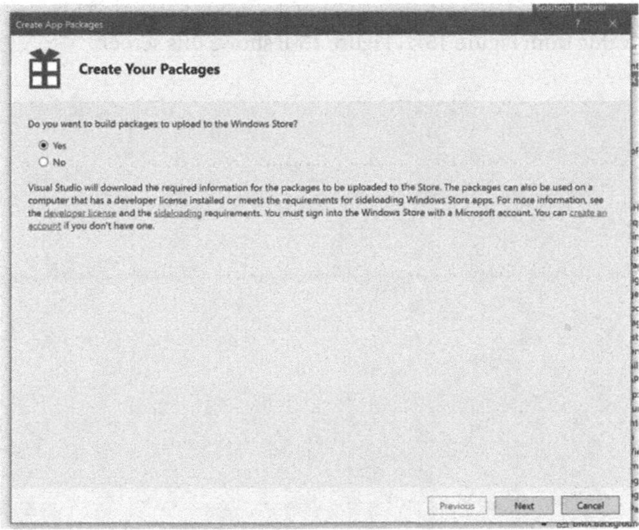

Figure 15-6. *Create package dialog*

Side Loading

Selecting "No" from this screen will put you on the path to creating a side-load capable app package ready to be installed on any developer machine or machine that supports this side loading. Figure 15-7 illustrates.

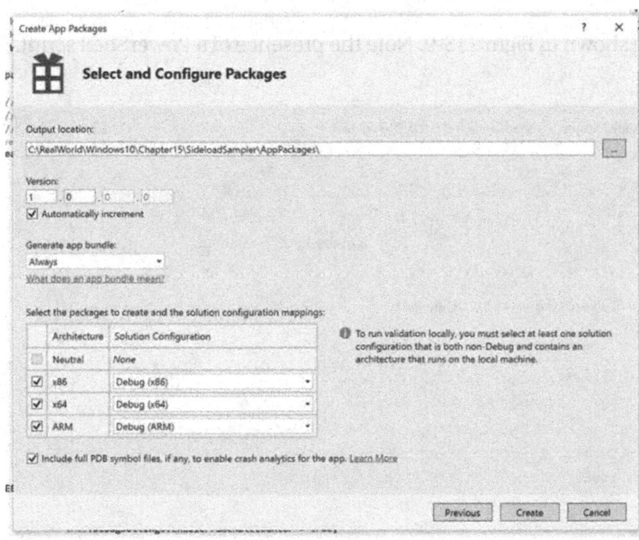

Figure 15-7. *Package selection dialog*

Once the packaging is complete, the dialog displays a link to the location of the published app. This can be modified if you change the Output location value from Figure 15-7. Figure 15-8 shows this screen.

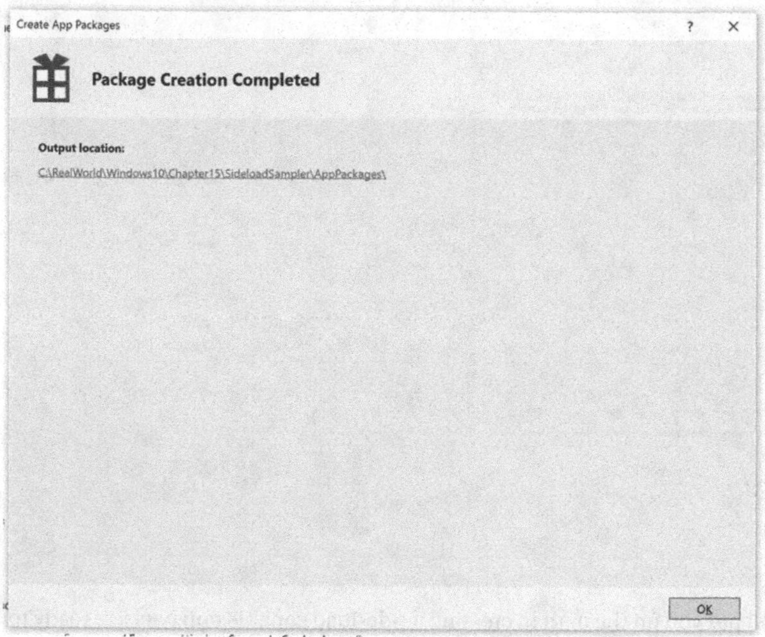

***Figure 15-8.** Package creation complete dialog*

The contents of the app package's folder are shown in Figure 15-9. Note the presence of a PowerShell script.

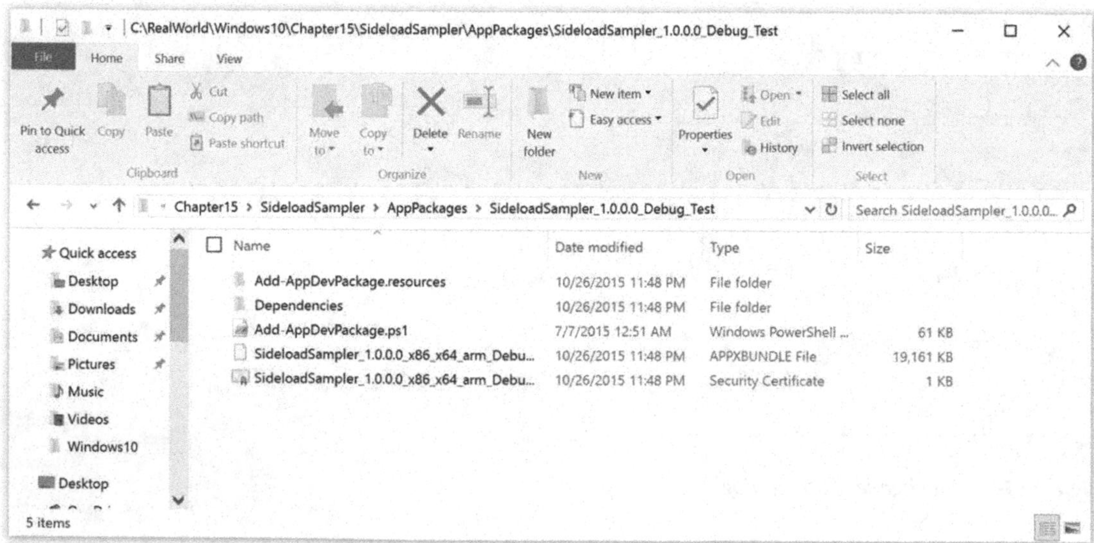

***Figure 15-9.** Local package folder structure*

Unlike Win32 applications, you can't just install UWP apps on any old machine. UWP apps require the device that the app is being side-loaded onto to specifically declare that it supports such app types. To declare a device as supporting developer or side-loaded apps, go to Settings ➤ Update & Security ➤ For Developers, and then select the developer feature you want enabled. Figure 15-10 illustrates.

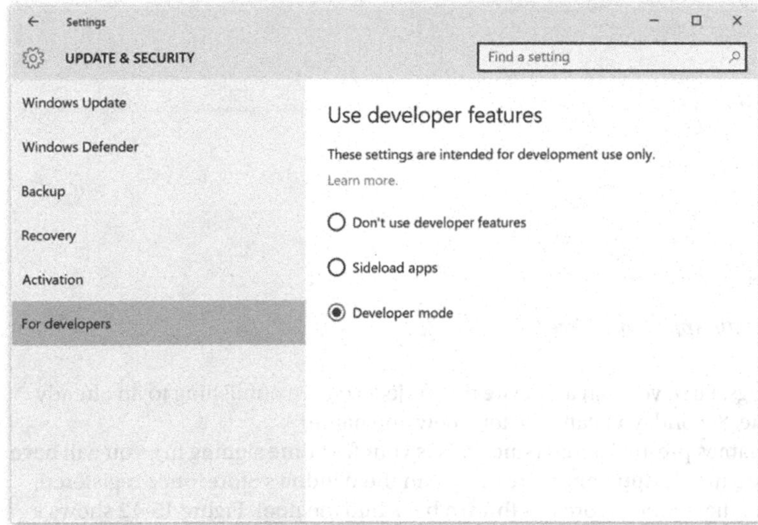

Figure 15-10. *Setting up Windows 10 Developer mode*

To install the app, navigate to the location of the file (using PowerShell) and then run the following command: `.\add-appdevpackage.ps1`.

You might have to initially set the execution policy for PowerShell using the command `Set-ExecutionPolicy RemoteSigned`.

Windows Store Distribution

Select the option to build the app package for the Windows Store and you will be prompted to sign into the Store with your Windows Developer account first. Once signed in, you will be directed to a screen where you can select the app name you want your app package to utilize. Figure 15-11 illustrates.

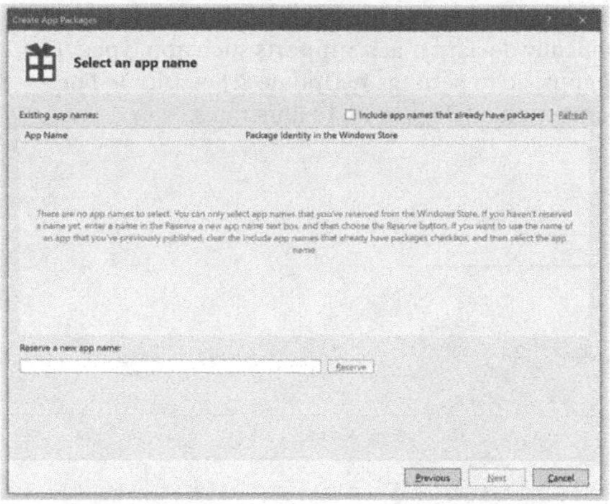

Figure 15-11. *Visual Studio's Select an App Name screen*

This screen allows for two things. First, you can associate the project you are publishing to an already registered Windows Store app name. Second, you can register a new app name.

As you undoubtedly have no names pre-registered (since this is your first time signing in), you will have to take the initial step of registering a name. App names are unique in the Windows Store; once registered, you have a year to publish an app to that name before it is thrown back into the pool. Figure 15-12 shows a new app name; once registered, the page refreshes and the app now shows in the App Name list.

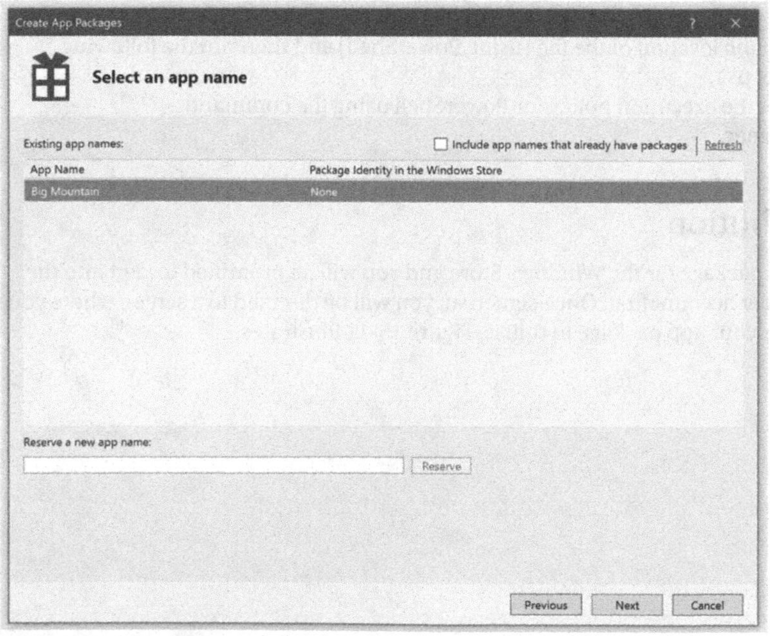

Figure 15-12. *Selecting an app name from the Windows Store*

As stated earlier, the Windows Store app names listed in Figure 15-12 are names you must have previously registered through the Windows Store developer center or through the "Reserve a new app name" command in the dialog box. Selecting one of these names associates the project you are working on with that particular app. In the case of Figure 15-12, it will make Big Mountain the app name for your Big Mountain X project. Doing this also pulls down all the identity information from the Windows Store and overrides the temporary settings in your app with them. As an example of this, open the app manifest for BigMountainX and navigate to the Packaging tab. You should now see new values all around, values that map to the name you have associated with the project. Figure 15-13 illustrates.

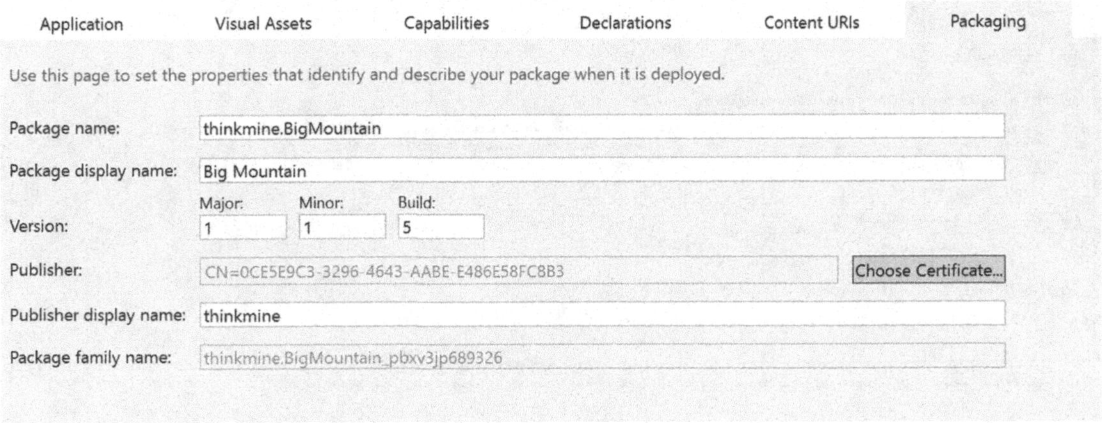

***Figure 15-13.** App manifest after Widows Store association*

Click Next, and you are shown a package settings screen where you specify the package output location, the version number, and the build configuration (see Figure 15-14). This is the same sort of screen you saw in Figure 15-13 but in this case a few extra items (relevant only to the Windows Store distribution model) are included.

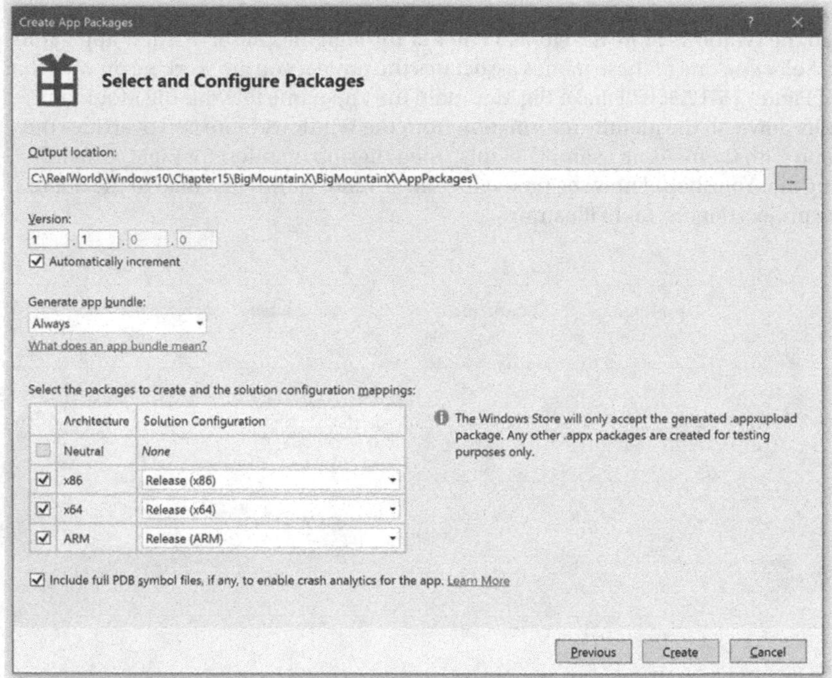

Figure 15-14. *Package settings screen*

App packages use a `.zip`-compliant appxupload packaging format for Windows 10 app publishing. An APPX package is what is downloaded to your machine when you install an app from the Windows Store; it is also the format you use for submission to the Windows Store. APPX packages can be deployed as x86 (for 32-bit operating systems), x64 (for 64-bit Windows 10 versions), ARM (for ARM-based phones, tablets, and PCs like the Lumia 950, Microsoft Surface, and Asus VivoTab). For Windows 10 deployment, you must explicitly specify all supported processor architectures. At the time of this writing, you can no longer specify the Neutral processor architecture.

Once you are done configuring how you want your app package to be created, click the Create button to build the package. Visual Studio compiles your project into the appropriate executable formats and packages them into an appxupload (this package will typically include all necessary certificates and package manifest files). At this point, the wizard is complete. The final step is to present you with the location where you can find the packaged file. Figure 15-15 shows this final screen (showing the path to the Big Mountain X package on our machine). You may run into a bizarre error during publishing, as we did.

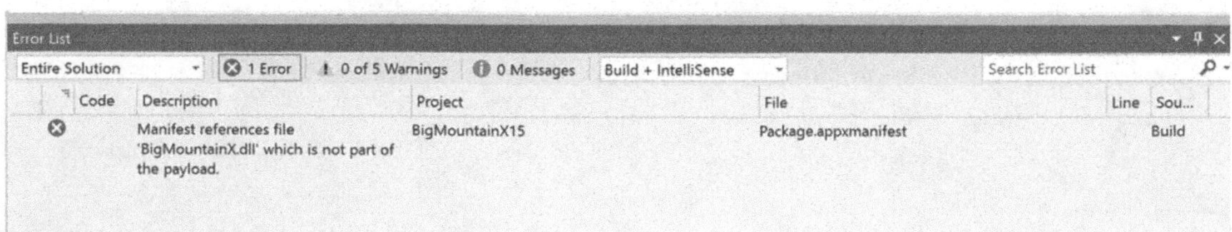

Figure 15-15. *Error screen*

We won't waste time explaining the convoluted reasons behind why it happens or what it means. It is a bug in Visual Studio 2015; that's really all you need to know. To work around this issue, follow these steps.

1. Right-click BigMountainX and select Unload project.
2. Right-click BigMoutainX again and select Edit Project File from the context menu.
3. Right underneath the first PropertyGroup node in the project XML, add the following XML:

```
<ItemGroup>
    <AppxSystemBinary Include="<assembly that shows in error>" />
</ItemGroup>
```

   So in this case the XML would be

```
<ItemGroup>
    <AppxSystemBinary Include="bigmountainx.dll" />
</ItemGroup>
```

4. Right-click BigMountainX and select Reload project.
5. Go through the steps to regenerate the app package. See Figure 15-16.

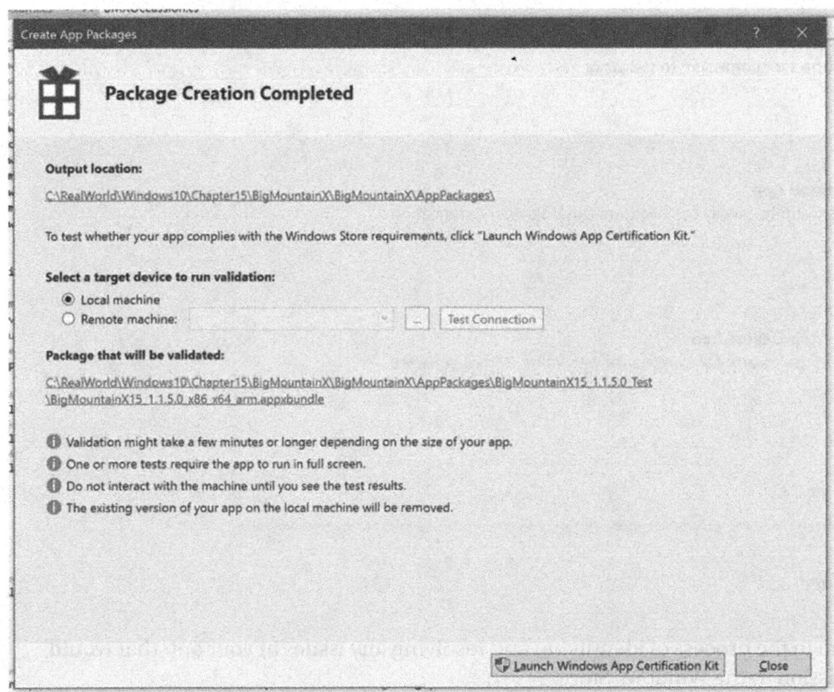

Figure 15-16. *The wizard's final screen*

Verifying Your App Package

In order for you to submit your app to the Windows Store, it must meet certain criteria identified by Microsoft. This ensures that apps in the Windows Store are safe for end users to install. It also means that there is a good chance that verified apps will work seamlessly on all platforms they target without exception. Microsoft expects your apps to utilize a standardized API surface area that is approved for use; they would also like for apps to follow design, style, and content guidelines that match the theme of the Windows Store, although this requirement has been loosened quite a bit since Windows 10 launched. Validating the content and style components requires human input; but as part of the app-submission process, the Windows Store automatically inspects the app package to determine which APIs and programming patterns you used. If the package doesn't meet the necessary requirements, it isn't accepted, and you will be unable to continue the submission process.

Microsoft provides a useful certification tool called the Windows App Certification Kit (WACK) that runs your app locally and performs a series of tests designed to find common and easily detected app certification failures. To launch it, simply use the Cortana and enter its name. You should also note that a button that activates it is available on the "Create an app package" completion screen. Figure 15-17 shows the WACK interface.

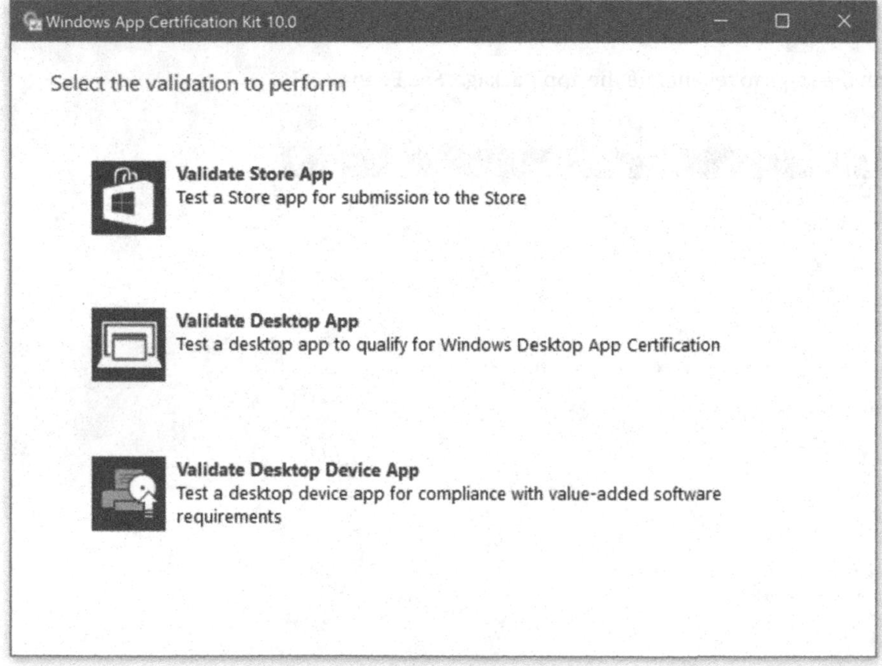

Figure 15-17. *WACK interface*

The WACK tool aids you in the process of identifying and resolving any issues in your app that would otherwise prevent its submission to the Windows Store.

The WACK test runs either in the background or in a small application window, depending on how you launched the tool. You will see your app appear and disappear several times over the few minutes WACK takes to run the complete set of tests. Whatever you do, don't attempt to interact with your app during the test, or your computer may overheat and explode.

Well, not quite, but your app will close, and you will not be allowed to interact with it. Once the WACK tool completes its tests, a results screen appears. If the test fails, the WACK tool report relays the reasons for the failure. If the WACK test passes, you can either head right to the Windows Store to continue your app submission, or look at the detailed report linked from the results window.

Built-in tests identify support-inclusion for support in previous versions of Windows (Windows 7, Windows 8, Windows 8.1) as well as identify and confirm compatibility with future versions of the Windows operating systems (Platform Version Launch Test). This new test flow will detect the app type and apply its corresponding test workflow as needed.

Enhancements since Windows 8 include an added check to rule out any wildcards in the domain information for top level domains in the App manifest test. App packages will fail if the wildcard is present. Also, the Application count is now its own test and has been removed from the App manifest test. Also removed from the API test is the App Notification Service Usage, which is now standalone as well.

Table 15-1 lists the tests performed by the WACK tool.

Table 15-1. *WACK App Tests*

Test	Description
Adherence to system restart manager messages	Ensures that the application exits as quickly as possible when notified of a system shutdown
Clean reversible install	Installs and uninstalls the app, checking for residual files and registry entries
Support x64 Windows	Ensures the .exe is built for the platform architecture onto which it will be installed
OS Version check	Determines how the app checks for the version of Windows on which it's running
Compatibility and resiliency	Verifies that the app doesn't use any Windows compatibility fixes
Crashes and hangs	Checks the app for crashes or hang-ups by performing startup, run, and shutdown processes
User account control (UAC)	Verifies unnecessarily elevated permissions aren't needed to run the app
Digital signed file	Verifies a valid digital signature
Safe mode	Verifies the driver or service is configured to start in safe mode
Installation and writing to the correct folder	Ensures writing of program and data files to the correct folders
Multiuser session	Tests how the app behaves when run in multiple sessions at the same time
Windows security best practices	Verifies that the app doesn't alter the default Windows security setting
Windows security features	Confirms there's no tampering with default Windows security protections
High DPI	Validates Win32 apps to be DPI aware

Submitting Your App

At the end of the previous section, you should have a verified app that you are sure can be submitted to the Windows Store without issue. You are sure of this because before attempting to submit it, you used the WACK tool to verify that the app meets the minimum criteria necessary to be allowed in the Windows Store.

This section covers using the developer dashboard to upload this verified app package to the Windows Store and completing the process by submitting your app for certification by the Store. Again, if you have existing apps on the Windows 8 platform or if you had apps on both Windows and Windows Phone, here you will experience the new Unified Developer Dashboard in which all your accounts are merged. Other functionality previously handled in the other developer dashboards associated with Windows Phone, such as managing ads and promoting your apps, are now located in the Dev Center, your single, unified place in which to manage your apps.

You can access the Windows Store Dev Center by navigating to `http://dev.windows.com`. Once there, you sign in with your Windows Store account (typically a `Hotmail/Live/Outlook.com` e-mail address). Figure 15-18 shows the Dev Center landing page.

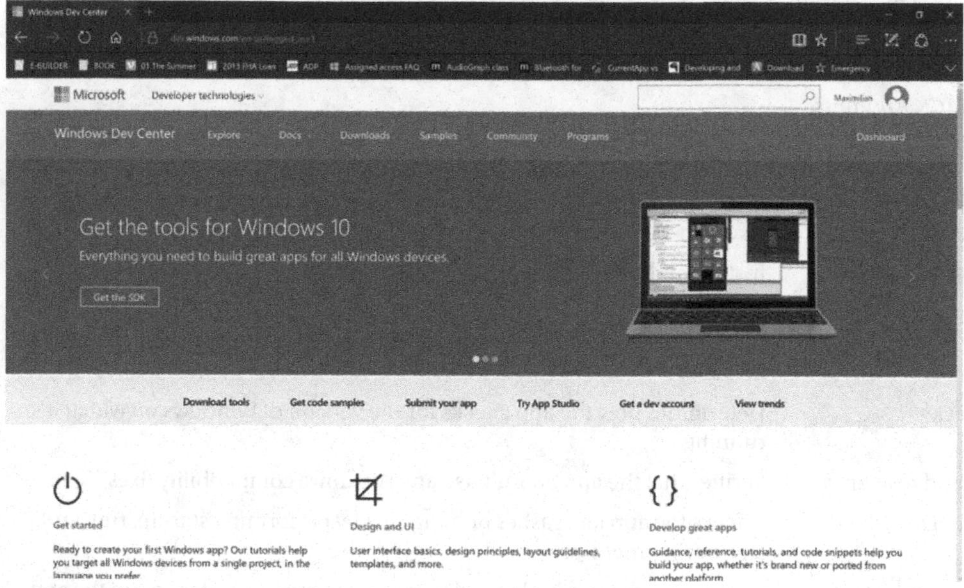

Figure 15-18. *Dev Center landing page*

Nothing you have done so far requires you to sign up for anything, but you need a developer account to reserve app names and submit applications to the Windows Store.

Once you are signed up and signed in, clicking the Dashboard link (shown in Figure 15-17) takes you into your Windows Store dashboard for Windows 10 apps. Figure 15-19 shows the Windows Store dashboard.

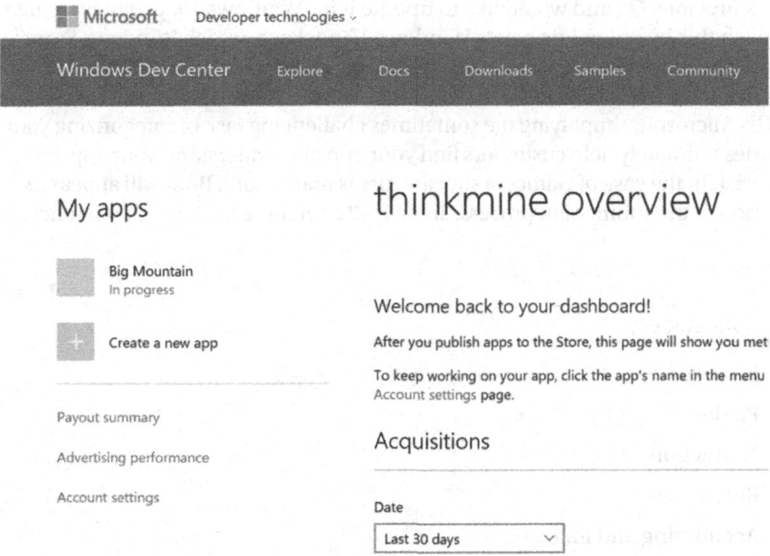

Figure 15-19. *Windows Store dashboard*

The primary means of submitting an app to the Windows Store is through the "Create a new app" link on the Dev Center dashboard (if you have already started a submission through Visual Studio or the dashboard, you can also continue it from here). Clicking this link puts you in a workflow that takes you all the way from giving your application a name to providing a detailed description for it. As part of the submission process, you must also provide selling details for your application, tying in everything you learned in Chapter 13. This means not only providing pricing for the app as a whole but also providing pricing for features that exist within the app (in-app offers are included in the IAPs section of the app configuration area, and Figure 15-20 illustrates).

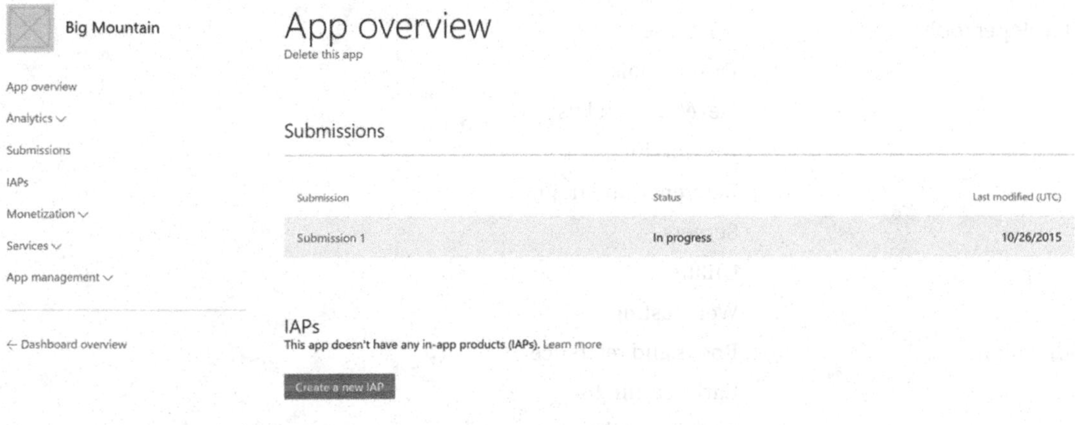

Figure 15-20. *App overview screen*

If you have an existing app in a previous OS and would like to update it for Windows 10, you may update your submission. You can accomplish this by uploading a new Windows 10 package, which Windows Store will automatically add to your apps. The Store then automatically selects the most compatible version for each customer's device from your available app packages.

Types of apps are categorized by Microsoft, simplifying the sometimes challenging task of categorizing your creation. Categories and subcategories ultimately help customers find your app and understand your app. For some categories, no subcategories exist. In the case of Games, a subcategory is mandatory. Both will appear in separate drop-downs for your selection in the submission process. Table 15-2 contains a list for your reference.

Table 15-2. *App Categories*

Category	Subcategory
Books and reference	E-reader
	Fiction
	Nonfiction
	Reference
Business	Accounting and finance
	Collaboration
	CRM
	Data and analytics
	File management
	Inventory and logistics
	Legal and HR
	Project management
	Remote desktop
	Sales and marketing
	Time and expenses
Developer tools	Database
	Design tools
	Development kits
	Networking
	Reference and training
	Servers
	Utilities
	Web hosting
Education	Books and reference
	Early learning
	Instructional tools
	Language
	Study aids

(*continued*)

Table 15-2. *(continued)*

Category	Subcategory
Entertainment	(None)
Food and dining	(None)
Games	Action and adventure
	Card and board
	Casino
	Educational
	Family and kids
	Fighting
	Music
	Platformer
	Puzzle and trivia
	Racing and flying
	Role playing
	Shooter
	Simulation
	Sports
	Strategy
	Word
Government and politics	(None)
Health and fitness	(None)
Kids and family	Books and reference
	Entertainment
	Hobbies and toys
	Sports and activities
	Travel
Lifestyle	Automotive
	DIY
	Home and garden
	Relationships
	Special interest
	Style and fashion
Medical	(None)
Multimedia design	Illustration and graphic design
	Music production
	Photo and video production

(*continued*)

Table 15-2. *(continued)*

Category	Subcategory
Music	(None)
Navigation and maps	(None)
News and weather	News
	Weather
Personal finance	Banking and investments
	Budgeting and taxes
Personalization	Ringtones and sounds
	Themes
	Wallpaper and lock screens
Photo and video	(None)
Productivity	(None)
Security	PC protection
	Personal security
Shopping	(None)
Social	(None)
Sports	(None)
Travel	City guides
	Hotels
Utilities and tools	Backup and manage
	File managers

The final step, providing your app description, may seem trivial, but it will most likely be the most engaging part of the processes (particularly if you don't have a graphic designer and well-defined iconography in place). In this step you must not only provide a textual description for your application but also include various screenshots of your running app, promotional images of varying resolutions, a privacy policy URL, e-mail address, and many more details. Figure 15-21 shows the Submit an App screen.

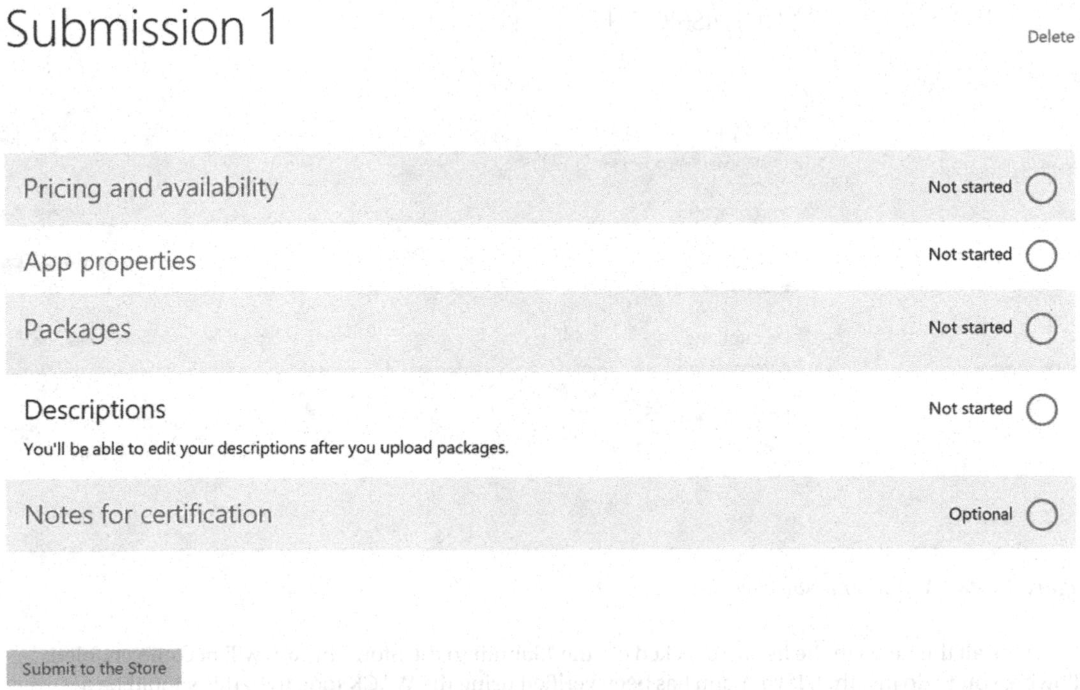

Submission 1

Delete

Pricing and availability — Not started

App properties — Not started

Packages — Not started

Descriptions — Not started

You'll be able to edit your descriptions after you upload packages.

Notes for certification — Optional

Submit to the Store

Figure 15-21. *App submission screen*

With the new Dev Center, the submission workflow is now sort of a check-list. You can step into any one of the areas that needs completing without having to complete a previous step. This allows developers to complete the submission process in a manner that they are most comfortable with. Some might want to take the time to get the pricing information done first; others might upload the app package and focus more on the description first. It all depends. Figure 15-22 shows a larger view of a submission process that is in the works.

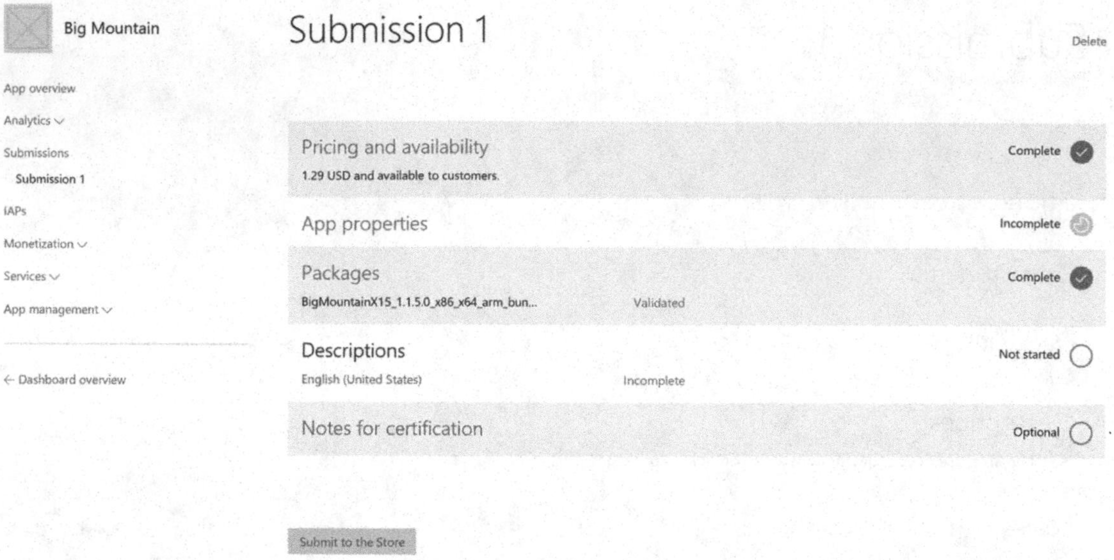

Figure 15-22. *App submission checklist*

Once all the items in the list are checked off, the "Submit to the Store" button will become enabled, allowing you to do just that. If your app has been verified using the WACK tool, then this should be a formality; otherwise it may turn out to be an extremely frustrating process, given the added upload time due to running the tool. (Note that app certification doesn't happen during upload but rather is run before anything else as part of the overall submission). In the following sections, we go through some of the key aspects of the app submission checklist.

Naming Your App

The pre-condition to getting to the submission checklist screen is naming your app. This is the entry point into the submission process as all other steps are presented in terms of this first one. As with web domains, app names are first-come, first-served. Luckily, in the world of apps the real estate is prime for buying.

When you click the "Create a new app" button, you are taken to a simple screen with a single input box in which to enter the name you wish your app to have (see Figure 15-23). Enter the name of your choosing, and click the "Reserve app name" button (you can use the Check availability link to the right of the TextBox to see if the name has been taken). If the name isn't available, you will be presented with an error message.

Create your app by reserving a name

Once you reserve a name, your app will be provisioned for services like push notifications and you can start defining IAPs (in-app products).

Make sure you have the rights to use any name you reserve. You must submit this app to the Store within one year, or you'll lose your name reservation. Learn more

My App Name × Check availability

Reserve app name Cancel

Figure 15-23. *Reserving an app name*

If the name is available, a new app is created, and you are launched into the app overview screen. From here you can manage multiple aspects of your app as well as start a new app submission. Figure 15-24 illustrates.

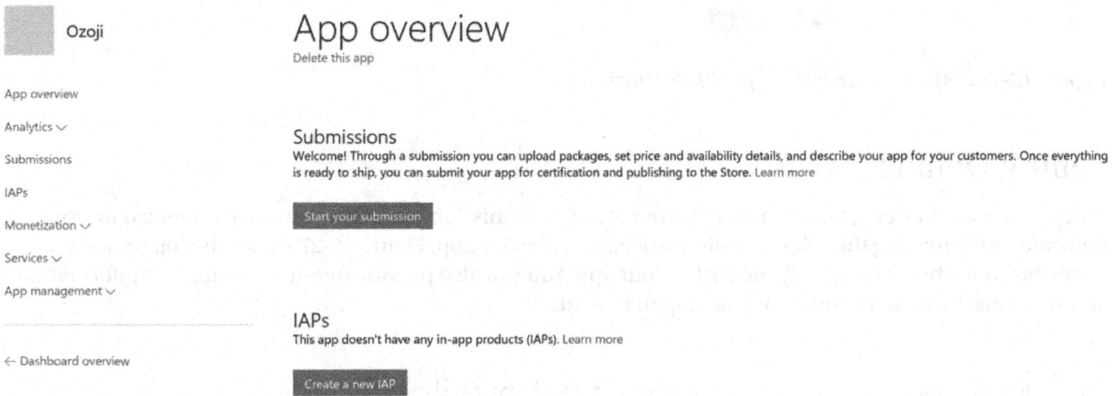

Figure 15-24. *App overview for newly created app*

In Figure 15-25, you can see the updated app list after you reserve two more app names.

My apps

Figure 15-25. *Developer app list*

Once a name is reserved, you have a one-year deadline to submit an app package to it. After that, the name goes back into the pool. Click the "Start your submission" button to begin the submission process (and enter into the app submission checklist discussed earlier). Future trips into the App overview screen will now show a list of submissions rather than the "Start your submission" button. This allows you to spread your app submission task out over time. Figure 15-26 illustrates.

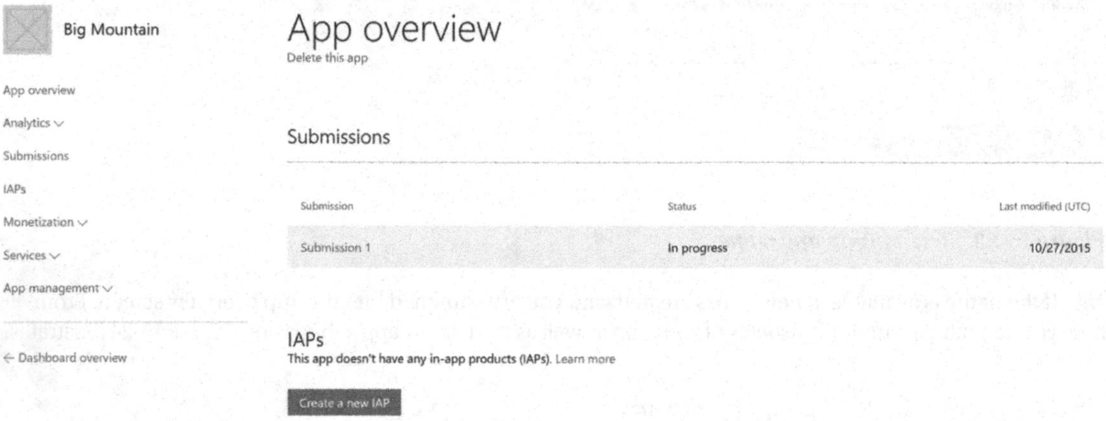

Figure 15-26. *App overview for app with submissions*

Selling Details

When you select "Pricing and availability' from the app submission checklist, you will be directed to a screen dedicated to managing the selling details associated with your app. Figure 15-27 shows the top part of this page, the area where you specify the cost of your app. You can also provide free-trial details and information about the markets where you want your app to be sold.

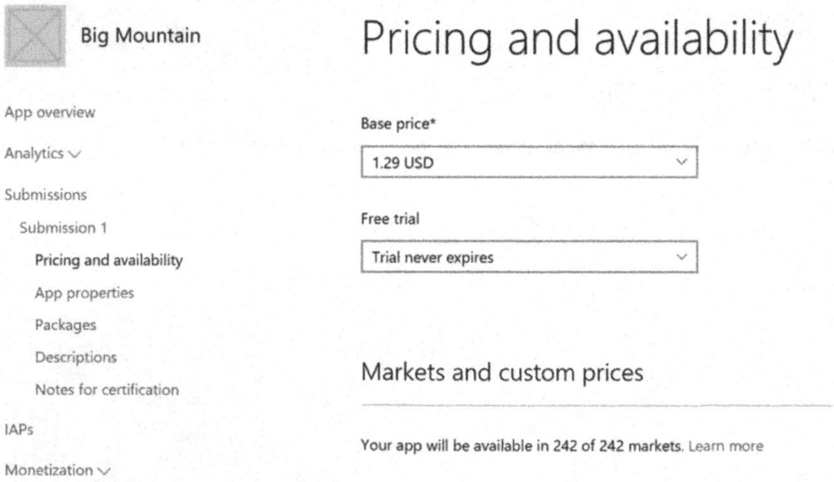

Figure 15-27. *Upper portion of the Pricing and availability screen*

Figure 15-28 shows the bottom part of the screen. Here you indicate when your app is to be released, the device families your app targets, and the degree to which your app is discoverable.

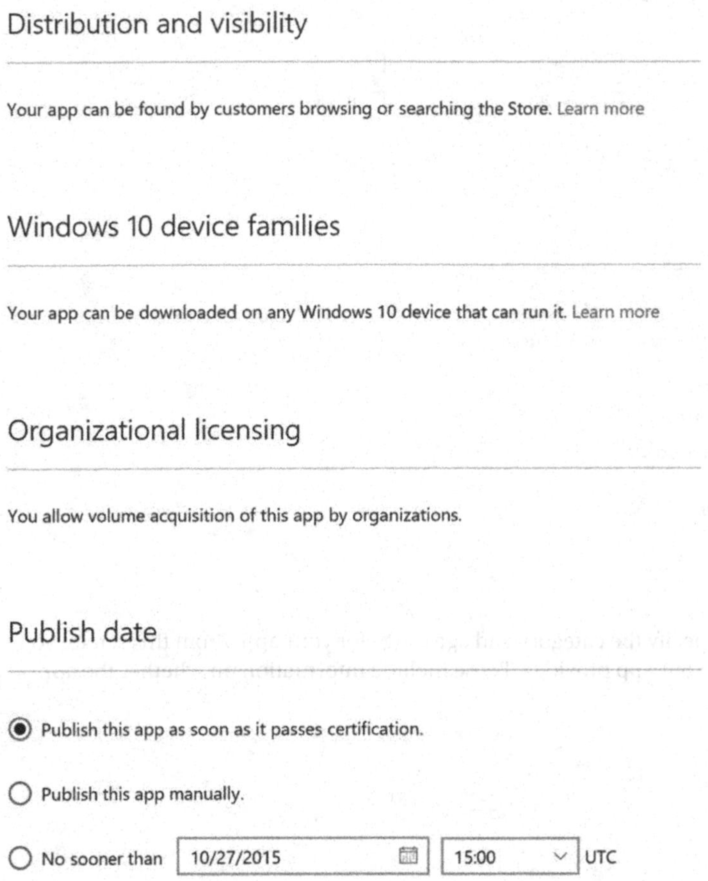

Distribution and visibility

Your app can be found by customers browsing or searching the Store. Learn more

Windows 10 device families

Your app can be downloaded on any Windows 10 device that can run it. Learn more

Organizational licensing

You allow volume acquisition of this app by organizations.

Publish date

(●) Publish this app as soon as it passes certification.

( ) Publish this app manually.

( ) No sooner than 10/27/2015 15:00 UTC

Figure 15-28. *Lower part of the Selling Details screen*

In-app purchases (IAPs) have been moved to their own dedicated screen. If you would like additional services tied to your app, this is where to do it (products are part of the in-app purchase functionality discussed in Chapter 13). They let you offer pieces of functionality that the user can purchase while using your app. Figure 15-29 shows more of the App properties screen from the Windows Store developer dashboard. For features such as push notification and map integration, look under the Services section of the main navigation area to the left of the screen.

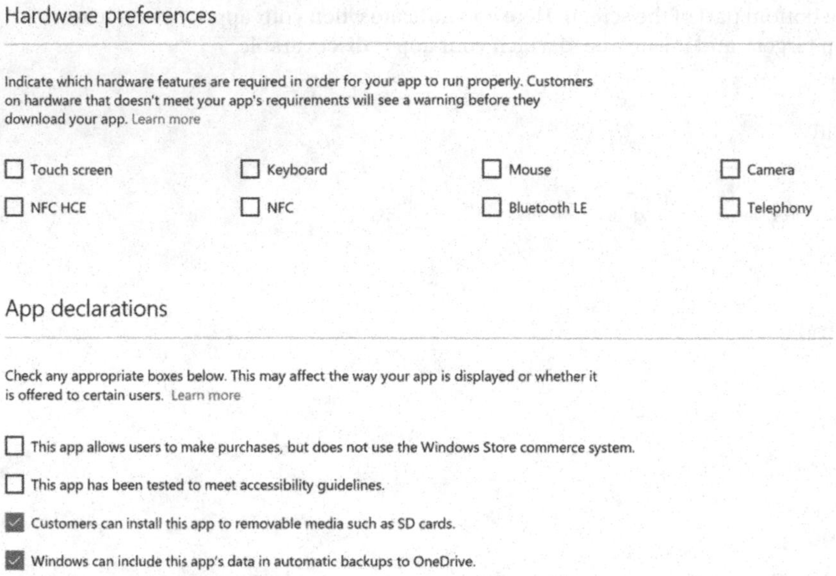

Hardware preferences

Indicate which hardware features are required in order for your app to run properly. Customers on hardware that doesn't meet your app's requirements will see a warning before they download your app. Learn more

☐ Touch screen ☐ Keyboard ☐ Mouse ☐ Camera

☐ NFC HCE ☐ NFC ☐ Bluetooth LE ☐ Telephony

App declarations

Check any appropriate boxes below. This may affect the way your app is displayed or whether it is offered to certain users. Learn more

☐ This app allows users to make purchases, but does not use the Windows Store commerce system.

☐ This app has been tested to meet accessibility guidelines.

☑ Customers can install this app to removable media such as SD cards.

☑ Windows can include this app's data in automatic backups to OneDrive.

Figure 15-29. *Advanced Features screen*

Advanced Properties

In the App Properties screen, you can specify the category and age range for your app. From this screen you can also specify any advanced features your app provides. These include information on whether the app requires the following hardware:

- Touch screen
- Keyboard
- NFC
- Mouse
- Camera
- Bluetooth
- Telephony

Figure 15-29 illustrates.

Age Rating and Rating Certificates

Next, you need to select an age rating for your app from among the choices listed in Table 15-3. These ratings are required for games. However, even if your app isn't a game, if contains adult content, it is best to stay on the cautious or conservative side and provide a rating. Doing so will help to ensure that you don't fail certification simply because of its absence. If you aren't sure how to rate the content you provide, we recommend using the highest age rating that makes sense for the provided content. (Again, it is beneficial to be conservative when it comes to this.)

Table 15-3. *Windows Store App Ratings*

Rating	Description
3+ Suitable for Young Children	These applications are considered appropriate for young children. There may be minimal comic violence in nonrealistic, cartoon form. Characters should not resemble or be associated with real-life characters. There should be no content that could be frightening, and there should be no nudity or references to sexual or criminal activity. Apps with this age rating also can't enable features that could access content or functionality unsuitable for young children. This includes, but is not limited to, access to online services, collection of personal information, or activating hardware such as microphones or webcams.
7+ Suitable for Ages 7 and Older	Apps with this age rating have the same criteria as the 3+ applications, except these apps can include content that might frighten a younger audience and can contain partial nudity, as long as the nudity doesn't refer to sexual activity.
12+ Suitable for Ages 12 and Older	Choose this rating if you aren't sure which age rating to select for your app. Apps with this age rating can contain increased nudity of a nonsexual nature, slightly graphic violence toward nonrealistic characters, or non-graphic violence toward realistic human or animal characters. This age rating might also include profanity, but not of a sexual nature. Also, apps with this age rating may include access to online services and enable features such as microphones and webcams.
16+ Suitable for Ages 16 and Older	Apps with this age rating can depict realistic violence with minimal blood, and they can depict sexual activity. They can also contain drug or tobacco use and criminal activities, and more profanity than would be allowed in a 12+ app, within the limits laid out in the certification requirements.
18+ Suitable for Adults Only	Apps with this age rating may contain intense, gross, or specific violence, and blood or gore that is only appropriate for an adult audience, in addition to content that is appropriate for a 16+ app.

Also note that there are varying age requirements for things like gaming, online access, and online interaction that may not be immediately evident to you (and may vary by country). For instance, even though social networking apps are inherently benign, they require higher ratings in general because there is no way to fully control the content that users ultimately view. If you are building such an application, it is important to present warnings that explicitly prohibit children. This is especially important in apps where there is a potential for interactions between adults and minors. Having a higher rating allows parents and guardians to restrict access to such apps.

Finally, if your plan is to publish this app internationally, you might consider specifying the app's age rating for other age rating systems. As stated earlier, other countries have varying age requirements. Figure 15-30 shows part of the App properties screen.

Big Mountain

App overview
Analytics
Submissions
Submission 1
Pricing and availability
App properties
Packages
Descriptions
Notes for certification
IAPs
Monetization
Services
App management

← Dashboard overview

App properties

Category and subcategory

Pick the category (and subcategory, if applicable) that best describes your app. Learn more

Pick a category | None

Store age rating

The Windows Store uses age ratings to help your customers find apps that meet their needs. Pick the age rating that pertains to the suitability of the content in your app, rather than the age of the user to which the content is directed. Some countries and regions require that you also rate your app through a specific ratings board. We recommend you choose the 3+ or 7+ rating only if your app contains content that is suitable for children. Apps that have these ratings have additional restrictions. Learn more

- 3+ (Suitable for young children) Show details
- 7+ (Suitable for ages 7 and older) Show details
- 12+ (Suitable for ages 12 and older) Show details
- 16+ (Suitable for ages 16 and older) Show details
- 18+ (Suitable for adults) Show details

Figure 15-30. *App properties screen*

Provided your app is a game or, based on discretion, requires a rating, the next step is to submit and save your rating. The submitted app's content is evaluated against the rating you give it during the certification process. For Windows 10 apps classified as games, a rating board is presented in which there is a certificate for every geographic market in which the app is listed. Based on these geographic markets—specifically, Brazil, Korea, South Africa, and Taiwan—the listed certificates must be obtained should you plan to make the gaming app available worldwide. Naturally, you have the option to forego sales in certain markets, should obtaining the certificates prove problematic.

Uploading Your App

The Packages checklist item is the step where app packages are actually uploaded to the Windows Store. The package to be dropped here is the appxupload package created as part of the Visual Studio publishing process. You can find the file using a File dialog, or you can drag and drop the appxupload file for your current version into the drop zone on the Packages page (see Figure 15-31). To ensure that all the needed files and resources are included in the package, the system performs a validation, which completes with an error or a success message. Until the Packages task is completed, the Description and Notes for certification task will not be available.

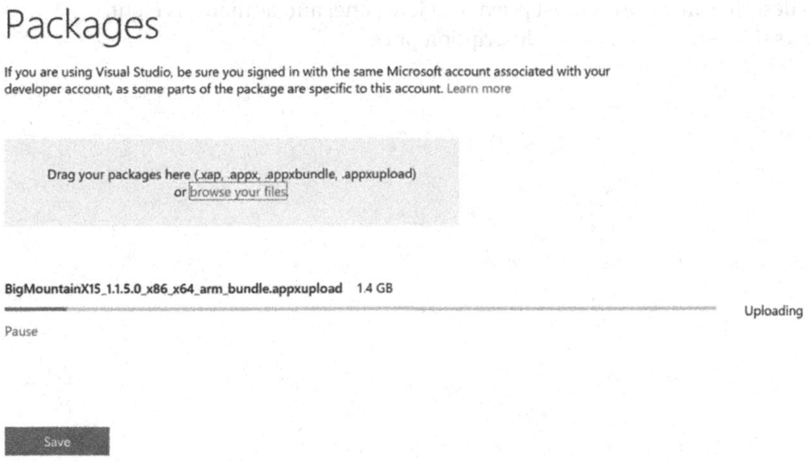

Packages

If you are using Visual Studio, be sure you signed in with the same Microsoft account associated with your developer account, as some parts of the package are specific to this account. Learn more

Drag your packages here (.xap, .appx, .appxbundle, .appxupload)
or browse your files

BigMountainX15_1.1.5.0_x86_x64_arm_bundle.appxupload 1.4 GB

Uploading

Pause

Save

Figure 15-31. Packages screen

Description

With the app package uploaded, it is now time for the fun part. Take a little pride in your hard work and enter a description of your app on the Description page. You also need to enter the app's features, keywords, and screenshots, accompanied by brief descriptions. This is the same information that will be visible to potential users and approvers, so the content should be accurate, concise, and compelling. Figure 15-32 shows the top part of the App description page, where you provide the description and application features.

App description - English (United States)

Enter the text and images that customers will see in your app's listing. At least one screenshot is required. Learn more

Description*

- Character limit: 10000
- Learn how to write a good description

Release notes

- Character limit: 1500

Figure 15-32. Top part of the App description page

In addition to the textual description, all apps must provide at least one, and as many as eight, screenshots. Figure 15-33 shows this section of the App description page.

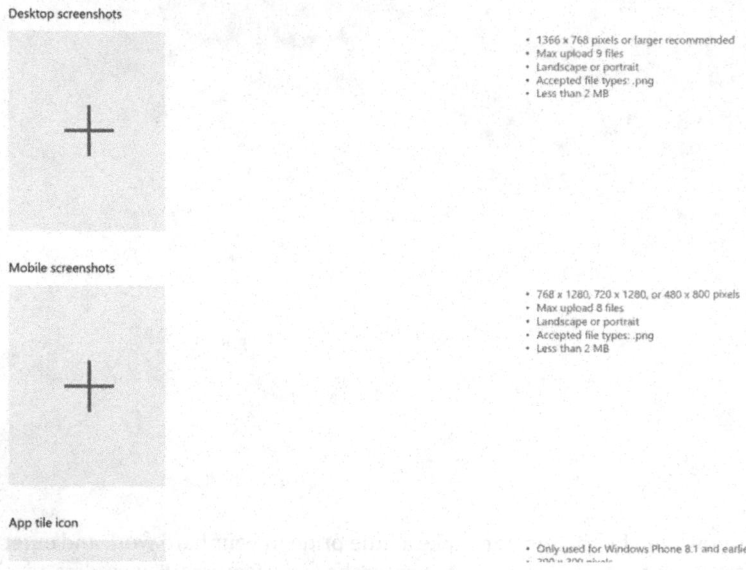

Figure 15-33. *The screenshots section of the App description page*

The next part of the App description page allows you to provide search keywords and extra information like the app's license terms, copyright information, and required or recommended hardware. If at some point you go back and edit your app submission (for instance, if you have a new version), you're required to include a separate description of the update. The hardware field is where you specify whether your app requires the existence of sensors or devices in order to operate. Figure 15-34 shows this section of the App description page.

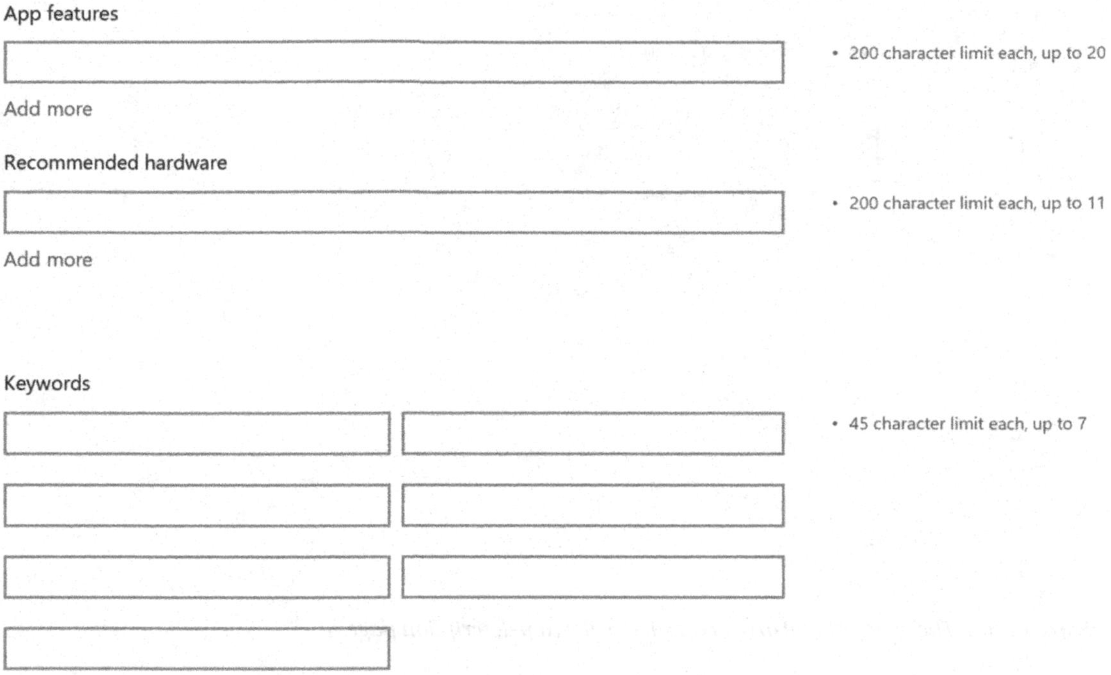

App features

• 200 character limit each, up to 20

Add more

Recommended hardware

• 200 character limit each, up to 11

Add more

Keywords

• 45 character limit each, up to 7

Figure 15-34. *Extra description information on the App description page*

Finally, you are allowed to upload promotional images for your app. This includes any images to be used for the purposes of marketing in the Windows Store. You can enter the website associated with your app or company, if you have one. You can also provide all those final yet important details, including a support contact address and URL and the link to your online privacy statement. See Figure 15-35.

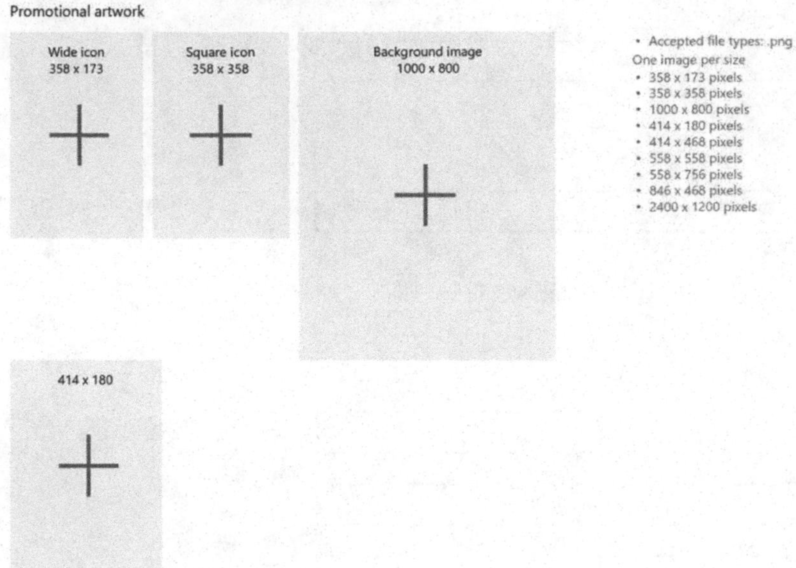

Figure 15-35. *The Promotional artwork section of the App description page*

Notes to Testers

The next and final screen, shown in Figure 15-36, lets you to enter any other information you choose to make available to the testers. Note that this is the place to enter login test credentials.

Notes for certification

Provide any info that helps testers use and understand your app.
Customers won't see this info.
Include the following (if applicable):

- Username and password for a test account
- Steps to access hidden or locked features
- Steps to verify background audio usage

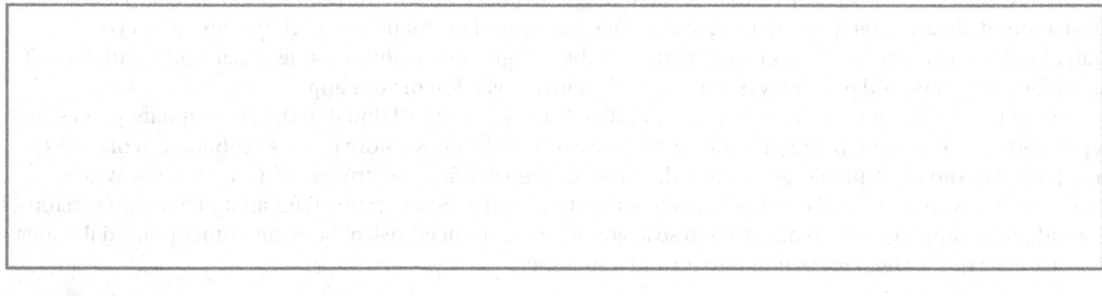

Save

Figure 15-36. Notes to Testers box

Getting Your App Certified

Now comes the easiest—or hardest, depending on how you look at it—part: monitoring your dashboard as you wait for certification, and subsequent publication, of your app. Following submission, you'll receive a confirmation e-mail from the Windows Store team so you know it wasn't all just a dream. This e-mail also provides the link to your dashboard for tracking the app's progression through the approval process.

This process requires six steps and an estimated wait time of six days. If at any point a test results in a fail, you're notified through your dashboard and via e-mail, and you are allowed to resubmit when you've addressed the error.

1. The submitted app is run through a series of automated tests.
2. The app proceeds to security testing. (Everyone appreciates downloading secure apps to their Windows 10 devices, after all.)
3. The app is put through a technical compliance test, which, if you had no problems running the WACK tool, should be smooth sailing, because Microsoft runs the WACK tool on its own servers. This completes the automated testing of the app.
4. Your humble creation is sent to an actual tester (what a fun job!) for compatibility testing. Your dashboard provides an estimate in terms of days, but because this is the most subjective stage of the approvals, there can be some leeway in this estimation. Once it passes this step, your app is ready to be published.

5. The app receives digital signage and proceeds to the Windows Store servers and on to release in the Windows Store!

6. But, ugh, there is still a potential for post-publication failure during what's called the Manual Content Compliance test. In this environment, your app is tested for bugs, security, and appropriateness. You'll receive an e-mail if the app fails this final step, directing you to the report detailing the fail reasons and actions to resolve them in the Dev Center.

Updating Your App

Hopefully, your app will do so well that, as technology advances, so will the need for updated app features. Rest assured, dear reader, you will receive feedback from your faithful users—perhaps more than you bargained for! This user feedback can provide valuable insight into usability issues, what works and doesn't work for your users, and what may be lacking in the current version of your app.

When development is complete on your updated version, you will find that the Store update process is a pared-down version of the initial submission process. The Windows Store requires submission of a new app package, and app updates go through the same six-step verification process. You can run the WACK tool again for your own local test. Fortunately, submitting and gaining approval for an updated app version should prove simpler as far as adhering to style guidelines, a reduced risk of bugs, and other potential issues.

Here's a quick checklist of things to do and remember:

- Click the Update button to initiate a new update on the app page.
- Before submitting a new version 2.0, remember to create the new version number in the Create App Package Wizard.
- Grab your updated app package, and head back to the dashboard.
- Before submitting for certification, I recommend providing a brief description of the changes or added features. The update page looks similar to the submission page for a new app, except that most of the information is already provided.
- If you need to update any of the information about your app, from its features or licensing terms to screenshots or in-app purchase offers, you can revisit the relevant sections and update the information accordingly. Otherwise, you can head right to the Upload Package step and upload the latest version of your app. Once the upload is complete, go to the Details step to complete the Description of Update field, which is required.

Summary

Congratulations! You made it not only through the book, but also through the final fulfilling step of getting your Windows 10 app into the Windows Store. From reading this chapter, you know that the steps in the process are straightforward and simple, but this may be a tense experience that may result in a lot of debugging or error fixes. Once you've made it to this step, don't give up or get frustrated! If anything, take a break from your code and revisit it with fresh eyes. Now, here's a brief review of the key points covered in this chapter:

- After reserving a name for your app, you have a year to get your app published under this name. After that, the name is redistributed into the pool.
- You submit your app and the tools you use in the Windows Store submission process, which includes the Create App Package Wizard, the Dev Center, and your developer dashboard.
- There's a certification tool called the Windows App Certification Kit (WACK) tool, which you can use to test your app.
- You now know the certification process, including automated testing, human testing, and Manual Content Compliance testing.
- Consider creating updates for your app by releasing new versions. This is an important aspect of keeping your app relevant, keeping your users satisfied, and maintaining an app that is at the forefront of technological advancement.

Index

■ B

■ C

D, E

F

■ M, N

■ O

■ P

■ Q

■ R

■ S

■ T

■ U

V

W

X, Y, Z

Printed in the United States
By Bookmasters